Critical Issues in Crime and Justice

Third Edition

Critical Issues in Crime and Justice

Thought, Policy, and Practice

Third Edition

Editors

Dan Okada
California State University Sacramento

Mary Maguire
California State University Sacramento

Alexa Sardina
California State University Sacramento

Los Angeles | London | New Delhi
Singapore | Washington DC | Melbourne

FOR INFORMATION:

SAGE Publications, Inc.
2455 Teller Road
Thousand Oaks, California 91320
E-mail: order@sagepub.com

SAGE Publications Ltd.
1 Oliver's Yard
55 City Road
London EC1Y 1SP
United Kingdom

SAGE Publications India Pvt. Ltd.
B 1/I 1 Mohan Cooperative Industrial Area
Mathura Road, New Delhi 110 044
India

SAGE Publications Asia-Pacific Pte. Ltd.
3 Church Street
#10-04 Samsung Hub
Singapore 049483

Acquisitions Editor: Jessica Miller
Editorial Assistant: Rebecca Lee
Production Editor: Jane Martinez
Copy Editor: Jared Leighton
Typesetter: C&M Digitals (P) Ltd.
Proofreader: Laura Webb
Indexer: Robie Grant
Cover Designer: Dally Verghese
Marketing Manager: Jillian Ragusa

Printed in the United States of America

Library of Congress Cataloging-in-Publication Data

Names: Okada, Dan editor.

Title: Critical issues in crime and justice : Thought, policy, and practice / editors, Dan Okada, Mary Maguire, Alexa Sardina, California State University Sacramento.

Description: Third Edition. | Los Angeles, California : SAGE, [2018] |

Previous edition: 2015. | Includes bibliographical references and index.

Identifiers: LCCN 2018013055 | ISBN 9781544307992 (pbk : acid-free paper)

Subjects: LCSH: Criminal justice, Administration of. | Criminology.

Classification: LCC HV7419 .C758 2018 | DDC 364—dc23 LC record available at https://lccn.loc.gov/2018013055

This book is printed on acid-free paper.

19 20 21 22 10 9 8 7 6 5 4 3 2

BRIEF CONTENTS

DETAILED CONTENTS

PART III • POLICING/LAW ENFORCEMENT

PART IV • COURTS/LAW/JURISPRUDENCE

PREFACE FOR THE THIRD EDITION

An old Chinese curse threatens its recipients, "May you live in interesting times." Clearly, in the world that beguiles us, from the broadest of considerations to the specificity of criminal justice, minimally, we all face interesting times. Other verbs also come to mind as we gather in front of the daily news cycle. It is impossible not to pay attention to the events as they transpire and realize the effect they have on us all.

It is important for those about to enter into the practical world of criminal justice and criminal justice scholarship to be aware of the issues, thought, and consideration that affects and is affected by these issues. It should also be recognized that taking a stand one way or another about which issues and point of view are relevant and meaningful—or even irrelevant or superfluous—is also important.

This volume continues our attempt to challenge advanced students in criminal justice and its allied disciplines, with both content and perspective. Crime happens in real time, and those involved and the situations that frame the event adapt to the conditions that influence them. Attempts to be comprehensive concerning what may be "contemporary criminal justice" would soon not be. Instead, what is presented here is our continued effort to include interesting and representative material from experts devoted to resolving the inconsistencies found in the pursuit of criminal justice and criminal justice education.

It should be mentioned that this collection contains work not found anywhere else. Each author was individually approached and asked to craft an essay about a particular topic in his or her area of expertise. Their instruction was simply to not attempt to be comprehensive about what they wished to say. A discussion that might be a "mile wide and an inch deep," reading more as a compendium of information offering no real point of view, would ultimately leave both reader and author frustrated. They were encouraged to entice the reader with provocative conversations about important issues within their topic's breadth so that the reader would become engaged and seek out more material and analysis on his or her own interest.

We are proud that SAGE and previous readers/users of this collection believe that the contributors, information, and message provided within these pages have been worthy of consideration and thus have led to the production of another edition. We have witnessed literally earth-shaking revelations, assaults on our psyche, tragedies of epic proportion, and, of course, opportunities to exercise creativity and resolve since our second edition was produced. Remembering what happened yesterday illustrates the fallacy of attempting to highlight what will happen tomorrow.

Regardless, we have amended, included, and reconsidered, as have our contributors, in our attempt to engage our classes. What is presented here is a wonderful evolution of our continuing pursuit to provide perspective, information, and an opportunity to interact with provocative subject matter. We hope you enjoy the read and continue your own pursuits to secure justice for us all.

—Dan Okada, Mary Maguire, and Alexa Sardina
Editors

NEW TO THIS EDITION:

- NEW and updated chapters offer a survey and examination of contemporary issues impacting the criminal justice system.

- Updated data and statistics in every chapter highlight current trends and research in criminal justice and criminology today.

- A NEW chapter on sex offender policies (Chapter 11) explores the intentions and unintended consequences behind these policies.

- A NEW chapter on human trafficking (Chapter 12) offers insights and case studies on the critical issue of sex and labor trafficking around the world.

- A NEW chapter on terrorism (Chapter 13) looks at mass-casualty terrorism in our modern era and its destabilizing influence on the global community.

- A NEW chapter on the involvement of the mentally ill in the criminal justice system (Chapter 21) examines key questions about the prevalence of mentally ill offenders.

- A NEW chapter on community corrections (Chapter 24) explores challenges around rehabilitation, reintegration, and reentry.

ACKNOWLEDGMENTS

That an acknowledgement page for a third edition of this collection is necessary is cause for hilarity. Way back in 2009, when the first edition was being conceived, one of the reasons that the editors worked so diligently to ensure the quality of the work considered for inclusion was to support the retention, tenure, and promotion process for which the editors would be undergoing. Mary Maguire is now an associate dean in the School of Health and Human Services at California State University Sacramento, having easily been tenured and promoted and having gone through the faculty progression of assistant to associate to full professor. She managed to serve as the chair of the Division of Criminal Justice as well. She was always destined for bigger and brighter accomplishments. Dan Okada had given up rank and tenure earlier in his career to come to Sac State and then also followed a similar line of progress: assistant to associate to full professor. In this edition, Alexa Sardina has lent her presence and is just beginning her journey through the rigors of the academy and is one of Sac State's Division of Criminal Justice's newest faculty. Her work with sex offenses and offenders is destined for academic prominence, and she will quickly be recognized as an influential voice in criminal justice teaching, scholarship, and public awareness. We are proud of the work found in this edition and are grateful for the efforts and attention made by each contributor and the large and mostly publicly unrecognized cadre of students, colleagues, professionals, SAGE Publications staff, friends, and families whom we are thankful for and whom we cannot possibly praise loud or long enough.

To our contributors: Big thanks for the effort, consideration, and skill you put in to make this product what it is. Your integrity and talent are a gift to us all.

To our students: Thanks for engaging us and encouraging us to provide you with professorship worthy of your futures.

To our colleagues: Your support and affection regularly goes unrecognized, not this time . . . You know who you are, but more importantly, we know who you are. Thanks!

To the reviewers: There is a wide number of personalities to whom we are unequivocally grateful for their guidance: Robert B. Jenkot, Coastal Carolina University; Brian A. Kinnaird, PhD, Bethany College; Tamara J. Lynn, Fort Hays State University; and April Terry, Fort Hays State University. Our appreciation is extended for their keen eye, critical analysis, counsel, and support.

Our friends: Beverages and hugs all around for the comfort you gave eagerly and the criticism you gave reluctantly (albeit thoughtfully).

Our families: Our gratitude and appreciation will be given to each of you privately, but publicly, we are fully aware that our lives would not be possible without you in them.

Gone (retired) but certainly not forgotten is the SAGE executive editor who was the gentle prodder and mauling muscle in pushing, goading, and getting this and many other scholarly balls rolling, Mr. Jerry Westby. Seemingly, there was no one in the academic discipline that is criminal justice that he did not know and have some life anecdote about. He was the referee who put this work into place and made it possible for this edition to even be a consideration. Ave Jerry!

That SAGE found a remarkable successor to fill its managing editor vacancy is testament to the professionalism and luck found in Thousand Oaks. Jessica Miller's patience, wisdom, and administration were essential in guiding (i.e., hammering) this work to completion. Working with Jessica has been wonderful. She has skillfully and effectively and with a much different touch seized Jerry's spot. Sincerest thanks, Jessica. Her remarkable and supportive crew at SAGE also committed themselves to make a quality product better.

Thank you to all of you.

Namaste.

INTRODUCTION

Is It Possible to Prepare for a Criminal Justice Future?

Dan Okada

One of the leading social demographers of his day, Philip Hauser (1961) wrote a warning to those who would listen:

> America is in the midst of a population crisis that threatens our traditional way of life. It is a crisis that becomes more severe with every day of the 1960s. It promises to become a national catastrophe and is already costing us heavily in money, terrible social problems, and lost liberty. (p. 31)

Of course, he was talking about the generation that would become known as the *baby boomers*. Birth rates ballooned as it was noted that between 1940 and 1960, the U.S. population grew by 48 million (Easterlin, 1962). It was the largest growth spurt in the country since its founding.

While those populating these numbers were looked upon with suspicion by society's elders (as they always have) and those basking in the glow of VE (Victory in Europe) and VJ (Victory over Japan) Days, Hauser's observations were prescient. They were followed by one of the pioneers of cohort analysis, Princeton University social demographer Norman Ryder, in a report to the President's Science Advisory Committee (cited in Wilson, 1975, pp.13–14), who warned:

> 'There is a perennial invasion of barbarians who must somehow be civilized and turned into contributors to fulfillment of the various functions requisite to societal survival.' That 'invasion' is the coming of age of a new generation of young people. . . . In 1950, and still in 1960,

the 'invading army' (*those aged fourteen to twenty-four*) (italics added) were outnumbered three to one by the size of the 'defending army' (those aged twenty-five to sixty-four).

What Hauser and Ryder were both suggesting was that the country was unprepared for what would accompany the birth rate boom. This new generation would realize shortages in schools, teachers, hospitals, doctors, nurses, housing, sanitation, and other social services; the list went on but clearly included the growth of the criminal justice system as well. Eventually, cultural awareness and technology caught up and some semblance of zero population growth flat-lined the population curve (Ryder & Westoff, 1971) in the later 1960s. But the numbers included the multitude who would then avail themselves to the field of cohort analysis and demography and give quantitative support to the reality that available social resources lagged behind the need of those who would require those services.

The social science caution of correlation not equaling causation is relevant here. It is true that given their numbers alone, even if their activity and behavior only remained constant with earlier generations, they would still have necessitated expansion and increased attention to those interactions that caused harm and necessitated societal response. Still, in this context, it was the standard that a low-end minimum age for juvenile delinquency is 7 years of age, and it is widely acknowledged that juveniles become most active as teenagers (i.e., Ryder's invading army of Barbarians).

If the baby boom can have an agreed-upon start as approximately a calendar year after the end of World War II (summer–fall 1945), the first boomers came into the world 9 months later, in spring–summer 1946, which they did. If this is then juxtaposed to the social scientific reality that delinquency and subsequent criminal activity has its own onset around adolescence, then sometime around the fall of 1960 would mark the onset of the boomer crime wave. That is, if a grossly oversimplified explanation for what happened is offered.

What is relevant here is that the overall crime rate did increase over the last three decades of the 20th century. Street gangs, problem-oriented policing, stop-and-frisk, prison overcrowding, mass incarceration, and more became part of contemporary cultural awareness and the scientific lexicon (and fodder for big-dollar grant subsidies to study these issues) as crime rose to proportions not seen previously. Another less often discussed truth emerged as well. Federal funding through programs such as the Law Enforcement Assistance Administration and the Law Enforcement Education Program encouraged colleges and universities to create and rush into place academic certification offerings in the study, practice, and examination of crime and criminal justice. Degree programs soon gained credibility, popularity, and FTEs as scholars emerged, or were anointed, to address this new interest and take advantage of

FIGURE 1.1 ■ United States Crime Rate (gray line) Over United States Incarceration Population

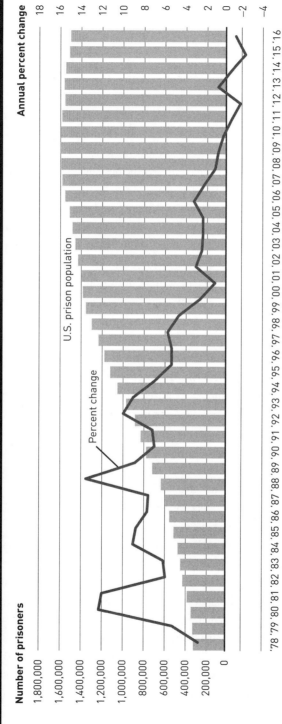

Source: Bureau of Justice Statistics (2016). National prisoner statistics, 1978–2015.

the economic boon that was also a feature of this epoch. And then something mystical and unexpected happened. In the early 1990s, crime rates started to come down—not just decrease but dramatically fall. The slope of the curve became precipitous.

The above figure (see Figure 1.1) is provided for illustration purposes. In spite of the bimodal peaks and valleys that bracket the 1980s' generally upward slope, a positive increase can be seen from the start of this graph in 1978, but the actual increase began much earlier, in 1960. As contested by Wilson (1975), the increase can be attributed to the emergence of the baby boom cohort who matured into Ryder's Barbarians and then persisted through their generation, approximately the ensuing 30 to 35 years. It took society a while to react and develop the tools and technology required to effect remedies to the onslaught. But the reality is that no one really knows why the drop happened.

Attention yielded results. Scholarship produced theory and recommendations to combat crime, more intrusive police surveillance and processing techniques arose; better investigation techniques led to more arrests; the Supreme Court turned back some of the more controversial offender's rights precedents and instructed criminal justice practices to be, at minimum, equally as involved with the rights of victims; more convicts were incarcerated; the prison-industrial complex mushroomed across the country; and more attention and social resources were directed to those urban arenas where critical population mass and crime often centered. Economists Donohue and Levitt (2001) even attributed the decline in crime to the unintended consequences that those potential criminals simply did not exist because of legalized abortion, simply an outcome of ersatz regulated birth control. Many suggestions were made, and many on this list likely interacted, albeit unknowingly, to affect change. However, the most reasonable explanation lies with the combined implementation, in part, of all of these efforts in concert.

This figure is further included to illustrate another issue regarding criminal justice policy and practice over this period. That is, that while there has been a demonstrable decrease in crime commission, likewise it has been accompanied by a steady and disproportionate increase in the incarceration rate (represented here as the histogram). In spite of fewer crimes being committed, nationwide, the national incarceration rate has increased unabated. Crime spikes have occurred periodically but were followed by similar many depreciations, leading to the reality that the overall crime rate is nowhere near what it was at the end of the 20th century, while the incarceration rate remains distressingly robust.

Perception is critical to crime recognition and criminal justice practice. Beccaria's (1963) delineation of crime categories informs the type of punishment that follows: (1) most serious: crime against the state; (2) most prevalent: crime that injures or affects the security of and/or the property of individuals; and (3) most recognized: crime that affects the public peace. Crime occurs by people against people. These tenets influenced our founding fathers and led to the criminal justice system existing today. This is also a reminder that as Quinney (2001) suggests, society creates definitions of crime based on its own ethnocentric criteria, and thus, cultural attention and law evolves, ebbs and flows, and is both quick and slow, simultaneously, to care or not care.

Attempting to link theory construction to policy creation to the world of criminal justice is challenging. Crime spans the breadth of human endeavor and interaction, from the seemingly irrelevant to the dramatically profound. Science is an active, problem-solving endeavor but predicting future events is beyond its scope or reach. Moral panics—societal reactions to wrongs—have everything to do with the creation of criminal justice and crime policy. Individual senses of justice, fairness, right, and wrong, as well as level of response, retribution, and retaliation, are all tied into jurisprudence, law creation, and social identity. There is also a link to the intrinsic need of people to do something. Ignoring or passively watching a disagreeable behavior be committed when it is in one's ability to stop, mitigate, neutralize, or prevent any ensuing harm to another is not what we do or who we are.

Approaching the end of first quarter of the 21st century underscores the reality that crime, its explanation, and any attempt to frustrate, or curb its existence, remains a worthwhile goal. There are several contemporary concerns that have attracted the attention of popular culture and have influenced the focus, deliberation, and context of criminology and crime policy. Colorado, Washington, and California have responded to the failure of prohibitions to effectively curtail marijuana use by enacting legislation that legalizes not only its medicinal but recreational use. The opioid crisis reminds us that villains are not only found lurking in society's dark corners (see Quinones, 2015). Or even that society's dark corners can be found in the open in myriad public locations. Sexual predation has been encountered in virtually every arena in which people interact. The entirety of corporate (broadly defined) entrepreneurs and public policy laborers and decision makers must be held accountable for the need to create predation-safe environments. These latest realizations have seized media attention away from what has long been the central concern of criminal justice, race and crime, race and criminal justice, and race and criminal justice practitioners. A discussion of crime in all of its orientations must include a discussion of race matters.

One of the Nixon administration's landmark legislative enactments was the Juvenile Justice and Delinquency Prevention Act of 1974. It demanded that four critical provisions be instituted in the handling of juvenile offenders. First, it called for the deinstitutionalization of status offenders. That is, because of the demonstrated overreach of the juvenile justice system, the Act stipulated that juveniles, whose offenses were based specifically on their age (i.e., status), could not be detained in youth detention facilities or adult jails. So truants, runaways, and incorrigibles were systematically removed from juvenile custody and system attention.

Next, the act demanded that any juvenile being detained for investigation or for his or her own protection could not be held in the same space as an adult offender. In fact, they must be separated by "sight and sound" from each other. A rider to this provision called for "jail removal." If facilities could not be provided and juveniles had to be detained in adult jails, this was allowable only as an exception and not the rule of jurisdictional policy.

The last provision is significant to this discussion. The act called for a resolution to the justice system's recognized disproportionate minority confinement (DMC). No gainsayers existed arguing a contrary position. It was universally accepted that however the examination was framed, juveniles of color were much more likely to be apprehended, processed, and incarcerated than their white counterparts. This obviously then produced a similar effect on the clientele of the adult system. Of interest here, is that the act has been reauthorized a number of times by Congress, and while the first three provisions have been addressed, all that has happened to the last is that the letter "C" in DMC was changed from *confinement* to *contact*. Georgetown University's Center for Juvenile Justice Reform has taken a further step and rebranded DMC and is offering training to jurisdictions so that they may become RED (reducing ethnic disparities) certified. Funding and hand-wringing on how to address this long-standing situation continues.

Taking a step back chronologically, what can further be tied to these recognitions is one of the fundamental findings of the 1965 President's Commission on Law Enforcement and the Administration of Justice report, *The Challenge of a Free Society* (1967). Arising from the turmoil witnessed in virtually every metropolitan area in the country in the 1960s, President Johnson recruited criminal justice experts to examine and then, based on their best analysis and interpretations (an early form of evidence-based practices), offer recommendations on how to improve literally every aspect of the criminal justice system. Along with producing task force reports in nine areas of concern—police, courts, corrections, juvenile delinquency and youth crime, organized crime, science and technology, assessment of crime, narcotics and drugs, and drunkenness—suggestions on how to remedy the confrontation problems law enforcement personnel and citizens were experiencing their cities were included in the report. Regarding policing, a very specific recommendation was this:

> The ultimate aim of all police departments should be that all personnel
> with general enforcement powers have baccalaureate degrees (p. 109).

Simply, the commission called for college graduate police officers. Almost universally, this recommendation has been ignored by the law enforcement community. While the benefits of a college education and the practice of policing have been demonstrated over a range of scientific investigations, data on how many departments actually have a 4-year degree as a baseline hiring qualification are impossible to find (Paoline, Terrill, & Rossler, 2014). A small minority of departments report having an education requirement beyond high school equivalency, some ask for completion of 60 college credits. Finding any department that requires a bachelor's degree is grueling. This standard must be considered in context with another reality in that possession of a college degree does not insure that that candidate will succeed as an effective/efficient law enforcement officer. While the 4-year college experience clearly provides the advantages of: a broad-ranged education, diverse social interaction, and decision-making and critical-thinking opportunities that are critical to contemporary policing, there are other intangible, practical assets not taught in a college classroom.

The commission further called for better police–citizen relations. A clear benefit of a liberal arts college education is the diversity of (in some cases, forced) interactions with a range of social others. Not simply tolerance but acceptance that solipsism is acceptable must be assertively rejected.

These two public policies can be juxtaposed here as a discussion of the range of concerns that are brought into focus with the recognition that finding examples throughout the social media or the nightly news of inappropriate police and citizen interactions is not difficult to do. Race and crime could potentially have very different outcomes if the educational quality of those engaged in a dissolute encounter were greater. Tough, dangerous decisions that have undergone immediate critical examination or even that are the product of rigorous evidence-based practice analysis could produce radically different results. Blame or fault is not the goal here; solutions that may lead to more positive outcomes are. If you have not had a chance to read *Los Angeles Times* reporter Jill Leovy's (2015) remarkable account of homicide investigators and the cases that they investigate, spending time with *Ghettoside* would very much be worth your effort with these considerations in mind.

Why Hauser and Ryder's observations about our collective future began this conversation is that the decade of the 2010s leading into the 2020s has seen a modest uptick in crime. While it may appear that violence, oppression, and avarice have remained unimpeachable in many venues and situations, the overall rate of crime and any connection to most of the sociodemographic variables that inspire the social sciences has not produced the dramatic criminal increases found by "The Greatest Generation." The progeny of the baby boomers have now reached or are now reaching the age of Ryder's Barbarians; we will see what the years reveal.

References

Beccaria, C. (1963). *On crimes and punishments* (translated by Henry Paolucci). New York, NY: Macmillan.

Bureau of Justice Statistics. (2016). National prisoner statistics, 1978–2015. Retrieved from https://www.bjs.gov/content/pub/pdf/p15.pdf

Donohue, J. D., & Levitt, S. D. (2001). The impact of legalized abortion on crime. *Quarterly Journal of Economics, 66*(2), 379–420.

Easterlin, R. A. (1962). *The American baby boom in historical perspective*. New York, NY: National Bureau of Economic Research.

Hauser, P. M. (1961, November 21). America's population crisis. *Look Magazine*, 29–31.

Juvenile Justice and Delinquency Prevention Act of 1974. Public Law 93-415; 88 Stat. 1109.

Leovy, J. (2015). *Ghettoside: A true story of murder in America*. New York, NY: Random House.

Paoline, E. A., Terrill, W., & Rossler, M. T. (2014). Higher education, college degree, major, and police occupational attitudes. *Journal of Criminal Justice Education, 26*(1), 49–73.

President's Commission on Law Enforcement and Administration of Justice. (1967). *The challenge of crime in a free society*. Washington, DC: United States Government Printing Office.

Quinney, R. (2001). *The social reality of crime*. New York, NY: Routledge.

Quinones, S. (2015). *Dreamland: A true tale of America's opiate epidemic*. New York, NY: Bloomberg Press.

Ryder, N. B., & Westoff, C. F. (1971). *Reproduction in the United States, 1965*. Princeton, NJ: Princeton University Press.

Wilson, J. Q. (1975). *Thinking about crime*. New York, NY: Basic Books, Inc.

ORIENTATION

PART I

THE IMPORTANCE OF ETHICS IN CRIMINAL JUSTICE

Cyndi Banks

I n criminal justice systems, the application of *ethical norms* has come to be recognized as a crucial part of the process of doing justice. Whether an action is performed by law enforcement, corrections, judges, lawyers or justice policy makers, we expect that decision-making will be ethical, and when it is not, we anticipate that those who violate ethical norms will be held accountable. The field of *normative ethics* sets standards of conduct to assist in determining how to act, and it draws on sources such as religions, natural law, and written law in shaping ethical standards. *Applied ethics* is concerned with resolving issues that raise questions concerning what is right or wrong and what is good or bad. Criminal justice professionals, who often possess the right to control others through the application of force and coercion, must understand how to act in situations where ethical dilemmas arise if they are to avoid accusations of abuse of their powers. Ethical theories about how to act and the rightness or wrongness of acts provide a foundation from which to analyze ethical dilemmas and arrive at a correct conclusion or resolution.

POLICE ETHICS

Of all the elements in criminal justice systems, policing is the most likely to provoke ethical dilemmas. In the early days of law enforcement in the United States, the police relied unhesitatingly on physical force and coercion to maintain control of the streets and paid little attention to ethical standards. An institutional culture, comprising the values, attitudes, and norms of law enforcement, developed throughout policing, and this culture encouraged and condoned corruption and the use of force, including lethal force, within the community. Research on policing began to identify the nature of policing and developed models and expectations of the crime fighter, the emergency operator, the social enforcer, and the social peacekeeper (Kleinig, 1996). Above all, commentators suggested that police themselves developed the notion that the cause of crime fighting was noble and therefore sometimes justified unethical conduct.

Police culture supported corruption, excessive use of force, a cynical and suspicious approach to the community, and the notion that police themselves were victims. Codes of ethics were devised, published, and promoted but were often flouted in favor of the noble cause (Crank & Caldero, 2000). Frequently, police managers reasoned that police abuse and corruption was caused by the individual acts of "rotten apples" and rejected explanations that these acts were indicative of systemic abuse. However, studies have shown that corruption and racism, in particular, are systemic within law enforcement, including, in particular, the tendency of police to stereotype persons in a practice known as *racial profiling* (Reiner, 1985; Skolnick, 1966; Walker et al., 2000, p. 95).

How do we explain instances of noble cause corruption within law enforcement? To a great extent, it can be linked to the extensive discretionary powers possessed by law enforcement that can be employed for good or bad ends and purposes. While opponents of broad police discretionary powers contend that the police should be limited by laws and internal rules, regulations, and codes of ethics, others argue that that curtailing discretion will impede crime fighting and endanger the community.

Generally, public opinion accepts broad policing discretionary powers, as long as those powers are not directed at them. Police misuse of force is a major issue in the exercise of police discretion and despite codes and rules of ethics that regulate its use, many situations place law enforcement in the position of having to make a determination about the degree and application of force and coercion. Of course, police may subsequently be accountable for rule violations, but by that time, innocent persons may have fatally suffered at their hands. Police culture and the influence of past histories of violence play an important part in determining the level of violence that law enforcement considers acceptable in any given policing situation. As well as force and coercion on the streets, police have powers over individual citizens during interrogation and investigation, and here, questions may arise about entrapment, the rights of persons apprehended by police, and practices like police lying and deception, which tend to be accepted modes of policing. Indeed, some argue that the public has no choice but to accept a certain level of police corruption and abuse in the interest of public safety and in serving the noble cause.

CASE STUDY: VIDEO SHOWS POLICE OFFICER USING BATON TO HIT MAN

On June 18, 2010, jurors in Manhattan watched a video showing a police officer, charged with assault, hitting a suspect with a baton over and over as he lay handcuffed on the floor of a housing project on West 93rd Street, Manhattan. Nevertheless, as the police officer's lawyer also pointed out, the video footage (shot from five different angles from lobby cameras) also shows the suspect, Walter Harvin, struggling with the officer David London, resisting his directions, and shoving him with his hands before the officer hit him.

Officer London has been charged with second-degree assault, filing false reports, falsifying business records, and making a false written statement; if convicted, he could face up to 7 years in prison.

The video shows Officer London in uniform, closing the door of the building and then opening it as he saw Mr. Harvin approaching. The prosecution claimed Mr. Harvin did not have his key, but when the officer asked him whether he lived there, Mr. Harvin ignored his questions. They exchanged words, and then Mr. Harvin pushed the officer's hand away and entered the building. The video then shows Mr. Harvin turning and pushing the officer with both hands as

he followed him in and tried to stop him. Officer London's partner came into the building, and then as Mr. Harvin stepped into the elevator, Officer London grabbed him and tried to spin him around. Mr. Harvin drew himself up, but Officer London took out his baton and struck Mr. Harvin near the face, causing him to fall to the ground. There, the officer began hitting him repeatedly with more than a dozen blows from his baton.

Mr. Harvin tried to avoid the blows until he was handcuffed by the two officers, and even after that, Officer London struck him again with the baton a few times. Officer London's lawyer claimed that Mr. Harvin had threatened to kill Officer London, but the prosecution said that even though Mr. Harvin should have cooperated with him, the fact that he did not was no justification for the beating he suffered and that Officer London used excessive force.

On June 28, 2010, Officer London was acquitted of the charges. Mr. Harvin, an Iraq war veteran, did not give evidence at the trial because he could not be located. Prosecutors indicated he had suffered some mental problems after returning to the United States from Iraq.

Source: Eligon, John. 2010, June 18. "Jurors Watch Video of Officer Hitting Man With a Baton." *The New York Times*, A16.

DISCRIMINATION

There is a consistent belief among many that racism exists in multiple forms within the justice system at certain decision-making points. This can be seen in decisions about who and when to arrest, in granting alleged offenders bail, in jury selection, and in conviction and sentencing. Numerous studies have shown that while there may not be systemic racism, individual acts of discrimination do take place at certain points within the criminal justice system where decisions are made and also that racism may be present in complex forms that are hidden from obvious view (Georges-Abeyie in Russell, 1998, p.32; Pope & Feyerherm, 1990). This means that all those who exercise decision-making powers within the system should always act ethically and make decisions that are free from explicit or implicit racial bias and discrimination.

CASE STUDY: IN DALLAS, DISMISSAL OF BLACK JURORS LEADS TO APPEAL BY DEATH ROW INMATE

Thomas Miller-El is an African American charged with shooting two white hotel clerks during a robbery in 1985. One of the hotel clerks died, and Miller-El, age 50, was due to be executed by the State of Texas in 2002. The 2005 Supreme Court case decided in Miller-El's favor (Death Penalty Information Center 2015). In 2002, he had asked the Texas Board of Pardons to commute his sentence and appealed his case to the U.S. Supreme Court on the grounds that the jury that convicted him was chosen using racial discriminatory standards that have been applied by the Dallas County district attorney's office in many cases. The district attorney's office opposed the appeal, arguing that there is no evidence of any racial discrimination.

The jury in the original trial comprised nine whites, one Filipino, one Hispanic, and one African American. Three other African Americans were excluded from the jury by prosecutors, as were seven of eight other African Americans interviewed as prospective jurors.

Racial discrimination in jury selection is prohibited by the Constitution, and until 1986, to establish race discrimination, an accused had to meet a heavy burden of proof because he or she had to show a pattern of discrimination. In 1986 in *Batson v. Kentucky*, the U.S. Supreme Court lowered the standard, determining that if the accused was able to show that the prosecution appeared to be using its peremptory challenges to jurors to exclude minorities, the trial judge could call for an explanation.

Miller-El was convicted and sentenced 1 month before the Batson ruling, but the decision applies to his case retroactively. To date, both state and federal courts have upheld his death sentence, determining that no racial discrimination occurred during jury selection. Miller-El's argument is that the courts considered only the number of challenges to jurors (10 out of 11 prospective African American jurors) and failed to consider other evidence showing that prosecutors in Dallas County had for years excluded blacks from juries as a matter of routine practice. This argument is supported by four former prosecutors whose terms of office cover the period from 1977 to 1989 and who confirmed that the Dallas County office did apply a policy of excluding blacks from juries. Further supporting this argument is a 1986 article in a local newspaper citing a 1963 internal memo in the district attorney's office advising prosecutors not to include "Jews, negroes, Dagos, Mexicans or a member of any minority race" as a jury member. Further, in the early 1970s, the prosecutor's office employed a training manual that contained advice on jury selection to the effect that a prosecutor should not include any member of a minority group because "they almost always empathize with the accused."

The *Dallas Morning News* has examined 15 capital murder trials from 1980 through 1986 and has revealed that prosecutors excluded 90% of African Americans qualified for jury selection. Nevertheless, the assistant district attorney in the Miller-El case disclaimed any notion that he had challenged the 10 African American jurors on grounds of race. He claimed that he was trying to assemble the best possible jury and that his office had no policy of racial discrimination. Despite these claims, at least three of the potential African American jurors challenged in the Miller-El case supported capital punishment and wanted to be on the jury.

Source: Rimer, Sara. 2002. February 13. "In Dallas, Dismissal of Black Jurors Leads to Appeal by Death Row Inmate." *The New York Times*.

LEGAL ETHICS

As professionals, lawyers are subject to detailed rules and codes about how to act in relation to their clients and to the justice system generally. For example, their duty to the court is specified, and there are particular rules about how prosecutors must conduct prosecutions and what tactics and strategies defense lawyers may or may not employ in representing their clients. Ethical norms are therefore highly developed within the legal profession, and accountability for violations is ensured through professional associations and the courts, both of which have the power to discipline and even disbar lawyers for unethical conduct. In cases where an ethical rule is unclear, a lawyer can seek advice from within the profession, which facilitates the task of keeping standards within the permissible boundaries regulating a lawyer's conduct and practice.

Among the general public, however, there is only very limited awareness of professional ethical rules and significant misunderstandings exist about the operation of the common law adversarial system of justice, a system that gives lawyers a good deal of control over the court process. For example, the public routinely faults defense lawyers for "defending persons they know to be guilty" based on a lack of understanding of the linkage between the protection of an accused persons rights and the role of the defense lawyer in ensuring those protections are enforced. Lawyers are required to adhere to the principles of partisanship and neutrality. They must put the interests of the client above the public good and, in representing a client, disregard questions of personal morality so that the client's interests always take precedence over those of the lawyer.

The primary duty of a prosecutor is not merely to secure a conviction but to ensure that justice is done. Prosecutorial work brings into play a special set of ethical issues that result from the wide discretion that prosecutors (like

CASE STUDY: PROSECUTOR WITHHOLDS EVIDENCE

In 2004, Ernest Ray Willis was released from death row after spending 17 years there for a crime he did not commit. He was convicted in 1987 of setting a house on fire and killing two women. During his trial, the prosecutor referred to him as a "rat," "an animal," "a mean vicious dog," and "a satanic demon." Jurors had to decide during the sentencing procedure whether Willis posed a future danger to society, and they answered in the affirmative and sentenced him to death.

It was discovered during a postconviction investigation that a state psychologist had examined Willis before trial and reported that he would not present much of a future danger to society, but this information, which could have helped him avoid a death sentence, was never given to his lawyer. However, the prosecutor did know of this report because a FedEx record showed that it had been delivered to his office; additionally, the psychologist remembered personally meeting with the prosecutor and advising him that Willis would not make a convincing death penalty case. The prosecutor has denied lying about the psychologist or the report.

A federal judge ordered the state to retry Willis or set him free, determining that suppressing the report plus other factors violated his rights. Following the investigation, the new district attorney requested Willis's immediate release from jail. The original prosecutor maintains that Willis was guilty and has no second thoughts about his prosecution of the case.

Source: Gier, Kelly. 2006. "Prosecuting Injustice: Consequences of Misconduct." *American Journal of Criminal Law,* 33(2), 192.

the police) enjoy in the operation of functions such as deciding what crime to indict persons with and the practice of plea bargaining. As well, the right of the prosecutor to determine, within a limited framework of rules, what evidence is to be put before the court and what evidence is made available to the defense can give rise to serious ethical conflicts. In the United States, many prosecutors are elected officials, and this raises further ethical issues including community pressures about how to exercise the prosecutorial function in the context of promises made and expectations raised during the election process. Whether the primary concern is for the victim, the community, reelection, or discovering "the truth," prosecutors must make choices and decide their constituency, either generally or in a particular case. The likelihood that judges and prosecutors may become corrupt or act unethically likely increases according to the extent to which they enjoy wide discretionary powers. However, because judges generally perform their functions transparently and in public, the risks of impropriety are reduced. The same cannot be said about prosecutors who conduct much of their business behind closed doors and do not open processes such as plea bargaining to public scrutiny.

PUNISHMENT

What is the ethical rationale for punishment and how do we justify its imposition? The sociological approach to understanding why we punish focuses on how the current modes of thinking affect the climate of tolerance and intolerance. Social theories about punishment treat it as a social phenomenon and explore relations between punishment and society. Philosophical theories apply utilitarian and retributive theories asking questions about the goals of punishment and its overall purpose. According to these theories, punishment is justified according to theories of deterrence, retribution, just deserts, rehabilitation, incapacitation, and restorative justice. Many believe that punishment deters crimes of both repeat offenders and potential offenders. Deterrence theory was first proposed by utilitarian philosophers who contended that it is the fear of the consequences of criminal actions that deters crime. However, numerous studies have failed to show conclusively that deterrence works, partly based on the fact that much crime does not seem to be committed based upon a rational decision weighed on the basis of the potential consequences (Beyleveld, 1979, cited in Hudson, 1996, p. 23; Ten, 1987, p. 9; Blumstein, Cohen, & Nagin, 1978, p. 66).

The theory of retribution contends that punishment can be justified because it is deserved and that persons ought to be held accountable for acts that harm society. Retributionists argue that the punishment imposed should always be proportionate to the wrongdoing, a standpoint known as *just deserts*. Retribution is considered justified in terms of criminals owing and paying a debt to society, that society ought to censure those who violate its norms and rules and that punishment has an expressive function (in that society is expressing its condemnation of an offender) that ought to be communicated to an offender.

Retribution or just deserts theory, began to gain ground over alternative versions of the purpose and justification of punishment in the 1980s. It has emerged as the premier rationale for punishment and, consistent with its emphasis on proportionality, has led to the development of sentencing guidelines and sentencing commissions charged with determining the extent of punishment that ought to be imposed for a particular crime. It focuses only on the harm involved in the crime and the culpability of the offender. Critics of just deserts argue that it lacks any principled basis for determining commensurate sentences for crimes and completely ignores social and other factors that ought to be taken into account in arriving at an appropriate sentence (Hudson, 1996, p. 46; Tonry, 1994, p. 153). Critics of retribution argue that it is nothing more than vengeance, but Nozick (1981, p. 366) points out that unlike retribution, revenge possesses no limits and may be inflicted on an innocent person, perhaps a relative, and not necessarily on the offender.

The concept of rehabilitation is that punishment ought to be concerned with healing an offender so that he or she may return to society after punishment with little or no chance of becoming a repeat offender. Crime is regarded as a social disease to be treated and cured. In order to determine the appropriate punishment the offender's social and economic background must be fully taken into consideration.

Previously, indeterminate sentences were imposed that made the release of the offender contingent on the successful completion of rehabilitation programs. The decision to release was exercised by boards based on their assessment of an individual's progress through rehabilitation and was not determined exclusively by the court. In the 1970s, opinion turned against rehabilitation as the proper rationale and basis for determining punishment when meta-studies of rehabilitation programs purported to show that "nothing works" (Martinson, 1974). The discredited rationale of rehabilitation was replaced with the now dominant theories of just deserts and incapacitation.

Incapacitation theorists argue that the public ought to be protected from the chance of future offending by those who are already convicted criminals and that placing offenders in custody for lengthy periods of time is justified in pursuit of this end. Opponents of incapacitation contend that offenders are therefore being punished on the basis of predictions of their likely future conduct and that this is arbitrary, unfair, and entirely speculative (Morris, 1994, p. 241). They question the ethics of punishing persons for crimes they have yet to commit.

Restorative justice proponents emphasize community involvement in determining an appropriate punishment and maintain that a process through which a victim confronts the offender with the harm suffered will help restore that offender to the community with an enhanced capacity to support social cohesion and not reoffend. Restorative justice calls for a return to community punishment practices that disappeared with the emergence of the state as the exclusive authority for administering punishment and providing solutions to crime. This form of justice has generally been employed to deal with minor offenses but has been accepted in some jurisdictions as the most appropriate means of punishing juvenile delinquency.

CORRECTIONAL ETHICS

Over the last two decades, criminal justice policies focusing on crime control, including so-called "zero-tolerance" practices and incapacitating offenders for very lengthy periods of time under laws such as "three strikes and you're out" have caused an explosion in the size of the prison population (Harrison & Beck, 2003). Commentators now regularly describe U.S. policy as favoring "mass imprisonment" (Christie, 2000).

Within justice systems, police and corrections officers have always been empowered to exercise a degree of physical control over citizens, and now, contemporary crime control strategies bring even greater numbers of citizens into direct contact with law enforcement and corrections staff. Heightened tensions between the public and criminal justice officials arising from policies of mass imprisonment make it essential that ethical standards of treatment and conduct are observed in prisons and jails.

Similar to law enforcement, corrections work possesses an institutional culture that has developed over time in conjunction with changes in prison operations, staffing, and disciplinary regimes. An understanding of that culture is vital to an appreciation of the ethical challenges faced by corrections staff. The organization and management of corrections developed from early individualistic methods of controlling persons in custody to fully fledged bureaucratic and managerialist regimes of control with detailed rules and procedures covering both prison staff and those incarcerated and the permitted interactions between them. Historically, prisoners had few rights and were treated harshly and with high levels of brutality, but in the contemporary period, prisoners regularly test the scope and content of their rights in the courts. How does ethics relate to corrections when prisoners are in custody, sometimes under maximum-security conditions and sometimes within lightly guarded facilities? Commentators argue that a person is sent to prison "as" punishment and not "for" punishment, and this means that practices such as highly controlled visitation, strip searches, and punishing prisoners through removal of so-called privileges should be prohibited because they amount to the imposition of additional and unauthorized sanctions (Kleinig, 2001, p. 7). Adopting an ethical standard would therefore mean respecting the dignity, humanity, and rights of prisoners, as well as refraining from imposing any further forms of punishment.

The nature of the relationship between guards and prisoners and between guards and their coworkers also raises questions about normative conduct. It is obvious that there is a significant power dynamic between inmates and guards. Guards, in the absence of rules that incorporate ethical standards and norms, potentially have the power to seriously abuse prisoners (Kleinig, 2001, p. 10). Guards are required to demonstrate an ability to manage prisoners but must also accept that they are dependent on having good relations with prisoners in order to protect their personal safety. Guards possess a personal authority derived from character and personality, as well as a legal authority, the source of which are institutional rules and regulations. Therefore, an ethical framework that regulates these interactions is required. One extreme school of thought argues, however, that the nature of incarceration is such that it is virtually impossible to apply ethical standards of conduct and that degradation and brutality are inescapable (Smith, 2001, p. 30).

Research has revealed the prison guard code and the "gray wall of silence" that incorporate key tenets of the business of guarding, including, "always aid an officer in distress," "don't rat," and "never make a fellow officer look bad in front of inmates" (Kauffman, 1988, pp. 86–117). The institutional culture of corrections valorizes the dangers and tensions of incarceration and how these elements combine to engender a sense of suspicion about events in a facility that are out of the ordinary or seem to be violations of prison rules. However, research reveals that guards, despite their apparent absolute dominance, in fact, must negotiate the extent of their domination with inmates through a process of contestation (Lombardo, 1989, p. 94). This process can result in the "corruption of authority" and means that rulebooks are often jettisoned in the interests of flexibility and of establishing a modus vivendi. Similar to law enforcement, individual discretion and its exercise are an important part of being a guard and are influenced by the guard culture and by relevant rules and the overall prison disciplinary regime. Studies of this culture reveal that corrections industry recruits are socialized into adhering to the elements of the prison guard code, which focuses on solidarity between coworkers against inmates (Kaufman, 1988, p. 198).

The use of force by corrections staff is a major ethical issue within corrections. In the past, violence was prevalent and expected. Nowadays, despite rules regulating the application of force and accountability, including actions in the courts, some prison systems continue to permit extralegal levels of coercion and force against inmates. The guard culture contends that force is always justified because only the threat of violence or violence itself will ensure control within the facility, and violence deters inmate attacks on guards (Kaufman, 1988, p. 141).

Reprisals for attacks by inmates are considered essential and entirely appropriate within the guard culture. Nevertheless, there is also an appreciation within corrections that violence begets more violence and that inmate resistance cannot be repressed by the constant application of force (Kaufman, 1988, p. 71). Nowadays, the use of force is regulated by rules and by the courts, the state, and the federal government. Other forms of conduct that violate ethical norms include institutional and guard attitudes toward rape in prison and the promotion of corruption through smuggling, drug trafficking, and similar activity.

CASE STUDY: SEXUAL ASSAULT AT WOMEN'S PRISON IN ALABAMA

In May 2015, the U.S. Department of Justice announced it had reached an agreement with the state of Alabama to compel the state to carry out reforms at the maximum-security Julia Tutwiler Prison for Women at Wetumpka, Alabama, where inmates had for many years been subjected to sexual assaults, including rape, sodomy, forced oral sex, and fondling at the hands of prison staff. The Tutwiler Prison opened in 1942 and was named after Julia Tutwiler, a prison reformer and advocate for improved conditions in women's prisons.

In January 2014, the Justice Department issued a letter with its findings that the prison had subjected female prisoners to a "pattern or practice" of sexual abuse in violation of the Eighth Amendment's prohibition on cruel and unusual punishment.

Justice Department investigators found that prison staff helped organize a "strip show" for prisoners, that male staff openly watched women shower and use toilet facilities, that women who reported abuse were commonly placed in segregation with limited or no access to a telephone or visitors, and that complaints of abuse often resulted in punishment and threats of physical abuse by staff. It was found that prison staff treated women who reported sexual abuse "with the presumption that they were lying, subjecting them to polygraph examinations as a prerequisite to investigating the allegation."

Source: "Justice Department Acts to End Sexual Assault at a Women's Prison in Alabama," Sari Horwitz, *The Washington Post*, May 28, 2015.

Probation and parole were originally linked to plans for the individualized treatment of prisoners, but in their contemporary form, they are focused almost exclusively on punishment and enforcement of court sanctions (Petersilia, 1999, p. 480). Parole officers have always been closer to law enforcement. Now, probation officers are adopting a police posture toward probationers, as many are now armed and often collaborate with law enforcement officers in raiding premises. Accordingly, both probation and parole officers exercise substantial degrees of control over probationers and parolees and face ethical concerns similar to those in corrections and law enforcement.

ETHICAL CRIMINAL JUSTICE POLICY MAKING

Crime control and how to punish offenders are key elements of justice policy making. For example, the development of private prisons as an option for punishment is an important issue in criminal justice policy and raises significant ethical issues, such as whether the state or government should ever permit outside agencies to punish citizens, whether the profit motive is compatible with the exercise of the right to inflict punishment through incarceration, and how private prisons resolve issues connected with the use of force.

Ethical considerations ought to play a significant role in criminal justice policy making, but since the 1970s, this enterprise has typically been more concerned with formulating punitive policies rather than with examining alternative options for punishment and exploring the ethical basis for certain policy approaches.

Most policy making is the outcome of a cost–benefit analysis, and that process does not generally incorporate ethical models or arguments. Normally, it is essential in designing policies to advance a justification for a particular approach to a policy issue. Policies may be justified on ideological, empirical, or ethical grounds. Those grounded in an ethical approach are analyzed under a process that has determined the "rightness or wrongness," or the "good or bad" of a particular approach.

There are two central concerns. First, it is necessary that policy makers should always act ethically in formulating policies, and secondly, there exists an ethical responsibility in making policy about subjects like punishment that have inherently ethical requirements. This latter kind of policy making can be termed "morality policy making," and there is a clear linkage in contemporary policy making between morality policy making and so called "moral panics" (Mooney 2001, p. 116). A moral panic arises when an event is constructed and portrayed as a danger or menace to society and its values. Good examples are the various "wars" declared by different administrations—for example, the war on poverty, the war on drugs, and the war on terrorism. Media—and therefore, public attention to particular forms of criminality—have influenced mandatory minimum sentencing, the war on drugs, truth-in-sentencing laws, and legislation designed to combat sexual predators and superpredators. The media frequently construct issues like drug abuse as moral panics, and the outcome is often badly conceived laws that are fundamentally unethical. The present mass incarceration of offenders is the result of policy choices based on converging policies and decisions that cannot be said to represent a rational and coherent response to crime.

Elected officials and representatives who react hastily to perceived constituency concerns and to the views of the general public, which are themselves, heavily influenced by media representations of an issue as a moral panic, usually formulate policies. Surveys have revealed that the public has a general tendency toward favoring punitive measures toward offenders. In the U.S., imprisonment is generally regarded as the appropriate form of punishment for most criminality but this is not so in other western countries where minor crimes are punished much more leniently. As for the ultimate penalty of capital punishment, which is a major moral issue for many, it has found steady support since the 1970s, and this is usually reflected in political platforms and in legislative approaches to punishment.

An ethical responsibility includes an obligation to act with integrity. For example, a legislator can be said to act unethically when he or she proposes changes in legislation in the expectation that such action will ensure his or her reelection, knowing that it is unlikely to achieve its aims and might even cause fresh injustice. Other acts of policy making that could be considered unethical include

CASE STUDY: PRISON AND AMENITIES

What standards and conditions should be applied to imprisonment? The topic of what level of amenities should be supplied to prisoners resurfaces in the media periodically. Those politicians who wish to demonstrate a "tough-on-crime" approach protest that prisoners are provided access to weight-lifting equipment, televisions, radios and "good" food (Banks, 2005, p. 137). In Maricopa County, Arizona, former sheriff Joe Arpaio's policies of housing inmates in tents without air conditioning in the more than 110°F summer weather, clothing inmates in pink underwear and striped uniforms, chain gangs for both men and women, and providing basic and unappealing food such as bologna on dry bread exemplify this attitude. Such politicians argue that if prisoners have standards of incarceration that are superior to the standard of living of the man on the street, then they cannot be said to be suffering punishment. The media fuel this debate by reporting that prisons are "holiday resorts" where prisoners enjoy extravagant amenities and conditions (see Lenz, 2002). In response to this political discourse, the No Frills Prison Act was passed in 1996; it bans televisions, coffeepots, and hot plates in the cells of federal prisoners. It also prohibits computers, electronic instruments, certain movies rated above PG, and unmonitored phone calls (Lenz, 2002).

The underpinning assumption to this legislation is that a deterrent effect will be achieved "by making a sentence more punitive, that is, making the inmate suffer more" (Banks, 2005, p. 138). Thus, it is assumed that an inmate will be "less inclined to reoffend knowing the harsh conditions in prison" (p. 138). The problem is that there is no existing research that can support this assumption. Some have argued that state costs are saved to the prison system and to the taxpayers through this approach, but again, this is not supported given that the 31 states that allow inmates televisions in their cells do not pay for them (prisoners or their relatives pay for them), and cablevision is paid for out of profits from the prison commissary, vending machines, and long-distance telephone charges (Finn, 1996, pp. 6–7).

Interestingly, prison administrators are often in favor of permitting amenities in the prisons because staff rely heavily on a system of rewards and punishments to maintain control in their institutions (Lenz, 2002, p. 506). They recognize that keeping inmates busy provides important benefits to inmate order and inmate activities. In other words, bored and unhappy prisoners are more likely to cause security problems that staff who are in short supply will have to respond to.

Placing telephone calls from prison to wives, husbands, and relatives used to be an inexpensive process, and until the 1990s, inmates could place and receive calls at rates similar to those charged outside. This might be considered a basic amenity for all inmates. Now, however, the prison telephone system has been turned over to private enterprise and is a $1.2-billion-a-year industry. Companies in this business commonly set rates and fees greatly in excess of those charged by commercial providers to persons outside prisons. After a series of complaints, the Federal Communications Commission (FCC) commenced an investigation. The practice is for phone companies to pay hundreds of millions of dollars ($460 million in 2013) in concession fees to state and local correctional systems for exclusive contracts to control the telephone services offered in prisons. According to the FCC, the fees, which are legal, are used to fund a range of prison costs from inmate welfare to salaries, and some end up in the revenue funds of the state concerned. Eliminating the fees has been fiercely opposed by prison and jail officials. In one case, a company fee for using its prison phone service included a charge for processing the bill and another charge if the bill was paid over the telephone (Williams, 2015).

responding to a particular event or series of events by formulating policies that are arbitrary, lack reason or good judgment, and have failed to take account of relevant ethical considerations.

CASE STUDY: ANTI-MUSLIM RACIAL PROFILING ON PLANES MUST STOP

- Khairuldeen Makhzoom, a student at the University of California Berkeley, was kicked off a Southwest Airlines flight after a fellow passenger complained about his use of Arabic. An Arabic-speaking Southwest employee allegedly asked him, "Why would you speak in Arabic on the airplane? It's dangerous. You know the environment around the airport. You understand what's going on in this country." Makhzoom was then searched publicly while a crowd in the airport terminal watched, and he was interrogated by the FBI.

- Hakima Abdulle, who was wearing a hijab, was removed from a Southwest Airlines flight after a flight attendant told her she could not switch seats with another passenger. The flight attendant later said she "did not feel comfortable" with Abdulle.

- Three Muslim passengers and one Sikh passenger were removed from an American Airlines flight after the captain and crew reportedly "felt uneasy and uncomfortable with their presence on the flight and as such, refused to fly unless they were removed from the flight."

Source: CREDO Action. https://act.credoaction.com/sign/Stop_Airline_Profiling

The so-called "war on terrorism" provokes significant ethical questions and issues. A central issue concerns the normative considerations applicable to the war on terrorism. Questions include why the U.S. declared such a war after September 11, and created a special prosecution and detention regime for alleged terrorists instead of giving the criminal justice system the responsibility for responding to those acts. After all, terrorist acts normally constitute offenses under the criminal law and can be prosecuted and punished as such. Another issue concerns the extent to which, if at all, torture or so-called "enhanced interrogation" can be applied to alleged terrorists in custody, even in the cause of averting further acts of terrorism.

Third, there is the question of the extent to which rights and freedoms ought to be restricted within the U.S. in order to fight the war on terrorism. The argument in this case is that we ought to be prepared to surrender some or even all of those rights and freedoms in the interest of reducing the risk of further acts of terrorism. Those rights include privacy and freedom from intrusive surveillance. Furthermore, pursuing the war on terrorism requires the establishment of specially constituted courts or military commissions to undertake the trials of alleged terrorists raising the further question of what legal protections and rights those accused should enjoy before such courts or commissions. These are complex issues that impact fundamental values and ethical norms.

The difficulties of ethical terrorism policy making are compounded by questions concerning the fact that there is no single "correct" definition of terrorism and that the nature of the war on terrorism has been shaped almost entirely by the events of September 11. It is clear that although termed a "war" in the same way that previous initiatives were described as a war on crime or a war on drugs, the war on terrorism is aligned much more to a conventional war but lacks its attributes. Policy makers have constructed the war on terrorism not as an issue of crime control but as involving issue of national security and, in doing so, have sought to justify exceptional measures, such as illegal international rendition and techniques that some have termed torture (Ackerman, 2004). By defining the campaign against terrorists as a war, the Bush administration justified measures such as the USA PATRIOT Act, which significantly increased surveillance powers over citizens and diminished individual rights and freedoms. The debate is concerned with whether such measures are ethically appropriate in all its circumstances. Some argue that such measures are immoral simply because they disregard customary and international rules concerning the treatment of detainees (by categorizing them as "unlawful combatants"), the rules of war, humanitarian laws of war, and prohibitions against torture and degrading treatment (Emcke, 2005, p. 237).

It has also been argued that depicting a counterterrorist strategy as warfare has the effect of elevating the level of activity inferior to that normally required by actual conventional warfare as if it were a conventional war between states. Thus, through this process of categorization, the U.S. has somehow been empowered to conduct "battles" within the ambit of a never-ending war. For example, in the pursuit of the war on terrorism, the U.S. deploys unmanned aircraft or drones in the air space of another state's territories, without that state's knowledge, in order to conduct assassinations of "known" terrorists. Sometimes these attacks cause so-called "collateral damage" to civilians, and some ask whether it is ethically correct to cause injury and death to innocent civilians in this way and whether the effects of this strategy actually mimic the acts of the terrorists themselves (Wilkinson, 2001, p. 23). Therefore, some argue that the war on terrorism might, in fact, constitute an evil that is greater than terrorism itself (Wilkinson, 2001, p. 115). In defending the war and its consequence, some suggest that so long as citizens can rely on the legislature and the courts for oversight, there is sufficient protection against excess (Ignatieff, 2004, p. 8). Yet others point to the lack of executive transparency and the administration's active concealment of surveillance activities that have only come to light through the activities of whistleblowers. In other words, the modern state has the capacity, if it possesses the will, to conduct a wide range of activities in pursuit of a goal that it alone deems critical to public interest and that many would judge illegal—and certainly immoral or unethical.

ANALYZING ETHICAL DILEMMAS

Ethical theories attempt to provide a means to respond to critical ethical questions such as, "How ought I to act in this situation?" Thus, for criminal justice professionals, ethical theories provide a foundation and a source of knowledge about how to go about the business of acting ethically in everyday situations. They help provide structure in an otherwise complex environment. A number of ethical theories exist, each offering a varying perspective and approach to ethical dilemmas. It is necessary, therefore, to be aware of the various arguments and perspectives to fully engage with the analysis and resolution of ethical issues. The principal ethical theories are deontology and consequentialism (also termed utilitarianism). However, more recently, virtue ethics has gained a foothold in ethical theorizing. Less significant theories include the Greek theories of hedonism, stoicism, and ethical egoism. Contemporary theorists such as John Rawls (1973) and Carol Gilligan (1982) have added social justice and feminist ethics (also termed the ethics of care) to the theoretical vocabulary.

Principles, Consequences, or Character?

The principal theories of deontology and consequentialism take contrasting positions on the question of how we ought to conduct ourselves in varying situations when faced with the question, "How ought I to act?" Consequentialists believe that the task of identifying the right way to act in a given situation always depends on the goodness of the consequences of acting in a particular way for everyone affected. Therefore, consequentialism always looks at outcomes in determining the proper course of action.

In contrast, deontology rejects consequentialism and argues that rules and principles that place limits on our activities and actions ought to guide us in making ethical decisions. Thus, it argues that certain acts are always wrong in themselves and lack moral support and cannot be employed to justify pursuing any ends, even those ends that are morally sound. For example, deontologists absolutely reject the act of lying and argue that lies are wrong because of their nature even if they result in or produce good consequences. Deontologists emphasize notions of obligation and duty and believe, for example, that it is right to keep promises regardless of the effects of carrying them out. Often, applying the primary theories will result in similar moral outcomes. For example, a deontologist will argue that stealing goods or breaking promises is always wrong and a consequentialist would come to the same conclusion but for different reasons, arguing that it is the consequences of such acts on the public welfare that renders them wrong, not their inherent wrongness. Conflicts will arise between these theories, however, when performing an act normally considered unethical results in an increase in the utility achieved in the result.

Aristotle's virtue ethics has enjoyed resurgence in ethical theorizing partly because the two principal theories seem to offer little except a choice between a focus on the consequences or a set of absolute rules about how to act. Virtue theories aim to provide us with a picture of the good life and how it can be realized. A good life was seen as one in which one's full potential as a human person is satisfied. This contrasts with more modern ethical theories, which see the good life and morality as separate notions. To the ancient Greek virtue theorists, the chief goal was to achieve a good life and realize our true nature, and to them, satisfying this aim was the test of the moral worth of a particular act.

From the 16th century onward, these concepts were abandoned, and modern ethical thinking has discouraged notions of final ends and purposes and the concept of the good life. Postmodernism has also impacted ethical thinking, and Bauman (1993), for example, argues that there are few ethical choices that can be considered as absolutely good or correct and that such choices are largely based on the application of impulses. He argues that uncertainty and ambivalence, which are the characteristics of postmodernism, apply equally to morality (itself diverse in nature, irrational, and subject to the exercise of power relations) so that moral codes are often the outcome of political claims of universalism. Richard Rorty goes further than this, arguing that philosophy itself is dead in the sense that claims to universal rules and principles are no longer possible or accepted in contemporary societies (Rumana, 2000, p. 4).

A Matter of Principle

Immanuel Kant is regarded as one of the greatest modern philosophers and as most responsible for shaping and explaining deontology. In answering the question, "What ought I to do?" Kant believed that a person should categorically act in a rational manner and in accordance with duty and obligation and take no account of the consequences of acting (Benn, 1998, p. 172). Kant expressed this notion as the *categorical imperative* and contended that all other considerations were irrelevant. This notion gives rise to the question of how to determine the nature and extent of a duty or obligation. Kant's response to this was to state that it could be determined by applying the test of whether an individual is willing that a particular act be followed by *all* persons at all times. If so, this gives the act the status of a rule, and it withstands the test of a universal law. Although this seems straightforward, it can pose difficulties. For example, Kant stated that the rule against lying was a categorical imperative, and therefore, it was wrong to lie under any circumstances (Rachels, 1999a, p. 125). In reality, however, a person may lie when faced with moral choices about how to act, such as when it is both wrong to lie and wrong to allow innocent people to be murdered. Thus, two categorical imperatives may conflict with each other. How then should this conflict be resolved? One suggestion is to treat moral rules not as absolute categorical rules but as generalizations. This would mean that while we should generally always refrain from telling lies, we may abrogate this rule if factors exist that should override this imperative.

Kant advanced the important notion that we should always respect others because they are rational human beings with dignity (Hill, 2000, p. 64). Thus, a person should not be treated as a means to an end but as an end in himself or herself. Thus, we ought not to use people to satisfy our own ends; we should always respect others' rights, promote their welfare, and avoid causing them harm. In this way, we will be promoting the worth and dignity of every person, as, for example, in the criminal justice process, where the right to a fair trial is afforded. This rule would also require that prisoners be treated with dignity, compassion, and humanity.

Considering the Consequences

Consequentialists or utilitarians look to the consequences of an act to determine their rightness or wrongness and disregard all other considerations. The question to ask when faced with an ethical question or dilemma is, therefore, which action will bring about the best possible consequences for everyone affected? This principle is known as the principle of utility, and it imposes a duty to act in ways that produce the greatest happiness for everyone affected. Underlying this theory is the thinking of the classical utilitarians, Bentham and Mill, who regarded happiness as equivalent to pleasure and believed that humans look for pleasure and try to avoid pain, which explains how we make choices about how to act (Rachels, 1999b, p. 65). More recent thinking substitutes the idea of "preference satisfaction" for "happiness," so that we should not aim for pleasure over pain but instead should determine how we can best satisfy human preferences, interests, or desires.

Utilitarians can be categorized as *act utilitarians* and *rule utilitarians*. The former argue that it is possible to measure whether an act causes more pleasure than pain and therefore whether it has more "utility." Given the complications in applying such a rule, act utilitarians follow rules of thumb that rely on past experience. Rule utilitarians link consequentialism with moral rules and contend that following specific moral rules will result in better consequences. Thus, rule consequentialism aligns, to an extent, with deontology. An example of rule utilitarianism is that it is generally better to follow the rule that one should speak the truth even when it means that doing so in a specific instance would cause more pain than pleasure on the basis that, in the long term, telling the truth produces greater benefits overall. Consequentialism is criticized for placing the outcome of an action above the ideals of justice. Also, critics argue that it would require us to give all our resources to others because such an act would promote the general welfare and pleasure of others.

It can be seen that the choice between duty and consequences involves evaluating absolute rules about conduct against a calculation as to which act will provide the most pleasure for the greatest number of people. Consequentialism enjoys a primary role in punishment policy making in the form of the theory that argues that punishment deters crime. It is claimed that imposing more severe penalties for certain crimes to deter others from committing similar crimes benefits everyone.

A Question of Character?

Virtue ethics does not ask, "What ought I to do?" but, "What kind of person should I become?" According to virtue theorists, the correct course of action can only be determined once that question has been answered. Virtues comprise those personal qualities that we develop through habitual action and that aid us to become persons of excellent character during our lives. Virtues are natural and acquired qualities, such as intelligence, honesty, generosity, loyalty, integrity, dignity, and self-control.

In contrast to deontology's absolute prohibition on lying and consequentialism's acquiescence in lying if the consequences are beneficial, virtue ethics takes the position that lying is dishonest and that dishonesty is a vice, not a virtue. Virtue ethics can, however, be problematic. For example, when a suicide bomber gives his life for a cause he or she believes in, is he or she acting courageously? If being generous is a virtue, how generous is one required to be? Aristotle believed that a good life included happiness in the form of well-being or flourishing and that virtues promote such happiness (Tessitore, 1996, p. 20). Aristotle thought that we should always act in ways that will bring about flourishing, and he advanced the notion of the mean or the golden mean, which means that when required to make decisions, we should seek the mean or the average between extremes. An example is not being too stingy or too lavish but generous, that is to say, the golden mean. It is easy to see how this idea can be applied to everyday ethical behavior. When applied to questions of conduct, this idea would advocate a middle course between forms of radical action.

Aristotle also advocated the notion of practical wisdom, which involves thinking about the circumstances, reasoning correctly, and making the right choices. Those who live with practical wisdom are said to have a kind of insight or perception that guides them in making the right decisions (Darwell, 1998, p. 213). Critics argue that virtue ethics has to be regarded as contextually and historically tied to an ancient time period, namely Athenian society of the fifth century, which took it for granted that virtues were possessed only by those with great wealth and high social status (MacIntyre, 1984, p. 11). Women and slaves were not considered human, and therefore, virtue ethics could not apply to them. Even so, modern philosophers attracted by virtue ethics and its focus on character link it to modern-day social life and the community, emphasizing the need to learn virtues within the family and the community (Blum, 1996, pp. 232–233). As for Aristotle's list of virtues, while some see it as arbitrary, others argue for the universality of virtue, whatever the nature of a society or its culture (Hinman, 1998, pp. 334–335).

A major criticism of virtue ethics is that it gives us no guidance about how to act in relation to ethical issues. For example, it provides no assistance about ethical questions like the imposition of capital punishment. However, in favor of virtue ethics, it can be argued that it fulfills an essential role in supplementing other ethical approaches that provided us guidance in deciding how to act (Rachels, 1999a, p. 189). It is also claimed that developing and possessing a virtuous character or a moral self is a prerequisite for resolving ethical dilemmas. Some modern philosophers argue that virtue ethics can stand alone as the ethical basis for ethical action because an action will be correct and moral if taken by a virtuous person acting in character in particular circumstances (Hursthouse, 1999, p. 26). Of course, virtue ethics seems very relevant to the criminal justice system, where power and authority are susceptible to abuse.

Indifference, Pleasure, or Selfishness?

The ethical theories of stoicism, ethical egoism, and hedonism do not enjoy much support among moral philosophers, despite the fact that egoism and hedonism, in their celebration of self-gratification, might be said to resonate with the values of modern consumer society. Stoicism is historically specific, like virtue ethics, and contends that the path to virtue lies in adopting an attitude of indifference toward external differences and in cultivating a life of indifference, accepting that while some things are within our power to change and influence, others are not (Prior, 1991, p. 209). Stoics believe in predestiny and the notion that whatever happens has a rational explanation and is always for the best. In some respects, stoicism echoes the claims of virtue ethics about individual character because stoics argue that developing the appropriate stoic frame of mind leads to virtue.

Hedonism comes in the forms of psychological hedonism and ethical hedonism. The former imagines a life devoted to the pursuit of pleasure and assumes that all action aims to achieve pleasure and avoid pain. Ethical hedonism is a moral version of hedonism and asserts that seeking pleasure is right conduct because pleasure alone is good (Feldman, 1997, p. 109). In this sense, hedonism seems unsatisfactory because it is difficult to accept that seeking pleasure can constitute the sole basis for deciding ethical issues. The theory of ethical egoism contends that right action is action that promotes one's own self-interest regardless of the interests or concerns of others.

Egoism is categorized as psychological egoism and ethical egoism. The former holds that all persons are motivated by and act according to egoist concerns. It rejects all altruistic explanations of behavior and contends that acts that may seem unselfish are always performed for egotistical reasons. An ethical egoist argues similarly that morality and reason are satisfied by promoting one's own greatest good and self-interest before anyone else's. The focus on self-interest does not exclude action that might help others as long as the primary goal is our own interests.

Ethical egoism as a theory seems to lack a principled foundation, and some argue that it resembles racism in its attention to the interests of one group alone (Rachels, 1999a, p. 94). Others suggest that it precludes any development of sustained relations between persons because an ethical egoist is so focused on his or her own good that this precludes acts such as assisting those in need unless such action first served a self-interest (Hinman, 1998, p. 154). In terms of criminal justice, ethical egoism would seem to supply justification for acts that are corrupt or inhumane.

Social Justice

John Rawls's (1973) theories seek to fix fundamental principles that would govern a morally good society, and in this sense, his search for a set of rules is Kantian in nature. His concern is not with the individual ethical actor so much as with justice in the sense of fairness, and he regards justice as a founding principle capable of providing guidance concerning how a society should conduct itself. According to Rawls, a moral person is one who possesses a sense of justice and the potential to pursue a concept of good (p. 121). Achieving this potential requires us to create a just society and to agree on its governing principles.

Rawls (1973) imagines a group of persons who collectively agree on the nature of this society from a position of ignorance about their class or social position and without taking account of any natural assets or abilities. His argument is that they would choose two principles of justice, one concerned with the equal right to basic liberties and the other with social and economic inequalities (p. 60). The first principle would provide personal liberties such as the right to vote and stand for public office and freedom of speech and assembly. The second principle, part of which is known as the *difference principle*, would comprise an equal distribution of primary goods and services, as well as burdens and responsibilities. However, certain inequalities would be considered just if they benefit everyone, especially the least advantaged (p. 75). Thus, there would be no injustice if the least advantaged were better off in an unequal situation than they would be with equality. Consequently, a just society that desires to treat all with equality would give more attention to those victimized by injustice or to those who enjoy a less favorable position because of unfair treatment. This echoes the Kantian principle that persons should always be treated as ends in themselves and not as means to an end.

Rawls (1973) sees his principles as purely hypothetical but nevertheless argues that they would be accepted by free and rational persons and would make explicit his notion of "justice as fairness" (p. 11). Rawls describes three stages of moral development in a life, beginning with the *morality of authority* developed by parents, then the *morality of association* arising through contact with the school and the neighborhood, and then the *morality of principles* where individuals follow moral positions as a result of earlier moral development and because they seek the approval of the wider society (pp. 473–476). Rawls suggests that in a society that seeks to achieve social justice, his principles will create harmony and cooperation and reduce injustice. In terms of relevance to the criminal justice system and its institutions, Rawlsian notions of social justice assist in overcoming inequalities in access to justice, as well as forms of discrimination within the system.

The Ethic of Care

Feminist ethical theories focus on the centrality of gender and are critical of other established theoretical approaches for giving too much prominence to the individual, to impartiality, and to universality (Hinman, 1998, pp. 367–369). Feminist theories give importance to relationships, care, and connectiveness. Seminal research by Carol Gilligan and Lawrence Kohlberg argue that moral development varies according to gender and that gender shapes the nature of moral inquiry (Hinman, 1998, p. 370). Thus, Gilligan contends that women see moral life in terms of care and responsibility, asking if relationships would be maintained or harm suffered because of an intended action, whereas men see the application of rules in a fair, impartial, and equal manner as the prime consideration (Flanagan & Jackson, 1993, p. 70). Men also show a concern for individual rights and autonomy, but women are more likely to resolve ethical issues by applying solutions that affirm relationships and minimize harm. This does not mean that women should be regarded as inherently emotional beings entirely lacking rational attributes. Both men and women are the products of social conditioning, and gender is socially constructed so that men too may follow an ethic of care rather then an individualistic ethical approach (Rachels, 1999a, p. 168).

Some question whether the ethic of care possesses the weight and dimensions sufficient for an ethical theory and suggest that it is best viewed as complementing virtue ethics (Blum, 1994, p. 208). Also problematic is the scope of the care ethic itself because while it is obvious that the ethic of care applies in close family relationships, the question is to what extent does it, for example, apply to the needy throughout the world? While some regard the familial obligation as absolute and other obligations as secondary, others emphasize the depth of a relationship outside the family circle. Still others argue that our duty can be broad enough to include a communal identity, such as membership in an ethnic group (Blum, 1994, p. 249).

Robin West (1997) advocates linking the ethic of care with the ethic of justice so that public institutions will be obliged to exercise compassion or care when dispensing justice (p. 9). She contends that a combined project of care and justice would mean reading and interpreting the law compassionately, for example, taking account of the life circumstances of an accused in a death penalty case. The notion of peacemaking has close links with the ethic of care but represents a distinct ethical philosophy variously termed peacemaking, peacekeeping, or peacemaking criminology (Braswell & Gold, 1998, p. 26). Peacemaking also calls attention to relationships, caring, and mindfulness (thinking about our actions and the needs of others in the long term). In terms of criminal justice policy making, peacemaking claims nonviolence as a fundamental principle and argues that violence and coercion in forms such as capital punishment or the excess use of force in policing should be rejected.

CONCLUSION

This exploration of ethics in criminal justice highlights the importance of the theoretical underpinnings of normative and applied ethics to the resolution of ethical issues and dilemmas and reveal the nature and scope of the multiple ethical questions that arise in "doing justice." In law enforcement and corrections, in particular, where there is daily direct interaction with suspected offenders and inmates, the level of ethical practice of an agency is greatly influenced by its institutional culture. Codes of ethics and accountability mechanisms, such as civilian oversight and the courts, can resolve individual cases of improper conduct, but systemic racism, corruption, or abuse conduct has proved difficult to eradicate. Sometimes, as in the case of terrorism, questions about "how ought I to act" are fundamentally about human rights and human dignity. Theoretical approaches toward ethical dilemmas and issues apply various mechanisms to evaluate and test the questions that arise, and fresh postmodern perspectives now challenge long-established theories. Shifts in both ethical practice and theory congruent with those in the social order ensure that the incorporation of ethical norms and standards will continue to be a testing and challenging field of endeavor in criminal justice.

Discussion Questions

1. Is there any relationship between the style of policing chosen by a department and the ethical practices it feels are legitimate for its officers to use in carrying out their duties? Which style of policing would support racial profiling, and why?

2. In an ethical correctional system, all prisoners would be treated with humanity. Explain how prisoner humanity would be respected in the use of force to deal with violence, including prisoner rape, and in the conditions of confinement.

3. One criminal justice policy that many states have supported is prisoner disenfranchisement.

Comment on this policy in light of the fact that, for example, if disenfranchisement is permanent, more than 40% of the African American male population will have no say in the policies and laws that have a significant effect on them and on their communities.

4. Is it ever ethically acceptable to torture a person in the war on terrorism? Support your argument by referring to the criteria of at least one ethical philosophy.

5. Why do modern philosophers regard virtue ethics as an alternative to deontological and consequentialist ethical decision-making approaches? Explain with examples.

References

Ackerman, B. (2004). This is not a war. *Yale Law Journal, 113*, 1871–1908.

Banks, C. (2005). *Punishment in America: A reference handbook*. Santa Barbara, CA: ABC-Clio.

Bauman, Z. (1993). *Postmodern ethics*. Oxford, UK: Blackwell.

Benn, P. (1998). *Ethics: Fundamentals of philosophy*. Montreal, Canada: McGill-Queen's University Press.

Blum, L. (1994). *Moral perception and particularity*. Cambridge, UK: Cambridge University Press.

Blum, L. (1996). Community and virtue. In R. Crisp (Ed.), *How should one live? Essays on the virtues* (pp. 231–250). Oxford, UK: Clarendon Press.

Blumstein, A., Cohen, J., & Nagin, D. (Eds.). (1978). *Deterrence and incapacitation: Estimating the effects of criminal sanctions on crime rates*.

Washington, DC: Panel on Research on Deterrent and Incapacitative Effects.

Braswell, M., & Gold, J. (1998). Peacemaking, justice and ethics. In M. Braswell, B. McCarthy, & B. McCarthy (Eds.), *Justice, crime and ethics* (3rd ed., pp. 25–39). Cincinnati, OH: Anderson.

Christie, N. (2000). *Crime control as industry: Towards gulags, Western style?* London, UK: Routledge.

Crank, J., & Caldero, M. (2000). *Police ethics: The corruption of noble cause*. Cincinnati, OH: Anderson.

CREDO Action. (n.d.). Anti-Muslim racial profiling on planes must stop. Retrieved January 28, 2018, from https://act.credoaction.com/sign/Stop_Airline_Profiling

Darwall, S. (1998). *Philosophical ethics*. Boulder, CO: Westview Press.

Eligon, J. (2010, June 18). Jurors watch video of officer hitting man with a baton. *New York Times*, A16.

Emcke, C. (2005). War on terrorism and the crises of the political. In G. Meggle (Ed.), *Ethics of terrorism & counter-terrorism* (pp. 227–244). Frankfurt, Germany: Ontos.

Feldman, F. (1997). *Utilitarianism, hedonism, and desert: Essays in moral philosophy*. New York, NY: Cambridge University Press.

Finn, P. (1996). No-frills prisons and jails: A movement in flux. *Federal Probation, 60*, 35–44.

Flanagan, O., & Jackson, K. (1993). Justice, care, and gender: The Kohlberg–Gilligan debate revisited. In M. J. Larrabee (Ed.), *An ethic of care: Feminist and interdisciplinary perspectives* (pp. 69–86). New York, NY: Routledge.

Gier, K. (2006). Prosecuting injustice: Consequences of misconduct. *American Journal of Criminal Law, 33*(2), 191–222.

Gilligan, C. (1982). *In a different voice: Psychological theory and women's development*. Cambridge, MA: Harvard University Press.

Harrison, P., & Beck, A. (2003, July). *Prisoners in 2002*. Bureau of Justice Statistics Bulletin NCJ 200248. Washington, DC: U.S. Department of Justice.

Hill, T. E. (2000). *Respect, pluralism, and justice: Kantian perspectives*. Oxford, UK: Oxford University Press.

Hinman, L. (1998). *Ethics: A pluralistic approach to moral theory*. Fort Worth, TX: Harcourt Brace.

Horwitz, S. (2015, May 28). Justice Department acts to end sexual assault at women's prison in Alabama. *Washington Post*.

Hudson, B. (1996). *Understanding justice: An introduction to ideas, perspectives and controversies in modern penal theory*. Buckingham, UK: Open University Press.

Hursthouse, R. (1999). *On virtue ethics*. Oxford, UK: Oxford University Press.

Ignatieff, M. (2004). *The lesser evil: Political ethics in an age of terror: The Gifford Lectures*. Princeton, NJ: Princeton University Press.

Kauffman, K. (1988). *Prison officers and their world*. Cambridge, MA: Harvard University Press.

Kleinig, J. (1996). *The ethics of policing*. New York, NY: Cambridge University Press.

Kleinig, J. (2001). Professionalizing incarceration. In J. Kleinig & M. L. Smith (Eds.), *Discretion, community, and correctional ethics* (pp. 1–15). Lanham, MA: Rowman & Littlefield.

Lenz, N. (2002). "Luxuries" in prison: The relationship between amenity funding and public support. *Crime & Delinquency, 48*(4), 499–525.

Ly, L. (2016, January 18). 3 Muslims, Sikh kicked off flight because of their looks, lawsuit says. CNN.

MacIntyre, A. (1984). *After virtue: A study in moral theory*. Notre Dame, IN: University of Notre Dame Press.

Martinson, R. (1974). What works? Questions and answers about prison reform. *Public Interest, 35*, 22–54.

Mooney, Christopher. (2001). Introduction: The public clash of private values: The politics of morality policy. In C. Mooney (Ed.), *The public clash of private values: The politics of morality policy* (pp. 3–18). New York, NY: Chatham House.

Morris, H. (2016, March 9). Muslim women removed from plane after staring at flight attendant. *The Telegraph*.

Morris, N. (1974). *The future of imprisonment*. Chicago, IL: University of Chicago Press.

Nozick, R. (1981). *Philosophical explanations*. Cambridge, MA: Harvard University Press.

Petersilia, J. (1999). Parole and prisoner reentry in the United States. In M. Tonry & J. Petersilia (Eds.), *Prisons* (pp. 479–529). Chicago, IL: University of Chicago Press.

Pope, C., & Feyerherm, W. (1990). Minority status and juvenile justice processing: An assessment of the research literature, Part I and II. *Criminal Justice Abstracts, 22*(2; 3), 327–385; 527–542.

Prior, W. (1991). *Virtue and knowledge: An introduction to ancient Greek ethics*. London, UK: Routledge.

Rachels, J. (1999a). *The elements of moral philosophy* (3rd ed.). Boston, MA: McGraw-Hill College.

Rachels, J. (1999b). *The right thing to do: Basic readings in moral philosophy* (2nd ed.). Boston, MA: McGraw-Hill College.

Rawls, J. (1973). *A theory of justice*. Oxford, UK: Oxford University Press.

Reiner, R. (1985). The police and race relations. In J. Baxter & L. Koffman (Eds.), *Police: The Constitution and the community* (pp. 149–187). London, UK: Professional Books.

Rimer, S. (2002, February 13). In Dallas, dismissal of Black jurors leads to appeal by death row inmate. *New York Times*. Retrieved January 29, 2018, from http://www.nytimes.com/2002/02/13/national/13DEAT.html

Rumana, R. (2000). *On Rorty*. Belmont, CA: Wadsworth.

Russell, K. (1998). *The color of crime: Racial hoaxes, White fear, Black protectionism, police harassment, and other macroaggressions*. New York, NY: New York University Press.

Skolnick, J. (1966). *Justice without trial*. New York, NY: Wiley.

Smith, M. L. (2001). The shimmer of reform: Prospects for a correctional ethic. In J. Kleinig & M. L. Smith (Eds.), *Discretion, community, and correctional ethics* (pp. 17–37). Lanham, MA: Rowman & Littlefield.

Stack, L. (2016, April 17). College student is removed from flight after speaking Arabic on plane. *New York Times*.

Ten, C. L. (1987). *Crime, guilt, and punishment: A philosophical introduction*. Oxford, UK: Clarendon Press.

Tessitore, A. (1996). *Reading Aristotle's ethics: Virtue, rhetoric, and political philosophy*. Albany, NY: State University of New York Press.

Tonry, M. (1994). Proportionality, parsimony, and interchangeability of punishments. In A. Duff & D. Garland (Eds.), *A reader on punishment* (pp. 133–160). Oxford, UK: Oxford University Press.

Walker, S., Spohn, C., & DeLone, M. (2000). *The color of justice: Race, ethnicity and crime in America*. Belmont, CA: Wadsworth.

West, R. (1997). *Caring for justice*. New York, NY: New York University Press.

Wilkinson, P. (2001). *Terrorism versus democracy: The liberal state response*. London, UK: Frank Cass.

Williams, T. (2015, March 30). Steep costs of inmate phone calls are under scrutiny. *New York Times*. Retrieved from http://www.nytimes.com/2015/03/31/us/steep-costs-of-inmate-phone-calls-are-under-scrutiny.html

UNLEASHING THE POWER OF CRIMINAL JUSTICE THEORY

Peter B. Kraska

Three serious concerns about how criminology and criminal justice approach theory are addressed. First, although theorizing about the why of crime is a recognized and institutionalized endeavor, theorizing about criminal justice/crime control is unrecognized, underdeveloped, and in need of an infrastructure and legitimation. Second, due to the dominance of the positivist social science model, the power of theory has been severely diminished as an educational tool. Criminal justice theory harbors tremendous transformative powers when used to cultivate critical-thinking skills and as a means to raise consciousness. This classic role of academic theorizing, however, has been displaced more often than not by the assumption that the single, ultimate goal of theory is to develop universal causal laws. Third, the academy has taken exclusive ownership of theory and, in doing so, inappropriately tended to define any theorizing that occurs in the public sphere as mere ideology or pointless rhetoric. The assumption that theorizing is an activity conducted by academics for other academics diminishes its educative power in public discourse and hence its ability to affect how we collectively make theoretical sense of crime and justice issues.

THE POWER OF CRIMINAL JUSTICE THEORY FOR OUR DISCIPLINE

As a graduate student, I was required to take numerous theory courses. At the same time, I became keenly interested in the intensely punitive turn taken by the

American criminal justice system (i.e., the war on crime and the war on drugs). What I noticed was that all of the "theory" instruction I was receiving focused on the why of crime; very little explanatory attention was paid to the why of criminal justice and crime control behavior. My experiences were typical of our field, even today, and I made an early and unsettling observation: The only recognized theoretical infrastructure and theoretical project we acknowledge in crime and justice studies is crime theory.

Over the years, I have come to recognize this as a serious disciplinary deficiency—one that some have attempted to remedy (Bernard & Engel, 2001; Duffee & McGuire, 2007; Kraska, 2004, 2006; Kraska & Brent, 2011). Our discipline assumes that theory work is reserved for the why of crime and crime rates. Within our leading scholarly journals, theory development and testing is targeted primarily at explaining crime. Our theory textbooks focus almost exclusively on the why of deviance, crime, and delinquency. Even the majority of our introductory criminal justice textbooks, which have the criminal justice system as their explicit object of study, dedicate nearly all of their discussion of theory to theories of criminal behavior. Our undergraduate and graduate degree programs assume that the theory component of their curriculum should concentrate only on the why of crime. And teaching theory, as part of these curricula, refers universally to teaching crime causation.

Overall, then, it is taken for granted that the central object of our theorizing in crime and justice studies is crime. Pursuing a recognized and usable theoretical infrastructure about criminal justice/crime control—despite the frustration with this state of affairs voiced by leading scholars in the field over the last three decades—has not been an acknowledged priority and certainly does not constitute a recognized theoretical project (Bernard & Engel, 2001; Duffee & McGuire, 2007; Hagan, 1989; Kraska, 2004, 2006; Kraska & Brent, 2011; Marenin & Worrall, 1998).

In fact, to make matters worse, studying criminal justice is usually framed as merely a "practical" endeavor, with little concern for theory development or high-level causal/intellectual thinking. Theory work is relevant to criminal justice studies only insofar as theories of crime causation lead to more effective crime control policies and tactics. (Again, criminal justice behavior is treated as simply the independent variable that affects crime.) Embedded in this thinking is the presumption that studying crime control and criminal justice is limited to policy and evaluation research focusing on how to control crime.

Many criminologists, therefore, see little need for criminal justice theory, since for them, crime theory already provides enough of a theoretical foundation for what the criminal justice system should and should not do about crime. Of course, distinguishing between theorizing crime and theorizing criminal justice is not difficult; most crime and justice scholars can appreciate the qualitative difference between explaining crime and explaining crime control. The latter concentrates on making theoretical sense of criminal justice and crime control phenomena, such

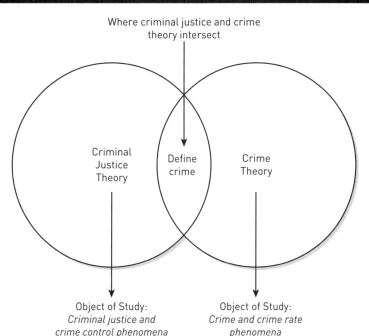

FIGURE 3.1 ■ Venn Diagram of Criminal Justice Theory and Crime Theory

Where criminal justice and crime theory intersect

Criminal Justice Theory

Define crime

Crime Theory

Object of Study:
Criminal justice and crime control phenomena

Object of Study:
Crime and crime rate phenomena

Source: Kraska, P. B., & Brent, J. (2011). *Theorizing criminal justice: Eight essential orientations* (2nd ed.). Prospect Heights, IL: Waveland Press.

as the behavior of the state, the behavior of criminal justice organizations (police, courts, corrections, and juvenile justice organizations), overall trends in the entire criminal justice apparatus, and the private sector's crime control activities.

Clearly, then, we need different theoretical infrastructures for understanding the nature of crime behavior versus the nature of crime control/CJ behavior. And although the two no doubt intersect (see Figure 3.1) in the realm of law creation, the study of criminal justice behavior and crime behavior require quite different theoretical tools.

The thinking that crime theory constitutes our intellectual core is so reified that many bright and capable academics have difficulty understanding that there is even a need for criminal justice theory. One reason is that theorizing criminal justice is inherently a more critical endeavor than theorizing crime. When our object of study shifts from crime to criminal justice—and we are forced to examine, for example, the why of the drug war as opposed to drug use or the why of the war on terrorism as opposed to terrorism itself or the why of police behavior as opposed to the commission of crime—we are essentially problematizing crime control activities and the criminal justice institution, as opposed to crime itself. Doing so necessitates the scrutiny of state behavior, private-sector crime control activities, or societal shifts in criminal justice punitiveness (e.g., explaining the rise of mass incarceration).

This is precisely why the "critical" theories found in traditional crime theory textbooks are an odd fit, if not conspicuously misplaced. In examining the state's oppression of marginalized groups (women, the poor, racial minorities, and homosexuals) via the criminal justice system, the truth is that these theories do not belong—because their explanatory gaze is directed less at crime than at the state's creation of and reaction to crime.

CRIMINAL JUSTICE: A WORTHY OBJECT OF THEORIZING

Another difficulty is, when we theorize criminal justice, our central object of study is even more complex than it is for crime. The terrain of possible foci is vast: ranging theorizing criminal justice practitioner behavior to the system's subcomponents or its historical development or perhaps explaining the system's steep growth in power and size over the last 30 years (a central objective of Garland's [2001] well-regarded book, *The Culture of Control*). Theorizing could also focus on contemporary trends and issues in crime control practices, such as privatization, militarization, federalization, the expansion of surveillance, racial profiling, erosion of constitutional safeguards, or trends and issues related to the "wars" on terrorism and drugs. More conventionally, criminal justice theory could seek to explain the behavior of criminal justice policy, agency behavior, and the why of practitioner and organizational decision making.

These varied and important objects of explanation should demonstrate that explanatory frameworks, other than those provided by crime theories, are not only possible but needed. Traditional criminological theories, despite their obvious interconnection with criminal justice practice, are not designed to explain nor are they beneficial to our understanding of criminal justice system or crime control behavior.

Please note that the claim here is not necessarily a lack of theorizing about the criminal justice system and crime control activities but, rather, the lack of a recognized infrastructure, the lack of recognition that a body of theory separate from crime theory even exists, the lack of desire to articulate criminal justice theory, and, due to all of these, the lack of access to these theories for students and academics alike.

DEVELOPING A USEFUL THEORETICAL INFRASTRUCTURE

To begin the large task of remedying this situation, an avenue is presented for developing an infrastructure (Kraska, 2004, 2006; Kraska & Brent, 2011). The approach

TABLE 3.1 ■ Criminal Justice Theoretical Orientations

Major Features	Rational/ Legal	System	Packer's Crime Control vs. Due Process	Politics	Social Construction	Growth Complex	Oppression	Late Modernity
Intellectual Tradition	neoclassical; legal formalism	structural-functionalism; biological sciences; organizational studies	liberal legal jurisprudence; legal realism; sociolegal studies	political science; public administration	interpretive school; symbolic interaction; social construction	Weber; Frankfurt School; critical public administration	Marx; feminism; critical sociology; race studies	Foucault; governmentality literature; postmodernism
Approaches to Knowledge Production	technical legal research; status quo positivism	mainstream positivist social science (critical and status quo focus)	academic legal research; sometime positivist	historical; comparative; positivist social science; theoretical synthesis research	interpretive social science; critical social science; content analysis	critical social science; theoretical synthesis research	critical social science; critical ethnography; feminist approaches	critical social science; theoretical synthesis research; minimal interpretive social science and positive social science
Key Concepts Employed	rational-legalistic, rulebound; taken for granted	functional; equilibrium; efficiency; technology; external forces; open system; closed system	value-cluster; efficiency, crime control values; due process values; needs-based values	ideology; conflict; symbolic politics; policymaking/implementing; state, community	myth; reality; culture; symbols; legitimacy; moral panic; impression management; institutional theory	bureaucracy building; privatization profit; complex; technical rationality; merging complexes	dangerous classes; gender; patriarchy; racism; class bias; conflict model; structural thinking; dialectics; praxis	actuarial justice; neoliberalpolitics; exclusive society; safety norm; incoherence in criminal justice policy

(Continued)

TABLE 3.1 ■ (Continued)

Major Features	Rational/Legal	System	Packer's Crime Control vs. Due Process	Politics	Social Construction	Growth Complex	Oppression	Late Modernity
Reasons for Rapid Criminal Justice Expansion in Last 30 Years	legal reaction to increased law-breaking (forced reaction theory)	criminal justice system reacting to increases in crime (forced reaction theory)	pendulum swing toward crime control values; choosing punitiveness	politicians exploiting problem; politicized drug war; shift in ideology	moral panics; media exploitation; runaway cultural process; crime as scapegoat	dynasty building; growth complex; merging private with public, criminal justice with military	control of threatening groups; marginalized used as scapegoats; crisis in state legitimacy	crisis in state sovereignty; risk-aversive society; growth complex; moral indifference; social exclusivity paradigm
Assumptions About Agency and Practitioner Motives	well-intended; protecting; serving; rule following; law abiding; professionalism	rational decision makers; efficient; adapting to external forces	role/goal conflict; mixed messages; mimic the value messages provided from public	responsive to politics; interest based; ideological pulls; power players	constructing problems for existing solutions; reacting to moral panics; culturally bound; managing appearances	self-serving; power building; quest for immortality; means over ends; bureaucratic survival; technical over moral thinking	institutional racism, sexism, classism; often unaware of oppressive end result of their own activities	navigating through massive transformations, late-modern forces; good intentions, disturbing results
Issues of Concern	deterrence; defending the virtues and honor of the criminal justice system	abuse of discretion; cutting-edge technology; streamline/centralize operations	erosion of constitutional rights; governmental intrusiveness	federalization; symbolic politics; ideological intensification	media/bureaucrat/political exploitation; mythology	exponential growth; private/public, military/police blur	violence against women; drug war's impact on marginalized; racial profiling	growth of system; changes in social control; rise of surveillance society

Source: Kraska, P. B., & Brent, J. (2011). Theorizing criminal justice: Eight essential orientations (2nd ed.). Prospect Heights, IL: Waveland Press.

is fairly straightforward: A large volume of existing theoretical scholarship about our reaction to crime is organized around eight explanatory constructs called theoretical orientations. These orientations are a type of theoretical lens, framed as metaphors, through which criminologists view and make sense of criminal justice and crime control phenomena. Formally defined, a theoretical orientation is an interpretive construct that includes a logically coherent set of organizing concepts, causal preferences, value clusters, and assumptions that work to orient our interpretations and understanding of criminal justice phenomena (similar to a paradigm).

The goal is not to develop a single, testable criminal justice theory; on the contrary, the objective is to illuminate the multiple theoretical lenses crime and justice scholars can employ to help us understand the behavior of the criminal justice system and trends in crime control. Table 3.1 provides a schematic of the eight theoretical orientations.

These metaphors are routinely employed in our field of study. They include criminal justice as (a) rational legalism, (b) system, (c) crime control versus due process, (d) politics, (e) the social construction of reality, (f) growth complex, (g) oppression, and (h) late modernity. The features of each theoretical orientation are noted beneath it.

Several theoretical orientations in our field are easily identified, the system perspective being the most obvious. Most would agree that the system's framework has dominated our field's thinking and research about criminal justice. The network of governmental agencies responding to our crime problem is universally known as the criminal justice system. The system's framework is derived from the biological sciences, Parson's structural functionalism, and organizational studies. It has a strong reformist element, emphasizing the importance of enhancing criminal justice coordination, efficiency, rational decision-making, and technology.

Another not-so-common explanatory framework is referred to as the *late-modern theoretical orientation*. This lens situates the criminal justice apparatus (broadly defined) within macro-shifts associated with the current era of social history labeled late modernity. Criminal justice and crime control phenomena are best explained as adaptations to late-modern social conditions. An impressive body of scholarship has emerged in this area (a few examples include Garland, 2001; O'Malley, 1999; Simon, 2007; and Young, 1999). Five late-modern conditions frame this orientation:

- The rise of actuarial justice and the influence of the risk society

- The neoliberal shift in macropolitics

- Increasing contradictions and incoherence in crime control policy

- The decline of the sovereign state's legitimacy

- The ascendance of an exclusion paradigm for managing those perceived to pose a safety threat in an increasingly security-conscious society

The late-modern orientation is probably the most theoretically vigorous pursuit of criminal justice and crime control phenomena in the literature today. As shown in Figure 3.1, there are many other possible theoretical lenses through which to view criminal justice behavior. Space limitations inhibit a more detailed examination; further elaboration can be found in Kraska (2004) and Kraska and Brent (2011).

THE POWER OF THEORY TO TRANSFORM CONSCIOUSNESS

As a result of constructing this infrastructure, I have been teaching criminal justice theory, instead of crime theory proper, to students for the last 15 years. I have come to realize the very real power of theory—and particularly criminal justice theory—to affect students' thinking. Theory work, if approached in the right spirit, harbors tremendous transformative powers through cultivation of critical-thinking skills and as a means to raise consciousness.

To fully appreciate its potential, we have to recognize the integral part theory plays, not just in such journals as *Criminology* but in our everyday lives. When my daughter Cora was only 3, she asked me, completely out of the blue, "How does a butterfly get the dust on its wings?" After I recovered and made a feeble attempt to cultivate her theoretical skills, I asked her what she thought. She responded first by positing that "the butterflies are just born that way" (i.e., an inherent part of their biological makeup). I told her that was correct—but then she demonstrated the early signs of a keen theoretical and creative mind. She said, "Daddy, I knew that was the right answer, but I was hoping it was because they pick up different colors of dust from flowers."

This anecdote demonstrates that the activity of theorizing is essential to everything we think and do, beginning in our earliest years. We craft theory throughout our lives as a way to make sense of our surroundings. The way in which we make theoretical sense of things guides the decisions we make so that we can navigate those surroundings competently and decently—to solve problems, to think through complex phenomena, to make accurate predictions, to understand others (empathy) and feel compassion or anger, and to make sense of our workplaces and organizational environments. Thousands of times a day, we either assume or assess the why of things, and these assumptions and assessments frame our thinking and actions. Theory is integral not only in everyday life but also to all those who work in organizations that deal with criminal or social justice.

Our field's traditional approach to teaching theory diminishes its pedagogical power and practical strength. Overall, the accepted approach involves (a) empirically testing existing crime theories, making minor modifications along the way, and (b) teaching students about these crime theories and examining the evidence that supports and/or refutes them.

Theory is something, therefore, owned by academics for academics, for the exclusive purpose of developing universal causal laws for the explanation of crime through testing relationships between clearly operationalized independent and dependent variables. Of course, this critique is not meant to diminish the importance of this activity; those of us who do this kind of work are a great asset to our field. What I question is whether this approach *alone* is the most efficacious for teaching and educating our students.

I have learned a lot about teaching theory in the last 20 years that I did not really recognize for the 10 years before. I now concentrate on teaching criminal justice theory in a way that enhances students' theoretical skills and sensitivities and that cultivates their critical-thinking abilities. My views about theory have matured while teaching graduate students in an in-service leadership program to police practitioners.

I have taught these nontraditional students theory by exposing them to some of the major theoretical orientations that help make sense of criminal justice/crime control phenomena (their everyday work). I present each of these orientations as lenses, or theoretical filters, that provide ideas and organizing concepts guiding their work and the police institution. We talk about how they each harbor a personal theoretical framework that has developed over their lifetime based on what they have learned through direct experience, entertainment, news media, significant others, and the educational system.

These students come to realize that their personal theoretical frameworks are always under construction and that the process of learning to interpret their surroundings through differing theoretical filters is a vital part of their educational experience. I concentrate on the eight theoretical lenses noted earlier. The idea is for students to read, think deeply about, and apply, through numerous engagement-oriented exercises, these varying theoretical lenses. The objective is to develop critical theoreticians who can

- raise vital questions and problems, formulating them clearly and precisely;

- gather and assess relevant information;

- use abstract ideas to make theoretical sense of things effectively;

- come to well-reasoned, explanatory-based conclusions and solutions and test them against relevant criteria and standards;

- think open-mindedly, empathetically, reflectively, and creatively, with an ability to view their objects of theorizing with multiple theoretical lenses;

- communicate effectively with others in figuring out explanations and solutions to complex problems; and

- more competently navigate their way through an increasingly complex social and criminal justice environment.

I have found that these in-service police students have a tremendous capacity for developing their own personal theoretical frameworks. One explanatory framework I have found particularly enlightening is the metaphor of a "growth complex." The growth complex theoretical orientation illuminates the possibility that organizations (or entire institutional systems) can devolve into entities more motivated by their own bureaucratic interests than by the public good. The underlying assumption is that any bureaucracy's most basic instinct is to survive and grow, to survive.

Growth complex thinking, therefore, casts the criminal justice apparatus in an intensely critical light. The criminal justice growth complex is an entity comprising numerous interrelated and interdependent parts—an intricate structural matrix of criminal justice and non–criminal justice governmental bureaucracies, politicians, private companies, media agencies, academic institutions, and myriad interests. Although not operating in harmony necessarily by design or even by intent, the net effect is nonetheless a complex of loosely and tightly connected organizations and interests that generate a synergy ideal for expansion.

In the quest for survival, growth, and influence building, the overall goal of pursuing the public interest through democratic processes and values (participation, accountability, fairness, and a concern for human dignity) is relegated to the back burner. The growth complex orientation views the criminal justice apparatus as an entity that seeks out and constructs new problems for its solution, that actively pursues its own self-serving agenda as opposed to working toward the public good, and that is increasingly influenced by the private-sector objectives of profit and growth. In its simplest terms, garnering power and size becomes not a means to a laudable end but an end in itself. (Please recall that this is only one lens and therefore only illuminates one potential dimension of criminal justice functioning.)

I have found that the reason this theoretical orientation resonates with police practitioners is that its theoretical premises coincide with their real-world experiences. (Data and theory are consistent.) The growth complex lens influenced one police administrator in dramatic fashion. He was in charge of securing grants for his department and apparently good at his job. He wrote an excellent paper during the semester, applying growth complex thinking to his work. A year or so after the class was over, he contacted me informing me that he was under a lot of pressure in his department from other administrators to renew a federal grant that his department had secured based on false premises. (I'm being purposely vague.) He argued against renewal, won the battle, and attributed his action to the new theoretical lenses he had recently adopted. Modifying his personal theoretical framework, of course, affected his values and his value choices. He acted against what he called "mindless bureaucracy building."

This example demonstrates that it is vital to value the everyday and real-world relevance of theory and not approach it merely as a body of scientific work found in books and articles. It is indeed an activity, something we do. Theorizing is part of what ought to be happening in a theory class: the application and even crafting of theory—approaching it as an activity, as opposed to simply learning a body of work (Frauley, 2005). Remember, we have been crafting theory since the day we were born. We have tested our theories in the real world. Some of us have done a good job, others not as good. The key is to not just have students learn about theory and famous theorists but to apply what they have learned to differing objects of study—like the way many of us conduct a research methods class—we ask them to conduct research.

The overall point here is that we should not limit the power of theory. It has the potential to foster creativity, empathy, the expansion of our cognitive gaze, a rethinking or at least a clarification of value preferences, and a serious questioning of and introspection about our taken-for-granted reality. Learning theory should be replete with great many "aha!" experiences. The purposes of learning theory should include enabling individuals to know themselves and their situation through retrospection and a raising of their consciousness about our complex social world.

THE POWER OF THEORY TO AFFECT PUBLIC EXPLANATIONS

My third and final concern is directly related to the second: Academe has taken complete ownership of theory and, as a result, has diminished its significant potential to shape public discourse. I fully realized the gravity of this concern while watching the now historic (2005) Hurricane Katrina disaster and its aftermath unfold.

Catastrophic natural disasters, despite all the suffering and pain they inflict, often play out ultimately as stories of human triumph, heroism, and community solidarity. We construct them as testaments to the true decency of humankind. The urgent task at hand, to take care of each other's most basic needs, trumps, at least temporarily, some of our uglier societal faults, such as class, race, and gender divisions and prejudices; self-centeredness; entrenched political conflict; and a lack of social caring.

Hurricane Katrina, which hit the coasts of Alabama, Louisiana, and Mississippi on August 29, 2005, was different. While human triumph and decency were evident, the lasting legacy of Katrina will be that it washed away the veil of denial and neglect and laid bare the ugly societal faults that are usually pushed to the periphery. It stirred up and inflamed some of our deepest contemporary fears: poor racial minorities free to loot and victimize others, a sign of things to come as the result of global warming, and a government so inept in homeland security matters that it failed on almost all accounts.

Just as with the terrorist attack of September 11, 2001, we have a strong collective desire to make sense of these types of catastrophic events, both for therapeutic reasons and to prevent or minimize the harm they cause. What exactly does making sense mean, though? Making sense, for some people, means resorting to religious explanations (e.g., "It must be God's will"); for others, it means filtering the event through a rigid ideology in order to reaffirm the truth of that ideology (e.g., "It's the fault of our welfare system; only those dependent on welfare would be unable to get out of New Orleans"). For the social scientist, it means using theory and research to examine rigorously the many unanswered questions.

Each of these endeavors seeks explanation, or a theoretically based narrative—an attempt to construct and find meaning in a highly complex and unsettling event. Traumatic events, such as 9/11 and Katrina, bring about a state of collective cognitive dissonance in which reality as previously constructed and perceived comes into serious question. Comfortable ideas, expectations, and assumptions are shattered, creating what Garfinkel called a temporary state of "meaninglessness." Theory helps us to put the pieces back together (Kraska & Neuman, 2008, p. 65).

Kishonna Gray and I examined real-world theorizing found in the public sphere after Hurricane Katrina (Gray & Kraska, 2006). Examining this catastrophe provided a valuable opportunity to study how theory operates in the real world. Katrina exposed a host of theoretical questions that are rarely examined, at least outside of academe, and generated an incisive public discourse about power structures, economic inequalities, racial injustice, governmental ineptitude and corruption, and accountability. Contrast this rich, contextualized coverage during Katrina with the public theorizing following 9/11, an insular and uncritical discourse emphasizing themes of xenophobia and evildoers.

Many regarded as unpatriotic any theorizing that criticized or fell outside these narrow parameters. The unique example of real-world theorizing found in the post-Katrina public sphere was essential to study, both for theoretical and practical reasons. Unfortunately, the social science community has constructed a disciplinary straitjacket around the notion of theory, limiting theory to testing the relationship between measurable variables by academics and generally for other academics.

Academics have unwisely taken exclusive ownership of theory, rendering it an entity separate from everyday thinking. Not only is this an untenable position, for most, if not all, social science theory emanates from real-world thinking and ideas, but it ignores as well the fact that public theorizing is of far greater consequence than what we do in academe. Indeed, the field of crime and justice studies tends to lose sight of what ought to be the premier goal of academic theory: the influencing and shaping of public thinking (i.e., public theory).

One particularly revealing theoretical moment emerged soon after Katrina hit. Kanye West, a music industry icon, was standing next to comedian Mike Myers and said the following on live national television during a post-Katrina fundraising event:

> I hate the way they portray us in the media. You see a black family, it says, "They're looting." You see a white family, it says, "They're looking for food." It's been five days waiting for federal help because most of the people are black. . . . So anybody out there that wants to do anything to help . . . please.

After Myers made another comment, West concluded his analysis by saying, "George Bush doesn't care about black people."

West's comments instantly became the cultural flash point for those who agreed and disagreed with his assertion. It is critical to note that West never said (despite the assertions of many reactionaries and some in the mainstream media) that George Bush hated Black people. Several news reports even misquoted West by using the word "hate." This popular culture moment highlighted the prominent role that race-based explanations played in public dialogue about the Katrina disaster. It would be a mistake to discount West's narrative as mere "sounding off" with little theoretical significance.

Of course, had he said hate, it would have implied a type of overt prejudice, a type of intentional racism that most would agree has diminished significantly in the last 75 years and is widely condemned as illegitimate in mainstream society (although we have witnessed a disturbing public resurgence of intentional racism during and after the 2016 presidential elections). Framing and interpreting West's assertion, therefore, as one of overt bigotry made it easy to delegitimize.

The phrase, "doesn't care about black people," however, connotes something entirely different. It embodies what is called structural racism—in which, even though intentional bigotry is not evident, the historical patterns and arrangements of race-based exclusion continue. Long after the majority of White people have ceased to actively hate racial minorities, there still exists an array of social and economic arrangements, constructed during a time of explicit hatred, that work to the disadvantage of racial minorities.

Where racial prejudice is kept alive by hate, structural racism thrives under conditions of indifference. West emphasized a lack of caring, positing that the abysmal response to the disaster was due to a lack of concern for African Americans. He captured succinctly an important theoretical organizing concept: that the enduring legacy of hate-based racism is a new form of racism, that operates alongside the old racism, and one based in conscious and unconscious indifference, neglect, apathy, and uncaring. It took indifference for our government at many levels to ignore a federally funded task force of scientists who predicted this fate for the population of poor African Americans living in New Orleans. It took indifference for Michael Chertoff, the director of Homeland Security at the time, to go to a conference the day after the disaster and not attend to a single detail of the relief operation (and for President Bush to remain on vacation). It took indifference to wait 5 days to provide any type of substantive humanitarian relief to those stuck in New Orleans while, in the meantime, the area was being "secured" by military and militarized police forces.

The purpose of this example is to illustrate that our field of study needs to broaden our perspective of theory and to recognize that we should not divorce our academic theorizing from public theory. This is true for both criminal justice theory and crime theory. The aftermath of Katrina gave a small glimpse of the potential of theoretical discourse within the public sphere to make a difference—a difference brought about by cracking the veneer of taken-for-granted ideology to reveal other possible explanations and richer theoretical narratives.

CONCLUSION: EMBRACING CRIMINAL JUSTICE THEORY

The transformative powers of theory, both in our private lives and in the public sphere, should be acknowledged and cultivated. We should find ways to encourage our theoretical curiosity and the creation of multiple theoretical lenses. This can assist us in seeing through reified and counterproductive dominant explanations, not just about terrorism but the war on terrorism, not just about drugs but the war on drugs—explanations that will help us discuss the undiscussable, confront the uncomfortable, and reveal the taken-for-granted. Competent, meaningful, accurate, and deep theorizing is an essential precursor for thoughtful, substantive, humane solutions.

Marenin and Worrall (1998) once asserted that "criminal justice is an academic discipline in practice but not yet in theory" (p. 465). Our field has not placed high value on this endeavor for two primary reasons. The first has already been discussed: the assumption that crime theory suffices. The second is more difficult to overcome: while exploring the why of crime has *prima facie* importance, our field has neither articulated nor acknowledged the value provided us by theorizing criminal justice and crime control. Some assume, in fact, that studying criminal justice is inherently and necessarily atheoretical because it concentrates on practice. The notion that practice can somehow be severed from theory has been thoroughly debunked in most other major fields of study. Theory and practice are implied in one another; no policy analysis, implementation, strategic plan, or practitioner action is devoid of theory. To deny the integral role theory plays in all of these instances is to remain ignorant of its influence.

As noted, theorizing criminal justice/crime control behavior is an inherently critical endeavor providing important insights into the system's irrationalities, missteps, and disconcerting implications. Theoretically based scrutiny focused on our reaction to crime should not be misconstrued as inappropriately critical. It simply approaches criminal justice as a research problem—similar to the way we study crime.

Nor should theorizing criminal justice phenomena be viewed as an endeavor intended exclusively for practical change. Many studying society's reaction to crime find it intellectually stimulating in and of itself, much like biologists who study the animal kingdom or astronomers who study the solar system. Studying humans and organizations that attempt to control wrongdoing (and that sometimes engage in wrongdoing in the attempt) yields intriguing insights about the nature of society, our political landscape, and cutting-edge cultural trends. In short, how we react to crime tells us a lot about ourselves and where our society might be headed.

I am certain criminal justice theory will eventually become a normalized presence in our criminal justice and criminology degree programs, our text-books, and our doctoral training. The realization is growing that nothing less than our disciplinary integrity is at stake. However, as this process unfolds, it is critical to avoid the shortcomings evident in the development of crime theory. In order for criminal justice theory to reach its full potential, we must (a) develop its infrastructure in a manner that renders it both intellectually stimulating and accessible, (b) teach it in a way that acknowledges our positivist tradition yet allows space for the classic function of transforming consciousness, and (c) apply it to the real world through policy prescriptions based on research find-ings yet attempt, as well, to actively influence public theories about criminal justice issues. Criminal justice theory holds significant potential power; let us hope it is wielded constructively—and soon.

Discussion Questions

1. Is it really possible for criminal justice students to theorize? Or is it more appropriate that they read and learn about preexisting theories and the research that tests their veracity?

2. Why is it likely that the field of criminal justice will proceed slowly and with many obstacles in developing the idea of criminal justice theory?

3. What types of public theorizing typify such major criminal justice efforts as the war on terror or the war on drugs?

4. What is structural racism, and how is it still relevant to the operations of the criminal justice system today?

References

Bernard, T., & Engel, R. (2001). Conceptualizing criminal justice theory. *Justice Quarterly*, *18*(1), 1–30.

Duffee, D. E., & Maguire, E. R. (2007). *Criminal justice theory: Explaining the nature and behavior of criminal justice*. New York, NY: Routledge.

Frauley, J. (2005). Representing theory and theo-rising in criminal justice studies: Practising theory considered. *Critical Criminology*, *13*(3), 245–265.

Garland, D. (2001). *The culture of control: Crime and social order in contemporary society*. Chicago, IL: University of Chicago Press.

Gray, K., & Kraska, P. B. (2006, February). *Hurri-cane Katrina meltdown: Examining the relevance of everyday theory*. Paper presented at the meeting of the Academy of Criminal Justice Sciences, Balti-more, MD.

Hagan, J. (1989). Why is there so little criminal justice theory? Neglected macro- and micro-level links between organizations and power. *Journal of Research in Crime and Delinquency*, *26*(2), 116–135.

Kraska, P. B. (2004). *Theorizing criminal justice: Eight essential orientations*. Prospect Heights, IL: Waveland Press.

Kraska, P. B. (2006). Criminal justice theory: Toward legitimacy and an infrastructure. *Justice Quarterly*, *23*(2), 167–185.

Kraska, P. B., & Brent, J. (2011). *Theorizing criminal justice: Eight essential orientations* (2nd ed.). Prospect Heights, IL: Waveland Press.

Kraska, P. B., & Neuman, L. (2008). *Criminal justice and criminology research methods*. Boston, MA: Pearson.

Marenin, O., & Worrall, J. (1998). Criminal justice: Portrait of a discipline in progress. *Journal of Criminal Justice*, 26(6), 465–480.

O'Malley, P. (1999). Volatile and contradictory punishment. *Theoretical Criminology*, 3(2), 175–196.

Simon, J. (2007). *Governing through crime*. Boston, MA: Oxford University Press.

Young, J. (1999). *The exclusive society: Social exclusion, crime and difference in late modernity*. London, UK: Sage.

OFFENSES AND OFFENDERS

VICTIMOLOGY

Leah E. Daigle

Victimology includes the etiology (or causes) of victimization, the consequences of victimization, how the criminal justice system accommodates and assists victims, and how other elements of society, such as the media, deal with crime victims. Victimology is the study of victims. For example, instead of simply wondering or hypothesizing why younger people are more likely to be victims than older people, victimologists examine why younger people appear to be more vulnerable than the elderly.

Each year, the Bureau of Justice Statistics publishes Criminal Victimization in the United States, which publishes findings from the National Crime Victimization Survey (NCVS) (Truman & Morgan, 2016). In 2015, more than 19,600,000 victimizations were experienced (Truman & Morgan, 2016). Of these, 5 million violent crime victimizations were experienced; however, 14.6 million property crime victimizations were reported. The most common type of property crime experienced was theft, while simple assault was the most common violent crime.

THE TYPICAL VICTIMIZATION AND VICTIM

Of some concern was the realization that most often victims identified their attacker as a friend or acquaintance. Strangers accounted for only about one third of all violent victimizations in the National Crime Victimization Survey (NCVS) (Truman & Morgan, 2016). This may be one of the reasons why most victimizations are not reported to the police. In fact, less than half of all victimizations are reported to the police. Reporting varies by type of victimization. Almost 70% of motor vehicle thefts are reported to the police, compared with 33% of rapes and sexual assaults (Truman & Morgan, 2016). In about 58% of incidents, the offender had a weapon, and about 55% of violent crimes resulted in the victim being physically injured (Truman, Langton, & Planty, 2013).

Gender

The NCVS has shown that for all violent victimization, males were actually less likely to be violently victimized than females. Females are more likely than males to be victimized by an intimate partner. In 2010, 22% of all violent victimizations against females were perpetrated by an intimate partner, compared with only 5% of incidents involving male victims (Truman, 2010).

Race and Ethnicity

Respondents who are non-Hispanic Blacks have higher victimization rates than persons who are White or Hispanic (22.6 per 1,000 persons 12 or older compared to 17.4 per 1,000 and 16.8 per 1,000 respectively) (Truman & Morgan, 2016). Persons who reported being another race (25.7 per 1,000 persons 12 or older) had the highest rates of violent victimization in 2015 (Truman & Morgan, 2016).

Age

Respondents who are young face the greatest risk of becoming a victim of violent crime. Those between the ages of 12 and [the dash indicates a range of ages, so it is preferable for these] 17 years of age have the highest violent victimization rate, followed by 18 to 24 year olds. Those 65 and older have the lowest rate of victimization (Truman & Morgan, 2016).

Household Characteristics

Households having low income are more likely to experience a property victimization. Households in the lowest income categories—those earning less than $7,500 or between $7,500 and $14,999 annually—faced the greatest risk of burglary and theft. Households earning less than $7,500 had a burglary victimization rate that was twice the rate of households with incomes $75,000 per year or higher (Truman, 2010). It was also reported that the greater the number of occupants per household, the greater the property crime victimization rate. In fact, households with six or more occupants had a property crime victimization rate that was almost 2.5 times higher than single-headed households (Truman, 2010).

THE COSTS OF VICTIMIZATION

Victimization is a public health issue. Economic costs can result from property losses; costs associated with medical care; time lost from work, school, and housework; physical and emotional pain, suffering, and reduced quality of life; and legal costs. In 2008, the total economic loss from crimes was estimated to be $17.4 trillion, as reported by the NCVS (BJS, 2008).

Direct Property Losses

Generally, when determining property losses, the value of property that is damaged or taken and not recovered, as well as insurance claims administration costs, are taken into consideration. According to the 2008 NCVS, 94% of all property crimes resulted in economic losses (BJS, 2011). Miller, Cohen, and Wiersema (1996) estimated the property loss or damage experienced per crime victimization event and concluded that arson victimizations resulted in an estimated $15,500 per event. Motor vehicle thefts cost approximately $3,300 for each incident. It is rare for a victim of a violent or property offense to recover even some of his or her losses. Only about 29% of victims of personal crime and 16% of victims of property crime recover all or some property (BJS, 2011).

Medical Care

Results from the 2008 NCVS indicate that 542,280 violent crime victims received some type of medical care (BJS, 2011). Of those victims, slightly over one third received care at a hospital emergency room or an emergency clinic, while 9% were hospitalized. Receiving medical care oftentimes results in victims incurring additional medical expenses. Almost 6% of victims of violent crimes reported having medical expenses as a result of their victimization. About 63% of injured victims report having health insurance or eligibility for public medical services.

Although crime victims often do not require hospitalization, even if they are treated in the emergency room, the Office for Victims of Crime (Bonderman, 2001) showed that gunshot victims make up one third of those requiring hospitalization. Victims who are shot and admitted to a hospital are likely to face numerous rehospitalizations and incur medical costs across their lifetime. In 1994, for all victims of firearm injuries, the lifetime medical costs totaled $1.7 billion.

Mental Health Care Costs

It is estimated that between 10% and 20% of all total mental health care costs in the United States are related to crime (Miller et al., 1996). Most of this cost is a result of crime victims seeking treatment to deal with the effects of their victimization. Between one quarter and one half of all rape and child sexual-abuse victims receive mental health care (Miller et al., 1996). Sexual victimizations, of both adults and children, result in some of the largest mental health care costs for victims.

Pain, Suffering, and Lost Quality of Life

The most difficult cost to quantify is the pain, suffering, and loss of quality of life that crime victims experience. This cost is the largest that crime victims sustain. For example, Miller et al. (1996) estimated the cost of rape to victims in out-of-pocket expenses to be slightly less than $5,100 per incident.

Another cost that crime victims may experience is a change in their daily routine and lifestyle. To illustrate, victims of stalking may change their phone number, move, or change their normal routine. Some may stop going out alone or start carrying a weapon when they do so. Although these changes may reduce risk of being victimized again, for victims to bear the cost of crime is unjust.

SYSTEM COSTS

When including costs for law enforcement, juridical processing, and corrections, the direct expenditures of the criminal justice system are over $214 billion annually (BJS, 2006). The criminal justice system employs over 2.4 million, with a payroll over $9 billion a year.

Insurance companies pay approximately $45 billion annually due to crime (Guns, Money, & Medicine, 1996). Additionally, the federal government pays $8 billion annually for restorative and emergency services to crime victims (Guns, Money, & Medicine, 1996). Gunshot victims alone cost taxpayers over $4.5 billion dollars annually (Guns, Money, & Medicine, 1996). These costs are not distributed equally across society. Some communities have been hit particularly hard by violence and gun violence in particular. Some 96% of all hospital expenses associated with gun violence at King Drew Medical Center in Los Angeles, California (the city emergency care facility located in what popular culture identifies as "South Central"), are paid by public funds (Bonderman, 2001).

MENTAL HEALTH CONSEQUENCES AND COSTS

It is likely that the way people deal with victimization is tied to their biological makeup, their interactional style, their personal coping style and resources, and the context in which the incident occurs. Some responses can be quite serious and long term while others are more transitory.

Three affective responses that are common among crime victims are depression, reduction in self-esteem, and anxiety. The way in which depression manifests itself can include sleep disturbances, changes in eating habits, feelings of guilt and worthlessness, and irritability. Generally, those who are depressed will have a general decline in interest in activities they once enjoyed, feelings of distress, or both.

Victimization may be powerful enough to alter the way in which a crime victim views himself or herself. Self-esteem and self-worth are reduced in some crime victims, particularly females. There may also be a difference in crime's impact on self-appraisal based on the type of victimization experienced. For example, victims of both child and adult sexual abuse are likely to suffer long-term negative impacts to their self-esteem (Turner et al., 2006).

Post-Traumatic Stress Disorder

One of the recognized disorders associated with a patterned response to victimization is post-traumatic stress disorder (PTSD). Commonly associated with returning war and combat veterans, PTSD is a psychiatric condition that has been recognized as a possible consequence of other traumatic events, such as criminal victimization. To be diagnosed with PTSD, a victim must have experienced or witnessed a traumatic event involving actual or threatened death, injury, or sexual violence. A person may also have learned about such experiences happening to their family member or friend. The victim must have at least one intrusion symptom, such as recurrent, involuntary, and intrusive distressing memories of the event, connected to the traumatic event that started after the event occurred. The victim must also have negative alterations in cognitions and mood connected to the traumatic event that either begin or worsen after the incident. Finally, the victim must also have marked changes in arousal and reactivity associated with the traumatic event that begin or worsen after it happens (APA, 2013).

To be diagnosed, the symptoms must be experienced for more than 1 month and must cause significant distress or impairment in social, occupational, or other functional areas (APA, 2013). PTSD can be debilitating and can impact a victim's ability to heal, move on, or thrive after being victimized. Depression also commonly co-occurs in victims who suffer PTSD (Kilpatrick & Acierno, 2003). The occurrence of PTSD in rape victims has been estimated to be almost 1 in 3 (Kilpatrick, Edmunds, & Seymour, 1992)

Self-Blame, Learned Helplessness, and the Brain

After victimization, the victim may blame himself or herself for his or her victimization. One type of self-blame, characterological self-blame, occurs when the victim ascribes blame to a nonmodifiable source such as his or her own character (Janoff-Bulman, 1979). Characterological self-blame involves believing that the victimization was deserved. Behavioral self-blame occurs when a modifiable source—behavior—is ascribed (Janoff-Bulman, 1979). When a person turns to behavioral self-blame, future victimization can be avoided, so long as his or her behavior changes. Victims can learn that responding is futile and become passive and numb (Seligman, 1975). Thus, victims may not take appropriate defensive action in the face of danger and, instead, risk subsequent victimization.

Although learned helplessness, as originally proposed by Seligman, is not alone sufficient in explaining victimization, research on animals shows that exposure to inescapable aversive stimuli (such as shocks to rats' tails) is related to behavioral changes that are likely related to fear—changes in eating and drinking, changes in sleep patterns, and not escaping future aversive stimuli when possible. These behavioral changes are linked to changes in brain chemistry, and researchers have hypothesized are similar to the neurochemical and behavioral changes seen in humans who suffer from major depressive disorders (Hammack, Cooper, & Lezak, 2012). In this way, then, it is possible that people who have been exposed to serious trauma and who interpret this trauma as being unavoidable may become depressed and experience behavioral changes that are then linked to future risk of victimization.

FEAR OF CRIME

Fear is an emotional response to a perceived threat (Ferraro & LaGrange, 1987). Victimization is not a requirement for being fearful. For example, females (Ferraro, 1995, 1996; Haynie, 1998; May, Rader, & Goodrum, 2010; Rountree, 1998) have higher levels of fear of crime than do males. For females, this elevated fear of crime has been attributed to their overarching fear of sexual assault. In what is known as the shadow hypothesis, the fear of sexual assault actually serves to increase females' fears of other types of crimes (Ferraro, 1995, 1996; Warr, 1984, 1985). Older persons have been shown to have elevated levels of fear as compared with younger persons as well, but this finding is dependent on question wording. When asked about specific worry about specific crime types, younger persons tend to express greater fear levels (Jackson, 2009).

In response to fear of crime, some may engage in proactive behavior modification to prevent harm. Avoidance behaviors are restrictions that are placed on behavior as protection from harm, for example, staying home at night. Others may engage in defensive or protective behaviors to guard themselves from victimization, such as purchasing a gun or installing security lights (Ferraro & LaGrange, 1987).

RECURRING VICTIMIZATION

Unfortunately, those who are victimized once are at greater risk of being victimized again. In fact, any victim is more likely than nonvictims to be victimized again.

Extent of Recurring Victimization

Recurring victimization occurs when a person or place is victimized with any type of victimization more than once. Repeat victimization occurs when a person or place is victimized more than once by the same type of offense. Revictimization refers to a recurring victim—the "trade" term is *recurring victim* and refers to someone whose victimization is perpetual, constant, albeit even if irregular across a relatively wide span of time—like from childhood to adulthood.

Recent research has also documented that victimization may also be a near-repeat victimization. A near-repeat victimization occurs when a place is victimized that is close by or near in proximity to a place that was previously victimized. Near repeats occur because of crime displacement within a relatively small geographical area after an initial victimization has occurred (Johnson et al., 2007). Near repeats are often studied in reference to burglary incidents. Consider a home that experiences a burglary. The homeowner decides to install an alarm and security lighting after the burglary, thus "hardening" the home from future burglary. Other homes without alarms, however, are not similarly protected. As a result, a burglar who returns to the location may find the first home an unattractive target and choose to burglarize a nearby home instead. In this way, near-repeat victimization happens to a new place but is considered recurring victimization because it is believed that the initial place that was victimized would have been targeted again had it not been for its target hardening.

The Crime Survey for England and Wales, a victimization survey similar to the NCVS, revealed that of those who were victimized, 28% experienced two or more incidents during the same year (Office for National Statistics, 2015). Victims of intimate partner violence, rape, and assault are all at risk of experiencing a subsequent incident following their initial victimization.

These recurring victims experience a disproportionate share of all victimization events. Daigle, Fisher, and Cullen (2008) found that 7% of college women they surveyed had experienced more than one different sexual victimization incident during the previous academic year, and these women experienced almost three fourths of all sexual victimizations reported.

Characteristics of Recurring Victimization

For recurring victims, it is likely that their next incident will happen quickly. For college sexual victims, Daigle et al. (2008) found that most subsequent incidents happen within the same month or 1 month after the initial incident. Fortunately, over time, the risk of experiencing another victimization wanes. Near repeats are most likely to occur within 2 weeks. After a burglary occurs, burglaries within 200 meters of the burgled home are at greatest risk of being burgled for a 2-week period (Johnson et al., 2007). Reiss (1980) found that when a person is victimized a subsequent time, she or he is likely to experience the exact same type of victimization. For example, a theft victim is likely to revisit that theft experience a second time.

Theoretical Explanations of Recurring Victimization

While painting a picture of what recurring victimization "looks" like, the literature does not address why some people are victimized a single time and others find themselves victimized again.

There are two theoretical explanations that have been proffered to explain recurring victimization. The first is risk heterogeneity. This explanation focuses on the qualities or characteristics of the victim. Those qualities or characteristics that place a victim at risk of being a victim, initially, will keep him or her at risk of experiencing a subsequent victimization if he or she does not change.

The second theoretical explanation of recurring victimization is known as state dependence. This suggests that it is not the qualities or characteristics of a victim that are important for recurring victimization so much as what happens during and after the victimization. How the victim acts and reacts during and after the incident and the information gleaned during and after the incident will influence the likelihood of revictimization. For example, a burglar who successfully enters a home and steals a television has learned that the home does not have a security system, how to enter and leave the home, and that the home has a nice television. This information may lead to an increased likelihood of the burglar returning to the home in hopes of stealing a replacement television. To be clear, neither of these explanations should be used to blame or hold responsible the victim or place for the victimization. The offender is solely responsible for his or her actions. These explanations are, however, tools to help understand why some people are targeted over and over again.

Recent theoretical developments have been made in the recurring victimization literature to better understand the interplay between risk heterogeneity and state dependence. According to the compounding vulnerability argument, those with the highest levels of underlying propensity for victimization will be at risk for future victimization because of state dependence processes. For example, those with low income who are victimized may be more likely to show signs of depression following a victimization. These signs of depression are signals to offenders of vulnerability that then increase risk of future victimization. A different perspective is a victimization salience one. In this perspective, state dependence processes will be most salient among those with the lowest underlying risks. Because a target has initially low risk, it makes sense statistically that their risk has more potential than other targets to increase after an initial victimization. Because their risk was initially low, the information that an offender gains about the target (consider a burglar and the house he successfully stole from) is particularly useful and serves to increase risk for future victimization. Contrast this with a target that has a risk that is initially fairly high—the information gained may not be of that much use or needed as the target cannot be that much more at risk anyways! A third perspective is the negative state dependence perspective, which suggests that low-risk persons experience negative state dependence. In this way, a victimization event would serve to reduce victimization risk because a person would become more aware of his or her risk and would take steps to reduce the chances of being victimized in the future (see Clay-Warner, Bunch, & McMahon-Howard, 2016).

THEORIES OF VICTIMIZATION

The Role of the Victim in Crime: Victim Precipitation, Victim Facilitation, and Victim Provocation

The first studies of crime victims did not perceive victims to be innocents who were wronged at the hands of an offender. Rather, concepts such as victim precipitation, victim facilitation, and victim provocation were developed from these investigations. Victim precipitation is the extent to which a victim is responsible for his or her own victimization. The concept of victim precipitation is rooted in the notion that although some victims may not be responsible at all for their victimization, others are, in fact, responsible. In this way, victim precipitation acknowledges that a victimization involves at least two people—an offender and a victim—and that both are acting and oftentimes reacting before, during, and after the incident. Identifying victim precipitation does not necessarily lead to negative outcomes. It is problematic, however, when it blames the victim while ignoring the offender.

Victim facilitation occurs when a victim makes it, unintentionally so, easier for an offender to commit the crime. A victim may, in this way, be a catalyst for victimization. Facilitation helps explain why a one person may be victimized over another, but it does not affix blame or responsibility.

Victim provocation occurs when someone actually does something to incite someone else to commit a crime. Provocation suggests that without the victim, the crime would not have occurred. Provocation, then, most certainly connotes blame. In fact, the offender bears little responsibility.

Hans von Hentig. Von Hentig (1948) looked at the criminal–victim dyad, recognizing the importance of considering the victim and the criminal not in isolation but together. He attempted to identify the characteristics of a victim that might effectively influence victimization risk. He argued that crime victims could be placed into one of 13 categories based on their propensity for victimization: (a) young, (b) female, (c) old, (d) immigrant, (e) depressed, (f) mentally defective or deranged, (g) the acquisitive, (h) dull normal, (i) minority, (j) wanton, (k) the lonesome and heartbroken, (l) tormentor, and (m) the blocked, exempted, and fighting. Each of these types of victims is targeted and contributes to his or her own victimization because of his or her characteristics.

Benjamin Mendelsohn. Known as the father of victimology, Mendelsohn (1968) coined the term *victimology* in the 1940s. He created a classification scheme based on culpability or the degree of victim blame. His classification entailed the following features:

1. Completely innocent victim—a victim who bears no responsibility at all for his/her victimization; becomes a victim simply because of his/her nature such as being a child

2. Victim with minor guilt—a victim who is victimized due to ignorance; a victim who inadvertently places him/herself in harm's way

3. Victim as guilty as offender or a voluntary victim—a victim who bears as much responsibility as the offender; a person who, for example, enters into a suicide pact

4. Victim as more guilty than offender—a victim who instigates or provokes his or her own victimization

5. Most guilty victim—a victim who is victimized during the perpetration of a crime or as a result of crime

6. Simulating or imaginary victim—a victim who actually was not victimized at all but instead fabricates his or her victimization event

Stephen Schafer. One of the earliest victimologists, Schafer (1968) located victims in groups based on how responsible they were for their own victimization using social characteristics and behaviors. He argued that victims have a functional responsibility to not provoke others into victimizing or harming them and that they also should actively attempt to prevent victimization from occurring. His seven categories and responsibilities are:

1. Unrelated victims—no responsibility

2. Provocative victims—share responsibility

3. Precipitative victims—some degree of victim responsibility

4. Biologically weak victims—no responsibility

5. Socially weak victims—no responsibility

6. Self-victimizing—total responsibility

7. Political victims—no responsibility

Menachem Amir. The crime of rape is not immune from victim blaming either today or in its history. Amir (1971) conducted an empirical investigation on rape incidents reported to the police. He examined the extent to which victims precipitated their (i.e., victims were always female) own rapes and also identified commonalities to that type of rape. He concluded that almost 1 in 5 rapes were victim precipitated. He determined that these rapes likely involved alcohol, the victim likely engaged in seductive behavior, she likely wore revealing clothing, likely used risqué language, and likely had a peccant reputation.

Amir also determined that the offender's interpretation of the victim's actions was important rather than what the victim actually did. The offender may view the victim—her actions, words, and clothing—as immodest, against his perception of appropriate female behavior. In this way, the victim is viewed as salacious and provocative. He may then rape her because of his misguided view of appropriate feminine behavior; she then deserves it—she had it coming. Amir's research was quite controversial—and was attacked for blaming victims for their own victimization.

ROUTINE ACTIVITIES AND LIFESTYLES THEORIES

A victimization theory is a set of testable propositions designed to explain why anyone is victimized. Both routine activities and lifestyles theories propose that victimization risk can best be understood by the extent to which the victim's routine activities or lifestyle creates opportunities for a motivated offender to offend.

In developing routine activities theory, Cohen and Felson (1979) argued that a person's daily routines impacted his or her risk of being a crime victim. Insomuch as anyone's routine activities brings him or her into contact with motivated offenders, victimization risk abounds. Cohen and Felson believed that motivated offenders are plentiful, and their motivation to offend does not need explaining. Rather, their selection of particular victims is more interesting. They noted that some factor of an individual or place encourages selection by a motivated offender. In fact, suitable targets are based on their attractiveness by the motivated offender. Attractiveness relates to qualities about the target, such as ease of transport, which is why a burglar may break into a home and leave with an iPod or laptop computer rather than a couch. Attractiveness is further evident when the target does not have capable guardianship, that is, the means by which a target can be effectively guarded so that a victimization is prevented. Guardianship is considered to be social, when the presence of another person makes the potential victim a less attractive target. Guardianship can also be provided through physical means, such as a home equipped with a burglar alarm or a person who carries a weapon for self-protection. When these three elements—motivated offenders, suitable targets, and lack of capable guardianship—coalesce in time and space, victimization is likely to occur.

When Cohen and Felson originally developed their theory, they focused on predatory crimes and were originally interested in explaining changes in rates of these types of crimes over time.

As people spent more time interacting with others, they were more likely to come into contact with motivated offenders. They also linked the increase in crime to the production of durable goods. Electronics began to be produced in sizes that were portable, making them easier to steal. Similarly, cars and other expensive items that could be stolen, reused, and resold became targets. As they saw it, social prosperity produces an increase in criminal victimization.

Hindelang, Gottfredson, and Garofalo (1978) posited that certain lifestyles or behaviors place people in situations in which victimization is likely to occur. A lifestyle that includes going to bars or working late at night in relative seclusion increases risk of victimization. As a person comes into contact—via lifestyle and behavior—with potential offenders, she or he is creating opportunities for crime victimization. Probability of victimization comes from associates, working outside of the home, and engaging in leisure activities. In this way, a person who associates with criminals, who works outside of the home, and who participates in activities, particularly at night, away from home, and with nonfamily members, is a more likely target for personal victimization than others. Hindelang et al. used the principle of homogamy, in which the more frequently a person comes into contact with persons in demographic groups with likely offenders, the more likely victimization will occur. This frequency is thought to be a function of demographics or lifestyle.

One of the reasons that routine activities and lifestyles theories have been the prevailing theories of victimization for over 30 years is because of the wide empirical support found when testing them. It has been shown that a person's routine activities and lifestyles impact risk of being sexually victimized (Cass, 2007; Fisher, Daigle, & Cullen, 2010; Mustaine & Tewksbury, 1999, 2007; Schwartz & Pitts, 1995); auto theft (Rice & Smith, 2002); stalking (Mustaine & Tewksbury, 1999); cybercrime victimization (Holt & Bossler, 2009); adolescent violent victimization (Lauritsen, Laub, & Sampson, 1992); theft (Mustaine & Tewksbury, 1998); victimization at work (Lynch, 1997); and street robbery (Groff, 2007).

STRUCTURAL CAUSES OF VICTIMIZATION

Some areas are so crime prone that they are considered to be "hot spots" for crime. First identified by Sherman, Gartin, and Buerger (1989), hot spots are areas that have a concentrated amount of crime. He found through examining police call data in Minneapolis that only 3% of all locations made up most calls to the police. If a person lived in or frequented a hot spot, she or he would be putting herself or himself in danger. The features of these hot spots and other high-risk areas create opportunities for victimization that, independent of a person's lifestyle or demographic characteristics, enhance his or her chances of being victimized.

What is it about certain areas that make them related to victimization? A body of recent research has identified many features, particularly of neighborhoods. One factor that is related to victimization is family structure. Sampson (1985), in his seminal piece on neighborhoods and crime, found that neighborhoods that have a large percentage of female-headed households have higher rates of theft and violent victimization. He also found that structural density, as measured by the percentage of units in structures with five or more units, is positively related to victimization. Residential mobility, or the percentage of persons 5 years and older living in a different house from 5 years earlier, also predicted victimization.

Living in a neighborhood that is disadvantaged places individuals at risk of being victimized, even if they do not have risky lifestyles or other characteristics related to victimization (Browning & Erickson, 2009). Using collective efficacy, it makes sense that neighborhoods that are disadvantaged are less able to mobilize effective sources of informal social control (Sampson, Raudenbush, & Earls, 1997). Informal social controls are oftentimes used as mechanisms to maintain order, stability, and safety in neighborhoods. When communities do not have strong informal mechanisms in place, violence and other deviancy are likely to abound. Such communities are less safe; hence, its residents are more likely to be victimized than residents of more socially organized areas.

CARING FOR THE VICTIM

Victim's Rights

Once essentially ignored by the criminal justice system and the law, victims are now granted a range of rights. The first such law guaranteeing victims' rights and protections was passed in Wisconsin in 1979; now, every state has some form of victims' rights legislation (Davis & Mulford, 2008). Despite each state having laws that afford victims rights, each differs according to whom the law applies, when the rights begin, what rights victims have, and how these rights can be enforced. Common, however, is the goal of victims' rights—to enhance victim privacy, protection, and participation (Garvin, 2010).

Slightly fewer than half of all states grant all victims rights (Howley & Dorris, 2007). In all states, the right to compensation, notification of rights, notification of court appearances, and ability to submit victim impact statements (VISs) before sentencing is granted to at least some class of victims (Dees, 1999). Other common rights given to victims in the majority of states are the right to restitution, to be treated with dignity and respect, to attend court and sentencing hearings, and to consult with court personnel before plea bargains are offered or defendants released from custody (Davis & Mulford, 2008).

VICTIM REMEDIES AND SERVICES

Victim Compensation

One way that victims receive financial compensation for their economic losses is through state-run victim compensation programs. First begun in 1965 in California, victim compensation programs now exist in every state. Funding for compensation comes from a variety of sources. A large portion derives from criminals themselves—fees and fines imposed on those charged with criminal offenses. These fees are attached to the normal court fees that offenders are expected to pay.

In addition, the Victim of Crime Act of 1984 (VOCA) authorized funding for state compensation and assistance programs. Today, the VOCA Crime Victims Fund provides over $700 million annually to states to assist victims and constitutes about one third of each program's funding (National Association of Crime Victim Compensation Boards, 2009). Not only did VOCA increase funding for state programs, but it also required states to cover all U.S. citizens victimized within the state's borders, regardless of the victim's residency.

Not all victims, however, are eligible for compensation from the Crime Victims Fund. Only victims of rape, assault, child sexual abuse, drunk driving, domestic violence, and homicide are eligible, since these crimes are known to create an undue hardship on victims (Klein, 2010). In addition to the type of victimization, victims must meet other requirements to be eligible:

- Must report the victimization promptly to law enforcement; usually within 72 hours unless "good cause" can be shown, such as being a child or incarcerated or otherwise incapacitated

- Must cooperate with law enforcement and prosecutors in the investigation and prosecution of the case

- Must submit application for compensation within a specified time, generally 1 year from the date of the crime that includes evidence of expenses

- Must show that costs have not been compensated from other sources, such as insurance or other programs

- Must not have participated in criminal conduct or significant misconduct that caused or contributed to the victimization

Victims can be compensated for a wide variety of expenses, including medical care costs, mental health treatment costs, funeral costs, and lost wages. Other expenses for which victims may be able to be compensated include the replacement or repair of eyeglasses or corrective lenses, dental care, prosthetic devices, and forensic sexual assault exams. Note that property damage and loss are not compensable expenses (Office for Victims of Crime, 2010), and only two states currently pay for pain and suffering (Evans, 2014). States have caps in place that limit the amount of money a crime victim may receive from the Crime Victims Fund, generally ranging from $10,000 to $25,000 per incident. On average, the maximum victims can receive is $26,000 (Evans, 2014). Some states also allow for monies for catastrophic injuries and permanent disability, ranging from $5,000 to $150,000 (Evans, 2014).

Of some import is that there is little evidence that persons who receive compensation are any more satisfied than others (Elias, 1984) or that they are more likely to participate in the criminal justice process (Klein, 2010).

Victim Impact Statements

As previously discussed, criminal trials involve two parties in an adversarial system that reflects that a crime is a harm against the state. As such, victims seldom play more than the role of witness in the trial. It was not until the 1970s that victims received rights that guaranteed them at least some voice in the criminal trial process. One of these rights was first adopted in 1976 in Fresno, California, giving victims an opportunity to address the court through a victim impact statement (VIS).

The VIS can be submitted by direct victims or by those who are indirectly impacted by the crime, such as family members. The VIS can be submitted in writing or presented orally (victim allocution).

Victim/Witness Assistance Programs

Victim/witness assistance programs (VWAPs) provide victims with assistance as they navigate the criminal justice system. These programs are designed to ensure that victims know their rights and have the resources necessary to exercise them. At its heart, however, is a goal to increase victim and witness participation in the criminal justice process, particularly by being witnesses, with the notion that victims who have criminal justice personnel assisting them will be more willing to participate in and be satisfied with their experience.

In the *President's Task Force on Victims of Crime: Final Report* (Office of Justice Programs, 1982), the task force recommended that prosecutors better serve victims. Specifically, prosecutors should work more closely with crime victims and receive their input as their cases are processed. It also noted that victims needed protection and their contribution should be valued—prosecutors should honor scheduled case appearances and return personal property as soon as possible. To this end, VWAPs have been developed, most commonly administered through prosecutors' offices but some also run through law enforcement agencies. At the federal level, each U.S. attorney's office has a victim witness coordinator to help victims of federal crimes.

Today, these programs most commonly provide victims with background information regarding the court procedure and their basic rights as crime victims. Notification about court dates and changes to those dates is also made. Information regarding victim compensation and aid for victims in applying for compensation if eligible is also provided. A victim who wishes to make a VIS can receive assistance from the VWAP. Another service offered by a VWAP is making sure the victims and witnesses have separate waiting areas in the courthouse so that they have privacy. In some instances, VWAP personnel will attend court proceedings and trials with the victim and his or her family.

Despite the effort of VWAP programs, research shows that some of the first of these programs did little to improve victim participation. The Vera Institute of Justice's Victim/Witness Assistance Project that ran in the 1970s provided victims with a wide range of services—day care for children while parents went to court, counseling for victims, assistance with victim compensation, notification of all court dates, and a program that allowed victims to stay at work rather than come to court if their testimony was not needed—to little "success" (Herman, 2004). Herman (2004) showed that victims were no more likely to show up at court. It was not until the Vera Institute developed a program that used victim advocates to go to court with victims that positive outcomes emerged. Few programs provide services that have been identified as most critical in the research literature; instead, VWAPs are largely oriented toward ensuring that witnesses cooperate and participate in court proceedings rather than ensuring that crime victims receive needed services (Jerin, Moriarity, & Gibson, 1996).

Family Justice Centers

Because crime victims often need a variety of services, family justice centers are designed to provide many "one-stop" services. These centers provide counseling, advocacy, legal services, health care, financial services, housing assistance, employment referrals, and other services (National Center on Domestic and Sexual Violence, 2011). The advantages to doing so are many—victims can receive a plethora of services without having to navigate the maze of health and social service agencies throughout their jurisdiction. Instead, these services can be found in one central location.

Victim–Offender Mediation Programs

Some victims may not wish to sit in the background and only interact on the periphery of the criminal justice system. Instead, they may want to have face-to-face meetings with their offender. As a way to allow such a dialogue between victims and offenders, victim–offender mediation (VOM) programs have sprouted up throughout the United States, with over 300 such programs in operation today (Umbreit & Greenwood, 2000). With the American Bar Association endorsing the use of VOM and what appears to be widespread public support for these programs, victim–offender mediation has become almost commonplace in U.S. courts (Umbreit & Greenwood, 2000). Victim–offender mediation is already widely used internationally, with more than 700 programs in operation in Europe (Umbreit & Greenwood, 2000).

Mediation in criminal justice cases most commonly occurs as a diversion from prosecution. This means that if an offender and victim agree and complete mediation and if the offender completes any requirements set forth in the mediation agreement, then the offender will not be formally prosecuted in the criminal justice system. Mediation can also take place as a condition of probation. For some offenders, if they formally admit guilt and are adjudicated, they may be placed on probation by the judge with the stipulation that they participate in mediation.

In all instances, it is up to the victim to ultimately participate in VOM programs (Umbreit & Greenwood, 2000). Most victims who are given the opportunity to participate in victim–offender mediation do so (Umbreit & Greenwood, 2000); it is the offender who is more likely to be reluctant.

Victim–offender mediation programs are designed to provide victims—usually property and minor assaults victims—a chance to meet their offenders in a structured environment. Sessions are led by a third-party mediator whose job it is to facilitate a dialogue through which victims are able to directly address their offenders and tell them how the crime impacted their lives. The victim may also question the offender. To achieve the objectives of restorative justice, mediation programs use humanistic mediation, dialogue rather than settlement driven (Umbreit, 2000). The mediator is there to be impartial and to provide unconditional positive concern and regard for both parties, with minimal interruption.

As noted by Umbreit (2000), humanistic mediation emphasizes healing and peacemaking over problem solving and resolution. One tangible product often but not always created from VOM is a restitution plan for the offender that the victim plays a central role in developing. This agreement becomes enforceable with the court, whereby when an offender does not meet his or her requirements, he or she can be remanded to court.

What happens after an offender and victim meet? Do offenders and victims both receive a benefit? What about the community? Collectively, research shows that there are many benefits to VOM programs. Participation has shown a reduction in fear and anxiety among crime victims (Umbreit, Coates, & Kalanj, 1994) including PTSD symptoms (Angel, 2005) and a desire to seek revenge against or harm offenders (Sherman et al., 2005; Strang, 2002). In addition, both offenders and victims report high levels of satisfaction with the VOM process (McCold & Wachtel, 1998; see Umbreit & Greenwood, 2000). Victims who meet their offenders report higher levels of satisfaction with their results than do victims of similar crimes who have their cases formally processed (Umbreit, 1994a). In addition to satisfaction, research shows that offenders are more likely to complete restitution required through VOM (Umbreit et al., 1994). More than 90% of restitution agreements from VOM programs are completed within 1 year (Victim–Offender Reconciliation Program Information and Resource Center, 2006). Reduction in recidivism rates for offenders has also been found (Nugent & Paddock, 1995; Umbreit, 1994b).

SUMMARY

The field of victimology emerged during the mid-1900s. Similar to criminology, victimology studies the causes and consequences of victimization and of how the criminal justice system and other social service agencies respond to crime victims.

We know from official data sources and victimization surveys that the victimization rate had been steadily declining since 1994 with only slight increases from 2010 to 2014 and a decline again in 2015. We also know who faces the greatest risk of being a crime victim. Young persons who are Black (Truman & Morgan, 2016). We also know that households that are low income and those having a greater number of occupants living in them are more likely to experience a property victimization than lesser populated households (Truman, 2010).

Once a person is victimized, she or he often experiences a range of consequences. For some victims, there are economic costs associated with victimization. These economic costs can result from property losses; from money spent on necessary medical or mental health care; from costs associated with losses in productivity or time lost from work, school, or housework; from pain and suffering; from reduced quality of life; and from legal costs. In 2008, the total economic loss from crimes was estimated to be $17,297 billion. Victimization also impacts other entities. In the United States, direct expenditures of the criminal justice system are over $214 billion annually (BJS, 2006). Insurance companies also pay claims associated with crime—annually, these costs top $45 billion (Guns, Money & Medicine, 1996). When uninsured individuals are injured from crime and seek medical attention, society absorbs the cost.

Economic costs are not the only expenses incurred by crime victims.

Many victims experience affective responses to victimization. The most common are depression, reductions in self-esteem, and anxiety. More recently, PTSD has been recognized as a possible outcome to severe trauma, including victimization. PTSD is characterized by exposure to a traumatic event, intrusion symptoms, negative alterations in cognitions and mood, and marked alterations in arousal and reactivity. These symptoms must cause clinically significant distress or impairment in social, occupational, or other functional areas for more than 1 month (APA, 2013).

Many victims blame themselves for their own victimization or experience learned helplessness, whereby they have learned that responding to victimization is futile and so become passive and numb (Seligman, 1975). Another potential cost of victimization is fear. Women and the elderly are fearful, although their actual victimization risks are low (Ferraro, 1995).

Victims face the real risk of being victimized again. Although most who are victimized will not experience another victimization, there is a sizable portion who do, and they are most at risk in the time period immediately following their initial incident. Two competing explanations have been offered to explain this phenomenon: risk heterogeneity and state dependence (Pease, 1998). According to this perspective, characteristics that place an individual at risk, if left unchanged, will continue to keep a victim at risk for subsequent incidents. State dependence, on the other hand, argues that it is what happens during and after an incident that impacts risk. What the victim and offender do and learn during and after an incident will shape future risk. More recent theoretical developments argue that those with the highest levels of underlying propensity for victimization are at the greatest risk for future victimization because of state dependence processes (compounding vulnerability). In addition, a different explanation of recurring victimization is that state dependence processes will be most salient for those with the lowest underlying risk (victimization salience). A third explanation is that persons who are low risk experience negative state dependence—victimizations reduce future risk because a person becomes more aware of their risk and takes steps to avoid future victimizations (Clay-Warner, Bunch, & McMahon-Howard, 2016).

Initial explorations in the field of victimology were centered on determining how much a victim contributes to his or her own victimization. In this way, early researchers were interested in victim precipitation—the extent to which victims are responsible for their own victimization. They studied victim facilitation that makes it easier for an offender to commit a crime. Finally, victim provocation, which occurs when a person incites another person to commit a crime against him, was also examined. Early publications by von Hentig (1948), Mendelsohn (1968), and Schafer (1968) involved developing victim typologies based on the degree to which they were responsible for their own victimization. Empirical studies of victim precipitation were conducted by Amir (1971), who found that almost 1 in 5 rapes were victim precipitated.

The most widely used theories to explain victimization are routine activities and lifestyles theories.

According to routine activities theory, when a person's daily routine activities bring him or her into contact with motivated offenders, without capable guardianship, victimization risk is high. Cohen and Felson (1979) argued that it is the coalescence of time and space of motivated offenders and suitable targets without capable guardianship that predict victimization. Hindelang, Gottfredson, and Garofalo's (1978) lifestyles theory is closely related to routine activities theory. Accordingly, it is a person's lifestyle that shapes victimization risk. Lifestyles that involve spending time outside of the home, especially at night away from the family, are risky in that people come into greater contact with potential offenders. Others have suggested that place characteristics make certain areas ripe for victimization. Some areas, known as "hot spots," are particularly crime prone. Sampson (1985) argued that certain features of neighborhoods impact their risk: family structure, structural density, and residential mobility.

Given the interest in crime victims, it is not surprising to learn that victims now have many rights. Commonly, victims have the right to compensation, the right to notification, the right to attend court hearings, and the right to submit a VIS. Some states also provide the right to restitution, the right to be treated with dignity and respect, the right to consult with court personnel before bond hearings and plea bargaining decisions, the right to protection, and the right to a speedy trial (Davis & Mulford, 2008).

Victim compensation is financial compensation for victims, which is administered through the state. Often, these funds are paid through charges attached to court fees along with Victim of Crime Act funding from the federal government (National Association of Crime Victim Compensation Boards, 2009). To be eligible for compensation, in many states, victims must report the incident to the police in a timely fashion, cooperate with criminal justice personnel in the investigation and prosecution process, submit an application within a specified time, document actual costs and show that these costs have not been paid from other sources, and not have participated in criminal conduct that contributed to the victimization.

Victims (and those indirectly impacted by the crime) may also have the right to make a VIS, which is written or given orally. The VIS details the effects of being victimized and often includes the victim's recommendation for sentence or release (National Center for Victims of Crime, 1999).

Many of the rights that victims have are exercised through their work with victim-witness assistance programs (VWAPs). VWAPs are designed to assist victims in knowing their rights and making sure they have the ability to exercise these rights. Often through prosecutors' offices, VWAPs most commonly provide victims with information about court processes and their basic rights as crime victims. Newer programs to assist crime victims where victims receive a range of services in one place have developed. These family justice centers provide counseling, advocacy, legal services, health care, financial services, housing assistance, employment referrals, and other centrally located services (National Center on Domestic and Sexual Violence, 2011).

Some programs provided to victims allow them to play a more direct role with the criminal justice process. Victim–offender mediation involves face-to-face meetings between the victim and offender and a neutral, third-party mediator. During mediation sessions, the victim is allowed to tell the offender how the victimization impacted his or her life and ask the offender questions. Similarly, the offender is provided an opportunity to apologize and to explain his or her behavior. Sometimes, mediation results in agreed-upon outcomes for the offender, such as restitution to be paid to the victim, that are enforceable by the court.

Discussion Questions

1. Who is the "typical" crime victim? Given the characteristics of the typical crime victim, why do you think that these persons are more at risk than others of being victimized?

2. Using routine activities and lifestyles theories, evaluate your own risk of becoming a crime victim. What measures do you already take to avoid victimization? What could you do but do not? Why do you not do these things? Is it fair to ask victims to change their habits and behavior to reduce victimization? Why, or why not?

3. What other factors besides routine activities and lifestyles do you think increase victimization risk? Why would these factors increase victimization?

4. Why are some people more fearful of being a crime victim than others? Do you think that being fearful could be good for a person? Why, or why not?

5. Research suggests that victimization is a risk factor for future victimization. Why do you think that some people are victimized multiple times and others are not at all? Why might a person not alter their behavior after an initial victimization in order to reduce their future victimization risk?

6. What do you think is the most important right given to crime victims? Why is this the most important?

7. Investigate the rights given to crime victims in your home state. Is it clear what rights are given to victims? Who is responsible for notifying victims of their rights? What remedy do victims have in your home state if their rights are not being met?

8. What programs or resources are available to victims at your college campus? You may find these resources online.

References

American Psychiatric Association. (2013). *Diagnostic and statistical manual of mental disorders* (5th ed.). Washington, DC: Author.

Amir, M. (1971). *Patterns of forcible rape.* Chicago, IL: University of Chicago Press.

Angel, C. (2005). *Crime victims meet their offenders: Testing the impact of restorative justice conferences on victims' post-traumatic stress symptoms.* Doctoral dissertation, University of Pennsylvania.

Bonderman, J. (2001). *Working with victims of gun violence.* Washington, DC: U.S. Department of Justice, Office for Victims of Crime.

Browning, S., & Erickson, P. (2009). Neighborhood disadvantage, alcohol use, and violent victimization. *Youth Violence and Juvenile Justice, 7*(4), 331–349.

Bureau of Justice Statistics. (2006). *Criminal victimization in the United States: Statistical tables.* Washington, DC: U.S. Department of Justice.

Bureau of Justice Statistics. (2008). *National Crime Victimization Survey, 2005.* Ann Arbor, MI: Inter-University Consortium for Political and Social Research. Retrieved from http://www.ICPSR .umich.edu/icpsrweb/NACJD/studies/22746

Bureau of Justice Statistics. (2011). *Criminal victimization in the United States, 2008: Statistical tables.* Washington, DC: U.S. Department of Labor, Bureau of Justice Statistics.

Cass, A. I. (2007). Routine activities and sexual victimization: An analysis of individual and school level factors. *Violence and Victims, 22*(3), 350–366.

Cohen, L. E., & Felson, M. (1979). Social change and crime rate trends: A routine activities approach. *American Sociological Review, 44*(4), 588–608.

Clay-Warner, J., Bunch, J., & McMahon-Howard, J. (2016). Differential vulnerability: Disentangling the effects of state dependence and population heterogeneity on repeat victimization. *Criminal Justice & Behavior, 43*(10), 1406–1429. doi:10.1177/ 0093854816636415

Daigle, L. E., Fisher, B. S., & Cullen, F. T. (2008). The violent and sexual victimization of college women: Is repeat victimization a problem? *Journal of Interpersonal Violence, 23*(9), 1296–1313.

Davis, R. C., & Mulford, C. (2008). Victim rights and new remedies: Finally getting victims their due. *Journal of Contemporary Criminal Justice, 24*(2), 198–208.

Dees, P. (1999). *Victims' rights: Notification, consultation, participation, services, compensation, and remedies in the criminal justice process.* New York, NY: Vera Institute of Justice.

Elias, R. (1984). Alienating the victim: Compensation and victim attitudes. *Journal of Social Issues, 40*(1), 103–116.

Evans, D. N. (2014). *Compensating victims of crime.* New York, NY: Research & Evaluation Center, John Jay College of Criminal Justice, City University of New York. Retrieved from http://www.justice fellowship.org/sites/default/files/Compensating %20Victims%20of%20Crime_John%20Jay_ June%202014.pdf

Ferraro, K. F. (1995). *Fear of crime: Interpreting victimization risk.* Albany, NY: State University of New York Press.

Ferraro, K. F. (1996). Women's fear of victimization: Shadow of sexual assault? *Social Forces, 75*(2), 667–690.

Ferraro, K. F., & LaGrange, R. L. (1987). The measurement of fear of crime. *Sociological Inquiry, 5*(7), 70–101.

Fisher, B. S., Daigle, L. E., & Cullen, F. T. (2010). What distinguishes single from recurrent sexual victims? The role of lifestyle-routine activities and first incident characteristics. *Justice Quarterly, 27*(1), 102–129.

Garvin, M. (2010). Victim's rights movement, United States. In B. S. Fisher & S. P. Lab (Eds.), *Encyclopedia of victimology and crime prevention* (Vol. *2*, pp. 1019–1020). Thousand Oaks, CA: Sage.

Groff, E. R. (2007). Simulation for theory testing and experimentation: An example using routine activity theory and street robbery. *Journal of Quantitative Criminology, 23*(2), 75–103.

Guns, money & medicine. (1996, July 1). *U.S. News & World Report,* pp. 31–40.

Hammack, S. E., Cooper, M., & Lezak, K. R. (2012). Overlapping neurobiology of learned helplessness and conditioned defeat: Implications for PTSD and mood disorders. *Neuropharmacology, 62,* 565–575.

Haynie, D. L. (1998). Explaining the gender gap in fear of crime over time, 1970–1995: A methodological approach. *Criminal Justice Review, 23*(1), 29–50.

Herman, S. (2004, April 28). *Supporting and protecting victims: Making it happen.* Keynote address at the National Victims Conference, London. Retrieved from http://www.ncvc.org/NCVC/main.aspx?dbNa me=DocumentViewr&DocumentI=38044

Hindelang, M. J., Gottfredson, M. R., & Garofalo, J. (1978). *Victims of personal crime: An empirical foundation for a theory of personal victimization.* Cambridge, MA: Ballinger.

Holt, T. J., & Bossler, A. M. (2009). Examining the applicability of lifestyle-routine activities theory for cybercrime victimization. *Deviant Behavior, 30*(1), 1–25.

Howley, S., & Dorris, C. (2007). Legal rights for crime victims in the criminal justice system. In R. C. Davis, A. J. Lurigio, & S. Herman (Eds.), *Victims of crime* (3rd ed., pp. 299–314). Thousand Oaks, CA: Sage.

Jackson, J. (2009). A psychological perspective on vulnerability in the fear of crime. *Psychology, Crime, and Law, 14,* 1–25.

Janoff-Bulman, R. (1979). Characterological versus behavioral self-blame: Inquiries into depression and rape. *Journal of Personality and Social Psychology, 37*(10), 1798–1809.

Jerin, R. A., Moriarty, L. J., & Gibson, M. A. (1996). Victim service or self-service: An analysis of prosecution-based victim-witness assistance programs and services. *Criminal Justice Policy Review, 7*(2), 142–154.

Johnson, S. D., Bernasco, W., Bowers, K. J., Elffers, H., Ratcliffe, J., Rengert, G., & Townsley, M. (2007). Space-time patterns of risk: A cross national assessment of residential burglary victimization. *Journal of Quantitative Criminology, 23,* 201–219.

Kilpatrick, D. G., & Acierno, R. (2003). Mental health needs of crime victims: Epidemiology and outcomes. *Journal of Traumatic Stress, 16*(2), 119–132.

Kilpatrick, D. G., Edmunds, C. N., & Seymour, A. K. (1992). *Rape in America: A report to the nation.* Arlington, VA: National Victim Center & Medical University of South Carolina.

Klein, L. (2010). Victim compensation. In B. S. Fisher & S. P. Lab (Eds.), *Encyclopedia of victimology and crime prevention* (Vol. *2*, pp. 971–974). Thousand Oaks, CA: Sage.

Lauritsen, J. L., Laub, J. H., & Sampson, R. J. (1992). Conventional and delinquent activities: Implications for the prevention of violent victimization among adolescents. *Violence and Victims, 7*(2), 91–108.

Lynch, D. R. (1997). The nature of occupational stress among public defenders. *Justice System Journal, 19*(1), 17–35.

May, D. C., Rader, N. E., & Goodrum, S. (2010). A gendered assessment of the "threat of victimization": Examining gender differences in fear of crime, perceived risk, avoidance, and defensive behaviors. *Criminal Justice Review, 35,* 159–182.

McCold, P., & Wachtel, B. (1998). *Restorative policing experiment: The Bethlehem Pennsylvania Police Family Group Conferencing Project.* Pipersville, PA: Community Service Foundation.

Mendelsohn, B. (1968). Rape in criminology. In S. Schafer (Ed.), *The victim and his criminal.* New York, NY: Random House.

Miller, T. R., Cohen, M. A., & Wiersema, B. (1996). *Victim costs and consequence: A new look.* Washington, DC: U.S. National Institute of Justice.

Mustaine, E. E., & Tewksbury, R. (1998). Predicting risks of larceny theft victimization: A routine activity analysis using refined lifestyle measures. *Criminology, 36*(4), 829–857.

Mustaine, E. E., & Tewksbury, R. (1999). A routine activity theory explanation for women's stalking victimizations. *Violence Against Women, 5*(1), 43–62.

Mustaine, E. E., & Tewksbury, R. (2007). The routine activities and criminal victimization of students: Lifestyle and related factors. In B. S. Fisher & J. J. Sloan (Eds.), *Campus crime: Legal, social, and policy perspectives* (pp. 147–166). Springfield, IL: Charles C. Thomas.

National Association of Crime Victim Compensation Boards. (2009). National conference to mark 25 years of VOCA grants to states. *Crime Victim Compensation Quarterly, 2,* 1. Retrieved from http://www.nacvcb.org/NACVCB/files/ccLibrary Files/Filename/000000000024/20093.pdf]

National Center Domestic and Sexual Violence. (2011). Family justice centers. Retrieved from http://www.ncadv.org/files/DomesticViolenceFact Sheet(National).pdf

National Center for Victims of Crime. (1999). Victim impact statements. Retrieved from http://www.ncvc.org/ncvc/main.aspx?dbName=document ID=32347

Nugent, W. R., & Paddock, J. B. (1995). The effect of victim offender mediation on severity of re-offense. *Mediation Quarterly, 12*(4), 353–367.

Office for Victims of Crime. (2010, April). *Crime Victims Fund: OVC fact sheet.* Retrieved from http://ovc.ncjrs.gov/Publications.aspx?SeriesID=70

Pease, K. (1998). *Repeat victimisation: Taking stock.* London, UK: Home Office, Police Research Group.

President's Task Force on Victims of Crime in 1982. Researchomatic. Retrieved from http://www.researchomatic.com/Presidents-Task-Force-On-Victims-Of-Crime-In-1982-153152.html

Rice, K. J., & Smith, W. R. (2002). Sociological models of automotive theft: Integrating routine activity and social disorganization approaches. *Journal in Research in Crime and Delinquency, 39*(3), 304–336.

Reiss, A. (1980). Victim proneness in repeat victimization by type of crime. In S. Fienberg & A. Reiss (Eds.), *Indicators of crime and criminal justice: Quantitative studies* (pp. 41–53). Washington, DC: U.S. Department of Justice.

Rountree, P. W. (1998). A reexamination of the crime-fear linkage. *Journal of Research in Crime and Delinquency, 35*(3), 341–372.

Sampson, R. J. (1985). Neighborhood and crime: The structural determinants of personal victimization. *Journal of Research in Crime and Delinquency, 22*(1), 7–40.

Sampson, R. J., Raudenbush, S. W., & Earls, F. (1997). Neighborhoods and violent crime: A multilevel study of collective efficacy. *Science, 277*(5328), 918–924.

Schafer, S. (1968). *The victim and his criminal: A study in functional responsibility.* New York, NY: Random House.

Schwartz, M. D., & Pitts, V. L. (1995). Exploring a feminist routine activities approach to explaining sexual assault. *Justice Quarterly, 12*(1), 9–31.

Seligman, M. (1975). *Helplessness*. San Francisco, CA: Freeman.

Sherman, L. W., Gartin, P. R., & Buerger, M. E. (1989). Hot spots of predatory crime: Routine activities and the criminology of place. *Criminology, 27*(1), 27–55.

Sherman, L. W., Strang, H., Angel, C., Woods, D., Barnes, G. C., Bennett, S., & Inkpen, N. (2005). Effects of face-to-face restorative justice on victims of crime in four randomized, controlled trials. *Journal of Experimental Criminology, 1*(3), 367–395.

Strang, H. (2002). *Repair or revenge: Victims and restorative justice*. Oxford, UK: Clarendon.

Truman, J. L. (2010). *Criminal victimization, 2010*. Bureau of Justice Statistics. Retrieved from www.bjs.gov

Truman, J. L., Langton, L., & Planty, M. (2013). *Criminal victimization, 2012*. Washington, DC: U.S. Department of Justice, Bureau of Justice Statistics.

Truman, J. L., & Morgan, R. E. (2016). *Criminal victimization, 2015*. Washington, DC: Bureau of Justice Statistics, Office of Justice Programs, U.S. Department of Justice. Retrieved from https://www.bjs.gov/index.cfm?ty=pbdetail&iid=5804

Turner, H. A., Finkelhor, D., & Ormrod, R. K. (2006). The effect of lifetime victimization on the mental health of children and adolescents. *Social Science & Medicine, 62*, 13–27.

Umbreit, M. S. (1994a). Crime victims confront their offenders: The impact of a Minneapolis mediation program. *Research on Social Work Practice, 4*(4), 436–447.

Umbreit, M. S. (1994b). *Victim meets offender: The impact of restorative justice and mediation*. Monsey, NY: Criminal Justice Press.

Umbreit, M. S. (2000). *Peacemaking and spirituality: A journey toward healing and strength*. Saint Paul, MN: Center for Restorative Justice and Peacemaking, University of Minnesota. Retrieved from http://www.cehd.umn.edu/ssw/rjp/Resources/Forgiveness/Peacemaking_and_Spirituality_Journey_Toward_Healing.pdf

Umbreit, M. S., Coates, R., & Kalanj, B. (1994). *Victim meets offender: The impact of restorative justice and mediation*. Monsey, NY: Criminal Justice Press.

Umbreit, M. S., & Greenwood, J. (2000). *Guidelines for victim-sensitive victim offender mediation: Restorative justice through dialogue*. Washington, DC: Office for Victims of Crime, Office of Justice Programs.

Victim–Offender Reconciliation Program Information and Resource Center. (2006). About victim offender mediation and reconciliation. Retrieved from http://www.vorp.com/

von Hentig, H. (1948). *The criminal and his victim: Studies in the sociobiology of crime*. Oxford, UK: Yale University Press.

Warr, M. (1984, September). Fear of victimization: Why are women and the elderly more afraid? *Social Science Quarterly, 65*, 681–702.

Warr, M. (1985). Fear of rape among urban women. *Social Problems, 32*, 238–250.

JUVENILE DELINQUENCY

David L. Parry

Available statistics reveal that persons under 18 years of age accounted for approximately 8% of all arrests in the United States in 2016, a percentage that has declined steadily since reaching its peak level of 19% in 1996 (Federal Bureau of Investigation, 1996–2016, 2017; Office of Juvenile Justice and Delinquency Prevention, 2017). As in previous years, most arrested youth fell within the delinquency-prone 15–17 age group, and the vast majority were charged with theft, minor assaults, vandalism, drug offenses, liquor law violations, disorderly conduct, or status offenses, such as curfew violations and loitering. Contrary to the overblown myths and hysterical rhetoric fueling what Howell (2009) has dubbed a "moral panic" over supposedly escalating juvenile violence, Columbine-style school shootings, and a wave of juvenile superpredators, no more than about 6% of juveniles arrested in 2016 were charged with serious violent crimes, and the total number of juvenile arrests in that year—estimated at roughly 856,130—had decreased 58% in the preceding 10 years (Federal Bureau of Investigation, 1996–2016, 2017; Office of Juvenile Justice and Delinquency Prevention, 2017).

So who are these delinquents? Where do they come from, and why do they do it? What pathways do they follow into delinquency and—for most—back out as they mature into young adults? What is "delinquency" anyway, and how much of it *really* occurs? These are among the many questions raised in this chapter. The answers are elusive, and the literature exploring them is voluminous. The goal, therefore, is not to present an exhaustive review but rather to selectively examine several key aspects of the delinquency problem, highlighting exemplary statistics and research findings as a vehicle for exploring some of the central issues that must be confronted if we are to better understand and more effectively respond to the delinquency around us and the young people engaged in it.

WHAT IS DELINQUENCY?

Let's begin by taking a look at the meaning of the term *juvenile delinquency*. Traditionally, juvenile courts have exercised jurisdiction in three distinct types of cases. Although statutory language varies, the *delinquency jurisdiction* of these courts generally authorizes intervention in any case involving a minor charged with an act that would be a crime if committed by an adult. It is thus differentiated from their jurisdiction over *status offenders* (youth who engage in activities that would be permissible for an adult but are prohibited for children) and *neglected or dependent* youth (those who have no parent or are the victims of parental neglect or abuse).

This deceptively straightforward definition of juvenile delinquency as a legal category masks significant state-by-state variations that make it exceedingly difficult to pin down exactly who and what we are studying when we try to *understand* delinquency. First, who falls within the delinquency jurisdiction of the juvenile court varies tremendously across states. The Illinois statute, commonly heralded as the first anywhere in the world to authorize creation of a separate court for juveniles, for example, limited the delinquency jurisdiction of juvenile courts to "any child under the age of 16 years who violates any law of this State or any city or village ordinance" (An Act to Regulate the Treatment and Control of Dependent, Neglected and Delinquent Children, 1899). Today, however, only two states continue to restrict delinquency jurisdiction so severely. Most now cap it at the 18th birthday, while seven states limit it to youth under 17 (Zang, 2017; National Center for Juvenile Justice, n.d.). But change is in the air yet again, as legislation already passed in four states (including the two with the lowest age caps) will soon reduce to five the total number of states that systematically prosecute 17- or even 16-year-olds as adults when they break the law (Zang, 2017; National Center for Juvenile Justice, n.d.).

Further complicating matters, juvenile courts have almost universally retained authority to transfer youth under the age cap to criminal court for prosecution as adults if the judge deems the child unamenable to effective treatment within the juvenile justice system, and many states also automatically (i.e., by statute) exclude certain categories of youth (usually those above a specified age) who are charged with very serious offenses from juvenile court jurisdiction and/or grant prosecutors discretion to file such cases directly in criminal court if they choose to do so (see discussions in Griffin, Addie, Adams, & Firestine, 2011; National Center for Juvenile Justice, n.d.). At the other extreme, statutes in most states allow for extended juvenile court jurisdiction over adjudicated delinquents placed on probation or committed to a juvenile correctional facility until well beyond the age at which original jurisdiction ends—most commonly until the youth turns 21 or even, in a handful of states, to age 25 or possibly longer (Zang, 2017; National Center for Juvenile Justice, n.d.). The term—the label—thus applies not only to the *act* but also to the *person* (the teenager or, occasionally, the child) who committed it and even to the young adult still under juvenile court jurisdiction despite advancing age.

The definition of juvenile delinquency gets even murkier when we consider the offenses that underlie the delinquency label. For example, underage drinking is regarded by many as a status offense because it is prohibited only for those under 21 years of age. In most states, however, it is prosecutable as a misdemeanor for "minors" who are younger than 21 but above the maximum age for juvenile court jurisdiction, rendering it a delinquent act for those under that age. A similar dilemma confronts us regarding possession of marijuana, a misdemeanor under federal law and the laws of most states and therefore a delinquent offense for juveniles in those jurisdictions. But in the past several years, eight states and the District of Columbia have legalized possession of small amounts of the drug for recreational use by adults over 21, while in several others, marijuana possession has been reclassified as a noncriminal infraction subject only to a monetary fine, and initiatives elsewhere suggest that sentiment favoring elimination of criminal penalties is gaining traction in still more states across the country (see discussion in National Conference of State Legislatures, 2017). These and other variations in statutory provisions applicable to the delinquency jurisdiction of juvenile courts have significant implications for efforts to understand delinquency as a *social* problem. We saw, for example, that even preteens may sometimes be convicted and punished as adult criminals in the eyes of the law, whereas other young people may technically remain "juvenile delinquents" until their mid-twenties. Does this mean researchers seeking to gauge the extent of delinquency or to understand its causes should rely on after-the-fact decisions by juvenile justice system officials or on legislatively established age caps for juvenile court jurisdiction in determining whether to regard particular behaviors as delinquency or as adult crime? Similarly, do variations in state laws mean we should consider teenaged marijuana smokers to be delinquent if they live in California but not if they live in Massachusetts? What about underage drinking—delinquency or not?

HOW MUCH DELINQUENCY?

These definitional challenges become especially problematic in any effort to gauge the extent of juvenile delinquency and the characteristics of juvenile offenders, even more so given the monumental obstacles to accurate measurement. Nonetheless, we can gain at least a general sense of the frequency and distribution of juvenile offenses by examining data derived from official arrest records, and we can further flesh out the picture by examining additional information gleaned from unofficial sources based on surveys tapping self-reported delinquency.

ARREST DATA

Frequency and rate estimates for arrests of persons under 18 years of age—the closest feasible approximation of youth whose delinquent behavior actually falls within the jurisdiction of juvenile courts in their respective home states—are developed annually by researchers at the National Center for Juvenile Justice (NCJJ), based on Uniform Crime Reports (UCR) data compiled by the Federal Bureau of Investigation and distributed in its *Crime in the United States* series. Prepared under a cooperative agreement with the U.S. Justice Department's Office of Juvenile Justice and Delinquency Prevention (OJJDP) and disseminated online via the *OJJDP Statistical Briefing Book*, the NCJJ estimates for 2016 peg nationwide arrests of "juveniles" as thus defined at 856,130 that year (Office of Juvenile Justice and Delinquency Prevention, 2017). Among the eight "Part I" offenses (formerly the "Crime Index"), the comparative infrequency of violent offenses is striking. While juvenile arrests for one such offense—rape—are not included in the NCJJ estimates because of definitional inconsistencies (i.e., since 2013, law enforcement agencies may submit arrest data to the FBI using either the outdated "legacy" definition of *forcible* rape or a broader "new" definition emphasizing lack of consent rather than force), the other three Part I violent offenses (murder, robbery, and aggravated assault) together accounted for just 5.6% of juvenile arrests in 2016; arrests of juveniles for murder, despite their prominence in news reports and in popular culture, occurred just once in every 1,000 juvenile arrests. Part I property offenses (burglary, larceny-theft, motor vehicle theft, and arson) constituted a much greater share of juvenile arrests—about 21.5%—with the large assortment of generally less serious Part II offenses making up the remainder. Representation of juveniles among *all* persons arrested in 2016 ranged as high as 26% for arson, 20% for robbery and vandalism, and 18% for motor vehicle theft and disorderly conduct. But for other offenses, it was considerably lower: 16% for liquor law violations; 15% for burglary; 12–13% for larceny-theft, weapons offenses, minor assaults, and possession of stolen property; just 6–7% for murder, aggravated assault, and drug abuse violations; and no more than 4% for any of the remaining Part II offenses specified in the NCJJ analysis (Office of Juvenile Justice and Delinquency Prevention, 2017).

Females accounted for 29% of all juvenile arrests in 2016 and for 34% of arrests for Part I property offenses, but among Part I violent offenses, their representation dropped to 26% for aggravated assault, 11% for robbery, and just 9% for murder (Office of Juvenile Justice and Delinquency Prevention, 2017). In contrast with the underrepresentation of females, African American youth, representing about 15% of the under-18 population, were substantially overrepresented, both among juveniles arrested for Part I property offenses (38%) and, even more so, among those arrested for Part I violent offenses for which NCJJ estimates are available: 43% of those arrested for aggravated assault, 61% of murder arrestees, and an astronomical 69% of all juveniles arrested for robbery.

Turning briefly to trends over time, juvenile arrests declined by 58% overall between 2007 and 2016 and by 36% or more for every offense included in NCJJ's analysis (Office of Juvenile Justice and Delinquency Prevention, 2017). In contrast, the FBI's Uniform Crime Reports data reveal that arrests of adults decreased by just under 14% over the same 10-year span and that arrests fell by no more than 16.5% for *any* Part I offense during the same period (Federal Bureau of Investigation, 1996–2016, 2017).

SELF-REPORT SURVEYS

Although arrest data offer important insights about delinquency patterns, they are of questionable reliability as barometers of the frequency with which young people actually engage in delinquent behavior (see discussions in Brame et al., 2004; Krohn, Thornberry, Gibson, & Baldwin, 2010; McCord, Widom, & Crowell, 2001). Alternative measures—especially those based on surveys tapping participants' self-reported involvement in unlawful behaviors—have therefore become an essential adjunct to official records in assessing the extent of delinquency.[1] Self-report data reveal levels of participation in at least minor forms of delinquency that in some studies approach or even exceed 90% (see Moffitt, 1993; Thornberry, Huizinga, & Loeber, 2004), and the cumulative prevalence of self-reported involvement (i.e., the proportion of youth admitting *any* past engagement) in acts characterized as serious violence runs as high as 30–40% of males and 16–32% of females in some accounts (see discussion in Office of the Surgeon General, 2001). Self-report data also tend to indicate smaller race and gender differences in rates of juvenile offending than do arrest statistics, although the extent of such differences varies tremendously across studies, with some researchers finding no differences at all, and others reporting even wider gaps than those found in officially recorded arrests (see discussions in Lauritsen, 2005; Loeber et al., 2015; Piquero, Schubert, & Brame, 2014; Zahn et al., 2008).

ADOLESCENT DEVELOPMENT, RISK FACTORS, AND PATHWAYS TO DELINQUENCY

Several strands in contemporary delinquency research warrant our attention here, insofar as they offer valuable insights about ways in which delinquency is conditioned by the nature of adolescent development, risk factors that increase the likelihood of escalating antisocial behavior, and pathways leading toward increasingly serious delinquency that carry important practical implications for delinquency prevention and juvenile justice policy.

Moffitt's (1993) well-known distinction between adolescence-limited and life course–persistent offenders provides a useful starting point for discussing the place of delinquency in the life course trajectories of youth. While large proportions of youth engage in delinquent behavior during adolescence, only a small minority continue their antisocial behavior into adulthood. Even fewer develop into career offenders, cycling in and out of jails and prisons while most of their peers "grow out of it" as they mature and take on law-abiding adult social roles. In contrast with the *discontinuity* displayed in the transitory delinquency of adolescence-limited offenders, who commit their first offenses as young teenagers and then *desist* as they enter adulthood, Moffitt describes a pattern of striking *continuity* across the entire lifespan in the antisocial behavior of life course–persistent offenders. These offenders—estimated at roughly 5–6% of the population[2]—are likely to exhibit "difficult" temperaments and aggressive tendencies even in infancy, have their first police contacts for delinquent before reaching puberty, become immersed in delinquency as teenagers, and develop into career offenders in adulthood.

NORMAL ADOLESCENT BEHAVIOR?

Many delinquency researchers share Moffitt's belief that some level of engagement in delinquent or otherwise antisocial behavior is an entirely normal part of adolescent development. Some, like Moffitt, view adolescence-limited offending through a social learning lens, as a self-reinforcing way for adolescents to cope with the uncomfortable paradox of attaining biological maturity years before the autonomy and privileges of adult status are extended to them, a temporary digression that is soon cast off as the transition to young adulthood brings new opportunities and altered contingencies that make desistance increasingly rewarding (Moffitt, 1993). Others, looking to the lessons of developmental psychology for answers, have sought an explanation in the still-developing decision-making capabilities of adolescents (see discussions in Scott & Steinberg, 2008; Bonnie, Johnson, Chemers, & Schuck, 2013). In one such approach reflecting broadly shared insights, researchers examining the impact of psychosocial immaturity on adolescents' competence to stand trial (an initiative of the MacArthur Foundation Research Network on Adolescent Development and Juvenile Justice) have systematically explored the ways in which teenagers differ from adults in cognitive capacity (reasoning ability) and judgment (common sense). Although developmental neuroscientists generally believed until roughly the dawn of the 21st century that the cognitive abilities of most youth approximated those of adults by mid-adolescence, more recent research has demonstrated that, while basic cognitive capability matures by about age 16, the brain nonetheless continues to develop beyond adolescence and into young adulthood, with significant structural changes in the frontal lobes and especially the prefrontal cortex that have important implications for impulse control and ability to assess the potential consequences of one's actions (see discussions in Bonnie et al., 2013; Scott & Steinberg, 2008; Steinberg, Cauffman, Woolard, Graham, & Banich, 2009).

Even as their brains are still developing and partially (but not entirely) in consequence of their immature cognitive functioning, the decision making of adolescents is also deeply impacted by heightened sensitivity to peer influence, comparatively cavalier attitudes toward risk, and a temporal perspective emphasizing short-term benefits over longer term consequences (Grisso et al., 2003; Scott & Grisso, 1997;

Steinberg & Scott, 2003; see also Grisso & Schwartz, 2000; Scott & Steinberg, 2008). This cluster of psychosocial factors is argued to affect adolescents' judgment in ways that lead them to use information differently, deploy their reasoning skills differently or less reliably, and weigh costs and benefits of their actions differently than would an adult in a comparable situation, thus increasing their vulnerability to external pressures supporting delinquent behavior (Scott & Grisso, 1997; see also Scott & Steinberg, 2008; Bonnie et al., 2013).

RISK AND PROTECTIVE FACTORS

The efforts of Moffitt (1993) and others to isolate characteristics that can help predict the direction a young offender's life will take—toward persistent offending in adulthood or toward desistance as he or she matures—have spawned extensive research seeking to identify *risk factors* that are predictive of later patterns of serious, violent, and/or chronic offending and the *pathways* leading toward escalating antisocial behavior.

A sense of the wide variety of factors that have been found to place a child at increased risk for later involvement in such behavior can be gathered from the following enumeration of individual, family, school, peer, and community characteristics that researchers participating in the Office of Juvenile Justice and Delinquency Prevention's Study Group on Serious and Violent Juvenile Offenders determined to be at least somewhat predictive of later violence, based on their findings in a groundbreaking and, at the time, exhaustive meta-analysis of 66 rigorous, separately conducted longitudinal studies published between 1959 and 1997:

- Individual Factors—pregnancy and delivery complications; low resting heart rate; internalizing disorders; hyperactivity, concentration problems, restlessness, and risk taking; aggressiveness; early initiation of violent behavior; involvement in other forms of antisocial behavior; beliefs and attitudes favorable to deviant or antisocial behavior.

- Family Factors—parental criminality; child maltreatment; poor family management practices; low levels of parental involvement; poor family bonding and family conflict; parental attitudes favorable to substance use and violence; parent–child separation.

- School Factors—academic failure; low bonding to school; truancy and dropping out of school; frequent school transitions.

- Peer-Related Factors—delinquent siblings; delinquent peers; gang membership.

- Community and Neighborhood Factors—poverty; community disorganization; availability of drugs and firearms; neighborhood adults involved in crime; exposure to violence and racial prejudice. (Hawkins et al., 2000, p. 2; see also Hawkins et al., 1998)

Not surprisingly, risk factors have been found to differ substantially in their predictive value, and research has shown that particular factors may be stronger—or weaker—predictors of later behavior when observed in young children, as compared with adolescents. In another pioneering meta-analysis by members of the Study Group on Serious and Violent Juvenile Offenders, Lipsey and Derzon (1998) found that the predictive value of particular factors differed considerably for young children, as compared with adolescents. For children aged 6–11, commission of a general juvenile offense (i.e., *any* juvenile offense committed by a child in this age group) was found to be the single strongest predictor of serious or violent behavior at age 15–25, followed by substance abuse and, in a second rank of predictive variables, gender (i.e., being male), family SES (socioeconomic status), and antisocial parents. For 12- to 14-year-olds, the strongest predictors were weak social ties and antisocial peers, with commission of general offenses following in the second rank but having noticeably less predictive value than was observed for the younger group. By contrast, antisocial peers had very little impact on later behavior for 6–11 year olds while substance abuse and family SES carried only minimal predictive value for the older group. Curiously, broken homes and abusive parents were ranked among the weakest predictors for both groups, although later research has emphasized the importance of child maltreatment as a predictor of various forms of violence and other antisocial behavior—especially if it occurs during adolescence (Maas, Herrenkohl, & Sousa, 2008; Thornberry et al., 2004).

Many of the risk factors identified here have found additional support in more recent studies, and other factors not specifically examined in the earlier studies have also been identified (see Loeber & Farrington, 2012). Researchers have also observed a *cumulative* effect of risk factors, such that exposure to multiple risk factors increases the likelihood of later antisocial behavior (Farrington, 1997; Herrenkohl et al., 2000). Other research has shown that the deleterious effects of exposure to one or more risk factors may be mitigated by the presence of *protective* factors that help insulate the child from negative influences—for example, intolerant attitudes toward deviance, supportive relationships with parents or other adults, or a strong commitment to school (see discussions in Office of the Surgeon General, 2001; Loeber & Farrington, 2012).

PATHWAYS TO DELINQUENCY

Considerable attention has been paid in recent years to the developmental "pathways" followed by adolescents as they progress toward deeper involvement in delinquency. Perhaps the most ambitious research to date in this regard has taken place within the broader context of three coordinated longitudinal research projects undertaken in furtherance of yet another major Office of Juvenile Justice and Delinquency Prevention initiative—the Program of Research on the Causes and Correlates of Delinquency. Based on an initial analysis of the offense trajectories of boys tracked over an extended period in the Pittsburgh Youth Study, project director Rolf Loeber and his associates identified three distinct patterns of escalating delinquency (Kelley, Loeber, Keenan, & DeLamatre, 1997):

- **Authority Conflict** is the first and earliest pathway. The pathway begins with stubborn behavior (stage 1) and can be followed by defiance (stage 2), such as refusal and disobedience. This, in turn, can be followed by authority avoidance (stage 3), such as truancy and running away from home. The authority conflict pathway applies to boys prior to age 12, because after that age some youth are likely to enter the pathway at the highest levels with behaviors such as truancy and staying out late at night.

- **Covert** acts and their escalation are addressed in the second pathway. This pathway tends to start with minor covert behaviors (stage 1), such as lying and shoplifting, and can be followed by property damage (stage 2), including vandalism and firesetting, and later by more serious forms of property crimes (stage 3), such as burglary.

- **Overt** or increasingly aggressive acts make up the third pathway. This sequence starts with minor aggression (stage 1), such as annoying others and bullying. This can be followed by physical fighting (stage 2), including gang fighting, and then by violence (stage 3), such as attacking someone, strong-arming, and rape (pp. 8–9).

The three-pathway model has been replicated in a variety of contexts, including various subsets of the Pittsburgh sample and in both the Rochester Youth Development Study and the Denver Youth Survey. Summarizing some of the key findings from this research, the project directors of the three causes and correlates studies later reiterated the conclusion that youth tend to follow an orderly sequence as they move from less serious to more serious delinquency, even in those instances where they progress on multiple pathways, engaging in a wider variety of delinquent behaviors as they get older (Thornberry et al., 2004; see also Thornberry & Krohn, 2003). Referencing related aspects of the studies, they emphasize the predictive importance of early onset (i.e., childhood aggression beginning before age 13), child maltreatment, and gang membership as precursors of escalating involvement in delinquent behavior. But they also caution that accurate differentiation between those whose behavior persists and escalates over time and those who desist following a period of experimentation remains distressingly elusive.

DIFFERENT FOR GIRLS?

Seeking to remedy the general dearth of attention paid to delinquent girls even as the gender gap in arrest rates narrows (see Chesney-Lind, Chapter 6 of this book;

Zahn et al., 2008), researchers have begun compiling an empirical record addressing the developmental pathways girls follow and the risk and protective factors that influence their delinquent involvement. While some have concluded that girls tend to follow the same developmental pathways as boys and that the risk factors for male and female delinquency are similar, others have found girls to follow distinctive routes and to respond differently to particular risk factors and protective factors (see discussions in Hawkins, Graham, Williams, & Zahn, 2009; Howell, 2009; Huizinga et al., 2013; Zahn et al., 2010).

With remarkable consistency, research on female delinquency points to a cluster of life circumstances shared by large proportions of delinquent girls. For example, in one study of girls in the California juvenile justice system, 92% of offenders reported a history of physical, emotional, and/or sexual abuse; 95% lacked a stable home environment; 91% had experienced some form of school failure; and 75% had a history of drug or alcohol abuse (Acoca & Dedel, 1998; see also Acoca, 1999). In another, focus groups with system-involved girls in 10 California counties revealed a set of risk factors for delinquency including the following: family issues (family conflict, parental absence, parental criminality or drug abuse, poor communication); sexual, physical, and emotional abuse; running away from home; substance abuse; gang involvement and fighting; school difficulties and negative attitudes toward school; and early and inappropriate sexual behavior (Bloom, Owen, Rosenbaum, & Deschenes, 2003).

The themes of sexual victimization, family disruption, educational failure, substance abuse, and running away also permeate Saar, Epstein, Rosenthal, and Vafa's (2015) haunting and strikingly well-documented account of "the sexual abuse to prison pipeline" and Chesney-Lind's examinations of the lives of female delinquents and the ways in which gender stratification and its consequences condition not only their delinquency but also their "invisibility" once drawn into the juvenile justice system (see especially Chesney-Lind, Morash, & Stevens, 2008; Chesney-Lind & Shelden, 2014). Finally, many of these same themes reemerge as "stepping-stones" in Howell's (2009) elucidation of a more-or-less sequential pathway leading girls toward escalating delinquency. Linking together findings from numerous studies of female delinquents, OJJDP's former deputy administrator and long-time director of research and program development builds the case for a sequence of six such stepping-stones for girls following a pathway toward serious, chronic, and/or violent delinquency. Describing a process grounded in the notion that the "gendered" nature of risk factors girls experience in common with boys may exacerbate the impact on girls, Howell traces a pathway leading from physical and/or sexual child abuse to mental health problems, drug abuse, running away from home, youth gang activity, and, finally, juvenile justice system involvement.

DISCUSSION

This brief overview has taken a highly selective look at several aspects of the delinquency problem that have recently drawn the attention of delinquency researchers. As indicated at the outset, the goal has been to highlight statistics and research findings that help point the way toward more effective ways of preventing and responding to delinquency. But the lessons of research are not always straightforward, and the policy implications of studies addressing one aspect of research may lead us in very different directions from those emerging from a different line of research or point us in different directions depending upon other considerations.

We have learned, for example, that delinquency is "normal" in adolescence but that most of us desist from illegal activity as we enter adulthood. In fact, age consistently ranks among the strongest correlates of criminal behavior (Farrington, 1986; Federal Bureau of Investigation, 1996–2016, 2017; Hirschi & Gottfredson, 1983), and the pervasiveness of delinquent involvement during adolescence followed by desistance in early adulthood is now well documented (see Moffitt, 1993; Thornberry et al., 2004). Even among serious juvenile offenders, a life course trajectory leading toward desistance or sharply reduced illegal activity in adulthood appears to be the norm rather than the exception (Mulvey et al., 2004; Rocque, 2017; Sampson & Laub, 2003). These patterns offer at least a modicum of support for the arguments of labeling theorists that juvenile court intervention is unnecessary or even counterproductive for most youthful law violators (Lemert, 1967; Schur, 1973). Does this mean we should follow their advice and avoid intervention altogether or intervene only if it is absolutely essential in order to protect public safety? Or does it direct us to heed the findings of research on risk factors and pathways to escalating delinquency, doing our best to identify potential life course–persistent offenders as early as possible so we can steer them in a different direction while leaving the adolescence-limited offenders alone as much as possible?

As those examining the causes and correlates discovered, early intervention is crucial to the success of efforts to divert youth from pathways leading to increasingly serious and persistent delinquency; so a "this too will pass" approach risks waiting until the opportunity to intervene effectively is long past (Kelley et al., 1997, p. 17; see also Thornberry et al., 2004). But categorizing young offenders based on the presence of known risk factors is not a panacea either. Aside from questions about the fairness of treating youth differently based on personal characteristics rather than the nature of the offense, even the most sophisticated research still lacks the ability to accurately distinguish "persisters" from "experimenters" (Kelley et al., 1997; Schubert, Mulvey, & Pitzer, 2016). Statistical association between a particular characteristic and later antisocial behavior cannot be taken as an indication that a youth exposed to that risk factor or even to a constellation of factors will necessarily become a serious or chronic offender later in life. It also bears emphasis that the findings of individual studies or even of a combination of studies cannot be taken as definitive with respect to factors that predict later delinquent behavior. Aside from variations in the overall quality of study design and execution that impact results, the focus of research varies considerably from one study to the next. Some studies investigate predictors of *violent* behavior, while others expand the focus to encompass predictors of *serious* delinquency, whether violent or otherwise, or even to *any* delinquent involvement. Yet others investigate predictors of *chronic* antisocial behavior continuing into adulthood or narrow the focus to risk factors for engagement in particular *types* of delinquent activity or other antisocial behavior (e.g., gang membership, sex offenses, and intimate partner violence). Likewise, the independent variables that are tested differ across studies, and study samples differ in ways that greatly affect results (e.g., risk factors may be very different for males and females or for youth of different racial groups, so findings based on a study of one group cannot be generalized to others). Even the measures of delinquency (arrest data, self-reports, etc.) differ tremendously from one study to the next in ways that impact results.

These observations offer just a hint of the many ways in which delinquency research can be used to stimulate consideration of policy innovations carrying the potential to divert youth from deeper involvement in delinquent behavior. But they should also serve as a caution against thoughtlessly translating research into policy without recognizing the probabilistic nature of the findings and the potentially conflicting implications for preventing or responding to delinquency arising from different lines of research.

Discussion Questions

1. If delinquent behavior is really a normal part of adolescent development that most youth engage in to some degree, what should be done about those who are caught, and what characteristics of the offense and the offender do you think should be taken into consideration in deciding how to respond in a particular case?

2. In light of what we know about adolescent development, the pervasiveness of adolescence-limited delinquency, and the distribution of crime across age groups (i.e., the correlation between age and crime), what maximum age for juvenile court jurisdiction would you consider most appropriate?

3. Given the importance of early onset as a risk factor for later involvement in serious, violent, and chronic offending, should young children who are caught committing delinquent acts be treated differently from adolescents who commit comparable offenses?

4. Based on what we know about risk factors and pathways to delinquency, what element would you recommend including in a prevention program in order to maximize its effectiveness in steering young people away from delinquency? What differences would you recommend in prevention programs targeting youth in each of the groups contrasted below?

    a. adolescents versus preteens

    b. males versus females

    c. youth at high risk to become life course–persistent offenders versus those likely to remain adolescence-limited offenders

5. How might research on adolescent development, risk factors, and pathways to delinquency be used to facilitate correctional intervention with youth who have been caught committing delinquent acts?

Notes

1. Although the many shortcomings of early self-report studies have not been entirely alleviated, increasing sophistication of the sampling frames, measures of delinquency, and question formats employed in contemporary survey instruments has greatly enhanced their utility as indicators of delinquent behavior (see discussions in Brame et al., 2004; Krohn et al., 2010; Hindelang, Hirschi, & Weis, 1981; Huizinga & Elliott, 1986; Thornberry & Krohn, 2000).

2. This figure is commonly traced to Wolfgang, Figlio, and Sellin's (1972) seminal finding that about 6% of boys born in Philadelphia in 1945 were responsible for over half of all offenses committed by youth in the "birth cohort." Moffitt (1993) cites a broad array of subsequent studies that have obtained comparable results with respect to various measures of serious and chronic antisocial behavior among children, adolescents, and adults.

References

Acoca, L. (1999). Investing in girls: A 21st century strategy. *Juvenile Justice, 6*(1), 3–13. Retrieved from https://www.ncjrs.gov/pdffiles1/ojjdp/178254.pdf

Acoca, L., & Dedel, K. (1998). *No place to hide: Understanding and meeting the needs of girls in the California juvenile justice system*. San Francisco, CA: National Council on Crime and Delinquency.

An Act to Regulate the Treatment and Control of Dependent, Neglected and Delinquent Children. (1899). Illinois Juvenile Court Act Approved April 21, 1899. Laws of the State of Illinois, enacted by the Forty-First General Assembly at the regular biennial session. 1899 Ill. Laws 131.

Bonnie, R. J., Johnson, R. L., Chemers, B. M., & Schuck, J. (Eds.). (2013). *Reforming juvenile justice: A developmental approach*. Washington, DC: National Academies Press.

Bloom, B., Owen, B., Rosenbaum, J., & Deschenes, E.P. (2003). Focusing on girls and young women: A gendered perspective on female delinquency. *Women & Criminal Justice, 14*(2/3), 117–136.

Brame, R., Fagan, J., Piquero, A. R., Schubert, C. A., & Steinberg, L. (2004). Criminal careers of serious delinquents in two cities. *Youth Violence and Juvenile Justice, 2*(3), 256–272.

Chesney-Lind, M., Morash, M., & Stevens, T. (2008). Girls' troubles, girls' delinquency, and gender responsive programming: A review. *Australian and New Zealand Journal of Criminology, 41*(1), 162–189.

Chesney-Lind, M., & Shelden, R. G. (2014). *Girls, delinquency and juvenile justice* (4th ed.). Hoboken, NJ: Wiley-Blackwell.

Farrington, D. P. (1986). Age and crime. In M. Tonry & N. Morris (Eds.), *Crime and justice: An annual review of research* (Vol. 7, pp. 189–250). Chicago, IL: University of Chicago Press.

Farrington, D. P. (1997). Early prevention of violent and nonviolent youthful offending. *European Journal on Criminal Policy and Research, 5,* 51–66.

Federal Bureau of Investigation. (1996–2016). *Crime in the United States, 1995–2015*. Retrieved from https://ucr.fbi.gov/ucr-publications.

Federal Bureau of Investigation. (2017). *Crime in the United States, 2016*. Retrieved from https://ucr.fbi.gov/crime-in-the-u.s/2016/crime-in-the-u.s.-2016

Griffin, P., Addie, S., Adams, B., & Firestine, K. (2011). *Trying juveniles as adults: An analysis of state transfer laws and reporting*. Washington, DC: Office of Juvenile Justice and Delinquency Prevention. Retrieved from https://www.ncjrs.gov/pdffiles1/ojjdp/232434.pdf

Grisso, T., & Schwartz, R. G. (Eds.). (2000). *Youth on trial: A developmental perspective on juvenile justice.* Chicago, IL: The University of Chicago Press.

Grisso, T., Steinberg, L., Woolard, J., Cauffman, E., Scott, E., Graham, S., . . . Schwartz, R. (2003). Juveniles' competence to stand trial: A comparison of adolescents' and adults' capacities as trial defendants. *Law and Human Behavior, 27*(4), 333–363.

Hawkins, J. D., Herrenkohl, T., Farrington, D. P., Brewer, D., Catalano, R. F., & Harachi, T. W. (1998). A review of predictors of youth violence. In R. Loeber & D. P. Farrington (Eds.), *Serious and violent juvenile offenders: Risk factors and successful interventions* (pp. 106–146). Thousand Oaks, CA: Sage.

Hawkins, J. D., Herrenkohl, T. I., Farrington, D. P., Brewer, D., Catalano, R. F., Harachi, T. W., & Cothern, L. (2000). *Predictors of youth violence.* Washington, DC: Office of Juvenile Justice and Delinquency Prevention. Retrieved from https://www.ncjrs.gov/pdffiles1/ojjdp/179065.pdf

Hawkins, S. R., Graham, P. W., Williams, J., & Zahn, M. A. (2009). *Resilient girls—Factors that protect against delinquency.* Washington, DC: Office of Juvenile Justice and Delinquency Prevention. Retrieved from https://www.ncjrs.gov/pdffiles1/ojjdp/220124.pdf

Herrenkohl, T. I., Maguin, E., Hill, K. G., Hawkins, J. D., Abbott, R. D., & Catalano, R. F. (2000). Developmental risk factors for youth violence. *Journal of Adolescent Health, 26*(7), 176–186.

Hindelang, M. J., Hirschi, T., & Weiss, J. G. (1981). *Measuring delinquency.* Beverly Hills, CA: Sage.

Hirschi, T., & Gottfredson, M. R., (1983). Age and the explanation of crime. *American Journal of Sociology, 89*, 552–584.

Howell, J. C. (2009). *Preventing and reducing delinquency: A comprehensive framework* (2nd ed.). Thousand Oaks, CA: Sage.

Huizinga, D., & Elliott, D. S. (1986). Reassessing the reliability and validity of self-reported data. *Journal of Quantitative Criminology, 2*(4), 293–327.

Huizinga, D., Miller, S., & the Conduct Problems Prevention Research Group. (2013). *Developmental sequences of girls' delinquent behavior.* Washington, DC: Office of Juvenile Justice and Delinquency Prevention. Retrieved from https://www.ojjdp.gov/pubs/238276.pdf

Kelley, B. T., Loeber, R., Keenan, K., & DeLamatre, M. (1997). *Developmental pathways in boys' disruptive and delinquent behavior.* Washington, DC: Office of Juvenile Justice and Delinquency Prevention. Retrieved from https://www.ncjrs.gov/pdffiles/165692.pdf

Krohn, M. D., Thornberry, T. P., Gibson, C. L., & Baldwin, J. M. (2010). The development and impact of self-report measures of crime and delinquency. *Journal of Quantitative Criminology, 26*(4), 509–525.

Lauritsen, J. L. (2005). Racial and ethnic differences in juvenile offending. In D. Hawkins & K. Kempf-Leonard (Eds.), *Our children, their children: Confronting race and ethnic differences in American criminal justice* (pp. 83–104). Chicago, IL: University of Chicago Press.

Lemert, E. M. (1967). The juvenile court: Quest and realities. In The President's Commission on Law Enforcement and Administration of Justice, Task Force on Juvenile Delinquency (Eds.), *Task force report: Juvenile delinquency and youth crime—Report on juvenile justice and consultants' papers* (pp. 91–106). Washington, DC: U.S. Government Printing Office.

Lipsey, M. W., & Derzon, J. H. (1998). Predictors of violent or serious delinquency in adolescence and early adulthood: A synthesis of longitudinal research. In R. Loeber & D. P. Farrington (Eds.), *Serious and violent juvenile offenders: Risk factors and successful interventions* (pp. 86–105). Thousand Oaks, CA: Sage.

Loeber, R., & Farrington, D. P. (Eds.). (2012). *From juvenile delinquency to adult crime: Criminal careers, justice policy and prevention.* New York, NY: Oxford University Press.

Loeber, R., Farrington, D. P., Hipwell, A. E., Stepp, S. D., Pardini, D., & Ahonen, L. (2015). Constancy and change in the prevalence and frequency of offending when based on longitudinal self-reports or official records: Comparisons by gender, race, and crime type. *Journal of Developmental and Life-Course Criminology, 1*(2), 150–168.

Maas, C., Herrenkohl, T. I., & Sousa, C. (2008). Review of research on child maltreatment and violence in youth. Trauma, Violence, & Abuse: A Review Journal, 9(1), 56–67.

McCord, J., Widom, C. S., & Crowell, N. A. (Eds.). (2001). Juvenile crime, juvenile justice. Washington, DC: National Academies Press. Retrieved from https://www.nap.edu/catalog/9747/juvenile-crime-juvenile-justice

Moffitt, T. E. (1993). Adolescence-limited and life-course-persistent antisocial behavior: A developmental taxonomy. Psychological Review, 100, 674–701.

Mulvey, E. P., Steinberg, L., Fagan, J., Cauffman, E., Piquero, A. R., Chassin, L., & Losoya, S. H. (2004). Theory and research on desistance from antisocial activity among serious adolescent offenders. Youth Violence and Juvenile Justice, 2(3), 1–24.

National Center for Juvenile Justice. (n.d.). Jurisdictional boundaries. Juvenile Justice Geography, Policy, Practice & Statistics (JJGPS). Pittsburgh, PA: National Center for Juvenile Justice. Retrieved from http://www.jjgps.org/jurisdictional-boundaries.

National Conference of State Legislatures. (2017). Marijuana overview. Washington, DC: National Conference of State Legislatures. Retrieved from http://www.ncsl.org/research/civil-and-criminal-justice/marijuana-overview.aspx.

Office of Juvenile Justice and Delinquency Prevention. (2017). OJJDP statistical briefing book. Retrieved from https://www.ojjdp.gov/ojstatbb/

Office of the Surgeon General. (2001). Youth violence: A report of the Surgeon General. Washington, DC: U.S. Department of Health and Human Services, Office of Public Health and Science, Office of the Surgeon General. Retrieved from https://www.ncbi.nlm.nih.gov/books/NBK44294/

Piquero, A. R., Schubert, C. A., & Brame, R. (2014). Comparing official and self-report records of offending across gender and race/ethnicity in a longitudinal study of serious youthful offenders. Journal of Research in Crime and Delinquency, 51(4), 526–556.

Rocque, M. (2017). Desistance from crime: New advances in theory and research. New York, NY: Palgrave Macmillan.

Saar, M. S., Epstein, R., Rosenthal, L., & Vafa, Y. (2015). The sexual abuse to prison pipeline: The girls' story. Washington, DC: Center for Poverty and Inequality, Georgetown University Law Center. Retrieved from https://www.law.georgetown.edu/academics/centers-institutes/poverty-inequality/upload/2015_COP_sexual-abuse_layout_web-2.pdf

Sampson, R. J., & Laub, J. H. (2003). Life-course desisters? Trajectories of crime among delinquent boys followed to age 70. Criminology, 41(3), 555–592.

Scott, E. S., & Grisso, T. (1997). The evolution of adolescence: A developmental perspective on juvenile justice reform. Journal of Criminal Law and Criminology, 88(1), 137–189.

Scott, E. S., & Steinberg, L. (2008). Rethinking juvenile justice. Cambridge, MA: Harvard University Press.

Schubert, C. A., Mulvey, E. P., & Pitzer, L. (2016). Differentiating serious adolescent offenders who exit the justice system from those who do not. Criminology, 54(1), 56–85.

Schur, E. M. (1973). Radical nonintervention: Rethinking the delinquency problem. Englewood Cliffs, NJ: Prentice Hall.

Steinberg, L., & Scott, E. (2003). Less guilty by reason of adolescence: Developmental immaturity, diminished responsibility, and the juvenile death penalty. American Psychologist, 58(12), 1009–1018.

Steinberg, L., Cauffman, E., Woolard, J., Graham, S., & Banich, M. (2009). Are adolescents less mature than adults? Minors' access to abortion, the juvenile death penalty, and the alleged APA "flip-flop." American Psychologist, 64(7), 583–594.

Thornberry, T. P., Huizinga, D., & Loeber, R. (2004). The causes and correlates studies: Findings and policy implications. Juvenile Justice Journal, 9(1), 3–19. Retrieved from https://www.ncjrs.gov/pdffiles1/ojjdp/203555.pdf

Thornberry, T. P., & Krohn, M. D. (2000). The self-report method for measuring delinquency and crime. In D. Duffee (Ed.), *Criminal Justice 2000: Vol. 4. Measurement and analysis of crime and justice* (pp. 33–84). Washington, DC: National Institute of Justice. Retrieved from https://www.ncjrs.gov/criminal_justice2000/vol_4/04b.pdf

Thornberry, T. P., & Krohn, M. D. (Eds.). (2003). *Taking stock of delinquency: An overview of findings from contemporary longitudinal studies.* New York, NY: Kluwer-Plenum.

Wolfgang, M. E., Figlio, R. M., & Sellin, T. (1972). *Delinquency in a birth cohort.* Chicago, IL: University of Chicago Press.

Zahn, M. A., Agnew, R., Fishbein, D., Miller, S., Winn, D., Dakoff, G., & Chesney-Lind, M. (2010). *Causes and correlates of girls' delinquency.* Washington, DC:

Office of Juvenile Justice and Delinquency Prevention. Retrieved from https://www.ncjrs.gov/pdffiles1/ojjdp/226358.pdf

Zahn, M. A., Brumbaugh, S., Steffensmeier, D., Feld, B. C., Morash, M., Chesney-Lind, M., & Kruttschnitt, C. (2008). *Violence by teenage girls: Trends and context.* Washington, DC: Office of Juvenile Justice and Delinquency Prevention. Retrieved from https://www.ncjrs.gov/pdffiles1/ojjdp/218905.pdf

Zang, A. (2017). *U.S. age boundaries of delinquency 2016.* JJGPS StateScan. Pittsburgh, PA: National Center for Juvenile Justice. Retrieved from http://www.ncjj.org/pdf/JJGPS%20StateScan/JJGPS_U.S._age_boundaries_of_delinquency_2016.pdf

GENDER MATTERS

Trends in Girls' Criminality

Meda Chesney-Lind

CRIME WAVE?

In 2016, girls accounted for nearly a third (29%) of juvenile arrests (OJJDP, 2016). From the 1960s to the 1980s, girls accounted for between 17% and 22% of juvenile arrests, one fifth of the total (Chesney-Lind & Shelden, 2004, pp. 9–11). This is a remarkable increase in their "share" of official delinquency and one that requires exploration.

The forces that lead to criminal behavior may be different for adolescents, and we now suspect that this has always been the case. Neuroscience (Jensen & Nutt, 2015; Raine, 2002) and social science (Moffitt, 1993) research have produced remarkable insight into the world of adolescence that was only suggested earlier. If one were to use arrests as a gauge of delinquency trends, female activity has been trending differently from that of their male counterparts. The much discussed "crime drop" in juvenile delinquency in the 1990s was more correctly a boy crime drop, fueled by a decline in gun- and drug-related violence among boys and young men (Blumstein & Wallman, 2000).

Looking specifically at national arrest data, it appears that boys' arrests peaked in 1993 and have dropped, but during the same period, girls' arrests continued to climb. According to FBI reports (FBI, 2003, p. 275, Table 33), between 1993 and 2002, girls' arrests increased 6.4%, whereas boys' arrests decreased by 16.4%. Between 2006 and 2015, the data do not show a stark increase in female offenses; nonetheless, their arrests decreased by a smaller percentage than boys', 56.1% compared to 51.6% (FBI, 2016, Table 33).

Juvenile delinquency has long been assumed to be a male problem, and girls were either ignored or excluded from consideration, particularly by researchers who worked during the formative years of criminological theory building. For instance, Hirschi (1969) distinctly excluded self-report data on females from analysis in his classic *Causes of Delinquency*. Others regarded delinquency as quintessentially male; the delinquent was the "rogue male," as can be seen in Cohen's (1955) noted *Delinquent Boys*.

Seminal criminological theories assume delinquency to be a male enterprise and therefore focus on male offenders. With this, research settings typically accessed boys and young men involved in their typically male offenses (see Chesney-Lind & Shelden, 2004). As a result, prevention and rehabilitation programs were aimed at male delinquency and intervention (see Girls Incorporated, 1996; Lipsey, 1992). Yet in spite of this lack of attention at virtually all levels within the juvenile justice system, more girls than ever are making their presence known. The academic, policy, and programmatic neglect of girls' issues, coupled with recent arrest trends, suggest that it is clearly time to consider female delinquency in its own right, not as an afterthought to boys' misconduct.

DELINQUENCY: GENDER MATTERS

The picture of female delinquency that emerges from the available data reflects the existence of substantial gender differences in both self-reported and official delinquency. For starters, girls are demonstrably less "serious" offenders than are boys. If one examines gender differences in court populations around the country, for example, girls differ from boys in that their instances of delinquency are less chronic and less serious. Based on an in-depth study of one large, urban court system, Snyder and Sickmund (1999, p. 80) found that 73% of females (compared with 54% of males) who enter the juvenile justice system never return to court on a new referral. They also noted that, of the youth who came to court for delinquency offenses, only 3% of females had committed a violent offense by the age of 18, compared with 10% for boys; likewise, only 5.5% of girls, compared with 18.8% of boys, had more than four referrals to court (p. 81).

The significant role played by minor offenses in girls' delinquency also emerged in the Annie E. Casey Foundation study of youth in detention in several cities. It was found that many more girls than boys were detained for "minor" offenses, such as public disorder, probation violations, status offenses, and traffic offenses. Finally, it was also learned that "rather than histories of violence, detained girls had more status offenses and misdemeanors in their histories" (American Bar Association & National Bar Association [ABA & NBA], 2001, pp. 18–19). This research documented that race as well as gender matters in girls' detentions; African American girls make up half of those in secure detention, according to this study, and Latinas, 13% (ABA & NBA, 2001, pp. 20–21).

The American Correctional Association's (1990) earlier study of girls held in state training schools found that substantial numbers of girls were incarcerated for probation or parole violation (15%), followed by aggravated assault (9.5%), larceny-theft (9%), and runaway (6.5%). Roughly half the girls were White (50.5%), nearly a third were Black or partly Black (31.7%), 6.2% were Hispanic, and 7.7% were Native American (p. 47). Most were between 16 and 17 years of age, and 18.6% were mothers at the time of their incarceration.

That same study found disconcertingly high rates of sexual abuse among incarcerated girls; over 60% had been the victim of some form of physical abuse, and 54% reported being the victim of sexual abuse. This finding may or may not explain why over 80% of the girls in training schools report that they have run away from home at least once, and a staggering 50% have run away from home six or more times.

The ACA (1990) study also found that 60% of this population needed substance abuse treatment at intake and that over half were multiply addicted. They also reported that many of these girls took drugs (34.4%) or drank alcohol (11.4%) as a form of self-medication to make themselves feel better. In addition, a majority stated that they used alcohol (50%) and marijuana (64%) regularly. Of the girls who were substance dependent, most started using between the ages of 12 and 15 (pp. 59–60). Although models that delineate the relationship between delinquency and substance abuse have largely involved adolescent males, evidence for females also indicates that substance abuse is highly correlated with disruptive behavior (Girls Incorporated, 1996).

These portraits of officially delinquent girls, particularly in the ACA study, point out two important themes in girls' delinquency, particularly the activities that bring girls into the juvenile justice system. First, although most girls' delinquency involves offenses that are not as legally serious as those committed by boys, this does not mean that they do not have serious problems, particularly those who stay in the system. Just because girls are arrested and referred to juvenile courts for legally less serious offenses gives a false impression. These "trivial" offenses often mask significant and ongoing problems, like sexual abuse, for which gender-responsive programming might well be appropriate but is infrequently available.

GIRLS' CRIME, GIRLS' OFFENSES

An overview of girls' arrest patterns reflects the themes found in the portraits of official delinquents (see Table 6.1) and is a logical starting point in discussing key themes in girl delinquency. In 2015, girls were most frequently arrested for larceny-theft, a property offense that, as we shall see, for girls means engaging in shoplifting (FBI, 2016, Table 33; Campbell & Harrington, 2000; Chesney-Lind & Shelden, 2004).

TABLE 6.1 ■ Rank Order of Arrests for Juveniles, 2006 and 2015

	Males				Females			
	2006		2015		2006		2015	
	Offense	Number of Arrests	Offense	Number of Arrests	Offense	Number of Arrests	Offense	Number of Arrests
1.	All Other Offenses (except traffic)	180,909	1. Arson (property crime)	87,184	1. Arson (property crime)	84,149	1. Arson (property crime)	46,128
2.	Arson (property crime)	171,301	2. All Other Offenses (except traffic)	77,354	2. Larceny-Theft	74,117	2. Larceny-Theft	41,533
3.	Larceny-Theft	106,506	3. Larceny-Theft	60,365	3. All Other Offenses (except traffic)	67,920	3. Other Assaults	30,807
4.	Other Assaults	101,366	4. Other Assaults	52,882	4. Other Assaults	51,030	4. All Other Offenses (except traffic)	29,896
5.	Drug Abuse Violations	93,508	5. Drug Abuse Violations	49,170	5. Disorderly Conduct	42,850	5. Drug Abuse Violations	16,303

Source: FBI, *Uniform Crime Reports: 2015 Crime in the United States* (2016, Table 33, "Ten-Year Arrest Trends").

Note: "All Other Offenses" refers to a variety of offenses, usually against state and local ordinances. Among the most common are public nuisance, trespassing, failure to appear on warrants, contempt of court, and, for juveniles especially, violation of various court orders (e.g., probation, parole) and certain status offenses. This category does not include traffic offenses. Status offenses other than runaway and curfew also account for a large proportion of girls' arrests for other offenses (Chesney-Lind & Shelden, 2004).

Girls also were arrested in large numbers for running away from home, an offense for which only juveniles can be taken into custody. Finally, a large numbers of girls, particularly in recent years, were arrested for the seemingly nontraditional girl offenses of simple assault and disorderly conduct. Boys' arrests are more diffuse, meaning that the most often committed offenses account for slightly over half of all boys' arrests (58.9%), whereas for girls over two-thirds (68.4%) of their arrests are accounted for by these five offense categories. The data also indicate that arrests for girls for arson (property crime) have replaced arrests for larceny-theft as the prevailing theme in girls' official delinquency.

GIRLS' VIOLENCE: WHEN SHE WAS BAD

Reports of increases in female aggression and violence have been widely, albeit not necessarily correctly, highlighted over the past few decades. Whether it was the female radical revolutionary of the 1970s, the girl gang banger (i.e., female gang member) of the 1980s, the violence-prone girl of the 1990s, or the mean girls who ushered in the new millennia, the past several decades have seen a cavalcade and spectacle of girls' acting out in ways that are far beyond merely unfeminine (see Chesney-Lind & Irwin, 2008). Quite often, the media frame, what is now the emerging area of visual criminology, is one that juxtaposes girls' aggression or violence with stereotypical images of a girlhood contrary to this emerging reality.

In many ways, this gender juxtaposition makes sense when considering Longfellow's (1992, p. 513) poem about his daughter: "When she was good, she was very, very good, but when she was bad she was horrid." Of course, the reality is much more complex. First, in spite of "common knowledge," it turns out that self-report data routinely show that girls act out violently and have been since the earliest self-report data were published (Elliot & Voss, 1974). Second, there appears to be very little evidence that these patterns have changed dramatically over the last decade, despite the media frenzy on the topic.

The Centers for Disease Control and Prevention (CDC) have monitored youthful behavior in a national sample of school-aged youth in a number of domains (including violence) at regular intervals since 1991 in a biennial survey titled the Youth Risk Behavior Survey. As an example, a review of the data collected over the 1990s and into the 2000s reveals that although 34.4% of girls surveyed in 1991 said that they had been in a physical fight in the previous year, 10 years later, by 2001, that figure had dropped to 23.9%, a 30.5% decrease in girls' fighting; boys' violence also decreased during the same period but less dramatically—from 50.2% to 43.1%, a 14.1% drop (Centers for Disease Control and Prevention, 1992–2004).

While girls had long reported that they were acting out violently, their arrests, particularly in the 1960s and 1970s, did not necessarily reflect that reality. Instead, girls' arrests tended to emphasize petty and status offenses; by the 1990s, that had changed dramatically, as more girls were arrested, particularly for such seemingly "masculine" offenses as simple assault. Between 1997 and 2006, despite an overall decrease in girls' arrests, girls' arrests for simple assault continued to climb, increasing by 18.7%, while boys' arrests for the same offense declined by 4.3%.

Chesney-Lind and Irwin (2008) suggest that increasingly, these shifts in girls' arrests are not products of a literal change in their behavior, with girls becoming "more" violent. Not only do most measures of girls' criminality fail to show an increase in girls' violence, but there is ample evidence also that girls are being more heavily policed, particularly at home and in school. Specifically, girls are being arrested for assault because of arguments with their parents, often their mothers (see Buzawa & Hotaling, 2006), or for "other assault" activities such as fighting in school because of new zero-tolerance policies enacted after the Columbine High School shootings (see New York Civil Liberties Union [NYCLU], 2007). In decades past, this "violence" would have been ignored or labeled as a status offense, like being "incorrigible" or a "person in need of supervision." Now, law enforcement is much more likely to effect an arrest.

Once introduced into the juvenile justice system, girls are also staying in the system after being arrested for these new "violent" offenses. Between 1985 and 2002, the number of girls' delinquency cases referred to juvenile courts increased by 92%, compared with a 29% increase for males (Snyder & Sickmund, 2006). Arrests of girls for crimes of violence clearly played a role in this pattern: "For females, the largest 1985–2002 increase was in person offense cases (20%)." Finally, like the pattern seen in girls' arrests, girls have proportionately more person offense referrals than boys: 26% compared with 23% (Snyder & Sickmund, 2006, p. 160).

Girls arrested for crimes of violence have also ushered in a dramatic increase in their rates of incarceration. Between 1991 and 2003, girl detentions rose by 98%, compared with a 29% expansion by boys (Snyder & Sickmund, 2006, p. 210). Girls detained for violent offenses were far more likely to be held for other person offenses, like simple assault. Well over half (57.3%) of the girls but less than a third of the boys (32.4 %) were held for these minor forms of violence (Sickmund, Sladky, & Kang, 2004). Likewise, girls' commitments to facilities increased by an alarming 88% between 1991 and 2003, while boys' commitments increased by only 23% (Snyder & Sickmund, 2006, p. 210).

Media sensationalization aside, girls' behavior, including violence, must be placed within a larger discussion of girls' place in a society, one that expects and normalizes aggression and violence from boys while encouraging girls and women to be nice, pretty, and feminine. It is important to describe the contexts that produce violence in girls (see Morash & Chesney-Lind, 2008).

Some hints of these issues can be found in the backgrounds of girls who act out violently. In her analysis of self-reported violence of girls in Canada, Artz (1998) noted that girls who reported problems with violence likewise reported significantly greater rates of victimization and abuse than did their nonviolent counterparts, and girls who were violent reported greater fear of sexual assault, especially from their boyfriends. Specifically, 20% of these violent girls stated that they were physically abused at home, compared with 10% of the violent males and 6.3% of nonviolent girls. Patterns for sexual abuse were even starker; roughly 1 in 4 violent girls had been sexually abused, compared with 1 in 10 nonviolent girls (Artz, 1998). Follow-up interviews with a small sample of violent girls found that they had learned at home that might makes right and had engaged in horizontal violence directed against other powerless girls. Certainly, these findings provide little ammunition for those who would contend that the new violent girl is a product of any form of "emancipation." Histories of physical and sexual abuse, then, may be an indication of girls' physical aggression, just as it is in their runaway behavior.

Aggressive and violent girls are, ironically, often quite comfortable with the "ideology of familial patriarchy . . . [which] supports the abuse of women who violate the ideals of male power and control over women" (DeKeseredy, 2000, p. 46). This ideology is acted out by those males and females who insist that women be obedient, respectful, loyal, dependent, sexually accessible, and sexually faithful to males. Artz (1998) builds on that point by suggesting that violent girls, more often than not, buy into these beliefs and "police" other girls' behaviors, thus preserving the status quo, including their own continued oppression.

Such themes are particularly pronounced among girls who have the most serious problems with delinquency. Artz, Blais, and Nicholson (2000, p. 31) found that the majority of their girl respondents were also male focused, expressed hostility to other girls, and wanted very much to have boyfriends—always making sure that they had at least one, both in and out of jail. One girl strongly identified with the boys and saw herself as "one of the guys," also admitting that she had "always wanted to be a boy." Only one girl spoke little about boys—at 18 years of age, she was the oldest girl in this sample. All of the girls used derogatory terms to describe other girls, and when they spoke about girls, their words reflected views of females as "other." Many saw other girls as threats, particularly if they were physically attractive or "didn't know their place." A "pretty" girl, or a girl who drew the attention of the boys, was a primary target for girl-to-girl victimization because she had the potential to unseat those who occupied higher rungs on the "pretty power hierarchy" (Artz et al., 2000, p. 124). An "ugly" or "dirty" girl (a girl designated a slut) was also targeted for girl-to-girl victimization because she "deserved" to be beaten for her unappealing looks and for her "unacceptable" behavior.

Such a perspective is puzzling, but the sad reality is that marginalized girls who have been the victims of male power often see that sort of agency as the only source of power available to them. Most of these girls regarded their victims as "responsible" for the violence that they committed, since they were acting as "sluts," "total bitches," or "assholes" (Artz et al., 2000, p. 189). Clearly, where these girls reside, "you've gotta watch your back" because "the world is a piece of shit" (p. 189). Those girls who have problems with violence suggest that both girls' and women's victimization, as well as girls' violence toward other girls, are really twin products of a system of sexual inequality that valorizes male violence as agency and has girls growing up "seeing themselves through the eyes of males" (Artz, 1998, p. 204).

RUNNING AWAY: GIRLS COPING WITH TRAUMA AND ABUSE

Running away from home and prostitution are the only two arrest categories in which more girls than boys are arrested. Of these, many more girls are arrested for running away than for prostitution, despite the public fascination with the latter. In 2006, there were 38,461 girls arrested for running away, whereas fewer than 1,000 were arrested for prostitution. In 2006, girls constituted over half (56.4%) of those arrested for this one status offense. This means that, despite the intention of the Juvenile Justice and Delinquency Prevention Act of 1974, which, among other things, encouraged jurisdictions to divert and deinstitutionalize juveniles charged with status offenses, arrests for these offenses remained substantial. Having said this, it should be noted that the arrest rates for runaways have been decreasing significantly for both girls and boys. From 1997 to 2006, these arrests decreased by 47.1% for girls during the same period that arrests of girls for simple assault increased by 18.7% (FBI, 2007, Table 33).

For many years, statistics showing significant numbers of girls arrested and referred to court for status offenses were taken as representative of the difference between male and female delinquency. Yet studies of actual delinquency show that girls and boys run away from home about equally. As an example, Canter (1982) found that in the National Youth Survey there was no evidence of greater female involvement, when compared with males, in any category of delinquent behavior. Indeed, males were significantly more likely than females to commit status and most other offenses. A study of inner-city adolescents who had been referred to one diversion program found that while youth showed considerable and expected gender differences in official arrests, with males being referred for law violations and girls being referred for status offenses and "personal problems," Rhodes and Fisher (1993) determined that self-report data from the same group "found that girls did not actually commit more status offenses than boys" (p. 884). National self-report data collected from youth aged 12 to 16 also showed no gender difference in runaway behavior; roughly 10% of both boys and girls reported that they had "ever" run away from home (Snyder & Sickmund, 1999, p. 54).

Thorne (1994), in an ethnography of gender in grade school, found that girls used "cosmetics, discussions of boyfriends, dressing sexually, and other forms of exaggerated 'teen' femininity to challenge adult, and class- and race-based authority in schools." She also found that "the double standard persists, and girls who are overtly sexual run the risk of being labeled sluts" (p. 156).

Other ethnographies of school life echo the validity of these parental perceptions. Orenstein's (cited in Thorne, 1994) observations also point to the durability of the sexual double standard; at the schools, she observed that sex "ruins girls" but "enhance[s] boys" (p. 57). Parents, too, according to Thorne (1994), have valid reasons to enforce the time-honored sexual double standard. Concern about sexual harassment and rape, to say nothing of sexually transmitted diseases, along with HIV/AIDS, if their daughters are heterosexually active, have caused "parents in gestures that mix protection with punishment, (to) often tighten control of girls when they become adolescents, and sexuality becomes a terrain of struggle between the generations" (Thorne, 1994, p. 156; see also Lamb, 2003). Finally, Thorne notes that, sadly and ironically, as girls use sexuality as a proxy for independence, they reinforce their status as sexual objects seeking male approval—ultimately ratifying their status as the subordinate sex. Whatever the reason, parental attempts to adhere to and enforce the sexual double standard continue to be a source of conflict between parents and their daughters.

Another reason for different responses to running away from home speaks to differences in boys' and girls' home experiences, family interactions, and gender realities. Girls are, for example, much more likely than boys to be the victims of child sexual abuse. According to the Executive Summary of the Third National Incidence Study, girls are sexually abused 3 times more often in their lives than boys (Sedlak & Broadhurst, 1996). Sexual abuse typically starts early; both boys and girls are most vulnerable to abuse between the ages of 7 and 13 (Finkelhor, 1994). Not surprisingly, the evidence also suggests a link between this problem and girl delinquency—particularly running away from home, since girls are more likely to be the victims of intrafamilial abuse (Finkelhor, 1994). More problematic however, is that this abuse lasts longer and has more serious consequences over their lifetimes than does stranger abuse (Finkelhor, 1994).

Widom (1995) found that victims of child sexual abuse are 27.7 times more likely than nonvictims to be arrested for prostitution as adults. It is speculated that some victims become prostitutes (if female) or abusers (if male) because they have a difficult time relating to others except on sexual terms. Not all studies find a link between sexual abuse, running away, and prostitution, however. In a comparison of prostitute and nonprostitute youth, Nadon, Koverola, and Schludeermann (1998) found that prostitute youth were not significantly more likely than an appropriate comparison group to report sexual abuse. However, adolescent prostitutes ran away from home significantly more often than adolescent nonprostitutes. Nadon et al. state that "it was determined prostitution may be a particular survival strategy for girls in very difficult circumstances" (p. 206).

Another study that tracked the gendered consequences of running away for girls and boys (Tyler, Hoyt, Whitbeck, & Cauce, 2004) showed that for females, running away from home for the first time was associated with engaging in deviant subsistence strategies, for instance, survival sex and victimization by a "friend or acquaintance." For boys, survival sex was associated with stranger victimization; for homosexual boys, though, victimization came at the hands of an acquaintance or friend (Tyler et al., 2004, p. 153).

Most girl runaways flee homes where abuse, including sexual abuse, is a prominent occurrence. Yet ironically and tragically, their lives on the streets are almost always even more abusive because, as with most other aspects of social life, street life and culture is also gendered. Once on the streets, girls recognize both the dangers involved in daily interactions and the paucity of survival options available to them. Many also quickly discover that they are in possession of a form of sexual capital that benefits them, whereas boys tend to engage in a wider variety and typically more criminal array of survival strategies.

The tragedy here is that girls who run away from physical and sexual abuse they experience at home, are forced to confront equally horrific options—returning to an intolerable home, inability to legally change or stop going to school, inability to gain legal employment, or inability to find alternative housing without parental permission—and are thus risking return to home. In short, their viable options, along with their practical survival methodologies, are criminalized by a system that unapologetically encourages them to return home and the purview of their parents. Even human assistance systems that want to explore other sorts of placement possibilities face numerous challenges, not the least of which is a paucity of programs for girls (Freitas & Chesney-Lind, 2001). Faced with abysmal choices, some girls turn to survival sex, which they may not even recognize as sexual exploitation or trafficking (Beyette, National Network for Youth, 2008), or some other form of sex work. For some—but not necessarily all—girl runaways, survival sex and possibly prostitution become a way to survive in the absence of few other earning skills (Campagna & Poffenberger, 1988; Miller, 1986). Current attention to this issue has given rise to various organizations such as a Women Escaping a Violent Environment (WEAVE, Inc.) in California and the National Center for Missing and Exploited Children.

WILD IN THE STREETS: GIRLS, DRUGS, AND ALCOHOL

Trends in girls' arrests for substance abuse also reveals a gendered pattern. Specifically, girls' arrests have increased for most offenses during the last decade, whereas boys' arrests have decreased. As an example, the FBI (FBI, 2007, Table 33), reports that girls' arrests for disorderly conduct increased by 19.0%, while boys' arrests decreased by 22.1%. Likewise, girls' arrests for driving under the influence showed a 39.3% increase, as compared with a 6.4% decrease seen in boys' arrests.

Reviews of self-reported drug use, like data from the Youth Risk Behavior Surveillance System, indicate that male and female use of alcohol has actually declined in the most recent decade for which data are available (1991–2004), while marijuana and cocaine use has actually increased slightly among respondents. Moreover, there is an apparent gender convergence. In 1993, 50.1% of boys reported "current alcohol use," whereas 45.9% of girls did; in 2003, only 43.8% of boys and 45.8% of girls reported use. With marijuana, 20.6% of boys reported use in 1993, compared with 25.1% in 2003; for girls, 14.6 % reported use in 1993, compared with 19.3% in 2003 (CDC, 1992; 2004).

In considering drug use at the point of arrest, in 1997, 29% of arrested girls tested positive for one or more illegal drugs, compared with 57% of boys, largely due to marijuana use (Belenko, Sprott, & Petersen, 2004, p. 6). Subsequent interviews with arrested youth revealed that 33% of arrested and detained girls and 34% of boys reported some alcohol use, and 61% of girls, compared with 75% of boys, were drug involved (Belenko et al., 2004, p. 6). With delinquent girls, depression is a major problem, whether in discussing runaways, aggressive youth, or youth with substance abuse issues. In fact, girls in general are more likely to report problems of depression and anxiety than boys, and these findings are magnified among girls in the juvenile justice system (Belenko et al., 2004, p. 21).

Kataoka et al. (2001) found that female juvenile offenders were 3 times more likely than girls who were not in the system to show clinical symptoms of anxiety and depression. As noted previously, many of the girls in the justice system have extensive histories of abuse, which can explain their choices to self-medicate in response to their traumatic history. The links between post-traumatic stress disorder (PTSD) and drug use are clearly more pronounced in girls than in boys. Deykin and Buka (1997) found that almost half (40%) of reported substance-abusing girls exhibited prevalence of PTSD, compared with slightly more than one tenth of boys (12.3%).

SHOPLIFTING: YOU SHOPLIFT AS YOU SHOP

Property crimes, particularly larceny-theft, accounted for 1 out of 4 girls' arrests in 2015; in contrast, this offense accounted for only 1 in 7 boys' arrests (FBI, 2016, Table 33). There is evidence that this offense is particularly gendered, as the bulk of girls' larceny-thefts involving shoplifting, while boys are more involved in buying stolen goods, stealing from cars, or committing bicycle theft (Campbell & Harrington, 2000; Chesney-Lind & Shelden, 2004). Girls' frequency of this offense has also increased over time, from 34.1% to 40.8% (FBI, 2007).

Such a gender shift is also apparent in the self-report data. Data collected from high school seniors suggest that while roughly a quarter (25.9%) of girls claim they had taken something from a store without paying for it at least once in the past year, which was about the same as a decade earlier (25.2%), for boys, the comparable figures were 30% in 2002 and 36% in 1994. Thus, although male shoplifting has been decreasing, these data suggest that female involvement has remained mostly constant (Bureau of Justice Statistics, 2003, Table 3.47). These data show that larceny-theft committed by boys has declined over time, possibly as a result of increased surveillance in shopping malls (Hayward, 2004, p. 189), though it is not clear why this would have affected boys' but not girls' levels of shoplifting.

Increasingly, discussions of women's crime and changes in the volume of female offending have focused on the role played by economic marginalization and patterns of women's employment in property crimes (see English, 1993; Heimer, 2000). Specifically, females have greater experience as employees in retail settings and, as a consequence, often have more knowledge of the security and enforcement routines that characterize these establishments, even if they work elsewhere (English, 1993). As retail employees and more frequently customers than their male counterparts, they are also likely to augment often minimum wage salaries by stealing or shoplifting where they work (Franklin, 1979). Because of gender bias in this industry as well, men, if they steal from the workplace, tend to be employed in higher level positions; if they steal, they are less likely to be caught (because they are less heavily supervised), steal larger amounts, and are often reprimanded and not prosecuted (Franklin, 1979).

According to Morris (1987), ironically, males are more likely to shoplift. She learned that males outnumbered females by a 2:1 ratio. Recall, though, that recent U.S. data show that while the gender gap has closed, that is because boys report doing less shoplifting. Males were found to be more likely than females to shoplift, but the male–female ratio for youths "cautioned by the police" or actually sentenced was only 1.7:1 (p. 31). Morris further suggests that a form of self-fulfilling prophecy exists as females are more often detected by store personnel because they are expected to shoplift more than men and therefore are watched with greater resolve.

Explanations of male and female shoplifting have generally been simplistic and gender biased. A common explanation, according to Morris, is that it is "a result of subconscious motivations (kleptomania), depression (for example, resulting from the menopause) or poverty (for example, mothers on welfare who steal food)" (p. 65). A common explanation of male shoplifting is that it results from "peer-group pressure and the search for excitement" (p. 65).

One consideration that rarely appears in the literature on shoplifting is that young people, especially girls, may be inordinately sensitive to the consumer culture: They steal things they feel they need or indeed may actually need but cannot afford. For example, Campbell (1981) notes that women—young and old—are the targets of calculated enormously expensive advertising campaigns for a vast array of personal products. They also constitute the greater proportion of those who shop, spend more time doing so, and, consequently, are exposed to greater consumer temptation (Campbell, 1981, pp. 122–123). Temptation is likely most pronounced for girls, who consider popularity to be tied very closely to physical appearance and possession of popular fashions and participation in current fads (see Adler & Adler, 1998).

Participation in the teen consumer subculture is costly, and if girls cannot afford participation, they are likely to steal their way in. It is no surprise, then, that they are more likely than boys to fall prey to shoplifting activities (Campbell, 1981, pp. 122–123). Moreover, because girls spend more time shopping, they undergo more scrutiny by store detectives, who report they are suspicious of young people in groups, particularly if they are not dressed well in the first place (May, 1978). In short, the girl subculture, where popularity is based on an appearance and contemporary consumerism, may weigh particularly heavy on girls with fewer avenues of access to resources.

In general, shoplifting by girls must be placed within the context of girls' lives in a youth- and consumer-oriented culture. Here, the drawbacks of not having money are evident, and for girls, there are few avenues to success. Shoplifting, then, is a social cost attributable to goods attainable only with money that many of them do not have.

CONCLUSION

Girls are contributing more and more to those being arrested. For instance, the arrest data show large numbers of girls arrested for assault, yet there are reasons to suspect that these increases do not reflect actual behavior but rather changes in law enforcement practices and philosophies. That said, girls' aggression and violence are best understood from within the context of their situations in their families, in their schools, and on the streets. Research suggests that violent girls have often themselves been victims as well as the victimizers.

At one time, arrests for running away were actually proxies for suspected sexual activity in girls, and there is still some evidence that the gender difference in girls' and boys' arrests for these offenses are products not of actual behavior but rather of parenting problems, where reports of daughters running away were filed but not sons. Girls on the run are often forced by current laws to live like fugitives. They are unable to attend school, get a job, or even live apart from their abusive families; they are forced into criminal behavior simply to survive. Sometimes, that behavior further criminalizes them and compels them to engage in other risky behaviors, like survival sex, prostitution, and/or drug use. Shoplifting, for instance, accounts for many girls' arrests, as research indicates that girls shoplift as a reflection of a youth culture that, particularly for girls, stresses the importance style over substance.

Those who study and work with girl delinquents must consider not only economics but also gender and race when crafting explanations of behavior. Those who hope to effectively prevent and intervene in their behavior would do well to consider the gendered way in which they experience adolescence and interact with their culture. In short, delinquency theory, which has often been uncritical in its acceptance of boys' delinquency with a particular emphasis on the role of class and social status, would do well to consider gender both in crafting an approach to the problem and in developing responses that will help rather than further stigmatize and victimize.

Girl incarcerations rise at a time when no such comparable increase is seen in the incarceration of boys. These trends, driven largely by the arrest and referral of girls for simple assault, threatens to undo more than 3 decades of efforts to remove youth from institutional settings. It also means that the mass incarceration that has so heavily impacted adult women, particularly women of color, might well be visited upon their younger sisters unless a vigorous campaign of education and advocacy is not launched.

Discussion Questions

1. Do females engage in crime for reasons different from their male counterparts and therefore require justice system treatment that is also different? Does this also cause them to engage in different sorts of crime activities?

2. Are girls subject to situations and conflict in their homes from which their brothers are excluded?

3. Must the justice system amend its previous practices to account for the influx of gender differences that were not present in previous decades? What should the justice system do?

4. What is the role of social patriarchy in the handling of female offenders versus male offenders? Are girls subjected to judicial treatment that is different from that faced by their brothers or other male offenders? Is there a remedy for this discrepancy?

References

Adler, P. A., & Adler, P. (1998). *Peer power: Preadolescent culture and identity*. New Brunswick, NJ: Rutgers University Press.

American Bar Association and the National Bar Association. (2001). Justice by gender: The lack of appropriate prevention, diversion and treatment alternatives for girls in the justice system. Chicago, IL: American Bar Association.

American Correctional Association. (1990). *The female offender: What does the future hold?* Washington, DC: Author.

Artz, S. (1998). *Sex, power and the violent school girl*. Toronto, ON: Trifolium Books.

Artz, S., Blais, M., & Nicholson, D. (2000). *Developing girls' custody units*. Unpublished report.

Belenko, S., Sprott, J. B., & Petersen, C. (2004, March). Drug and alcohol involvement among minority and female juvenile offender: Treatment and policy issues. *Criminal Justice Policy Review, 15*(1), 3–36.

Beyette, B. (1988, August 21). Hollywood's teenage prostitutes turn tricks for shelter, food. *Las Vegas Review-Journal*, p. A4.

Blumstein, A., & Wallman, J. (2000). *The crime drop in America*. Cambridge, UK: Cambridge University Press.

Bureau of Justice Statistics. (2003). *Sourcebook on criminal justice statistics*. Retrieved February 14, 2008, from http://www.albany.edu/sourcebook/pdf/t347.pdf

Buzawa, E. S., & Hotaling, G. T. (2006). The impact of relationship status, gender, and minor status in the police response to domestic assaults. *Victims and Offenders, 1*(4), 323–360.

Campagna, D. S., & Poffenberger, D. L. (1988). *The sexual trafficking in children*. Dover, MA: Auburn House.

Campbell, A. (1981). *Girl delinquents*. New York, NY: St. Martin's Press.

Campbell, S., & Harrington, V. (2000). *Youth crime: Findings from the 1998/1999 youth lifestyles survey* (Home Office Research Findings No. 126). London, UK: Her Majesty's Stationery Office.

Canter, R. J. (1982). Sex differences in self-report delinquency. *Criminology, 20*(3–4), 373–393.

Centers for Disease Control and Prevention. (1992–2004). *Youth risk behavior surveillance—United States, 1991–2004* (CDC Surveillance Summaries). U.S. Department of Health and Human Services. Atlanta, GA: Author.

Chesney-Lind, M., & Irwin, K. (2008). *Beyond bad girls: Gender, violence, and hype*. New York, NY: Routledge.

Chesney-Lind, M., & Shelden, R. (2004). *Girls, delinquency, and juvenile justice* (2nd ed.). Belmont, CA: Thompson/Wadsworth.

Cohen, A. K. (1955). *Delinquent boys: The culture of the gang*. New York, NY: The Free Press.

DeKeseredy, W. (2000). *Women, crime, and the Canadian criminal justice system*. Cincinnati, OH: Anderson.

Deyken, E. Y., & Buka, S. L. (1997). Prevalence and risk factors for posttraumatic stress disorder among chemically dependent adolescents. *American Journal of Psychiatry, 154*(6), 752–757.

Elliot, D., & Voss, H. (1974). *Delinquency and dropout*. Lexington, MA: D. C. Heath.

English, K. (1993). Self-reported crimes rates of women prisoners. *Journal of Quantitative Criminology, 9*(4), 357–382.

Federal Bureau of Investigation. (2004). *Crime in the United States, 2003* (Table 33, Ten-year arrest trends). Washington, DC: Government Printing Office. Retrieved from http://www.fbi.gov/about-us/cjis/ucr/crime-in-the-u.s/2003/03sec4.pdf

Federal Bureau of Investigation. (2007). *Crime in the United States, 2006* (Table 33, Ten-year arrest trends). Washington, DC: Government Printing Office. Retrieved from http://www.fbi.gov/about-us/cjis/ucr/crime-in-the-u.s/2006

Federal Bureau of Investigation. (2016). *Crime in the United States, 2015* (Table 33, Ten-year arrest trends). Washington, DC: Government Printing Office. Retrieved from https://ucr.fbi.gov/crime-in-the-u.s/2015/crime-in-the-u.s.-2015/tables/table-33

Finkelhor, D. (1994). Current information on the scope and nature of child sexual abuse. *The Future of Children, 4*(2), 31–53.

Franklin, A. (1979). Criminality in the workplace: A comparison of male and female offenders. In F. Adler & R. Simon (Eds.), *The criminality of deviant women* (pp. 167–170). Boston, MA: Houghton Mifflin.

Freitas, K., & Chesney-Lind, M. (2001, August/September). Difference doesn't mean difficult: Workers talk about working with girls. *Women, Girls, & Criminal Justice, 2*(5), 65–78.

Girls Incorporated. (1996). *Prevention and parity: Girls in juvenile justice*. Indianapolis, IN: Girls Incorporated National Resource Center.

Hayward, K. J. (2004). *City limits: Crime, consumer culture, and the urban experience*. London, UK: Glasshouse Press.

Heimer, K. (2000). Changes in the gender gap in crime and women's economic marginalization. In G. Lafree (Ed.), *Criminal justice 2000: Vol. 1. The nature of crime: Continuity and change* (pp. 427–483). Washington, DC: National Institute of Justice.

Hirschi, T. (1969). *Causes of delinquency*. Berkeley, CA: University of California Press.

Jensen, F. E., & Nutt, A. E. (2015). *The teenage brain: A neuroscientist's survival guide to raising adolescents and young adults*. New York, NY: HarperCollins Publishers.

Kataoka, S., Zima, B., Dupre, D., Moreno, K., Yang, X., & McCracken, J. (2001). Mental health problems and service use among female juvenile offenders. *Journal of the American Academy of Child and Adolescent Psychiatry, 40*(5), 549–555.

Lamb, S. (2003). Not with my daughter: Parents still have trouble acknowledging teenage sexuality. *Psychotherapy Networker, 27*(May/June), 44–49.

Lipsey, M. (1992). Juvenile delinquency treatment: A meta-analytic inquiry in the variability of effects. In T. A. Cook, H. Cooper, D. S. Cordray, H. Hartmann, L. V. Hedges, & R. J. Light (Eds.), *Meta-analysis for explanation: A casebook* (pp. 83–127). New York, NY: Russell Sage.

Longfellow, H. W. (1992). "There was a little girl." In J. Bartlett & J. Kaplan (Eds.), *Familiar quotations* (16th ed., p. 513). Boston, MA: Little, Brown.

May, D. (1978, May). Juvenile shoplifters and the organization of store security: A case study in the social construction of delinquency. *International Journal of Criminology and Penology, 6*(2), 137–160.

Miller, E. M. (1986). *Street woman*. Philadelphia, PA: Temple University Press.

Moffitt, T. E. (1993). Adolescence-limited and life-course persistent antisocial behavior: A developmental taxonomy. *Psychological Review, 100*(4), 674–701.

Morash, M., & Chesney-Lind, M. (2008). Girls' violence in context. In M. Zahn (Ed.), *The delinquent girl* (pp. 182–206). Philadelphia, PA: Temple University Press.

Morris, A. (1987). *Women, crime, and criminal justice*. New York, NY: Blackwell.

Nadon, S., Koverola, C., & Schludeermann, E. (1998). Antecedents to prostitution: Childhood victimization. *Journal of Interpersonal Violence, 13*(2), 206–221.

National Network for Youth. (2008). *Consequences of youth homelessness*. Retrieved March 6, 2008, from https://www.nn4youth.org/wp-content/uploads/IssueBrief_Youth_Homelessness.pdf

New York Civil Liberties Union. (2007). *Criminalizing the classroom: The overpolicing of New York City schools*. New York, NY: Author.

Office of Juvenile Justice and Delinquency Prevention. (2016). Demographic characteristics of juvenile arrests, 2016. In *Statistical Briefing Book*. Retrieved from http://www.ojjdp.gov/ojstatbb/crime/qa05104.asp?qaDate=2016

Raine, A. (2002). Biosocial studies in antisocial and violent behavior in children and adults: A review. *Journal of Abnormal Child Psychology, 30*(4), 311–326.

Rhodes, J. E., & Fischer, K. (1993). Spanning the gender gap: Gender differences in delinquency among inner-city adolescents. *Adolescence, 28*(112), 879–889.

Sedlak, A., & Broadhurst, D. (1996). *Executive summary of the Third National Incidence Study of Child Abuse and Neglect*. Washington, DC: U.S. Department of Health and Human Services, National Center on Child Abuse and Neglect.

Sickmund, M., Sladky, T. J., & Kang, W. (2004). *Census of juveniles in residential placement databook*. Washington, DC: U.S. Department of Justice. Retrieved February 14, 2008, from http://www.ojjdp.ncjrs.org/ojstabb/cjrp

Snyder, H. N., & Sickmund, M. (1999). *Juvenile offenders and victims: 1999 national report*. Washington, DC: U.S. Department of Justice, Office of Justice Programs, Office of Juvenile Justice and Delinquency Prevention.

Snyder, H. N., & Sickmund, M. (2006). *Juvenile offenders and victims: 2006 national report*. Washington, DC: U.S. Department of Justice, Office of Justice Programs, Office of Juvenile Justice and Delinquency Prevention.

Thorne, B. (1994). *Gender play: Girls and boys in school*. New Brunswick, NJ: Rutgers University Press.

Tyler, K., Hoyt, D., Whitbeck, L., & Cauce, A. (2004). The impact of childhood sexual abuse on later sexual victimization among runaway youth. *Journal of Research on Adolescence, 11*(2), 151–176.

Widom, C. S. (1995). *Victims of childhood sexual abuse: Later criminal consequences*. Washington, DC: U.S. Department of Justice, National Institute of Justice.

RACE AND CRIME

Helen Taylor-Greene

The concepts of race and crime have been inextricably linked in the study of criminology and criminal justice since the late-19th century. Today, many colleges and universities that offer undergraduate and graduate degrees in criminology/ criminal justice have either a required or an elective course that explores the economic, historical, political, and sociological contexts of race and crime. Some also include analyses of ethnicity, class, gender, and comparative perspectives. Most of these courses focus on issues that continue to challenge justice practitioners and researchers including race and the extent of crime, police, courts, corrections, juvenile justice, bias and hate crimes, immigration and crime, racial profiling, and sentencing disparities. Many of these issues will focus this discussion.

DEFINITIONAL COMPLEXITIES

What is race? Its definition is complex. Historically, race was conceptualized biologically and primarily based on one's physical characteristics. Beliefs about the superiority of Whites and inferiority of others, especially people of color, prevailed. Over time, according to the American Anthropological Association (1997), the concept of race acquired a cultural and ideological context in the United States and elsewhere in the world that

> magnified the differences among Europeans, Africans, and Indians, established a rigid hierarchy of socially exclusive categories, underscored and bolstered unequal rank and status differences, and provided the rationalization that the inequality was natural or God-given. (p. 1)

Biological differences between individuals, especially their color and hue, provide the foundation for what many refer to as the social construction of race

(Aguirre & Turner, 2011). Are individuals that look different on the outside different on the inside? If not, why are race and ethnicity (used here interchangeably with minorities) at the center of so many controversies nationally and internationally?

In 2000, the U.S. Bureau of the Census noted that racial categories were sociopolitical constructs and not scientific or anthropological in nature (Gabbidon & Greene, 2015). The U.S. Census Bureau recognizes five racial categories, including American Indian or Alaskan native, Black or African American, Native Hawaiian or other Pacific Islanders, and White; Latino or Hispanic origin is recognized as an ethnic category. A category for "some other race" with numerous combinations to choose from was added in 2000 as well. In 2010, "more than 9 million Americans considered themselves multiracial and self-identified with two or more races" (Gabbidon & Greene, 2013, p. 7). Persons of Hispanic or Latino ethnicity, the largest minority group in the population, also are of very diverse origins (Gabbidon & Greene, 2015). All members of a racial/ethnic-minority group are not the same; there are cultural, subcultural, and class differences.

Consider President Barack Hussein Obama. His mother was White, his father was African, and he was raised for many years by his White grandparents in Honolulu, Hawaii. Does that make him White? African? African American? His race—and that of many other Americans—is not easily categorized as either Black, White, or other. At an earlier time in our country, President Obama would be classified as Black and, depending on the time period, referred to as either mixed, mulatto, colored, Negro, or African American because of his skin color. In the past, Americans with any African blood, especially if they did not look White, were considered Black. Today, racial categories in the U.S. Census recognize several mixed-race categories, including two, three, four, or more races. Another example is someone from another country that may look Black but does not identify with the Black (American) subculture. Rather she or he identifies with the subculture of her or his country of origin. In spite of more multiracial categories included in the Census, identifying one's race does not capture heterogeneity, that is, differences between and within racial and ethnic groups.

Unlike race (and ethnicity), crime is easier to define. In the early 20th century, Paul Tappan (1947) defined crime as "an intentional act in violation of the criminal law (statutory law and case law) committed without defense or excuse, and penalized by the state as a felony or misdemeanor" (p. 99). Over time, even though behaviors that are illegal change, some, including murder, rape, burglary, and theft, always have been considered crimes. In the past and present, many factors, including values, industrialization, immigration, and technological developments, have led to both the criminalization and decriminalization of many behaviors. For example, when legislative efforts to outlaw the sale and use of alcohol failed (the Volstead Act), it was decriminalized. Decades later, as the use of automobiles increased, so did the problem of driving under the influence of alcohol or drugs. Due to increased attention, especially from Mothers Against Drunk Driving (MADD), penalties for vehicular homicides by drunk drivers have increased.

Even though marijuana has not been decriminalized nationwide, several states and municipalities have made it legal to use for medicinal purposes and recreational use and to possess small amounts.

Even though Whites commit numerous crimes—in fact, most crimes—the study of race and crime has been concerned primarily with those committed by Blacks and other minorities. In the past, acts considered criminal for Blacks were not necessarily viewed as such when committed by Whites. For example, prior to the Civil War, slave owners were rarely punished for beating, branding, raping, and killing their slaves. According to Kennedy (1997), the law protected Whites in order to maintain their supremacy. Both before and after the Civil War, the law was used to maintain social control and "keep the Negro in his place" (Work, 1937, p. 111), as well as to control immigrant Whites and other minorities at the time viewed as undesirable.

Some of the focus on minorities in the study of criminology/criminal justice evolves from their disproportionate involvement in crime, especially violent personal crimes. According to Young (1996),

> The concept of disproportionality, has become the mainstay of discussions of race and crime. . . . When authors review trends and patterns of crime and introduce the "variable" race the comparisons are between Blacks, whites and others and the emphasis is on the disproportionate involvement of nonwhites, in particular Blacks. (p. 74)

Even though Whites commit violent crimes, especially bias or hate crimes, they do not receive as much attention as Blacks and other minorities. White-collar crimes committed by Whites do not receive much attention either. This fixation on Black crime contributes to the racialization of crime (Covington, 1995), a belief that the majority of Blacks (and perhaps other minorities) commit crimes.

The overreliance on official statistics, such as the Federal Bureau of Investigation's Uniform Crime Reports (UCR), contributes to misperceptions about race and crime in the United States. For example, most students are often surprised to learn that (a) most Americans, regardless of race, are not arrested and that (b) even though Blacks are vastly overrepresented in arrest statistics, most persons arrested are White.

Arrests and Victimization

The two major sources of statistics on crime and victimization are the UCR, collected and compiled by the Federal Bureau of Investigation (FBI), and the National Crime Victimization Survey (NCVS), compiled for the Bureau of Justice Statistics (BJS) by the U.S. Bureau of the Census. Both the UCR and NCVS collect and report information on race that is available online. The BJS provides statistics and data analysis tools that provide information on many justice topics that include race and ethnicity. Many other governmental and nongovernmental sources provide information that permit analyses by race as well, such as the Death Penalty Information Center and the Sentencing Project.

FBI Uniform Crime Reports

The FBI UCR includes information on crimes reported, arrests, clearance trends, and police employment data. In the "Crimes Reported" section of the 2016 FBI UCR, the estimated size of the United States population was 320,896,618, and an estimated 1,248,185 violent crimes were reported, about 386.3 violent crimes per 100,000 inhabitants. There were an estimated 7,919,035 property crime offenses reported in 2016, a rate of about 2,450.7 offenses per 100,000 inhabitants. Larceny-theft offenses accounted for over 71.2% of all property crimes in 2016 (FBI, 2017). Violent crimes increased by about 4%, while property crimes decreased about 1% (compared with 2015).

In the "Persons Arrested" section of the UCR, information is provided by race in five categories: (1) Whites, (2) Blacks, (3) American Indian or Alaskan Native, (4) Asian, and (5) Native Hawaiian or other Pacific Islander. In 2016, there were an estimated 8,421,481 arrests, most for drug abuse violations (1,242,630), other assaults (853,493), and larceny-theft (833,558). It is estimated that 69.6% of all persons arrested were White, and about 27% were Black; other races accounted for about 3.6% of arrests, and Latinos accounted for 18.4% of arrests (see Table 7.1).

For the traditional Part I offenses (murder/non-negligent manslaughter, aggravated assault, robbery, forcible rape, burglary, larceny-theft, motor vehicle theft, and arson), most persons were arrested for larceny-theft, regardless of race, followed by arrests for aggravated assault and burglary. When examining the percentage distribution by race, Blacks are overrepresented in reported arrests for all Part I crimes, Whites for arson, and Hispanics for aggravated assault, rape, and motor vehicle theft (see Table 7.1). Though not shown in Table 7.1, Whites, Blacks, and Hispanics are overrepresented in several of the Part II offenses, including sex offenses (Whites, Blacks, Hispanics), driving under the influence, liquor law violations and drunkenness (Whites), weapons (Blacks), and gambling (Blacks and Hispanics) (FBI, 2017).

How do the UCR arrest data contribute to understanding race and crime? The answer to this question is unclear and requires taking the following weaknesses of the UCR data into consideration:

- Arrests of Hispanics and/or Latinos were included in the White category until 2015, and some may still be recorded in that category.

- Many (crimes and) arrests are not reported (often referred to as the dark figure of crime), and others are not recorded by the police.

- The UCR utilize estimates of the total population, crimes reported, and persons arrested that might be inaccurate.

- Police biases can result in different arrests for different individuals of different ages, classes and races.

TABLE 7.1 ■ Persons Arrested by Race and Ethnicity for Part I Crimes, 2016

Arrests By Race and Ethnicity, 2016
[13,049 agencies; 2016 estimated population 257,112,535]

Offense Charged	Total Arrests — Race						Total Arrests — Ethnicity		
	Total	White	Black or African American	American Indian or Alaska Native	Asian	Native Hawaiian or Other Pacific Islander	Total[1]	Hispanic or Latino	Not Hispanic or Latino
Total	8,421,481	5,858,330	2,263,112	171,185	103,244	25,610	6,647,012	1,221,066	5,425,946
Murder and nonnegligent manslaughter	9,374	4,192	4,935	108	109	30	6,882	1,374	5,508
Rape[2]	18,606	12,571	5,412	233	309	81	13,896	3,758	10,138
Robbery	76,267	33,095	41,562	663	659	288	60,116	12,657	47,459
Aggravated assault	304,626	191,205	101,432	6,374	4,678	937	250,762	61,073	189,689
Burglary	164,641	112,651	47,991	1,613	1,925	461	130,179	27,113	103,066
Larceny-theft	833,558	575,105	231,199	14,933	10,277	2,044	624,800	91,210	533,590
Motor vehicle theft	68,170	44,970	20,955	1,018	895	332	52,786	14,160	38,626
Arson	7,767	5,593	1,813	218	120	23	5,495	910	4,585

Source: FBI UCR, Crime in the United States 2016, "Arrests," Table 21 A, B, C (2017).

Note: Because of rounding, the percentages may not add to 100.0.

Note: Violent crimes are offenses of murder and nonnegligent manslaughter, rape, robbery, and aggravated assault. Property crimes are offenses of burglary, larceny-theft, motor vehicle theft, and arson.

1. The ethnicity totals are representative of those agencies that provided ethnicity breakdowns. Not all agencies provide ethnicity data; therefore, the race and ethnicity totals will not equal.

2. The rape figures in this table are aggregate totals of the data submitted based on both the legacy and revised Uniform Crime Reporting definitions.

To overcome some of the weaknesses of the UCR, the National Crime Victimization Survey (NCVS) described in the next section was created as an alternative source of information on the extent of crime and victimization.

The National Crime Victimization Survey

The Bureau of Justice Statistics (BJS) publishes an annual bulletin titled *Criminal Victimization*. Participants are asked about their experiences as victims of personal and household crimes. The survey has been redesigned several times, most recently in 2016, to improve data collection. In the 2016 bulletin, the reported victimization rate for violent crimes was 21.1 per 1,000 persons (Morgan & Kena, 2017). The overall rate of violent crime for Blacks was 24.1; Whites, 20.5; Hispanics, 22.2; and other, 23.0. Unlike in the past, persons of two or more races are included in the "other" category. Rates were highest for persons aged 25 to 34 (31.8) followed by those 12–17 (30.9) and 18 to 24 (30.9) (see Table 7.2).

Like the UCR, the NCVS also has limitations:

- It only includes persons over the age of 12.

- Victimization data are based on the respondent's recall about the incident either he or she or someone in the household was involved in.

- Minorities are probably underrepresented since they are underrepresented in population statistics and may be reluctant to participate in the survey.

In spite of the limitations of both sources, they both seem to indicate that crime and victimization are important to any discussion of race and crime because both sources show patterns that require explanation. Some of these explanations found in the race and crime theoretical research are presented next.

TABLE 7.2 ■ Rates of Violent Victimization and Percentage Reported to Police by Sex, Race/Hispanic Origin, and Age of Victims				
	Rate of total violence per 1,000 persons age 12 or older		Percentage of violence reported to police	
Victim demographic characteristic	Violent crime[a]	Serious violent crime[b]	Violent crime[a]	Serious violent crime[b]
Total	21.1	7.0	42.1%	51.3%
Sex				
Male*	21.4	6.5	44.3%	60.5%
Female	20.8	7.5	40.0	43.7 t

Victim demographic characteristic	Rate of total violence per 1,000 persons age 12 or older		Percentage of violence reported to police	
	Violent crime[a]	Serious violent crime[b]	Violent crime[a]	Serious violent crime[b]
Race/Hispanic origins				
White	20.5	6.3	40.1%	45.0% t
Black*	24.1	8.2	39.8	59.8
Hispanic	20.2	8.2	51.6 t	64.8
Other[c]	23.0	8.5	42.9	47.8
Age				
12–17	30.9	8.6	27.7%	48.1%
18–24*	30.9	11.0	35.7	51.5
25–34	31.8	12.8	38.9	37.8 #
35–49	22.9 t	6.8 t	49.8 t	58.6
50–64	16.1 t	5.2 t	49.1 t	65.2 #
65 or older	4.4 t	1.1 t	60.4 t	62.0

Source: Adapted from Morgan, R. E. and Kena, G. (2017). Bureau of Justice Statistics. *Criminal Victimization, 2016.* Table 8.

Note: Victimization rates are per 1,000 persons age 12 or older.

Note: White, Black, and other race categories exclude persons of Hispanic or Latino origin.

*Comparison group.

t Significant difference from comparison group at 95% confidence level.

Significant difference from comparison group at 90% confidence level.

a. Includes rape or sexual assault, robbery, aggravated assault, and simple assault. Excludes homicide because the NCVS is based on interviews with victims and cannot measure murder.

b. In the NCVS, serious violent crime is a subset of violent crime and includes rape or sexual assault, robbery, and aggravated assault.

c. Includes American Indian or Alaska Native; Asian, Native Hawaiian, or Other Pacific Islander; and persons of two or more races.

THEORETICAL PERSPECTIVES ON RACE AND CRIME

Why do African Americans and some other minorities continue to be overrepresented in crime and victimization statistics? This question has perplexed criminologists and other scholars for decades. Why do we downplay the role of justice professionals, especially police and prosecutors and their discretionary decisions concerning arrest, charges, and negotiating pleas? In the criminological research, explanations include biological, sociological, and psychological explanations that focus on either the individual, the environment, or both. Although criminal justice theoretical research is more limited, it focuses on the fairness of the criminal justice system raised by the second question. According to Duffee and Allan (2007), "Theories of criminal justice raise questions about why the government is doing what it is doing" (p. 18). Justice, including just processes, outcomes, and the just use of state power, is central to criminal justice theory (Castellano & Gould, 2007). Classical and positivist criminological theories have predominated in the study of criminology for hundreds of years. Classical and neoclassical theories focus on several key concepts, including utilitarianism, hedonism, free will, and rational choice, and do not address race and crime specifically. Positivists believe that criminal behavior is determined by biological, psychological, and/or sociological factors. Cesare Lombroso's research on physical characteristics was influential in the United States, where beliefs about the inferiority of Blacks and Native Americans already existed. Though less popular, biological research continues in the United States today (Moffitt, 1993; Rowe, 2007; Rushton, 1995; Walsh & Beaver, 2008; Wilson & Herrnstein, 1985).

W. E. B. Du Bois, Monroe N. Work, Clifford R. Shaw, and Henry D. McKay were among the earliest scholars to refute the biological approach and its fixation on the individual. Instead, they focused on the role of the environment and social disorganization on crime (Du Bois, 1899/1973; Work, 1900; Shaw & McKay, 1942). Du Bois (1899/1973) and Work (1900) noted the impact of slavery, discrimination, and segregation on Black criminality and pointed to social, economic, and political conditions that contributed to Blacks' involvement in crime. Shaw and McKay (1942), who were affiliated with the University of Chicago Department of Sociology, examined delinquency areas in Chicago and concluded that "within similar areas, each group, whether foreign-born or native, recent immigrant or older immigrant, black or white, had a delinquency rate that was proportional to the rate of the overall area" (as cited in Vold & Bernard, 1986, p. 170).

Unlike other immigrants who found themselves in "delinquency areas" and eventually were able to relocate, many Blacks seemed to be unable to leave and were trapped there, creating the "truly disadvantaged," a term coined by William Julius Wilson (1987). These areas experience concentrated indicators of social disorganization, including poverty, crime, school dropouts, drug use and sales, inadequate housing, high incarceration rates, teen pregnancies, and unemployment. Over time, these and other factors, including housing inequality and socially isolated residents, foster cultural adaptations that undermine both social organization and the control of crime (Sampson & Wilson, 1995).

One criticism of social disorganization theory is that all minorities in socially disorganized communities are not involved in criminal behavior (Gabbidon, 2015; Gabbidon & Greene, 2015; Gabbidon, Unnever, & Gabbidon, 2011). Several researchers have examined social capital and/or collective efficacy to explain variations in levels of crime. Social capital refers to social ties, levels of trust, and the ability of individuals to work together for the good of the community. Unlike communities with high levels of social capital (Hawes, 2017), those with low levels of positive social capital and cohesion are more apt to succumb to negative social networks that value criminal behavior (Poteyeva, 2009). Many other sociological explanations, such as subcultural theories, the colonial model, conflict theory, critical race theory, the general theory of crime, racial socialization, social control, strain theory, and social inequality, are useful to understanding race and crime.

Theoretical research on other minorities, including Latinos, Native Americans, and Asian Americans, is limited. Is social disorganization theory or any other theory applicable to these groups or Whites? All theories have their strengths and weaknesses, and none fully explain patterns of race, arrests, and victimization. Another explanation for the disproportionate representation of Blacks and other minorities in the criminal justice system is discrimination. Discretion, that is, decisional latitude, permits justice practitioners to be guided by not only the official policies of their agencies but also their own values and perhaps implicit biases as well. As a result, even though discrimination and injustices that existed in the past are less prevalent today, vestiges of racial and ethnic disparities still exist in criminal justice (Walker, Spohn, & DeLeone, 2018). Disparities in juvenile justice, pretrial release, sentencing, traffic stops, and use of force continue.

CONTEMPORARY ISSUES IN THE STUDY OF RACE AND CRIME

What are the five most important issues in the study of race and crime today? Gangs, mass incarceration, police use of force, policing illegal immigrants, racial profiling, violent juvenile offenders, the war on drugs, and wrongful convictions are often identified. While there is a considerable amount of research on these topics, many that identify "what works," "best practices," and offer policy recommendations, each of these issues continue to challenge individuals, families, communities, and justice agencies, as do the issues presented next.

Police Killings

On July 2014, Eric Garner, a father and grandfather, was killed on a street corner in Staten Island by a New York City police officer who put him in a choke hold. At the time, Garner, 44, had a long history of arrests for various crimes, including unlawfully selling cigarettes. His killing resulted in several demonstrations and the slogan "I can't breathe," which he is said to have repeatedly uttered before dying. A month later, on August 9, 2014, Michael Brown Jr., an unarmed teenager in Ferguson, Missouri, was killed by a police officer. In Ferguson, demonstrations, civil unrest, and the police department's militarized response were seen in real time on television and social media. Since 2014, many other incidents have occurred and stakeholders, including citizens, researchers, police, and other practitioners, have tried to understand police killings, especially the disproportionate killings of unarmed Black males. Even though police killings are rare events and most officers are never involved in these incidents, they have an impact on citizens' level of confidence in the police, police–community relations, police recruitment efforts, and police work itself.

In 2015, the United States Department of Justice (DOJ) released the results of its investigation of the Ferguson, Missouri, police department that found,

> Bias against African-Americans was routine and thorough, affecting "nearly every aspect of Ferguson police and court operations. . . . For blacks distrust and fear of the police was well-founded." (Andrews, DeSantis, & Keller, 2015)

Before and after *The Ferguson Report*, the DOJ found racial bias in policing in many other locales including Los Angeles, California; Maricopa County, Arizona; Baltimore, Maryland; and Chicago, Illinois.

Surprisingly, there was no national data on police killings readily available in 2014. Some police agencies reported justifiable homicides by the police to the FBI on a voluntary basis. *The Guardian*, the *Washington Post*, and an online database, Killed by Police, began compiling data on fatal force by police in 2015. That year the *Washington Post* identified 991 incidents. In 2016, 963 were identified, and 987 in 2017 were identified. The majority of those killed were White (457), Black (223), Latino (179), and others (44) (almost half of killings), and 84 were listed as race unknown. Nineteen unarmed Black males were killed in 2017, two more than in 2016, and fewer than 36 killed in 2015 ("Police shootings 2017 database," 2018). How can the killings of unarmed Black (and brown) males be explained?

Makarechi (2016) analyzed several studies of police and racial bias that included police killings. One study found that the probability of Black unarmed males being killed by the police was 3.4 times greater that the probability for White males. Another found that the only variable that mattered was whether or not the person was Black, not crime variables. There was no correlation between levels of violent crime and that area's police killing rate. According to the *Washington Post* ("Police shootings 2017 database," 2018), in 2015, the FBI agreed to develop a database of police killings that might be available in 2018. In order to improve citizen's confidence in and trust of the police and improve police–community relations, departments will need ongoing communication with them and to hold police involved in fatal incidents accountable.

Prisoner Reentry

In 2016, there were 1,505,400 prisoners in state and federal prisons (Carson, 2018). The National Reentry Resource Center (2016) estimates that 95% of these prisoners will eventually be released. The overrepresentation of racial and ethnic groups in prison means that their communities will be burdened more by returning ex-offenders (see Table 7.3). Over a decade ago, Jeremy Travis, the former director

TABLE 7.3 ■ Sentenced Prisoners Under Jurisdiction of State or Federal Correctional Authorities, by Jurisdiction, Sex, Race, and Hispanic Origin, December 31, 2006–2016

Year	Total	Federal[a]	State	Male	Female	White[b,c,d]	Black[b,c,d]	Hispanic[c,d]
2006	1,504,598	173,533	1,331,065	1,401,261	103,337	507,100	590,300	313,600
2007	1,532,851	179,204	1,353,647	1,427,088	105,763	499,800	592,900	330,400
2008	1,547,742	182,333	1,365,409	1,441,384	106,358	499,900	592,800	329,800
2009	1,553,574	187,886	1,365,688	1,448,239	105,335	490,000	584,800	341,200
2010	1,552,669	190,641	1,362,028	1,447,766	104,903	484,400	572,700	345,800
2011	1,538,847	197,050	1,341,797	1,435,141	103,706	474,300	557,100	347,800
2012	1,512,430	196,574	1,315,856	1,411,076	101,354	466,600	537,800	340,300
2013	1,520,403	195,098	1,325,305	1,416,102	104,301	463,900	529,900	341,200
2014	1,507,781	191,374	1,316,407	1,401,685	106,096	461,500	518,700	338,900
2015	1,476,847	178,688	1,298,159	1,371,879	104,968	450,200	499,400	333,200
2016[e]	1,458,173	171,482	1,286,691	1,352,684	105,489	439,800	486,900	339,300
Average annual percent change								
2006–2015	−0.2%	0.3%	−0.3%	−0.2%	0.2%	−1.2%	−1.7%	0.6%
2015–2016	−1.3	−4.0	−0.9	−1.4	0.5	−2.3	−2.5	1.8

Source: Table 3 in Carson, E. A. (2018). *Prisoners, 2016.*

Note: Jurisdiction refers to the legal authority of state or federal correctional officials over a prisoner, regardless of where the prisoner is held. Counts are based on prisoners with sentences of more than 1 year.

a. Includes prisoners held in nonsecure, privately operated community corrections facilities and juveniles held in contract facilities.

b. Excludes persons of Hispanic or Latino origin and persons of two or more races.

c. Race and Hispanic origin counts for all years have been reestimated using a different method and will not match previously published estimates. See *Methodology.*

d. Rounded to the nearest 100.

e. Total and state estimates include imputed counts for North Dakota and Oregon, which did not submit 2016 NPS data. See *Methodology.*

of the National Institute of Justice and president of John Jay College of Criminal Justice in New York City, was instrumental in drawing attention to the issue of prisoner reentry in his book titled *But They All Come Back: Facing the Challenges of Prisoner Reentry*. According to Travis (2005), the growth of the prison population (mass incarceration) at that time resulted in large numbers of ex-offenders returning to families, communities, and often crime. The most recent reentry data indicate that almost 641,000 prisoners were released from state prisons and about 9 million from jails (National Reentry Resource Center, 2016). In 2006, when an estimated 750,000 prisoners were released, institutional and community corrections agents were not prepared for "mass reentry," and few resources and employment opportunities were available. Today (as in the past), ex-offenders face barriers to not only employment but also education, housing, restoration of rights, transportation, and health care. These barriers contribute to recidivism, another challenge. Too many ex-offenders will return to crime when they are released. However, misinformation about ex-offenders' recidivism contributes to their stigma. Rhodes et al. (2016) address this issue and conclude that the extent of recidivism is much lower than previously believed. They found that 2 out of 3 persons released from prison in 17 states did not return to prison.

During the past decade, there have been federal, state, and local initiatives to improve ex-offenders' transition back into society. In 2008, the Second Chance Act began funding state, local, and nonprofit organizations to provide reentry assistance to those released (National Reentry Resource Center, 2016). Today, stakeholders, including corrections officials (in facilities and in the community), law enforcement, faith organizations, families, communities, and ex-offenders, continue to address reentry challenges and their collateral consequences. According to the Restoration of Rights Project (2018), recent legislative reforms include laws to reduce barriers to employment (for example, Ban the Box) and limiting access to criminal history information. Several successful reentry programs have also been identified by the What Works in Reentry Clearinghouse.

While reentry reforms are helpful, current sentencing policies, including mandatory sentencing and three-strikes laws, guarantee that prisoner reentry will continue to be a problem requiring innovative solutions for decades. Even though the number of inmates and those leaving prison have decreased in the last several years, about 10,000 are still released everyday (Hughes & Wilson, 2003). These returning prisoners will not be fully reintegrated into their families and communities until the stigma of incarceration can be lessened.

Disproportionate Minority Contact and Confinement

Disproportionate minority contact and confinement (DMC) refers to the overrepresentation of minorities at various stages in adult and juvenile justice systems. Initially, the term was used to describe overrepresentation of minority youth in secure facilities (confinement) but later was revised to include overrepresentation at other decision points (contact). If you have ever visited a juvenile probation office, a juvenile court, or a juvenile correctional facility, then you know that they are full of youth of color, especially in metropolitan areas. In 2016, there were 674,820 juvenile arrests, 62.1% White, 34.7% Black, and 22.8% Hispanic (see FBI, 2018, Table 21B). Since Hispanics are separate from Blacks and Whites in the FBI arrest tables, the disproportionality is less visible than it is in the secure confinement data. In 2015 (the most recent data available), there were 48,043 youth in confinement, 15,024 White, 20,136 Black, 10,545 Hispanic, 839 American Indian, 402 Asian, and 1,097 Other (Sickmund, Sladky, Kang, & Puzzanchera, 2017). According to the Sentencing Project (2018),

> Racial and ethnic disparities weaken the credibility of a justice system that purports to treat everyone equally. . . . Across the country juvenile justice systems are marked by disparate racial outcomes at every stage of the process.

Why do racial disparities continue to persist even though there have been fewer juvenile arrests and fewer youth placed in secure confinement? First, for some youth, involvement in crime is acceptable. This is often referred to as the differential involvement explanation. The other explanation, differential treatment, recognizes how discretion of the police, probation officers, judges, and others, coupled with racial bias, results in different outcomes for youth of color (The Sentencing Project, 2018).

Disproportionate minority contact in the juvenile justice system is most problematic at arrest, confinement, and waivers to adult courts (Jones & Greene, 2015). Since 1988, the U.S. Congress has legislated core requirements in revisions to the Juvenile Justice and Delinquency Prevention Act of 1974 in an effort to address DMC. At that time, states were required to identify and address the problem in order to receive federal funding through formula grants (Gabbidon & Greene, 2015). The Office of Juvenile Justice and Delinquency Prevention (OJJDP) is responsible for monitoring DMC progress and providing technical assistance to the states. It also collects data from states and maintains a DMC website. Unfortunately, progress in reducing and preventing DMC has been limited, as it continues to exist at many stages and in most states.

Some recent initiatives to address DMC include addressing crossover youth that are in both child welfare and juvenile justice systems, dealing with the school-to-prison pipeline, and reducing implicit bias among practitioners. Information on best DMC practices and evidence-based DMC model programs is necessary as well.

FUTURE ISSUES IN THE STUDY OF RACE AND CRIME

The history of racial discrimination, racism, and racial bias in our country continues to impact people of color and the justice system. One of the most important developments in the future is the changing demographic trends in the United States. Latinos, now the largest minority in the United States, have composed the majority in several cities and counties, especially in the southwestern United States. Researchers should resolve the dilemma of counting members of this group so that we have a better understanding of ethnic trends in crime and victimization. In spite of the fixation on illegal immigrants, especially from Mexico, the role of Latinos in justice agencies will garner more attention in the next decade. Arguably, as their representation in justice agencies increases, outcomes for people of color, especially Latinos, could change as social distance between practitioners and clients is reduced.

As long as social and economic disparities exist, "street crime" will occur. It is important to continue to invest in crime and delinquency prevention, youth development, restorative justice, and other strategies that may result in better outcomes than some of the current ones. Justice agencies must also continue to develop cultural competencies of employees to overcome hidden biases.

Other important issues in the future study of race and crime are DNA analysis, human trafficking, and women of color. DNA databanks and the role of DNA in solving crimes and identifying wrongful convictions requires more research. Human trafficking requires greater emphasis on how this global problem relates to race, ethnicity, crime, and justice since the majority of human trafficking victims are women of color. Lastly, women of color as leaders in justice agencies, other practitioners, offenders, and victims require more attention in the study of race and crime.

Discussion Questions

1. Do you think the historical context of the problem of race and crime in the United States is still relevant today? Explain your answer.

2. What do arrest and victimization statistics tell us about race and crime?

3. What is the best explanation of the overrepresentation of some minorities as crime perpetrators and victims?

4. Do you think that police officers are justified in shooting unarmed persons that they question during traffic stops?

5. What recommendation would you make to an elected official to reduce disproportionate confinement of people of color?

Web Resources

Bureau of Justice Statistics: www.bjs.gov

Death Penalty Information Center: www.death penaltyinfo.org

Sentencing Project: www.sentencingproject.org

What Works in Reentry Clearinghouse: whatworks. csgjustice.org

References

Aguirre, A., Jr., & Turner, J. H. (2011). *American ethnicity: The dynamics and consequences of discrimination* (7th ed.). New York, NY: McGraw-Hill Higher Education.

American Anthropological Association (1997). AAA's statement on race. Retrieved February 7, 2009, from http://www.understandingrace.org/about/statement.html

Andrews, W., DeSantis, A., & Keller, J. (2015, March 4). Justice Department's report on the Ferguson Police Department. *New York Times.* Retrieved from https://www.nytimes.com/interactive/2015/03/04/us/report-what-happened-in-ferguson.html

Banks, D., & Kyckelhahn, T. (2011). *Characteristics of suspected human trafficking incidents, 2008–2010.* Retrieved March 18, 2014, from http://www.bjs.gov/content/pub/pdf/cshti0810.pdf

Carson, E. A. (2018). *Prisoners in 2016.* Retrieved from https://www.bjs.gov/content/pub/pdf/p16.pdf

Castellano, T. C., & Gould, J. B. (2007). Neglect of justice in criminal justice theory: Causes, consequences and alternatives. In D. E. Duffee & E. R. Maguire (Eds.), *Criminal justice theory: Explaining the nature and behavior of criminal justice* (pp. 71–92). New York, NY: Routledge Taylor & Francis.

Covington, J. (1995). Racial classification in criminology: The reproduction of racialized crime. *Sociological Forum, 10*(4), 547–568.

Du Bois, W. E. B. (1973). *The Philadelphia Negro.* Millwood, NY: Kraus-Thomson. (Original work published 1899)

Duffee, D. E., & Allan, E. (2007). Criminal justice, criminology and criminal justice theory. In D. E. Duffee & E. R. Maguire (Eds.), *Criminal justice theory: Explaining the nature and behavior of criminal justice* (pp. 1–26). New York, NY: Routledge Taylor & Francis.

Federal Bureau of Investigation. (2013). *Crime in the United States, 2012.* Retrieved March 18, 2014, from http://www.fbi.gov

Gabbidon, S. L. (2015). *Criminological perspectives on race and crime* (3rd ed.). New York, NY: Routledge.

Gabbidon, S. L., & Greene, H. T. (2013). *Race and crime* (3rd ed.). Thousand Oaks, CA: Sage.

Gabbidon, S. L., & Greene, H. T. (2015). *Race and crime* (4th ed.). Thousand Oaks, CA: Sage.

Gabbidon, S. L., & Higgins, G. E. (2007). Consumer racial profiling and perceived victimization: A phone survey of Philadelphia area residents. *American Journal of Criminal Justice, 32*(1–2), 1–11.

Greene, H. T., & Gabbidon, S. L. (2000). *African American criminological thought.* Albany, NY: State University of New York Press.

Hawes, D. P. (2017). Social capital, racial contexts, and incarcerations in the American states. *State Politics and Policy Quarterly, 4,* 393–417.

Hughes, T., & Wilson, D. J. (2003). *Reentry trends in the United States.* Washington, DC: Bureau of Justice Statistics. Retrieved from https://www.bjs.gov/content/pub/pdf/reentry.pdf

Kennedy, R. (1997). *Race, crime, and the law.* New York, NY: Vintage Books/Random House, Inc.

Moffitt, T. E. (1993). Adolescence-limited and life-course-persistent antisocial behavior. A developmental taxonomy. *Psychological Review, 100*(4), 674–401.

Morgan, R. E., & Kena, G. (2017). *Criminal victimization, 2016.* Retrieved January 19, 2018, from https://www.bjs.gov/content/pub/pdf/cv16.pd.

National Reentry Resource Center. (2016). NRRC facts & trends. Retrieved from https://csgjusticecenter.org/nrrc/facts-and-trends

Police shootings 2017 database. (2018). *Washington Post.* Retrieved from https://www.washingtonpost.com/graphics/national/police-shootings-2017

Rhodes, W., Gaes, G., Luallen, J., Kling, R., Rich, T., & Shively, M. (2016). Following incarceration, most released offenders never return to prison. *Crime and Delinquency, 62*(8), 1003–1025.

Rowe, D. C. (2007). *Race and crime.* New York, NY: Oxford University Press.

Rushton, J. P. (1995). Race and crime: International data for 1989–1990. *Psychological Reports, 76,* 3607–3612.

Sampson, R. J., & Wilson, W. J. (1995). Toward a theory of race, crime, and urban inequality. In J. Hagan & R. D. Peterson (Eds.), *Crime and inequality* (pp. 37–54). Stanford, CA: Stanford University Press.

Shaw, C., & McKay, H. D. (1942). *Juvenile delinquency and urban areas: A study of rates of delinquents in relation to different characteristics of local communities in American cities*. Chicago, IL: University of Chicago Press.

Sickmund, M., Sladky, T. J., Kang, W., & Puzzanchera, C. (2017). Easy access to the Census of Juveniles in Residential Placement. *Retrieved on* January 23, 2018, from https://www.ojjdp.gov/ojstatbb/ezacjrp/asp/Age_Race.asp

Tappan, P. (1947). Who is the criminal? *American Sociological Review, 12*(10), 96–112.

Travis, J. (2005). *But they all come back: Facing the challenges of prisoner reentry*. Washington, DC: The Urban Institute Press.

United States Department of Justice, Faith-Based and Community Initiatives. (n.d.). *Prisoners and prisoner reentry*. Retrieved on January 23, 2018, from https://www.justice.gov/archive/fbci/progmenu_reentry.html

Unnever, J., & Gabbidon. S. L. (2011). *A theory of African American offending*. New York, NY: Routledge.

Vold, G. B., & Bernard, T. J. (1986). *Theoretical criminology* (3rd ed.). New York, NY: Oxford University Press.

Walker, S., Spohn, C., & DeLone, M. (2018). *The color of justice* (6th ed.). Belmont, CA: Wadsworth.

Walsh, A., & Beaver, K. (Eds.). (2008). *Contemporary biosocial criminology*. New York, NY: Routledge.

Wilson, J. Q., & Herrnstein, R. (1985). *Crime and human nature: Intelligence and crime construction*. Cambridge, MA: Harvard University Press.

Wilson, W. J. (1987). *The truly disadvantaged*. Chicago, IL: University of Chicago Press.

Withrow, B. L. (2006). *Racial profiling: From rhetoric to reason*. Upper Saddle River, NJ: Prentice-Hall.

Work, M. N. (1900). Crime among Negroes in Chicago. *American Journal of Sociology, 6*(2), 204–223.

Work, M. N. (1937). Problems of adjustment of the race and class in the South. *Social Forces, 16*(1), 108–117.

Young, V. D. (1996). The politics of disproportionality. In A. T. Sulton (Ed.), *African-American perspectives on crime causation, criminal justice administration and crime prevention*. Boston, MA: Butterworth-Heinemann.

POPULAR CULTURE, MEDIA, AND CRIME

Richelle S. Swan

The interrelationship between popular culture, the media, and crime is a complicated one that can be approached from many angles. For years, scholars interested in these issues focused on a few different questions related to whether particular forms of popular culture influence delinquency and crime, and how the news media and other forms of mass media construct issues of crime, delinquency, and social control. These questions are still important ones that drive a great deal of research, but our contemporary social world requires us to ask newer questions as well. For example, do the ever-popular television reality shows about crime issues impact viewers' behavior? What is the significance when people share examples of their own misbehavior or crime via the Internet or through social media? How do people resist or challenge unjust media representations of their or others' behaviors? Although it is difficult to make any conclusive statements about the answers to these questions, one thing that is clear when we consider the relationship between contemporary media, popular culture, and crime: The lines between fictional and nonfictional representations of crime are becoming less rigid. As a result, the need to interrogate existing social practices and mediated materials related to crime is more important than ever.

POPULAR THEORETICAL APPROACHES TO THE STUDY OF POPULAR CULTURE, MEDIA, AND CRIME

In order to study issues of popular culture, crime, and media, scholars often use theoretical approaches that turn a critical eye towards issues of meaning making as they transpire within the larger institutions of the media, the criminal justice system, and overarching sociopolitical structures. Insights from social constructionism (Berger & Luckmann, 1966), a theory that forwards the idea that people create their reality based on their individual interpretation of symbols exchanged in social interactions, are often central to such analyses. In the fifth edition of Ray Surette's well-known book, *Media, Crime, and Criminal Justice: Images, Realities, and Policies* (2014), he explains that individuals make sense of the world by means of our personal experiences (i.e., our *experienced reality*) and from information obtained from significant others; social institutions, such as schools, government agencies, religious groups, and unions; and the mass media (i.e., our *symbolic reality*). The mass media can be especially powerful influences in terms of symbolic reality because they offer easy access to information that most of us are not privy to firsthand, and they have the ability to selectively shape or *frame* images and stories.

Many of the insights from studies on the media, popular culture, and crime are based on analyses of these media frames and their impact (e.g., Altheide, 2002; Chermak, 1995; Fishman & Cavender, 1998; McCormick, 2010). The social constructionist lens is often used in conjunction with conflict theory, feminist theory, and critical race theory to uncover how the mass media frame messages about socioeconomic class, gender, sexuality, and race and ethnicity and their relationship to crime and social control (e.g., Bissler & Conner, 2012; Covington, 2010; Mann & Zatz, 2002; Rome, 2004; Russell-Brown, 2008).

Cultural criminology, a theoretical approach that first emerged in the 1990s, builds on insights from earlier sociological and criminological theories, such as symbolic interactionism, labeling theory, and the work of British criminologists from the Birmingham School (Ferrell, Hayward, Morrison, & Presdee, 2004). According to Ferrell (2013), the social construction of meaning related to crime and social control is fundamental to its analysis.

We see the power of meaning sometimes by its absence—when, for example, the harms wrought by powerful individuals or groups are allowed

> to remain meaning-less as regards to legal culpability or moral panic (Jenkins, 1999). We find meaning being made when we listen to the shared argot of marginal groups, or notice the stylistic codes around which illicit subcultures organized and define themselves. And every day, in newspaper headlines and television news feeds, we see meaningful accounts of crime and criminal justice assigned to certain stories, and differently to others. . . . Meaning can be seen to be a constitutive element of human actions and a foundation of human culture—an ongoing, everyday process of sense-making, symbolic communication, and contested understanding. (p. 258)

Cultural criminological theory is used to examine the reasons behind people's engagement in popular cultural activities (e.g., street art or graffiti, raves and electronic music events) that are labeled as criminal, deviant, or socially problematic. It is also used to examine the meanings that risky and/or criminal behaviors have to individuals who participate in them as a means of better understanding their genesis.

The various ways that people use popular culture and media outlets to resist stereotyping and criminalization by social control agents (through means such as the creation of music, critiques on blogs and social media, and the widespread dissemination of videos) is also facilitated by cultural criminological theory. When used in tandem with other theoretical approaches that generally come from a conflict or critical perspective, cultural criminology challenges the ways in which some meanings are legitimized in popular culture while others are delegitimized and the implications this has for crime, justice, and social control. Those using critical frameworks often focus on unveiling the structural factors that shape media production in our increasingly globalized world. Such scholarly examinations often consider the implications of the fact that only a small number of media corporations dominate the various communication formats (print, internet, film, radio/music, and television/satellite) and the global media industry (Arsenault & Castells, 2008; Potter & Kappeler, 2012). Other cultural criminological scholarship examines the importance of race (Cunneen & Stubbs, 2008), gender (Naegler & Salman, 2016), religion (Williams & Kamaludeen, 2017), and/or nationality and geographic location (Joe Laider, Lee, & Wong, 2017) to the analysis of law, crime, and popular culture.

Although works originating from a social constructionist or cultural criminological vein are arguably the most commonly employed by scholars analyzing issues of popular culture and crime today, it is important to note that a multitude of other criminological theories come into play when we consider the specific messages of crime communicated through news stories, books, songs, video games, and other media.

Rafter and Brown (2011) assert that a number of traditional theories are apparent in popular cinema, and this is significant when we consider that most of the messages that people receive about crime and crime control are derived from popular culture as a whole. Thus, to understand what messages are being conveyed, a working knowledge of the range of criminological theories—from the individualistic to the sociological—is needed. Rafter and Brown labeled the space in which academic criminology and popular culture intersect *popular criminology* and claimed that the consideration of the crime discourse found there can eventually enrich the development of academic criminological theory and popular culture. According to their perspective, students of criminology and seasoned scholars alike can benefit from turning a critical eye to the mass-produced messages of crime and social control that we are subjected to on a daily basis. Although some criminological theories have fallen out of favor among criminologists, they tend to be recycled and reproduced by the media (Surette, 2014).

POPULAR METHODOLOGICAL APPROACHES USED IN THE STUDY OF POPULAR CULTURE, MEDIA, AND CRIME

An assortment of methods is used in studies of popular culture, media, and crime. Quantitative studies using experimental designs and surveys are commonly used alone or in conjunction with qualitative methods, such as interviews, content analysis, and ethnography. Statistical surveys that examine media consumption patterns and attitudes towards crime and/or past delinquent or criminal behavior are used to examine the nature of the relationship between them. Because the analysis of social constructions and meanings is a primary concern of many scholars in the field, qualitative methods, such as content analyses of media texts and discourse, the deconstruction of public messages about crime and justice in the news and entertainment media, and interviews with those who create mediated messages about crime and those who consume the messages, are commonly employed (Ferrell, 2013).

Ethnography, which often employs long-term participant observation in a chosen setting, is also a popular method used by scholars who either want to understand the workings of individuals and groups who are engaging in popular culture to commit acts of crime and/or transgression or those who are resisting stereotyping and criminalization of their social group or others'. Sometimes engaging in an ethnographic study translates into law-breaking by researchers or otherwise risky behaviors as a means of better understanding a group's behavior or a cultural phenomenon (Ferrell & Hamm, 1998; Landry, 2013), but this is not commonly the case.

IMPORTANT RESEARCH THEMES IN STUDIES OF POPULAR CULTURE, MEDIA, AND CRIME

Painting a Punitive Picture: Traditional Media Frames of Crime Issues in Popular Culture and News

Studies of media, popular culture, and crime have often focused on an analysis of media frames, "the focus, a parameter or boundary for discussing a particular event" (Altheide, 2002, p. 45) and the ways in which frames are used to define social problems and then to implicitly or explicitly suggest solutions to those problems. Many research studies on the frames used to present information about crime and justice issues show that they tend either to perpetuate a punitive crime control ideology and/or provide misleading or incomplete information about crime and criminal justice issues (Altheide, 1996, 1997; Barak, 1994;

Sasson, 1995; Surette, 2014). This has been found to be true across a variety of forms of popular and news media.

For example, fictional and animated characters in cartoons, comic books, television shows, and films are often shown to be crime fighters who are obsessed with obtaining some sort of punishment for or retribution against wrongdoers (Giddens, 2015; Phillips & Strobe, 2013). In Kort-Butler's (2013) examination of depictions of justice in superhero television cartoons (i.e., Batman, Spider-Man, and the Justice League) over a 15-year time period, she found that viewers are often presented with depictions of the criminal justice system and the actors within it as flawed and unequipped to properly address crime. The superheroes in the cartoons are often shown pursuing crime fighting themselves, claiming that it is their moral duty to do so and employing methods that that usually involve breaking the very legal system's rules that they are defending. Ultimately, the messages of these cartoons is that harsh punishment of wrongdoers is uniformly necessary and that the criminal justice system has its limitations but should be respected by people who are not in possession of superpowers. There is little attention paid to the possibility of rehabilitation of wrongdoers or to the necessity of reforming or overhauling a flawed criminal justice system, which sends a message that it is futile to pursue such alternatives.

Mainstream constructions of crime and justice are often reinforced in media forms that focus upon the lives of nonfictional situations and characters as well (Fishman & Cavender, 1998). As a means of contextualizing the relevance of such work, Cecil (2010) explains that viewers of such media often believe them to unblemished reflections of reality and accept them on face value. The editing behind the images presented may go unnoticed and the message crafted through the presentation of material by those behind the scenes may go unquestioned. Her analysis of the social construction of crime and justice in reality-based television shows and documentaries about U.S. jails follows in the tradition of other such examinations of prisons and correctional institutions (e.g., Cecil, 2007; Cecil & Leitner, 2009). She finds that the vignettes that are pieced together in these forms of media tend to emphasize inmate violence, unpredictability, and the need to socially control them by any variety of means. By ignoring the more common activities of the jail day—such as watching television, reading, and exercising—in favor of showing scenes of violence, reality shows and documentaries tend to conflate jails with prisons and send a confusing message about what jails entail, while paying little attention to underlying factors, such as substance use problems and mental health challenges. Consequently, viewers are left with little information that might lead them to consider alternatives to punitive responses to inmates or reform of correctional institutions.

Similarly, studies of media frames used by various forms of news sources, including written forms such as news magazines and newspapers, as well as television news and radio news, show that a skewed framing of crime and justice issues is the norm (e.g., Altheide, 1976, 2009a; Chermak, 1995; Cohen & Young, 1973).

Collins et al.'s (2011) analysis of news magazines in both the United States and the United Kingdom demonstrates that the United States' sources tend to only focus on state crime or governmental crime when the country itself is not involved. This focus on other nations shapes the U.S. public's perceptions of the acts of wrongdoing of those in power in the various levels of government. This is in keeping with the well-backed assertion that "a steady diet of sensationalist crimes hides more mundane and harder-to-detect crimes, just as a focus on street crime hides corporate crime" (McCormick, 2010, p. 11). For example, the typical characteristics of a given crime may be consistently ignored and/or misrepresented in news stories. This often happens in the case of rape, which gets a great deal more attention in the news media when it is perpetrated by a stranger than it does in the much more common case of being perpetrated by someone who is known to a rape victim (Carrabine, 2008; McCormick, 2010).

The analysis of multiple forms of crime reporting has demonstrated that sensationalistic and/or partial crime reporting often works to stoke the fears of the general public (Altheide, 2002, 2009b; Chiricos, Padgett, & Gertz, 2000; Potter & Kappeler, 2012; Schlesinger & Tumber, 1994) and fuels other strong emotional reactions as well, including disgust and apathy (McCormick, 2010), which may increase support for punitive crime policies. By the same token, those crimes that are ignored, often crimes of those with some degree of social power, are more likely to go unaddressed in light of little public concern.

FRAMING GONE EXTREME: MORAL PANICS ABOUT CRIME, DELINQUENCY, AND POPULAR CULTURE

Social scientists have revealed that the framing of crime issues often results in a strong public reaction that can be analyzed as moral panic or scares about crime and delinquency (Cohen, 1972; Goode & Ben-Yehuda, 2009). These scares typically share a number of elements: The news and/or entertainment media spread exaggerated information about the prevalence and seriousness of crime and/or an alleged source of crime in the community, interested community members and politicians pick up on the information, and attempts are made to fuel some sort of change or reform to the system. Regardless of whether any meaningful change is accomplished, the particular characterization of the problem tends to fade away and subsequently reemerges in another form (Ferguson & Olson, 2010; Gauntlett, 1995).

These panics not only are fueled by the publicity generated by media sources, such as television shows, news stories, and print journalism, but often, the very focus of the scares is the *consumption and/or use* of different means of communication and entertainment and how they allegedly lead to crime and delinquency.

In the late 1700s, there was a burgeoning concern about the dangers of "explicit" songs and photos as inspirations for law breaking (Bates & Swan, 2017). This was soon followed by panics related to the consumption of a number of different media forms and cultural practices and their hypothesized links to delinquency and/or crime. A few examples of these panics include the uproar over attending the theatre and acting in the 1800s; listening to or playing jazz music (see McMahon, 1921), reading dime novels (Park, 2002), and watching talking films (Gilbert, 1986) in the early decades of the 1900s; and reading comic books (Goode & Ben-Yehuda, 2009) and listening to rock music in the 1950s.

In the later decades of the 20th century, there were uproars about the connection between listening to psychedelic music in the late 1960s and early 1970s and crime, as well as with heavy metal and rap beginning in the 1980s and violent crime (Binder, 1993). In the 21st century, concerns about the dangers of some forms of cultural consumption, such as listening to electronic and other forms of music at raves, are not always characterized by moral outrage but, instead, are highly bureaucratized efforts at "quiet regulation" (Tepper, 2009). In spite of the different form of claims making present in these regulatory efforts, like moral panics, they ultimately facilitate the social control of media and cultural forms, as well as their consumers.

A contemporary moral panic that centers on a proposed link between popular culture, media consumption, and crime is related to playing video games, or "gaming." Fears that playing violent and crime-ridden video games that are increasingly realistic (e.g., the *Grand Theft Auto* series) led to public discussions among politicians and community members in the early 2000s, following years of concerns that were voiced about gaming since the 1980s. News media and other forms of media were used to spread messages linking violence, crime, and gaming, and eventually, laws were passed prohibiting the sale of extremely violent video games in states such as California. Later, the U.S. Supreme Court ruled that it was unconstitutional to pass such laws and cited the problematic history of moral panics in their ruling (see *Brown v. Entertainment Merchants Association*, 2011).

Fears about video games continue to resurface after major crimes with perpetrators that played them, such as after Adam Lanza's 2012 mass shooting in Newtown, Connecticut (Bates & Swan, 2017). Critics of the video game panic note that most young men have played violent video games, and the attempt to craft a direct relationship between gaming and violent crime distracts from more important factors, such as mental illness (e.g., Ferguson, 2015).

EFFECTS OF POPULAR CULTURE AND MEDIA CONSUMPTION ON CRIME

An area of research that is related to the recognition of a moral panic is focused on the effects of popular culture and media consumption. Studies on the possible effects of violent media have been the most prevalent, and they point to what have been labeled as the aggressor, victim, bystander, and appetite effects (Bickham, 2006).

In sum, children who engage in violent media consumption are often found to have an increased likelihood to demonstrate aggressive forms of thought or behavior; to have an exaggerated fear of victimization and to experience the world as a scary place; to be desensitized to violence and less likely to care about victims or victimization; and to have an increased appetite for exposure to more violent media. Although many draw on insights from learning theory and assert that these effects will amount to an increase in violent delinquency or crime, there is no conclusive evidence in this regard. Given that most crime that is committed is nonviolent crime, even if media-influenced social aggression inspires some violent crime, it may not inspire a great deal of the crime that occurs today (Surette, 2014).

Current research on media and criminal behavior is hampered by a number of methodological challenges, including the fact that it is difficult to conduct experiments on media effects on crime; the media could be affecting crime in any number of different ways (e.g., influencing people who never committed crime to commit crime; influencing those who have committed crime to commit more crime, to learn new techniques, or to become more violent in their acts; influencing media consumers to become more greedy and to engage in seemingly condoned acts of crime and violence; etc.), and effects of media consumption are likely intertwined with a number of other social factors affecting crime for only a small subset of people (Savage, 2008; Surette, 2014). Research on copycat crimes, crimes in which the offender mimics or imitates a criminal act presented in a media portrayal, is limited, but generally demonstrates that they are committed by a subset of people who have previously committed an offense. These individuals tend to be primed to accept media-generated scripts and ideas about criminals and crimes more readily than most other media consumers (Gunter, 2008).

Surette (2013) found in his study of over 500 anonymous surveys of inmates that young men were the most at risk to commit copycat crimes based on both real world and media influences. Based on his analysis, he concluded that the media more likely serves as a *rudder* for crime, providing examples for how to commit crimes, rather than a direct influence or *trigger*.

Studies on the effects of crime-related media on crime *prevention* behaviors have typically looked at the effects of crime prevention campaigns on the community—such as the "Take a Bite Out of Crime" public service announcement campaign of the 1980s or current anti–drunk driving media campaigns, such as "Buzzed Driving Is Drunk Driving" (see Flexon & Guerette, 2009; Mazerolle, 2003). The general findings about such campaigns show that people are more likely to change their perceptions about crime than their behaviors, and the effectiveness of the campaigns varies among people depending on their resources. For example, only people with sufficient free time can participate in the neighborhood patrolling activities recommended by many crime prevention campaigns (Flexon & Guerette, 2009).

Another less common type of study related to media effects on crime prevention is related to the actions of "real-life superheroes" (RLSH). Fishwick and Mak (2015) studied comic enthusiasts in North America and Asia who don costumes or uniforms who walk the streets engaging in various forms of do-gooding in the name of justice. They found that this norm-breaking behavior, or "edgework," allowed participants to escape their everyday lives and identities and made them feel as though they were putting some of the comic superheroes' skills into action. The RLSHs were motivated by superhero comics' messages that retribution against potential "criminals" was necessary, but voluntary community patrolling showed them that crime problems were exaggerated by the media.

BEING FRAMED: THE SKEWED REPRESENTATION OF SOCIAL GROUPS IN CRIME MEDIA AND ENTERTAINMENT

The bulk of the research on media, popular culture, and crime indicates that the presentation of crime issues in either fictional, "reality," or nonfictional forms tends to perpetuate the various social inequities and privileges that characterize a given society. The news stories that predominate are those that focus on lower income men of color, and they tend to exaggerate the likelihood of victimization of White, economically privileged members of society, elders, and children (Chiricos, Eschholz, & Gertz, 1997; Potter & Kappeler, 2012). The racialized and class-based messages of reality shows (Beckett & Sasson, 2000; Fishman & Cavendar, 1998; Mann & Zatz, 2002) and video games (Leonard, 2009) follow suit.

Rome (2004) found that Black men are often mistakenly linked to the perpetuation of violent crimes against White people and members of other racial and ethnic groups due, in part, to racist stereotypes communicated in various types of crime media, which leads to unjust law enforcement practices, such as racial profiling. Other people of color tend to be met with a variety of problematic experiences as well: Latinos and Asian boys and men are commonly stereotyped as criminals who prey on others in their own ethnic/racial groups, and American Indians are faced with stereotypes related to drinking alcohol, gambling, and vice crimes. Additional scholarly examinations of media representations of Black people have found that the repeated perpetuation of images of Black men as violent criminals and Black women as irresponsible, oversexualized, and lazy works to further conservative political agendas within criminology and the larger society (Covington, 2010). Video games (Leonard, 2009) and YouTube videos (Guo & Harlow, 2014; Lee, 2017) have been shown to convey messages about race and racism by portraying youth of color as dangerous criminals or potential criminals. Nationality and status also come into play in the replication of social inequities in the media, as immigrants and refugees have often been framed by media sources as potential terrorists and imminent threats (Esses, Medianu, & Lawson, 2013).

MEDIATING ONESELF: USING MEDIA AND POPULAR CULTURAL FORMS TO COMMUNICATE MESSAGES ABOUT CRIME AND JUSTICE

Although the framing of crime and justice issues in the mainstream media generally reinforces the need for punitive methods of crime control, fuels moral panics related to crime, and reinforces the marginalization of social groups, the creation of new media forms expand the possibilities for communicating messages about crime and justice.

Yar (2012) explained that scholars have long assumed that to understand the relationship between media and crime, one needs to analyze the media's production and dissemination crime representations and the effects of exposure to those messages by their respective audiences. But unlike traditional forms of media (e.g., print, records/CDs, radio, film, and television) that involve the communication of messages of a few to many others with accompanying high production costs, the various forms of new media (e.g., digital audio-visual recordings, computer-generated animation, desktop publishing, and image manipulation) are largely computerized communication technologies that allow many people to distribute their ideas to many others for little cost. For example, today there is widespread access to easily portable technologies, such as smartphones and video cameras, which allow people to record themselves in audio and/or video form with merely a touch of a finger and then to share their creations electronically with audiences big or small.

As a result of these technological innovations, people have begun to publicize information about their own crimes and/or acts of misbehavior through the use of videos and photography on YouTube and other online sites and social networking applications, such as Snapchat and Twitter. Sometimes the acts they share are minor ones, and other times they are quite serious, such as acts of sexual violence (Dodge, 2017).

The new dynamics of social media raise the question of whether the motivation to present a particular image to the world is increasingly serving as an impetus to commit crimes or acts of wrongdoing. As Yar (2012) noted, the examination of acts of people *mediating messages about themselves* is a necessary reversal of the assumption that the general public are acted upon by media and is a fruitful subject of inquiry for criminological research. He cited acts such as "happy slapping," youth recording themselves hitting or slapping their peers and then distributing the video via multimedia text messages, and "train surfing," people filming themselves or being filmed while standing on the outside of a moving train and jumping off of it, as transgressions that appear to be motivated by the desire to convey a particular image to the world. Once these images are widely shared through electronic social networks, the actor ostensibly feels some satisfaction and/or notoriety that may or may not inspire similar acts on the part of viewers. Similarly, researchers have studied other self-mediated framings, such as those related to gang involvement.

New media forms are used to boast about gang activity and/or status (King, Walpole, & Lamon, 2007), communicate threats between gangs (Pyrooz, Decker, & Moule, 2012), and distribute videos showing violence between and within groups (Patton, Eschmann, & Butler, 2013). Recent scholarship has shown that regardless of the type of crime or misbehavior, the desire to share it through new media forms is not surprising given that we are in the "age of the selfie" and during a time in history in which the humiliation of others is reinforced through technology (Sandberg & Ugelvick, 2017, p. 1036).

Although popular media and cultural forms are often used to stoke longstanding stereotypes about the criminality of marginalized groups, they also serve as a means of communicating messages of societal resistance (Alvarez, 2009; Hall & Jefferson, 1976; Martinez, 1997; Negus, 1999; Tepper, 2009). As Ferrell, Hayward, and Young (2008) explained, "Marginalization and criminalization certainly produce internecine predation, but they also produce, sometimes in the same tangled circumstances, moments in which outsiders collectively twist and shout against their own sorry situations" (p. 21). In her work, "Crime, Resistance and Song: Black Musicianship and Black Criminology," Saleh-Hanna (2010) found that a variety of reggae, Afrobeat, and hip hop songs created by Black artists demonstrate such moments in their lyrical challenges to current U.S. criminal justice policies. Many hard-core fans of rap music have been found to view rap music as a form of protest music (Dyson, 2004; Kitwana, 2005; Quinn, 2005; Tanner, Ashbridge, & Wortley, 2009). Fans of acid house music have used alternative media, such as e-mail campaigns, gay-focused media, mass mailings, and nonmainstream broadcasting to counter stereotypes about the dangers of raves and to stop measures to pass ordinances against raves (Tepper, 2009).

Although girls and women who overtly stand up against gender oppression and victimization are often labeled delinquent or criminal, research has shown that they have persisted in using music and zines (self-published magazines) (Leblanc, 1999; Schilt, 2003) and social media (Tan, 2017) as means of resistance. In addition, activist groups have used media tools in their campaigns against media messages about crime that they deem questionable, such those supporting the use of shock incarceration methods for juveniles in the television show, *Beyond Scared Straight* (Bates & Swan, 2017). Social media has also been used to conduct "trials by media" that allow people to publish information and/or pictures about harms they experience and harness public responses to address their victimization outside of the criminal justice system (Chagnon & Chesney-Lind, 2015).

Some filmmakers have created both feature and documentary films to challenge criminal and juvenile justice systems (Tang, 2017) and to expose government and corporate crimes (Cavender & Jurik, 2016). Similarly, a subset of mainstream and online journalists has worked to counter mainstream narratives about crime. An example of this was the generally positive Western news representations of the feminist punk rock group Pussy Riot, their resistance against the Russian government, and their imprisonment (Seal, 2013). All of these examples of resistance demonstrate that the relationship between popular culture, media, and crime continues to be a complex one that escapes simple characterizations and requires additional scholarly examination.

Discussion Questions

1. Pick your favorite television show or film related to crime, and consider how the issues of crime and social control are framed. What is/ are the implied causes of crime? How are the "solutions" to the crime problem framed?

2. Analyze any experiences you may have had with the various forms of "new media" that allow for the easy dissemination of images and ideas about crime, criminalization, and social control to audiences of your choosing. How did you learn about these tools of communication? How have you used them in the past and to what effect(s)?

3. When people make claims about the relationship between the consumption of violent media and crime, what factors do they need to take into consideration according to the existing research?

4. List and analyze at least three pieces of popular culture (e.g., songs, poems, books, blog posts, tweets, etc.) that have messages of resistance related to unjust stereotyping and/or injustice in the criminal justice system. Consider what audiences are generally exposed to these media forms, what their messages are, and their possible impacts.

References

Altheide, D. L. (1976). *Creating reality: How TV news distorts events.* Beverly Hills, CA: Sage.

Altheide, D. L. (1996). *Qualitative media analysis.* Thousand Oaks, CA: Sage.

Altheide, D. L. (1997). The news media, the problem frame, and the production of fear. *Sociological Quarterly, 38,* 647–668.

Altheide, D. L. (2009a). *Terror post 9/11 and the media.* New York, NY: Peter Lang Publishers.

Altheide, D. L. (2009b). The Columbine shootings and a discourse of fear. *American Behavioral Scientist, 52*(10), 1354–1370.

Alvarez, L. (2009). *The power of the zoot: Youth culture and resistance during World War II.* Berkeley, CA: University of California Press.

Arsenault, A. H., & Castells, M. (2008). The structure and dynamics of global multimedia business networks. *International Journal of Communication, 2,* 707–748.

Barak, G. (Ed.). (1994). *Media, process, and the social construction of crime*. New York, NY: Garland Press.

Bates, K. A., & Swan, R. S. (2017). *Juvenile delinquency in a diverse society* (2nd ed.). Thousand Oaks, CA: Sage.

Beckett, K., & Sasson, T. (2000). *The politics of injustice*. Thousand Oaks, CA: Pine Forge Press.

Berger, P., & Luckmann, T. (1966). *The social construction of reality: A treatise in the sociology of knowledge*. New York, NY: Anchor Books.

Bickham, D. (2006, March 29). *Testimony before the Senate Judiciary Committee on the Constitution, Civil Rights and Property Rights*. Retrieved from https://www.judiciary.senate.gov/imo/media/doc/Bickham%20Testimony%20032906.pdf

Binder, A. (1993). Constructing racial rhetoric: Media depictions of harm in heavy metal and rap music. *American Sociological Review, 58*(6), 753–767.

Bissler, D. L., & Conners, J. L. (2012). (Eds.). *The harms of crime media: Essays on the perpetuation of racism, sexism, and class stereotypes*. Jefferson, NC: McFarland and Company.

Carrabine, E. (2008). *Crime, culture and the media*. Cambridge, UK: Polity Press.

Cavender, G., & Jurik, N. (2016). Film review: *The big short*. *Crime Media Culture, 12*(2), 283–286.

Cecil, D. K. (2007). Looking beyond 'Caged heat': Media images of women in prison. *Feminist Criminology, 2*, 304–306.

Cecil, D. K. (2010). Televised images of jail: Lessons in controlling the unruly. *Sociology of Crime, Law & Deviance, 14*, 67–88.

Cecil, D. K., & Leitner, J. L. (2009). Unlocking the gates: An examination of MSNBC Investigates—Lockup. *Howard Journal of Criminal Justice, 48*(2), 184–199.

Chagnon, N., & Chesney-Lind, M. (2015). "Somebody's been in the house": A tale of burglary and a trial by media. *Crime Media Culture, 11*(1), 41–60.

Chermak, S. (1995). *Victims in the news: Crime and the American news media*. Boulder, CO: Westview Press.

Chiricos, T., Eschholz, S, & Gerz, M. (1997). Crime, news, and fear of crime. *Social Problems, 44*(3), 342–357.

Chiricos, T., Padgett, K. & Gerz, M. (2000). Fear, TV news, and the reality of crime. *Criminology, 38*, 755–785.

Cohen, S. (1972). *Folk devils and moral panics*. London, UK: MacGibbon & Kee.

Cohen, S., & Young, J. (Eds.). (1973). *The manufacture of news: Deviance, social problems, and the mass media*. London, UK: Constable.

Collins, V. E., Farrell, A. L., McKee, J. R., Martin, F. A., & Monk-Turner, E. (2011). The state of coverage: The media's representation of international issues and state crime. *International Criminal Justice Review, 21*(1), 5–21.

Covington, J. (2010). *Crime and racial constructions: Cultural misinformation about African Americans in media and academia*. Lanham, MD: Lexington Books.

Cunneen, C., & Stubbs, J. (2008). Cultural criminology and the engagement with race, gender and post-colonial identities. *University of Sydney Law School*, Legal Studies Research Paper No. 8/15.

Dodge, A. (2017). Digitizing rape culture: Online sexual violence and the power of the digital photography. *Crime Media Culture, 13*(1), 65–82.

Dyson, M. E. (2004). *The Michael Dyson reader*. New York, NY: Basic Civitas Books.

Esses, V. M., Medianu, S., & Lawson, A. S. (2013). Uncertainty, threat, and the role of the media in promoting the dehumanization of immigrants and refugees. *Journal of Social Issues, 69*, 518–536.

Ferguson, C. J. (2015). Clinicians' attitudes toward video games vary as a function of age, gender and negative beliefs about youth: A sociology of media research approach. *Computers in Human Behavior, 52*, 379–385.

Ferguson, C. J., & Olson, C. K. (2010). The Supreme Court and video game violence: Will regulation be worth the costs to the first amendment? *The Criminologist, 35*(4), 18–21.

Ferrell, J. (2013). Cultural criminology and the politics of meaning. *Critical Criminology, 21*, 257–271.

Ferrell, J., & Hamm, M. (1998). *Ethnography at the edge: Crime, deviance, and field research*. Chicago, IL: Northeastern University Press.

Ferrell, J., Hayward, K., Morrison, W., & Presdee, M. (2004). Fragments of a manifesto: Introducing *Cultural criminology unleashed*. In J. Ferrell, K. Hayward, W. Morrison, & M. Presdee (Eds.), *Cultural criminology unleashed* (pp. 1–9). London, UK: Glasshouse Press.

Ferrell, J., Hayward, K., Morrison, W., & Presdee, M. (Eds.) (2004). *Cultural criminology unleashed*. London, UK: Glasshouse Press.

Ferrell, J., Hayward, K. & Young, J. (2008). *Cultural criminology: An invitation*. Thousand Oaks, CA: Sage.

Fishwick, E., & Mak, H. (2015). Fighting crime, battling injustices: The world of real-life superheroes. *Crime Media Culture, 11*(3), 335–356.

Fishman, M., & Cavender, G. (Eds.). (1998). *Entertaining crime*. New York, NY: Aldine de Gruyter.

Flexon, J. L., & Guerette, R. T. (2009). Differential effects of an offender-focused crime prevention media campaign. *Journal of Criminal Justice, 37*, 608–616.

Gauntlett, D. (1995). *Moving experiences: Understanding television's influences and effects*. Luton, UK: John Libbey.

Giddens, T. (Ed.). (2015). *Graphic justice: Intersections of comics and law*. New York, NY: Routledge.

Gilbert, J. B. (1986). *A cycle of outrage: America's reaction to the juvenile delinquency in the 1950s*. New York, NY: Oxford University Press.

Goode, E., & Ben-Yehuda, N. (2009). *Moral panics: The social construction of deviance* (2nd ed.). Malden, MA: Wiley-Blackwell.

Gunter, B. (2008). Media violence: Is there a case for causality? *American Behavioral Scientist, 51*(8), 1061–1122.

Guo, L., & Harlow, S. (2014). User-generated racism: An analysis of stereotypes of African Americans, Latinos, and Asians in YouTube videos. *Howard Journal of Communications, 25*(3), 281–302.

Hall, S., & Jefferson, T. (1976). *Resistance through rituals*. London, UK: Hutchinson.

Jenkins, P. (1999). Fighting terrorism as if women mattered: Anti-abortion violence as unconstructed terrorism. In J. Ferrell & N. Websdale (Eds.), *Making trouble: Cultural constructions of crime, deviance, and control* (pp. 319–346). New York, NY: Aldine de Gruyter.

Joe Laider, K., Lee, M., & Wong, G. P. F. (2017). Doing criminology on media and crime in Asia. *Crime Media Culture, 13*(2), 135–151.

King, J. E., Walpole, C. E., & Lamon, K. (2007). Surf and turf wars online: Growing implications of Internet gang violence. *Journal of Adolescent Health, 41*(6), S66– S68.

Kitwana, B. (2005). *Why White kids love hip hop: Wankstas, wiggers, wannabes, and the new reality of race in America*. New York, NY: Basic Civitas Books.

Kort-Butler, L. (2013). Justice league?: Depictions of justice in children's superhero cartoons. *Criminal Justice Review, 38*, 50–69.

Landry, D. (2013). Are we human? Edgework in defiance of the mundane and measurable. *Critical Criminology, 21*, 1–14.

LeBlanc, L. (1999). *Pretty in punk: Girl's gender resistance in a boy's subculture*. New Brunswick, NJ: Rutgers University Press.

Lee, D. (2017). *"It's just a prank, bro!": A sociological analysis of new media, race, and horrid humor*. Master's thesis. San Marcos, CA: California State University San Marcos.

Leonard, D. (2009). Young, black (& brown) and don't give a fuck: Virtual gangstas in the era of state violence. *Cultural Studies-Critical Methodologies, 9*, 248–272.

Mann, C. R., & Zatz, M. S. (Eds.). (2002). *Images of color, images of crime* (2nd ed.). Los Angeles, CA: Roxbury.

Martinez, T. A. (1997). Popular culture as oppositional culture: Rap as resistance. *Sociological Perspectives, 40*, 265–286.

Mazerolle, L. (2003). The pros and cons of publicity campaigns as a crime control tactic. *Criminology and Public Policy, 2*, 531–540.

McCormick, C. (2010). *Constructing danger: Emotions and the mis/representation of crime in the news*. Black Point, Nova Scotia, Canada: Fernwood Press.

McMahon, J. R. (1921). Unspeakable jazz must go. *Ladies Home Journal, 38*, 116.

Naegler, L., & Salman, S. (2016). Cultural criminology and gender consciousness: Moving feminist theory from margin to center. *Feminist Criminology, 11*(4), 354–374.

Negus, K. (1999). *Music genres and corporate cultures*. London, UK: Routledge.

Park, D. (2002). The Kefauver comic book hearings as show trial: Decency, authority, and the dominated expert. *Cultural Studies, 16*(2), 259–288.

Patton, D. U., Eschemann, R. D., & Butler, D. A. (2013). Internet banging: New trends in social media, gang violence, masculinity and hip-hop. *Computers in Human Behavior, 29*, A54–A59.

Phillips, N. D., & Strobl, S. (2013). *Comic book crime: Truth, justice and the American way*. New York, NY: New York University Press.

Potter, W. J., & Kappeler, V. E. (2012). Introduction: Media, crime and hegemony. In D. L. Bissler & J. L. Conners (Eds.), *The harms of crime media: Essays on the perpetuation of racism, sexism, and class stereotypes* (p. 3017). Jefferson, NC: McFarland and Company.

Pyrooz, D. C., Decker, S. H., & Moule, R. K. (2015). Crime and routine activities in online settings: Gangs, offenders and the Internet. *Justice Quarterly, 32*(3), 471–499.

Quinn, E. (2005). *Nuthin' but a "G" thang*. New York, NY: Columbia University Press.

Rafter, N., & Brown, M. (2011). *Criminology goes to the movies: Crime theory and popular culture*. New York, NY: New York University Press.

Rome, D. (2004). *Black demons: The media's depiction of the Black male criminal stereotype*. Westport, CT: Praeger Publishers.

Russell-Brown, K. (2008). *The color of crime: Racial hoaxes, White fear, Black protectionism, police harassment, and other microaggressions* (2nd ed.). New York, NY: New York University Press.

Saleh-Hanna, V. (2010). Crime, resistance and song: Black musicianship's Black criminology. *Sociology of Crime, Law & Deviance, 14*, 145–171.

Sandberg, S., & Ugelvik, T. (2017). Why do offenders tape their crimes? Crime and punishment in the age of the selfie. *British Journal of Criminology, 57*, 1023–1040.

Sasson, T. (1995). *Crime talk: How citizens construct a social problem*. Hawthorne, NY: Aldine de Gruyter.

Savage, J. (2008). The role of exposure to media violence in the etiology of violent behavior: A criminologist weighs in. *American Behavioral Scientist, 51*(8), 1123–1136.

Schilt, K. (2003). "I'll resist with every breath": Girls and zine making as a form of resistance. *Youth and Society, 35*, 71–97.

Schlesinger, P., & Tumber, H. (1994). *Reporting crime: The media politics of criminal justice*. Oxford, UK: Oxford University Press.

Seal, L. (2013). Pussy riot and feminist criminology: A new "femininity in dissent?" *Contemporary Justice Review, 16*, 293–303.

Surette, R. (2013). Cause or catalyst: The interaction of real world and media crime models. *American Journal of Criminal Justice, 38*, 392–409.

Surette, R. (2014). *Media, crime, and criminal justice: Images, realities, and policies* (5th ed.). Belmont, CA: Wadsworth.

Tanner, J., Asbridge, M., & Wortley, S. (2009). Listening to rap: Cultures of crime, cultures of resistance. *Social Forces*, *88*(2), 693–722.

Tan, J. (2017). Digital masquerading: Feminist media activism in China. *Crime Media Culture*, *13*(2), 171–186.

Tang, D. T. (2017). Feeling alive: Voices of incarcerated youth in 'We are alive'. *Crime Media Culture*, *13*(2), 153–170.

Tepper, S. J. (2009). Stop the beat: Quiet regulation and cultural conflict. *Sociological Forum*, *24*(2), 276–306.

Williams, J. P., & Kamaludeen, M. N. (2017). Muslim girl culture and social control in Southeast Asia: Exploring the hijabista and hijabster phenomena. *Crime Media Culture*, *13*(2), 199–216.

Yar, M. (2012). Crime, media and the will-to-representation: Reconsidering relationships in the new media age. *Crime Media Culture*, *8*(3), 245–260.

9

CRIME AND ECONOMICS

Consumer Culture, Criminology, and the Politics of Exclusion

Stephen L. Muzzatti and Maggie Reid

A SPECTER IS HAUNTING CRIMINOLOGY . . .

The connections between crime and economics are complex and multifaceted. Perhaps because of this density, thorough coverage of the topic "crime and economics" has proven to be so elusive to mainstream or "administrative" criminology, particularly in the United States, despite some ostensibly elaborate and occasionally very high-profile attempts at addressing it. In some respects, the topic is an anathema to criminology. While such an assertion may read as "sacrilegious" to orthodox criminologists, it is not anywhere near as wildly unsubstantiated as some of orthodoxy's high priests might retort.

As any devoted reader of the indecipherable articles that fill journals such as *Criminology* and *Justice Quarterly* (to say nothing of moribund textbooks and stale government reports) can undoubtedly attest, there is a plethora of criminological studies purporting to address the matter of crime and economics. However, many of these studies, if they indeed address economics at all, do so in a disjointed, limited, and myopic way. These studies, in various degrees, attempt to account for the impact of economics on crimes rates, ethno-racial or subcultural variations in offending, policing practices, criminogenic age cohorts, victimization risks, incarceration, recidivism, and a host of other issues. They do so in a sophisticated and nuanced fashion; symbolically representing crime's factors with *lamda* and *chi*, employing elaborate multiple regression models and the latest statistical alchemy (see Ferrell, Hayward, & Young, 2015; Muzzatti, 2010, Muzzatti & Smith, 2018). They ultimately tell us very little about crime and economics. While we do not mean to cast any aspersions on the researchers involved or question the countless hours of work and effort they devote to these projects, most fall victim to a fatal ontological flaw; they fail to address *capitalism*.

It seems that capitalism is a bad word in criminology. It is not something to be discussed in polite company (such as found or heard at the American Society of Criminology's annual meetings) lest you be labeled a leftist ideologue, or worse, a "reductionist," and it is certainly not something to be committed to print (except occasionally, in esoteric European-based criminology journals). Academic criminology's gatekeepers are aware of the potential consequences associated with allowing an unbridled thrashing of the "C-word" and work diligently to prevent it from sullying the good name of the discipline.[1]

Aside from a few serpentine flashes, any emancipatory potential to be found in criminology is met with the Marcusian repressive tolerance of program committees, blind reviewers, institutional ethics boards, tenure and promotion committees, and outside funding sources such as the National Institute of Justice (NIJ). It is far easier and more respectable to facilitate work on "nuts, sluts, and perverts" and "the exotic, the erotic, and the neurotic" under the aegis of "value-free" voodoo criminology and the numbers game than to risk the ire of editors, publishers, and granting agencies, to say nothing of the grief that one will undoubtedly suffer at the hands of orthodox criminology's high priests and most of the lesser clergy who totter along in ideological lockstep (see Hall & Winlow, 2015; Liazos, 1972; Muzzatti, 2003; Young, 1999, 2004).

We are fortunate that Dan Okada, Mary Maguire, and Alexa Sardina were not only open to but enthusiastic about including an ontological and epistemological challenge to the "crime and economics" canon in this collection. For that, we are grateful. Of course, readers should note that any shortcomings or foibles are ours alone. Readers should also be aware that in addition to "capitalism," they will encounter throughout this chapter a number of other *profanities* well outside criminology's polite lexicon (e.g., political economy, late modernity, etc.) as we attempt to historically and genealogically reconstruct a criminology of capitalism.

READING THE PROFANE: THEORIZING CRIME AND CAPITALISM

While it is true that many contemporary American criminologists fail to address the role of capitalism in matters of crime (whether causation, creation, reification, or commodification), some late-19th-century and early 20th-century European scholars paid it considerable attention. In the following section, we will briefly address the work of two often overlooked "criminological theorists," Germany's

Karl Marx and Holland's Willem Bonger, as a means of contextualizing extant issues of crime and capitalism in 21st-century America.

Karl Marx (1818–1883)

Considering his vast corpus of work, it is not surprising that many criminologists overlook Karl Marx's writing on crime. With the exception of his piece on "Debates on the Law on the Thefts of Wood" in 1842[2] and a couple of articles for the *New York Daily Tribune*[3] in the 1850s, Marx rarely addressed the topic of crime specifically. However, he wrote extensively about capitalism as an economic and political system and the way this system essentially produced two classes of people: *capitalists* and *proletarians*. Because capitalists owned the means of production, they also were able to exert almost total control over social institutions (including but not limited to what we today understand as the criminal justice system) and were able to entrench their beliefs and values as *the* beliefs and values of society. In contrast, the proletarians owned and controlled nothing and, hence, were obliged to exchange their ability to work for a wage at the discretion of the capitalists. For Marx, the social production of concrete material relations—relations by which people secured their material existence—permeated all aspects of life. Because of this, the capitalist ruling class was able to translate its economic power into political and ideological power. Through his endeavor to illustrate that the material basis for systemic inequality produced conflict (which can manifest itself as crime), Marx provided the requisite conceptual tools through which questions about crime could be answered.

At the risk of oversimplifying, Marx theorized that "the criminal" and "criminal law" are inextricably bound to the larger economic order. In *The German Ideology* (1846), Marx and Friedrich Engels describe crime as the struggle of the isolated individual against the prevailing conditions. In other words, it was the economy, specifically industrial capitalism, that determined crime's incarnations. The creation and enforcement of law was at the discretion of the capitalist class. Though this posit was ignored by most American criminologists, these correlates of crime and inequality are certainly no less true today than when Marx and Engels first described them.

Willem Adriaan Bonger (1876–1940)

Between the time of Marx's death and the first decade of the 20th century, a criminology of the capitalist economic system was emerging in several European nations, notably France, Germany, and Italy.[4] The late 1880s, in particular, saw a proliferation of these works by Italian criminologists such as Bruno Battaglia, Napoleone Colajanni, and Filippo Turati. However, to the considerable detriment of Anglo-American criminology, few of these stellar contributions were ever translated into English.[5] A notable and instructive exception was the translation of Dutch criminologist Willem Bonger's book, *Criminalite et Conditions Economiques* (1905).

As a young man, Bonger studied law at the University of Amsterdam. It was here that he became well acquainted with the work of Marx and was inspired to study the political economy of crime by G. A. van Hamel, a renowned penologist who was his criminal law professor. While Bonger made several major contributions to criminology in the areas of racism and criminal justice, suicide, penal philosophy, militarism, and war, it was the English translation of *Criminality and Economic Conditions* (1916) that proved to be his most enduring and the one most relevant to this chapter.

According to Bonger, capitalism is criminogenic. Put simply, capitalism's brutality creates conditions under which crime is not only produced but flourishes. For Bonger, crime and capitalism are connected in three fundamental ways. Bonger employed the historical materialism of Marx and Engels in illustrating the first of these connections: the development of criminal law in unison with the aggrandizement of property rights. Hence, for Bonger, the history of theft is the history of private property. Much of criminal law was created to protect the property of the *haves* from the *have nots*. Connected to this was Bonger's second major posit: that crime is engendered by the miserable conditions forced upon the working class in the emergence of industrial capitalism. Finally—and most prescient for the consideration of crime under late modernity—Bonger theorizes that the economic logic of capitalism promotes endless greed and fosters crime.

Both Marx and Bonger addressed the myriad ways capitalism produces crime, including the miserable conditions under which the majority of the population languished, the biased creation and application of law, as well as the destructive values of avarice and individualism that permeated industrial society. However, with the notable exception of what came to be known as the "conflict criminology"[6] of William Chambliss, Elliot Currie, Julia and Herman Schwendinger, Steven Spitzer, Tony Platt, and Richard Quinney in the 1970s and 1980s, few American criminologists took up these themes with vigor.[7]

Tragedy of the Commons

Imperative to understanding the relationship between capitalism and crime is that the development of capitalism was premised on crime, albeit state "authorized" theft. For example, the enclosure of common lands in the British Isles between the 15th and 19th centuries, converting them from public lands into private property controlled by a single landholder, was one of the earliest crimes by the capitalist state. Taking the common lands out of the public domain and assigning their property rights to the landed gentry was justified on the basis that their public status made the lands susceptible to overuse and underdevelopment of their productive capacities (Boyle, 2008). This made the initial theft of the lands legal but any subsequent theft or unauthorized use by the common people illegal. Defenders of privatizing the commons wonder how they will stop the lands from being over-grazed if everyone has the right to use them?

Critics wonder if one has the right to control the lands, why make them to the benefit of the many? Thomas More argued that greed is what led to the enclosure of the common lands and envisioned that the disruption this caused in the lives of poor farmers would lead to crime and violence. For More, the enclosure movement of the common lands, despite its rational and functional justifications, actually facilitated social dysfunction.

In the current epoch, society has entered what James Boyle (2008) has characterized as a "second enclosure movement" or "enclosing of the commons of the mind," which refers to the extension of new property rights to things formerly viewed as uncommodifiable or common. He is referring more specifically about the broad umbrella of intellectual property rights and their intensification over the last 25 years. The Lockean possessive individualism of late modernity is ever present in the proliferation of intellectual property regimes, where creators are rewarded rights for their original genius rather than recognizing works as being built on the backs of other texts that have come before them (McLeod, 2001). Like the first enclosure movement, the argument goes that without strict intellectual property laws, lacking the ability to exclude will dull the incentive to create and stifle innovation (Boyle, 2008; David, 2017). Private property is apparently the efficient solution to the 'problem' of public ownership. However, as new forms of property emerge, so do new ways to contest intellectual property frameworks. Unlike the common lands in England, intellectual property is, for the most part, nonrival. This is particularly true in a digital context, where the cost of copying approaches zero.

BANALITY AND VICIOUSNESS IN LATE MODERNITY

Whilst the conditions of 21st-century America are very different than those experienced by More, Marx, and Bonger, capitalism rages on, leaving a broad swath of destruction and human suffering, including but not limited to what is narrowly defined as "crime." Contrary to the vociferous pronouncements of capitalist running dogs, market order cheerleaders and neoliberal apologists, globalization, deindustrialization, austerity measures, and the so-called sharing economy have not made the American landscape a better, safer, or more humane environment. Massive transnational corporations the size and scope of which the authors of the Sherman Antitrust Act could nary imagine continue to steal and murder with impunity, street crime is ever more racialized, minor transgressions increasingly come to be addressed through the criminal justice system's formal and punitive mechanisms, and living wage jobs are nearly impossible to find and even more difficult to keep.

Under such conditions, it is little wonder that people are adrift and cling desperately to anything that promises more stability than late modernism's liquidity (see Bauman, 2000). Unfortunately, there is relatively little available on which people, particularly young people, can moor themselves. As Hall (2012) illustrates with great aplomb, because the global capitalist project is increasingly reliant upon *finance* capital rather than *productive* capital, material reality has readily been displaced by a fictitious realm of fleeting visceral pleasure and ephemeral amelioration. Hence, unlike pre-deindustrialized generations in which social worth was determined through the relationship to the means of production and other stratified forms of social meaning, under late modernity, our selves and our subjectivities are increasingly determined through our consumption practices (Ewen, 1977, 1988; Hayward & Yar, 2006; Muzzatti, 2013, 2017).

In his seminal work on crime and consumer culture, Hayward (2004) illustrates that the products and services we acquire and access through our consumer exercises are the primary indices of identity. While there is nothing inherently new about capitalism's unapologetic promotion of consumerism as a gateway to social integration, the process has accelerated rapidly over the past 2 decades, reaching gargantuan proportions. Today, the creation and expression of identities via the celebration of consumer goods have all but supplanted other, more traditional forms of identity expression. This, in combination with the aforementioned withdrawal of meaningful, living wage employment opportunities seriously undermines the life world, moral codes, and habitus of ordinary people (Bordieu, 1984; Hall et al., 2008).

CONSUMING CRIME AND CULTURE

Scything through capitalism's veneer, it is evident that lives of late modern subjects have been so thoroughly colonized by consumerism that the goals–means discrepancy (i.e., "strain") Merton described over 70 years ago seems almost benign in comparison. Indeed, living in a world where work, if it exists at all, is increasingly deskilled, wages are pitifully low, and growing segments of the former "middle classes" slip into a vortex of unsecured debt, it is little wonder that consumption itself is now *the* strategy employed to demarcate, compartmentalize, and control the general public (see relatedly, Bauman, 2000, 2007; Wilson, 1987). This transformation has only served to intensify capitalism's inequality. According to Bauman, late modern consumer society is now polarized between, on the one hand, indemnified, privileged, and dutiful consumers, and, on the other, the increasingly swollen ranks of the marginalized and criminalized classes, who, either as a result of inability or unwillingness, have failed to acquiesce to the hegemonic dictates of consumerism. The first of these groups, the "Seduced," exhibit the requisite desire and fixation required by unmediated consumer societies. More importantly, though, they are in a position to satisfy their desire through continual cycles of unreflexive hyperconsumption. Importantly, in late consumer society, this type of consumption is becoming ever more possible to the masses as counterfeit products and cheap commodities predicated on exploited labor are readily available.

The consumption of counterfeited goods is particularly interesting, as it accounts for roughly 5% to 10% of global trade (Rojek, 2017). As seduced consumers descend into criminal underground markets to purchase their counterfeited luxury handbags, watches, and perfumes, Rojek (2017) argues that "when viewed from the logic of the general consumption process under capitalism, it is also the rational extension of consumer activity into 'hyper consumerism'" (p. 31). In other words the desire to consume supersedes legality in order to achieve social status at a killer price.

The same is true for the violation of other forms of intellectual property. Much to the chagrin of the entertainment industries, the digital age has enabled access to free cultural products at alarming rates due to the ease of copying and sharing information. Property and law are easily overlooked by Internet users to have free access to music and other forms of entertainment. On the one hand, digital piracy challenges the economic power and monopoly control of major media companies (David, 2017), who have rigidly controlled their properties in the analog age. Ad campaigns that liken digital files to physical objects, like "You wouldn't steal a car," in an appeal to Internet users to refrain from digital piracy, have fallen flat as users understand that digital files are nonrival. As the entertainment industries claim that they have lost billions in global movie piracy and song downloads (Rojek, 2017), which, of course, is predicated on the assumption that digital pirates would otherwise be consumers, digital culture positions itself as somewhat antithetical to private property; the Internet is about sharing. On the other hand, the ideological functions of the entertainment industries are alive and well and reaching more audiences than ever as their content reaches not only the good, paying customers but also the degenerate pirates. Digital piracy simultaneously challenges and disrupts while also promoting the consumer mediation of identity.

Standing in stark contrast to the "Seduced" are the "Repressed," a group that embodies what one might describe as the *collateral damage* of consumerism. This throng of uncommoditized or failed consumers represent an ever-growing, marginalized mass who, through negligence or willfulness, fail to adequately acquit themselves of their consumer "duties." The "Repressed's" insufficient and/or disreputable consumption patterns do not satisfactorily integrate them into the acceptable echelons of consumer society (Muzzatti, 2004, 2010). The musings of "Elliot Alderson," the antisocial cybersecurity engineer and protagonist of American television drama *Mr. Robot* well capture the illusory "free will" of late capitalism and the ensuing nihilism of living under such social conditions.

> How do we know if we're in control? That we're not just making the best of what comes at us, and that's it. Trying to constantly pick between two options. Like your two paintings in the waiting room. Or Coke and Pepsi. McDonald's or Burger King? Hyundai or Honda? It's all part of the

same blur, right? Just out of focus enough. It's the illusion of choice. Half of us can't even pick our own cable, gas, electric. The water we drink, our health insurance. Even if we did, would it matter? You know, if our only option is Blue Cross or Blue Shield, what the fuck is the difference? In fact, aren't they the same? No, man, our choices are prepaid for us, long time ago.[8]

To move beyond Bauman's "Seduced" and the "Repressed," we could consider a group that we might call the "Liberated." The "Liberated" constitute a group that seek to de-commodify informational goods in order to reduce barriers to technology. Beyond the consumption (and piracy) of commodities are real struggles for access to information and computer software that are increasingly becoming important tools for employability and social mobility. Much like other forms of content, digital piracy accounts for a large portion of software that is acquired and installed (Rojek, 2017). There is a tension between commercial software developers who build digital rights management (DRM) to lockout unlawful users technologically from utilizing their software and "hactivists" who attempt to break those systems of control.

David (2017) argues that all attempts to encrypt and lock down software have failed as they have been cracked by open-source hackers. The collaborative culture among open-source hackers, or "networked autonomy" of sharing of tips and ideas renders hackers more efficient at writing (and therefore cracking) software than teams in corporate settings (David, 2017). Soderberg (2008) argues that free sharing cultures online constitute a form of "dot.communism." Hackers today appropriate technology in order to tap into its "potential to overcome the alienation of labor in a capitalist society" (David, 2017, p. 61). The growth of online hacktivism has illustrated that the sharing of intellectual resources is what fosters creativity and motivation, rather than strict intellectual property rights. David (2017) contends that the tragedy of the commons is a myth, which is evidenced by how sharing and hackivism are implicated in innovation, as well as struggles for equality and access to information and software.

LATE MODERNITY, CRIME, AND PSEUDOPACIFICATION

What is of importance in terms of this chapter (and something overlooked by Bauman) is the way in which late modernity's ideological work serves not only to incessantly remind us of this compartmentalization but also acts to control and manipulate us by illustrating the consequences of lax or ineffectual consumption work (Muzzatti, 2010, 2013). As Hall and his colleagues poignantly illustrate, late capitalism systematically organizes conditions of social insecurity while simultaneously lauding aggressive competition and individual hubris (Hall, 2012; Hall et al., 2008).

Unlike the "norms" of the Mertonian framework, late modernity's norms are created in fantasy world of venture capitalism, hyperwealth, and unlimited personal and natural resources. Such arrangements are potentially criminogenic, as they detach people from reality, breed frustration, and undermine any true sense of community and solidarity by fostering irresponsible and wholly instrumental attitudes toward other people (Hall, 2012; Hall et al., 2008). A rank, dog-eat-dog individualism and fortress mentality are vital components of late modernity's de-politicalization process that lulls the populace into a state of false insecurity. Alternately described as *anelpis* (Hall & Winlow, 2004, p. 277, quoting Taylor) and *vertigo* (Young, 2007, p. 12), this malaise of late modernity is characterized by total cynicism, no opinions (except as they relate to the incontrovertibly mundane), no hope, a sense of entitlement, unrealistic expectations, giddiness, unsteadiness, uncertainty, and insecurity. Perhaps most significantly, it is evidenced by misplaced fear, not a legitimate fear of government, corporations, or other authority but a misplaced and unrealistic fear of other people.

Capitalism produces numerous contradictions. In late modernity, we live in isolation from our neighbors and cut ourselves off from all but a small number of intimates yet pay high monthly fees to have media conglomerates pump highly stylized images of the outside world into our homes. We distrust strangers and move briskly to maintain our physical distance from those we do not recognize on the street but loudly discuss our most intimate personal details on mobile phones in shopping malls and post the prosaic intricacies of our lives on social networking sites for anyone to see. We are suspicious of those who migrate to our shores because they may "take our jobs" or not work and "live off our tax dollars." We fear terrorism but fail to scrutinize the foreign policy of our own government dare we be labeled un-American. Perhaps capitalism's greatest obfuscation is found in the fact that we continually feed our cravings for inexpensive consumer goods but fail to consider the real costs—economic, social, and environmental, at home and abroad—of doing so.[9]

SELLING CRIME, MARKETING TRANSGRESSION, AND COMMODIFYING VIOLENCE

Even in their most surreal nightmares, it is unlikely that either Marx or Bonger could have envisaged the leviathan proportions and seemingly infinite tentacles of 21st-century capitalism. However, given their respective historical contexts, both offered some discerning commentary on the saleability of crime. In the first volume of *Theories of Surplus Value* (1861), Marx's insights into the marketability of crime are perhaps even more poignant under today's conditions of late modernity than when it was first written.

According to him,

> The criminal produces not only crime but also criminal law, and even the inevitable text-book in which the professor presents his lectures as a commodity for sale in the market . . . but also art, literature, novels and the tragic drama, as *Oedipus* and *Richard III*, . . . (quoted in Greenberg, 1981, pp. 52–53).

In a similar vein, Bonger, in stark contrast to most contemporary criminology textbooks, begins *Criminality and Economic Conditions* not with the conventional hyperbolic pieties about "the current state of crime and justice" but instead devotes several pages to Thomas More's fictional account of the traveller Raphael Hythloday.[10] While these examples focus on suffering under petty mercantilism and other precapitalist economic formations, they do address the narcissistic individualism that capitalism has exacerbated under late modernity.

While several early British "conflict" criminologists examined the way the news media used crime to sell (see Cohen, 1972; Cohen & Young, 1973; Hall, Critcher, Jefferson, Clarke, & Roberts, 1978), it has only been in last 20 years or so that criminologists have seriously investigated the connection between crime and the entertainment media. A new wave of cultural criminologists have applied the contributions of Frankfurt School theorists such as Max Horkheimer and Theodor Adorno (1946) to an understanding of the role played by the culture industries in transmitting corporate consumerism's destructive values. Ferrell and Sanders (1995) were among the first of this new wave to examine on how "mass" or "common culture" (p. 7) is recast as crime. They theorize that the criminalization of everyday life is a cultural enterprise of the powerful and must be investigated as such.

Similarly, Presdee's (2000) analysis of carnival desire and the sensuality of wickedness demonstrates how our everyday/night responses to late modernity come to be defined as criminal. Analogizing mediated crime to the board game *Monopoly*, Presdee examines the way in which crime, like monopoly capitalism, is dehistoricized, whitewashed, and transmogrified into mass-marketed pleasure. Citing a range of examples from Internet bondage sites and arson to racing stolen cars and weapon bazaars, Presdee explores the contradictions and irrationality of a commodity-oriented society from which criminalized culture emanates.

More recently, cultural criminologists have been attentive to the processes and products associated with what they have variously described as the "marketing of transgression" (Hayward, 2004) and the "commodification of violence" (Ferrell, Hayward, & Young, 2015). This visual representation of crime and transgression is, they argue, not only central to the production of news but is now a vital component of the entertainment media—gripping the collective imagination of television viewers, moviegoers, Internet browsers, video gamers, and other audiences. To a certain extent, of course, there is nothing intrinsically new about the use of this type of imagery in the service of consumerism—certainly crime and violence have been used to sell cinema passes, TV programs, video games, and music for decades. However, what is new, as Ferrell, Hayward, and Young (2015) illustrate, is the force and range of these "illicit" messages and the effect this has had on the tectonic landscape of the late modern entertainment media. In particular, there appears to be a far greater willingness among *mainstream corporations* to utilize allusions to crime and transgression to give their products edgy appeal while still serving the conservative interests of consumer capitalism and its control functions. Considering late capitalism's oligopolistic media ownership patterns, it is perhaps not surprising that the same racialized and class-biased images of the new "dangerous classes" that are meant to frighten the public on the news are also now employed to entertain us and sell us a host of products and services.

CONCLUSION: NOTHING TO LOSE BUT OUR CHAINS

What does the American Dream mean today? For Niko Bellic, fresh off the boat from Europe, it is the hope he can escape his past. For his cousin, Roman, it is the vision that together they can find fortune in Liberty City, gateway to the land of opportunity. As they slip into debt and are dragged into a criminal underworld by a series of shysters, thieves and sociopaths, they discover that the reality is very different from the dream in a city that worships money and status, and is heaven for those who have them and a living nightmare for those who don't.[11]

Rockstar Games, Grand Theft Auto IV. Website copy.

The preceding quote from the enormously popular video/PC game Grand Theft Auto IV poignantly illustrates the harsh and unforgiving landscape of late modernity. While the narrative framing of the Cousins Bellic is fictional, the brutality of capitalism that undergirds the story-bound Liberty City is all too real in 21st-century America. Inexplicably, orthodox criminology continually fails to address this criminogenesis.

Irrespective of whether we conceptualize such a paucity of attention as obstinacy or benign neglect, the end result differs little—the material conditions that influence our lives and, indeed, the single most influential factor not only in the production, distribution, and consumption of crime but a driving force that has transformed human existence more in the last 200 years than anything in the previous millennia remains unstudied by our discipline.

If there is a silver lining to this cloud, it is that late modern capitalism's multiple appendages coupled with orthodox criminology's inability/unwillingness to address it leaves many openings available to those inclined to challenge the hegemony of these twin sacred cows. Certainly, from environmental racism and the prison–industrial complex through the disappearance of work and crimes of globalization, the fissures are legion.

The intention of this chapter, as astute readers likely surmised several pages back, was not to provide a comprehensive assessment nor for that matter a general overview of the literature on crime and economics. In fact, some readers may be uncomfortable with this chapter's leap from Marx and Bonger to a 21st-century criminology of capitalism. We are among them.[12] However, our intention here was not to produce a "definitive" piece but rather a heuristic tool through which readers can intellectually and politically confront the intersecting convenient fictions of late capitalism and orthodox criminology.

Discussion Questions

1. Identify and describe some of the ways that the brutal cultural climate of late capitalism in the USA contributes to crime and victimization.

2. The authors cite Grand Theft Auto IV as a crime–capitalism narrative. Draw on your own experiences with other forms of popular culture to provide additional examples.

3. Make a list of several street crimes and white-collar, corporate, or state crimes, and illustrate their connections to capitalism.

4. The authors enumerate several examples of how capitalism fosters contradictory forms of human behavior. Provide examples of other such contradictions.

5. Why has American criminology failed to adequately address the question of capitalism?

Notes

1. See, for example, William Chambliss (1989).

2. The article was the third of three that Marx was commissioned to write on the Proceedings of the Sixth Rhine Province Assembly for *The Rheinische Zeitung*. The paper published only the first and the third.

3. "Capital Punishment" (February 18, 1853) and "Population Crime and Pauperism" (September 16, 1859).

4. See Bonger (1916, pp. 673–700).

5. Sadly, instead of translations of these, English-language criminology was introduced to the racist, misogynistic, and bigoted work of Lombroso and other biodeterminist European criminologists. The seeding of this "pathological" theory to the American criminological canon was certainly fueled by and served as an accelerant for the eugenics movement and facilitated the growth of a homegrown pathological school (e.g., Henry Goddard, Ernest Hooton, Eleanor and Sheldon Glueck, etc.).

6. In the intervening years, the paradigm alternately came to be known as "radical" criminology. Today, it is generally referred to as "critical criminology" and encompasses a variety of traditions including left realist, peacemaking, anarchist, convict, state, feminist, and cultural and ultrarealist criminologies.

7. A parallel but perhaps slightly more effervescent trajectory also emerged in the UK at this time, including the work of Stanley Cohen, Stuart Hall, Carol Smart, Ian Taylor, Paul Walton, and Jock Young.

8. Mr. Robot (2015–) Season 1, Episode 2, titled "eps1.1_ones-and-ser0es.mpeg," written by Sam Esmail.

9. Many of the same structural conditions that facilitate the crimes by the capitalist state abroad also contribute to the social harms it inflicts on people in America (see Tifft & Sullivan, 1980).

10. Published as a novel in 1516, St. Thomas More's *Utopia* described a land of economic equality.

11. Grand Theft Auto IV, www.gta4.net.

12. Among our most egregious offenses herein is relegating the rich, vibrant work of many of America's founding "conflict" criminologists to passing references and footnotes. So too, aside from a few citations, we failed to adequately address the stellar contributions of contemporary ultrarealist criminologists, particularly the work of Steve Hall and Simon Winlow. These were conscious decisions made in keeping with space limitations.

References

Bauman, Z. (2000). *Liquid modernity*. Cambridge, UK: Polity Press.

Bauman, Z. (2007). Collateral casualties of consumerism. *Journal of Consumer Culture*, 7(1), 25–56.

Bonger, W. A. (1905). *Criminalite et conditions economiques*. Amsterdam, Netherlands: G. P. Tierie.

Bonger, W. A. (1916). *Criminality and economic conditions* (F. H. Norcross, Trans.). Boston, MA: Little, Brown and Company.

Bourdieu, P. (1984). *Distinction: A social critique of the judgement of taste*. Cambridge, MA: Harvard University Press.

Boyle, J. (2008). *The public domain: Enclosing the commons of the mind*. New Haven, CT: Yale University Press.

Chambliss, W. (1989). On trashing Marxist criminology. *Criminology*, 27(2), 231–238.

Cohen, S. (1972). *Folk devils and moral panics: The creation of the mods and rockers*. Oxford, UK: Basil Blackwell.

Cohen, S., & Young, J. (Eds.). (1973). *The manufacture of news*. Beverley Hills, CA: Sage.

Currie, E. (1997). Market, crime and community: Toward a mid-range theory of post- industrial violence. *Theoretical Criminology*, 1(2), 147–172.

David, M. (2017). *Sharing: Crime against capitalism*. Cambridge, UK: Polity Press.

Engels, F. (1973). *The condition of the working-class in England*. Moscow, Russia: Progress Publishers. (Original work published 1845)

Ewen, S. (1977). *Captains of consciousness: Advertising and the social roots of consumer culture*. Toronto, ON: McGraw-Hill.

Ewen, S. (1988). *All consuming images: The politics of style in contemporary culture*. New York, NY: Basic Books.

Ferrell, J., Hayward, K., & Young, J. (2015). *Cultural criminology: An invitation* (2nd ed.). London, UK: Sage.

Ferrell, J., & Sanders, C. (Eds.). (1995). *Cultural criminology*. Boston, MA: Northeastern University Press.

GrandTheftAuthoIVwebpage:https://www.rockstar
games.com/games/info/IV

Greenberg, D. (Ed.). (1981). *Crime and capitalism.*
Palo Alto, CA: Mayfield Publishing Company.

Hall, S., Critcher, C., Jefferson, T., Clarke, J., &
Roberts, B. (1978). *Policing the crisis: Mugging, the
state and law and order.* London, UK: Macmillan.

Hall, S., & Winlow, S. (2015). *Revitalising criminological theory: Toward a new ultra-realism.* Oxon,
UK: Routledge.

Hall, S. (2012). Don't look up, don't look down:
Liberal criminology's fear of the supreme and the
subterranean. *Crime, Media, Culture, 8*(2), 197–212.

Hall, S., & Winlow, S. (2004). Barbarians at the
gate: Crime and violence in the breakdown of
the pseudo-pacification process. In J. Ferrell,
K. Hayward, W. Morrison, & M. Presdee (Eds.),
Cultural criminology unleashed (pp. 275–286).
London, UK: Glasshouse Press.

Hall, S., & Winlow, S. (2015). *Revitalizing criminological theory: Towards a new ultra-realism.* New
York, NY: Routledge.

Hall, S., Winlow, S., & Ancrum, C. (2008). *Criminal
identities and consumer culture: Crime, exclusion and
the new culture of narcissism.* Devon, UK: Willan.

Hayward, K. (2004). *City limits: Crime, consumer
culture and the urban experience.* London, UK:
Glasshouse Press.

Hayward, K., & Yar, M. (2006). The chav phenomenon: Consumption, media and the construction of
a new underclass. *Crime, Media, Culture, 2*(1), 9–28.

Hayward, K., & Presdee, M. (2009). *Framing crime:
Cultural criminology and the image.* London, UK:
Routledge.

Horkheimer, M., & Adorno, T. (1972). *Dialectic of
enlightenment.* New York, NY: Herder and Herder.
(Original work published 1946)

Lasch, C. (1979). *The culture of narcissism:
American life in an age of diminishing expectations.*
New York, NY: Norton.

Marx, K., & Engels, F. (1976). *The German ideology.*
Moscow, Russia: Progress Publishers. (Original
work published 1846)

McLeod, K. (2001). *Owning culture: Authorship,
ownership and intellectual property law.* New York,
NY: Peter Lang.

Merton, R. K. (1938). Social structure and anomie.
American Sociological Review, 3(5), 672–682.

More, T. (1965). *Utopia* (P. Turner, Trans.).
Harmondsworth, UK: Penguin Books. (Original
work published 1516)

Muzzatti, S. (2003). Anarchy against the curriculum.
In M. Schwartz & M. Maume (Eds.), *Teaching the
sociology of deviance* (5th ed., pp. 9–14). Washington,
DC: American Sociological Association.

Muzzatti, S. (2004). Criminalising marginality
and resistance: Marilyn Manson, Columbine and
cultural criminology. In J. Ferrell, K. Hayward,
W. Morrison, & M. Presdee (Eds.), *Cultural criminology unleashed* (pp. 143–153). London, UK:
Glasshouse Press.

Muzzatti, S. (2005). Bits of falling sky and global
pandemics: Moral panic and severe acute respi-
ratory syndrome (SARS). *Illness, Crisis and Loss,
13*(2), 117–128.

Muzzatti, S. (2010). Drive it like you stole it: A
cultural criminology of car commercials. In
K. Hayward & M. Presdee (Eds.), *Framing crime:
Cultural criminology and the image* (pp. 138–155).
London, UK: Routledge.

Muzzatti, S. (2013). They sing the body ecstatic:
Television commercials and captured music. In
M. Pomerance & J. Sakeris (Eds.), *Popping culture*
(7th ed., pp. 191–201). Toronto, ON: Pearson.

Muzzatti, S. (2017). Terrorism and counter-terrorism
in popular culture. In *Oxford Research Encyclopedia
of Criminology* (pp. 1–26). New York, NY: Oxford
University Press.

Muzzatti, S., & Smith, E. (2018). Cultural criminology. In W. DeKeseredy & M. Dragiewicz (Eds.),
Routledge handbook of critical criminology (2nd ed.,
pp. 107–120). Oxon, UK: Routledge.

Presdee, M. (2000). *Cultural criminology and the
carnival of crime.* London, UK: Routledge.

Rojek, C. (2017). Counterfeit commerce: Relations
of production, distribution and exchange. *Cultural
Sociology, 11*(1), 28–43.

Selke, W., Corsaros, N., & Selke, H. (2002). A working class critique of criminological theory. *Critical Criminology, 11*(2), 93–112.

Soderberg, J. (2008). *Hacking capitalism*. Abingdon, UK: Routledge.

Taylor, I. (1983). *Crime, capitalism and community*. Toronto, ON: Butterworths.

Taylor, I. (1999). *Crime in context: A critical criminology of market societies*. Boulder, CO: Westview Press.

Wilson, W. J. (1987). *The truly disadvantaged: The inner city, the underclass and public policy*. Chicago, IL: University of Chicago Press.

Sullivan, D., & Tifft, L. (1980). The struggle to be human: Crime, criminology and anarchism. Orkney, Scotland: Cienfuegos Press.

Young, J. (1999). The exclusive society. London, UK: Sage.

Young, J. (2007). *The vertigo of late modernity*. London, UK: Sage.

10

SERIOUS GANG PROBLEMS IN THE UNITED STATES

What to Do?

James C. Howell and Megan Qually Howell

The history of street gangs in the United States begins with their emergence on the East Coast, in New York City in the 1820s (Haskins, 1974). Gang formation in the Northeast was fueled by immigration and poverty, first by two waves of largely White and poor families from Europe. City social services were overwhelmed, and large groups of immigrants were isolated in slums (Riis, 1902/1969). Conflict was therefore imminent, and gangs grew in these environments as groups of adolescents and young adults fought one another over scarce resources, while striving to create a wedge of safety among social disorder, squalor, and chaos. Subsequent migrations of Europeans to the U.S. led to even greater social disorganization and subsequent gang formation, first in the Northeast cities (New York, in 1825, followed by Boston and Philadelphia), then in the Midwest, led by Chicago, in the 1860s (Howell, 2015a). In many respects, gang emergence in Chicago replicated the Eastern region process, following immigrant invasion and conflict; though one-half century later because of the delayed influx of large migrant groups into the U.S. heartland. Gangs next formed in the west region (Los Angeles) in the 1930s and were not reported in the Southern region (San Antonio and Miami) until the 1970s and continuously emerged in that region (notably in Atlanta and New Orleans) up to the mid-1990s (Howell, 2015a).

The Great Migration of Blacks from the rural South northward between 1910 and 1930 was a major contributing factor to White-on-Black conflict and gang formation and expansion among Black youth in Chicago (Haskins, 1974). In contrast, gangs grew out of the preexisting Mexican culture in the Western region (first in Los Angeles, in the 1930s), and their growth was fueled by subsequent Mexican American migrations (McWilliams, 1948/1990)—and the later arrival of a large population of Blacks (Howell, 2015a). The Mexican Revolution that began in 1910 sent large numbers of Mexican peoples northward toward both Los Angeles and Chicago, populating those areas with Mexican Americans and fueling gang growth following conflicts with local youths. Gangs emerged in the Southern states a generation later following steady Mexican American immigration and large-scale return migration of Blacks from Northern cities after decades of disappointment from presumed opportunities to better their lives in those urban areas (Spergel, 2007).

In the 1950s and 1960s, two social policies boosted gang growth and expansion. First, the establishment of high-rise public housing complexes in many large cities isolated poor Black and Mexican American families. This policy provided gangs an operational base, a virtual kingdom, as these buildings became gang strongholds in Chicago (Venkatesh, 2002). One enormous public housing project built there (Robert Taylor Homes), consisting of 28 16-floor buildings, was home to several gangs and soon deemed too dangerous for police to enter. Hence, gangs themselves informally policed several of these buildings on an everyday basis.

Next, "wars on gangs," led by federal law enforcement and local police in many cities, put many gang leaders and members in prisons, which led to the further development of prison gangs, and these later expanded into formidable criminal operations with enormous growth in prison populations that commenced in the 1960s (Schlosser, 1998). In the mid-1970s, Latino gangs, Black gangs, and Caucasian gangs in Illinois prisons formed loose alliances, the largest of which were the People and the Folk. As prison gang members began returning to neighborhoods from whence they came, this inadvertently strengthened local gangs and led to multiple gang alliances, creating what some called "supergangs" (Chicago Crime Commission, 1995). This continuing massive flow of returning gang inmates remains a major contributor to local gang violence and this factor soon became more prominent (Egley & Howell, 2013).

The 1970s and 1980s brought another large wave of migrants to the United States, around 7 million people (Pincus & Ehrlich, 1999). Before the end of the 20th century, Miller's (1982/1992) research shows that the South region matched the other major regions in the prevalence of gang activity. Youth gang problems in the United States grew dramatically between the 1970s and the 1990s, with the prevalence of gangs reaching unprecedented levels in the mid-1990s (W. Miller, 2001). New York City, Chicago, and Los Angeles served as gang epicenters, spawning gang culture outward via youth subcultures. The growing availability of automobiles, coupled with the use of more lethal weapons, fueled the growth of drive-by shootings, a tactic that previously took the form of on-foot, hit-and-run forays.

Gangs of the late-20th century seemed to have both younger and older members than before and more members with prison records or ties to prison inmates, and there clearly was a substantial increase in the availability, sophistication, and use of firearms in ongoing gang violence (Miller, 1982/1992). By the mid-1990s, 40% of local law enforcement agencies nationwide reported youth gang problems in the National Youth Gang Survey (Figure 10.1).

This chapter draws attention to the most serious gang activity in the United States because of its contributions to criminal justice system caseloads. First, we examine the key gang magnitude indicators of serious gang violence: the number of gangs, gang members, and homicides. Second, we discuss the distinguishing features of the most violent gangs. Third, these discussions provide a backdrop for consideration of solutions to serious gang activity. Before proceeding, gang definitions are presented next that guide our focus in this chapter.

GANG DEFINITIONS

There is no single, universally accepted definition of a *gang*. Federal, state, and local jurisdictions in the United States tend to develop their own definitions. By the end of 2016, all 50 states and the District of Columbia (D.C.) had enacted some form of legislation relating to gangs or gang-related activity. A total of 44 states and Washington, D.C., had legislation that defines *gang*, 15 states had legislation that defines *gang member*, 31 states defined *gang crime/activity*, 29 states had passed gang prevention laws, 34 states had laws that provide for enhanced penalties for gang-related criminal acts, 32 states had laws against graffiti, 28 states and D.C. had legislation on gangs and schools, and 12 states had enacted laws that deal with gang-related databases (National Gang Center, 2018). The term *street gang* is often used to reference gangs composed of older members to underscore their active involvement in murder, robbery, aggravated assault, and firearm offenses in street settings, where most such offenses occur. In cities with populations of 50,000 or more, two thirds of the gang members are over age 18 (Howell & Griffiths, 2018).

Law enforcement respondents to the National Youth Gang Survey define *gangs* as groups of youths who (1) commit crimes together, (2) hang out together, (3) have a name, (4) have a leader, (5) display common colors or symbols, and (6) claim turf. Each of these criteria is judged "moderately important" or "very important" in defining gangs among respondents in larger cities, suburban counties, smaller cities, and rural areas (Howell & Griffiths, 2018). National Youth Gang Survey (NYGS)[1] results (Figure 10.1) show that in 2012 (the final year of the survey), gangs were active in more than one fourth (28%) of cities, towns, and counties across the U.S. (Howell & Griffiths, 2018). This national estimate has remained fairly stable since 2005, fluctuating by only 9 percentage points through 2012.

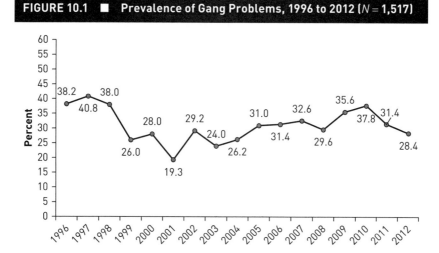

FIGURE 10.1 ■ Prevalence of Gang Problems, 1996 to 2012 (N = 1,517)

Source: Howell & Griffiths, 2018, p. 2. Copyrighted by Sage Publications.

KEY INDICATORS OF SERIOUS GANG ACTIVITY

The number of gang members, number of gangs, and occurrence of gang-related homicides are key indicators of the magnitude of serious gang activity in large cities. NYGS data for 2011 indicate that more than half (56%) of all gangs and three-fourths (75%) of all gang members are located in metropolitan areas,[2] and almost 9 out of 10 (87%) gang-related homicides occur in these areas (Egley & Howell, 2013).

Number of gang members. It goes without saying that gang members are far more numerous in more densely populated cities that report a persistent gang problem. The number of gang members reported in the NYGS is a strong correlate of nationwide gang homicides (Decker & Pyrooz, 2010). To illustrate the importance of the number of gang members, in the early 1990s, the Chicago Police Department estimated that membership in four very large gangs numbered about 19,000 (the Black Gangster Disciples Nation, the Latin Disciples, the Latin Kings, and the Vice Lords), and from 1987 to 1990, they accounted for 69% of all street gang–motivated crimes and for 56% of all street gang–motivated homicides, although they represented just 10% of the "major" Chicago gangs and 51% of the city's gang members (Block & Block, 1993).

Number of gangs. The number of gangs present in an area is significantly related to the area's overall level of violence and, particularly, nationwide gang homicides (Howell, 2015a). A case in point, Block's (2000) citywide Chicago research on the spatial distribution of gang violence found that "the relationship between the number of gangs that are active in an area and the levels of assaults and drug-related incidents is remarkably high" (p. 379). To be sure, numerous other gang studies support this pattern (Howell & Griffiths, 2018).

Number of homicides. Of course, gang homicides characterize serious gang problem cities, along with the number of gangs and gang members. Overall, approximately one quarter of all homicides in cities with populations greater than 100,000 are gang related each year (Howell, Egley, Tita, & Griffiths, 2011). More than two thirds (70%) of these large cities consistently report that between 20% and 40% of their homicides are gang related. By the 1980s, gangs had considerably more firearms, including semiautomatic weapons, of greater lethality than ever before (Howell, 1999). Therefore, it is important to consider the history and dangerousness of gangs in large cities (of 100,000 population or more) in crafting strategies for reducing their violence.

CONTEXTS OF SERIOUS GANG VIOLENCE

Intergroup rivalries produce what Block and Block (1993) identify as "peaks and valleys" in homicides and other violence. Escalating and de-escalating stages create a feedback loop where each killing requires a new killing. Nearly 2 decades later, Papachristos and colleagues identified co-offending networks citywide in Chicago, beginning with the cataloguing of arrest events that involved more than one person among the nearly 1 million arrests that occurred during a 6-year period (Papachristos, Wildeman, & Roberto, 2015). In total, more than 400,000 unique individuals were identified in the arrest records, of which 41% had been arrested in an incident involving two or more individuals. About 70% of all nonfatal gunshot victims during the observation period were positioned in co-offending networks composing less than 6% of the city's population—one third of whom were gang members.

Owing to the geographic orientation of these well-established networks, Tita, Cohen, and Endberg (2005) mapped places where gangs came together as a sociological group—that is, their *set space*. The gang set space is usually a very small geographic area, much smaller than neighborhoods or even census tracts, perhaps one block or only one side of a block.

The nexus between gangs and the geography of violent crime is explained by two defining features of gangs (Tita & Radil, 2011). First, gangs are geographically oriented in that they have a strong attachment to the territory, or turf, under their direct control. Second, behaviors associated with the control of that territory, including communicating turf boundaries, regulating activities within turf, and defending turf against rivals, are important contributors to the emergence and diffusion of violence. In Figure 10.2, which depicts relationships

FIGURE 10.2 ■ The Network Structure of Two Chicago Street Gangs

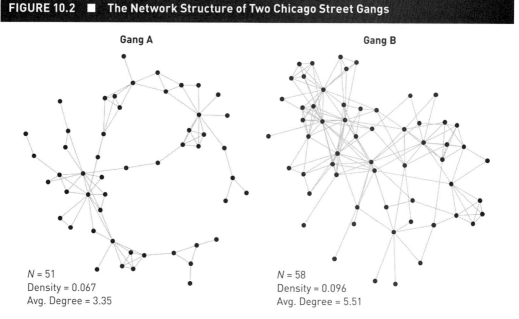

Gang A

Gang B

N = 51
Density = 0.067
Avg. Degree = 3.35

N = 58
Density = 0.096
Avg. Degree = 5.51

Source: Papachristos, A. V. (2013). The importance of cohesion for gang research, policy, and practice. *Criminology and Public Policy, 12,* 49–58. Reprinted with permission from the American Society of Criminology.

between members of two Chicago gangs (Papachristos, 2013), each node (dot) represents a unique individual in the gang, with Gang B having slightly more members (N = 58) than Gang A (N = 51). Each line represents a social connection (friendship or association link) between the individuals as determined from existing police data that reveals co-offenders in recorded crimes. The difference in density (and possibly cohesion) of the two gangs in this figure is apparent: There are more connections among members in Gang B, creating a network that looks more cohesive (i.e., more people regularly interact with one another). In contrast, Gang A is sparser than Gang B; that is, fewer people regularly interact with one another in Gang A. Of course, Gang B is expected to be more heavily involved in local gang violence, owing in large part to greater cohesion among its member network.

The claiming and defense of turf or territory is a key characteristic of street gangs in serious gang problem cities. From the point of their origin in the United States, control over turf has been the basis of street gangs' social honor (Adamson, 1998). In these areas, the gang's very existence sometimes depended on its capacity to stand its ground and ward off incursions from hostile groups. An East Los Angeles study found that violence strongly clusters along the boundaries between 13 criminal street gangs, accounting for 75% of all lethal violence in this area—in 563 between-gang shootings involving during a 3-year period (Brantingham, Tita, Short, et al., 2012).

OTHER FACTORS ASSOCIATED WITH GANG VIOLENCE

Eight out of ten law enforcement agencies nationwide contend that drug trafficking is the most predominant influence on local gang violence (Egley & Howell, 2013). The dynamics of this relationship are not straightforward, however. The so-called "crack cocaine epidemic" said to have occurred in the late 1980s and early 1990s was overstated and was most prevalent in only a few cities (Howell, 2015a; Reeves & Campbell, 1994). Most street gangs—largely made up of adolescents—lack the necessary organizational characteristics to effectively manage drug distribution operations (Howell & Decker, 1999). Still, violence is most likely to occur where gang activity, drug trafficking, and firearm ownership or use intersects (Howell & Griffiths, 2018). Lizotte and colleagues (2000) explain, "If one travels in a dangerous world of youth armed illegally and defensively with firearms, it only makes sense to carry a gun. Therefore, peer gun ownership for protection increases the probability of gun violence" (p. 830). In turn, during late adolescence, "involvement in serious drug trafficking, independent of gang involvement, is a much stronger factor explaining hidden gun carrying—typically after gang involvement has ended" (p. 829). In other words, many gang members who do not desist from gang involvement continue to carry guns, and many of them advance into street-level drug trafficking (Gordon, Rowe, Pardini, et al., 2014).

JUVENILE AND CRIMINAL JUSTICE SYSTEM INVOLVEMENT OF GANG MEMBERS

Because of their elevated offending rates, gang members are very prevalent in both juvenile and adult criminal justice systems. Youth gang involvement at least doubles the odds of being arrested (Curry, 2000), thus probation and correctional caseloads is another context in which criminal involvement of gang members is quite evident. For example, statewide North Carolina data showed that youth gang members represent the following:

- 7% of all juveniles on whom delinquent complaints are filed,

- 13% of juveniles adjudicated,

- 21% of juveniles admitted to short-term detention, and

- 38% of juveniles committed to secure residential facilities (M. Q. Howell & Lassiter, 2011).

Gang membership is a strong predictor of entry into the correctional system for juveniles and adults. In two large statewide multiyear samples of adjudicated serious and violent juvenile offenders in North Carolina and Florida, gang members were about 3 times more likely than other offenders to be chronic serious property and violent juvenile delinquents (Baglivio, Jackowski, Greenwald, & Howell, 2014; M. Howell & Lassiter, 2011). Moreover, there are more than 7 times as many high-risk offenders among gang members than among nongang youth (M. Howell & Lassiter, 2011). Gang membership is one of the strongest predictors of homicide (Decker & Pyrooz, 2010). Continuous offending often leads to imprisonment, especially given gang backgrounds. A 2009 survey of federal and state prison systems estimated that 19% of all inmates were gang members (Winterdyk & Ruddell, 2010). Without any doubt, the proportion is higher in states with multiple very large gang-ridden cities, such as California and Illinois (Howell et al., 2011). Unfortunately, the number of prison gangs cannot be established at this time because these are included in the broader category of "Security Threat Groups" (American Correctional Association, 2009). In the early 1980s, a national survey of prison systems identified 112 individual prison gangs with a total membership of 12,634 (Camp & Camp, 1985). Research has established that prison gangs are responsible for a disproportionate amount of prison violence (Griffin & Hepburn, 2006).

WHAT WORKS IN COMBATING GANG VIOLENCE

This chapter concludes with consideration of program implications of the foregoing research and data on gang crime. The leading program for addressing youth gang problems community-wide or encompassing cities or counties is the federal Office of Juvenile Justice and Delinquency Prevention's Comprehensive Gang Prevention, Intervention, and Suppression Program Model (commonly known as the Comprehensive Gang Program Model). This three-pronged model guides jurisdictions of any size in forming a continuum of gang prevention, intervention, and suppression programs and strategies. Prevention programs target children and adolescent youth at risk for gang involvement and reduce the number of youth who join gangs. Intervention programs and strategies provide sanctions and services for adolescents and young adults who are actively involved in gangs. Law enforcement suppression strategies target the most violent gangs and older, criminally active gang members.

When implemented with high program fidelity, this program reduced gang violence and also gang affiliations (i.e., hastened gang disengagement) in multiple cities, including both Chicago and Los Angeles (Cahill & Hayeslip, 2010; Hayeslip & Cahill, 2009; Hodgkinson, Marshall, Berry, et al., 2009; National Gang Center,

2010; Spergel, Wa, & Sosa, 2006). "Some youth changed from leaders to core members or regular members, peripherals, or nonmembers" (Spergel et al., 2006, p. 214). In addition, "effective [police] suppression contacts, as perceived by police (and indicated in outreach worker's activity reports) were related to a reduction in a program youth's degree of affiliation with his gang" (p. 214). In a similar fashion, "the greater the dosage [frequency] of worker contacts and services, the greater the reduction in the number of gang friends among [program] youth" (p. 214). Most noteworthy, however, is that Spergel's program proved effective in the Little Village community of Chicago, a city that Spergel did not select (Howell, 2015b) because at that time it was a "Wounded City," dubbed as such by Vargas (2016) because city agencies and police often worked at cross-purposes. Remarkably, gang violence was allowed to thrive as a result of their pursuit of organizational self-interest above public safety concerns.

Cure Violence (CV) works to identify, engage, and promote change among those gang members most likely to be involved in shootings or killings; detect and interrupt events that could lead to violence or retaliation; and change norms about the acceptance and use of violence. Cure Violence outreach workers concentrate on changing the behavior and risky activities of a small number of selected members of the community who have a high chance of either "being shot" or "being a shooter" in the immediate future. Violence interrupters (mostly former gang members) work alone or in pairs mediating conflicts between gangs and high-risk individuals on the streets and in hospital emergency rooms. With reality therapy, they interject themselves into on-the-spot decision making by individuals at risk of shooting others, helping potential shooters weigh the likely disastrous, life-changing outcomes against perceived short-term gains. Long-term change agents (outreach workers) address key immediate causes of violence, including norms regarding violence, and serve as positive role models for young people, steering them to resources such as jobs or educational training and needed services. An independent study found significantly reduced homicides and shootings in six of the seven CV sites in some of the most violent, gang-ridden communities in Chicago. A later research update found that the program worked to decrease violence with 40 of the most violent gangs in Chicago (Ransford, Kane, Metzger, Quintana, & Slutkin, 2010). An evaluation of a sister program in Baltimore drew similar conclusions (Webster, Whitehill, Vernick, & Curriero, 2013).

The Group Violence Intervention (GVI) program concentrates on enhanced and aggressive investigation and prosecution of gun offenders and gun traffickers. Chronic gang members or violent offenders are notified at call-in meetings by high-level local, state, and federal policy makers, influential community members, and social service providers that gun violence will no longer be tolerated. Long sentences are given to repeat offenders and are well publicized. The primary purpose of a call-in is to deliver the strategy's key messages clearly to the group/gang members and, through them, back to the entire group/gang with which they are associated. During the call-in, a moral message from the community is communicated to the group of offenders from the same gang/group that the

violence must stop, that these individuals are valued, and that the community wants them to succeed. During the call-in, help is offered to those who want to change their violent lifestyles. The Operation Ceasefire component of the Boston Gun Project was responsible for a 63% reduction in youth homicide victimization (Wellford, Pepper, & Petrie, 2005) and has since been effectively implemented as the Group Violence Intervention. The typical impact is a 35% to 60% reduction in community-wide levels of homicides and a significant but sometimes lesser reduction in nonfatal shootings citywide (National Network for Safe Communities at John Jay College, n.d.). The Boston Ceasefire working group designed an intervention that created spillover effects on other gangs and neighborhoods via its communication strategy (Braga, Apell, & Welsh, 2013). Replications of the Boston strategy demonstrated evidence of effectiveness in reducing serious violence generated by street gangs or criminally active street groups in Cincinnati, Ohio; Indianapolis, Indiana; Los Angeles, California; Lowell, Massachusetts; Chicago, Illinois; and Stockton, California (Braga & Weisburd, 2012).

Network analysis powers the Group Violence Intervention model. As Papachristos (2013) explains, "In the social network literature, cohesion often is measured as the density of a network—the extent to which individuals in a group are more or less connected to each other" (p. 52). Utilizing Chicago police arrest data, co-offending networks were created citywide, beginning with the cataloguing of arrest events that involved more than one person among the nearly one million arrests that occurred during a 6-year period (Papachristos, Wildeman, & Roberto, 2015). In total, more than 400,000 unique individuals were identified in the arrest records, of which 41% had been arrested in an incident involving two or more individuals. As expected, the greater the extent to which one's social network is saturated with gunshot victims, the higher one's probability of also being a victim. For individuals with two or fewer immediate associates, their likelihood of victimization is 2–3 times greater if one of their associates is a victim than if they have no exposure to victims.

In an evaluation of a similar strategy, the Group Violence Reduction initiative in Chicago that targeted small gang factions, consisting of active offenders and victims, Papachristos and Kirk (2015) found that the Chicago VRS produced significant reductions in both shooting behavior and gunshot victimization in Chicago—despite the challenge in intervening with co-offending networks, which is a first in gang programming (see also Howell, 2015c). The reported success is also attributable to emphasis on service access and matching these to offenders' needs on a case-by-case basis. These services included health, mental health, housing, drug treatment, education, and employment services, all of which are made available to those in attendance free of charge.

It may come as a surprise to many readers that there is much resistance to addressing gang activity with a community-wide long-term strategy (Gebo & Bond, 2012; Huff, 1990; Vargas, 2016). Short-term suppression strategies are more appealing for their directness and toughness—and the supporting media attention these may draw (Hagedorn, 2008). In addition, many mayors, school administrators, and other public officials sometimes deny the obvious existence of gang problems because doing so may not be deemed in their best interest in the near term. As an example of a collaborative approach that engages partners county-wide, utilizing the Comprehensive Gang Program Model, the Multnomah County Local Public Safety Coordinating Council (LPSCC) is a county-wide, long-term model that blends prevention, intervention, and suppression strategies. Following a well-executed county-wide gang assessment that most other jurisdictions in the United States can emulate, the LPSCC Youth and Gang Violence Steering Committee developed an implementation plan (a living document that is open to ongoing revision of goals and objectives) that facilitates the development of primary prevention, secondary prevention, intervention, suppression, and reentry activities while using effective services.[3]

An intervention team is an essential component of the CGPM (National Gang Center, 2010). The following key agencies are crucial to an effective intervention team's success: law enforcement representatives involved in gang investigation and enforcement; juvenile and adult probation or parole officers who will have frequent contact with program clients; school officials who can access student educational data for program clients and leverage educational services; appropriate social service or mental health providers who can leverage services and provide outcome information to the team; a representative who can assist in preparing program clients for employment and find jobs for them; and outreach workers who can directly connect to program clients on the street, in their homes, or at school. The intervention team should engage both JJSs and CJSs in systematically identifying active gang members who require intensive supervision coupled with equally intensive services, especially cognitive-behavior therapy; the most potent evidence-based model is Aggression Replacement Training (Goldstein, Glick, & Gibbs, 1998; for implementation guidance, see Goldstein & Glick, 1994).

In sum, several potentially effective programs and strategies are now available for responding to gang violence on a city, county, or statewide basis. The choice of particular options must be based on a thorough assessment of the key features of gang violence in those contexts. Recent research suggests that long-term trajectories of gangs and city gang problem histories can be modified, thereby producing potentially important public safety benefits. We should not expect large benefits, however. Reducing violence among institutionalized gangs with long histories in major cities is a daunting enterprise. The modest success of Spergel's program—against all odds in Chicago (Vargas, 2016) and the Los Angeles area—gives basis for optimism that well-designed interventions can be effective, even in such a challenging setting, when implemented with fidelity (Spergel et al., 2006, pp. 216–217).

There is no quick fix, no magic bullet that can produce measurable and sustainable reductions in institutionalized gang violence. Each of these three leading programs has favorable features. A key feature of Cure Violence is the presence of "violence interrupters" who seek to truncate the transmission of violence between individuals and groups and change community norms that encourage retaliation. This is a fundamental public health model with potential long-term cost-benefits. The Group Violence Reduction program strategically breaks up networks of chronic violent offenders who often are united in gangs by virtue of the experience they share in common: violent victimization. The particularly unique feature of the CGPM is that it promotes a continuum of program options along the life course of gang involvement, including desistance.

Primary prevention (also called *universal* prevention) targets the entire population (all youths and families and other members) in communities.

Secondary prevention identifies young children (ages 7 to 14) at high-risk, and—drawing on the resources of schools, community-based organizations, and faith-based groups—intervenes with appropriate services before early problem behaviors turn into serious delinquency and gang involvement.

Intervention targets active gang members and close associates and involves active outreach coupled with services, as well as support for gang disengagement.

Suppression focuses on identifying the most dangerous gangs and reduces their threat by removing the most criminally active and influential gang members from the community.

Discussion Questions

1. What are some examples of conditions associated with the formation of violent gangs across the country, and are there any similarities?

2. What are the key structural features of violent gangs found nationwide?

3. What is the connection between gangs and the geography of violent crime?

4. Describe the concept of "cohesion." How does it apply to gangs and their members and influence their levels of violence?

5. How can social networks aid our understanding of the observed uneven risk of homicide in high-risk communities?

6. How are network analyses typically used to study gang-related homicides?

7. Compare and contrast the three leading programs for combatting gang violence.

Notes

1. For a description of the NYGS study population and sample methodology, see www.nationalgangcenter.gov/Survey-Analysis/Methodology. Independent evaluations have confirmed and demonstrated the validity and reliability of the NYGS data.

2. Cities with populations greater than 100,000 and suburban county sheriffs' and police departments.

3. Program implementation details can be accessed at www.multco.us/lpscc/multnomah-county-comprehensive-gang-assessment-and-implementation-plan

References

Adamson, C. (1998). Tribute, turf, honor and the American street gang: Patterns of continuity and change since 1820. *Theoretical Criminology*, 2, 57–84.

American Correctional Association. (2009, Spring). Gangs/security threat groups in the U.S.A. and Canada. *Corrections Compendium*, 22–37.

Baglivio, M. T., Jackowski, K., Greenwald, M. A., & Howell, J. C. (2014). Serious, violent, and chronic juvenile offenders: A statewide analysis of prevalence and prediction of subsequent recidivism using risk and protective factors. *Criminology and Public Policy*, 13, 83–116.

Block, C. R., & Block, R. (1993). Street gang crime in Chicago. *Research in Brief*. Washington, DC: U.S. Department of Justice, National Institute of Justice.

Block, R. (2000). Gang activity and overall levels of crime: A new mapping tool for defining areas of gang activity using police records. *Journal of Quantitative Criminology*, 16, 369–383.

Braga, A. A., Apell, R., & Welsh, B. (2013). The spillover effects of focused deterrence on gang violence. *Evaluation Review*, 37, 314–342.

Braga, A. A., & Weisburd, D. L. (2012). The effects of focused deterrence strategies on crime: A systematic review and meta-analysis of the empirical evidence. *Journal of Research in Crime and Delinquency*, 49, 323–358.

Brantingham, P. J., Tita, G. E., Short, M. B., & Reid, S. (2012). The ecology of gang territorial boundaries. *Criminology*, 50, 851–885.

Cahill, M., & Hayeslip, D. (2010). *Findings from the evaluation of OJJDP's Gang Reduction Program* (Juvenile Justice Bulletin). Washington, DC: U.S. Department of Justice, Office of Juvenile Justice and Delinquency Prevention.

Camp, G. M., & Camp, C. G. (Eds.). (1985). *Prison gangs: Their extent, nature and impact on prisons.* Washington, DC: U.S. Department of Justice.

Curry, G. D. (2000). Self-reported gang involvement and officially recorded delinquency. *Criminology*, 38, 1253–1274.

Decker, S. H., & Pyrooz, D. C. (2010). On the validity and reliability of gang homicide: A comparison of disparate sources. *Homicide Studies*, 14, 359–376.

Egley, A. E., & Howell, J. C. (2013, September). Highlights of the 2011 National Youth Gang Survey. *OJJDP Fact Sheet*. Washington, DC: Office of Juvenile Justice and Delinquency Prevention.

Gebo, E., & Bond, B. J. E. (2012). *Beyond suppression: Community strategies to reduce gang violence.* Lanham, MD: Lexington Books.

Goldstein, A. P., & Glick, B. (1994). *The prosocial gang: Implementing Aggression Replacement Training.* Thousand Oaks, CA: Sage.

Goldstein, A. P., Glick, B., & Gibbs, J. C. (1998). Aggression Replacement Training: A comprehensive intervention for aggressive youth (Rev. ed.). Champaign, IL: Research Press.

Gordon, R. A., Rowe, H. L., Pardini, D., Loeber, R., White, H. R., & Farrington, D. (2014). Serious delinquency and gang participation: Combining and specializing in drug selling, theft and violence. *Journal of Research on Adolescence*, 24, 235–251.

Griffin, M. L., & Hepburn, J. R. (2006). The effect of gang affiliation on violent misconduct among inmates during the early years of confinement. *Criminal Justice and Behavior*, 33, 419–448.

Hagedorn, J. M. (2008). *A world of gangs: Armed young men and gangsta culture.* Minneapolis, MN: University of Minnesota Press.

Haskins, J. (1974). *Street gangs: Yesterday and today.* Wayne, PA: Hastings Books.

Hayeslip, D., & Cahill, M. (2009). *Community collaboratives addressing youth gangs: Final evaluation findings from the Gang Reduction Program.* Washington, DC: Urban Institute.

Hodgkinson, J., Marshall, S., Berry, G., Reynolds, P., Newman, M., Burton, E., Dickson, K., & Anderson, J. (2009). *Reducing gang related crime: A systematic review of 'comprehensive' interventions.* Summary report. London, UK: EPPI-Centre, Social Science Research Unit, Institute of Education, University of London.

Howell, J. C. (1999). Youth gang homicides: A literature review. *Crime and Delinquency, 45,* 208–241.

Howell, J. C. (2015a). *The history of street gangs in the United States: Their origins and transformations.* Lanham, MD: Lexington Books.

Howell, J. C. (2015b). The legacy of Irving A. Spergel. In S. Decker & D. C. Pyrooz (Eds.), *The Wiley handbook of gangs* (pp. 424–439). Hoboken, NJ: John Wiley & Sons.

Howell, J. C., & Decker, S. H. (1999). *The youth gangs, drugs, and violence connection* (Juvenile Justice Bulletin. Youth Gang Series). Washington, DC: Office of Juvenile Justice and Delinquency Prevention.

Howell, J. C., Egley, A., Jr., Tita, G., & Griffiths, E. (2011). *U.S. gang problem trends and seriousness.* Tallahassee, FL: Institute for Intergovernmental Research, National Gang Center.

Howell, J. C., & Griffiths, E. (2019). *Gangs in America's Communities* (3rd ed.) Thousand Oaks, CA: Sage.

Howell, M. Q., & Lassiter, W. (2011). *Prevalence of gang-involved youth in NC.* Raleigh, NC: North Carolina Department of Juvenile Justice and Delinquency Prevention.

Huff, C. R. (1990). Denial, overreaction, and misidentification: A postscript on public policy. In C. R. Huff (Ed.), *Gangs in America* (pp. 310–317). Thousand Oaks, CA: Sage.

Lizotte, A. J., Krohn, M. D., Howell, J. C., Tobin, K., & Howard, G. J. (2000). Factors influencing gun carrying among young urban males over the adolescent-young adult life course. *Criminology, 38,* 811–834.

Lore Joplin Consulting. (2014). Multnomah County Comprehensive Gang Assessment: A collaborative project sponsored by the Multnomah County Local Public Safety Coordinating Council. *Portland, OR.* Retrieved from https://multco.us/file/34749/download

McWilliams, C. (1990). *North from Mexico: The Spanish-speaking people of the United States* (Rev. ed.). New York, NY: Greenwood. (Original work published 1948)

Miller, W. B. (1992). *Crime by youth gangs and groups in the United States.* Washington, DC: U.S. Department of Justice, Office of Juvenile Justice and Delinquency Prevention. (Original work published 1982)

Miller, W. B. (2001). *The growth of youth gang problems in the United States: 1970–1998.* Washington, DC: Office of Juvenile Justice and Delinquency Prevention.

National Gang Center. (2010). *Best practices to address community gang problems: OJJDP's Comprehensive Gang Model.* Washington, DC: Author.

National Gang Center. (2018). Retrieved from https://www.nationalgangcenter.gov/Legislation/Highlights

National Network for Safe Communities at John Jay College. (n.d.). FAQs. Retrieved from http://nnscommunities.org/our-work/faqs#7

Papachristos, A. V. (2006). Social network analysis and gang research: Theory and methods. In J. F. Short & L. A. Hughes (Eds.), *Studying youth gangs* (pp. 99–116). Lanham, MD: AltaMira Press.

Papachristos, A. V. (2009). Murder by structure: Dominance relations and the social structure of gang homicide. *American Journal of Sociology, 115,* 74–128.

Papachristos, A. V. (2013). The importance of cohesion for gang research, policy, and practice. *Criminology and Public Policy, 12,* 49–58.

Papachristos, A. V., & Kirk, D. S. (2015). Changing the street dynamic: Evaluating Chicago's group violence reduction strategy. *Criminology & Public Policy, 14,* 525–558.

Papachristos, A. V., Wildeman, C., & Roberto, E. (2015). Tragic, but not random: The social contagion of nonfatal gunshot injuries. *Social Science & Medicine, 125,* 139–150.

Pincus, F. L., & Ehrlich, H. J. (1999). Immigration. In F. L. Pincus & H. J. Ehrlich (Eds.), *Race and ethnic conflict* (pp. 223–228). Boulder, CO: Westview Press.

Ransford, C., Kane, C., Metzger, T., Quintana, E., & Slutkin, G. (2010). An examination of the role of CeaseFire, the Chicago police, Project Safe Neighborhoods, and displacement in the reduction in homicide in Chicago in 2004. In R. J. Chaskin (Ed.), *Youth gangs and community intervention: Research, practice, and evidence* (pp. 76–108). New York, NY: Columbia University Press.

Reeves, J. L. & Campbell, R. (1994). *Cracked coverage: Television news, the anti-cocaine crusade, and the Reagan legacy.* Durham, NC: Duke University Press.

Riis, J. A. (1969). *The battle with the slum.* Montclair, NJ: Paterson Smith. (Original work published 1902)

Schlosser, E. (1998, December 6). The prison-industrial complex. *Atlantic Monthly,* 282, 51–77.

Spergel, I. A. (2007). *Reducing youth gang violence: The Little Village Gang Project in Chicago.* Lanham, MD: AltaMira Press.

Spergel, I. A., Wa, K. M., & Sosa, R. V. (2006). The comprehensive, community-wide, gang program model: Success and failure. In J. F. Short & L. A. Hughes (Eds.), *Studying youth gangs* (pp. 203–224). Lanham, MD: AltaMira Press.

Tita, G., Cohen, J., & Endberg, J. (2005). An ecological study of the location of gang set space. *Social Problems,* 52, 272–299.

Tita, G. E., & Radil, S. M. (2011). Spatializing the social networks of gangs to explore patterns of violence. *Journal of Quantitative Criminology,* 27, 521–545.

Vargas, R. (2016). *Wounded city: Violent turf wars in a Chicago barrio.* New York, NY: Oxford University Press.

Venkatesh, S. A, (2002). *American project: The rise and fall of a modern ghetto* (2nd ed.). Cambridge, MA: Harvard University Press.

Vigil, J. D. (1998). *From Indians to Chicanos: The dynamics of Mexican-American culture* (2nd ed.). Prospect Heights, IL: Waveland.

Webster, D. W., Whitehill, J. M., Vernick, J. S., & Curriero, F. C. (2013). Effects of Baltimore's Safe Streets program on gun violence: A replication of Chicago's CeaseFire Program. *Journal of Urban Health,* 90, 27–40.

Winterdyk, J., & Ruddell, R. (2010). Managing prison gangs: Results from a survey of U.S. prison systems. *Journal of Criminal Justice,* 38, 730–736.

SEX OFFENDER POLICIES

Good Intentions and Unintended Consequences

Alexa Sardina

Sexual assault is a significant problem in the United States and has a significant impact on survivors. According to the U.S. Department of Justice, there were an estimated 300,170 rapes and sexual assaults in 2013 (Truman & Langton, 2014). Thus, it is clear that the public and lawmakers have understandable concern and outrage about sex crimes and those who commit them.

The overlapping systems of sex offender registration, community notification, and residence restrictions were initially designed to help police capture the names and addresses of previously convicted adult sex offenders on a list, which could then be referred to when a new sexual offense was perpetrated. Initially, this was a well-intentioned attempt to protect children and communities from future instances of sexual assault. In reality, however, these policies were based on a misconception that those found guilty of a sexual offense are likely to commit new sex offenses. However, available research indicates that sex offenders are among the *least* likely to reoffend. According to recent research, the recidivism rate for all offenses (sexual and nonsexual combined) was 40%, whereas the recidivism rates for sex offenders has been reported to be between 13% and 14% (Hanson & Bussiere, 1998; Hanson & Morton-Bourgon, 2005).

SEX OFFENDER REGISTRATION AND COMMUNITY NOTIFICATION LAWS

In part as a result of high-profile cases of sexual abuse in the late 1980s and 1990s, state and federal policy makers passed an array of registration, community notification, and residence restriction laws for individuals convicted of sex offenses.

- **Registration** requires sex offenders to provide certain information to law enforcement and periodically update it so it remains current.

- **Community notification** requires law enforcement to notify the public or portions of the public that a sex offender is living nearby. In some states, law enforcement proactively notifies the public. In other states, the information is made available to the public upon request.

- **Residence restriction laws** refer mostly to state and local ordinances that limit registered sex offenders' ability to reside or spend time in specific locations, usually where children spend time.

There are several examples of memorial legislation, but the Jacob Wetterling Crimes Against Children and Sexually Violent Offender Act of 1994, Megan's Law, the Lyncher Act, and the Adam Walsh Act are pieces of legislation based on highly unusual cases in which a child was abducted, sexually assaulted, and murdered by a stranger offender. Furthermore, each of the cases involved parents or family members who advocated for changes in public policy regarding sex offenders (see Case Studies: Memorial Legislation Backround).

The first federal law addressing sex offender registration, the **Jacob Wetterling Crimes Against Children and Sexually Violent Offender Registration Act of 1994** established a national database of sex offenders. Specifically, it required states to create registries of offenders convicted of sexually violent offenses or crimes against children and to establish increased registration requirements for offenders that were designated as highly dangerous. If states implemented the law, they received federal funds. The majority of states passed notification and registration statutes for sex offenders between 1994 and 1996 (CSOM, 1999).

Congress passed the first community notification law in 1996 in response to the abduction and murder of 7-year-old Megan Kanka. Under **Megan's Law**, community notification requirements applied only to individuals identified as "potentially dangerous sex offenders." Community notification systems multiplied quickly through several amendments to Megan's Law. Some form of community notification for adult sex offenders has been established in all 50 states and the District of Columbia since 1996. State notification laws establish public access to registry information by mandating the creation of online registries that provide a former offender's criminal history, current photograph, current address, and other information, such as place of employment. In many states, everyone who is required to register is included on the online registry.

The Lyncher Act was also passed in 1996. It amended the federal community notification laws and provided for a national sex offender database and mandated that certain sex offenders be required to register for life. Today, federal law and the laws of all 50 states require adults to register with enforcement.

CASE STUDIES: MEMORIAL LEGISLATION BACKGROUND

Jacob Wetterling was 9 in 1989. Jacob, his younger brother, and a friend rode their bikes to rent a movie at a local store. They were riding back on a country road in St. Joseph, Minnesota, when a man approached them, brandished a gun, and ordered them off their bikes. The man took Jacob and ordered the others to ride away without looking back. No one saw Jacob again. Although, at the time, no direct evidence indicated that a sex offender kidnapped Jacob, it was widely assumed that was what had occurred. It was later discovered that halfway houses in the city provided housing for sex offenders after their release from prison. Subsequently, Jacob's mother, Patty Wetterling, became an advocate for missing children. She was appointed to a governor's task force, which led to tougher laws, including the Wetterling Act. Recently, a convicted sex offender named Danny Heinrich admitted to molesting and killing Jacob and led law enforcement officials to his remains.

Source: Louwagie, Pam and Brooks, Jennifer. "Danny Heinrich confesses to abducting and killing Jacob Wetterling." *Star Tribune.* 7 September 2016.

Megan Kanka was 7 in 1994 when she was abducted and killed by a neighbor in New Jersey. The neighbor, a twice-convicted child molester, lured Megan by asking her if she wanted to see a puppy. Megan was raped, killed, and dumped in a nearby park. Her parents, devastated, indicated that they would never have left Megan unsupervised in their neighborhood if they had known a sex offender lived nearby. Megan's killer Jesse K. Timmendequas had been convicted for two previous sexual assaults of girls ages 5 and 7.

Source: Glaberson, William. "'Megan' Prosecution Rests After Rape Is Described." *The New York Times.* 23 May 1997.

Pam Lyncher was a real estate agent in the Houston, Texas, area. One day she received a phone call from a man who was interested in seeing a property. Pam asked her husband to come along to the showing. She stayed in the kitchen while her husband went to another part of the house. A man that Pam had hired to clean the house entered at the time of the appointment claiming he had returned to finish the job. When Pam turned her back, he grabbed her from behind, put his hand over her mouth, and attempted to rape her. Hearing the struggle, Pam's husband ran to help his wife. The man was arrested, convicted, and eventually sent to prison for 20 years. The man turned out to be a convicted rapist and child molester who had been released from state prison under a mandatory early release policy designed to ease prison overcrowding.

Source: Pennsylvania State Police: Megan's Law—History of the Law and Federal Facts.

In July 1981, 7-year-old Adam Walsh and his mother went to a department store in Hollywood, Florida. Adam saw a small group of children playing a video game in the store. His mother left him with the other children and shopped in another part of the store, approximately 75 feet away. When she returned, Adam was gone. A security guard said there had been a small skirmish, and the children were told to leave. Sixteen days after he went missing, Adam's severed head was found floating in a canal off the Florida turnpike. Adam was taken by Ottis Toole, a serial killer, who confessed but was never convicted. Toole ended up dying in prison in 1996 while serving five life sentences for other crimes. Adam Walsh's father, John Walsh, became an advocate for abducted children. He later became the star of *America's Most Wanted*. The show encourages people to share information that could lead to the possible capture of offenders. The show last aired in 2011 and claimed responsibility for the arrest over 1,000 offenders.

Source: Waxman, Olivia B. "The U.S. Is Still Dealing With the Murder of Adam Walsh." *TIME.* 10 August 2016.

In an effort to standardize the vast and growing number of state offender registration systems, Congress passed the **Adam Walsh Child Protection and Safety Act** in 2006. Title I of the Adam Walsh Act, also known as the **Sex Offender Registration and Notification Act (SORNA)**, provides a set of federal guidelines that further expands the extent of sex offender registration and notification in the 50 states, the District of Columbia, U.S. territories, and federally-recognized tribal territories. SORNA made several broad changes to existing federal guidelines on sex offender registration that include the following:

- Creating a state and federal offense of "failure to register," which is punishable by a term of imprisonment

- Requiring registration for offenses that may not be considered sexual offenses, including public urination, indecent exposure, and possession of child pornography

- Requiring jurisdictions to reclassify the risk level of each sex offender based only on the crime for which he or she was convicted and not on individual risk assessment

To comply with SORNA, states must also require registered sex offenders to keep their information updated with law enforcement in the jurisdictions in which they live, work, or attend school. Jurisdictions that fail to enact the SORNA guidelines risk losing federal funding (McPherson, 2007). The deadline to comply with SORNA was July 2011. Currently (as of the publication of this text), no jurisdiction has completely implemented SORNA, and only 18 states have fully implemented the law (U.S. Department of Justice, 2008).

SORNA also established a tier classification system of sex offenders. Each tier has specific registration guidelines. Tier III includes the most serious offenders. These offenders are subject to lifetime registration. Additionally, they are required to renew or update their registration information every 3 months with law enforcement. Anyone who is designated a Tier II offender, will be reclassified as a Tier III offender if they commit any subsequent sex offense. The sex offenses that qualify a person as Tier III are punishable by at least 1 year of incarceration (U.S. Department of Justice, 2008). They include the following:

- Sex with a person under force or threat

- Sex with another person who has been made unconscious or was involuntarily drugged or who is incapable to consent to sexual acts

- Sex with a child under the age of 12

- Nonparental kidnapping of a minor

Tier II offenses are less serious than Tier III offenses yet are considered more serious than Tier I offenses. Tier II offenders are required to register for 25 years. Again, anyone who was a Tier I offender and commits a subsequent felony sex offense will become a Tier II sex offender, regardless of the tier level of their subsequent felony sex offense. Tier II sex offenses include child prostitution and child pornography (U.S. Department of Justice, 2008).

Tier I sex offenders are considered the least serious. They are required to register for 15 years and must renew their registration on a yearly basis. This tier includes people who have committed misdemeanor and felony sex offenses that meet the criteria of a sex offense as defined by federal law.

In addition to establishing the tier system, with regard to the information required for the registry, all registered sex offenders are required to submit, *at least*, the following information to law enforcement officials:

- Name and aliases

- Date of birth

- Social Security number

- Photograph

- Fingerprints

- Passport information

- Home, work, school address

- Home/cellular phone numbers

- License plate number/description of vehicles

- E-mail addresses

- Pseudonyms used for messaging online

- Offense and date of conviction

- Punishment received

Additionally, when sex offenders travel for more than 7 days, they are required to notify their local law enforcement officials for the purpose of notifying officials in the jurisdiction to which they plan to travel (U.S. Department of Justice, 2008).

Individuals can request to be exempt from registration requirements. However, the request can only be made after the offender has been registered for a significant period of time. For example, Tier III offenders must wait 25 years. Additionally, offenders can only make the request that their registered time be reduced after maintaining a clean record (U.S. Department of Justice, 2008).

SORNA specifically allows for the retroactive application of the law for some sex offenders. For example, offenders who are in prison or are under criminal justice supervision (i.e., probation or parole) for a registerable offense or for another crime are required to register under SORNA. Also, those who were already subject to a former registration requirement (i.e., the Wetterling Act) and any people who were rearrested for any other offense are required to register (McPherson, 2007).

DOES THE REGISTRY PREVENT SEX OFFENSES?

Despite the massive growth in the number of registered sex offenders, studies of states that have implemented registration requirements are inconclusive as to whether the registries have any effect on the number of sexual offenses that are reported to law enforcement (Bandy, 2015). One study of 10 states with registries concluded that "the results do not offer a clear unidirectional conclusion as to whether sex offender notification laws prevent rapes" (Vasquez, Maddan, & Walker, 2008). Another study conducted in New Jersey found that sex offense rates have consistently decreased since 1985. The data showed that the greatest decrease in sex offending occurred prior to 1994 (the year registration laws were passed) and the least rate of decline occurred in 1995 (the year registration laws were implemented) (Zgoba, Witt, Dalessandro, & Veysey, 2008). As such, there are at least three flaws of sex offender registration that researchers suggest explain the ineffectiveness of sex offender registration in deterring sex crimes.

First, sex offender registries are focused on preventing recidivism, when instead, the focus should be on preventing sexual offenses from happening in the first place (Association for the Treatment of Sexual Abusers, n.d.). As previously mentioned, the focus on recidivism is misguided because sex offenders are among the least likely to reoffend. Individuals labeled as "sex offenders" have extremely low recidivism rates when compared with persons convicted of robbery, nonsexual assault, burglary, larceny, motor vehicle theft, fraud, drug offenses, and public order offenses. The only type of offense with lower recidivism rates is homicide (Letourneau, Levenson, Bandyopadhyay, Sinha, & Armstrong, 2010).

Second, sex offender registration overburdens law enforcement. Officers are often required to make home visits to registered sex offenders. Focusing attention and limited resources on an overly broad group of ex-offenders can detract attention from the smaller number of active sexually violent offenders that require the closer attention of law enforcement. This may leave communities vulnerable to sexual abuse, create a false sense of security, and exhaust valuable resources by tracking the wrong offenders—individuals who are not likely to reoffend (Center for Sex Offender Management, 2007).

Third, registration does not target resources where they are most needed. Federal guidelines adopted under SORNA may worsen the problem by mandating that states stop using individual risk assessments to determine which offenders are likely to recidivate. Instead, SORNA guidelines require states use the tier system based on the crime of conviction only as the way to classify offenders. The focus on the crime of conviction is problematic as sex offenders are a heterogeneous group that differ in their level of impulsiveness, persistence, risk, and willingness to change their behavior (Center for Sex Offender Management, 2007). These factors contribute to the addition of more low-risk offenders to the registry. The sex offender registry database continues to grow, but funding for monitoring sex offenders is decreasing (Harris, Lobanov-Rostovsky, & Levenson, 2015).

UNINTENDED CONSEQUENCES OF REGISTRATION, NOTIFICATION, AND RESIDENCE RESTRICTIONS LAWS

In addition to the failures of sex offender legislation to prevent or reduce sexual offenses, there are several reported unintended consequences of sex offender registration, notification, and residence restrictions. Sex offenders have reported that registration decreases the chances they will reenter their communities successfully (Levenson et al., 2007), which may put them at a greater risk of reoffending. For example, one study reported that the majority of sex offenders in the sample suffered negative consequences attributable to registration, such as depression, shame, and hopelessness. Additionally, a majority of sex offenders reported job loss as a result of registration (Levenson et al., 2007). Thus, researchers report that sex offender registration laws can often lead to limited access to education, housing, and employment (Bonnar-Kidd, 2010).

Registered sex offenders have also reported being harassed. This includes threats of harassment and property damage (Levenson et al., 2007). Many of these incidents even involve serious bodily harm and death (see Case Study: Sex Offenders and Vigilantism). Sex offender registration laws can result in negative, collateral consequences that affect relatives of registered sex offenders (Farkas & Miller, 2007; Levenson & Tewksbury, 2009). Family members may also experience depression, frustration, and hostility from other members of their own family and people in the community (Levenson & Tewksbury, 2009).

Residence restrictions typically forbid registered sex offenders from living in and sometimes just being in the vicinity of places where children congregate, such as schools, daycares, and parks (Mustaine, 2014). Such restrictions are also based on unsupported assumptions that sex offenders locate victims from these types of locations (Mustaine, 2014). Instead, sex offenders typically choose victims who are their acquaintances or relatives (Colombino, Mercado, & Jeglic, 2009). Registered

CASE STUDY: SEX OFFENDERS AND VIGILANTISM

In 2012, Patrick Drum, 34, of Washington State killed two sex offenders, Gary Lee Blanton (28) and Jerry Wayne Ray (57). Drum shot the men multiple times near their homes. Drum had planned to kill 60 other sex offenders before he was apprehended. Drum told officers that the killings "had to be done." He admitted his plan had been to live in the wild and continue to attack sex offenders for as long as he could.

Drum was severely abused as a child, and both of his parents were drug addicts. His father was also convicted of statutory rape. Although Drum never claimed that his father sexually abused him, he asserts that he was sexually abused by an adult male when he was about 10 years old. In the early 2000s, a girl name Melissa Carter was killed in the Port Angeles area of Washington. Police believe she was raped and then strangled to death. Drum says it was then that he decided to kill sex offenders.

Drum claimed that what he did was for the betterment of the community. "I believe that my experiences with sex offenders, my father and the abuse gave me firsthand empathy for the issue, but my actions were not about me. They were about the community. I suffered many failures and my overall view of things was one of hopelessness. I took that hopelessness and in turn threw myself away to a purpose. I gave myself to something bigger than myself."

Many residents showed support for Drum. Some rape survivors wrote to him and called him a hero. Other people seemed unsure how to feel. They disliked sex offenders but were not sure if murder was the solution. Vigilantes, especially those that target sex offenders, often believe that they are protecting others from harm. For Drum's supporters, any objections to murder outweighed the need to protect children. When Drum was given the opportunity to give a statement before his sentencing, he refused to apologize for the murders. "It was never my intent to hurt the families . . . it's like collateral damage." The Judge S. Brooke Taylor sentenced Drum to two life sentences without parole.

A week after sentencing, Drum stabbed a fellow inmate. The 19-year-old sex offender was serving time for failure to register. Drum would not know until later that his victim had committed the offense when he was only 13 years old.

Source: Pandell, Lexi. "The Vigilante of Clallam County." *The Atlantic.* 4 December 2013.

sex offenders subjected to residence restrictions report a high degree of frustration and stress relative to housing (Tewksbury & Mustaine, 2009). Nearly one third of surveyed registered sex offenders in one study reported having to move because of either social pressure from the community or financial problems. In some cases, sex offenders subject to residence restrictions may be forced to live in high-crime areas (Mustaine & Tewksbury, 2011).

In extreme cases, residence restrictions can lead to homelessness for some sex offenders. Reporters in Miami, Florida, highlighted the problem of homelessness among registered sex offenders. Pictured in many newspapers were groups of tents underneath a highway occupied by sex offenders who believed they had no choice but to live there. This situation was the result of Miami legislation that included a 2,500-foot residence restriction, preventing sex offenders from living near schools. Additionally, many organizations in the area legally had their status changed to "school," which excluded many parts of the city as a place for sex offenders to live.

In 2014, the Florida Civil Liberties Union filed a lawsuit challenging these laws. The lawsuit alleged that criminal justice officials were aware of the problem and actually directed sex offenders to the tent cities (Flatow, 2014).

Some state and local officials have begun to recognize the negative consequences of sex offender legislation. For example, in December 2015, California reversed previous laws forbidding sex offenders from living near parks, schools, or other places where children congregate. The current law only forbids those who had molested children from living near such areas. Thus, more than 4,200 of the nearly 6,000 sex offenders will not be subjected to residence restrictions (Associated Press, 2015).

THE CIVIL COMMITMENT OF SEXUALLY VIOLENT PREDATORS

Civil commitment laws have been used in the U.S. for about 20 years, and they vary from state to state. They allow for individuals who meet certain criteria to be involuntarily institutionalized, usually in psychiatric institutions. These laws have been typically applied to people with mental illnesses who were in need of treatment. Most states require that there is an imminent danger that a mentally ill person will kill himself or herself or someone else to be civilly committed (Brooks, 2007). It has not been until recently that sex offenders have been civilly committed in the U.S. This allows for sex offenders who have already served a prison sentence to be civilly committed and their institutionalization continued. The offender can be continuously committed and, therefore, indefinitely institutionalized (Szabo, 2013).

The U.S. Supreme Court established that civil commitment could be used for offenders classified as sexually violent predators. The Court specifically examined the constitutionality of civilly committing a sexually violent offender on the basis of due process and double jeopardy. With regard to due process, it was specifically questioned whether a law could be created ex-post facto (after the fact). Second, with regard to double jeopardy, the U.S. Constitution prohibits more than one prosecution of the same defendant for the same crime in the same jurisdiction. Ultimately, the U.S. Supreme Court found that the civil commitment of sexually violent predators is constitutional because it is a civil proceeding, not a criminal one (Vandiver, Braithwaite, & Stafford, 2017)

Given that the U.S. Supreme Court has found that it is constitutional to civilly commit sex offenders, states are allowed to develop and implement similar legislation. Twenty states have done so, including Arizona, California, Florida, Illinois, Iowa, Kansas, Massachusetts, Minnesota, Missouri, Nebraska, New Hampshire, New Jersey, New York, North Dakota, Pennsylvania, South Carolina, Texas, Virginia, Washington, and Wisconsin (Association for the Treatment of Sexual Abusers, 2010). Although the states vary in how civil commitments are carried out, many have been criticized for the few offenders who are deemed rehabilitated through treatment and subsequently released (Association for the Treatment of Sexual Abusers, 2010).

CONCLUSION

As noted throughout this chapter, sex offender legislation is often based on inaccurate assumptions regarding this group of offenders and was developed as a knee-jerk response to high-profile, emotionally charged cases of child abduction, sexual assault, and murder by recidivist, stranger offenders. Furthermore, there is little empirical evidence that such restrictive laws lead to fewer sex crimes, and in some cases, these reactionary policies may do more harm than good (Ackerman, Sacks, & Greenberg, 2012).

Discussion Questions

1. The goal of sex offender legislation is to prevent sexual offending and recidivism. Do you think current sex offender legislation achieves this goal? If yes, what evidence supports your claim? If not, what changes would you recommend to achieve this goal?

2. What should happen in circumstances where sex offenders are harassed by community members? Putting aside legal issues, is it reasonable for registered sex offenders to expect law enforcement to protect them?

Would you favor prosecuting the harassers? Why, or why not?

3. What do you think should happen to the hundreds of thousands of people who committed sex offenses and have completed their sentences?

4. Do you think labeling some offenders as "sexually violent predators" is appropriate? Should it be applied to every person who has committed a sexual offense? Why, or why not?

Web Resources

Association for the Treatment of Sexual Abusers (ATSA): www.atsa.com

Center for Sex Offender Management (CSOM): www.csom.org

Darkness to Light: www.d2l.org

National Center for Missing and Exploited Children: www.missingkids.com

National Center for Victims of Crime: www.victimsofcrime.org

National Institute of Justice (NIJ) Sex Offenders: www.nij.gov/topics/corrections/community/sex-offenders

National Sex Offender Public Website (NSOPW): www.nsopw.gov

National Sexual Violence Resource Center: www.nsvrc.org

Office of Sex Offender Sentencing, Monitoring, Apprehending, Registering, and Tracking (SMART): www.smart.gov

Rape, Abuse, and Incest National Network (RAINN): www.rainn.org

Sex Offender Management Assessment and Planning Initiative (SOMAPI): www.smart.gov/SOMAPI

Stop it Now!: www.stopitnow.org

References

Ackerman, A. R., Sacks, M., & Greenberg, D. F. (2012). Legislation targeting sex offenders: Are recent policies effective in reducing rape? *Justice Quarterly, 29*(6), 858–887.

Adam Walsh Sex Offender Registration and Notification Act (2006).

Associated Press. (2015, December 14). *California's sex offenders free to live near parks and schools.* Retrieved December 26, 2017, from http://nypost.com/2015/12/14/california-sex-offenders-free-to-live-near-parks-and-schools

Bandy, R. (2015). The impact of sex offender policies on victims. In R. Wright (Ed.), *Sex offender laws: Failed policies, new directions* (2nd ed.). New York, NY: Springer.

Bonnar-Kidd, K. K. (2010). Sexual offender laws and prevention of sexual violence. *Journal of Public Health, 100*(3), 412–419.

Brooks, R. (2007). Psychiatrists' opinions about involuntary civil commitments: Results of a national survey. *Journal of American Academy of Psychiatry and the Law, 35*(2), 219–228.

Center for Sex Offender Management. (1999). Sex offender registration: Policy overview and comprehensive practices. Retrieved December 28, 2017, from http://csom.org/pubs/sexreg.pdf

Center for Sex Offender Management. (2007). Managing the challenges of sex offender reentry. Retrieved December 28, 2017, from http://www.csom.org/pubs/reentry_brief.pdf

Colombino, N., Mercado, C. C., & Jeglic, E. L. (2009). Situational aspects of sexual offending: Implications for residence restriction laws. *Justice Research and Policy, 11*(1), 27–44.

Farkas, M. A., & Miller, G. (2007). Reentry and reintegration: Challenges faced by the families of convicted sex offense recidivism. *Criminal Justice and Behavior, 35*(4), 484–504.

Flatow, N. (2014, October 23). Inside Miami's hidden tent city for 'sex offenders.' Retrieved December 27, 2017, from http://thinkprogress.org/justice/2014/10/23/3583307/in-miami-dade-sex-offenders-are-relegated-to-outdoor-encampments

Freeman-Longo, R. E. (1996). Feel good legislation: Prevention or calamity. *Child Abuse & Neglect, 20*(2), 95–101.

Glaberson, W. (1997, May 23). 'Megan' prosecution rests after rape is described. *The New York Times.* Retrieved from https://www.nytimes.com/1997/05/23/nyregion/megan-prosecution-rests-after-rape-is-described.html

Hanson, R. K., & Bussiere, M. T. (1998). Predicting relapse: A meta-analysis of sexual offender recidivism studies. *Journal of Consulting and Clinical Psychology, 66*(2), 348–362.

Hanson, R. K., & Morton-Bourgon, K. E. (2005). The characteristics of persistent sexual offenders: A meta-analysis of recidivism studies. *Journal of Consulting and Clinical Psychology, 73*(6), 1154–1163.

Harris, A., Lobanov-Rostovsky, C., & Levenson, J. S. (2015). *Law enforcement perspectives on sex offender registration and notification: Preliminary survey results.* Lowell, MA: University of Massachusetts Lowell.

Jacob Wetterling Crimes against Children and Sexually Violent Offender Registration Act, Public Law 103-322. (1994).

Letourneau, E. J., Levenson, J. S., Bandyopadhyay, D., Sinha, D., & Armstrong, K. (2010). Effects of South Carolina's sex offender registration and notification policy on community reentry for sex offenders. *Criminal Justice Policy Review, 21*(4), 587–602.

Levenson, J. S., D'Amora, D. A., & Hern, A. L. (2007). Megan's Law and its impact on community re-entry for sex offenders. *Behavioral Sciences and the Law, 25*(4), 587–602.

Levenson, J. S., & Tewksbury, R. (2009). Collateral damage: Family members of registered sex offenders. *American Journal of Criminal Justice, 34*(1), 54–68.

Louwagie, P., & Brooks, J. (2016, September 7). Danny Heinrich confesses to abducting and killing Jacob Wetterling. *Star Tribune.* Retrieved from http://www.startribune.com/danny-heinrich-confesses-to-abducting-and-killing-jacob-wetterling/392438361/

McPherson, L. (2007). Practitioner's guide to the Adam Walsh Act. *National Center for the Prosecution of Child Abuse, 20*(9 & 10), 1–7.

Megan's Law of 1996, Public Law 104-145 (2000).

Mustaine, E. E. (2014). Sex offender residency restrictions: Successful integration or exclusion? *Criminology and Public Policy, 13*(1), 169–177.

Mustaine, E. E., & Tewksbury, R. (2011). Assessing the informal social control against the highly stigmatized: An exploratory study of differential experiences and resulting stress of registered sex offenders. *Deviant Behavior, 32*(10), 944–960.

Office of Sex Offender Sentencing, Monitoring, Apprehending, Registering, and Tracking. (2017). Sex Offender Registration and Notification Act (SORNA): State and territory implementation progress check. Retrieved December 28, 2017, from http://www.smart.gov/pdfs/SORNA-progress-check.pdf

Pam Lychner Sexual Offender Tracking and Identification Act of 1996, Public Law 104-236 (1996).

Pennsylvania State Police. (n.d.). Megan's Law Website. Retrieved December 28, 2017, from http://www.pameganslaw.state.pa.us

Szabo, L. (2013, January 7). *Committing a mentally ill adult is complex.* Retrieved December 30, 2017, from http://www.usatoday.com/story/news/nation/2013/01/07/mental-illness-civil-commitment/1814301

Tewksbury, R., & Mustaine, E. E. (2009). Stress and collateral consequences for registered sex offenders. *Journal of Public Management and Social Policy, 15*(2), 215–239.

Truman, J. L., & Langton, L. (2014). *Criminal victimization 2013.* Retrieved December 30, 2017, from https://www.bjs.gov/index.cfm?ty=tp&tid=317

U.S. Department of Justice. (2008). Frequently asked questions: The Sex Offender Registration and Notification Act (SORNA) final guidelines. Retrieved December 30, 2017, from http://ojp.gov/smart/pdfs/faq_sorna_guidelines.pdf

Vandiver, D., Braithwaite, J., & Stafford, M. (2017). *Sex crimes and sex offenders: Research and realities.* New York, NY: Routledge.

Vasquez, B. E., Maddan, S., & Walker, J. T. (2008). The influence of sex offender registration and notification laws in the United States. *Crime & Delinquency, 54*(2), 175–192.

Waxman, O. B. (2016, August 10). The U.S. is still dealing with the murder of Adam Walsh. *TIME.* Retrieved from http://time.com/4437205/adam-walsh-murder/

Zgoba, K., Witt, P., Dalessandro, M., & Veysey, B. (2008). Megan's Law: Assessing the practical and monetary efficacy. Retrieved December 30, 2017, from https://www.ncjrs.gov/pdffiles1/nij/grants/225370.pdf

12

ISSUES IN THE FIGHT AGAINST HUMAN EXPLOITATION

A Look at Labor and Sex Trafficking

Casey Branchini

HUMAN TRAFFICKING DEFINED

The Trafficking Victims Protection Act (TVPA) of 2000 represents the first comprehensive federal law to combat human trafficking. Reauthorized through the Trafficking Victims Protection Reauthorization Acts (TVPRAs) of 2003, 2005, 2008, and 2013, it applies a three-pronged approach that includes *prevention*, *protection*, and *prosecution* (i.e., the 3 Ps). At the release of the 2009 *Trafficking in Persons (TIP) Report*, the U.S. Secretary of State, Hillary Rodham Clinton, announced the addition of a "fourth P" (*partnership*) in order to ensure that the government at all levels (federal, state, and local) and other key stakeholders (e.g., nongovernmental organizations, international organizations, academic institutions, survivor networks, health care providers, etc.) were committed to addressing the problem of human trafficking.

According to the TVPA of 2000, as amended (22 U.S.C. § 7102), "severe forms of trafficking in persons" include both sex and labor trafficking:

- *Sex trafficking* is the recruitment, harboring, transportation, provision, obtaining, patronizing, or soliciting of a person for the purposes of a commercial sex act, in which the commercial sex act is induced by force, fraud, or coercion, or in which the person induced to perform such an act has not attained 18 years of age (22 USC § 7102).

- *Labor trafficking* is the recruitment, harboring, transportation, provision, or obtaining of a person for labor or services, through the use of force, fraud, or coercion for the purposes of subjection to involuntary servitude, peonage, debt bondage, or slavery (22 USC § 7102).

MAGNITUDE OF THE PROBLEM

The International Labor Organization (ILO) estimates that approximately 24.9 million people are trafficked globally. Victims of labor trafficking make up the largest proportion of trafficking victims (64.3%; 16 million), followed by victims of sex trafficking (19.3%; 4.8 million) and victims of state-imposed forced labor (16.5%; 4.1 million). Relative to males, females are disproportionately impacted, accounting for a significantly larger share of total victims (57.6% versus 42.4% respectively). Among the cases of labor trafficking in the private economy for which the type of work is known, the domestic work sector composes the largest proportion (25%), followed by the construction (18%), manufacturing (15%), and agriculture and fishing (11%) sectors (ILO, 2017).

Unfortunately, despite increased attention paid to exploitative labor in the past decade, there remains a dearth of evidence on the needs of labor trafficking victims, specifically their treatment in the criminal justice system. To date, the overwhelming majority of trafficking research has focused on women and girls in the commercial sex industry, despite the fact that they compose fewer than 20% of all victims globally (ILO, 2017). Hardly any research focuses on how the lack of protections for labor trafficking victims, particularly undocumented migrants, impacts their participation in the criminal justice process and, ultimately, their ability to exercise their basic human rights. This research to evidence gap poses a major barrier to the development of an effective criminal justice response for this large yet overlooked population of 16.1 million victims globally (ILO, 2017).

CASE STUDIES: VICTIM'S STORIES—SEX TRAFFICKING

Syria | Lebanon

Maya was 22 when she fled her home country of Syria due to conflict in the region. She was promised a job working in a factory in Lebanon, but when she arrived, she was forced into commercial sex along with more than 70 other Syrian women. They endured severe physical and psychological violence. Eventually, police raided the apartment units the women lived in and arrested 10 men and eight women who had been part of the sex trafficking scheme.

Venezuela | Trinidad and Tobago

Working with a recruiter in Venezuela, Sarah accepted a job in a nursing home in Trinidad and Tobago. She was thrilled by the chance to earn more money yet nervous that she had to leave her home and did not have enough experience in elder care. When Maria arrived in Trinidad and Tobago, she realized she had been deceived. The recruiter informed her she owed a large debt, and instead of working at a nursing home, she was forced into prostitution at a local hotel bar. Her recruiter confiscated most of her earnings each night.

Cambodia

After Lai's family fell into debt to loan sharks, her mother asked her to help the family earn more money. Lai, just 12 years old, was examined by a doctor and issued a certificate of virginity. Her mother then delivered her to a hotel where a man raped her repeatedly. For nearly 2 years, Lai's mother continued to sell her to make money to pay off their debts. After learning her mother was planning to sell her again, this time for a 6-month stretch, Lai fled her home and found sanctuary in a residence for sex trafficking victims.

United States

Amy was 12 when her father, an alcoholic and drug addict, began abusing her physically and sexually. When she was 17, Amy began staying with her friend, Lisa, to escape her father's abuse. Lisa told Amy that she knew an agent who could help her become a model—something Amy had always dreamed of. Instead, the man forced Amy into prostitution and kept all of the money she made, locking her in a hotel room for weeks, giving her very little food. He threatened to kill her if she ever left. Amy was finally able to escape and now hopes to train to become a certified nursing assistant so she can help others.

Source: Trafficking in Persons Report June 2017, 2017. U.S. State Department.

PROSECUTION OF TRAFFICKING CRIMES

In examining the human trafficking problem from an equity perspective, one cannot help but notice the discrepancy between the number of prosecutions of sex and labor trafficking offenses. In not only the United States but globally, sex trafficking crimes are prosecuted at a much higher rate, and impunity for labor traffickers persists. Traditionally, efforts to improve the criminal justice response to trafficking have focused on women and girls, specifically those trafficked for sex. It was not until the last decade or so that the focus has begun to shift toward labor trafficking, as well as to boys and men.

According to the most recent *Trafficking in Persons (TIP) Report* published by the U.S. Department of State in 2017, a total of 66,520 trafficking victims were identified globally. This translates to less than 0.3% of the world's estimated 24.9 million victims. Less than one quarter (22.4%) of those identifications led to prosecution (U.S. Department of State, 2017; ILO, 2017). The number of prosecutions for sex trafficking ($N = 13,184$) crimes was 12 times greater than the number of prosecutions for labor trafficking crimes ($N = 1,083$), which constituted less than 7% of the all prosecutions that year. This number pales in comparison to the estimated 16.1 million estimated victims globally (U.S. Department of State, 2017).

Restricting data to the United States only, a similar upward trend can be observed. The notable increase in the number of victims identified and the number of cases prosecuted has largely been attributed to steps taken by the U.S. government to improve coordination of efforts against trafficking in persons, specifically the establishment of the Human Trafficking Prosecution Unit (HTPU) within the U.S Department of Justice's (U.S. DOJ's) Civil Rights Division (see Figure 12.1).

FIGURE 12.1   ■   Trafficking Victims Protection Act (TVPA) Tier Map

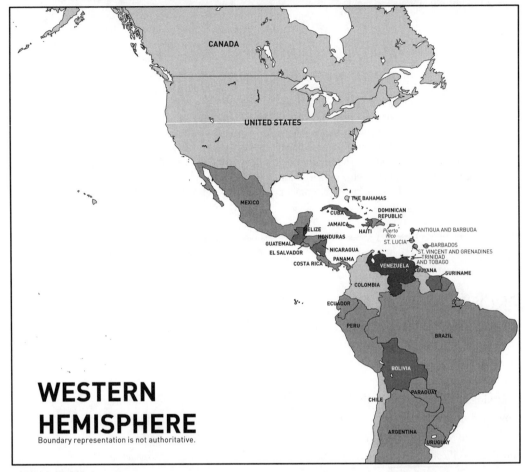

TIER PLACEMENTS

TIER 1 Countries whose governments fully meet the Trafficking Victims Protection Act's (TVPA) minimum standards.

TIER 2 Countries whose governments do not fully meet the TVPA's minimum standards, but are making significant efforts to bring themselves into compliance with those standards.

TIER 2 WATCH LIST Countries whose governments do not fully meet the TVPA's minimum standards, but are making significant efforts to bring themselves into compliance with those standards AND:

a) The absolute number of victims of severe forms of trafficking is very significant or is significantly increasing;

b) There is a failure to provide evidence of increasing efforts to combat severe forms of trafficking in persons from the previous year; or

c) The determination that a country is making significant efforts to bring itself into compliance with minimum standards was based on commitments by the country to take additional future steps over the next year.

TIER 3 Countries whose governments do not fully meet the minimum standards and are not making significant efforts to do so.

YEAR	PROSECUTIONS	CONVICTIONS	VICTIMS IDENTIFIED	NEW OR AMENDED LEGISLATION
2010	732 (80)	293 (65)	6,681	6
2011	624 (17)	279 (14)	9,014 (2,490)	3
2012	1,077 (369)	402 (107)	7,639 (3,501)	8
2013	1,182 (207)	446 (50)	7,818 (3,951)	4
2014	944 (67)	470 (63)	8,414 (2,014)	5
2015	1,796 (83)	663 (26)	9,661 (2,118)	6
2016	1,513 (69)	946 (24)	8,821 (109)	2

The above statistics are estimates derived from data provided by foreign governments and other sources and reviewed by the Department of State. Aggregate data fluctuates from one year to the next due to the hidden nature of trafficking crimes, dynamic global events, shifts in government efforts, and a lack of uniformity in national reporting structures. The numbers in parentheses are those of labor trafficking prosecutions, convictions, and victims identified.

Source: Trafficking in Persons Report June 2017, 2017. U.S. State Department.

The goal of the HTPU is to capitalize on the unique expertise of the country's leading prosecutors to improve the investigation and prosecution of the most complex trafficking cases. The unit also serves as the coordinator of critical intra- and inter-agency initiatives involving governmental and nongovernmental partners at all levels (local, state, and federal). By strengthening critical coordination mechanisms, over a 5-year period (fiscal year [FY] 2011 to FY 2015), the number of human trafficking prosecutions increased by more than 60% (62%) (325 vs. 201 from FY 2006 to FY 2010) (U.S. Department of Justice, 2017).

By FY 2015, the number of trafficking prosecutions and convictions handled reached a record high. The U.S. Department of Homeland Security (DHS) reported opening 1,034 investigations into possible human trafficking. The U.S. Department of Justice (DOJ) formally opened 802 cases, and an additional 1,011 investigations were initiated by its Enhanced Collaborative Model Taskforce. The DOJ initiated a total of 257 prosecutions, charging close to 400 defendants ($N = 377$). Although this represents an increase from the year prior (208 prosecutions; 335 defendants), labor trafficking cases still make up 4% ($N = 9$) of the total cases. Similarly, less than 2% of the 297 traffickers convicted were convicted of labor trafficking offenses (U.S. Department of State, 2016).

CASE STUDIES: VICTIMS' STORIES—LABOR TRAFFICKING

India | United Kingdom

Vihaan, a maritime machinist, accepted a job in the oil industry on a boat off the coast of the United Kingdom, thinking the sacrifice of leaving his family would be worth the money he could send home to support them. Once he arrived, the job was not as promised. Vihaan was not paid and had to work long hours under difficult conditions. When the Indian owner of the vessel abandoned the ship due to unpaid debts, he left the crew stranded with their wages unpaid. Vihaan and his crewmates decided they would not desert the ship until they had been paid, and waited 7 months before the Indian bank that owned the ship agreed to settle the unpaid wages.

India | New Zealand

Rajiv arrived in New Zealand on a student visa to enroll in a business management program. Before courses started, he traveled to the Bay of Plenty, where he knew there was agricultural work, to earn extra money for school expenses. He soon found himself in a situation he could not leave. His employers forced him to use fake identification documents so he could work 80-hour weeks illegally in kiwi fruit orchards. Rajiv and other migrant workers lived in fear of being deported or kidnapped if they complained about the grueling work. Rajiv's employer refused to give him his promised wages. After several months, Rajiv escaped the orchards and sought assistance from the New Zealand authorities.

Kuwait

Nicole left her impoverished family to work as a maid in Kuwait with the intention of sending her earnings back home. For 9 months she worked constantly, suffered physical and verbal abuse, and received no pay. When her work visa expired, her employer took Nicole to the police and falsely accused her of a petty crime. Nicole tried to explain her innocence and reported that she had not been paid and had been abused over the past 9 months. The police did not listen and instead jailed Nicole for 6 months. After her time in jail, Nicole was deported and returned home without any compensation.

Source: Trafficking in Persons Report June 2017, 2017. U.S. State Department.

In FY 2016, the number of trafficking investigations remained relatively unchanged ($N = 1,029$); however, the number of prosecutions dropped slightly, to 241, while labor trafficking cases still composed only 5.4% of the total prosecutions. Furthermore, although the number of individuals charged (from 377 to 531) and convicted (from 297 to 439) of a trafficking crime increased, individuals convicted of labor trafficking crimes still composed less than 4% (3.2%) of the total (U.S. Department of State, 2017).

OBSTACLES TO THE PROSECUTION OF TRAFFICKING CRIMES

Although these data demonstrate a continuous effort over the past 5 years to bring traffickers to justice, the number of victims identified and traffickers convicted is minor when compared with the scope of the problem, particularly in terms of labor trafficking crimes. Research has identified a plethora of factors that impede the effective and timely identification and investigation of trafficking crimes, including a lack of coordination among agencies across all levels of government (i.e., federal, state, and local); inadequate distribution of resources, skills and commitment to handle cases; as well as an extreme focus on sex trafficking relative to labor trafficking (Farrell, McDevitt, & Fahy, 2010; Wilson, Williams, & Kleuber, 2006). These obstacles are even more pronounced when it comes to labor trafficking, as evidenced by the fact that the overwhelming majority of human trafficking investigations involve sex trafficking, specifically of U.S. citizens under 18 years of age (Banks, Duren, & Kyckelhahn, 2011).

An analysis of 479 state human trafficking prosecutions (2003–2012) revealed that less than 10% (8.0%) of all suspects arrested for labor trafficking were charged with a state human trafficking offense (Bouche, Farrell, & Wittmer, 2015). This suggests a low level of understanding of the appropriate application of state trafficking statutes among lawmakers, particularly in terms of proving the presence of force, fraud, and coercion, as U.S. law leaves all three of these terms open to interpretation. These analyses also show that the likelihood of being convicted of a trafficking crime or any state crime was higher among labor trafficking suspects, relative to sex trafficking suspects. Bouche, Farrell, and Wittmer (2015) attribute this to lower levels of awareness of labor trafficking, compared with sex trafficking. Even among law enforcement agencies that demonstrate an awareness of human trafficking and possess substantial resources to combat the crime, the number of labor trafficking victims identified remains low (Newton, Mulcahy, & Martin 2008). Many law enforcement officials, in fact, do not truly understand what human trafficking is and, thus, are not able to identify victims. Pointedly, many perceive trafficking as a crime that they are not likely to encounter on a routine basis.

Further evidence of low levels of knowledge of trafficking laws and their application to labor trafficking comes from a recent assessment of human trafficking cases prosecuted at the state level across 12 counties in the U.S. It found that many state prosecutors were unfamiliar with their state trafficking laws while not a single prosecutor sampled had experience charging a labor trafficking case. Bouche et al. (2016) attribute this to the differences in the legal elements that must be present in labor versus sex trafficking cases, once again, pointing to the need for increased efforts to educate state and county prosecutors on trafficking laws and how to apply them to labor trafficking in particular.

Under the TVPA, only those individuals who are considered victims of a "severe form of trafficking" are eligible to receive benefits, including social services and legal immigration status. To be considered as such, an individual must be induced by "force, fraud, or coercion." While these three components are the cornerstone of the definition of trafficking, identifying and proving such terms remains a major challenge in guaranteeing victims the protections and benefits they rightly deserve (Sheldon-Sherman, 2012). The TVPA specifies that only those individuals who cooperate with law enforcement in the prosecution of their traffickers are eligible to receive services (Wooditch, 2009). Under domestic law, trafficking is the only crime where the reception of government benefits and the guaranteeing of basic human rights (i.e., access to health care, housing, etc.) hinges upon the participation of victims in the criminal justice process (Siskin & Wyler, 2012). More often than not, the benefits guaranteed under the TVPA are the only means of access to these rights immigrants have. Thus, if they fail to participate in the criminal justice proceedings, they are left with no means to exercise their right to basic protection and services (Riegler, 2007).

In addition to improved awareness, greater collaboration is needed between state and federal law enforcement and local nonprofit organizations. Perhaps most critically, the key role that governmental and nongovernmental actors play throughout each step of the criminal justice process, particularly in terms of support for victims, must be recognized and emphasized. While some traffickers operate within large-scale, well-organized crime rings, others function independently (Simkhada, 2008). Regardless, one of the leading reasons why victims do not participate in criminal justice proceedings is fear of retaliation against either themselves or members of their family. Although victims are offered witness protection, the system fails to protect their families in their countries of origin who may be in immediate danger, as traffickers often have strong and volatile connections to the victims' home communities. Others may be unable to participate in the prosecution of their traffickers, as they are unable to relive the trauma experienced while in the trafficking situation. Many are at risk of being revictimized, which will severely impact their physical and psychological health (MacKinnon, 1989; Sadruddin, Walter, & Hidalgo, 2005). Many victims are so traumatized by their experiences that they are unable to accurately recall their experiences, thus failing to comply with the TVPA's cooperation requirement. Furthermore, requiring victims to either participate in the criminal justice process or be deported renders "choice" meaningless, augmenting their feelings of disempowerment and subordination. This is another area where NGOs and other local service providers can play a key role in terms of supporting victims in a manner and environment that is much more responsive to their needs.

CONCLUSION

As discussed throughout this chapter, labor trafficking remains a large yet overlooked problem. Although improvements have been made in the past decade, counter-trafficking strategies continue to focus predominantly on sex trafficking, allowing labor traffickers to operate without impunity. Moving forward, efforts must be made to increase proportional emphasis on preventing and responding to trafficking in its various forms.

Discussion Questions

1. Do you think that the current "4P" (prevention, protection, prosecution, and partnership) is sufficient to address trafficking crimes? If yes, provide evidence in support of your response. If no, what changes would you recommend to facilitate a more comprehensive response?

2. In your opinion, in order to ensure continued progress in the fight against trafficking, is it necessary to place equal weight on efforts to address labor and sex trafficking? If yes, provide evidence in support of your claim. If not, what recommendations do you have for maximizing the efficacy of the response?

3. As a global leader in the fight to combat trafficking, the United States must increase accountability for labor traffickers by incentivizing law enforcement and prosecutors to identify and investigate additional labor trafficking cases. What strategies would you recommend to ensure trafficking cases are identified and prosecuted proportionally across the board? In your opinion, what, if any, adverse consequences may result from the use of such incentives?

Additional Resources

U.S. Department of State, Office to Monitor and Combat Trafficking in Persons: www.state.gov/j/tip

U.S. Department of Justice: www.justice.gov/human trafficking

International Labour Organization: www.ilo.org/global/topics/forced-labour

The Polaris Project: www.polarisproject.org

Alliance to End Slavery & Trafficking (ATEST): www.endslaveryandtrafficking.org

Free the Slaves: www.freetheslaves.net

References

Banks, D., & Kyckelhahn, T. (2011). *Characteristics of suspected human trafficking incidents, 2008–2010.* Washington, DC: U.S. Department of Justice, Office of Justice Programs, Bureau of Justice Statistics.

Bouche, V., Farrell, A., & Wittmer, D. (2016). *Identifying effective counter-trafficking programs and practices in the US: Legislative, legal, and public opinion strategies that work.* Washington, DC: U.S. Department of Justice, NCJRS.

Farrell, A., McDevitt, J., & Fahy, S. (2010). Where are all the victims? Understanding the determinants of official identification of human trafficking incidents. *Criminology and Public Policy, 9*(2), 201–233.

International Labor Organization. (2017, September). *Global estimates of modern slavery: Forced labour and forced marriage.* Geneva, Switzerland: Author.

Kim, K., & Hreshchyshyn, K. (2004). Human trafficking private right of action: Civil rights for trafficked persons in the United States. *Hastings Women's Law Journal, 16*, 1.

MacKinnon, C. A. (1989). *Toward a feminist theory of the state.* Cambridge, MA: Harvard University Press.

Newton, P. J., Mulcahy, T. M., & Martin, S. E. (2008). *Finding victims of human trafficking.* Bethesda, MD: University of Chicago, National Opinion Research Center.

Riegler, A. (2007). Missing the mark: Why the trafficking victims protection act fails to protect sex trafficking victims in the United States. *Harvard Journal of Law & Gender, 30*, 231–256.

Sadruddin, H., Walter, N., & Hidalgo, J. (2005). Human trafficking in the United States: Expanding victim protection beyond prosecution witnesses. *Stanford Law & Policy Review, 16*, 379–401.

Sheldon-Sherman, J. A. (2012). The missing P: Prosecution, prevention, protection, and partnership in the Trafficking Victims Protection Act. *Penn State Law Review, 117*, 443–501.

Simkhada, P. (2008). Life histories and survival strategies amongst sexually trafficked girls in Nepal. *Children & Society, 22*(3), 235–248.

Siskin, A., & Wyler, L. S. (2012). *Trafficking in persons: US policy and issues for congress.* Washington, DC: Congressional Research Service.

Trafficking in Persons Report. (2017, June). Washington, DC: U.S. State Department. Retrieved from https://www.state.gov/documents/organization/271339.pdf

Trafficking Victims Protection Act of 2000, Public Law 106-386 [H.R. 3244], 22 U.S.C. §§7101–7110 (2000).

Trafficking Victims Protection Reauthorization Act of 2003, Public Law No. 108-193 (2003).

Trafficking Victims Protection Reauthorization Act of 2005, Public Law No. 109-164 (2006).

Trafficking Victims Protection Reauthorization Act of 2008, Public Law No. 110-457 (2008).

Trafficking Victims Protection Reauthorization Act of 2008, Public Law No. 110-457 (2008).

Trafficking Victims Protection Reauthorization Act of 2013, Public Law No. 113-114 (2013).

U.S. Department of Justice. (2017). Human Trafficking Prosecution Unit (HTPU). Retrieved from www.justice.gov/crt/human-trafficking-prosecution-unit-htpu

U.S. Department of State. (2016). *Trafficking in persons report 2016.* Washington, DC: Author.

Wilson, D., Williams, W., & Kleuber, S. (2006). Trafficking in human beings: Training and services among U.S. law enforcement agencies. *Police Practice and Research, 7*(2), 149–160.

Wooditch, A. C., DuPont-Morales, M. A., & Hummer, D. (2009). Traffick jam: A policy review of the United States' Trafficking Victims Protection Act of 2000. *Trends in Organized Crime, 12*(3–4), 235–250.

TERRORISM

C. Augustus Martin

At the outset, it must be understood that mass-casualty terrorism is a principal attribute of the modern era and has become a destabilizing influence in the affairs of the global community. There has been a marked escalation in lethality by dedicated extremists in the present era, as well as continuing progression in utilizing modern networking and technological resources by extremist movements. Terrorists are quite willing to use modern weapons technologies in ways guaranteed to increase the likelihood of mass casualties. Acceptable weapons technologies include weapons of mass destruction and innovative "stealth" weapons, such as suicide bombs and improvised explosive devices. Modern terrorists are no longer "surgical" in the deployment of such weapons—entire groups of people are declared to be the enemy and therefore attacked as legitimate targets. Thus, while terrorists in the past would justify civilian casualties by declaring that they represented inadvertent "collateral damage" to the intended target, terrorists in the present era declare that civilian populations *are* the intended and justifiable targets.

Events on the morning of September 11, 2001, profoundly impacted how the people of the United States perceived the quality of violence posed by modern terrorism. The United States had certainly experienced domestic terrorism for much of its history but never on the scale of the 9/11 attacks and never with the underlying understanding that Americans themselves were primary targets. After the September 11 attacks, a significant policy shift occurred in the American approach to domestic security. A new concept, *homeland security*, was adopted to coordinate preparedness and response initiatives at all levels of society. The new homeland security doctrine marshaled the resources of federal, state, local, and private institutions. The intention was to create an ongoing and proactively dynamic nationwide culture of vigilance.

THE CHALLENGE OF DEFINING TERRORISM

The effort to formally define terrorism is critical as government antiterrorist policy calculations must be based on criteria that determine whether a violent incident is indeed an act of terrorism. Governments and policy makers must piece together the elements of terrorist behavior and demarcate the factors that distinguish terrorism from other forms of conflict.

There is some consensus among experts—but no unanimity—on what kind of violence constitutes an act of terrorism. Governments have developed definitions of terrorism, individual agencies within governments have adopted definitions, private agencies have designed their own definitions, and academic experts have proposed and analyzed dozens of definitional constructs. This lack of unanimity is frustratingly accepted as reality in the study of political violence.

A significant amount of intellectual energy has been devoted to identifying formal elements of terrorism, as illustrated by Schmid and Jongman (2005), who identify more than 100 definitions.[1] Establishing formal definitions can, of course, be complicated by the perspectives of the participants in a terrorist incident, who instinctively differentiate freedom fighters from terrorists, regardless of formal definitions. Another complication is that most definitions focus on political violence perpetrated by dissident groups, even though many governments have practiced similar acts as both domestic and foreign policy.

The United States has not adopted a single definition of terrorism as a matter of government policy, instead relying on definitions that are developed from time to time by government agencies. These definitions reflect the United States' traditional law enforcement approach to distinguishing terrorism from more common criminal behavior. The following definitions are a sample of that approach.

The U.S. Department of Defense (2010) defines terrorism as "the unlawful use of violence or threat of violence, often motivated by religious, political, or other ideological beliefs, to instill fear and coerce governments or societies in pursuit of goals that are usually political." The U.S. Code (18 U.S.C. 3077) defines terrorism as illegal violence that attempts to "intimidate or coerce a civilian population; . . . influence the policy of a government by intimidation or coercion; or . . . affect the conduct of a government by assassination or kidnapping." The Federal Bureau of Investigation (1996) defines terrorism as "the unlawful use of force or violence against persons or property to intimidate or coerce a Government, the civilian population, or any segment thereof, in furtherance of political or social objectives." The U.S. Department of State (22 U.S.C. 2656f) has defined terrorism as "premeditated, politically motivated violence perpetrated against non-combatant targets by subnational groups or clandestine agents."[2]

Using these definitions, common elements can be combined to construct, for this discussion, a composite American definition:

Terrorism is a premeditated and unlawful act in which groups or agents of some principle engage in a threatened or actual use of force or violence against human or property targets. These groups or agents engage in this behavior, intending the purposeful intimidation of governments or people to affect policy or behavior, with an underlying political objective.

These elements indicate a fairly narrow and legalistic approach to defining terrorism. When this definition is assigned to individual suspects, they may be labeled and detained as terrorists. It must be emphasized that in evaluating the practical policy implications of this approach, labeling and detaining suspects as terrorists is not without controversy. Some counterterrorist practices have prompted strong debate as a consequence of the post–September 11, 2001, war on terrorism. For example, when enemy soldiers are taken prisoner, they are traditionally afforded legal protections as *prisoners of war*. This is well recognized under international law. During the war on terrorism, many suspected terrorists were designated by the United States as *enemy combatants* and were not afforded the same legal status as prisoners of war. Such practices have been hotly debated among proponents and opponents because of civil liberties concerns.

WHAT IS "NEW" ABOUT THE NEW TERRORISM?

In the modern world, states and targeted populations are challenged by the New Terrorism, which is characterized by the following:

- Loose cell-based networks, which, by design, have minimal lines of command and control

- Desired acquisition of high-intensity weapons and weapons of mass destruction

- Politically vague, religious, or mystical motivations

- Asymmetrical methods that maximize casualties

- Skillful use of the Internet and social networking media and manipulation of the mass media

New information technologies and the Internet create unprecedented opportunities for terrorist groups and violent extremists have become adept at bringing their wars into the homes of literally hundreds of millions of people. Those who specialize in suicide bombings, vehicular bombings, or mass-casualty attacks correctly calculate that carefully selected targets will attract the attention of a global audience. Thus, cycles of violence not only disrupt normal routines, they also produce long periods of global awareness. Such cycles can be devastating. These threats offer new challenges for policy makers about how to respond to the behavior of terrorist states, groups, and individuals.

Toward the end of the 20th century, two important developments came to characterize the terrorist environment, moving it into a new phase: a new morality and organizational decentralization. The definitions of who an enemy is, what a legitimate target can be, and which weapons to use have become much broader. This redefining of what constitutes a legitimate target, as well as the appropriate means to attack that target, led to a new kind of political violence. Modern terrorism is "new" in the sense that it is, "indiscriminate in its effects, killing and maiming members of the general public . . . , arbitrary and unpredictable . . . , refus[ing] to recognize any of the rules or conventions of war . . . [and] not distinguish[ing] between combatants and non-combatants" (Crosbie-Weston, 1979). Operationally, the new terrorist morality can be spontaneous and quite gruesome. When terrorists combine this new morality with an ever-increasing lethality of modern weapons, the potential for high casualty rates and terror on an unprecedented scale is very real.

A newly predominant organizational profile—the terrorist cell—has also emerged. Modern cell-based movements have indistinct command and organizational configurations. Similarly, terrorist networks are often composed of a "hub" that may guide the direction of a movement but exercises little direct command and control over operational units. The Internet, encrypted communications technologies, and social networking media allow fellow believers to remain linked to their movement and also receive general guidance and inspiration from leaders and networks. The operational units are typically autonomous or semiautonomous cells that act on their own, often after lying dormant for long periods of time as "sleepers" in a foreign country. The benefit of this type of organizational configuration is that if one cell is eliminated or its members are captured, they can do little damage to other independent cells.

Similarly, many incidents of terrorist violence have been committed by individuals or small groups of extremists who act independently without clearly identifiable associations with terrorist organizations or networks. Such individuals certainly profess an intellectual or ideological identification with extremist causes, but they are individual (i.e., "lone-wolf") or limited-number cell operators who act on their own initiative or are sent on unique/specific missions by extremist organizations. This phenomenon is known as the lone-wolf model.

In the modern era, lone-wolf terrorist violence is typically carried out by individuals and small cells motivated by racial, ideological, or international jihadist ideologies. Such attacks have been adopted as practical tactical operations by some extremist organizations. For example, present-day jihadist movements such as ISIS and al-Qaeda have specifically encouraged lone-wolf and small-cell attacks on Western nations. Messages broadcast by these groups on the Internet and other technologies are easily received by potential sympathizers, who declare allegiance to the movement prior to carrying out their attacks.

TERRORISM IN THE UNITED STATES: THE INTERNATIONAL SOURCES

International terrorism has been relatively less common in the United States than in other countries. During most of the postwar era (prior to the 1990s), international incidents in the United States were spillovers from conflicts in other Western countries and were directed against foreign interests with a domestic presence in the United States. Most of these spillovers ended after a single incident or a few attacks. Some terrorist spillovers were ongoing campaigns. Like many short-term incidents, these campaigns were directed primarily against non-American interests. The terrorist environment evolved during the 1990s, when American interests were directly attacked domestically by international terrorists. A new threat emerged from religious radicals who considered the United States a primary target in their global jihad.

War Comes to the Homeland: Jihad in America

The American people and government became acutely aware of the destructive potential of international terrorism from a pattern that emerged during the 1990s and culminated on September 11, 2001. The following incidents were precursors to the modern security environment:

- February 1993: In the first terrorist attack on the World Trade Center, a large vehicular bomb exploded in a basement parking garage; this was a failed attempt to topple one tower into the other. Six people were killed and more than 1,000 were injured. The mastermind behind the attack was the dedicated international terrorist Ramzi Yousef. His motives were to support the Palestinian people, to punish the United States for its support of Israel, and to promote an Islamic jihad. Several men, all *jihadis*, were convicted of the attack.

- October 1995: Ten men were convicted in a New York federal court of plotting further terrorist attacks. They had allegedly conspired to attack New York City landmarks, such as tunnels, the United Nations headquarters, and the George Washington Bridge.

These incidents heralded the emergence of a threat to homeland security that had not existed since World War II. The practitioners of what became known as the New Terrorism apparently concluded that assaults on the American homeland were desirable and feasible. The key preparatory factors for making these attacks feasible were the following:

- The attacks were carried out by operatives who entered the country for the sole purpose of carrying out the attacks.

- The terrorists received support from cells or individuals inside the United States. Members of the support group facilitated the terrorists' ability to perform their tasks with dedication and efficiency.

The support apparatus profile in the United States for these attacks was not entirely unknown; militants had been known to be in the United States since the late 1980s and 1990s. For example, aboveground organizations were established to funnel funds to the Middle East on behalf of Hamas, Hezbollah, and other movements. These organizations—and other social associations—were deliberately established in many major American cities. The fact is that since at least the late 1980s, anti-American *jihadi* sentiment has existed within the United States among some fundamentalist communities. Significantly, jihad has been overtly advocated by a number of fundamentalist leaders who have taken up residence in the United States.

The New Terrorism in the United States

The worst incident of modern international terrorism occurred in the United States on the morning of September 11, 2001. It was carried out by 19 al-Qaeda terrorists who were on a suicidal "martyrdom mission." They committed the attacks to strike at symbols of American (and Western) interests in response to what they perceived to be a continuing process of domination and exploitation of Muslim countries. These were religious terrorists fighting in the name of a holy cause against the perceived evil emanating from the West. Their sentiments had been born in the religious, political, and ethnonational ferment that has characterized the politics of the Middle East for much of the modern era. After the September 11 attacks, the activity profile of international terrorism in the United States shifted to cell-based religious terrorist spillovers originating in the Middle East. The threat from the New Terrorism in the United States included the very real possibility of a terrorist campaign using high-yield weapons to maximize civilian casualties.

Homegrown Jihadists. A significant threat to homeland security in the United States arose from an unanticipated source—homegrown sympathizers of the international jihadist movement. Domestic security became increasingly challenged in the aftermath of high-casualty terrorist incidents carried out by extremists residing in Western democracies. Such incidents were particularly problematic because many of the perpetrators were seamlessly woven into the fabric of mainstream society. Examples of attacks carried out by homegrown jihadists include the Fort Hood incident, the Boston Marathon bombing, and the San Bernardino attack.

- *The Fort Hood Incident.* On November 5, 2009, a gunman opened fire in the sprawling military base at Fort Hood, Texas, killing 13 people and wounding 29. The attack occurred inside a Fort Hood medical center, and the victims were four officers, eight enlisted soldiers, and one civilian. The shooter was Army major Nidal Malik Hasan, a psychiatrist assigned to treat returning veterans for combat stress.

- *The Boston Marathon Bombing.* On April 15, 2013, two bombs were detonated at the crowded finish line of the Boston Marathon. Three people were killed and more than 260 were wounded, many severely. The devices were constructed from pressure cookers and were detonated 13 seconds apart within approximately 210 yards of each other. They were packed with nails, ball bearings, and possibly other metal shards. Emergency response occurred swiftly, in part because medical personnel and emergency vehicles were already on hand to assist runners at the finish line. Law enforcement officers were also present as members of the race's security detail. Two brothers, Dzokhar and Tamerlan Tsarnaev, were held responsible for the attack. The Tsarnaevs were young immigrants from Chechnya who had resided in the United States since about 2002.

- *The San Bernardino Attack.* On December 2, 2015, 14 people were killed and 21 injured when two armed assailants—a married couple—attacked the Inland Regional Center in San Bernardino, California. The state-run center assisted people with developmental disabilities. The assailants were Syed Rizwan Farook, who had worked at the regional center for 5 years, and his wife Tashfeen Malik. Farook was born and raised in the United States, and his wife, Malik, was born in Pakistan. Farook previously traveled abroad to Pakistan and Saudi Arabia, where he participated in the Muslim hajj pilgrimage to Mecca. He returned to the United States in July 2014 with Malik, whom he subsequently married.

- *The Pulse Nightclub Attack.* On June 12, 2016, gunman Omar Mir Seddique Mateen shot 102 people at the Pulse nightclub in Orlando, Florida, with an assault rifle and semiautomatic handgun, killing 49 of his victims and wounding 53. Pulse was a popular nightclub frequented by members of the LGBT (lesbian, gay, bisexual, and transgender) community. Mateen was a first-generation Afghan American, born in Queens, New York City, and raised in Port St. Lucie, Florida. He deliberately selected an LGBT site to carry out his attack. He opened fire as he entered the nightclub, shooting patrons and exchanging gunfire with an off-duty police officer. He continued firing, retreating to a restroom when police officers began arriving on the scene. Mateen shot a number of patrons who had taken refuge in a restroom. While in the restroom, he dialed the local 911 emergency service and professed his allegiance to Islamic State of Iraq and the Levant (also known as Islamic State of Iraq and al-Sham, or ISIS). He also participated in three conversations with a crisis negotiation team, during which Mateen claimed he was an "Islamic soldier" demanding an end to American intervention in Iraq and Syria.

These incidents confirm the reality of a domestic threat environment in the United States that for years had existed in Europe and elsewhere: mass-casualty violence emanating from homegrown terrorists inspired by international terrorist movements.

TERRORISM IN THE UNITED STATES: THE DOMESTIC SOURCES

Domestic terrorism in the United States is rooted in extremist ideologies and behaviors emanating from the political right and left and from international sources. These attributes reflect political conditions unique to the United States, including American policies that are opposed from abroad by international actors. Unlike many terrorist environments elsewhere in the world, where the designations of *right* and *left* are not always applicable, political violence in the United States has often fallen within these designations. Even nationalist and religious sources of domestic political violence tend to reflect the attributes of U.S. rightest or leftist movements. It is only when we look at the international sources of political violence that the right and left designations lose their relevance in the United States.

Background to Homegrown Terrorism in America

The subject of domestic sources of terrorism in the United States is arguably a study in idiosyncratic political violence. Indigenous terrorist groups reflect the American political and social environments during historical periods when extremists chose to engage in political violence.

In the modern era, right-wing and left-wing political violence emanates from very different circumstances. Rightist violence originates from historical racial and nativist animosity, combined with modern applications of religious and antigovernment ideologies. Leftist violence evolved from a uniquely American historical activist environment that produced the civil rights, Black Power, and New Left movements. In the current political environment, threats originating from right-wing antigovernment and racial supremacist extremists pose the most immediate and plausible scenarios of political violence. In contrast, potential violence from leftist extremists is relatively lower when compared with the right.

Understanding Right-Wing Extremism and Terrorism in the United States

The American right traditionally encompasses political trends and movements that emphasize conventional and nostalgic principles. On the mainstream right, traditional values are emphasized. Examples include family values, educational content, and social order ("law and order") politics. It is also common on the American right (unlike in the European and Latin American rightist movements) to find an infusion of fundamentalist or evangelical religious principles. On the far and fringe right, racial, mystical, and conspiracy theories abound. There is also a great deal of antigovernment sentiment, with some fringe extremists encouraging other adherents to separate from mainstream society.

Terrorist violence has usually been racial, religious, or antigovernment in nature. With few exceptions, terrorism from the right has been conducted by self-isolated groups, cells, or individual lone wolves. Unlike most leftist attacks, many of the right's targets intentionally include people and occupied symbolic buildings. Most examples of ethnocentric "hate crimes"—regardless of whether or not they may be considered acts of terrorism or aggravated crimes—come from the far and fringe right wing. This type of ethnocentric violence has a long history in the United States.

Thus, the modern American right developed from cultural and grassroots sources. Unlike the left, whose characteristics reflected the activism of the 1960s, the right is characterized by self-defined *value systems*. These value systems are perceived by right partisans to be under attack and hence in need of protection—often through assertive defense. This tendency is rooted in newly emergent trends such as antigovernment and religious activism, as well as in historical cultural trends such as racial supremacy. Some political controversies, such as illegal immigration, have rallied extremists who promote their own agendas by claiming that such issues justify their extreme beliefs.[3]

The Patriot Movement. The Patriot movement came to prominence during the early 1990s. The movement considers itself to represent the true heirs of the ideals of the framers of the U.S. Constitution. Members hearken back to what they have defined as the "true" American ideals of individualism, an armed citizenry, and minimum interference from government. For many Patriots, government in general is not to be trusted, the federal government in particular is to be distrusted, and the United Nations is a dangerous and evil institution. To them, the American government no longer reflects the will of the people; it has become dangerously intrusive and violently oppressive. Likewise, the Patriot movement is not ideologically monolithic, and numerous branches have spread, such as the Common Law Courts and Constitutionalists.

Conspiracy theories abound within the Patriot movement. Some of them have long and murky origins, having been fused over decades. Other theories emerge and dissipate during periods of political or social crisis. Nevertheless, three phases of modern conspiracy beliefs can be identified:

- Cold War–era conspiracy theories

- New World Order conspiracies

- Post-9/11 conspiracy beliefs, also referred to as the "Truther" movement

Rightist conspiracy theories range from the fanciful to the paranoid. For example, Patriots cite evidence that non-American interests are threatening to take over—or have already taken over—key governmental centers of authority. This is part of an international plot to create a one-world government.

Two events from the 1990s served to invigorate paranoid political activism on the Patriot right, giving rise to new conspiracy theories. These events were the tragedies at Ruby Ridge, Idaho, and Waco, Texas.

- *Ruby Ridge.* In August 1992, at Ruby Ridge, Idaho, White supremacist Randy Weaver and his family, along with compatriot Kevin Harris, were besieged by federal agents for Weaver's failure to reply to an illegal weapons charge. Two members of the Weaver family were killed during the standoff, as was a U.S. marshal. Weaver's teenage son, Sammy, and Marshal William Degan were killed during a shootout that occurred when Sammy, Randy, and Harris were confronted as they walked along a wooded pathway. Weaver's wife, Vicky, was later fatally shot by an FBI sniper as she held her baby in the doorway of the Weaver home. The sniper had previously fired shots at Weaver and Harris. Members of the Patriot movement and other right-wing extremists, cite this incident as evidence of a broad government conspiracy to deprive freedom-loving "true" Americans of their right to bear arms and other civil liberties.

- *Waco.* In early 1993, in Waco, Texas, federal agents besieged the Branch Davidian cult's compound after a failed attempt in February to serve a search warrant for illegal firearms, ended in the deaths of four federal agents and several cult members. On April 19, 1993, during an assault led by the FBI, about 80 Branch Davidians—including more than 20 children—died in a conflagration that leveled the compound. As with Ruby Ridge, Patriots and other rightists considered this tragedy to be evidence of government power run amok.

Although the Patriot movement attracted a significant number of adherents during the 1990s, and although Patriot militias at one point recruited tens of thousands of members, no underground insurgent movement ensued. Few terrorist groups emanated from the Patriot movement—largely because many members were "weekend warriors" who did little more than train and because law enforcement agencies successfully thwarted a number of true plots. Thus, despite many implicit and explicit *threats* of armed violence from Patriots, terrorist conspiracies were rarely carried to completion.

According to the Southern Poverty Law Center's *Intelligence Report* (2001), the number of armed militias declined during the period between the April 1995 Oklahoma City bombing and the American homeland attacks of September 11, 2001. By 2000, the number of Patriot organizations was only one fourth of the 1996 peak, and this general decline continued after September 11, 2001 (Southern Poverty Law Center, 2002). This occurred for several reasons:

- First, the 1995 Oklahoma City bombing caused many less committed members to drift away.

- Second, the dire predictions of apocalyptic chaos for the new millennium that were embedded in their conspiracy theories did not materialize, especially the predicted advent of the New World Order.

- Third, the September 11, 2001, attacks shifted attention from domestic issues to international threats. (Barry, 2005)

Experts noted, however, that the most militant and committed Patriot adherents remained within the movement and that these dedicated members constitute a core of potentially violent true believers. This became evident after the 2008 presidential elections, when the number of Patriot organizations and identified armed militia groups increased markedly. Growth continued steadily, matching or exceeding previous peak numbers found during the 1990s.

Racial Supremacy. The history of racial supremacy in the United States began during the period of African chattel slavery and continued with the policy to remove Native Americans from ancestral lands. The racial dimensions of these practices became norms (accepted features) of the early American nation. As the nation grew, what had originated before the Civil War as a cultural *presumption* of racial supremacy became entrenched as cultural and political *policy* after the war. For example, African Americans were legally relegated to second-class citizenship, which meant that racial exclusion and social discrimination were practiced with impunity. Most Native Americans were simply removed from society and resettled on reservations.

Modern organized racial supremacist groups include the modern Ku Klux Klan, neo-Nazi movements, racist skinhead youth gangs, and some adherents of the neo-Confederate movement. Members of far- and fringe-right movements frequently justify their claims of racial supremacy and cultural purity by referencing underlying spiritual values—essentially claiming that they have a racial mandate from God. Racial supremacists in particular have developed mystical foundations for their belief systems, some of which are cult-like, such as the Christian Identity and Creativity movements.

Several events from the 2000s are examples of neo-Nazi and racial supremacist violence that were both acts of terrorism and hate crimes.

- *James Wenneker von Brunn.* James Wenneker von Brunn opened fire inside the entrance to the U.S. Holocaust Memorial Museum in Washington, D.C., on June 10, 2009. An African American security guard who opened the door for him was shot with a .22 caliber rifle and later died of his wounds. Other security guards returned fire, wounding von Brunn, who was a known racial supremacist and Holocaust denier—he believed that the Nazi-led genocide during World War II never occurred. Von Brunn had been previously arrested in 1981 when he entered a federal building armed with weapons.

- *Frazier Glenn Cross.* Frazier Glenn Cross shot and killed a 14-year-old Eagle Scout and his grandfather in the parking lot of a Jewish community center in the suburban community of Overland Park, near Kansas City on April 13, 2014. He then went to a nearby Jewish retirement home and killed another victim. It was reported that Cross shouted "Heil Hitler!" several times as the police took him into custody. The 73-year-old had a long history of racial supremacy activity, including leadership in a group originally affiliated with the Ku Klux Klan that eventually reformed as the White Patriot Party, a Christian Identity organization.

- *Dylann Roof.* Dylann Storm Roof shot 12 people who were attending a Bible study meeting at the Emmanuel African Methodist Episcopal Church in Charleston, South Carolina, on June 17, 2015. All victims were African Americans, and nine died during the assault. Roof was an avowed racial supremacist who carried out the attack even after being welcomed by the Bible study participants and sitting with them for approximately 1 hour. He confessed to the crimes and stated he sought to set an example by his actions, which he had intended to be a "spark" to ignite a race war.

Understanding Left-Wing Extremism and Terrorism in the United States

The American left traditionally references political trends and movements that emphasize group rights. Several trends characterize the American left: labor activism, "people's rights" movements, single-issue movements, and antitraditionalist cultural experimentation. Examples include the following:

- *Labor activism.* Historically, labor activism and organizing have promoted ideals frequently found on the left. The labor movement of the late-19th and early 20th centuries was highly confrontational, with violence emanating from management, the unions, and the state. Socialist labor activists such as Samuel Gompers were quite active in organizing workers.

However, the mainstream American labor movement was distinctive, as compared with those found in European labor movements, in that the dominant labor unions generally rejected Marxism and other socialistic economic ideologies.[1]

- *People's rights.* There have been a number of people's rights movements on the American left. In the modern era, activism on the left has generally promoted the interests of groups that have historically experienced discrimination or a lack of opportunity. Examples of people's rights movements include the civil rights, women's rights, Black Power, gay rights, and New Left movements.

- *Single issue.* Single-issue movements, such as the environmental and peace movements, have also been common on the left.

- *Questioning traditions.* One facet of the left has been a tendency toward antitraditionalist cultural trends. Manifestations of this includes experimentation with alternative lifestyles and the promotion of countercultural directions, such as drug legalization.[2]

The modern American left has been characterized by several movements that mostly originated from the political fervor of the 1960s. Bear in mind, none of these movements were fundamentally violent in nature, and they were not terrorist movements. However, extremist leanings within them led to factions that sometimes espoused violent confrontation, and a few did engage in terrorist-like violence. On the far and fringe left, elements of Marxist ideology and left-wing nationalist principles are situated.

Terrorist violence from the left has generally been ideological or nationalistic in nature. It has typically been carried out by covert underground organizations or cells that link themselves (at least ideologically) to leftist "rights" movements. Although there have been human casualties as a direct result of leftist terrorism, most violence has been directed at nonhuman symbols such as unoccupied businesses, natural resources, banks, or government buildings. Law enforcement officers have also been occasionally targeted, usually by ethnonationalist terrorists. The heyday of leftist terrorism in the United States was from the late 1960s to the mid-1980s.

Although left-wing terrorist violence is sporadic and not common, political activism from the far and fringe left has become resurgent in the modern political environment. For example, protests against a globalized economy have rallied activists ranging in ideology from liberal trade unionists to radical anarchists. Adherents of the far left are also increasingly opposed to perceived right-wing politics in the United States. Some leftists have violently challenged what they define as rightist policies such as anti-immigration and austerity programs. For example, in early 2017, far-left activists confronted police and engaged in vandalism in

Portland, Oregon, and Washington, D.C., to protest the presidential election of businessman and television personality Donald Trump. In January 2017, black-clad protesters committed acts of vandalism in Berkeley, California, to challenge a planned speech by a right-wing journalist at the University of California.

As occurred in Berkeley, members of the far left employ a strategy popularly dubbed "Black Bloc" to engage in confrontational street protests. Black Bloc is a confrontational tactic rather than a movement. Widely considered to be anarchistic, street protesters dress in black and mask their faces *en masse* at demonstrations. They find other similarly black-clad protesters, forming a Black Bloc, confront the authorities, and engage in acts of vandalism. This tactic is widely used at contemporary street demonstrations.

RESPONDING TO TERRORISM: HOMELAND SECURITY AND ANTITERRORISM LAWS

Homeland security is a dynamic concept that constantly evolves with the emergence of new terrorist threats. This evolution is necessary because counterterrorist policies must adapt to ever-changing political environments and new threat scenarios. Factors that influence the conceptualization and implementation of homeland security include changes in political leadership, demands from the public, and the discovery of serious terrorist plots (both successful and thwarted).

What Is Homeland Security?

Homeland security is a relatively new concept that, however defined, exists to safeguard the domestic security of the United States and broadly promote the stability of the state when man-made and natural disasters occur. Although originally configured to describe national responses to domestic terrorist incidents in the aftermath of the September 11, 2001, terrorist attacks, homeland security was conceptually expanded after Hurricane Katrina in 2005 to include preparedness and recovery from natural and hazard-related incidents that grew out of that catastrophe. Nevertheless, it is the domestic security mission of the homeland security enterprise that continues to be its fundamental and underlying tenet. An extraordinarily large amount of resources—human and financial—has been devoted to strengthening domestic security and coordinating this effort at all levels of government.

The threat of terrorism and other challenges to domestic security have significantly affected the missions of government agencies nationally and locally. Every level of domestic security organization, law enforcement agency, and emergency response institution incorporates attention to homeland security contingency planning and training. Homeland security has become endemic to modern domestic security and is arguably the domestic counterpart to international counterterrorist initiatives undertaken by national security and national defense institutions.

The Rule of Law and Counterterrorism

In 1996 and 2001, the United States Congress deliberated about and enacted counterterrorist legislation to the emerging terrorist environment. The Anti-Terrorism and Effective Penalty Act of 1996 and the USA PATRIOT Act of 2001 were written into law as seminal statutes in the United States' response to the modern terrorist environment. Within the context of domestic security considerations, norms of criminal justice and legal procedures are incorporated into such legislation to investigate and punish those who commit acts of political violence. Legislation, criminal prosecutions, and incarceration have become typical policy measures to strengthen domestic security.

- *The Anti-Terrorism and Effective Death Penalty Act of 1996.* During the Clinton administration, the United States passed its first comprehensive counterterrorism legislation, titled the Anti-Terrorism and Effective Death Penalty Act. The purpose of this act was to provide resources for counterterrorist programs, punish terrorism, and regulate activity that could be used to mount a terrorist attack. It was an omnibus bill in the sense that it contained a multiplicity of provisions to accomplish its underlying purpose. The law was passed after the terrorist attack at Centennial Park during the 1996 Atlanta Olympics and the explosion of TWA Flight 800 near Long Island, New York.

- *Uniting and Strengthening America by Providing Appropriate Tools Required to Intercept and Obstruct Terrorism Act of 2001 (The USA PATRIOT Act of 2001).* In the aftermath of the September 11, 2001, homeland attacks, the U.S. Congress quickly enacted legislation intending to address the new security threat. On October 26, 2001, President George W. Bush signed this legislation into law. Commonly known as the USA PATRIOT Act, it was also an omnibus law, similar to the Anti-Terrorism and Effective Death Penalty Act but even more comprehensive and omnipotent. Lawmakers included a sunset provision mandating that the USA PATRIOT Act's major provisions automatically expire unless periodically extended. Lawmakers required the Department of Justice to submit reports on the impact of the act on civil liberties.

- *The Department of Homeland Security Act of 2002.* In the immediate aftermath of the September 11 terrorist attacks, efforts to establish a homeland security enterprise quickly revealed a fractured and turf-oriented federal bureaucracy. To remedy publicized reports of political and operational disarray within the domestic security effort, President George W. Bush, in June 2002, completely reorganized the American homeland security community. A large, cabinet-level Department of Homeland Security was created by the new law.

- *The USA PATRIOT Improvement and Reauthorization Act of 2005.* Sunset provisions were integral components of congressional oversight and proactive management of renewal processes for the USA PATRIOT Act. The purpose of these provisions was to counterbalance enhanced authority granted to the executive branch under the act. Congress first renewed the USA PATRIOT Act in March 2006 after passage of the USA PATRIOT Improvement and Reauthorization Act of 2005.

- The *Uniting and Strengthening America by Fulfilling Rights and Ending Eavesdropping, Dragnet-collection and Online Monitoring Act of 2015 (The USA FREEDOM Act of 2015).* The USA PATRIOT Act was reauthorized, with modifications, in June 2015 with the passage of the USA FREEDOM Act. Key provisions of the USA PATRIOT Act were restored, and other provisions were either modified or eliminated. These statutes represent broad legalistic approaches to controlling emerging terrorist environments.

Civil Liberty and Homeland Security: What Is the Balance?

There is a natural tension between the desire to safeguard human rights and the necessity of securing the homeland. This tension is reflected in spirited political and philosophical debates about how to accomplish both goals. It is also reflected in the fact that during historical periods when threats to national security existed, sweeping security measures were undertaken as a matter of perceived necessity. The implementation of these policies was often politically popular, primarily because of the immediacy of the perceived threat—but questioned during reflection subsequently.

Civil liberties advocates contend that a careful balance must be struck between national security and civil liberties. To achieve security, government responses must be proportional to the perceived threat and measured in how they are implemented. At the same time, civil liberties advocates argue that because government responses are usually reactive after a threat arises, a more permanent solution may be found by countering extremism through reform—in effect, the creation of an environment that counters conditions conducive to encouraging radical sentiment.

Counterterrorist options occasionally involve controversial practices and procedures that recurrently inflame misgivings held by civil liberties advocates. This tension between homeland security necessities and civil liberty ideals is starkly highlighted when one considers several politically sensitive counterterrorist options. The underlying question is whether effective homeland security is a justifiable end for implementing controversial options. Examples of this tension include the following considerations.

- *Regulating the Media.* Freedom of the press is an ideal standard—and arguably an ideology—in the United States. The phrase embodies a conceptual construct that suggests that the press (and all news outlets) should enjoy the liberty to independently report information to the public, even when this information might involve national security or be politically sensitive. The counterpoint to absolute freedom of the press is regulation of the press. This issue becomes even more contested when the media publish information about subjects/issues that the public or the government would rather not consider. Regulation is theoretically a genuine option when matters of national security are at stake.

- *Electronic Surveillance.* Electronic surveillance has become a controversial practice in the United States and elsewhere. The fear is that civil liberties can be jeopardized by unregulated interception of telephone conversations, e-mail, telefacsimile, and other transmissions. Detractors argue that government use of these technologies can conceivably move beyond legitimate application against threats from crime, espionage, and terrorism. Absent strict protocols to monitor these technologies, a worst-case scenario envisions state intrusions into the everyday activities of innocent civilians.

- *Terrorist Profiling.* After the September 11, 2001, World Trade Center attacks, the Federal Bureau of Investigation (FBI) and other agencies created a terrorist profile similar to standard criminal profiles used in law enforcement investigations. Criminal profiles are descriptive composites that include the personal characteristics of suspects, such as their height, weight, race, gender, hair color, eye color, and clothing. Suspects who match these descriptions can be administratively detained for questioning. The new terrorist profile included these characteristics: Middle Eastern heritage, temporary visa status, Muslim faith, male gender, and young adult age. Based on these criteria—and during the serious post-9/11 security crisis—the FBI and Immigration and Naturalization Service administratively detained hundreds of men fitting this description. Material witness warrants, in some cases absent due process, were used to detain many of these men for questioning.

- *Labeling Detainees.* When enemy soldiers are taken prisoner, they are afforded legal protections as *prisoners of war.* This is well recognized under international law. During the war on terrorism, many suspected terrorists were designated by the United States as *enemy combatants* and were not afforded the same legal status as prisoners of war and were therefore technically ineligible to receive the right of legal protection. Such practices have been hotly debated among proponents and opponents.

These considerations emphasize the quality of complexity inherent in protecting domestic society from terrorist threat scenarios. The conversation and examination of this issue is dynamic and provocative.

Discussion Questions

1. What is the significance of the attacks on September 11, 2001?

2. Does an official American approach toward defining terrorism exist?

3. In your opinion, are rebels sometimes labeled too quickly as terrorists?

4. Discuss the ideology of the American extreme right wing. What are the sources of their ideology? What is their terrorist activity like?

5. Discuss the ideology of the American extreme left wing. What are the sources of their ideology? What is their terrorist activity like?

6. How can the effectiveness of a terrorist incident be measured?

7. Compare and contrast the Patriot movement with the racial supremacist right.

8. Discuss the effect of conspiracy theories on perpetuating far- and fringe-right-wing movements. Why do you think conspiracy theories persist?

9. In your opinion, does a viable threat exist in the United States of political violence from domestic sympathizers of al Qaeda and other jihadist movements?

10. In your opinion, what are the implications of the militia phenomenon in the United States?

11. Are repressive domestic laws an acceptable counterterrorist option?

12. In your opinion, are antiterrorist laws necessary?

13. Is torture an acceptable counterterrorist option?

Notes

1. The book reports the results of a survey of 100 experts asked for their definitions of terrorism.

2. See also Bureau of Counterterrorism and Countering Violent Extremism. *Country reports on terrorism 2015.* Washington, DC: U.S. Department of State, 2016. p. 406.

3. See Ressner, J. (2006, June 5). Rousing the zealots: Neo-Nazis, White supremacists and militamen are revivified by the furor over illegal immigration. *Time.*

References

Barry, E. (2005, April 13). It's the wilderness years for militias. *Los Angeles Times*.

Crosbie-Weston, R. (1979). Terrorism and the rule of law. In R. W. Cross (Ed.), *20th century* (p. 2715). London, UK: Purnell Reference Books.

Federal Bureau of Investigation, National Security Division, Terrorist Research and Analytical Center. (1996). *Terrorism in the United States 1995* (p. ii). Washington, DC: U.S. Department of Justice.

Schmid, A. P., & Jongman, A. J. (2005). *Political terrorism: A guide to actors, authors, concepts, data bases, theories, and literature* (2nd ed.). Piscataway, NJ: Transaction Publishers.

Southern Poverty Law Center, Intelligence Project. (2001, Summer). A patriot timeline. *Intelligence report*.

Southern Poverty Law Center, Intelligence Project. (2002, Summer). Patriot movement declining. *Intelligence report*.

U.S. Department of Defense. (2010, November 8). *Department of Defense dictionary of military and associated terms*. Washington, DC: Author. (As amended through June 15, 2014). At 266.

CRITICAL ISSUES IN CYBERCRIME

Johnny Nhan

The 2016 U.S. presidential race was marred by allegations of e-mail hacking, widespread voter manipulation through social media, and new terms that entered the public lexicon, such as "fake news." Once marginalized by many academics and the public as an "emerging crime" that only affected a limited number of victims, major events in the past decade have brought cybercrime to the forefront of public consciousness. A growing number of large data breaches that affected millions have occurred regularly. For instance, hackers accessed retail giant Target's server, stealing credit and debit card information from an estimated 110 million consumers in 2013. In 2017, a similar breach happened with credit bureau Equifax, which affected 143 million consumers. App-based transportation service Uber paid hackers $100,000 in 2016 in an attempt to keep secret a data breach that exposed personal information of 57 million users. This stolen sensitive information exposes millions of victims to identity thieves, who can use the data in a variety of crimes, ranging from filing fake tax returns to taking out fraudulent lines of credit. In other words, cybercrime was not only ubiquitous but caused real harm and fundamentally changed one's ability to guard against crime.

Understanding and dealing with computer crimes remains a challenge for academics and practitioners. As computer crimes become more sophisticated and converge with the ubiquitously connected world of networked comput-ers and computing devices, it tests our understanding of existing paradigms of crime, policing, law, and victimization. Some scholars describe cybercrime as a form of "old wine in new bottles" (see O'Neill, 1999; Graboski, 2001; Brenner, 2004), while others question the notion of having a "bottle" at all.

Wall (1999) stresses the uniqueness of the virtual environment in creating a social ecosystem that redefines acceptable and deviant behavior and the meaning of communities.

CRITICAL ISSUE: HACKING AND COMPUTER NETWORK SECURITY

When most people think of cybercrime, hacking and computer network intrusions come to mind—and with good reason. Some of the most consequential cybersecurity breaches occurred in 2016 and 2017. In August 2016, an unknown hacking group, the Shadow Brokers, obtained highly classified National Security Administration (NSA) information and some of the organization's most sophisticated hacking tools, leading many security professionals to believe it was a high-level hack or an internal leak. The *New York Times* described these leaks as "catastrophic" and potentially undermining the agency's ability to protect its cyberattack assets and ultimately national security (Shane, Perlroth, & Sanger, 2017). In March 2017, this information was made public when secret information publishing site WikiLeaks published the hacked NSA software and documentation codenamed "Vault 7," claiming to be a significant proportion of the NSA's digital spying tools (see www.wikileaks.org/ciav7p1). Hacking, however, did not start with this level of maliciousness and gainful utility.

The term hacking was derived from the origin term *hacker*, which was coined in the late 1950s early '60s at MIT to describe technically skilled hobbyists, motivated by learning and exploring, who advanced computing technology through creative software development that pushed the bounds and redefined the functions of the machine. Eventually, the term hacking evolved to encompass finding ways to use a device for an unintended purpose to include all technologies, beyond computers. Accordingly, a hacker became defined as someone who participates in these hacking activities.

Early hackers were driven by curiosity and desire to advance the nascent technology but also the thrill and utility of using computer and telecommunications technologies for deviant and often illegal activities. Early hackers, for instance, replicated routing tones that essentially produced free calls called *phone phreaking*. Hackers exploited the technology using a variety of methods, including impersonating phone company technicians in order to learn telecommunication systems that allowed them to develop circumventing devices to make free calls. Despite many hackers' perception of these activities as harmless fun justified by the purpose of learning and problem solving akin to a puzzle, many people today, including the law enforcement community, perceive their actions as simply criminal.

Hacking today is often slang for describing unauthorized access or use of a computer or network. Hackers employ a variety of technical and nontechnical methods in order to gain access to computer systems and networks. Arguably the most famous hacker is Kevin Mitnick, who used a variety low- and high-tech methods to gain access to government and company computer systems in the 1980s and '90s. Mitnick started engaging in mischievous behavior as a youth with activities such as getting free bus rides by exploiting the ticketing system and phreaking before getting caught stealing telephone manuals from Pacific Bell. He graduated into gaining unauthorized access to the California Department of Motor Vehicles and later the North American Defense Command (NORAD) and a variety of private technology companies before being arrested and sentenced in 1995 (see Mitnick & Simon, 2012).

Mitnick's most effective means of hacking was employing *social engineering*, or the use of deception, manipulation, and influence on others. One particular type of intrusion is called *spear phishing*, where a nefarious e-mail masquerades as coming from a legitimate source that tricks the recipient into opening a file that installs malicious software, or *malware*, that allows cybercriminals to gain access to the system and/or network. In an interview, Mitnick, who is now a security consultant, explains how he uses social networks to find out more about a potential target before launching a spear phishing attack, stating, "If I know you love Angry Birds, maybe I would send you an e-mail purporting to be from Angry Birds with a new pro version. Once you download it, I could have complete access to everything on your phone" (Luscombe, 2011).

Computer intruders often use broader *phishing* methods to attack based on similar deception and social engineering. Phishing uses widely distributed unsolicited e-mails, websites, and phone calls that are designed to convince the recipient under false pretenses to take some sort of action, such as installing software, downloading something from a website, or calling a phone number. The e-mails are often intended to cause some sort of victimization. The most notorious of these phishing scams are commonly known as *advance-fee scams*, such as the widespread *Nigerian 419 scam*, named after the Nigerian penal code for fraud, which typically involves false promises of large returns for a small money advance by the victim.

Researchers have found that victims, who are often blinded by greed, are susceptible to psychological trust-building manipulation (Holt & Graves, 2007; Nhan, Kinkade, & Burns, 2009). While many would ridicule these grammatically challenged scams as obvious and only effective on foolish people, consider the case of renowned psychiatrist Louis A. Gottschalk, who diagnosed Ronald Reagan with mental impairments and headed the University of California, Irvine's Gottschalk Medical Plaza, who was scammed over $3 million over a 10-year period (Lobdell, 2006).

Phishing attacks can be used as part of larger attacks against organizations. Victim systems can have software installed that discretely replicates itself by infecting other computers. Once there are enough infected computers, an attacker can launch a *distributed denial of service* (DDoS) attack using a network of infected computers (*botnet*) to overload and disable a website or network. The automated attack floods the target with unnecessary and excessive requests from multiple sources simultaneously, making it impossible to distinguish between attack and legitimate traffic and extremely difficult to stop.

Hackers can be motivated by a variety of reasons to deploy botnets, ranging from blackmail to revenge. The largest attack to date occurred in 2016, when Internet domain name system (DNS) service, Dyn, that translates Internet Protocol (IP) numbers into recognizable names, was attacked, which brought down service to sites such as Netflix, Twitter, CNN, and many others in the U.S. and U.K. Such major disruptions to business can mean millions in revenue lost per day (Woolf, 2016). More nefarious hackers can use the attack period to exploit security vulnerabilities, such as a temporary disabling of antivirus security software in order to restore site functionality, in order to gain entry into the network and, thus, private information that can be used for financial gain.

CRITICAL ISSUE: DARKNETS AND THE DEEP WEB

Successful network intrusions in the past have resulted in hackers gaining access to and exploiting a large amount of personal data for very lucrative gain. Hackers can exploit users' stolen private information, such as medical records, financial information, and Social Security numbers. This private information can be used to take out new lines of credit to filing fraudulent tax returns. Moreover, hackers can sell this personal information in illegal Internet black marketplaces, or *darknets*, in bulk or exploit the information themselves.

Darknets, sometimes today referred to as the *deep web*, are a collection of private secure networks used to mask a variety of malicious and illegal activities, as first coined by Microsoft researchers. Darknets, which were nonstandard software protocols that exploited existing the Internet physical infrastructure, were ideal for facilitating illegal activities due to (1) fewer users present, (2) allowing users to upload, copy, and permanently store files freely, (3) while allowing users to connect with high-bandwidth channels (Biddle, England, Peinado, & Willman, 2002). Early darknets facilitated illegal file sharing of copyrighted materials, such as software, music, movies, and books.

Darknets have evolved to facilitate more serious crimes and criminal activity. A number of extremists, among other groups, utilize darknets today as private communication channels for political dissent to terrorist and antiterrorist activities (Mansfield-Devine, 2009). More recently, more user-friendly software developed for darknets to create anonymous online marketplaces for the selling and purchasing of illegal goods and services. The most infamous of these "crypto-marketplaces" (see Martin, 2003) is the Silk Road, which drew national attention when thousands of users each month used the Amazon.com-like marketplace to purchase anything from illegal narcotics ranging from cocaine and pharmaceuticals (see Buskirk et al., 2016; Barratt, Ferris, & Winstock, 2014) to child pornography, illegal weapons, sex trafficking, and even assassination services (see Ball, 2013).

High demand for illegal goods and services coupled with anonymizing tools facilitates activities on the Silk Road and other darknet marketplaces. In order to log on to the marketplace, users must use an anonymizer called The Onion Router ("Tor") that is designed to shield users against surveillance and anyone knowing their physical locations, justified as protecting personal freedom and privacy (see www.torproject.org). In addition, crypto-currency, or encrypted currency that eliminates the need for financial institutions and is described as a "gold standard without gold" and "fiat money without a state," is used (Bjerg, 2016). Consequently, there is no recordkeeping for the currency, which ensures anonymous transactions in these marketplaces. To gauge the scope of the marketplace, in 2011, the Silk Road collected 9.5 million Bitcoin crypto-currencies out of only 11.75 million in existence, which was equivalent to over $1.2 billion in sales (Fernholz, 2013). In 2017, Bitcoin was worth more than $16,000 each.

Regularly occurring large-scale security breaches have put more users, even ones careful protecting their purses and wallets, at increasing risk. The Identity Theft Resource Center (ITRC) tracks known data breaches in seven categories: (1) insider theft, (2) hacking/computer intrusion, (3) data on the move, (4) physical theft, (5) employee error/negligence, (6) accidental Web exposure, and (7) unauthorized access (see www.idtheftcenter.org). The ITRC recorded 8,087 breaches that exposed 1.06 *billion* records that include private information ranging from Social Security numbers to user logins and passwords from January 2005 to November 2017. Despite the ITRC's compiled data, the full scope and harm of data breaches is not fully known.

According to the FBI, computer and network intrusions have larger national security implications. Attackers can disrupt or disable hospitals, banks, and 9-1-1 emergency services in addition to using these disruptions to further terroristic goals (see www.fbi.gov/investigate/cyber). As far back as the Clinton administration, the protection of critical infrastructures against cyber threats has been a top priority, even during the Internet's nascent stage when the threats were theoretical. In a 1996 executive order, the White House identified points of cyber protection to include telecommunication systems, electric power grids, energy storage and transportation, banking and finance, water supply, emergency services, and government continuity (Clinton, 1996). Subsequent presidents have issued similar orders.

Cyber threats to critical infrastructure are no longer theoretical in nature. By the end of 2016, nearly a quarter of cyberattacks were aimed at industrial targets, notably industrial control systems, which accounted for 40% of those attacks (Seals, 2017). The first known military cyber weapon was deployed against Iran's Natanz nuclear fuel enrichment facility in 2010. The Stuxnet virus, deployed by the U.S. and Israel, gave operators false readings of normal operation while overheating them and physically destroying approximately 20% of the centrifuges and setting the program back for years. Studying these critical infrastructure vulnerabilities and interdependencies has taken an interdisciplinary approach, with much of the literature produced in the computer sciences and engineering, as well as by security professionals (see Chen, 2011a; Langner, 2011). Some researchers have warned that Stuxnet can be perceived as an act of war and signaled the beginning of the potential of cyberwarfare between advanced nation states (Chen, 2011b; Farwell & Rohozinski, 2011; Fidler, 2011).

CRITICAL ISSUE: THE INTERNET CULTURE AND ETHOS

Hacking is more than just computer intrusions, but at its core, it represents a technological counterculture of the computer revolution. Much of hacking behavior can be understood as a derivative of an ethos or spirit of electronic discovery during the early days of computing. Coinciding with technological developments during the computer revolution was the emergence of an ethos that characterized the counterculture. MIT student hobbyists from a railroad club that modified train parts and circuits soon applied this "hacker" mentality toward new IBM computers acquired by the university. When these members were granted limited time with the system during off-hours, they quickly developed software that utilized the hardware beyond its intended scope. This spirit of open development tacitly became a hacker ethic, where all individuals working together in a free flow of information created more collective knowledge (Levy, 2010).

The hacker ethic is often at odds with the proprietary nature of software and digital media and the companies that own them. Early hackers felt that Internet was developed as an open platform for information sharing. Today's World Wide Web was developed in the 1960s at universities such as MIT and UCLA as part of a joint venture with the U.S. military's Defense Advanced Research Projects Agency (DARPA) to create a robust, noncentralized, wide-area information packet sharing computer network, ARPANET (Leiner, et al., 2009). When this network was eventually released to the public in the 1990s, it quickly became populated by users who saw the Internet as a last frontier for free thought and information and companies that saw not only commercial opportunities that included privatizing and monetizing parts of the Web.

The commercial threat to the Internet prompted *A Declaration of the Independence of Cyberspace* by cyber-libertarian and founder of the digital rights organization Electronic Frontier Foundation, John Perry Barlow. The declaration reflects the core ethos and Internet culture and warns entities that threaten the information sovereignty of the Web. For example, the declaration states, "We are creating a world where anyone, anywhere may express his or her beliefs, no matter how singular, without fear of being coerced into silence or conformity," adding, "Your legal concepts of property, expression, identity, movement, and context do not apply to us. They are all based on matter, and there is no matter here" (Barlow, 1996). One of the founders of the Internet, Leonard Kleinrock (2004), echoes this opinion with his Rules of Engagement, which list, among other Internet characteristics, as "no one controls it," "it serves everyone," "it is diversifying," and "it is empowering" (p. 199).

Many hackers today often use the principles of a free Internet in order to justify online criminal activity. While the Internet has opened opportunities for business and information sharing, it also has a "dark side." Kleinrock (2004) lists these darker characteristics to include, among other things, "It does not obey the laws of all countries" (p. 200). In other words, one can perceive the Internet as an unregulated space that is rampant with crime and criminal activity, much of which can be attributed to malicious hackers.

Today, a number of criminologists have looked at the "hacker subculture" in explaining deviant behavior. Ross (1990), for example, has questioned the focus on making rational, economic, and ethical explanations of the hacker behavior but instead looked at subcultural normative behaviors.

RESEARCH: UNDERSTANDING HACKERS' MOTIVATIONS

The sheer types and variety of motivations for hacking makes a singular explanation for motive impossible. Individuals and groups who hack for nefarious reasons are known as *black hat hackers*, also referred to as "crackers" or "dark-side" hackers. These individuals' activities range from breaking into computer systems and networks to creating harmful viruses and even demanding ransom (*ransomware*). On the other end of the spectrum are *white hat hackers*, who are often security professionals breaking into computer systems and networks looking for vulnerabilities ("penetration tests") for the purpose of fixing or patching them. In between are a variety of hacker types that include *gray hat hackers*, who compromise systems without evil intent and are essentially hackers for hire. Unfortunately for target systems and networks, the threat and activities are still the same and must be treated as a critical threat, including the possibility of an act of cyberwarfare by a nation-state.

A number of criminologists have applied existing theoretical paradigms to explain hacker behavior. There is no one theory that explains the motivation for hacking or a profile of a hacker, but there is empirical evidence to support theoretical claims. For instance, some criminologists and economists have looked at the rationality of hacking in terms of profit-driven motives. Leeson and Coyne (2005) compared the motives of fame and profits in shaping a policy framework.

Criminologists have applied social learning theory to explain hacker behavior. Morris and Backburn (2009) argue that since the newness of computer crimes gives it no learning reference point from parents, college students mimicked and neutralized computer crime using social learning through peer associations (see also Morris & Higgins, 2010). Pons and Perez-Pons (2015) examined whether college students taking courses in *ethical* hacking, which gives students hacking know-how, resulted in students taking that knowledge and applying it for nefarious reasons. The study found that despite having the tools to be able hack, students did not engage in illegal hacking activity. However, a statistically significant number of students were willing to receive payment for hacking into a computer network.

Morris (2010) empirically tested Sykes and Matza's (1957) neutralization theory. Neutralization theory categorizes five justifications or rationalization for criminal behavior that include (1) denial of responsibility, (2) denial of injury, (3) denial of victim, (4) condemning the condemners, and (5) appeals to higher authorities (Sykes & Matza, 1957). Morris's study of 785 college students found that neutralization techniques are statistically significantly related to some malicious computer hacking activities, reasoning that the disembodied victimization of the cyber environment versus face-to-face offenses makes unethical behavior easier to commit.

Bossler and Burruss (2011) applied self-control theory using Gottfredson and Hirschi's (1990) general theory of crime, which states that crime is a result of the inability to refrain from temptation and impulses. Using structural equation modeling, the researchers found a strong correlation using variables that measured deviant activity related to self-control among college students (Bossler & Burruss, 2011). Similarly, Holt, Bossler, and May (2010) found a positive correlation between hacking activity and measures of low self-control as measured by cyber defiance among students, such as surfing the Internet for nonacademic activities. Moon, McCluskey, McCluskey, and Lee (2013) examined gender differences and self-control with illegal software downloads and illegal use of others' resident registration numbers (RRN) with a sample of over 2,700 Korean middle school students and found that self-control and opportunities are significant predictors of computer crime activities.

Yar (2005) looked at the disproportionate amount of youth participation in computer hacking activity by mapping categories of expertise with causal factors that include moral development, family dysfunctions, as well as youth culture and peer associations. He asserts that hacking is a socially constructed expression that does not have a singular definition and motivations and while hackers typically fit a distinct profile of being male youths, their motivations are extremely varied, ranging from rational acts (See Clarke & Felson, 1993) to manifestations of Internet addiction associated with low self-control (See Grossman, 2001) and "thrill seeking" activities (See Katz, 1988).

A number of researchers have tried to profile hackers. Chiesa, Ducci, and Ciappi's (2009) Hacker Profile Project (HPP) go into great detail in examining hackers, include gender, age, places of residence, family background, education, psychological profiles, and other variables. Zhang, Tsang, Yue, and Chau (2015) classified hackers using online community forums into "knowledge exchange" behavioral categories of "gurus," who are knowledgeable and respectable; "casuals," who act as observers; "learners," who are experts but utilize hacker forums for learning; and "novices," who join the communities, which are a source for knowledge transfer, for a short period. This classification scheme can be viewed as more accurate by looking at community activities and expertise rather than self-professed profiles.

CRITICAL ISSUE: POLICING CYBERSPACE

Policing hacking activity has been a difficult task for the law enforcement community and individuals. State and local law enforcement agencies were not created to deal with abstract crime (Huey, 2002). Structurally, these agencies are bounded by functional bounds and physical jurisdictions (Nhan, 2010). In addition, state and local officers, with limited understanding of complex computer networks, prioritize individual victims where more localized computer forensics can be employed. Much of local law enforcement efforts have focused on crimes that have a connection to persons and physical spaces. Sexual predators, for instance, have garnered significant state and local police attention over more abstract cases of hacking.

Computer forensics fits well with the scope of state and local agencies that are more familiar with and prioritize crimes that are more traditional in nature using the online environment where there are clear victims and perpetrators. Police investigations function primarily to link abstract Internet space with the physical world. The goal of computer forensics remains grounded in traditional police work in identifying, locating, and apprehending a suspect that has committed harm against a person in preparation for court. In order to accomplish this task with computer forensics, there is only one primary step in transforming an abstract computer crime to a more traditional crime form.

An essential first step in computer forensics is finding the physical source of a computer system that was used for a crime. Investigators examine and trace a computer's Internet protocol (IP) address, a unique number assigned to a computer akin to a telephone number, back to a physical location. Oftentimes, this trace leads back to an IP address that is linked to an Internet service provider (ISP), such as a telecommunications or cable company that owns a range of these addresses, akin to an area code. In order to find out the exact address of a computer using a specific IP address within the ISP's network, investigators often present a subpoena to the ISP, who then releases the customer to the investigators.

Having an Internet protocol address that is linked to a physical address is not enough information for officers to arrest a suspect, who can simply claim he or she was not using the computer system at the time. At this point, investigations become "old-fashioned police work," where detectives often seize the computer and perform computer forensics (Nhan & Huey, 2013). Computer forensics requires investigators to carefully examine the contents of a computer system without compromising evidentiary integrity, looking at the different times of activity. For instance, if the crime was traced back to a coffee shop or Internet café, the investigator can analyze security camera footage to find the person actually on the keyboard.

Investigators can also establish motive by examining the digital content of a computer. A search of a person's Internet search history and activity can help establish motive. Investigators can invalidate a suspect's claim the he or she was not using the computer at the time of the crime, for example, by looking at e-mail logins immediately before or after the time of the crime.

Despite the seeming simplicity of computer forensics, it is difficult, expensive, and time-consuming for local police agencies. Typically, larger police departments usually employ specially trained detective units and task forces (see Nhan, 2010). Smaller departments without the in-house capacity for computer forensics can outsource such work to regional computer forensic labs or simply dismiss certain crimes, referring victims to federal agencies. The limited capacity of law enforcement is further strained by more abstract network intrusion cases, where there is no clear victim and perpetrator.

In the United States, the brunt of computer crimes, particularly computer network intrusions and hacking, have been under the purview of federal agencies. Five federal agencies have taken the brunt of enterprise-level cybersecurity: the FBI, the Federal Trade Commission (FTC), Department of Homeland Security (DHS), U.S. Secret Service, and the National Institute of Standards and Technology (NIST). These agencies often prioritize terrorism activities with cyberspace with fewer resources dedicated to individual victims.

Despite the efforts of local, state, and federal agencies, policing cyberspace remains woefully inadequate, leading to *crowdsourcing* to fill the security deficit. During the 2013 Boston Marathon bombing investigation, a number of online communities organically joined in, compiling and combing through thousands of photographs and surveillance videos looking for clues. Moreover, these varied individuals with different backgrounds and expertise applied their knowledge, from identifying baseball caps to pressure cooker models. While it was not successful in finding the suspects and often blurs the line of illegal vigilantism, crowdsourcing showed great potential in investigations (Nhan, Huey, & Broll, 2015).

CRITICAL ISSUE: DIGITAL PIRACY

Digital piracy is one area of cybercrime that can be described as a "cat and mouse" game between Hollywood music and movie studios and users. Digital media pirates have evolved from the days of hosting music on websites, to peer-to-peer (P2P) audio sharing service Napster, to more sophisticated and decentralized torrenting sites that do not host or store any pirated copies, such as the Pirate Bay (see Nhan, 2013). Despite legislative advancements, such as the Digital Millennium

Copyright Act (DMCA) that criminalizes the circumvention of copyright technologies, such as Digital Rights Management (DRM) and the distribution of unauthorized digital content, piracy is still prevalent today.

Digital piracy remains a massive problem despite the availability of relatively inexpensive legal music and movie streaming services. According to data from marketing research firm NPD, file sharing increased 44% from 2008 to 2015 (Steele, 2015). While some may argue that file sharing technology is neutral and used oftentimes as an efficient way of sharing data, the majority of file sharing activity is used for music (78.1%) and television (92.9%) piracy (Steele, 2015). For example, even with HBO NOW streaming service costing $14.99 and $9.99 for students, *Game of Thrones* season 7 was pirated more than 1 billion times, compared with the average 31 million who legally watched (Price, 2017). This phenomenon was backed by research data in music piracy that showed consumers who had favorable attitudes toward piracy were less likely to try subscription-based services (Cesareo & Pastore, 2014).

Hollywood music and movie studios and their respective trade associations, the Recording Industry Association of America (RIAA) and Motion Picture Association of America (MPAA), have employed a variety of methods to curtail the problem with relatively little success. The RIAA was infamous for suing users, which included a number of college students, beginning in 2003. It is estimated that the RIAA filed, settled, or threatened legal action on at least 30,000 individuals from 2003 to 2008 (Electronic Frontier Foundation, 2008). In 2006, the MPAA raided and took down the P2P torrent index the Pirate Bay in Stockholm, arresting key operators, only to have it reappear days later fully operational with the banner that read, "The World's Most Resilient Bittorrent Site." High levels of piracy are often driven by demand for pirated activity, which is often justified by downloaders' perceptions and attitudes towards pirated material.

Many researches have examined attitudes towards digital piracy, especially among teenagers. A study of high schoolers in Taiwan found that perceptions of factors such as prosecution risk, magnitude consequence, and social consensus, did not affect pro-piracy attitudes, but only singer or band idolization stopped them from pirating music (Chiou, Huan, & Lee, 2005). Al-Rafee and Cronan (2006) found that illegal downloaders felt digital media is overpriced, had no fear of getting caught, and did not feel that digital piracy is important. Moreover, research subjects reported feeling happiness and excitement when pirating.

Criminologists have applied criminological theories to explain piracy activity. Malin and Fowers (2009) applied Gottfredson and Hirschi's general theory of crime to examine high school students' level of self-control. The researchers found age, along with factors such as association with deviant peers, associated with lower levels of self-control were significant factors in music and movie piracy, suggesting the focus of research and policing efforts shift toward younger individuals. Similarly, Higgins, Fell, and Wilson (2006) integrated both self-control and social learning theories with digital piracy using three causal models measuring direct and indirect interactive effects of both theories using a sample of college students. Data analyzed through structural equation modeling shows statistically significant effects of both control and learning theories on digital piracy.

CRITICAL ISSUE: CYBERBULLYING

Cyberbullying is a growing trend among ubiquitously connected youths. According to National Crime Victimization Survey (NCVS) data, an estimated 1.7 million students are cyberbullied each year (U.S. Department of Education, 2015). This estimate may not be entirely accurate, given that cyberbullying is severely under-reported. A study by Smith et al. (2008) found that nearly 44% of victims aged 11 to 16 did not report the bullying activity.

Cyberbullying can include spreading harmful information online, via instant and text messaging, online gaming, and exclusion from online communities. Moreover, bullying can include *revenge porn*, or the unauthorized posting of explicit photos online in order to inflict shame and stigma as a form of retaliation. Websites dedicated to revenge porn gained popularity in 2010, when the site IsAnyoneUp.com became an instant hit before shutting down in 2012. The site got into legal trouble when it began posting victims' information, such as full names and social media profiles. Despite the demise of IsAnyoneUp, it was quickly replaced by Myex.com, which found a legal loophole to operate.

Unfortunately for victims of revenge porn, who are usually women whose photos were posted by former partners, there is a significant harm with little recourse. Sites like Myex post easily searchable personal information while allowing site visitor comments. Victims are usually shamed by descriptions as "sluts," "cheaters," and "whores." The permanence and ubiquity of the Internet make it virtually impossible to remove that presence and photos, potentially damaging victims' future reputations. Unfortunately for victims of revenge porn wanting to take legal action, revenge porn laws have not been adequately developed.

The criminalization of revenge porn has been met with resistance in the form of claims of civil immunity by site operators and claims of revenge porn as protected under freedom of expression (see Franklin, 2014) as well as other legal complications (see Calvert, 2014). As of 2017, 38 states and the District of Columbia have some form of revenge porn laws in place, in addition to civil penalties. At the time of this writing, no federal statutes exist for criminalizing revenge porn. However, the proposed Intimate Privacy Protection Act would criminalize the distribution of nonconsensual pornography and may standardize the law. Current laws mostly govern child pornography without much consideration for adult pornography. These legal complications highlight the rapid pace of cybercrime when interfacing with traditional institutions.

Cyberstalking is another form of cyberbullying. Since cyberstalking is often not mutually exclusive with offline stalking, it is often grouped together, which makes it very difficult to measure. However, researchers have found that cyberstalking is fundamentally different than traditional stalking (Sheridan & Grant, 2007). Victims who once found refuge at home do not have a safe place insulated from bullying. One study of 463 middle and high school students found that victims internalized psychological problems that included self-esteem, depression, anxiety, and stress (Aoyama, Terrill, & Fearon, 2011).

CONCLUSION

This chapter merely scratches the surface of critical issues in dealing with cybercrime and does not a represent a comprehensive list of issues. As with the dynamic nature of technology, it is constantly and rapidly changing, which creates a variety of problems for our justice and legal institutions, which are slow moving and steeped in legal, functional, and cultural boundaries. Society constantly finds itself in a cycle of new, emergent forms of computer crimes followed by delayed responses by slow-moving institutions in criminal justice and law. This has been highlighted throughout recent history with digital music, such as the case of music file-sharing service Napster and more recently, as illustrated, with revenge porn.

Nevertheless, researchers have made significant inroads in understanding certain behaviors and activities that take place online. The difficulty is getting the public, lawmakers, and even academics to recognize the realities of current harm through cybercrime and that everyone can be a potential victim. Without this acknowledgement, inadequate effort and resources will be allocated to fighting it. Edwin Lemert (2000) argued that ambivalence expressed in public attitudes can undermine collective action, stating, "Generalized culture conflict which affects such a large majority of the population that little consistent action is possible" can result in "community tolerance [that] is precariously stabilized just short of a critical point in the tolerance quotient at which collective action is taken" (p. 34).

Discussion Questions

1. Most security professionals stress that people protect themselves against computer crimes, such as safeguarding and frequently updating passwords; we have seen that companies have been hacked despite these efforts. What can you do, and whose responsibility is it to protect against cybercrime?

2. What can state and local police do to better equip themselves to police cyberspace given jurisdictional, functional, and cultural limitations? Should these agencies just stick to localized computer crimes?

3. Is media piracy still really a problem given the widespread availability of digital streaming services, such as Netflix and Hulu? Why are studios still pursuing pirates given the record profits in recent years?

4. How can one respond to the solution against cyberbullying as simply staying off the Internet and staying away from the bully? Why is that solution not as simple as it seems? How can activities such as revenge porn be addressed? Is it possible to undo an unauthorized picture or video that is released on to the Internet?

References

Al-Rafee, S., & Cronan, T. P. (2006). Digital piracy: Factors that influence attitude toward behavior. *Journal of Business Ethics*, *63*(3), 237–259.

Aoyama, I., Saxon, T. F., & Fearon, D. D. (2011). Internalizing problems among cyberbullying victims and moderator effects of friendship quality. *Multicultural Education & Technology Journal*, *5*(2), 92–105. doi:10.1108/17504971111142637

Ball, J. (2013, March 22). Silk Road: The online drug marketplace that officials seem powerless to stop. *The Guardian*. Retrieved from https://www.theguardian.com/world/2013/mar/22/silk-road-online-drug-marketplace

Barlow, J. P. (1996, February 8). *A declaration of the independence of cyberspace*. Davos, Switzerland: Electronic Frontier Foundation. Retrieved from https://www.eff.org/cyberspace-independence

Barratt, M. J., Ferris, J. A., & Winstock, A. R. (2014). Use of Silk Road, the online drug marketplace, in the United Kingdom, Australia and the United States. *Addiction*, *109*(5), 774–783. doi:10.1111/add.12470

Biddle, P., England, P., Peinado, M., & Willman, B. (2002). The Darknet and the future of content distribution. *ACM Workshop on Digital Rights Management*. Microsoft Corporation. Retrieved from http://msl1.mit.edu/ESD10/docs/darknet5.pdf

Bjerg, O. (2016). How is Bitcoin money? *Theory, Culture & Society*, *33*(1), 53–72. doi:10.1177/0263276415619015

Bossler, A. M., & Burruss, G. W. (2011). The general theory of crime and computer hacking: Low self-control hackers? In T. J. Holt & B. H. Schell (Eds.), *Corporate hacking and technology driven crime: Social dynamics and implications* (pp. 38–67). Hershey, NY: IGI Global.

Brenner, S. (2004). Cybercrime metrics: Old wine, new bottles? *Virginia Journal of Law & Technology*, *9*(13), 1–52.

Calvert, C. (2014). Revenge porn and freedom of expression: Legislative pushback to an online weapon of emotional and reputational destruction. *Fordham Intellectual Property Media and Entertainment Law Journal*, *24*(3), 674–702.

Cesario, L., & Pastore, A. (2014). Consumers' attitude and behavior towards online music piracy and subscription-based services. *Journal of Consumer Marketing*, *31*(6–7), 515–525. doi:10.1108/JCM-07-2014-1070

Chen, T. M. (2011a). Lessons from Stuxnet. *Computer*, *44*(4), 91–93. doi:10.1109/MC.2011.115

Chen, T. M. (2011b). Stuxnet, the real start of cyber warfare? *IEEE Network*, *24*(6), 2–3. doi:10.1109/MNET.2010.5634434

Chiesa, R., Ducci, S., & Ciappi, S. (2009). Profiling hackers: *The science of criminal profiling as applied to the world of hacking*. Boca Raton, FL: CRC Press.

Chiou, J.-S., Huan, C.-Y., & Lee, H.-H. (2005). The antecedents of music piracy attitudes and intentions. *Journal of Business Ethics*, *57*, 161–174. doi:10.1007/s10551-004-5263-6

Clarke, R., & Felson, M. (Eds.). (1993). *Routine activity and rational choice*. London, UK: Transaction Press.

Clinton, W. J. (1996). Executive Order 13010: Critical infrastructure protection. Retrieved from http://naturalenvironmentsociety-arizonasouthwest.com/references/PDFs/presidential-actions/outline1/Clinton_EO_13010.pdf

Electronic Frontier Foundation. (2008, September 30). RIAA v. the people: Five years later. Retrieved from https://www.eff.org/wp/riaa-v-people-five-years-later

Farwell, J. P., & Rohozinski, R. (2011). Stuxnet and the future of cyber warfare. *Survival: Global Politics and Strategy*, *53*(1), 23–40.

Fernholz, T. (2013, October 2). Silk Road collected 9.5 million bitcoin—and only 11.75 million exist. *Quartz*. Retrieved from https://qz.com/131084/silk-road-collected-9-5-million-bitcoin-and-only-11-75-million-exist

Fidler, D. P. (2011). Was Stuxnet an act of war? Decoding a cyber attack. *IEEE Security & Privacy*, *9*(4), 56–59. doi:10.1109/MSP.2011.96

Franklin, Z. (2014). Justice for revenge porn victims: Legal theories to overcome claims of civil immunity by operators of revenge porn websites. *California Law Review*, *102*(5), 1303–1336.

Gottfredson, M. R., & Hirschi, T. (1990). *A general theory of crime*. Stanford, CA: Stanford University Press.

Grabosky, P. N. (2001). Virtual criminality: Old wine in new bottles? *Social & Legal Studies, 10*(2), 243–249.

Grossman, W. (2001). *From anarchy to power: The net comes of age*. New York, NY: New York University Press.

Higgins, G. E., Fell, B. D., & Wilson, A. L. (2006). Digital piracy: Assessing the contributions of an integrated self-control theory and social learning theory using structural equation modeling. *Criminal Justice Studies, 19*(1), 3–22. doi:10.1080/14786010600615934

Holt, T. J., & Graves, D. C. (2007). A qualitative analysis of advance fee fraud e-mail schemes. *International Journal of Cyber Criminology, 1*(1), 137–154.

Holt, T. J., Bossler, A. M., & May, D. C. (2012). Low self-control, deviant peer associations, and juvenile cyberdeviance. *American Journal of Criminal Justice, 37*(3), 378–395. doi:10.1007/s12103-011-9117-3

Huey, L. J. (2002). Policing the abstract: Some observations on policing cyberspace. *Canadian Journal of Criminology, 44*(3), 243–254.

Katz, J. (1988). *The seductions of crime*. New York, NY: Basic Books.

Kleinrock, L. (2004). The Internet rules of engagement: Then and now. *Technology in Society, 26*(2–3), 193–207. doi:10.1016/j.techsoc.2004.01.015

Langner, R. (2011). Stuxnet: Dissecting a cyberwarfare weapon. *IEEE Security & Privacy, 9*(3), 49–51. doi:10.1109/MSP.2011.67

Leeson, P. T., & Coyne, C. J. (2005). The economics of computer hacking. *Journal of Law, Economics & Policy, 1*(2), 511–514.

Leiner, B. M., Cerf, V. G., Clark, D. D., Kahn, R. E., Kleinrock, L., Lynch, D. C., Postel, J., Roberts, L. G., & Wolff, S. (2009). A brief history of the Internet. *ACM SIGCOMM Computer Communication Review, 39*(5), 22–31. doi:10.1145/1629607.1629613

Lemert, E. M. (2000). *Crime and deviance: Essays and innovations of Edwin M. Lemert*. New York, NY: Rowman & Littlefield.

Levy, S. (2010). *Hackers: Heroes of the computer revolution*. Sebastopol, CA: O'Reilly Media.

Lobdell, W. (2006, March 2). UCI Psychiatrist bilked by Nigerian e-mails, suit says. *Los Angeles Times*. Retrieved from http://articles.latimes.com/2006/mar/02/local/me-nigerian2

Luscombe, B. (2011). 10 questions for Kevin Mitnick. *Time*. Retrieved from http://content.time.com/time/magazine/article/0,9171,2089344,00.html

Malin, J., & Fowers, B. J. (2009). Adolescent self-control and music and movie piracy. *Computers in Human Behavior, 25*(3), 718–722. doi:10.1016/j.chb.2008.12.029

Mansfield-Devine, S. (2009). Darknets. *Computer Fraud & Security, 12*, 4–6. doi:10.1016/S1361-3723(09)70150-2

Martin, J. (2003). Lost on the Silk Road: Online drug distribution on the 'cryptomarket.' *Criminology & Criminal Justice, 14*(3), 351–367. doi:10.1177/1748895813505234

Mitnick, K., & Simon, W. L. (2011). *Ghost in the wires: My adventures as the world's most wanted hacker*. New York, NY: Back Bay Books.

Moon, B., McCluskey, J. D., & McCluskey, C. P. (2010). A general theory of crime and computer crime: An empirical test. *Journal of Criminal Justice, 38*, 767–772. doi:10.1016/j.jcrimjus.2010.05.003

Moon, B., McCluskey, J. D., McCluskey, C. P., & Lee, S. (2013). Gender, general theory of crime and computer crime: An empirical test. *International Journal of Offender Therapy and Comparative Criminology, 57*(4), 460–478.

Morris, R. G. (2010). Computer hacking and techniques of neutralization: An empirical assessment. In *Cyber crime: Concepts, methodologies, tools and applications vol. 1* (pp. 457–473). Hershey, PA: Information Sources Management.

Morris, R. G., & Blackburn, A. G. (2009). Cracking the code: An empirical exploration of social learning theory and computer crime. *Journal of Crime and Justice, 32*(1), 1–34. doi:10.1080/0735648X.2009.9721260

Morris, R. G., & Higgins, G. E. (2010). Criminological theory in the digital age: The case of social learning theory and digital piracy. *Journal of Criminal Justice, 38*(4), 470–480. doi:10.1016/j.jcrimjus.2010.04.016

Nhan, J. (2013). The evolution of online piracy: Challenge and response. In T. Holt (Ed.), *Crime on-line: Correlates, causes, and context* (pp. 61–76). Durham, NC: Carolina Academic Press.

Nhan, J., & Huey, L. (2013). 'We don't have these laser beams and stuff like that': Police investigations as low-tech work in a high-tech world. In S. Leman-Langlois (Ed.), *Technocrime: Policing and surveillance* (pp. 79–90). New York, NY: Routledge.

Nhan, J., Huey, L., & Broll, R. (2015). Digilatism: An analysis of crowdsourcing and the Boston Marathon bombings. *British Journal of Criminology, 57*(2), 341–361. doi:10.1093/bjc/azv118

Nhan, J., Kinkade, P., & Burns, R. (2009). Finding a pot of gold at the end of the Internet rainbow: Further examination of fraudulent email solicitation. *International Journal of Cyber Criminology, 3*(1), 452–475.

O'Neill, M. E. (2000). Old crimes in new bottles: Sanctioning cybercrime. *George Mason Law Review, 9*(2), 237–288.

Pons, E. H., & Perez-Pons, A. (2015). *Social learning theory and ethical hacking: Student perspectives on hacking curriculum.* Proceedings of the Information Systems Education Conference, 32.

Price, R. (2007, September 7). 'Game of Thrones' season 7 was pirated more than 1 billion times. *Business Insider.* Retrieved from http://www.businessinsider.com/game-of-thrones-season-7-pirated-1-billion-times-torrents-streaming-muso-2017-9

Ross, A. (1990). Hacking away at the counterculture. *Postmodern Culture, 1*(1). doi:10.1353/pmc.1990.0011

Seals, T. (2017). 40% of ICS, critical infrastructure targeted by cyberattacks. *Info Security.* Retrieved from https://www.infosecurity-magazine.com/news/40-of-ics-critical-infrastructure

Shane, S., Perlroth, N., & Sanger, D. E. (2017, November 12). Security breach and spilled secrets have shaken the N.S.A. to its core. *New York Times.* Retrieved from https://www.nytimes.com/2017/11/12/us/nsa-shadow-brokers.html

Sheridan, L. P., & Grant, T. (2007). Is cyberstalking different? *Psychology, Crime & Law, 6,* 627–640.

Smith, P. K., Mahdavi, J., Carvalho, M., Fisher, S., Russell, S., & Tippett, N. (2008). Cyberbullying: Its nature and impact in secondary school pupils. *Journal of Child Psychology and Psychiatry, 49,* 376–385.

Sykes, G. M., & Matza, D. (1957). Techniques of neutralization: A theory of delinquency. *American Sociological Review, 22*(6), 664–670.

U.S. Department of Education. (2015). Student reports of bullying and cyber-bullying: Results from the 2013 School Crime Supplement to the National Crime Victimization Survey. NCES 2015-056. Retrieved from https://nces.ed.gov/pubs2015/2015056.pdf

Van Buskirk, J., Naicker, S., Bruno, R., Burns, L., Breen, C., & Roxburgh, A. (2016). Drugs on the Internet. *National Drug & Alcoholic Research Centre, 7.* Retrieved from https://ndarc.med.unsw.edu.au/sites/default/files/ndarc/resources/dnet bulletin_issue7_final.pdf

Wall, D. S. (1999). Cybercrimes: New wine, no bottles? In P. Davies, P. Francis, & V. Jupp (Eds.), *Invisible crimes: Their victims and their regulation* (pp. 105–139). London, UK: Palgrave Macmillan. doi:10.1007/978-1-349-27641-7_5

Woolf, N. (2016, October 26). DDoS attack that disrupted Internet was largest of its kind in history, experts say. *The Guardian.* Retrieved from https://www.theguardian.com/technology/2016/oct/26/ddos-attack-dyn-mirai-botnet

Yar, M. (2005). Computer hacking: Just another case of juvenile delinquency? *Howard Journal of Crime and Justice, 44*(4), 387–399. doi:10.1111/j.1468-2311.2005.00383.x

Zhang, X., Tsang, A., Yue, W. T., & Chau, M. (2015). The classification of hackers by knowledge exchange behaviors. *Information Systems Frontiers, 17,* 1239–1251. doi:10.1007/s10796-015-9567-0

POLICING/LAW ENFORCEMENT

PART III

POLICE THEORY

Major Perspectives

*Dawn M. Irlbeck, Connie M. Koski, and
John P. Crank*

The term *police theory* invites exploration in whatever imaginative direction we could conjure, past and future, that this coercive yet malleable normative world would take us. Would we best serve the field by following existing leads on theoretical development or by branching out on our own? Might we be so bold as to suggest new directions, trying to explore that further and unknown territory of theory-to-be?

Four ways of looking at theory that have a relatively long-standing history: normative-rational, institutional, conflict and critical, and postmodern are presented here. Each of these has something to offer the police scholar, and each has its current limitations. Importantly, they provide us a way to begin to organize this field called police scholarship and to think about where we go next.

NORMATIVE-RATIONAL THEORY

Why do we need police theory? It is obvious that the police exist to do something about crime—if not, then many citizens are being fooled, big time. It is not obvious that we need to know much more than that about them, unless we are looking for a job and want to become a police officer.

Normative-rational perspectives look at police organizations as independent entities and ask what do they do to achieve their mission. Normative means that their work is governed by broad societal norms, in this case, those norms that formally sanction behavior. Rational means that they make reasonable decisions and act on them, based on a rational assessment of their environment.

Two ways of looking at normative perspectives are presented here. The first is through an assessment of contingency theory, which is an explanation of the behavior of police organizations in terms of their environmental setting. The second is an overview of contemporary crime interdiction practices, those that represent the state of the art in police work today.

Contingency Theory

Contingency theory is a rational approach to theory building, but it is different from traditional perceptions of organizational rationality. The characteristic feature of contingency theory is that organizations adapt to the contingencies they face. Their efforts to achieve particular goals consequently depend on the nature of the community and organizational circumstances in which they find themselves.

Donaldson (2001) defined contingency theory as follows: "Organizational effectiveness results from fitting characteristics of the organization, such as its structure, to contingencies that reflect the situation of the organization" (p. 1). Structural contingency theory, which refers to theories or efforts to explain or change organizational structure, refers to perspectives that locate structure in terms of the three contingencies of environment, size, and strategy.

Contingency theory is not universalistic or, in today's jargon, does not lend itself to "best practices." Donaldson notes that contingency refers to adaptive processes: The relationship between any element of structure and its performance is mediated by contingencies that have to be recognized and addressed. A "contingency is any variable that moderates the effect of an organizational characteristic on organizational performance" (p. 7). Consequently, when we seek to understand organizational structure or the behavior of those structures, we take into consideration three issues:

1. There is a relationship between the contingency and the structure.

2. If the contingency changes, the structure changes.

3. The fit between the contingency and the organization determines organizational performance. The better the fit, the more effective will organizational performance be.

The police-community/political environment research is a good example of structural contingency theory where contingency is located in the environment. Since the seminal work of Wilson (1968), researchers have been interested in the relationship between characteristics of the community and policing structure (see Klinger, 2004; Maguire, 2003; Stucky, 2005).

Morabito (2008) hypothesized that particular community political structures would facilitate the adoption of community policing practices. She identified three political structures: (1) jurisdictions with city managers, (2) those with partisan elections, and (3) community characteristics, such as residential stability, diversity, and income that she used as a proxy for variations in district-based elections. She also included the contingencies of organizational size and formalization of structure. Her findings showed that form of government and district-based elections, as well as organizational formalization, emerged as significant predictors of innovation.

Morabito's work is community theory, which can be considered a subcategory of contingency theory. However, from a contingency theory perspective, there is an unasked question: What is the environment–organization mis-fit that structural innovations of community policing addresses? That is, what is the policing problem that community policing addresses and that extant forms of policing do not address? In terms of effectiveness, what is the inefficiency that organizational change toward community policing makes effective?

This is a three-part question: What is it that (1) community policing addresses, that (2) represents a change in the environment, and that (3) resulted from a mis-fit between community policing and the environment—it is not simply academic. It is an organizational issue that has haunted community policing since its inception. One can argue, from a contingency theory perspective, that the rapid rise and institutionalization of data-driven CompStat, with its focus on effectiveness in terms of arrest-driven results, is a result of the mis-fit in community and policing created by the community policing movement, visibly indicated by public perceptions that crime was inadequately addressed (cf., Willis, Mastrofski, & Weisburd, 2007).

In spite of this, contingency theory does not seem to work well for understanding police organizations. Maguire (2003) noted that because departments have unclear outputs and survive from public need in spite of their performance, changes in environmental contingencies have minimal effect on them. However, contemporary trends in policing, with their focus on the production of arrest statistics, increase the importance of such outputs.

Police Effectiveness

Police effectiveness refers specifically to police effort to do something about crime. This area also represents the most applied area of police theory today, in that a great deal of research has focused on the effectiveness of police practices in a wide variety of crime and disorder settings (for an interesting argument for a theory of "police effects," see Cullen & Pratt, 2016).

The signature work on police effectiveness is the tome "Preventing Crime: What Works, What Doesn't, and What's Promising" (Sherman et al., 1996). Sherman et al. (1996) represents a comprehensive evaluation of the effectiveness of Bureau of Justice grants to assist state and local law enforcement and communities in preventing crime. It is the most thorough overview of police practices yet undertaken. The work focuses on institutional settings, including labor markets, places, families, and schools and asks whether research carried out in these settings has had any significant effects on crime. Findings are organized according to two factors: (1) Did the interventions show success, and (2) was the methodology adequate for confidence in the conclusions of the research?

The study of police effectiveness today can be separated into two branches. The first assesses existing practices, and the second looks at innovations, although the difference between the two branches is subtle.

Existing Practices: Homicide

Homicide is perhaps the most important crime police deal with—it is the central focus of a great deal of media attention, and it carries the heaviest penal sanction. Yet the clearance rate for homicide has gone sharply down over the past 50 years. In 1965, the average clearance rate for homicide was 91%. By 2002, it had dropped to 64%. Why?

Cronin, Murphy, Spahr, Toliver, and Weger (2007) present a solid review and analysis of the many facets of police work related to homicide clearance rates. They tracked current organizational practices for homicide—the management of homicide units, the identification of eyewitnesses, interrogation practices, the use of crime labs, and how to deal with cold cases in the age of DNA. This research did not identify a single causative agent—police work by all accounts has substantially improved over the past 50 years—but provided a range of suggestions in each of these areas. For example, the authors, noting that as many as 75% of eyewitnesses misidentify suspects, provided a series of recommendations with regard to the use of eyewitness testimony and for the management and organization of line-ups. This work is an excellent review of many aspects of police work central to contemporary routine police practices.

New Directions: The Return to the Professional Model

Researchers interested in new directions in policing have voluminous materials that they can select. All of the practices listed below represent different ways the police have developed new directions in the past 30 years, and all focus on the mission of crime control:

CompStat—Crime control through managerial oversight and command responsibility.

Lever pulling—Crime control through using all available prosecutorial and police tools to threaten (and carry out) apprehension conviction.

Problem-oriented policing—Crime control by identifying and gaining control of underlying problems.

Broken windows/zero tolerance—Crime control through aggressive order maintenance activity.

Crime mapping—Crime control by visual representation of high crime areas and real-time response.

Third-party policing—Crime control through pressure on third parties who in some way facilitate crime.

Intelligence-led policing—Crime control through higher quality intelligence/information in real time.

Hot-spot policing—Crime control through greater presence/visibility in high-crime areas.

Crackdowns—Heavy use of arrest in areas associated with specific crimes or problems.

Interestingly, these changes have each been housed under community policing, yet none of them involve activities where the police reach out to the community in some pragmatic way, the *sine qua non* of community policing. To the contrary, all represent a rejection of a mission that is not meaningfully tied to crime suppression and prevention. They appear to have piggybacked on community policing's legitimacy and today are emerging as the functional center of a new police professionalism, with the community policing movement in decline. From a historical point of view, we witness in these practices two features: (1) the emergence and continuation of police effectiveness as a strong area of academic research and (2) the return of the field of policing to its professional roots, a neoprofessionalism movement, with a central focus on the law enforcement mission but with a stronger scientific and intelligence-based foundation for its work.

INSTITUTIONAL THEORY

Institutional theory of policing is traced to Mastrofski, Ritti, and Hoffmaster (1987) and theoretically elaborated by Crank and Langworthy (1992) and Crank (1994). Briefly stated, institutional theory is the idea that organizational structure and policy is about satisfying values carried by important constituencies in their environments. It represents a sharp challenge to contingency theories of police organizations. Put simply, organizations in highly institutionalized environments are about constituent values, not technical efficiency. Police organizations, instead of focusing on clear-cut outputs around a core product, such as arrests or traffic stops, for example, turn outward to their institutional environment to determine appropriate organizational structures. This has several meanings:

1. Police departments loosely couple their structures to the technical core so that they can satisfy legitimacy concerns without being held accountable for what they actually do.

2. Departments operate under a "logic of good faith" according to which members support each other and believe in the organization as a matter of faith rather than reliance on measurable outputs.

3. Organizational structures mirror turbulence in the external environment by becoming internally complex. Similarly, organizational complexity is a reflection of environmental conflict. For example, hiring processes tend to build in to their policies and practices broad controversies regarding civil service, gender and race equality, and meritoriousness.

4. Organizations respond to environmental change by adding layers of complexity. Hence, departments tended to respond to community policing by adding community policing units and specialized activities, rather than restructuring or simplifying organizational structures and processes.

Institutional theory itself is in the process of institutionalization in police theory. Yet it faces a broad set of issues.

Issue 1: Transmission of Institutional Expectations

How are institutional values transmitted to organizations? If an institution is a causal agent, the specification of that agent is critical. Giblin (2006), adapting DiMaggio and Powell's (1983) model, identified three means of institutional transmission: mimetic, normative, and coercive pressures. *Mimetic* pressures are those by which organizations borrow convenient items from member organizations in the organizational sector. *Normative* pressures are related to training, accreditation, and education and refer to pressures to conform to broad normative expectations in the institutional environment. *Coercive* pressures refer to compulsory pressures on organizations to conform to their environment. The law, particularly constitutional law, is an example of such a coercive pressure.

Crank (2003), adapting Scott's (1992) model of institutional transmission, identified six ways in which environmental elements are received by police organizations. The first, *imposition*, is the same as coercive noted earlier. *Authorization*, the second, is similar to normative, in that it refers to the way in which broad norms are defined and enforced. However, it refers to more formalistic sources of authority than the general "normative" category. Third, structure and policy may be *induced* in that it is accompanied with rewards for the organization. Crank and Langworthy (1996) described the adoption of community policing as a process of institutional inducement, through which community policing was induced into police organizations through large grants that helped pay for programs and for officer salaries. *Acquisition*, the fourth, is about how organizations deliberately choose elements from their institutional environment. It recognizes that organizations are autonomous actors. The transmission of CompStat across the institutional settings of police organizations can be described as a process of acquisition. *Imprinting*, fifth, occurs when organizations are first formed. For example, one could argue that a militaristic rank structure was imprinted on police organizations in that most of the early departments were post–Civil War and were staffed by Civil War veterans who brought a military posture to the newly minted field of urban policing. Finally, *incorporation* refers to the tendency of multipurpose organizations such as the police to internally map their external environment. Conflicts in that environment will be elaborated in terms of broad policy statements, as in the example of personnel policies mentioned before.

Issue 2: Legitimating Processes

How is it that the process of legitimacy occurs in concrete settings? Vitale (2005) argued that the adoption of quality-of-life policing in New York should be understood in terms of institutional processes. Bratton and Giuliani came to power in New York City in an environment in which police were seen as ineffectual in crime suppression. Bratton and Giuliani had a legitimizing mandate: a "quality of life" philosophy focusing on zero tolerance, frequent use of stop and frisk, broad use of civil enforcement practices, and the creation of other laws and regulations that aimed at controlling disorderly behavior. Through the ongoing commitments and very public support for quality-of-life policing, the mayor and chief led the NYPD through broad and profound change in its nature. Quality-of-life policing, with its intense law enforcement focus on arrest practices through command responsibility, was institutionalized across the organization. Vitale noted the unique historical circumstances behind the NYPD's transition, including the recognition that many elements of the new policing were already underway when Giuliani was elected. This is an excellent study of legitimacy lost and regained and how a department transformed itself and ultimately led the transformation of policing across the United States.

Others have noted the importance of legitimacy for organizational well-being. Crank and Langworthy (1994) argued that the legitimacy of police organizations was carried out as a ceremonial function. The loss of legitimacy was indicated by the firing of the chief and only restored after the selection of a new chief with a new legitimizing mandate. Katz (2001) discussed how a specialized gang unit emerged from constituency pressure and consequently placed greater stock on ceremonial aspects aimed at satisfying environmental "sovereigns" rather than on substantive efforts to actually do something about gangs.

Police Legitimacy and Procedural Justice Theory

More recently, attention has focused directly on legitimacy and the police–citizen encounter itself. This theoretical perspective, particularly highlighted by the significant and growing body of work of Tyler and various colleagues, argues that citizens' perceptions of fairness have the most influence over their attitudes toward criminal justice officials (Tyler 1990, 2001; Tyler & Folger, 1980). Importantly, the emphasis is on the interaction *process* versus its outcome, with citizens often placing greater importance on perceived treatment during the encounter than the final outcome of that encounter. Police legitimacy, or public confidence that the police are fair and equitable, is important to the police role in society and, when lost, can result in a general loss of trust, respect, and confidence. This, in turn, can negatively impact police effectiveness, resulting in a lack of citizen cooperation and decreased crime reporting. Thus, the individual behaviors of police officers and the institutional strategies adopted by police organizations in this regard are of critical importance (Sunshine & Tyler, 2003).

It is relevant to ponder how procedural justice theory can impact both the fairness of individual officers' actions, as well as institutional approaches that ensure a culture in which the effective execution of problem-solving and crime-fighting strategies (or "procedures") are fair and just. For instance, Gau and Brunson (2010) presented several recommendations that would assist law enforcement agencies in alleviating concerns over aggressive stop-and-frisk practices. Roberg and colleagues (2015) go a step further by suggesting that the "most straightforward approach would be for police departments to demand that officers always act in a courteous and respectful manner when interacting with the public—poor or rich, urban or rural—whether formally (legally) or informally" (p. 144) and conclude by suggesting a number of ways in which police managers could encourage such behavior within their organization. The application of this theoretical approach to the business of policing, while still evolving, has the potential to hold significant promise for the practice of policing, especially among communities with historically low levels of trust in the police as an institution.

Issue 3: Empirical Testing Against Contingency Theory

Few authors have taken on what might be called the institutional-contingency debate. This debate is whether police practices and organizational changes are better understood in terms of contingency theory or institutional theory. Two works are noted in this regard.

Willis, Mastrofski, and Weisburd (2001) provide a qualitative assessment of three police organizations that adopted CompStat practices. All three organizations took technical issues into consideration, but the speed and pattern of acceptance of CompStat elements suggested that CompStat was adopted in response to "institutional pressures to appear progressive and successful" (p. 148). Though not using the term, this study provided an excellent example of loose coupling, in that actual crime control practices remained fundamentally unchanged in spite of a broad administrative refocusing on crime control. This has important theoretical implications that deserve further consideration. The theoretical study of organizations should not posit institutional and technical perspectives as contradictory or categorical but should consider each as part of the overall contribution to organizational success. It may be that organizational well-being requires both. That is, it must attend to technical requirements in its work on its product core, formalized in the public sector in terms of the mission or charter of the organization, and also ceremonially dress up its product to impress audiences who would like to know why the public should continue to fund it.

Giblin (2006), looking at the expansion of crime analysis units nationally, used measures derived from both perspectives. Unfortunately, his findings provided little support for either perspective—none of his predictors were significant at the .05 level. However, his data trended in the direction of support for institutional predictors, an interpretation he indicated was justifiable based on relatively small sample sizes.

Issue 4: Understanding the Sweep of Police History

Institutional theory reminds us that there was not a "catechism" of police, as McEwen (1996) once noted, but that changes in police structure and practices are a consequence of broad changes in the environment of policing. Crank and Langworthy (1994) noted how the emergence of community policing, responsive to the urban conflicts of the 1960s, was initially aimed at building bridges between the African American community and the police. Yet with an increasingly conservative electorate in the 1980s, community policing had shifted to aggressive, public-order-oriented practices based on "broken windows" justifications for harsh treatment of minor crimes in spite of its alienating effects on minority communities.

Ritti and Mastrofski (2002), in what is likely the exemplar of empirical analysis of institutional research, described the spread of community policing across the American landscape as a three-phase institutional process. The first phase, growing dissatisfaction with a problem, reflected the concerns about policing emerging from the 1960s and early 1970s. The second phase, called "consensus about what to do about the problem," reflected the spread of community policing as an umbrella term, and its creative adaptation in many departments outside those associated with its emergence. The third phase, "effectiveness transmission of practices," was a period of intense assessment of community policing practices in a few large departments across the country. The fourth, "institutional transmission of practices," marked the period in which community policing practices were adopted, not because they were critically assessed but because they were the "right thing to do." They represented the new symbolic face of policing for the public and carried with them the appropriate discourse legitimizing the uncritical adoption of practices. Particularly useful was the way in which the authors operationalized their analysis. Ritti and Mastrofski's work is particularly helpful for researchers looking for ways of measuring institutional-level variables.

Institutional theory has been around in policing for 15 to 25 years, depending on where one locates its first efforts in policing. It has the support of a small but strong body of theorists and researchers. It is this paper's view that its success today is due largely to the works of Mastrofski who, working alone and with others, has provided a body of research aimed at the empirical measurement of institutional theory. Students are encouraged to look at the body of this work (Mastrofski &

Ritti, 1996, 2000; Mastrofski & Uchida, 1996; Mastrofski, Ritti, & Hoffmaster, 1987; Ritti & Mastrofski, 2002; Willis, Mastrofski, & Weisburd, 2007) to both examine efforts to quantify institutional theory and to empirically compare institutional and contingency theory. It is this body of work that has set the standard for the empirical assessment of institutional theory in policing in the current era.

CONFLICT THEORY

The Traditions of Conflict Theory

Conflict theory refers to a multifaceted set of perspectives loosely organized around the idea that strategies of crime control serve the interests of dominant groups (Holmes, 2000). Turk (1969) extended Blalock's (1967) work by suggesting that culturally and racially dissimilar subordinate groups are perceived as threatening to the social and political order and are therefore more disproportionally subject to arrest and punishment by the criminal justice system. Quinney (1970) expanded this further in arguing that law is the primary means of establishing order in heterogeneous communities in order to compensate for the declining significance of informal control mechanisms. Liska, Chamlin, and Reed (1985) drew upon Blalock's threat hypothesis to further argue that an increase in the percentage of non-Whites increases the threat of crime perceived by authorities, thereby leading to increases in both the size of the crime control apparatus and the pressure on that apparatus to control crime.

Law enforcement activities, from a conflict perspective, are a reaction to the threat that minority groups pose to the racial majority. As Jacobs (1979) explained, "Conflict theorists maintain that the control of crime and deviance proceeds in accord with the wishes of those with power who use this control to further their own narrow interests" (p. 913). For instance, conflict theorists have demonstrated strong relationships between the size of minority populations and police resources and expenditures (Jackson & Carroll, 1981), as well as the size of police forces (Jacobs, 1979).

Three primary variations of conflict theory, all of which affect police research, have emerged: The racial threat thesis, the inequality thesis, and the racial disturbance thesis. The racial threat thesis, initially put forth by Blalock, suggests that minority group threat increases with the size of the minority population. This relationship may be curvilinear: It increases until minority groups reach a certain level, beyond which it diminishes. Results have historically tended to demonstrate that relative strength of police forces in the early 1970s was positively impacted by the size of their Black population. The inequality thesis, on the other hand, is a slightly different version of conflict theory that focuses on economic inequalities in a community rather than on the presence of racial minorities as the source of the threat that generates social control efforts, such as heightened policing.

From this perspective, places where there are substantial economic resource inequalities are places where the advantaged have the resources and desire to defend against those who do not. Additionally, since the police constitute the primary governmental institution responsible for "the coercive maintenance of stability and order," enhanced police strength may be expected in areas where greater economic inequality is found (Jacobs, 1979, p. 914). Finally, the racial disturbance thesis asserts that potential threats influenced by minority group mobilizations, such as significant racial uprisings or riots, may directly affect the amount of resources devoted to policing. It is this facet of conflict theory that has been the least empirically supported in the literature (Jackson & Carroll, 1981; Sharp, 2006).

Overview: Research on Conflict Theory and the Police

Rational Choice and Conflict

Holmes, Smith, Freng, and Munoz (2008) provide an empirical analysis of police department expenditures and size, drawing on conflict and rational choice perspectives to construct contrasting hypotheses. The strength of their analysis is both the comparative analysis of two important and competing theoretical traditions and the recognition that the specification of a minority group—in this case, Latino—requires a greater degree of specificity than is usually done.

Rational choice theory maintains that resources are distributed in accordance with the need for crime control. Conflict theory counters that resources are allocated with the aim of controlling racial and ethnic minorities. In other words, the police are the principal agents of action for rational theorists, while for conflict theorists, the police serve as the principal agents of domestic coercion (Bittner, 1970), and resource allocations to police departments largely determine the crime control capacity of states (Liska, 1992). From rational choice, then, the distribution of resources to policing is tied to community crime rates. The central focus of the minority threat perspective, on the other hand, looks at distribution in terms of "percentage minority" from the total population (most often White/Black).

Holmes et al. (2008) note that the effects of minority threat "may depend on factors such as region and the degree of racial and ethnic tension" (p. 137). Previous research on the Hispanic minority threat has found that percentage Hispanic is related positively and strongly to the incidence of police brutality civil rights criminal complaints in large southwestern cities. Additionally, it has been found that the dominant group, whose anxieties are fueled by media portrayals and political rhetoric, would marshal their superior political power to ensure allocations of public resources to policing. From conflict theory, then, the authors hypothesized that the perceived threat potential of Hispanics in the Southwest should result in greater allocations of fiscal and personnel resources to policing in southwestern cities with relatively large and relatively poor Hispanic populations, particularly those in close proximity to the border with Mexico.

The key contribution of this study's analysis, beyond providing support for conflict perspectives, is the identification of within-group class distinctions as potentially more important indicators of minority threat, at least in the Southwest, than percentage Hispanic. Allocations of police resources appear to be tied to the presence of poor Hispanics on both sides of the border, pointing to the relevance of the intersection of class and ethnicity to public policy decisions in the region.

Agency Size and Race Conflict

Sharp (2006) presents hypotheses from racial threat, inequality, and racial disturbance theses to assess the growth of police organizations. It is a creative use of conflict theory to assess police organizational size, more typically studied in contingency theories of the police. He particularly focuses on the historical legacy of police force growth in the 1960s–1970s era of racial turmoil and the playing out of racial threat dynamics in that era. The latter may have led to a shift in the base levels of department size.

Sharp's findings indicate:

1. The baseline or legacy effect of the department's relative force size as of 1980 appeared to consistently be the most important predictor of contemporary organizational size.

2. A city's more contemporary experience with racial disturbances is consistently the next most important predictor of contemporary force size. (In other words, more significant than the "legacy" effect.)

3. Although the racial threat thesis is unsupported when it is assessed in terms of the prevalence of Blacks in the population, there is evidence for this thesis when all minority groups are included in the analysis.

Contemporary racial threat and racial insurgency, more than historical/legacy influences, are the key predictors of enhanced contemporary police strength (i.e., cities that have encountered recent race riots from 1980–2000). This alone does not explain the actual processes by which local policy makers react to race riots: A qualitative, case study approach is needed to possibly uncover what she describes as the "veiled discourse" (Sharp, 2006, p. 303) that may be at play. She also argues that future research needs to focus on minorities more broadly and move away from the White or non-Black versus Black dichotomies that have historically been analyzed.

The staffing of U.S. police agencies, the author concluded, appears to be an artifact of the "social control phenomenon of subduing a population perceived to be rebellious" (Sharp, 2006, p. 305). This research also showed that crime rates, though most often studied in terms of functionalism, could be incorporated into conflict perspectives. That is, police force size is an important part of the material frequently shaped and used by public officials in marketing the fear of crime (see Chambliss, 1999).

Drug Arrests and Conflict

This research provides an assessment of both conflict and social disorganization variables in the prediction of drug arrests in 187 U.S. cities. Mosher (2001) argued that "spatial differences in rates of drug arrests are particularly relevant to the central tenets of conflict theory" (p. 88). Narcotics legislation in the U.S., he noted, have been used to control minority populations, especially since the intensity in the "war on drugs" increased in the 1980s. Mosher also points out that social disorganization and conflict theories posit that numerous measures of inequality will be related to higher drug arrest rates. Social disorganization, however, generally predicts that the effect of a population's ethnic/racial composition is mediated through structural indicators of the relative disadvantage of minority groups when compared with Whites. Contrarily, conflict theory (especially the variation focused on minority threat—e.g., Blalock, 1967) predicts that racial/ethnic composition will have an independent positive effect on drug arrest rates that will hold true even when relative economic disadvantage is controlled for. Finally, conflict theory predicts that police strength would exert a strong independent effect on the drug arrest rate across cities.

Mosher found that the percentage African American is a statistically significant predictor of variation in possession arrest rates across cities, even when controlling for race-specific economic deprivation. And when he looked at trafficking arrests, Mosher found percentage African American was the strongest predictor of arrest rates. Additionally, cities with more police per square mile had higher trafficking arrest rates. In sum, Mosher's findings provide strong support for the predictions developed from conflict theory.

Conflict and Racial Profiling

One of the more controversial issues in the current era is racial profiling, which refers to the perception that police make decisions to act based on the race of an individual. Petrocelli, Piquero, and Smith (2003) carried out a micro-level analysis of police practices using census tract data from a single city to examine how neighborhood context may influence police behavior. To what extent, this research asked, are police stop, search, and arrest decisions function of neighborhood demographic and socioeconomic characteristics in this particular city? Findings indicated that the percentage of African American population was significantly related to the percentage of stops resulting in a search, and this was especially the case in Black neighborhoods. In addition, the number of police stops were significantly higher in neighborhoods with higher rates of Part I crime. Notably, however, in areas where there was a higher percentage of Black population, the chance of stops involving at least one arrest/summons is lower. Similarly, in high crime rate areas, the chance of a stop involving at least one arrest/summons is lower.

These findings describe a *hurdle effect*. The likelihood of being stopped seems to be more a function of the crime rate in the area than demographic and/or socio-economic characteristics. After the initial stop, however, searches appear to be more prevalent in neighborhoods with higher percentages of Black residents. They assert that this could be the result of one or two things: "ecological bias" (officer responses tied to neighborhood characteristics) or that officers are more likely to search African American residents based on general perceptions or stereotypes.

Hence, though finding support for a race effect, these findings do not overall tend to support a conflict explanation. Such would hold that officers would be more likely to profile poor, minority areas and to make a higher percentage of stops in such areas. Instead, the crime rate appears to be a more important factor in the decision to stop.

Conflict and Communicative Action

This final paper (Schneider, 1999) is based in grounded theory, which looks at conflict and communication among Vancouver, British Colombia, residents. This study is particular in that it represents an effort to look at Habermas's ideas of communicative action as a recipe for conflicts between the police and community groups. Schneider argued that police officers, despite an advocacy of community policing, might be undermining their policing programs through communication problems with residents of socially disadvantaged neighborhoods (SDNs). Schneider defined communication broadly, ranging from interpersonal, verbal or nonverbal personal communications to mass communication, such as the promotion of a crime prevention program by a police department.

He found that police officers in this jurisdiction engaged in "unilingual" communication, demonstrated a limited range of different cultures, showed a lack of empathy with special-needs groups, and overused technical jargon offensive or overtly authoritative. These communication practices perpetuated "the ongoing asymmetrical power relations" between the police and residents of these neighborhoods, ultimately undermining community policing efforts. Community policing programs, Schneider suggested, typically began with the broad assumption that society was pluralistic and that all communities had similar problems, needs, and access to political and economic resources. That assumption resulted in a law enforcement mindset that approached crime prevention and community policing programs with a language geared toward "stable, ethnically homogeneous (i.e., white) middle and upper income neighborhoods." In SDNs, however, this type of approach inevitably failed to address the unique, specific needs and demands of poorer, less empowered neighborhoods.

Schneider concluded that COP principles and practices required a revised theoretical framework oriented toward (1) reducing power relations between the police and SDNs and (2) avoiding the technical, authoritative approaches characteristic of community policing. A more effective approach would be an "affective-emotional model that places community safety in the broader context of community and social development," rather than the rational, detached, and objective approach typically followed in contemporary law enforcement (p. 362). The adoption of

Habermas's theory of communicative action would facilitate "undistorted communication as a means to reduce asymmetrical power relations between social groups, address[ing] the epistemological weaknesses inherent in liberal community policing theory" (p. 362) (see also Forester, 1993, 1989). Shifts in the power differential between SDNs and the police, however, will not be accomplished by improving communication alone. An effective critical approach of community policing must also include contributions to the social, economic, and political development of and sharing of control of crime prevention decision-making and resources with SDNs by law enforcement agents.

POSTMODERNISM

Postmodernism carries several meanings. In this discussion, we are interested in two: postmodernism as a philosophy of rejection of the modern and postmodernism as a time period, also sometimes called late modern, representing the rejection of or the fulfillment of modernism depending on whom one reads.

The Philosophy of Postmodernism

Postmodern theory is sometimes located under the umbrella of critical theory, gaining prominence in the mid-1970s. However, though postmodernism continues to look at social class as one of the major causes of crime, it adds other dimensions of inequality such as race and gender, which together are coproductive of the conditions of crime. Like critical criminology, postmodernism is less a theory about crime causation than an attempt to develop a more profound policy response to or deeper understanding of the causes of crime. In addition, postmodernism is interested in how structured inequalities (social class, race/ethnicity, and gender) contribute to and are reinforced by a culture that makes these divisions seem real. These social divisions, while faced as real and substantive, are socially constructed and can, if subjected to critical analysis, be deconstructed or dissolved (Lanier & Henry, 1998).

Postmodernism, as a philosophy, looks at the symbolic, everyday, and formal use of language that underpins the socially constructed nature of societies' rules, norms, and values. These languages represent discourses and are central to what is defined as criminal and to the way in which society is a source of crime (Lanier & Henry, 1998). Consequently, postmodernism highlights the significance of language and signs in the arena of crime and criminal justice and offers a source of concepts that capture elements of an emerging reality in the new context and set of conditions in which crime occurs, the current postmodern period (Schwartz & Friedrichs, 1994).

Postmodern is often questioned for its failure to provide answers to the questions it raises. Yet that expectation reveals a misunderstanding of much of postmodernism. One can look at the brooding works of Cesar Vallejo and Jean-Paul Sartre—not normally considered postmodernists—and see a great deal of what postmodernism is about in their dark existentialism. Postmodernism is a rejection—once discourse is shattered, it is unclear that anything remains underneath. Take away the meaning of a word, and sometimes all that is left is the jarring sound of mismatched consonants, conveying nothing. Only the most optimistic wing of postmodernism sees qualities of the human condition that somehow prevail with the deconstruction of the taken for granted.

Postmodernism as Historical Epoch

As explained by postmodern theorist T. R. Young (1997), premodern understanding of law and justice was based on the idea of "natural" laws, given by God. The existing social hierarchy—and the corresponding system of rights and privileges—was right and proper, natural. Modernism, carried in Enlightenment ideals, replaced the good of god with the good of the individual. The American justice system, for example, was founded upon a statement of natural law in its Declaration of Independence, and moved the basis of law-making from the gods and/or nature to human beings acting in democratic concert. The priest was replaced with the research scientist, and modern criminology pays homage to the data gatherer rather than the scriptural message. Postmodernism represents the dismantling or rejection of modern discourses. The legacy of modernism and its vanities of progress, far from a democratic peace, is the firebombing of Dresden and the annihilation of the citizens of Hiroshima in thermonuclear fire.

Some recognize the interplay between both the philosophy and the historical sweep of postmodernism: Young (1995), in this regard, noted that "whereas modern science privileges objectivity, rationality, power, control, inequality, and hierarchy, postmodernists deconstruct each theory and each social practice by locating it in its larger socio-historical context in order to reveal that human hand and the group interests which shape the course of self-understanding" (pp. 578–579).

Police and Postmodernism

Postmodernism literature on the police tends to view them in terms of adaptation to a postmodernist landscape. Whereas in the modern period, policing was dictated by a militaristic, hierarchical, technical-rational, bureaucratic model of authority, in the postmodern (sometimes called late modern) era, the role of the police is seen as more fluid and multilateral. Policing becomes much more complex, characterized by (1) the fragmentation of values and moralities; (2) globalization; (3) a rise in consumerism, including private policing; (4) a hollowing out of the nation-state (Reiner, 1992; Sheptycki, 1995); the emergence of a "risk society" (see, for example, Beck, 1986/1992; DeLint, 1999); and (6) adaptive risk-based policing strategies (see Ericson & Hagerty, 1997). One of the key implications for postmodern policing is the shift to a focus on discourse and mode of consumerism, where the community and community policing become coauthored in the same discourse (Reiner, 1992; see Clark, 2005).

Waters (2007) discusses how the rhetoric of police reform is consistent with postmodern notions of discourse. Official discourse about police reform and policing developments, he argues, is overwhelmingly couched in terms consistent with postmodern discourse. Sheptycki (2002) discusses contradictions between the modernist police setting and a postmodern one. The fragmented terrain of the policing field poses accountability problems not easily answered by the traditional model of constitutional control in a militaristic hierarchy.

Ericson and Haggerty (1997) focus on the communication systems that institutions develop to identify and manage risks and on how the police become involved in these systems. The police are seen as being in a complex, ambiguous, shifting, and contradictory field of risk management in relation to other institutions. This excellent work provides a sense of the fluid systems in which police find themselves and how they are adapting to those systems.

Manning and Singh (1997) focus on symbolic violence in the rhetoric of community policing. Using a case study of community policing in one western U.S. city, based on interviews with police, observations, and focus groups, they found that COP rhetoric is used as a public discourse. Yet the daily interdiction practices of patrol officers is relatively unchanged. Moreover, the absence of a crime control emphasis alters public perceptions of the police while undercutting police morale.

Miller (2007) argues that data collection, the primary response to concerns over racial profiling, is ineffective, largely because it is driven primarily by police concerns about developing and maintaining the perception of responsiveness to public desires. That is, profiling is a symbolic response to the public perceptions of crime and, hence, difficult to eradicate in view of contradictions between public and legal expectations of police behavior. Using LEMAS data, Miller assesses the extent to which "antiracial profiling policies" are implemented.

CONCLUSION

One can see through this tour of police theory that police provide an amazing, colorful, and richly detailed palate on which to paint a theory. They provide substantive analysis for policy and theory from institutions to individuals and encompass us in the sweep of history. We have only looked at a few of the many writings on the police—we leave it to the reader to explore from here. There is much to enjoy—and an unfair share of pain and suffering as well—on that journey. One thing you can be sure. You will be engaged in a study of people as they really are—sometimes without benefit of social custom and often layered in controversy—and in the end, you may learn much about yourself, as well as the complexities of social life, the quest for order and community safety, as well as the undeniable influence of human agency and the surety of social change.

Discussion Questions

1. What is police criminology? Is it similar to scientific criminology?

2. What is institutional theory? Why is legitimacy central to understanding institutional theory?

3. Are the police shifting from a community policing model to a different model (i.e., neoprofessionalism)? Justify your answer from

information presented in this chapter and from personal experience.

4. According to this chapter, what is the relationship between race and the police?

5. What is the link between conflict theory and profiling?

6. Identify three implications of postmodernism for the police.

References

Beck, U. (1992). *Risk society: Towards a new modernity* (M. Ritter, Trans.). Newbury Park, CA: Sage. (Original work published 1986)

Bittner, E. (1970). *The functions of police in modern society*. Washington, DC: Government Printing Office.

Clark, M. (2005). The importance of a new philosophy to the post modern policing environment. *Policing: An International Journal of Police Strategies and Management, 28*(4), 642–653.

Cronin, J., Murphy, G., Spahr, L., Toliver, J., & Weger, R. (2007). Promoting effective homicide investigations. *Office of COPS publication*. Washington, DC: Police Executive Research Forum.

Crank, J. P. (1994). Watchman and community: Myth and institutionalization in policing. *Law and Society Review, 28*(2), 325–351.

Crank, J. P. (2002). *Imagining justice*. Cincinnati, OH: Anderson Press.

Crank, J. P. (2003). *Understanding police culture* (2nd ed.). Cincinnati, OH: Anderson Press.

Crank, J. P., & Langworthy, R. H. (1992). An institutional perspective of policing. *Journal of Criminal Law and Criminology, 83*, 338–363.

Crank, J. P., & Langworthy, R. H. (1996). Fragmented centralization and the organization of the police. *Police and Society, 6*, 213–229.

Cullen, F. T., & Pratt, T. C. (2016). Toward a theory of police effects. *Criminology and Public Policy, 15*(3), 799–811.

DeLint, W. (1999). A post-modern turn in policing: Policing as pastiche? *International Journal of the Sociology of Law, 27*(2), 127–152.

DiMaggio, P., & Powell, W. W. (1983). The iron cage revisited: Institutionalized isomorphism and collective rationality in organizational fields. *American Sociological Review, 48*, 147–160.

Donaldson, L. (2001). *The contingency theory of organizations*. Thousand Oaks, CA: Sage.

Ericson, R., & Haggerty, K. (1997). *Policing the risk society*. Oxford, UK: Clarendon Press.

Forester, J. (1989). *Planning in the face of power*. Berkeley, CA: University of California Press.

Forester, J. (1993). *Critical theory, public policy and planning practice: Toward a critical pragmatism*. Albany, NY: State University of New York Press.

Gau, J., & Brunson, R. K. (2010). Procedural justice and order maintenance policing: A study of inner-city young men's perceptions of police legitimacy. *Justice Quarterly, 27*, 255–279.

Giblin, M. (2006). Structural elaboration and institutional isomorphism: The case of crime analysis units. *Policing: An International Journal of Police Practices and Management, 29*, 643–664.

Holmes, M. D., Smith, B. W., Freng, A. B., & Muñoz, E. A. (2008). Minority threat, crime control, and police resource allocations in the southwestern United States. *Crime & Delinquency, 54*(1), 128–152.

Jacobs, D. (1979). Inequality and police strength: Conflict theory and coercive control in metropolitan areas. *American Sociological Review, 44*(6), 913–925.

Katz, C. (2001). The establishment of a police gang movement: An examination of organizational and environmental factors. *Criminology, 39*, 37–74.

Klinger, D. (2004). Environment and organization: Reviving a perspective on the police. *ANNALS of the American Academy of Political and Social Science, 5931*, 119–136.

Lanier, M. M., & Henry, S. (1998). *Essential criminology*. Boulder, CO: Westview Press.

Liska, A. E. (1992). Introduction to the study of social control. In A. E. Liska (Ed.), *Social threat and social control* (p. 1–32). Albany, NY: State University of New York Press.

Liska, A., Chamlin, M., & Reed, M. (1985). Testing the economic production and conflict models of crime control. *Social Forces, 64*, 119–138.

Maguire, E. (2003). *Organizational structure in American police agencies*. Albany, NY: State University of New York Press.

Manning, P. K., & Singh, M. P. (1997). Violence and hyperviolence: The rhetoric and practice of community policing. *Sociological Spectrum, 17*(3), 339–361.

Mastrofski, S. D., & Ritti, R. R. (1996). Police training and the effects of organization on drunk driving enforcement. *Justice Quarterly, 13*, 291–320.

Mastrofski, S. D., & Ritti, R. R. (2000). Making sense of community policing: A theoretical perspective. *Police Practice and Research: An International Journal, 2*, 183–210.

Mastrofski, S. D., Ritti, R. R., & Hoffmaster, D. (1987). Organizational determinants of police discretion: The case of drinking-driving. *Journal of Criminal Justice, 15*, 387–402.

Mastrofski, S. D., & Uchida, C. D. (1993). Transforming the police. *Journal of Research in Crime and Delinquency, 30*(3), 330–358.

McEwen, T. (1996). National data collection on police use of force (Joint publication with National Institute of Justice). Washington, DC: Office of Justice Programs.

Miller, K. (2007). Racial profiling and postmodern society: Police responsiveness, image maintenance, and the left flank of police legitimacy. *Journal of Contemporary Criminal Justice, 23*(3), 248–262.

Morabito, M. (2008). The adoption of police innovation: The role of the political environment. *Policing: An International Journal of Police Strategies and Management, 31*, 466–484.

Mosher, C. (2001). Predicting drug arrest rates: Conflict theory and social disorganization perspectives. *Crime and Delinquency, 47*(1), 84–104.

Petrocelli, M., Piquero, A., & Smith, M. R. (2003). Conflict theory and racial profiling: An empirical analysis of police traffic stop data. *Journal of Criminal Justice, 31*(1), 1–11.

Quinney, R. (1970). *The social reality of crime*. Boston, MA: Little Brown.

Reiner, R. (1992). Policing a postmodern society. *Modern Law Review, 55*(6), 761–781.

Ritti, R., & Mastrofski, S. (2002). *The institutionalization of community policing*. Unpublished Manuscript.

Roberg, R., Novak, K., Cordner, G., & Smith, B. (2015). *Police & society* (6th ed.). New York, NY: Oxford University Press.

Schneider, S. R. (1999). Overcoming barriers to communication between police and socially disadvantaged neighbourhoods. *Crime, Law and Social Change, 30*, 347–377.

Schwartz, M., & Friedrichs, D. (1994). Postmodern thought and criminological discontent: New metaphors for understanding violence. *Criminology, 32*, 221–246.

Scott, R. (1992). Unpacking institutional arguments. In W. Powell & P. DiMaggio (Eds.), *The new institutionalism in organizational analysis* (pp. 164–183). Chicago, IL: University of Chicago Press.

Sharp, E. B. (2006). Policing urban America: A new look at the politics of agency size. *Social Science Quarterly, 87*(2), 291–307.

Sherman, L., Gottfredson, D., Mackensie, D., Eck, J., Reuter, P., Bushway, S., and the members of the graduate program. (1997). *Preventing crime: What works, what doesn't, and what's promising.* Washington, DC: U.S. Department of Justice.

Sheptycki, J. (1995). Transnational policing and the makings of a postmodern state. *British Journal of Criminology, 35,* 613–631.   .

Sheptycki, J. (2002). Accountability across the policing field: Towards a general cartography of accountability for post-modern policing. *Policing and Society, 12*(4), 323–338.

Snipes, J., & Maguire, E. (2007). Foundations of criminal justice theory. In D. Duffee & E. Maguire (Eds.), *Criminal justice theory: Explaining the nature and behavior of criminal justice.* New York, NY: Routledge.

Stucky, T. (2005). Local politics and police strength. *Justice Quarterly, 22,* 139–169.

Sunshine, J., & Tyler, T. R. (2003) The role of procedural justice and legitimacy in shaping public support for policing. *Law & Society Review, 37*(3), 555.

Turk, A. (1969). *Criminality and legal order.* Chicago, IL: Rand McNally.

Tyler, T. R. (1990). *Why people obey the law.* New Haven, CT: Yale University Press.

Tyler, T. R. (2001). Public trust and confidence in legal authorities: What do majority and minority group members want from the law and legal institutions? *Behavioral Sciences and the Law, 19,* 215–235.

Tyler, T. R., & Folger, R. (1980). Distributional and procedural aspects of satisfaction with citizen-police encounters. *Basic and Applied Social Psychology, 1,* 281–292.

Vitale, A. (2005). Innovation and institutionalization: Factors in the development of "quality of life" policing in New York. *Policing and Society, 15,* 99–124.

Waters, I. (2007). Policing, modernity and postmodernity. *Policing & Society, 17*(3), 257–278.

Willis, J., Mastrofski, S., & Weisburd, D. (2007). Making sense of CompStat: A theory-based analysis of organizational change in three police departments. *Law and Society Review, 41,* 147–178.

Wilson, J. (1968). *Varieties of police behavior.* Cambridge, MA: Harvard University Press.

Young, T. R. (1997). *A constitutive theory of justice: Architecture and content.* No. 004 Distributed as part of the Red Feather Institute Postmodern Criminology Series. Boulder, CO: The Red Feather Institute.

Young, T. R. (1995). *The Red Feather dictionary of critical social science.* Boulder, CO: Red Feather Institute.

16

A VISION OF CONTEMPORARY POLICING

Present Practices and Future Developments

Gennaro F. Vito

PARADIGMS IN POLICING

My mission here is to review present police practices, use them to predict what policing will focus upon, and get you to think about what you may do in law enforcement. To accomplish these tasks, let us begin by describing the dominant innovations in police operations in recent years to see where we may be going. Thus, our objectives are (1) to review paradigms of police operations, (2) to determine the origins of these approaches, (3) to determine where we are today, and (4) to consider where we are going.

A paradigm is "a mental screen or cognitive filter through which information must pass before it can be integrated into human thought processes and behaviors" (More, Vito, & Walsh, 2012, p. 139). While paradigms explain and guide operations, they also can impede progress by limiting our ability to recognize and develop new ways of doing things by restraining our thought processes to existing methods that have proven to be successful in the past (Covey, 2004, p. 26; More, Vito, & Walsh, 2012). In recent years, there has been a paradigm shift in police operations—innovative changes in practice that have shaken traditional organizational methods and tactics.

THE BRITISH PARADIGM: BALANCING DEMOCRATIC PRINCIPLES AND THE MILITARY MODEL

Mostly, modern police agencies developed in the 18th and 19th centuries as a response to the rise of industrialized, urban societies. In large cities, policing could no longer be the responsibility of all citizens. Urban policing is largely a modern phenomenon that was developed to deal with urban crime and disorder. In 1829, the Home Secretary, Sir Robert Peel, established and organized the first metropolitan police force in London. These actions were undertaken because of the passage of the Metropolitan Police Act—"An Act for Improving the Police In and Near the Metropolis." There were 10 essential elements of "Peelian Reform" (Johnson, 1981, pp. 59–60):

1. The police must be stable, efficient, and organized along military lines. Their policies must be independent of social and political influence.

2. The police must be under governmental control. Their basic mission is to prevent crime. The only alternative is the use of military force and severe legal punishments.

3. The police must secure and maintain the respect of the public to effectively maintain law and order. The best way to achieve this goal is to provide impartial service to all members of the community regardless of their wealth or social standing. Public support makes the exercise of force unnecessary.

4. The police should be ready to protect and preserve life while sacrificing their own. The police are also members of the community and should act in its best interests. In a sense, the police are paid to perform tasks that are the duty of every member of the community.

5. The police must refrain from seeming to act as agents of revenge, usurping the powers of the judiciary, judging guilt and punishing the guilty.

6. Physical force should be used only as a last resort when persuasion, advice, and warning have failed to result in cooperation. When force is exercised, it should be the minimum degree that is necessary to maintain order.

7. The test of police efficiency is the absence of crime and disorder, not the visible evidence of police action in dealing with them.

8. The distribution of crime news is essential.

9. The deployment of police strength both by time and area is essential.

10. The securing and training of proper persons is at the root of efficiency.

These themes have had a great influence upon the evolution of policing, especially the community policing paradigm. Many of them serve as guidelines today.

The London police were called "Bobbies" regarding their founder. Again, Peel believed the main mission of the police was crime prevention through patrol. These officers occupied the streets and patrolled their beats. Unlike the watchmen they replaced, their visibility discouraged law breaking through deterrence. Structured along military lines, these 1,000 officers wore uniforms but were unarmed. Their administrative structure was modeled after the military. Although ultimately responsible to the Home Secretary and Parliament, two commissioners were in charge of the police force.

The first two police commissioners were Colonel Charles Rowan and Richard Mayne. Naturally, the greatest fear among the public was that the police would become a "secret police" that would enforce political views. Therefore, it was crucial that the police obtained the support of the public. Rowan and Mayne insisted that the police force obtained its authority from the English Constitution and that their behavior was determined by rules of law (Uchida, 1993, p. 20). This approach tied the police to accepted and firmly established societal institutions that ensured their acceptance (Klockars, 1985, p. 49). They also developed a strong administrative structure with centralized authority. In addition, police officers were selected, retained, and promoted on the basis of merit. In 1856, Parliament passed a law that permitted justices of the peace to form police forces.

The newly established police force soon ran into serious problems. There was a threefold turnover of the officer population. Dismissals for corruption and drinking on duty were common (Klockars, 1985, p. 42). Despite these initial difficulties, the London policing experiment was adopted across the country and on the continent. Their development also profoundly influenced the structure and nature of policing in America.

This review of the British police paradigm reveals several basic themes. To be effective in a democratic society, the police must represent society in all of its segments. Policing began as a responsibility of citizens to keep the peace and respect the rights of others. Even when a police force is established, this responsibility cannot be shirked and simply passed on to government. In fact, Peel took pains to demonstrate that the police force was not an agency of the government and not a political force commanded by the party in power. To be accepted and effective, the police must be tied to the norms and institutions of the country. The police cannot fight crime without community aid and support. Ultimately, the police represent and are accountable to the people they serve.

While Peel's reforms led to development of a "professional" police force, they had several unintended consequences. The strong administrative structure and recognition of the police as specialized workers led to cutting the close community ties necessary to do the job. This image led to the feeling that only the police know how to do their job—or at least the best way to do it. Besides abuse of authority, the police face problems with corruption due to their work. Substance abuse (in this case, alcohol) was related to many of the crimes that the police commonly dealt with. Despite these limitations, the development of British police forces greatly influenced how this institution was formed in the colonies.

EARLY AMERICAN POLICE PARADIGMS

As in Britain, the key law enforcement agent in rural, colonial America was the county sheriff. The crux of the sheriff's job was tax collection, rather than law enforcement. Sheriffs were paid under a fee system for every arrest made or other action taken. Patrol was not a function of the sheriff. Instead, sheriffs responded to calls or complaints from the public when a crime occurred. Thus, the sheriff was a reactive force—responding only when called upon. They often used citizens to assist them but did not act on their own.

However, there was one critical difference between England and colonial America. While Britain was an island, America was a vast landmass with an ever-present frontier. When the population was scattered, the sheriff's system of law enforcement was effective. When people concentrated in towns and cities, the nature of policing had to adapt. In the 1600s, colonists adopted the constable and watch system from Britain. Again, the watch was considered to be the duty of every male citizen. The watch performed many functions, such as reporting fires, raising the "hue and cry," and maintaining street lamps (Uchida, 1993, p. 18).

In 1631, Boston formed a nightwatch to protect its citizens. They were called the rattlewatch because they used rattles to communicate with each other and announce their presence (Germann, Day, & Gallati, 1978, p. 64). As in England, these watchmen proved unreliable and unpredictable as colonial Americans evaded their duty. In 1658, New York replaced the rattlewatch with eight paid watchmen. In 1693, the first uniformed police officer was appointed, and the mayor of New York selected a 12-man watch (Law Enforcement Assistance Administration, 1976, p. 15).

On the frontier, vigilantes assumed control of crime duties. In Virginia, Charles Lynch led a band of men that took the law into their own hands against criminals, British sympathizers, and Indians. They were so notorious that unlawful hanging became known as lynching. In the "Wild" West, officials who interpreted the law in their own fashion were commonplace. Men such as Judge Roy Bean fought crime using their own methods (Law Enforcement Assistance Administration, 1976, p. 15). However, western law enforcement took a more traditional form with the establishment of the Texas Rangers in 1840.

THE POLITICAL ERA PARADIGM

Kelling and Moore (1988) offer a precise description of American police reform efforts across the centuries. Several American cities developed police departments following the British system in the 1800s. Beginning with organized watches, cities like New York (1844), Chicago (1851), Cincinnati and New Orleans (1852), Philadelphia (1854), Boston (1855), Newark and Baltimore (1857), and Kansas City and St. Louis (1861) established formal law enforcement agencies to deal with the dual trends of urbanization and industrialization. Factory owners wanted temperance—sober workers to operate machinery. Urbanization promoted unrest by bringing together people from diverse class, ethnic, and racial backgrounds who resented each other. What was needed now was crime prevention and order maintenance. Watchmen and constables became obsolete (Johnson, 1981, p. 17).

Although American cities faced similar pressures, they copied the London police force selectively, rather than literally. Both police departments attempted to maintain the support of the public—maintaining order under the rule of law. However, their officers were recruited and trained in different ways. London's police were carefully selected and trained, exercised little discretion, maintained strict discipline, and remained aloof from the public. Police in New York were selected from the masses and received only rudimentary training, exercised great discretion in enforcing the law, exhibited lax discipline, and were close to their fellow citizens. The "most notable carryover" from London was the adoption of the preventive patrol (Uchida, 1993, p. 21).

One of the major differences in the development of the police between Britain and the U.S. was the Americans' inability to remove the negative impact of political influence from policing. In New York (and other U.S. cities), local government controlled the police. Their membership, management, and organizational structure reflected the patterns of city politics and administration. As a political operative, the police officer owed his allegiance to the ward boss and the police captain who chose him. They were largely under the control of the ward bosses—a continuous source of corruption (Kelling & Stewart, 1981). Political domination was problematic. It controlled who was hired and undermined departmental discipline. New York State attempted to seize control of the department and run it through a board appointed by the governor. This system held for 13 years and was attempted by other states (Germann, Day, & Gallati, 1978, p. 66; Law Enforcement Assistance Administration, 1976, p. 18). The passage of the Pendleton Act in 1833 ended the "spoils system" and led to civil service examinations to select police officers and other public servants. It was the first of several attempts to remove the hand of political influence from police forces.

Other difficulties hampered the development of the police. By the late 1800s, corruption was commonplace. The police were also routinely involved in gambling and the drug trade in large cities. Naturally, they failed to command respect. Badges and uniforms became targets for gangs of ruffians who routinely beat up officers (Germann, Day, & Gallati, 1978, p. 66; Law Enforcement Assistance Administration, 1976, p. 18).

America became the land of opportunity for both legitimate and illegitimate enterprises. The cities created an environment that both promoted crime and made it more difficult to control. The size of cities made it impossible for the police to establish a presence on the streets to deter criminal behavior. Land use was specialized and thousands of strangers were thrown into close contact with one another (Johnson, 1981, pp. 34–36). The police officer was alone on the street and left to solve problems alone. This lack of direct supervision led not only to corruption but misuse of deadly force, ignorance of the law, and direct contact with victims.

THE REFORM ERA PARADIGM

In the 1890s, a reform movement swept America. The Progressive Movement sought to eliminate corruption and return government to the hands of the people. They believed in the power of the state to serve all of its members. In policing, Progressive reformers sought to eliminate the influence of political machines on departments and end corruption. Civil service appointments and the establishment of a rational, bureaucratic, and military organizational structure would improve the efficiency and effectiveness of policing. Police administrative boards would isolate departments from the negative influences of politics. Introducing technology would both improve the quality of police services and establish a line of supervision between the street cop and his supervisor. The aims were to centralize authority in the chief and provide better training, discipline, and selection. Policing would be "professionalized."

For example, the Wickersham Commission (1931) determined that police forces lacked the expertise and equipment to deal with large American cities. It concluded that Prohibition was unenforceable. Prohibition made corruption a continual threat and sponsored the rise of criminal organizations. It made several pronouncements on police administration. Officers should be hired on the basis of competence, including intelligence tests and physical requirements. It also advocated the formation of state police forces and bureaus of investigation. The commission noted that police officers needed both training and discipline to carry out their job (Uchida, 1993, p. 24).

Professionalism was viewed as the result of expertise and training that provided the ability to deal with a set of problems. It led to a redefinition of the primary mission of policing—crime fighting. This ideology also made organizational change a priority. Departments should have centralized bureaucratic authority and strict control over its members. Political influence should be minimized. Without it, reform would be impossible. Educational and physical standards should be coupled with effective training. In sum, policing is a profession that requires specialized knowledge (Johnson, 1981, pp. 67–71). The professional police department was one (1) where police officers were experts—the only ones who knew how to do their job, (2) that was autonomous from external influences—made its own rules and regulated their personnel, (3) that was administratively efficient—carried out its mandate through modern technology and businesslike practices (Uchida, 1993, p. 26). A cadre of police chiefs led this movement.

These law enforcement leaders included August Vollmer, the chief of police of Berkeley, California, from 1905 to 1932. He was the first to suggest that police officers should have college training and become well rounded. As a result, Vollmer helped develop the School of Criminology at the University of California, Berkeley in 1916 (Law Enforcement Assistance Administration, 1976, p. 22). He emphasized the application of *scientific management* to the police organization. His principles of criminal investigation, deployment of personnel, and crime prevention were widely emulated. In 1914, his entire patrol force was operating out of automobiles (Douthit, 1975, p. 121). By 1921, these police cars were outfitted with radios. He advocated the use of psychological testing to hire officers and promotion based on the evaluation of objective measures of performance, like clearance rate (by arrest) statistics. He also promoted the development of specialized police units (e.g., juvenile units). Vollmer felt that police officers should develop crime prevention programs that attack the social causes of crime since they had more direct contract with social problems than any other governmental agency. In sum, he promoted the ideal that police officers were professional crime fighters who enforced the criminal law (Kelling & Stewart, 1981).

A protégé of Vollmer, O. W. Wilson's ideas on the professional administration of police departments has influenced a generation of administrators and scholars. His career as a police chief began in Fullerton, California (1925), continued in Wichita, Kansas (1928–1935), and culminated as superintendent of the Chicago Police Department (1960–1967). In the academic world, he was a professor and dean of the University of California Berkeley's School of Criminology from 1939 to 1960.

He believed scientific principles of management could be applied to police departments, and he applied them to such problems as manpower deployment, crime analysis, and the functional division of the department (Carte & Carte, 1977, p. 213). Recognizing that organizational principles could apply to policing, Wilson tied organizational theory, personnel administration, and technology to police work. Wilson believed the police officer was subject to efficient and centralized control. He sponsored the development of motorized (rather than foot) patrol with single-man squad cars and improved methods of communication, such as the radio dispatch of police calls. These methods were central to Wilson's belief that the police could establish crime control through preventive patrol. Their dominant presence on the streets of the city would be a deterrent to crime.

J. Edgar Hoover, the director of the Federal Bureau of Investigation, introduced several innovations to law enforcement. He emphasized the scientific investigation of crime, the creation of the federal crime laboratory (1932), and the use of fingerprint technology in crime analysis. He raised the eligibility standards of his agents and founded the FBI National Academy in 1935 to train officers from local police departments around the country. In addition, he established the Uniform Crime Reports (UCR) as the dominant source of information about crime and the National Crime Information Center (NCIC), a computerized record bank of offenders and offenses that could be accessed by police agencies across the country. Although his long tenure led to abuses of power and authority, particularly in surveillance of citizens, Hoover's early reforms were clear examples of "enlightened, progressive law enforcement administration" (Murphy, 1977, p. 263).

The "Reform Era" sponsored by these leaders of the professionalism movement had many consequences (Kelling & Moore, 1988). Together, reformers and progressives wrested the control of police departments from ward politicians. Leaders like Vollmer brought scientific principles of management to police departments in the deployment of forces, techniques of investigation, and crime prevention. Personnel were screened and hired only after they had successfully completed a battery of psychological tests. Promotion was based on ratings achieved through the use of such objective measures as crime, arrest, and clearance rate statistics. Management authority was centralized, and police services were tailored to meet specific functions (e.g., juvenile units). Together with the bureaucratic command structure, civil service examinations isolated departments from the corrupting influence of politicians.

Technology also made a significant impact on police operations. Motorized patrol connected officers to their supervisors and simultaneously separated them from the improper influence of citizens and politicians. The telephone and the two-way radio made it possible for the police to respond to citizens without direct contact with them. Such technology "represented mobility, power, conspicuous presence, control of officers, and professional distance from citizens" (Kelling & Moore, 1988, p. 8).

The police rallied around their new, carefully crafted image of professional crime fighters—the impartial enforcers of the criminal law. This "thin blue line" metaphor was acceptable to the public and attractive to their peers. From 1940 to 1960, police executives built and maintained strong boundaries around their departments. Yet the creation of such "closed systems" had unintended, negative consequences. The community was not just a potential source of corruption. It was also the source of police legitimacy. The police became separated from the people they were supposed to serve. This isolation led to difficulties with communities that still affect policing.

Throughout this period, professionalization became the dominant rationale in police departments. By the end of the 1930s, the central features of modern American police administration had taken shape. Police organizations conformed to a single model: large bureaucratic structures organized along hierarchical, quasi-military lines. For the rank and file, police work was a lifelong career, and the officers themselves were increasingly drawn into a tight-knit subculture. Almost no new ideas or techniques were introduced in police administration from the 1940s through the mid-1960s. The national crisis over the role of the police that erupted in the 1960s was a direct consequence of several decades of police reform. As Walker states, the history of the police professionalization movement sheds new light on the origins of our contemporary police problems (Walker, 1977).

MINORITIES AND THE POLICE

The history of policing in America must consider the relationship between the police and minority groups. Here, we will focus on African Americans. Slavery, segregation, and racism have affected the development of police departments (Williams & Murphy, 1990, p. 1). As agents of the state, the police were charged with the enforcement of laws that were wholly discriminatory and were eventually recognized as unconstitutional. As a result, the police in America have been alienated from minority groups.

Although police in the South emerged from night watchmen, the history of policing in the South was much different than the North (Curry, 1974, p. 53). Police in the South were typically organized along military lines. The controls placed on private behavior led to the creation of a "new kind of police—consolidated, specialized, with a public mandate to enforce the laws, uphold certain standards of morality, and to ensure the security of persons and property" (Jordan, 1979, p. 123). For example, police in Charleston, South Carolina, evolved from the "City Guard." This quasi-military force was founded on the notion that Blacks were "domestic enemies" who had to be kept constantly under surveillance and subordinate. The perception was "that Negroes could be awed into tractability by military display" (Jordan, 1979, p. 123). Often, these "slave patrols" were instruments of oppression, designed to prevent slaves from running away. They had the authority to track down and punish runaway slaves with impunity. Reichel (1977) notes that these patrol were common in the South and represented a "transitional" force led by citizens before cities developed professional police departments.

The repression of African Americans did not cease with the Civil War. In response to the abolition of slavery, Southern states passed legislation to suppress free Blacks. To defend their slave property interests, individual states passed the Slave Codes, a notion of the African slave as property that was later reinforced by the United States Supreme Court in the *Dred Scott* decision. Despite specific legislation and several Constitutional Amendments, the legal status of African Americans was less than that of their White counterparts. The U.S. Supreme Court declared civil rights legislation unconstitutional and upheld laws that established segregation. For example, in the case of *Plessy v. Ferguson* (1896), the Court supported a Louisiana railroad law that required "separate but equal" accommodations for African and Euro-Americans. This decision led to the passage of "Jim Crow" laws that set up separate facilities for African Americans in all arenas of public life, including education and public facilities of all types (Mann, 1993, p. 124). The police were charged with the enforcement of these laws.

Thus, the history of policing is one of alienation from minority communities. The police were viewed as the agents of a tyrannical system of racism and injustice. As Mann (1993, p. 165) states, this is an *indelible impression*, rooted in a long and bloody history of minority oppression. As a result, police departments now find it difficult to find and develop the level of support necessary to institute reforms (like community policing) in urban areas. Despite official measures to eliminate police brutality, resentment still exists.

Throughout the '60s and '70s, the public and the police were brought into conflict under the civil rights and anti–Vietnam War movements. As a result, the professional model of policing was questioned for several reasons. First, the police failed to meet the promise of crime control and prevention. Crime rose dramatically during the 1960s. The fear of crime also soared. Citizens abandoned parks and public transportation and ultimately fled cities for the suburbs.

Racial and ethnic minorities felt that the police discriminated against them and made them the target of deadly force. Riots erupted in minority communities: New York City (1964), Los Angeles (1965), Detroit (1967), and Miami and Newark (1968). As a result, President Lyndon B. Johnson established the National Advisory Commission on Civil Disorders (the Kerner Commission) to investigate the causes of these disturbances. This commission uncovered several problems in police–community relations: (a) Police conduct included brutality, harassment, and abuse of power against minorities; (b) training and supervision was inadequate; (c) police–community relations were poor, and (d) the employment of Black police officers lagged behind the growth of the population. The "disconnected, impersonal style" dictated by the professional model helped create these problems (Uchida, 1993, pp. 29–30).

The civil rights and antiwar movements challenged the legitimacy of the police. A national television audience watched as students and minorities physically confronted the police and were shocked at what they saw (e.g., the "police riot" at the National Democratic Convention in Chicago, 1968). Using force against the public, coupled with mass arrests, gave credence to the belief that the police were agents of repression.

Internal weaknesses of the professional model were exposed. Research revealed that the use of discretion characterized policing at all levels and that law enforcement activity was only a small part of the police officer's job. These conclusions ran counter to conventional wisdom about policing and attacked the basis for such bulwarks as preventive patrol and rapid response to calls from citizens (Kelling & Stewart, 1981, p. 15). The model also failed to rally line officers treated as "grunts" rather than professionals in the department. Because of their low status, their work was routinized, standardized, and governed by rules aimed at their personal appearance and off-duty behavior. They were given few opportunities to make suggestions about their work and how it should be conducted. The hierarchy failed to promote officers who thought for themselves. Instead, the organizational atmosphere fostered the creation of a police subculture directed against citizens and their supervisors (Uchida, 1993, p. 30).

The police lost financial support with the fiscal crisis faced by cities. Not only were departments forced to do more with less. Competitors in the business of protecting the public arose in the form of private security and the community crime control movement (Johnston, 1992). The reform strategy promoted by the professional model could not adjust to the changing social circumstances of the 1960s and 1970s.

Several remedies were attempted during this period. In 1967, President Johnson's Commission on Law Enforcement and the Administration of Justice stated that the police needed to develop closer relations with citizens in all communities. As a part of the "War on Crime," President Johnson also sponsored the development of the Law Enforcement Assistance Administration (LEAA) to improve and support police departments through training and equipment. One element of this program, the Law Enforcement Education Program (LEEP) helped send police officers to college hoping education would benefit departments. However, these reforms did not address the structural changes that the reform of the professional model would require.

THE COMMUNITY AND PROBLEM-ORIENTED POLICING PARADIGMS

During the early 1980s, experts in policing looked for solutions to these problems and issues. Research on foot patrol programs in Flint, Michigan, and other cities proved promising. The research results led to the conclusion that the police could not "solve" the crime problem or even manage it effectively without active involvement and support from the community. The basic argument was that the police must get out of their cars and spend more time in public spaces, confronting and assisting citizens with their private troubles instead of driving around in cars waiting for a radio call (Moore & Kelling, 1983, p. 65).

Such sentiments became the basis for community policing. This concept was defined as both a philosophy and an organizational strategy that allows the police and community residents to work closely together in new ways to solve the problems of crime, fear of crime, physical and social disorder, and neighborhood decay. Law-abiding citizens deserve input into the police process. Solutions to contemporary community problems demand freeing both people and the police to explore creative new ways to address neighborhood concerns beyond a narrow focus on individual crime incidents (Trojanowicz & Bucqueroux, 1990, p. xii).

Community policing involves two interrelated concepts: problem solving and community involvement. Problem-solving policing focuses on identifying chronic incidents in the community and their elimination to halt calls for service (Goldstein, 1990). This organizational strategy requires a partnership between the police and the people they serve. The community helps the police identify, prioritize, and solve problems. The aim is to improve the quality of life in the area, introducing strategies designed to enhance neighborhood safety.

Problem-solving and community policing are strategic concepts that seek to redefine the ends and the means of policing. Problem-solving policing directs police attention to the problems that cause incidents, rather than to the incidents themselves. Community policing emphasizes establishing working partnerships between police and communities to reduce crime and enhance security (Moore, 1992).

Specifically, problem-oriented policing (POP) requires officers and crime analysts to identify the underlying conditions that produce crime and disorder problems and seek a thorough and detailed analysis of a problem before determining a possible, long-term resolution to it that eventually does not involve arrests. POP stresses that greater decision-making freedom should be given to line officers and that evaluation of the outcome of a solution is required to determine its success. POP outlines the use of the SARA model:

- Scanning—Identify recurring problems and how they affect community safety.

- Analysis—Determine the causes of the problem.

- Response—Seeking out, selecting, and implementing activities to solve the problem.

- Assessment—Determine if the response was effective, or identify new strategies.

Thus, the use of evidence-based information to guide operations is the key component of this process.

There is evidence that community policing lowers the fear of crime in communities when the level of interaction between citizens and officers increases. When police community stations and citizen contact patrol is used and when citizens are respected, they are more likely to comply with police requests (National Research Council, 2004, pp. 234–235).

These research findings were upheld by studies that followed this report. Research on Chicago's community policing program (Chicago Alternative Policing Strategy, or CAPS) determined that residents in areas served by the program had higher opinions of the ability of the police to fight crime than residents in matched comparison group neighborhoods. Overall, the CAPS experience documented that police departments need to tailor their approaches and responses to specific communities regarding their socioeconomic background to be effective in implementing community policing (Lombardo, Olson, & Staton, 2010).

Research on COP also addressed its impact upon arrests by the police. Tillyer (2017, p. 21) reports departments with more COP activities (i.e., including COP in the departmental mission statement, partnering with the community, use of technology, and having a COP plan in place) registered the highest Index Crime arrest rates—suggesting to influence arrests, departments should engage in multiple community policing activities. Chappell and her colleagues (2006, p. 300) determined that the overall number of arrests and violent crime arrests were not significantly higher in departments practicing community policing. Finally, a meta-analysis of the effectiveness of community policing addresses the results compiled from 25 studies containing 65 independent tests of this method. The results provided "robust evidence" that COP increased citizen satisfaction with the police (including their perceptions of police legitimacy) and their perceptions of neighborhood disorder. However, there was no evidence COP reduces fear of crime or officially recorded crime (Gill, Weisburd, Telep, Vitter, & Bennett, 2014, p. 423).

These goals are a key part of the community policing strategy—meeting the demands of citizens for police services and promoting feelings of safety in the community. The core idea of community policing encourages individual agencies to adapt it to meet the circumstances they face. Thus, "community policing is a philosophy that promotes organizational strategies which support the systematic use of partnerships and problem solving techniques to proactively address the immediate conditions that give rise to public safety issues such as crime, social disorder, and fear of crime" (Scheider, Chapman, & Schapiro, 2009, pp. 697–698).

THE COMPSTAT PARADIGM

Developed and implemented by the New York City Police Commissioner William Bratton in 1994, CompStat is a goal-oriented strategic management process that aims to control crime by holding police officials accountable for organizational performance. It has been recognized as a revolutionary police management paradigm (Henry, 2002; McDonald, 2002; Walsh, 2001).

CompStat enforced administrative responsibility to reduce the incidence of crime. Basically, it comprises a four-step process:

1. Accurate and Timely Intelligence—To reduce crime, you must know about it.

   - What type of crime is it (i.e., drug sales, robbery, burglary)?

   - Where crime is occurring (areas, types of location)?

   - When crime is happening (day of week, hour of day)?

   - Why crime is happening (motive, i.e., drug-related shootings)?

2. Rapid Deployment—By providing weekly crime statistics, the CompStat process allows administrators to assess this intelligence. Commanders can then deploy their resources as rapidly as possible to address crime conditions.

3. Effective Tactics—Focusing specific resources on specific problems.

4. Relentless Follow-Up and Assessment—The first three steps are only effective if commanders constantly follow up on what is being done and assess their results. If results are not what they should be, something needs to change.

Operational managers are held accountable for addressing the crime and disorder issues and trends associated with the CompStat data for their areas. They are empowered to focus, manage, and direct their unit's problem-solving process. Traditional, community, and problem-oriented policing strategies are integral parts of their operational tactics. A principle aim of the CompStat process is not to just displace crime but to reduce it and create a permanent change in the community. CompStat is not just about crime statistics but crime control (Safir, 1997).

The underlying concept of CompStat is that police officers and police agencies can have a substantial positive impact on crime and quality-of-life problems facing the communities they serve if managed strategically. It presents police executives and managers with a new way of looking at police organizations and police activities. It is radically different from the accepted concepts and practices that have guided police administration through most of it existence, and it points to new methods and strategies similar to those used by business managers that police agencies can use to fulfill their mission (Henry, 2002). CompStat emphasizes the vital link between information, operational decision-making, and crime control objectives (McDonald, 2002). However, as a management tool, its impact extends way beyond crime fighting and can apply to any organizational setting. Its strength is that it is a management process that can adapt to constantly changing conditions.

Operational managers are held accountable for addressing the crime and disorder issues and trends associated with the CompStat data for their areas. Under CompStat, operational managers are empowered to focus, manage, and direct their unit's problem-solving process. Traditional, community, and problem-oriented policing strategies are integral parts of their operational tactics. A principle objective of the CompStat process is not to just displace crime but to reduce it and create a permanent change in the community. CompStat is not just about crime statistics but crime control (Safir, 1997).

It is relevant to emphasize that the underlying concept of CompStat is that police officers and police agencies can have a substantial positive impact on crime and quality-of-life problems facing the communities they serve if managed strategically. It presents police executives and managers with a new way of looking at police organizations and police activities. It is a radically different concept and practice that has guided police administration through most of it existence, and it points to new methods and strategies similar to those used by business managers that police agencies can use to fulfill their mission (Henry, 2002

An exhausive analysis of the effectiveness of the CompStat program by Zimring (2012, p. 134) reveals that New York City experienced a decline in seven major crime categories (homicide, rape, robbery, assault, burglary, larceny, and auto theft) that was greater than the nine other largest U.S. cities during the period 1990–2009. For these crimes, the average decline in New York was 63% during the 1990s and 45 percent after 2000 (Zimring, 2012, p. 139). Specifically, Zimring (2012, p. 147) attributes this crime drop to the effective use of hot-spots emphases and tactics—"the most important of these is a data driven crime mapping and control strategy management program with many of the elements of CompStat." The use of a CompStat system in the White Plains (NY) Police Department between 2002 and 2005 led to a 69% increase in arrests that resulted in a 32% decrease in crimes against the person and a 33% decrease in property crime. In addition, vehicle and traffic summonses rose by 81%, and a 6.4% reduction in motor vehicle accidents occurred (despite an increase in traffic flow) (O'Connell & Straub, 2007, p. 19).

Other studies of CompStat have been less conclusive. In particular, the Committee to Review Research on Police Policy and Practices (2004, p. 185) noted in their literature review that the effectiveness of CompStat would be difficult to scientifically ascertain. Recent research on the impact of CompStat and its strategies in New York City have been mixed and qualified in its assessment of effectiveness (Rosenfeld & Fornango, 2014; Weisburd, Telep, & Lawton, 2014).

However, research by Braga and Weisburd (2011) provides empirical evidence that "police can control crime hot spots without displacing crime problems to other places" (p. 4) by utilizing problem-oriented policing and situational crime prevention techniques to address the "dynamics, situations and characteristics" of the location. To effectively implement and manage a hot-spot policing program, they recommend that police departments use a "CompStat-like accountability system that puts a premium on problem oriented policing and community policing" (Braga & Weisburd, 2010, p. 243).

THE INTELLIGENCE-LED POLICING PARADIGM

Another data-driven information system to guide police operations is known as intelligence-led policing (ILP) (Ratcliffe, 2008). Basically, it targets prolific and serious criminals to combat a specific crime problem and "triage out" most other crime from further investigation. It features the strategic use of surveillance and informants to make intelligence central to operational decision-making. In sum, ILP is a managerial model of evidence-based police resource allocation decisions through prioritization of problems. ILP components feature investigation to determine the existence and management of linked series of crime incidents (hot spots), the targeting of specific offenders, and the application of preventative measures to combat the crime problem.

Over the past decade, intelligence-led policing activities have been implemented in several cities. David Kennedy (2011) and his colleagues have helped police departments in Boston, Cincinnati, and other cities create and evaluate programs designed to deter specific criminal activity (e.g., gang violence and drug markets) without alienating the law-abiding residents in those areas. This program, now operating under the name National Network for Safe Communities, was adopted effectively in Boston (Operation Ceasefire—the Boston "Miracle"), Minneapolis;

Stockton, California; Indianapolis; Memphis; New Haven; Portland, Oregon; Baltimore; High Point, North Carolina; and Cincinnati. Consistent with the premises of deterrence theory, drug market thugs are viewed as rational actors who will respond to the threat of imminent punishment. They are scared and carry guns for protection. Thus, heavy enforcement is announced ahead of time, showing the offenders they are under police surveillance and showing the prison terms given to their convicted peers while asserting the necessity of punishment that is immediate and forthcoming (through the use of federal enforcement and sentencing). It is a plan of "focused deterrence" on one problem—strictly aimed at stopping the violence associated with the illegal drug trade.

In Cincinnati, homicides declined almost 20% overall—and 36% among Black males using handguns (University of Cincinnati Policing Institute, 2009). While previous crackdowns in Cincinnati had resulted in a backlash from law-abiding residents who felt harassed by police, this targeted crackdown was praised by community members. In High Point, North Carolina, an evaluation of the drug market policing strategy in that city found a statistically significant reduction in violent crime within the targeted neighborhoods compared to other High Point neighborhoods, although the violent crime rate actually increased after the interventions were implemented (Corsaro, Hunt, Hipple, & McGarrell, 2012). Implemented in this fashion, ILP has the potential to disrupt, enforce, and prevent crime problems previously believed to be intractable. A meta-analysis of 11 studies of focused deterrence operations determined that these strategies generated a statistically significant crime reduction effect, although they were not the result of randomized experimental evaluations (Braga & Weisburd, 2012). The findings did support the conclusion that focused deterrence operations alter offenders' perceptions of risk (Braga & Weisburd, 2012, p. 349).

THE SMART POLICING INITIATIVE

This initiative melds the methods of previous paradigms (POP, CompStat, and ILP) together by emphasizing the use of data analysis to effectively improve police operations and use evaluation research to assess the effectiveness of innovative approaches. According to the SPI website (http://www.smartpolicinginitiative .com), the Bureau of Justice Assistance has sponsored a number of Smart Policing Initiatives (SPI) in several cities. These initiatives feature approaches based upon hot-spot policing and focused deterrence, offender-based strategies (Coldren, Huntoon, & Medaris, 2013, p. 281).

The hot-spot policing tactic is an example of the SPI paradigm. Research evidence on hot-spot policing has been positive. For example, a problem-oriented approach to convenience store crime in Glendale, Arizona, resulted in a 42% decrease in crime at targeted stores (White & Katz, 2013, p. 305). In Boston, Safe Street Teams identified and targeted hot spots of violent crime, resulting in a 17% reduction in violent crimes, particularly robbery and aggravated assault (Braga & Schnell, 2013, p. 351). In Lowell, Massachusetts, the police indentified hot spots of property crime. Increased surveillence of these areas resulted in decreases in motor vehicle theft (61%), larceny (43% and 50%), and shoplifting (42% and 41%) (Bond & Hajjar, 2013, pp. 332–333). The Los Angeles (CA) Police Department (LAPD) targeted repeat violent offenders and gang members (Operation LASER) in its Newton Division—a hot spot of gun and gang-related violent crime. The removal of the targeted offenders resulted in a 5.2% decrease in gun crime per month in the hot-spot area (Uchida & Swatt, 2013, p. 297). Braga and Weisburd (2011) offer empirical evidence that "police can control crime hot spots without displacing crime problems to other places" (p. 4) by using problem-oriented policing and situational crime prevention techniques to address the "dynamics, situations and characteristics" of the location.

In Boston, a problem-oriented strategy focused on micro-level hot spots was able to reduce aggravated assaults by more than 15%, violent crime by over 17%, and robberies by over 19%. Target enforcement of crime hot spots in Baltimore reduced homicides by 27%. In addition, a related focused deterrence intervention reduced nonfatal shootings in one neighborhood by 40% and a gun offender registry reduced gun-related reoffending risks among participants by 92% (Braga, Webster, White, & Saizow, 2014, pp. ii–iii).

In sum, these SPI efforts have demonstrated that evidence-based strategies can effectively reduce crime in areas that have had long-term crime problems (Joyce, Ramsey, & Stewart, 2013, pp. 366–367).

CONCLUSION

This review of police operational paradigms leads to several conclusions concerning where we have been and where we are going. The original purposes of policing outlined by Sir Robert Peel have never lost their significance. To effectively prevent crime, the police must be tied to the community in a true democratic fashion. The reforms of the professional model were designed to prevent police corruption and promote police independence from political influence. However, the focus of the professional model had the intended results of isolating the police from the community and promoting methods of patrolling that proved ineffective in combating crime. Recent police paradigms have attempted to prevent these problems by reestablishing the vital linkage between the police and the communities they serve. They also use information to promote the implementation of operational methods to address identified crime problems.

What do these strategies have in common, and how do they differ from past policing paradigms? First, they use information to guide operations and meet the true purpose of policing: to prevent crime. Second, they also follow up to test and assess the effectiveness of these operations to determine whether they have been effective and, if not, how to alter operations so they can improve. Third, they seek the support of and input from the community and recognize that citizens are in partnership with the police in crime prevention efforts. The police departments of the future will be open and information-driven operations that are based upon community support.

The problem that remains is the same caution that Peel identified in the first place: The police must use unobtrusive and democratic methods of crime prevention that respect the rights of citizens and their autonomy. For example, the major force behind the implementation of CompStat, William Bratton, has been named police commissioner of New York City for the second time. Bratton also served as chief of the Los Angeles Police Department. Under his leadership, the LAPD met the requirements of a federal consent decree designed to repair the relationship between the department and its communities in light of the Rodney King episode and subsequent riots. Although New York City has enjoyed a reduction in crime rates since the CompStat implementation, the use of stop-and-frisk tactics by the police have been denounced by community leaders and declared unconstitutional by the courts. Bratton has now been called in to solve the same problem that he faced in Los Angeles—to rebuild the department's relationship with the public (Rashbaum & Goldstein, 2013). These new paradigms place an emphasis on the development of effective crime prevention tactics. However, they must be accompanied an ethos consistent with the requirements of democracy. To do otherwise is to invite the abuses of an authoritarian police state that is directly contrary to the founding values of our country.

Discussion Questions

1. What is a paradigm, and what purpose does it serve?

2. Which of Peels's principles is most important? Why?

3. What are the elements of the CompStat program? What does it seek to accomplish?

4. What are the aims of intelligence-led policing? What is different about it?

5. What are the aims of smart policing? What is different about it?

References

Bond, B. J., & Hajjar, L. M. (2013). Measuring congruence between property crime problems and response strategies. *Police Quarterly, 16*(3), 323–338.

Braga, A. A., & Weisburd, D. L. (2010). *Policing problem places: Crime hot spots and effective prevention.* New York, NY: Oxford University Press.

Braga, A. A., & Weisburd, D. L. (2012). The effects of focused deterrence strategies on crime: A systematic review and meta-analysis of the empirical evidence. *Journal of Research in Crime and Delinquency, 49*(3), 323–358.

Braga, A. A., Webster, D. W., White, M. D., & Saizow, H. (2014). *SMART approaches to reducing* gun violence: Smart Policing Initiative spotlight on evidence-based strategies and impacts. Washington, DC: Bureau of Justice Assistance.

Carte, G. E., & Carte, E. (1977). O. W. Wilson: Police theory in action. In P. J. Stead (Ed.), Pioneers in policing (pp. 207–218). Montclair, NJ: Patterson Smith.

Chappell, A. T., MacDonald, J. M., & Manz, P. W. (2006). The organizational determinants of police arrest decisions. Crime & Delinquency, 52(2), 287–306.

Coldren, J. R., Huntoon, A., & Medaris, M. (2013). Introducing smart policing: Foundations, principles, and practice. Police Quarterly, 16(3), 275–286.

Committee to Review Research on Police Policy and Practices. (2004). Fairness and effectiveness in policing: The evidence. Washington, DC: National Academies Press.

Connell, N., Miggans, K., & McGloin, J. (2008). Can a community policing Initiative reduce serious crime? Police Quarterly, 11(2), 127–150.

Corsaro, N., Hunt, E., Hipple, N., & McGarrell, E. (2012). The impact of drug market pulling levers policing on neighborhood violence: An evaluation of the High Point drug market intervention. Criminology and Public Policy, 11(2), 167–199.

Covey, S. R. (2004). The 8th habit. New York, NY: Free Press.

Curry, L. P. (1974). Urbanization and urbanism in the Old South: A comparative view. Journal of Southern History, 40(1), 43–60.

Douthit, N. (1975). August Vollmer, Berkeley's first police chief, and the emergence of police professionalism. California Historical Review, 54, 101–124.

Germann, A., Day, F., & Gallati, R. (1978). Introduction to law enforcement. Springfield, IL: Charles C. Thomas.

Gill, C., Weisburd, D., Telep, C. W., Vitter, Z., & Bennett, T. (2014). Community oriented policing to reduce crime, disorder and fear and increase satisfaction and legitimacy among citizens: A systematic review. Journal of Experimental Criminology, 10, 399–428.

Goldstein, H. (1990). Problem-oriented policing. New York, NY: McGraw Hill.

Henry, W. (2002). The CompStat paradigm: Management accountability in policing. New York, NY: Looseleaf Press.

Johnson, D. R. (1981). American law enforcement: A history. St. Louis, MO: Forum Press.

Johnston, L. (1992). The rebirth of private policing. London, UK: Routledge.

Jordan, L. W. (1979). Police power and public safety in antebellum Charleston: The emergence of a new police, 1800–1860. South Atlantic Urban Studies, 3, 122–140.

Joyce, N. M., Ramsey, C. H., & Stewart, J. K. (2013). Commentary on smart policing. Police Quarterly, 16(3), 358–368.

Kelling, G. L., & Stewart, J. K. (1981). The evolution of contemporary police management. In W. A. Geller (Ed.), Local government police management (pp. 3–19). Washington, DC: International City Management Association.

Kelling, G., & Moore, M. (1988). The evolving strategy of policing. Washington, DC: U.S. Department of Justice.

Kennedy, D. M. (2011). Don't shoot: One man, a street fellowship and the end of violence in inner-city America. New York, NY: Bloomsbury.

Klockars, C. B. (1985). The idea of police. Beverly Hills, CA: Sage.

Law Enforcement Assistance Administration. (1976). Two hundred years of American criminal justice. Washington, DC: U.S. Department of Justice.

Lombardo, R., Olson, D., & Staton, M. (2010). The Chicago alternative policing strategy: A reassessment of the CAPS program. Policing, 33(4), 586–606.

Mann, C. R. (1993). Unequal justice: A question of color. Bloomington, IN: Indiana University Press.

McDonald, P. P. (2002). Managing police operations: Implementing the New York crime control model—CompStat. Stamford, CT: Thomson.

Moore, M. H. (1992). Problem-solving and community policing. In M. Tonry, & N. Morris (Eds.), Modern policing (pp. 99–158). Chicago, IL: University of Chicago Press.

Moore, M. H., & Kelling, G. L. (1983). To serve and protect—Learning from police history. *Public Interest, 70*, 49–65.

More, H. W., Vito, G. F., & Walsh, W. F. (2012). *Organizational behavior and management in law enforcement.* Upper Saddle River, NJ: Prentice Hall.

Murphy, P. V. (1977). John Edgar Hoover: The federal influence in American policing. In P. J. Stead (Ed.), *Pioneers in policing* (pp. 255–263). Montclair, NJ: Patterson Smith.

National Research Council. (2004). *Fairness and effectiveness in policing.* Committee to Review Research on Police Policy and Practice. Committee on Law and Justice, Division of Behavior and Social Sciences and Education. Washington, DC: National Academies Press.

O'Connell, P. E., & Straub, F. (2007). *Performance-based management for police organizations.* Long Grove, IL: Waveland Press.

Rashbaum, W. K., & Goldstein, J. (2013, December 16). Bratton is expected to reshape police to rebuild relationship with the public. *New York Times,* A1, A7.

Ratcliffe, J. (2008). *Intellgence led policing.* Portland, OR: Willan Publishing.

Reichel, P. L. (1977). Southern slave patrols as a transitional police type. *American Journal of Police, 7,* 51–77.

Rosenfeld, R., & Fornango, R. (2014). The impact of police stops on precinct robbery and burglary rates in New York City, 2003–2010. *Justice Quarterly, 31*(1), 96–122.

Scheider, M. C., Chapman, R., & Schapiro, A. (2009). Towards unification of policing innovations under community policing. *Policing, 32*(4), 694–718.

Trojanowicz, R., & Bucqueroux, B. (1990). *Community policing: A contemporary perspective.* Cincinnati, OH: Anderson.

Tillyer, R. (2017). Assessing the impact of community policing on arrest. *Justice Quarterly.* doi:10.108 0/07418825.2017.1327609

Uchida, C. D. (1993). The development of American police: An historical overview. In R. Dunham & G. Alpert (Eds.), *Critical Issues in Policing: Contemporary Readings* (2nd ed., pp. 16–32). Prospect Heights, IL: Waveland Press.

Uchida, C. D., & Swatt, M. L. (2013). Operation LASER and the effectiveness of hotspot patrol: A panel analysis. *Police Quarterly, 16*(3), 287–304.

University of Cincinnati Policing Institute. (2009). *Implementation of the Cincinnati Initative to Reduce Violence (CIRV): Year 2 report.* Cincinnati, OH: University of Cincinnati.

Walker, S. (1977). *A critical history of police reform: The emergence of professionalism.* Lexington, MA: D.C. Heath and Company.

Walsh, W. (2001). CompStat: An analysis of an emerging police managerial paradigm. *Policing, 24*(3), 347–362.

Weisburd, D., Telep, C. W., & Lawton, B. A. (2014). Could innovations in policing have contributed to the New York City crime drop even in a period of declining police strength?: The case of stop, question and frisk as a policing strategy. *Justice Quarterly, 31*(1), 129–153.

White, M. D., & Katz, C. M. (2013). Policing convenience store crime: Lessons from the Glendale, Arizona Smart Policing Initiative. *Police Quarterly, 16*(3), 305–322.

Williams, H., & Murphy, P. V. (1990). *The evolving strategy of police: A minority view.* Washington, DC: U.S. Department of Justice.

Xu, Y., Fiedler, M., & Flaming, K. (2005). Discovering the impact of community policing: The broken windows thesis, collective efficacy, and citizen's judgment. *Journal of Research in Crime and Delinquency, 42*(2), 147–186.

Zimring, F. E. (2012). *The city that became safe: New York's lessons for urban crime and its control.* New York, NY: Oxford University Press.

17

POLICE ORGANIZATION AND ADMINISTRATION

Thomas Nolan

There are approximately 18,000 state and local law enforcement agencies in the United States employing over 800,000 police officers of various types: state and local police, sheriff's departments, agents of the federal government, constables and marshals, and special jurisdiction police (such as campus and tribal police). Seven percent of police agencies employ 100 or more officers, and these accounted for 64% of sworn personnel nationwide; almost half of all law enforcement agencies employ fewer than 10 officers. "Among these smaller agencies, about 2100 (12%) had just one full-time officer or part-time officers only" (Reaves, 2011). Additionally, 73 federal law enforcement agencies employ an additional 120,000 full-time law enforcement officers who carry firearms and who have the authority to make arrests, bringing the total number of law enforcement officers in the United States to approximately 885,000 (Reaves, 2012).

Contemporary observers have used the metaphors "juggernaut" (Gordon, 1990; Websdale, 2001) and "monolith" (Maguire, 2008; Morash, 2005) to describe the criminal justice system generally and policing in particular, and any examination of the ways that law enforcement organizations are organized and administered ought to be conducted through these insightful and illuminating prisms.

When considering the topics of the administration and organization of police and other law enforcement agencies in the 21st century, an enlightened and progressive inquiry and analysis will necessarily eschew the traditional emphasis on organizational charts and structures, the span of control, unity of command, line and staff functions, the deployment of field forces, and the various organizational theories of Weber, Hammer, Katz, Maslow, Herzberg, McGregor, and others. Of more critical import (and more informed insight) in understanding how police departments are actually organized and administered (formally and informally) will be an examination of the organizational culture (or subculture) of contemporary law enforcement agencies.

ORIGINS OF THE STRUCTURAL MODEL OF POLICE ORGANIZATIONS

What virtually all law enforcement agencies share, from the 561 departments consisting of but one officer to the New York City Police Department with over 36,000 officers, is an organizational model that is quasi-military, hierarchical, and rigidly structured along clearly delineated lines of authority and responsibility. This categorizes the *formal*, prescribed, and public organization of the police. The question arises as to how the organizational structure that we see present in virtually all police organizations came to assume its form, as the inchoate nature of urban policing during its dawn in the mid-19th century saw little, if any, "uniformity" (literally and metaphorically). "Police were involved in social service activities: they ran soup kitchens, provided lodging for indigents, and spurred moral reform movements against cigarettes and alcohol . . . [they] were union busters and political-machine enforcers" (Pollock, 2007, p. 191). Not yet established in the nascent days of policing were military ranks, uniforms, badges of office, or even the issuance and carrying of firearms. It is suggested here that the hierarchical and quasi-military structure of contemporary law enforcement agencies arose out of expediency and necessity when police departments, in their earlier incarnations, were confronted with rioting, looting, and hooliganism on a scale that was hitherto unprecedented.

The only organizational model available to those mid-19th century police administrative neophytes was that of the military: Easily recognized and identified, rapidly deployed, operating under a strict chain of command and span of control, trained in teamwork and coordination, the military structure seemed readily adaptable to the unprecedented exigencies confounding emerging police departments in New York, Boston, Philadelphia, and elsewhere. In London, the Metropolitan Police Act of 1829 created a police department founded on a military model that eventually met with a degree of success; this proved to be the form that would be emulated in the United States.

This model of police organization has been, throughout its history, a somewhat uneasy (if not unholy) alliance of philosophical underpinnings and operational strategies and policies. The contemporary emphasis on community policing and problem-oriented policing philosophies, for example, have often proven inimical and incompatible with the quasi-military model of police organization. The military emphasis on absolute deference and obedience to authority, rote conformity to group norms, the use of force and violence to overcome resistance, and closely monitored and orchestrated teamwork are all squarely at odds with the realities, practices, and expectations of policing in the 21st century, particularly as they relate to community and problem-oriented policing principles. These philosophies and principles privilege and endorse decision-making at the lowest levels of the organizational hierarchy—the street-level police officer—in clear contraindication to military practice. Community policing and problem-oriented policing also place responsibility for the identification and resolution of police-related issues squarely in the hands of the individual officer(s) assigned to a particular area or beat. The model of policing in operational practice in the United States today sees the vast majority of what the police actually engage in conducted not only out of the public eye but also absent any scrutiny, inspection, or observation from police supervisors or managers (and this is especially so in the ±3% of United States' police departments that are composed of but a single officer), again clearly contrary to the military model (U.S. Department of Justice, Office of Justice Programs, 2013).

THE POLICE AND MILITARIZATION

What police departments have adopted from the military, at least in part, is its hierarchical organizational rank structure. Consider this modified adaptation: Officers of rank in most American police departments are referred to as "corporal," "sergeant," "lieutenant," and "captain." Some of the more highly militarized departments (such as many state police agencies) use the higher military ranks such as "major" or "colonel," but chief executive officers of police departments in the United States are never referred to as "general," as they are in other countries where the organizational boundaries between the military and the police are somewhat blurred. Executive officers of American police departments typically use the title "chief," and the Western referent to this appellation lies in the Native American conception of the leader of a tribe or clan. Police chiefs often attire themselves in a somewhat conspicuous display of the trappings and symbols of their office: the hat (headdress) adorned with braided gold oak leaves, the gold stars, the gold shield, the embroidered epaulets, the velvet stripes—all serve to set the chief above and apart from his or her subordinates, not unlike their earlier historical counterparts who were tribal leaders (see more on the "tribe" referent in the police subculture section that follows).

The police have also adopted many of the organizational designations employed by the military: Squads, platoons, units, task forces, even battalions and regiments are commonly used in police organizational charts to describe function, lines of authority and accountability, numbers of sworn officers, duties, hours of work, and other identifying and organizationally pertinent information.

A more recent adaptation of military argot in describing police organizational tactics is manifested in the (now) ubiquitous use of the term *operation*. Consider "Operation Community Shield" (Immigration and Customs Enforcement targeting violent gangs), "Operation Would You Like Fries" (sheriffs undercover in fast-food restaurants to spot impaired drivers), "Operation Homefront" (police working with clergy and troubled youths), "Operation CARE" (police warning motorists about safety belts), and "Operation Falcon" ("Federal and Local Cops Organized Nationally" to round up 30,000 petty criminals). In fact, the city of Boston, Massachusetts, police department recently launched an incursion into that city's inner-city neighborhoods dubbed "Operation Rolling Thunder"[1] without any apparent awareness that its military counterpart and predecessor consisted of the aerial bombardment and "carpet bombing" of North Vietnam by the U.S. Air Force beginning in 1965 (Karnow, 1983). Even more recently, police in South Carolina have launched their own version of "Operation Rolling Thunder" in a law enforcement sledgehammer operation involving 21 different agencies and over 80 police officers.

In its 2014 report on the militarization of the police in the United States, "War Comes Home: The Excessive Militarization of American Policing," the American Civil Liberties Union found this:

> Policing—particularly through the use of paramilitary teams—in the United States today has become excessively militarized, mainly through federal programs that create incentives for state and local police to use unnecessarily aggressive weapons and tactics designed for the battlefield. The militarization of policing in the United States has occurred with almost no public oversight. (p. 5)

In 1990, Congress passed the National Defense Authorization Act, which authorized the Department of Defense, through the Defense Logistics Agency (DLA), to transfer surplus military equipment to domestic law enforcement agencies for their use in fighting the so-called "War on Drugs," in what became known as the "1033 Program." The belief at the time was that law enforcement agencies in the United States faced an unprecedented threat from heavily armed drug cartels and drug distributors that could only be countered by equipping police with military-grade weapons and vehicles. Since its inception, the 1033 Program has distributed over $5.1 billion worth of equipment to over 8,000 law enforcement agencies. In 2013 alone, $450 million worth of equipment was distributed to local, state, and county agencies. The equipment includes M-16 and M-4 military rifles; mine-resistant, ambush-protected (MRAP) vehicles; bayonets; night-vision goggles; military aircraft; watercraft; and tanks.

Additionally, the federal government disburses funds to law enforcement agencies through Department of Homeland Security's (DHS) "Homeland Security Grant Program" (HSGP) and the Department of Justice's (DOJ) Edward Byrne Memorial Justice Assistance Grant (JAG) program. These funds are used to purchase tactical weapons, armored vehicles, "battle-dress" uniforms (BDUs), and other military equipment in the domestic "War on Terrorism" that has emerged as the operating mandate for much of domestic law enforcement practice since the attacks on the World Trade Center towers and the Pentagon on September 11, 2001.

The 2014 ACLU report also uncovered widespread deployment of paramilitary SWAT teams in the execution of search warrants in private homes, most often involving drug possession and distribution cases where there was no information that the occupants of the home were armed or that there were weapons in the home. According to the ACLU (2014),

> SWAT teams were often deployed—unnecessarily and aggressively—to execute search warrants in low-level drug investigations; deployments for hostage or barricade scenarios occurred in only a small number of incidents. The majority (79 percent) of SWAT deployments the ACLU studied were for the purpose of executing a search warrant, most commonly in drug investigations. (p. 5)

Further, the ACLU (2014) discovered significant and troubling racial disparities in the use of SWAT units during drug searches:

> The use of paramilitary weapons and tactics primarily impacted people of color; when paramilitary tactics were used in drug searches, the primary targets were people of color, whereas when paramilitary tactics were used in hostage or barricade scenarios, the primary targets were white. Overall, 42 percent of people impacted by a SWAT deployment to execute a search warrant were Black and 12 percent were Latino. This means that of the people impacted by deployments for warrants, at least 54 percent were minorities. Of the deployments in which all the people impacted were minorities, 68 percent were in drug cases, and 61 percent of all the people impacted by SWAT raids in drug cases were minorities. (p. 5)

The metaphor of the modern-era police chief leading warriors into battle against criminals, gang-bangers, terrorists, and drug dealers is telling in its irony. For it is here that the military analogy gains the most traction, while at serious risk of running aground. At the turn of the 21st century, the police in America had largely been organized as the first wave of shock troops on the urban battlefield that too many of our cities had become. Klockars (2005) sees three compelling themes in this analogy:

> First . . . the military analogy sought to confer some honor and respect on the occupation of policing. Second, the idea of a war on crime struck a note of emergency [and] . . . a moral urgency and a rhetorical tone that was difficult to resist . . . Third, the military analogy sought to establish a relationship between local politicians and police chiefs that was analogous to the relationship between elected executives at the national level and the general of the U.S. military. (pp. 445–446)

In this role, the police were seen by many as an army of oppression and occupation (particularly in inner-city communities of color), and, in large part, the police themselves did little to discourage this perception. That no small number of police departments initiated policies arming the police with assault rifles and dressing them in military BDUs drove a wedge into solid gains that had been made under community policing and problem-oriented policing initiatives dating from the late 1980s. Community partnerships and coproduction initiatives that had been the hallmarks of community policing risked being scuttled as police departments reorganized themselves to meet what they perceived to be the law enforcement exigencies of the 21st century.

Thus the so-called "wars" on drugs (declared in 1984), gangs, terrorists, and the like, saw the police at the turn of the 21st century morph into a military monolith or "juggernaut" whose mission may seem somewhat conflicted when community policing's "three core elements: citizen involvement, problem solving, and decentralization" (Skogan, as cited in Weisburd & Braga, 2006, p. 28) square off against the more recent mandate to meet violent crime (particularly when it is gang related) with a formidable and well-organized display of force—"In the words of one officer: 'We kick ass'" (Wilson & Kelling, 1982, p. 34).

POLICE ORGANIZATION: SUBCULTURE, ETHOS, AND MILIEU

While the formal organization of contemporary police organizations is characterized by a quasi-military hierarchical structure that is governed by formalized rules, policies, procedures, and practices, it is perhaps an articulation and understanding of the *subculture* of policing that provides a richer and more elaborate understanding of the police organization and its membership, one not formally recognized and one rarely understood by the public.

Police and their organizations have been characterized as being insular, isolated, hidebound, conservative, masculinist, morally superior, autonomous, authoritarian, cynical, and ethnocentric (among other things). That the police subculture is insular owes much to the nature of the expectations that society has of its police: The police are organized in a fashion that clearly delineates them from other members of the communities that they police through their distinctive uniforms, badges of office, conspicuously marked modes of transport, and their being openly (and somewhat heavily) armed. The police are expected to maintain order, to prevent the occurrence of crime, and to ensure the safety of the public (among other duties) and, as a result, develop a self-image of a crime fighter engaged in a "noble cause." Waddington (1999) observes that the police, in the performance of their duties, do not confront an "enemy, but fellow citizens and that makes their position acutely marginal . . . It is why the police are so insular: they find social encounters with non-police friends, acquaintances, neighbours and others fraught with difficulty" (p. 298).

The police are isolated largely owing to the environment in which they work and the significant degree of discretion that they exercise. "Police officers often work alone or in pairs . . . there is no direct supervision. Also, a majority of police–citizen encounters occur in private places, with no other observers present . . . for this reason, policing has been described as low-visibility work" (Walker & Katz, 2005, p. 362). Thus, the means by which the police "work product" is organized contributes directly toward physically isolating officers from their constituent communities and indirectly toward perpetuating a tangible sense of isolation (within the context of the police subculture) that the police themselves experience.

The police subculture is hidebound in its resistance to change, and there is perhaps nowhere in recent evidence a more convincing example of this than the arguably abysmal results of community policing initiatives from the early 1990s to the present. Mastrofski (2006) attributes these failures to the organizational subculture of the police and observes that efforts to change what some observers have dubbed a "monolithic" police culture through community policing and other like-minded innovations are likely to "die on the vine" (p. 53), owing to skepticism on the part of rank-and-file officers who are extremely resistant to change. He goes on to suggest that "police socialization processes" are what influence officer behavior and the police subculture far more than hiring practices that emphasize diversity and cultural change (p. 51). These socialization processes are the mechanisms that serve to perpetuate, validate, and privilege the status quo. That status quo endorses behavioral practices that vehemently resist changes to the organizational subculture that would alter promotional practices, access to desirable assignments, the marginalization of women and minority officers, the tolerance of violence and brutality, and practices that turn a blind eye to minor acts graft, corruption, and deceit (Nolan, 2009).

The police endorse and validate a conservative worldview in the execution of their duties, and this conservatism is a cornerstone of the organizational subculture of policing. In an environment permeated in gray, the police are habituated to see black and white:

> The police tend to view their occupational world as comprised exhaustively of three types of citizens. These ideal types are: (1) 'suspicious persons'—those whom the police have reason to believe may have committed a serious offense; (2) 'assholes'—those who do not accept the police definition of the situation; and (3) 'know nothings'—those who are not either of the first two categories but are not police and therefore, according to the police, cannot know what the police are about. (Van Maanen, 2005, p. 281)

The police thus construct these conceptual categories as cognitive shorthand to deal with the myriad and occasionally overwhelming banalities and crises into which they are constantly being submerged. Under community policing initiatives, police organizational practice "privileges the law abider who cares for his home, his lawn, and his children, and the neighborhood merchant" (Harcourt, 2001, p. 127). The police are organized around a conservative ethic that "embraces and unmediated aesthetic of order, cleanliness, and sobriety" (Harcourt, 2001, p. 135) and one in which the "order or rules of civilian conduct . . . are geared toward producing a more harmonious social environment with strong moral bonds" (Harcourt, 2001, p. 140). The police organize their experiential practice into maintaining a conservative social agenda that embraces conformity and adherence to a middle-class ethic of adherence to tacitly understood canons of behavior and comportment. They value patriotism, religious practice, distrust of the media, loyalty, respect for tradition and authority, duty to family, and the unquestioned righteousness of the rule of law.

ORGANIZATION AND SUBCULTURE: INITIATION AND MASCULINISM

Masculinism is a social construct that "justifies and naturalizes male domination. As such, it is the ideology of patriarchy. It sanctions the political and dominant role of men in the public and private spheres" (Brittan, 2001, p. 53). The police subculture is, for the large part, created, maintained, and structurally organized by the men who establish the discourse, enforce the formal and informal rules, and who maintain and assign group and member roles: the leaders, the cadre, the plebeians, the novitiates, and the outsiders. Even though women have been mainstreamed into the ranks of the police since the latter decades of the 20th century, the latest available Bureau of Justice Statistics figures (2010) show that of the 706,866 full-time sworn personnel in all local and county police departments in 2009, approximately 11% were women.

The training that police officers receive at the intake level is an indoctrination and instills in the initiate the language, the behaviors, the symbols, and the rituals that will ensure effective adaptation and assimilation for the novice. Ritualistic forms of voice, gait, posture, demeanor, language, and dress are all prescriptive and representative of a certain form of tribal initiation. Likewise, the ritualistic assembly in the "roll call" is a highly masculinized throwback to a secret military convocation that dates to the Roman Legions. ("Roll calls" are organizational rituals where officers are inspected and given their assignments.) Outsiders are never allowed to watch or participate in a roll call, except on extremely rare occasions that are completely staged for the intrusion. The officers hardly see these assemblies as sites for bonding and reinforcing the subculture of policing; that what is said at roll call stays in the "guard room" (as the assembly point is referred to) seems only natural.

Revisit the particular form of masculinism that presents itself in the military representations of rank and vertical hierarchy. As in the military, those higher up in the vertical scale of rank, those bearing or wearing gold stars and bars, are accorded the respect and attention that the efficient operation of this masculinist enterprise mandates. Beyond that, officers of rank are viewed with mistrust, suspicion, and resentment, and a different construction of hierarchy emerges among the plebeians. For example, "street cops" (those who work more hazardous patrol duty) are depicted in the subculture as more masculine than officers who work in clerical positions or guarding prisoners. Likewise, police officers who work in what is (perhaps inaccurately) characterized as more dangerous duty in inner-city neighborhoods (i.e., communities of color) are held in higher masculine esteem than officers who work in the relative tranquility of a suburban or downtown community (Nolan, 2009).

A long-held (and equally misguided) subcultural stereotype would have those who perform the more glamorous functions associated with plainclothes and undercover police work as more masculine than officers who must perform their duties conspicuously and publicly in uniform. Officers assigned to uniform duty are "in the bag," a pejorative reference to being unable to conceal oneself from public view and to wear the fashionable clothes of a "made" detective or the street clothes of an undercover. Those who work in drug investigations are perceived as more "male" than those who work with sexual assault victims (who are largely female). What emerges thus is a fraternity of those engaged in what they perceive as duty fraught with danger, a battle against the underworld, replete with the bonding, the secrecy, the faux-loyalty, and the war metaphors that have historically accompanied those identified with the organizational subculture of policing (Nolan, 2009).

In an earlier writing (2001), I had described how certain highly masculinized police organizations (perhaps unwittingly) routinely objectified, degraded, and sexualized female officers in coercing them into posing as decoy prostitutes during sting operations targeting "johns." So culturally ingrained are many masculinized organizational practices in police departments that they are often hardly recognized as such, even by progressive administrators.

ORGANIZATIONAL SUBCULTURE AND MORAL SUPERIORITY

The police see their mission as organized around a trope that is imbued with a sense of moral superiority and one in which the police have designated themselves the arbiters of the right/wrong or good/bad dichotomies. Through the police use of discretion, they often decide in context-specific situations whether or not to invoke the provisions of the criminal law based on their assessment of the level of moral "injury" or offense present in a particular situation. This is particularly true in drug, gambling, prostitution, and other nonviolent and victimless crimes. The police believe themselves to be as follows:

Perpetually engaged in a struggle with those who would disobey, disrupt, do harm, agitate, or otherwise upset the order of the regime. And, that as policemen, they and they alone are the most capable of sensing right from wrong; determining who is and who is not respectable; and, most critically deciding what is to be done about it (if anything). Such heroic self-perceptions regarding moral superiority have been noted by numerous social scientists concerned with the study of the police. (Van Maanen, 2005, pp. 280–281)

In fact, during the last 2 decades, the vast majority of police organizational strategy and policy has been driven by community policing and problem-oriented policing strategies, the nexus of which has been Kelling and Wilson's so-called broken windows theory. Foundational to this "theory" that drove so much of police practice was that the police themselves "defined 'order,'" and they themselves identified it, and they decided who had violated local moral norms: "Not necessarily violent people, nor, necessarily criminals, but disreputable or obstreperous or unpredictable people: panhandlers, drunks, addicts, rowdy teenagers, prostitutes, loiterers, the mentally disturbed" (Kelling & Wilson, 1982, p. 2). Thus, the police have assumed for themselves the role of identifying morality and immorality and have organized their mission at the local level in an effort to enforce standards of good and bad behavior, as they understand it.

Ethnocentrism is "the tendency to reject and malign other ethnic groups and their members while glorifying one's own group and its members" (APA, 2007, p. 345). Several observers have seen police organizations as akin to such groups whose members have a strong identification with a common history, culture, belief system, means of communicating, shared values, world view, and designation of "out groups." It is suggested here that the ways in which the police are formally and informally organized are reflective of *in-group bias*:

> The tendency to favor one's own group, its characteristics, and its products, particularly in reference to other groups. The favoring of the in-group tends to be more pronounced than the rejection of the out-group, but both become more pronounced during periods of intergroup contact. (APA, 2007, p. 481)

Gendreau (2006) and Andrews and Bonta (2006) have described *theoreticism* as "the practice [that] involves accepting or rejecting knowledge on the basis of one's personal values and experiences" and one that "is a critical problem in the criminal justice field" (Gendreau, 2006, p. 226). In organizations (such as the police) that are insular and dogmatic, theoreticism can be especially pernicious in guiding organizational practice at the street level and organizational policy and philosophy at the administrative level. Police organizations collectively and the police themselves are very often skeptical of outsiders ("assholes") and of "knowledges" that do not originate within and conform to the police's worldview and experience. This is particularly true of academics and scholarly research.

POLICE ORGANIZATION: AUTONOMY AND AUTHORITARIANISM

That police organizations conduct the vast majority of their day-to-day operations out of the public eye and with little (if any) oversight by or input from the communities they serve has become routinized and normative as American law enforcement enters the second decade of the 21st century. The police are typically neither licensed nor controlled by any government or professional regulatory entity outside of the agency itself, unlike lawyers, doctors, haircutters, masseuses, acupuncturists, or even tattoo artists. For the large part, police organizations operate almost completely autonomously. For example, it was recently uncovered that in Massachusetts, "some 82 local police departments have obtained more than 1000 weapons over the last 15 years under a federal program that distributes surplus guns from the U.S. military" (Slack, 2009). The weapons ranged from M-16 assault rifles to M-79 grenade launchers, and they were acquired by university police departments and some departments with fewer than 10 officers. No input was sought from affected communities, and the proposal to equip 200 police officers in the Boston Police Department with the assault rifles was shelved after it was leaked to the news media and the public backlash made the proposal politically untenable. One police official, when questioned about equipping officers with the assault rifles stated "that decision belongs with police officials, not the public" and "likened community involvement in arms decisions to public involvement in hospitals' decisions on what type and how many heart stents to buy" (Slack, 2009).

In describing the work environment of policing, Skolnick (1994) observed that "police work constitutes the most secluded part of an already secluded system of criminal justice and therefore offers the greatest opportunity for arbitrary behavior" (p. 13). Thus, it is the organizational autonomy of the police that sets them distinctly apart from other "individual practitioners of a craft," as Bittner (2005) has described them. In acting autonomously, "most of what a policeman needs to know to do his work he has to learn on his own" (p. 169).

The perspective that it is the police who are the experts and the professionals in all matters pertaining to public safety and in the ensuing regulation of human behavior in the maintenance of public order assumes a standpoint that some have characterized as organizational authoritarianism and in police officers an

> authoritarian personality: a personality pattern characterized by
> (a) preoccupation with power and status, (b) strict adherence to highly
> simplified conventional values, (c) an attitude of great deference to authority
> figures while demanding subservience from those regarded as lower in
> status, and (d) hostility toward minorities and other outgroups and to people
> who deviate from conventional moral prescriptions. (APA, 2007, p. 89)

FEDERAL OVERSIGHT OF THE POLICE

As of 2017, there were approximately 24 police departments in the United States that had entered into consent decree agreements with the Department of Justice (DOJ), following DOJ investigations usually involving agency-wide excessive force and unconstitutional stop and search complaints. These legally binding agreements are court-approved plans for improving operational policies and procedures in police departments that have been found to have engaged in so-called "pattern and practice" violations of the constitutional rights and civil liberties protections of citizens, most often residents of communities of color. Police departments in Los Angeles, Miami, Pittsburgh, and Detroit have been under federal oversight in recent years, as well as in Albuquerque and Cleveland.

Following the 2014 shooting death of Michael Brown in Ferguson, Missouri, the DOJ's Civil Rights Division issued a scathing report that found that the Ferguson Police Department

> has engaged in a "pattern and practice of constitutional violations (that primarily target African Americans) in stopping people without reasonable suspicion, arresting them without probable cause, and using unreasonable force." The FPD's policies and practices were found to routinely violate the Fourth Amendment in racially profiling African Americans and disproportionally singling them out for "pedestrian checks," "Failure to Comply," and illegal "Stop and Identify" offenses. DOJ found that the FPD consistently uses excessive force in violation of the Fourth Amendment and that African Americans accounted for almost 90 percent of the use of force incidents from 2010 to 2014. FPD used force involving a canine bite 14 times during this time period and in all incidents the person bitten was African American. (Nolan, 2015)

In January 2017, the Department of Justice and the Baltimore Police Department (BPD) entered into a consent decree whereby the BPD agreed to stipulated changes in the ways that it conducts policing in the city, specifically in communities of color. In August of 2016, the DOJ had released the results of its investigation into the BPD where it found that the BPD "engages in a pattern or practice of conduct that violates the First and Fourth Amendments of the Constitution as well as federal anti-discrimination laws. BPD makes stops, searches and arrests without the required justification; uses enforcement strategies that unlawfully subject African Americans to disproportionate rates of stops, searches and arrests; uses excessive force; and retaliates against individuals for their constitutionally-protected expression."

Also in January of 2017, the DOJ announced the findings of its investigation into the Chicago Police Department (CPD), where it found that the CPD "engages in a pattern or practice of using force, including deadly force, in violation of the Fourth Amendment to the Constitution." The DOJ's investigation followed the 2014 shooting death of 17-year-old Laquan McDonald at the hands of then-police officer Jason

Van Dyke. Van Dyke shot McDonald 16 times, 14 times after his lifeless body had fallen to the ground, and conspired with his fellow officers to falsify reports on the shooting and the events that precipitated McDonald's death. Video footage of the shooting had been hidden from the public for over a year following the teenager's death and, when released, gave lie to the officers' version of what had transpired.

At the close of January 2017, the level of the continued oversight of police departments nationwide by the DOJ remains to be seen. Speaking at his Senate confirmation hearing, the nominee for attorney general, Jeff Sessions, testified, "These lawsuits undermine the respect for police officers and create an impression that the entire department is not doing their work consistent with fidelity to law and fairness, and we need to be careful before we do that."

POLICE ADMINISTRATION AND THE CIVIL SERVICE

The vast majority of the over 18,000 law enforcement agencies in the United States operate under some type of civil service or tenured intake and promotion system that serves to severely restrict and delimit the discretion that an administrator or appointing authority has in hiring and promoting individuals within a particular police agency. In theory, the civil service system was instituted around the turn of the 20th century in an effort to abolish patronage appointments to local police departments. In practice, it has created and sustained a complicated and convoluted system that is often encumbered in cronyism *adumbrated in administrivia*. For example, preference provisions written into many civil service laws have given entry-level and promotional preference to military veterans, survivors of police deemed to have died "in the line of duty," civilian "cadets," women, foreign language speakers, emergency medical technicians, and others. Further, tests and other instruments are administered to applicants that, to many observers, are in no way reflective or capable of measuring the skills necessary or the most qualified applicants for entry-level and promotional positions. Police administrators often complain about being hamstrung by outdated legal requirements that hamper their efforts to place the most desirable and qualified applicants into open positions, as well as to terminate the employment of those proven to be unsuitable in the police service.

POLICE ADMINISTRATION AND UNIONS

Police unions and the collective bargaining process can prove vexing and frustrating for police administrators. (Full disclosure: This author was a long-time elected constitutional officer of a large police union.) "Nationwide, 41% of local police departments, employing 71% of all officers, authorized collective bargaining for sworn personnel" (U.S. Department of Justice, Office of

Justice Programs, 2003, p. 12). Contemporary police unions began forming in the 1960s and 1970s in response to oppressive working conditions for many police officers that included abysmal compensation, lack of overtime pay, poor equipment, work schedules that permitted few days off, no vacation, mandatory unpaid call outs, and draconian residency and travel notification requirements.

Many of today's police unions have negotiated generous compensation packages for their members and have proven formidable adversaries in often contentious and confrontational relationships with police administrators. Protracted and fractured contract negotiations between police unions and the City of Boston threatened to shut down the Democratic National Convention in 2004 until the city's police unions won a significant wage increase from the city in an unprecedented contract package that offered no concessions from the unions to the city.[2]

THE POLICE

Students of criminal justice are offered here a glimpse into the realm of the lived experience and worldview of the police from the perspective of one who has lived it for over 30 years. It is a dominion that is in many ways mired in a perspective on society jaded by constant exposure to a sliver of the polity that is hardly representative of the society in which most of us live; yet it is all too often for the police their only tangible grasp on the netherworld that is, for them, all too real, all too pervasive, all too unrelenting. Progressive police administrators (and enlightened students) understand that therein lay the value and sacrifice of what the police provide to the rest of us and the price that they pay in serving our communities.

Discussion Questions

1. How does the formal organizational structure of contemporary police agencies contribute (if you believe that it does) to inconsistencies and difficulties in implementing community policing and problem-oriented policing philosophies and strategies?

2. Police organizations have been described as *masculinist* in nature and form. What are the manifestations of masculinism in contemporary police organizations? How has masculinism affected and informed the ways that police interact with their constituent communities? What are the implications of such masculinism for the future of police organizations?

3. The police are organized in a quasi-military form that employs military metaphors such as "war" and "operation" (among others) in descriptions of their purpose and mission. What are the implications of using military terms to describe strategies, policies, and tactics that the police employ in our communities? Are these descriptions compatible with community policing initiatives?

4. The police are organized around the enforcement not only of the criminal law but also of moral behavior generally. How do the police engage in the identification and enforcement of morality? What are the implications of having the police enforce standards of behavior? Do the police, in fact, decide what is appropriate moral behavior?

Suggested Readings

Alpert, G., Dunh, R., & Stroshine, M. (2006). *Policing: Continuity and change.* Long Grove, IL: Waveland Press.

Balko, R. (2013). *Rise of the warrior cop: The militarization of America's police forces.* New York, NY: Perseus Books Group.

Banks, C. (2012). *Criminal justice ethics: Theory and practice* (3rd ed.). Thousand Oaks, CA: Sage.

Bohm, R., & Walker, J. (2006). *Demystifying crime and criminal justice.* Los Angeles, CA: Roxbury Publishing.

Braswell, M., McCarthy, B., & McCarthy, B. (2011). *Justice, crime, and ethics* (7th ed.). Cincinnati, OH: Anderson Publishing.

Cohen, H., & Feldberg, M. (1991). *Power and restraint: The moral dimension of police work.* Westport, CT: Praeger Publishers.

Delattre, E. (1989). *Character and cops: Ethics in policing.* Washington, DC: American Enterprise Institute.

Friedman, B. (2017). *Unwarranted: Policing without permission.* New York, NY: Farrar, Straus and Giroux.

Gray, D., & Henderson, S. (2017). *The Cambridge handbook of surveillance law.* Cambridge, UK: Cambridge University Press.

Kleinig, J. (1996). *The ethics of policing.* Cambridge, UK: Cambridge University Press.

Leighton, P., & Reiman, J. (2001). *Criminal justice ethics.* Upper Saddle River, NJ: Pearson Prentice Hall.

Pogrebin, M. (2011). *About criminals: A view of the offender's world* (2nd ed.). Thousand Oaks, CA: Sage.

Rossmo, D. (2009). *Criminal investigative failures.* Boca Raton, FL: CRC Press.

White, M. (2007). *Current issues and controversies in policing.* Boston, MA: Pearson.

Williams, C., & Arrigo, B. (2011). *Ethics, crime, and criminal justice* (2nd ed.). Upper Saddle River, NJ: Pearson Prentice Hall.

Notes

1. Go to http://www.cityofboston.gov/news/Default.aspx?id=2621 to read the full press release.

2. See Greenhouse, S. (July 23, 2004), "Convention Near, Boston Police Win Raise," *The New York Times.* Available online at http://www.nytimes.com/2004/07/23/us/convention-near-boston-police-win-raise.html

References

American Civil Liberties Union. (2014). *War comes home: The excessive militarization of American policing.* Retrieved from https://www.aclu.org/report/war-comes-home-excessive-militarization-american-police

American Psychological Association. (2007). *The American Psychological Association dictionary of psychology.* Washington, DC: Author.

Andrews, D., & Bonta, J. (2006). *The psychology of criminal conduct* (4th ed.). Cincinnati, OH: Anderson Publishing.

Bittner, E. (2005). Florence Nightingale in pursuit of Willie Sutton: A theory of the police. In T. Newburn (Ed.), *Policing: Key readings* (pp. 150–172). Devon, UK: Willan Publishing.

Brittan, A. (2001). Masculinities and masculinism. In S. Whitehead & F. Barrett (Eds.), *The masculinities reader.* Cambridge, UK: Polity Press.

Bureau of Justice Statistics. (2010). Full-time law enforcement employees (Table 74). In *Crime in the United States, 2009.* Retrieved from https://www2.fbi.gov/ucr/cius2009/data/table_74.html

Gendreau, P. (2006). Offender rehabilitation: What we know and what needs to be done. In C. Bartol & A. Bartol (Eds.), *Current perspectives in forensic psychology and criminal justice* (pp. 223–229). Thousand Oaks, CA: Sage.

Gordon, D. (1990). *The justice juggernaut: Fighting street crime and controlling citizens*. Piscatawy, NJ: Rutgers University Press.

Harcourt, B. (2001). *Illusion of order: The false promise of broken windows policing*. Cambridge, MA: Harvard University Press.

Karnow, S. (1983). *Vietnam: A history. The complete account of Vietnam at war*. New York, NY: The Viking Press.

Kelling, G., & Wilson, J. (1982). The police and neighborhood safety: Broken windows. *Atlantic Monthly, 127*, 29–38.

Klockars, C. (2005). The rhetoric of community policing. In T. Newburn (Ed.), *Policing: Key readings* (pp. 442–459). Devon, UK: Willan Publishing.

Maguire, M. (2008). Merry Morash: Understanding gender, crime, and justice. *Journal of Critical Criminology, 16*, 225–227.

Morash, M. (2005). *Understanding gender, crime, and justice*. Thousand Oaks, CA: Sage Publications.

Nolan, T. (2001). Galateas in blue: Women police as decoy sex workers. *Criminal Justice Ethics, 20*(2), 63–67.

Nolan, T. (2009). Behind the blue wall of silence. *Journal of Men and Masculinities, 12*(2), 250–257.

Nolan, T. (2015). *Ferguson, the prequel*. American Constitution Society. Retrieved from https://www.acslaw.org/acsblog/ferguson-the-prequel

Pollock, J. (2007). *Ethical dilemmas and decisions in criminal justice* (5th ed.). Belmont, CA: Thomson Wadsworth.

Reaves, B. A. (2011). *Census of state and local law enforcement agencies, 2008*. Washington, DC: Bureau of Justice Statistics. Retrieved from https://www.bjs.gov/index.cfm?ty=pbdetail&iid= 2216

Reaves, B. A. (2012). *Federal law enforcement officers, 2008*. Washington, DC: Bureau of Justice Statistics. Retrieved from http://www.bjs.gov/index.cfm?ty=pbdetail&iid= 4372

Skogan, W. (2006). The promise of community policing. In D. Weisburd & A. Braga (Eds.), *Policing innovation: Contrasting perspectives* (pp. 27–43). Cambridge, UK: Cambridge University Press.

Skolnick, J. (1994). *Justice without trial* (3rd ed.). New York, NY: Macmillan.

Slack, D. (2009, June 15). Even small localities got big guns: some regulations for police enforced. *The Boston Globe*. Retrieved from http://www.boston.com/news/local/massachusetts/articles/2009/06/15/details_emerge_on_distribution_of_military_weapons_in_mass/

U.S. Department of Justice, Office of Justice Programs. (2013). Local police departments, 2013: Personnel, policies, and practices. Retrieved from https://www.bjs.gov/index.cfm?ty=pbdetail&iid=5279

Waddington, P. (1999). Police (canteen) subculture: An appreciation. *British Journal of Criminology, 39*(2), 287–309.

Websdale, N. (2001). *Policing the poor: From slave plantation to public housing*. Boston, MA: Northeastern University Press.

Van Maanen, J. (2005). The asshole. In T. Newburn (Ed.), *Policing: Key readings* (pp. 280–296). Devon, UK: Willan Publishing.

Walker, S., & Katz, C. (2007). *The police in America: An introduction* (6th ed.). Boston, MA: McGraw-Hill.

COURTS/LAW/ JURISPRUDENCE

PART IV

18

PUBLIC POLICY

Janice Ahmad

Public policy shapes much of our everyday social life, from the way we get to school or work, to the breaks that students and employees are granted, to the sanitary conditions of the restaurant in which we eat, to the taxes and fees we pay to maintain our infrastructure, law enforcement agencies, and virtually all of our social services. Public policy has an extensive impact at federal, state, and local levels. This is particularly true for the criminal justice system practiced in the United States.

There are two versions of public policy: the formal, *de jure* (according to law), and the way in which it is actually practiced, *de facto* (in reality). Both will be explained here, along with *three contemporary influences* on the creation of public policy and what we consider to be the future of public policy.

PUBLIC POLICY: THE FORMAL VERSION

Public policy is what the government chooses to do or not do (Dye, 2017). These actions or inactions are based on the social contract—what society expects from government. The social contract evolves and changes according to the interests and values of the public and policy makers. Changes in the social contract occur for such reasons as natural disasters, acts of terrorism, refugees, climate change, government corruption, principles held by new policy makers, or program evaluation results.

A more formal definition of public policy is the purposive governmental course of action or inaction. Policy makers make choices based on a review of an identified problem. These choices (policies) are then implemented and their outcomes observed. The outcomes are evaluated to determine if the impact and effectiveness are meeting the goals of the policy. This formal process of policy making follows a systems approach and is reviewed and revised to meet changes in the social contract. Under this model, one would expect public policy to be the product of a carefully considered process.

Public policy is generally created when a problem is identified and brought to the attention of policy makers. If the problem is perceived as fitting the policy makers' agenda, a public policy may be developed to resolve the problem. In criminal justice, policy agendas are generally based on one of the major goals of the criminal justice system: deterrence, incapacitation, punishment, rehabilitation, reintegration, and restoration (Marion & Oliver, 2012). Before a policy is adopted, the policy-making process is enacted to ensure that resources are effectively and efficiently expended.

When developing public policy, we must keep in mind that it is not developed in a vacuum; rather, a policy can impact several systems and agencies, as well as many people. Policy that does not account for this interconnectedness generally has unintended consequences and is ineffective. Recognizing this, Welsh and Harris (2016) separate the policy-making process into seven components, which can be merged into three for illustration: defining and examining the problem, developing goals and objectives, and creating and implementing the policy.

The first step in developing public policy is to define and examine the problem. What may seem like a widespread problem when first presented may not be, upon examination, as far reaching as thought. Thorough investigation into the problem will reveal its causes, impact, history, stakeholders, previous interventions and outcomes, agency interconnectivity, and the barriers to and support for change. This analysis will produce the goals and objectives that need to be met by the public policy, although more than one approach for resolving the problem may be revealed.

Early identification and involvement of the stakeholders—people who will be positively and negatively affected and the agencies that will be impacted—is vital in policy development. Their involvement is critical to help determine the problem, create the most effective goals and objectives, develop good policy, gain support for the policy, and implement it as intended.

The analysis of the problem will reveal the goals and objectives of the identified solution (i.e., policy). These goals and objectives drive policy development so that the target population, authorized entity, and details and implementation of the policy will resolve the identified problem. Also included in this policy-making process component is the determination of the cost, resources needed, and funding sources (Welsh & Harris, 2016). Finally, an evaluation component is developed.

Evaluation of the public policy helps to determine if the goals and objectives are being met. During the past several years, we have seen an evaluation component being included in public policies. For example, grant solicitations by the U.S. Department of Justice now require that performance measures (i.e., *evidence-based practices*) be included in the grant application and for funding. Evaluations also guide the review and reassessment process to determine if the policy should be revised, continued, or discontinued.

Criminal justice is both directly and indirectly impacted by public policies. Public policies that reduce fear of crime, punish or rehabilitate offenders, and develop more violent crime task forces can be identified as criminal justice policy initiatives and are created in consultation with criminal justice agencies. However, policies that involve other systems (mental health, education, the workplace) may also greatly impact criminal justice. For example, during the late 1960s and early 1970s, many mental health facilities were closed, as it was deemed that clients would be best served in their communities using community resources. However, this resulted in many mentally ill persons becoming involved in a criminal justice system that was not equipped to handle them and thus were subsequently treated as criminals rather than as mentally ill. Unfortunately, we are still seeing the impact of this. Had a policy-making process been thoroughly undertaken and the criminal justice system included in the process, perhaps more community resources for treating the mentally ill would have been established, thus reducing their number in jails and prisons. Therefore, thinking outside the proverbial box needs to be part of the policy-making process.

SOURCES OF CRIMINAL JUSTICE POLICY

Multiple sources create public policy that impacts criminal justice. These include the U.S. Constitution, court decisions, legislatures enacting statutes, administrative agencies issuing regulatory directives, and governmental agencies developing various procedures. All of these sources are duplicated at the federal, state, and local levels, increasing the number of criminal-justice-related policies.

The U.S. Constitution outlines the rights of the people and the responsibility of government. Ultimately, all public policies must conform to this doctrine. In the more than two centuries since the Constitution was ratified, amendments have been added, and its meaning has been debated and analyzed. The U.S. Supreme Court has impacted criminal justice public policy in such cases as *Miranda v. Arizona* (1966; the now famous "Miranda Warnings"), *In re Gault* (1967; beginning due process for juveniles), *Furman v. Georgia* (1972; overturning the death penalty), *Gregg v. Georgia* (1976; reinstating the death penalty under certain conditions), and *Roper v. Simmons* (2005; ending the death penalty for juveniles).

Federal and state statutes lead to criminal justice policy through the establishment of agencies (e.g., California Commission on Peace Officer Standards and Training, Federal Bureau of Prisons, and Texas Juvenile Justice Department); making certain behaviors illegal (speeding, taking someone else's property, possessing controlled substances, or killing another); or providing funds for crime-related initiatives (crime victim compensation, new prisons, or specialized courts).

Regulatory agencies are created through federal and state statutes and are authorized to develop and enforce directives to meet the agency's goals and objectives. These directives, in turn, can impact criminal justice policy. Examples include the California Board of State and Community Corrections, which regulates adult and juvenile detention facilities; the United States Department of Agriculture, which oversees the type of vegetation and animals that can be brought into the country; and the Wisconsin Office of Lawyer Regulation, which sets ethical standards for attorneys. Criminal justice agencies are required to fulfill policies issued by myriad regulatory agencies.

Federal and state legislatures pass bills each year, many of which affect the way criminal justice agencies operate. These statutes are based on policy makers' agendas and are public policy in that they reflect what the government has chosen to do or not do—the basic definition of public policy. Laws making a substance illegal, increasing the number of lower risk defendants released before trial, creating pretrial supervision, or collecting arrestee DNA for analysis are all criminal justice policies that involve making choices, having outputs, and impacting various stakeholders.

One of the most far-reaching public policies for criminal justice was the creation of the Department of Homeland Security (DHS). This decision reconstituted federal criminal justice agencies and affected their duties and responsibilities. The effects filtered down to local levels, creating new positions and interactions. Several evaluations have been conducted to determine if the department meets its various goals and objectives. These evaluations revealed mixed results. A public opinion survey revealed different levels of support for the Department of Homeland Security (Robinson, Xinsheng, Stoutenborough, & Vedlitz, 2013). Friedman (2011) explained that public support for the DHS may be driven by increased fear of terrorism and the perception of the need for more homeland security. In a bottom-up review of the DHS's programs and activities by its own personnel, it was determined that the department needs to work toward meeting its mission, improving leadership and management quality, becoming more accountable for resources, increasing partnership connections, and improving international engagement (DHS, 2010). In a more recent study, the Office of Inspector General of the Department of Homeland Security (2017) reported that the department continues to suffer from management challenges that interfere with meeting the department's goals, contributes to the lack of internal controls, and does not promote the unity of the many different agencies within the department. The evaluations and assessments of the DHS demonstrate the need for continual review and policy change.

Agency-level policy in criminal justice also reflects policy makers' agenda and principles. Policy at this level is generally specific to the agency and its employees, such policies affect those who are served by and interact with the agency. Some agency-level policies have produced their own problems, frequently because the policy-making process was not effectively implemented. These problems are then brought to the attention of other policy makers for remedy. Cases such as *Chimel v. California* (1969; permitting warrantless search incident to arrest), *Pell v. Procunier* (1974; limiting media access to prisoners), and *Riley v. California* (2014; searches incident to arrest exception does not apply to cell phones) are examples of agency policy that has been examined by other policy makers.

PUBLIC POLICY AS IT IS IN PRACTICE

Our description of public policy making in the formal sense is influenced (as is usually the case when it comes to actual practice in criminal justice matters) by elements inside and outside the system. There are four primary groups of policy-influencing elements: moral entrepreneurs, or moral crusaders; lobbyists, think tanks, and those otherwise politically and financially connected to powerful people; vested-interest groups; and the media.

Partisanship, Politicization, and Ideology

Any public policy is an outcome of the political process because it can only be created through that process. However, certain parties both inside and outside of the political arena attempt to exert power and influence so that the direction and content of public policy reflects their interests. Partisanship on certain issues results in setting aside the essential democratic process of our political system to ensure that issues near and dear to the hearts of political majorities (or at least those with substantial political power) are enacted into law. In some instances, it is sufficient that certain viewpoints hold sway and become the preferred view. In such cases, public policy is no longer a product of group consensus but instead a vehicle to force the values of a powerful group onto those less powerful. The recent history of partisanship and legislation in the U.S. Congress is testament to the process of influence leading to politicization. When issues can be politicized, values and sometimes influence itself become more important than their content. Values embedded in policies are frequently used to direct far-reaching purposes that have little to do with the policies themselves.

These values are sometimes referred to as *ideologies*. An ideology is a basic set of background assumptions that control the way a person or group views and judges a phenomenon. As a result, ideologies are rarely questioned by those who hold them and are often based on belief, not science (Walker, 2015). Indeed, to question an ideology would move it from the background of ideas to the foreground and therefore likely to abort its power to control thought. In one sense, we all have ideologies, but it is when they are thrust into the political arena that they become concerning for public policy. This discussion of partisanship suggests that there are at least two opposing ideologies in the U.S. political world today. Each group of adherents attempts to control how public realities are viewed. Public policy is used as an instrument to further that control. Thus, public policy, by itself, is not the important ingredient; the *control* of policy becomes a way to implement ideology, or core values.

Sources of Influence and Information

Moral entrepreneurs are among the most influential of these where the making of public policy is concerned. As described by Becker (1963), moral entrepreneurs who are rule creators seek to influence and define particular social norms. They do this for selfish reasons, but most likely their purpose is the product of a moral outrage and evil to be fought—or as Becker (1963) puts it, "a moral crusade" (p. 148). In one of the more common criminal justice scenarios, this is usually the product of a crime found abominable by some relative of the victim, the relative takes it upon himself or herself to campaign for a new law or approach to the crime. For example, the killing of Candy Lightner's 12-year-old daughter by a drunk driver resulted in her campaign against DWI and the subsequent creation of MADD in 1980.

Even if the crime is statistically rare, the pursuit of "righting the wrong" results in artificially inflated numbers and a claim of common occurrence to justify policy change. Common characteristics among moral entrepreneurs are dogged pursuit of the issue, grandstanding, making out-of-proportion claims, and appealing for sympathy as a victim. Somewhere along this process, many also begin to benefit from their cause, either financially or by celebrity. Some have become television personalities, and others have created foundations to disperse donated funds (resulting in employment by their own foundation). In this sense, they become vested participants in the public policy process, over and above their original interest.

These moral entrepreneurs are part of the process Cohen (1972) termed *moral panics* and known more generally as *constructed social problems*. The process is identical in all aspects to the process of recognizing social problems. Focusing on a real (or even imagined) issue, the moral entrepreneur brings the issue to the attention of the public with exaggerated claims of its frequency. Those with a vested interest (for example, an agency handling such issues and thereby having a financial stake) pick up the public claims and make public announcements designed to support the image of the problem as a relatively common occurrence. The media then circulate this information, again reporting claims and the frequency of the problem. The claims tend to escalate the exaggeration and stress the moral offensiveness of the problem. At this point, a politician or bloc of politicians, sensing a gain in both publicity and political image, become "saviors" by creating public policy against the heinous problem. Thus, public policy in the criminal justice arena is often a knee-jerk reaction to an exaggerated problem.

A factor in whether this reaction actually produces results is the timing with which others who have actual knowledge of the extent of the problem critique the exaggerations. If this happens fairly soon after the initial pronouncements, the creation of policy is less likely to occur. If the critique occurs later in the process, laws are frequently already passed, and the issue takes on a life of its own, regardless of the evidence against it. Once some organization or agency has gained responsibility for eliminating the issue, the financial incentives that go along with it virtually ensure that the problem will continue to exist. In fact, most documented cases have not only resulted in the survival of the problem but led to its expansion. In other words, organizations use social problems to gain funding and expand; to the extent they can gain control over these problems, they can redefine problems in ways that best suit their own agendas.

Some of the characteristics associated with moral panic leading to law and public policy generally have emotional attributes, including child victims, stranger offenders, and the randomness of crime. Of course, the political power and degree of vested interest of both the claims-makers and those potentially arrayed against the claims must be considered. The problem of these claims is twofold. First, public policy should deal with common occurrences, not exaggerated phenomena made to seem more pervasive than they are. And second, they absorb limited criminal justice system resources and distract attention from more frequent and more serious issues.

Aside from moral entrepreneurs, there are other common sources of people and organizations that push to have their agendas made into policy. Included among them are lobbyists, think tanks, and the power-elite, many groups with a single focus. There are a number of ways these groups affect public policy through their often self-serving efforts. Moreover, any of these can also serve as moral crusaders, including the media. The media, in particular, contribute to the agenda of other groups by reporting on any emerging policy initiatives. Media are frequently seen as disinterested bystanders, but because they are businesses, they have a vested interest in selling themselves. Thus, any topic imbued with the essence of sensationalism and the right combination of images (a child victim of sex abuse and an adult predator are ideal) will be given substantial coverage. This applies to Internet and digital sources (such as social media, Twitter, Instagram, and Snapchat), as well as the more traditional television, radio, and/or printed in newspapers. As of late, some media sources have even given up the attempt to appear objective and simply aired images of crime and victims, as other businesses might seek any high-profit item. Finally, it should be obvious that many criminal justice policy initiatives find most, if not all, of these influences coming together to support political agendas.

THE USE AND MISUSE OF PUBLIC POLICY

The use and misuse of criminal justice public policy is a virtual certainty. You can be sure that someone or some group has a vested interest in every public policy created in the criminal justice arena. This however, does not suggest that policy is being misused; it just means that public policy has untold utility.

One way to critically analyze any public policy is to think about its function. Merton (1936, 1968) distinguished between two types of functions, *manifest* and *latent*. Manifest functions are those that are intended. For example, in the public policy known as "three strikes," the manifest function was to make sure that dangerous felons were removed from the streets and kept in prison for at least 25 years. Latent functions are an action's unanticipated consequences, or those functions that are unintended. In the three-strikes example, latent functions might include application of the law to criminals who are not dangerous, the increased numbers of jury trials because of defendants' refusals to plead guilty or plea bargain, and costly new prison construction due to the increased numbers of inmates.

Another issue to look for in a proposed public policy is financial motive. Such motives do not usually surface in initial proposals and discussions, as legislative proposals rarely include immediate funding. Nonetheless, during the latter stages of policy making, an agency can gain funding by showing a need for added personnel, new programming, and/or technological innovations that will be needed for its implementation. For instance, the sex offender registration policies forced state agencies to develop real-time databases that are easily accessible to the public, while large police agencies developed new units to ensure timely registration and enforcement of the law. Therefore, these agencies were able to justify economic assistance to ensure their implementation. The increased budgetary expenses needed for sex offender registration laws, for example, are supported by policy makers who do not want to appear soft on crime or for favor further victimization of children by strangers.

Finally, there are cases of purposefully misleading the public to achieve policy goals. These, too, are exemplified in the victims' movement and how legislative bills and acts are named. While these titles maybe misleading, they serve the purpose of generating policy statements on (usually) related issues. The so-called PATRIOT Act is an example. Who would be against this law?

Examples of California Public Policy Overreach

The victims' movement in California provides three good examples of the creation of social policy to benefit victims, while actually having another purpose. In 1984, the state assembly approved the Roberti-Imbrecht-Rains-Goggins Child Sexual Abuse Prevention Act. With the words *children* and *sexual abuse* in the title, supporting the act was a "no-brainer" for politicians, and they literally lined up to be associated with it. The fact was that it did nothing to specifically support the prevention of child sexual abuse, and it was intentionally mislabeled to gain support (Iglehart, 1990), which was remarkable. The act provided funds for police and prosecutors, instituted harsher punishments for child molesters, extended the statute of limitations for filing charges, and allowed judges and prosecutors (both elected officials) to reap political benefits as they claimed to actively combat crime in the new get-tough atmosphere.

A second example of intentional mislabeling is the California Child Protection Act of 1984. Once again, there were no provisions to directly protect children, and the intended beneficiaries were prosecutors and legislators, both of whom could make political claims of their support (Iglehart, 1990). The primary nonpolitical benefits were that prosecutors (1) no longer needed to prove intent and (2) could confiscate property that was the fruit of child pornography profits, along with the equipment used in its production. The latter meant additional funding in their budgets as the confiscated property was auctioned off.

Finally, the California Crime Victims Justice Reform Initiative of 1990 (Proposition 115) was passed under the state's proposition process. As with the other two acts, the title was intentionally misleading (Iglehart, 1990). Victims gained little direct assistance with the passage of the proposition. On the other hand, judges, prosecutors, and politicians benefited tremendously. Because the public was caught up in a "crime wave" mentality and protecting victims was a popular cause, the proposition provided political gains to its supporters and made it easier for judges and prosecutors to increase conviction rates. Even better for politicians faced with campaign spending caps, campaign money was transferred to support the proposition (along with mention of the candidate's largesse), and thus, candidates were able to avoid legal spending limitations but still gain media coverage by "campaigning" for a popular issue.

THE POLICY IMPLICATIONS OF PUBLIC POLICY

Evidence-Based Policy

After decades of coaxing, criminal justice researchers have recently seen the adoption of *evidence-based decision-making* by criminal justice agencies. This has long been considered the gold standard of adopting policies and programs in other fields, especially medicine. Previously, most policy decisions in criminal justice were based on many of the elements examined here, including gut-level and instinctive decisions. Now, we are seeing the use of both research evidence and data from agency information systems to provide a more objective, reality-based and, certainly, more defensible way to determine what problems exist and what decisions might be made about them. Several criminal justice program-funding organizations, especially the Police Research Foundation, the Edna McConnell Clark Foundation, and the National Institute of Justice (NIJ), now require evidence-based program decisions when they are the funding sources.

The Obama administration used *evidence-based* as a mantra and insisted that it be used to guide policy decisions. Evidence-based policy making should result in better public policies and the laws to support them, particularly when compared with past examples of ideologically driven and gut-level policies. An example is a report from the National Academy of Sciences (2009), in which scientific experts evaluated current forensic science practice, technology, and interpretation. They found that a substantial amount of the work in police crime laboratories was based on faulty, discredited, and/or imprecise science and procedures to match evidence to individuals, in particular non-DNA tests, such as fingerprint comparison, tool analysis, and hair analysis. As a result, NIJ is requesting research to determine what directions need to be pursued in developing policy for handling, testing, interpreting, and presenting criminal evidence. Criminal justice agencies are adopting this standard when introducing new programs and when making changes to programs already in place. For example, when Harris County, Texas, was developing a felony mental health court, evidence-based models were included by the planning and development committee. This was to ensure that the data collected would be available in the evaluation of the court.

It will be interesting to watch the Trump administration's use or lack of use of evidence-based policies and programs. A November 2017 report written by the Department of Homeland Security included statements showing the desire and need to follow evidence-based practices. However, we have heard statements by members of this administration that several ideas that were previously adopted because of research and scientific findings are now being disclaimed due to junk science.

THE POLITICIZATION OF PUBLIC POLICY

Though evidence-based policy has been declared the gold standard of effective and efficient policy making and is being adopted across criminal justice practice, there is reason to believe that the informal elements and motivations involved in past policy making will reappear. Despite the acceptance of evidence-based policy making, we have seen a movement intended to subvert the use of scientific evidence in federal government agencies and congressional hearings. In the 1980s, the tobacco industry developed argumentative techniques in which "fringe science" was presented as "sound science" (Mooney, 2006). While *sound science* sounds reasonable, suggesting the use of the best available evidence and scientific positions, the opposite is true with antiscience pronouncements that all scientific opinion is equal. Rather, real science itself is highly skeptical, critical, and, above all, not democratic; quality and rigor are valued above all else. That very questioning and skepticism has been used to label real science as "uncertain," "fatally-flawed," and, thus, "junk science" (Mooney, 2006). Various vested-interest groups and ideologues in the federal government have pushed "sound science" as a pseudonym allowing fringe positions (those supportive of their positions) an equal voice with best available evidence (i.e., evidence-based research) in an effort to rig hearings and policy. Because real scientists are skeptical and critical, representatives of these interest groups or ideologies play up small disagreements and uncertainties in best available evidence as if there actually were no good evidence. Pseudoscientists asked to provide evidence in support of the vested-interest position have no such qualms and critical stance, thus they and their political supporters announce their fringe "evidence" as correct. Most recently, we have seen this applied to the Paris Climate Agreement, in which every country in the world has signed except the United States under the Trump administration.

Several years ago, this process played out in criminal justice as political operatives were appointed to positions in various agencies within the Department of Justice. Scientific research reports suddenly required approval by a deputy director who knew little about research. If findings did not match a desired conclusion, the wording of the report was changed. Those who objected found that their reports went unpublished. Even worse, the grant process was subverted to provide a substantial amount of money to those with business connections (criminal justice and homeland security technologies) and/or the correct political connections. Peer review of grants (the process of researcher experts being assigned to evaluate proposed research) was ignored so that funded "research" was often poorly constructed and incapable of producing a defensible result. If this subversion of scientific research reasserts itself, then there is reason to doubt that evidence-based policy making will actually produce better informed and more objective policies.

THE CONTRIBUTIONS OF ACADEMIC CRIMINAL JUSTICE

Another factor in the future of public policy development is the emerging majority of criminal justice agency personnel who have been educated in university criminal justice departments. This group is now developing into a critical mass and is much more likely to ask for research results and related evidence before making decisions. As a result, better agency policy decisions are being, and will be, made and better advice is available to lawmakers and governmental agencies. Similarly, academic criminal justice is now more likely to be asked to provide information for the development of legislation and public policy. This trend is favorable but threatens vested-interest groups, ideologists, lobbyists, and moral entrepreneurs. Because legislators and policy makers are ultimately public figures, loud public voices will continue to have a substantial say in criminal justice legislation and policy.

CONCLUSION

The use of evidence and research results in criminal justice decision making and the creation of agency policy have made great strides. Whether that will continue in the larger public policy realm is much in doubt. Simply put, there is too much at stake among those with moral positions, ideological agendas, and political futures for public policy to be made in a purely evidence-based, research-informed atmosphere. While there is reason to hope that future public policy will be more objective, perhaps the best that we can do now is to ask for a voice in the process and attempt to provide valid information. One way to do this is to supply the media with time-sensitive and objective information to counter exaggerated claims made in the early stages of the policy debate. Assuming that the best public policy is based on objective reality rather than subjective versions of reality, any increase in the consumption of objective information based on the scientific method can only serve to improve criminal justice policies.

Discussion Questions

1. How should public policy making be accomplished in a democracy? How closely does that description fit with your experience?

2. How do you see public policy being made in your state? Do various checks and balances come into play, or is it a product of rather unfettered influence? Are there any other ways to make public policy that you might find preferable?

3. When federal mental health agencies deinstitutionalized the mentally ill in favor of community treatment, there was a profound effect on local criminal justice agencies. Why are we still experiencing the impact of this policy decision?

4. What do you think of the concept of moral entrepreneurs and moral panics? Is it an overblown academic position, or does it represent reality? Identify current examples of potential moral panics that may call for new criminal justice policies.

5. What do you view as the effect of ideology on the making of public policy? Is there anything wrong with the interplay of ideology and policy making? How would one create any particular focus to guide policy making if ideologies did not exist?

6. Rather than affect public policy by public outcry, as moral entrepreneurs do, others attempt to directly influence both the making and the direction of public policy. How would you describe the effect of lobbyists and think tanks on policy making? In a philosophical vein, what do you think about the fairness of their efforts and subsequent effects in a democratic society?

7. How do you react to the statement that the discipline of criminal justice may ultimately have an effect on the quality of public policy in the crime and justice area? If you agree, how do you see this happening? If you disagree, what are your reasons?

Note From the Author

I am indebted to Frank P. Williams III for coauthoring this chapter in earlier editions of the book. He developed the theoretical framework, which I continue to use here. Dr. Williams has retired from the University of Houston–Downtown and is enjoying life as a woodworker and craft brew taste tester.

References

Becker, H. S. (1963). Moral entrepreneurs. In H. S. Becker (Ed.), *Outsiders: Studies in the sociology of deviance* (pp. 147–163). New York, NY: The Free Press.

Cohen, S. (1972). *Folk devils and moral panics: The creation of the Mods and Rockers.* Oxford, UK: Basil.

Department of Homeland Security. (2010, July). *Bottom-up review report.* Washington, DC: Author.

Dye, T. (2017). *Understanding public policy* (15th ed.). Upper Saddle River, NJ: Prentice Hall.

Friedman, B. H. (2011). Managing fear: The politics of homeland security. *Political Science Quarterly, 126*(1), 77–106.

Iglehart, R. (1990, October). *The impact of Proposition 115: The Crime Victims Initiative.* Keynote speech delivered to the Association of Criminal Justice Researchers (CA), Claremont, CA.

Marion, N. E., & Oliver, W. M. (2012). *The public policy of crime and criminal justice* (2nd ed.). Upper Saddle River, NJ: Prentice Hall.

McShane, M. D., & Williams, F. P., III. (1992). Radical victimology: A critique of the concept of victim in traditional victimology. *Crime & Delinquency, 38,* 258–271.

Merton, R. K. (1936). The unanticipated consequences of purposive social action. *American Sociological Review, 1,* 894–904.

Merton, R. K. (1968). Manifest and latent functions. In R. K. Merton (Ed.), *Social theory and social structure* (3rd ed., pp. 73–91). New York, NY: Free Press.

Mooney, C. (2006). *The Republican war on science* (Rev ed.). New York, NY: Basic Books.

National Academy of Sciences, Committee on Identifying the Needs of the Forensic Sciences Community. (2009). *Strengthening forensic science in the United States: A path forward.* Washington, DC: National Academies Press.

Office of Inspector General. (2017, November 3). *General major management and performance challenges facing the Department of Homeland Security* (OIG-18-11). Washington, DC: Department of Homeland Security.

Robinson, S. E., Xinsheng, L., Stoutenborough, J. W., & Vedlitz, A. (2013). Explaining popular trust in the Department of Homeland Security. *Journal of Public Administration Research and Theory, 23*(3), 713–733.

Walker, S. (2015). *Sense and nonsense about crime, drugs, and communities* (8th ed.). Stamford, CT: Cengage Learning.

Welsh, W. N., & Harris, P. W. (2016). *Criminal justice policy and planning* (5th ed.). New York, NY: Routledge.

AMERICAN COURTS

Cassia Spohn

The past 50 years have witnessed significant changes in the structure of the American court system and the procedures that courts use to adjudicate criminal cases and sentence convicted offenders. Some of these changes resulted from Supreme Court decisions that interpreted constitutional provisions regarding right to counsel, selection of the jury, cruel and unusual punishment, due process of law, and equal protection under the law. Other changes resulted from legislative attempts to toughen criminal sentences and reduce sentence disparity, to provide alternatives to prison and probation, or to handle certain types of cases such as drug offenses or cases involving mentally ill offenders more efficiently and effectively. Considered together, these changes have revolutionized the way American courts do business.

SUPREME COURT DECISIONS AND AMERICAN COURTS

The United States Supreme Court has played an important role in the development of the American court system, particularly with respect to such issues as right to counsel, jury selection, and sentencing. The decisions handed down by the Court in these areas have altered policy and practice and have led to fairer and less discriminatory court processing decisions.

The Right to Counsel

A series of court decisions broadened the interpretation of the Sixth Amendment's guarantee of the right to counsel and led to significant changes in requirements for provision of counsel for indigent defendants. The process began in 1932, when the Court ruled in *Powell v. Alabama* (287 U.S. 45 [1932]) that states must provide attorneys for indigent defendants charged with capital crimes. The Court's decision in a 1938 case, *Johnson v. Zerbst* (304 U.S. 458 [1938]), required the appointment of counsel for all indigent defendants in federal criminal cases, but the requirement was not extended to the states until *Gideon v. Wainwright* (372 U.S. 335 [1963]) was handed down in 1963. In subsequent decisions, the Court ruled that "no person may be imprisoned, for any offense, whether classified as petty, misdemeanor, or felony, unless he was represented by counsel"[1] and that the right to counsel is not limited to trial but applies to all "critical stages" in the criminal justice process.[2] As a result of these rulings, states must provide most indigent defendants with counsel, from arrest and interrogation through sentencing and the appellate process.

States moved quickly to implement the constitutional requirement articulated in *Gideon* and the subsequent cases, either by establishing public defender systems or by appropriating money for court-appointed attorneys. In 1951, there were only seven public defender organizations in the United States; in 1964, there were 136. By 1973, the total had risen to 573 (McIntyre, 1987), and by 2010, there were 957 public defender offices across the nation. A national survey of indigent defense services among all U.S. prosecutorial districts found that 21% used a public defender program, 19% used an assigned counsel system, and 7% used a contract attorney system; the remaining districts (43%) reported that a combination of methods was used (Bureau of Justice Statistics, 2006). Although some critics have questioned the quality of legal services afforded indigent defendants (Casper, 1971; "Gideon's promise," 2000), particularly in capital cases where the stakes are obviously very high (Bright, 1994), the findings of a number of methodologically sophisticated studies suggest that case outcomes for defendants represented by public defenders are not significantly different from those for defendants represented by private attorneys (Hanson & Ostrom, 2004; Williams, 2002). These results suggest that poor defendants are no longer "without a voice" (Myrdal, 1944, p. 547) in courts throughout the United States.

The Supreme Court also ruled that defendants must be provided with "effective assistance of counsel" (*Strickland v. Washington*, 466 U.S. 668 [1984]). According to this court ruling, to establish ineffectiveness, a defendant must prove, first, that counsel's performance was deficient and, second, that the deficiencies in the counsel's performance deprived the defendant of a fair trial. In two subsequent decisions, the Court ruled that the right to effective assistance of counsel applies to plea negotiations, as well as to trials. In one case, *Missouri v. Fyre* (132 S. Ct. 1399, 2012), the defense attorney failed to make the defendant aware of a plea offer from the prosecutor and the defendant subsequently pled guilty not knowing that the prosecutor had offered to reduce the seriousness of the charge. In a second case, *Lafler v. Cooper* (132 S. Ct. 1376, 2012), the defense attorney advised the defendant, who was charged with assault with intent to murder, to reject a plea offer that would have resulted in a sentence of 52–85 months in prison because, in his view, the prosecutor would be unable to prove intent to murder given that

Lafler had shot the victim below the waist. The defendant went to trial, was convicted, and was sentenced to 185–360 months in prison. In both of these cases, the Supreme Court ruled 5–4 that the defendants had not been provided effective assistance of counsel.

Jury Selection

Supreme Court decisions also have placed important restrictions on the jury selection process. The Court has consistently ruled against racial and ethnic bias in the selection of the jury pool and has made it more difficult for prosecutors and defense attorneys to use their peremptory challenges to exclude Black and Hispanic jurors. As the Court has repeatedly emphasized, the jury serves as "the criminal defendant's fundamental 'protection of life and liberty against race or color prejudice.'"[3] Reflecting this, in 1889, the Supreme Court ruled in the case of *Strauder v. West Virginia* (100 U.S. 303 [1880]) that a West Virginia statute limiting jury service to White males violated the equal protection clause of the 14th Amendment and therefore was unconstitutional.

The Court's ruling in *Strauder* made it clear that states could not pass laws excluding Blacks from jury service, but it did not prevent states—and particularly southern states—from developing techniques designed to preserve the all-White jury. In a series of decisions that began in the mid-1930s, the Supreme Court struck down these laws and practices, ruling, for example, that it was unconstitutional for a Georgia county to put the names of White potential jurors on white cards, the names of Black potential jurors on yellow cards, and then "randomly" draw cards to determine who would be summoned for jury service (*Avery v. Georgia*, 345 U.S. 559 [1953], at 562). As the Court stated in this case, "The State may not draw up its jury lists pursuant to neutral procedures but then resort to discrimination at other stages in the selection process."

Critics contend that the Court's decisions regarding the *peremptory challenge* do, in fact, open the door to discrimination in jury selection (Kennedy, 1997; Serr & Maney, 1988). The Supreme Court's insistence that the jury be drawn from a representative cross-section of the community and that race is not a valid qualification for jury service applies only to the selection of the jury pool. It does not apply to the selection of individual jurors for a particular case. As the Court has repeatedly stated, a defendant is *not* entitled to a jury "composed in whole or in part of persons of his own race."[4] Thus, prosecutors and defense attorneys can use their peremptory challenges—"challenges without cause, without explanation, and without judicial scrutiny"[5]—as they see fit. Critics of the process contend that, decisions handed down by the Supreme Court notwithstanding, prosecutors and defense attorneys can use their peremptory challenges to produce juries that contain few, if any, racial minorities.

The Supreme Court's rulings regarding racial discrimination in the use of peremptory challenges have evolved over time. The Court initially ruled that, although the prosecutor's use of peremptory challenges to strike all of the Black potential jurors in a jury pool did not violate the equal protection clause of the Constitution, a defendant could establish a prima facie case of purposeful racial discrimination by showing that the elimination of Blacks from a particular jury was part of a *pattern of discrimination* in that jurisdiction (*Swain v. Alabama*, 380 U.S. 202 [1965]). The problem, of course, was that the defendants in *Swain* and in the cases that followed could not meet this stringent test. As Wishman (1986) observed, "A defense lawyer almost never has the statistics to prove a pattern of discrimination, and the state under the *Swain* decision is not required to keep them" (p. 115). The ruling, therefore, provided no protection to the individual Black or Hispanic defendant deprived of a jury of his peers by the prosecutor's use of racially discriminatory strikes.

It was not until 1986 that the Court, in *Batson v. Kentucky* (476 U.S. 79 [1986]), rejected *Swain's* systematic exclusion requirement and ruled "that a defendant may establish a *prima facie* case of purposeful discrimination in selection of the petit jury solely on evidence concerning the prosecutor's exercise of peremptory challenges at the defendant's trial." The justices added that once the defendant makes a prima facie case of racial discrimination, the burden shifts to the state to provide a racially neutral explanation for excluding Black jurors.

Although *Batson* seemed to offer hope that the goal of a representative jury was attainable, an examination of cases decided since 1986 suggests otherwise. State and federal appellate courts have ruled, for example, that leaving one or two Blacks on the jury precludes any inference of purposeful racial discrimination on the part of the prosecutor[6] and that striking only one or two jurors of the defendant's race does not constitute a "pattern" of strikes.[7] Trial and appellate courts have also been willing to accept virtually any explanation offered by the prosecutor to rebut the defendant's inference of purposeful discrimination (Serr & Maney, 1988, pp. 44–47, but see the recent decision by the U.S. Supreme Court in *Foster v. Chatman*, 578 U.S. ____, 2016, in which the Court ruled that the defendant had established purposeful racial discrimination in the prosecutor's use of peremptory challenges).

Decisions such as these led Kennedy (1997) to characterize the peremptory challenge as "a creature of unbridled discretion that, in the hands of white prosecutors and white defendants, has often been used to sustain racial subordination in the courthouse" (p. 214). The Supreme Court's decisions notwithstanding, the peremptory challenge continues to be an obstacle to the creation of a racially neutral jury selection process.

Capital and Noncapital Sentencing

A third area that has been significantly reshaped by Supreme Court decisions is sentencing. The Court has handed down a series of important decisions on the capital sentencing process. Although the Court has never ruled that the death penalty per se is cruel and unusual punishment, it has said that the death penalty cannot be imposed on an offender convicted of the rape of an adult woman (*Coker v. Georgia*, 433 U.S. 584 [1977]) or child (*Kennedy v. Louisiana*, 554 U.S. 407 [2008]) and that the death penalty can be imposed on an offender convicted of felony murder if the offender played a major role in the crime and displayed "reckless indifference to the value of human life" (*Tison v. Arizona*, 481 U.S. 137 [1987], at 157). The Court also has ruled that the execution of someone who is mentally handicapped is cruel and unusual punishment in violation of the Eighth Amendment (*Atkins v. Virginia*, 536 U.S. 304 [2002]), that the Eighth and 14th Amendments forbid the imposition of the death penalty on offenders who were younger than age 18 when their crimes were committed (*Roper v. Simmons*, 543 U.S. 551 [2005]), and that the Constitution does not prohibit the use of lethal injection (*Baze v. Rees*, 553 U.S. 35 [2008]). With the exception of the felony murder and lethal injection rulings, these decisions all restrict the use of the death penalty by state and federal courts. In recent years, the Court also has overturned a number of death sentences due to ineffective assistance of counsel (see, for example, *Porter v. McCollum*, 130 S.C. 447 [2009] and *Sears v. Upton*, 130 S.C. 3,259 [2010]).

The Supreme Court also has addressed the issue of the role played by the jury at sentencing. The first case, *Apprendi v. New Jersey* (530 U.S. 466 [2000]), involved Charles Apprendi Jr., who fired several shots into the home of a Black family and made a number of statements, which he later retracted, suggesting that he had fired into the home because he did not want the family living in his neighborhood. Apprendi pleaded guilty to possession of a weapon for an unlawful purpose, a crime that carried a term of imprisonment of 5 to 10 years. The prosecutor then filed a motion for an enhanced sentence under the New Jersey hate crime statute. The judge in the case found by a preponderance of the evidence that the shooting was racially motivated and sentenced Apprendi to 12 years in prison. Apprendi appealed, claiming that the due process clause of the Constitution required the state to prove the allegation of bias to the jury beyond a reasonable doubt. The Supreme Court ruled in Apprendi's favor, stating that any fact that increases the penalty for a crime beyond the prescribed statutory maximum, other than the fact of a prior conviction, must be submitted to a jury and proved beyond a reasonable doubt. In 2002, the justices similarly ruled that a jury—not a judge—must find the aggravating circumstances necessary for imposition of the death penalty (*Ring v. Arizona*, 536 U.S. 584 [2002]).

The Court reiterated this position in subsequent decisions involving defendants who were challenging sentences imposed under state and federal sentencing guidelines. In 2004, for example, the Court ruled in *Blakely v. Washington* (542 U.S. 296 [2004]) that the judge's decision to impose a sentence more severe than the statutory maximum allowed under the Washington sentencing guidelines violated the defendant's Sixth Amendment right to trial by jury. The Court revisited this issue 6 months later. This time, the issue was the power of federal judges to impose sentences more severe than called for under the U.S. sentencing guidelines.

In *United States v. Booker* (543 U.S. 220 [2005]), the Court ruled, consistent with its decisions in *Apprendi* and *Blakely*, that the jury must determine beyond a reasonable doubt any fact that increases the defendant's sentence beyond the maximum sentence allowed under the sentencing guidelines.[8] The facts in this case were similar to those in *Blakely*. Booker was found guilty of a drug offense that, under the guidelines, carried a sentence of 210 to 262 months. At the sentencing hearing, however, the judge found additional facts that justified a harsher sentence; he sentenced Booker to 360 months in prison. The Court held that the 30-year sentence imposed by the judge violated the Sixth Amendment right to a jury trial and ordered the district court either to sentence Booker within the sentencing range supported by the jury's findings or to hold a separate sentencing hearing before a jury. The Court also ruled that the federal sentencing guidelines were advisory, not mandatory. In two cases decided in 2007,[9] the Court reiterated that the guidelines were advisory and ruled that the below-guidelines sentences imposed in each case were "reasonable" and that the judges who imposed the sentences had not abused their discretion. In the *Gall* decision, the Court noted that although the guidelines are the starting point and initial benchmark, they are not the only factors to be taken into consideration. A 2013 case, *Alleyne v. United States* (133 S. Ct. 2151 [2013]), added to this line of jurisprudence by ruling that facts that increase mandatory minimum sentences must be submitted to the jury (and proved beyond a reasonable doubt) or admitted to by the defendant.

The Supreme Court's decisions in these sentencing cases enhance the role played by the jury in both capital and noncapital cases. The decisions emphasize that the jury, not the judge, is to determine the facts in the case, that juries must determine the existence of aggravating factors that justify the imposition of the death penalty, and that sentences cannot exceed the maximum sentence based on the facts that were admitted in a guilty plea or found by the jury. Considered together, these decisions have transformed the landscape of sentencing in the United States.

THE SENTENCING REFORM MOVEMENT

In 1972, Marvin Frankel, U.S. district judge for the Southern District of New York, issued an influential call for reform of the sentencing process (Frankel, 1972). The focus of Judge Frankel's critique was the indeterminate sentence, in which the judge imposed a minimum and maximum sentence, but the parole board determined the date of release based on its assessment of whether the offender had been rehabilitated or had served enough time for the particular offense. Judge Frankel characterized the indeterminate sentencing system as "a bizarre 'nonsystem' of extravagant powers confided to variable and essentially unregulated judges, keepers, and parole officials" (p. 1). Frankel (1972), who maintained that the degree of discretion given to judges led to "lawlessness" in sentencing, called for legislative reforms designed to regulate "the unchecked powers of the untutored judge" (p. 41).

Judge Frankel's calls for reform did not go unheeded. Reformers from both sides of the political spectrum joined in the attack on indeterminate sentencing and pushed for reforms designed to curtail judicial discretion and eliminate arbitrariness and disparity in sentencing. In response, state legislatures and Congress enacted a series of incremental structured sentencing reforms. A number of jurisdictions experimented with voluntary or advisory sentencing guidelines. Other states adopted determinate sentencing policies and abolished release on parole. Still other jurisdictions created sentencing commissions authorized to promulgate presumptive sentencing guidelines. Most states and the federal government also enacted mandatory minimum sentences for certain types of offenses (especially drug and weapons offenses), "three-strikes-and-you're-out" laws that mandated long prison sentences for repeat offenders, and truth-in-sentencing statutes that required offenders to serve a larger portion of the sentence before being released.

This process of experimentation and reform revolutionized sentencing in the United States. Thirty years ago, every state and the federal government had an indeterminate sentencing system, and "the word 'sentencing' generally signified a slightly mysterious process which . . . involved individualized decisions that judges were uniquely qualified to make" (Tonry, 1996, p. 3). The situation today is much more complex. Sentencing policies and practices vary enormously on a number of dimensions, and there is no longer anything that can be described as the American approach.

Determinate Sentencing

In the mid- to late 1970s, several states abolished release on parole and replaced the indeterminate sentence with a fixed (i.e., determinate) sentence. Under this system, the state legislature established a presumptive range of confinement for various categories of offenses. The judge imposed a fixed number of years from within this range, and the offender would serve this term minus time off for good behavior. Determinate sentencing, which was first adopted in California, Illinois, Indiana, and Maine, was seen as a way to restrain judicial discretion and thus to reduce disparity and (at least in the minds of conservative reformers) preclude judges from imposing overly lenient sentences. However, the degree to which the reforms constrain discretion varies.

The California Uniform Determinate Sentencing Law, which took effect on July 1, 1977, provides that judges are to choose one of three specified sentences for persons convicted of particular offenses. The judge is to impose the middle term unless there are aggravating or mitigating circumstances that justify imposing the higher or lower term. Judges have considerably more discretion under the Illinois Determinate Sentencing Statute. Felonies are divided into six classifications and the range of penalties is wide, especially for the more serious offenses.

Murder and Class X offenses are nonprobationable, but judges can impose prison terms of 20 to 60 years or life for murder and 6 to 30 years for Class X offenses. If there are aggravating circumstances, the sentence range for Class X felonies increases to 30 to 60 years.

Although judges in jurisdictions with determinate sentencing retain control over the critical probation or prison decision, their overall discretion is reduced, particularly in states like California. Evaluations of the impact of the California law showed that judges complied with the law and imposed the middle term in a majority of the cases (Cohen & Tonry, 1983). Despite predictions that discretion would shift to the prosecutor and that plea bargaining would consequently increase, there were no changes in the rate or timing of guilty pleas that could be attributed to the determinate sentencing law. On the other hand, there was some evidence that prosecutors were increasingly likely to use provisions regarding sentence enhancements and probation ineligibility as bargaining chips. One study, for example, found that the sentence enhancement for use of a weapon was dropped in 40% of robbery cases and that the enhancement for serious bodily injury was struck in 65% to 70% of these cases (Casper, Brereton, & Neal, 1982). As Walker (1993) noted, "The net effect of the law seems to have been to narrow and focus the exercise of plea-bargaining discretion. Given the very restricted options on sentence length, the importance of the various enhancements and disqualifiers increased" (p. 129).

Partly as a result of research showing that determinate sentencing laws did not significantly constrain the discretion of judges, the determinate sentencing movement lost steam and eventually sputtered out. With the exception of the District of Columbia, no jurisdiction has adopted determinate sentencing since 1983. Moreover, in 2007, the Supreme Court addressed the validity of sentences imposed under California's determinate sentencing law. In the case of *Cunningham v. California* (127 S. Ct. 856 [2007]), the judge sentenced Cunningham to the higher term, based on six aggravating circumstances that the judge found by a preponderance of the evidence during a post-trial sentencing hearing. In striking down Cunningham's sentence, the Court reiterated that it had repeatedly held that facts that result in greater punishment for an offender must be found by a jury, not a judge, and using the standard of proof beyond a reasonable doubt. In response to this ruling, California changed its law and gave judges broad discretion to choose between the lower, middle, or upper term provided by the law for the particular crime; the judge does not need to show that there are aggravating factors that justify a sentence at the top of the range.

Presumptive Sentencing Guidelines and Mandatory Minimum Sentences

Since the late 1970s, presumptive sentencing guidelines developed by an independent sentencing commission have been the dominant approach to sentencing reform in the United States. About half of the states have adopted or are considering sentencing guidelines, and sentencing at the federal level has been structured by guidelines since 1987. In 1994, the American Bar Association (ABA) endorsed sentencing guidelines; it recommended that all jurisdictions create permanent sentencing commissions charged with drafting presumptive sentencing provisions that apply to both prison and nonprison sanctions and are tied to prison capacities (American Bar Association, 1994).

The guidelines systems adopted by Congress and by state legislatures have a number of common features (Stith & Cabranes, 1998). In each jurisdiction with presumptive guidelines, there is a permanent sentencing commission or committee composed of criminal justice officials and, sometimes, private citizens and legislators. The commission is charged with studying sentencing practices and formulating presumptive sentence recommendations. The commission is also authorized to monitor the implementation and impact of the guidelines and to recommend amendments. A second common feature is that the presumptive sentence is based primarily on two factors: the severity of the offense and the seriousness of the offender's prior criminal record. Typically, these two factors are arrayed on a two-dimensional grid; their intersection determines whether the offender should be sentenced to prison and, if so, for how long.

Jurisdictions with presumptive sentencing guidelines, as opposed to voluntary or advisory guidelines, require judges to follow them or provide reasons for failing to do so. (Judges in the U.S. District Courts, where guidelines have been advisory since 2005, are also required to provide reasons for departing from the guideline range.) Judges are allowed to depart from the guidelines and impose harsher or more lenient sentences if there are specified aggravating or mitigating circumstances. Some jurisdictions also list factors that should not be used to increase or decrease the presumptive sentence. For example, both the federal guidelines and the Minnesota guidelines state that the offender's race, gender, and employment status are not legitimate grounds for departure. In North Carolina, on the other hand, judges are allowed to consider the fact that the offender "has a positive employment history or is gainfully employed" (Bureau of Justice Assistance, 1996, pp. 79–80). In most states and in the federal system, a departure from the guidelines can be appealed to state appellate courts by either party. If, for example, the judge sentences the defendant to probation when the guidelines call for prison, the prosecuting attorney can appeal. If the judge imposes 60 months when the guidelines call for 36, the defendant can appeal.

Concomitant with the push toward sentencing guidelines, most jurisdictions enacted mandatory penalty statutes. These statutes, which require judges to impose minimum sentences on offenders convicted of certain types of crimes, proliferated during the war on crime that was waged during the 1970s, 1980s, and early 1990s. Candidates from both political parties campaigned on tough-on-crime and zero tolerance of drug use platforms and decried "lenient sentences" imposed by "soft" judges; they championed reforms designed to ensure that offenders "who do the crime will do the time." State and federal legislators responded enthusiastically (for a more detailed discussion of these laws, see Beckett & Sasson, 2000; Mauer, 2006; Tonry, 1995, 1996). Despite the fact that evaluations of these statutes revealed that they had not achieved their objectives, the mandatory penalty movement continued unabated. By the mid-1990s, mandatory penalties had been enacted in every state, and Congress had passed over 60 mandatory sentencing laws covering more than 100 federal offenses (Tonry, 1996, Chapter 5).

The Impact of Sentencing Guidelines

A detailed discussion of the impact of sentencing guidelines would consume many pages; there have been literally dozens of studies focusing on compliance with the guidelines and attempting to determine whether the guidelines (and mandatory minimum sentences) resulted in more punitive sentences and reduced disparity and discrimination in the sentencing process. Although the evidence is somewhat mixed, it does appear that sentences are more punitive today than in the past (Austin & Irwin, 2001; Engen & Steen, 2000; Frase, 1997; Kramer & Lubitz, 1985; Marvel & Moody, 1995; Moore & Miethe, 1986; Spohn, 2000; U.S. Sentencing Commission, 1991a, 1991b, 2004). The movement away from indeterminate sentencing and the rehabilitative ideal to determinate sentencing and an emphasis on just deserts—coupled with laws mandating long prison terms—have resulted in harsher sentences. As a result of these changes in sentencing policy, offenders convicted of felonies in state and federal courts face a greater likelihood of incarceration and longer prison sentences than they did in the prereform era. These changes, in turn, have led to dramatic increases in the nation's prison population.[10]

The evidence regarding the question of whether sentences today are fairer or more equitable in the past also is mixed. Critics of sentencing reform contend that members of the courtroom workgroup have been able to circumvent—or even sabotage—the reforms enacted during the past 30 years; they argue that this makes it difficult to assess the impact of the reforms. Nonetheless, most studies of sentences imposed under federal and state guidelines conclude that guideline sentences are more uniform and less disparate (Anderson, Kling, & Stith, 1999; Anderson & Spohn, 2010; Ashford & Mosbaek, 1991; Hofer, Blackwell, & Ruback, 1999; Knapp, 1987; Kramer & Lubitz, 1985; Stolzenberg & D'Alessio, 1994; U.S. Sentencing Commission, 1991a; Washington State Sentencing Guidelines Commission, 1992; Wright, 1998). There is less interjudge disparity in jurisdictions with sentencing guidelines, and sentences are more tightly linked to the seriousness of the offense and the offender's prior criminal record.

The evidence regarding the effect of legally irrelevant offender characteristics—race, gender, age, education, and employment status—is less inconsistent and, unfortunately, more negative. There is a lack of longitudinal research comparing the effect of offender characteristics on sentence outcomes before and after the implementation of guidelines; this makes it difficult to assess the degree to which the guidelines have reduced unwarranted disparities in sentencing. Nonetheless, the studies of sentences imposed in federal and state jurisdictions operating under sentencing guidelines showed that racial minorities and women were sentenced differently from Whites and men (Albonetti, 1997, 2002; Demuth & Steffensmeier, 2004; Everett & Wojtkiewicz, 2002; Griffin & Wooldredge, 2006; Kramer & Steffensmeier, 1993; Kramer & Ulmer, 1996; LaFrentz & Spohn, 2006; Mustard, 2001; Spohn, 2000; Stacey & Spohn, 2006; Steen, Engen, & Gainey, 2005; Steffensmeier & Demuth, 2000, 2006; Steffensmeier & Hebert, 1999; Steffensmeier, Kramer, & Streifel, 1993; Steffensmeier, Ulmer, & Kramer, 1998). This suggests that attempts to constrain judicial discretion have not eliminated unwarranted disparities in sentencing. The guidelines notwithstanding, judges mete out harsher sentences to Black and Hispanic offenders than to similarly situated White offenders. They impose more lenient sentences on females than on males, and the unemployed and less educated receive harsher sentences than their counterparts.

These conclusions apply to sentences imposed under both federal and state sentencing guidelines. They imply that judges and prosecutors are reluctant to place offenders into cells of sentencing grids defined only by crime seriousness and prior criminal record and, thus, that statutorily irrelevant factors such as race, gender, age, employment status, and social class may be factually relevant to criminal justice officials' assessments of dangerousness, threat, and culpability. In sum, these conclusions attest to the validity of Tonry's (1996) assertion, "There is, unfortunately, no way around the dilemma that sentencing is inherently discretionary and that discretion leads to disparities" (p. 180).

SPECIALIZED OR PROBLEM-SOLVING COURTS: A FOCUS ON DRUG COURTS

The last three decades have witnessed another important change in the American court system: the development of specialized or problem-solving courts. These are limited-jurisdiction courts specializing in certain crime problems, such as drugs, guns, and domestic violence. These courts are like traffic courts in that they address a specific problem, but several factors set them apart (Berman & Feinblatt, 2001). The typical specialized court focuses on case outcomes—for example, getting offenders off drugs or protecting women from further intimate partner abuse— rather than case processing, and judges closely supervise offenders and monitor their progress. Specialized courts also are characterized by collaboration among criminal justice and social service agencies, nontraditional roles for participants, and a focus on systemic change.

The Drug Court Movement

The development of specialized courts is best illustrated by the drug court movement. Increases in the number of drug offenders appearing in state and federal courts—coupled with mounting evidence of both the linkages between drug use and crime and the efficacy of drug treatment programs—led a number of jurisdictions "to rethink their approach to handling defendants charged with drug and drug-related offenses" (Drug Court Clearinghouse and Technical Assistance Project, 1999, p. 3). Some jurisdictions, such as Cook County (Chicago), Illinois, established specialized dockets designed to manage the drug caseload more efficiently and to alleviate stress on the felony court system (Inciardi, McBride, & Rivers, 1996). Other jurisdictions, such as Dade County (Miami), Florida, created "drug treatment courts," which incorporated intensive judicial supervision of drug offenders, mandatory drug treatment, and rehabilitation programs providing vocational, educational, family, and medical services.

The drug treatment court concept spread rapidly during the 1990s.

As of June 1999, there were 377 drug courts operating, and an additional 217 drug courts were in the planning stages in 49 of the 50 states, the District of Columbia, Puerto Rico, Guam, several Native American tribal courts, and two federal district courts (Drug Court Clearinghouse and Technical Assistance Project, 1999, p. 1). By June of 2015, there were more than 3,000 adult and juvenile drug courts operating in jurisdictions throughout the United States and its territories.

Although the nature and characteristics of drug courts throughout the United States vary widely, they share several key elements (National Association of Drug Court Professionals, 1997):

- Integration of substance abuse treatment with justice system case processing

- Use of a nonadversarial approach

- Early identification and prompt placement of eligible participants

- Access to a continuum of treatment, rehabilitation, and related services

- Frequent testing for alcohol and illicit drugs

- A coordinated strategy among judge, prosecutor, defense, and treatment providers to govern offender compliance

- Ongoing judicial interaction with each participant

In the typical preadjudication drug court, drug offenders who meet the eligibility criteria for the program are given a choice between participation in the drug court and traditional adjudication. Although the eligibility criteria vary, most programs exclude offenders who have prior convictions for violent offenses or whose current offense involved violence or use of a weapon. They target offenders whose involvement with the criminal justice system is due primarily to their substance abuse. The program may last 12 months, 18 months, or longer. Offenders who are accepted and agree to abide by the requirements of the program are immediately referred to a substance abuse treatment program for counseling, therapy, and education. They also are subject to random urinalysis and are required to appear frequently before the drug court judge. Offenders who do not show up for treatment sessions or drug court or who fail drug tests are subject to sanctions. Repeated violations may result in termination from the program and in adjudication and sentencing on the original charges. The charges against the offender are dismissed upon completion of the program.

The Effectiveness of Drug Courts

There is mounting evidence that drug courts reduce offender recidivism and prevent drug relapse. A report by the U.S. General Accounting Office (GAO, 1997) summarized the results of 20 evaluations of 16 drug courts that had been completed by early 1997. The GAO report indicated that these early evaluations generally concluded that drug courts were effective in reducing drug use and criminal behavior. A later review by Belenko (1998) summarized the results of 30 evaluations of 24 drug courts that had been completed by May 1998. Belenko observed that most of these evaluations concluded "that criminal behavior was substantially reduced during participation in the program" (p. 29). For example, an evaluation of a Ventura County, California, drug court, which tracked recidivism over an 8-month period, found that only 12% of the drug court participants were rearrested, compared with 32% of those in a comparison group. A Jackson County, Missouri, evaluation similarly revealed 6-month rearrest rates of 4% for program participants and 13% for nonparticipants.

Belenko's review also included studies that assessed the impact of drug court participation on postprogram recidivism. Eight of the nine evaluations reported lower recidivism rates for the drug court group, compared with a group of similarly situated offenders who did not participate in the drug court program. An evaluation of the Multnomah County, Oregon, drug court, for example, found statistically significant differences between drug court participants (0.59 new arrests) and drug court–eligible nonparticipants (1.53 new arrests) over a 24-month tracking period. Belenko concluded that "drug use and criminal behavior are substantially reduced while clients are participating in drug court, [and] criminal behavior is lower after program participation" (p. 18).

More recent and methodologically sophisticated studies also provide evidence that drug courts are effective in preventing recidivism. An evaluation of the Baltimore City Drug Treatment Court, for example, used an experimental design in which eligible offenders were randomly assigned either to the drug court or to traditional adjudication (Gottfredson & Exum, 2002). The results of the evaluation revealed that offenders assigned to the drug court were less likely than offenders placed in the traditional adjudication group to be rearrested during the 12-month follow-up period. A follow-up study using 3 years of recidivism data showed similar results; this study also showed that the positive effects of participation in the drug treatment court extended past the offenders' involvement in the drug court (Gottfredson, Najaka, Kearley, & Rocha, 2006).

CONCLUSION: POLICY IMPLICATIONS

The American court system has undergone significant changes over the past three decades. Criminal procedure has been reformed as a result of Supreme Court decisions that broadened the rights of criminal defendants, established rules for the selection of juries and the use of peremptory challenges, and placed restrictions on judges' sentencing discretion. Sentencing policies and practices in state and federal jurisdictions have undergone important modifications, and specialized or problem-solving courts have spread throughout the United States.

The question, of course, is whether these changes have produced a fairer and more equitable court system. It seems clear that the Supreme Court's decisions for broadening the right to counsel and restricting the use of race in the jury selection process have resulted in fairer treatment of poor defendants and defendants who are racial minorities and that the Court's decisions on limiting the use of the death penalty have made it more likely that capital punishment will be reserved for particularly heinous crimes. Less clear are the effects of the Court's decisions for enhancing the role of the jury in sentencing and making the federal sentencing guidelines voluntary. Although these decisions, which place significant restrictions on judicial discretion, may produce less disparity in sentencing, it also is possible that discretion will simply shift downstream to prosecutors. In other words, the source of disparity, including unwarranted disparity, in the new regime may be prosecutors' charging and plea-bargaining decisions.

The impact of specialized or problem-solving courts is also less evident. Research evaluating these courts is limited, and the research that does exist suffers from a number of methodological problems (Belenko, 1998). Nonetheless, there is mounting evidence that drug courts, domestic violence courts, and other specialized courts do reduce recidivism rates, and there is some evidence that these courts also lead to improvements in offenders' education and employment status, physical and mental health, and cognitive functioning. As research on problem-solving courts accumulates, our conclusions regarding their effectiveness will become less tentative.

Discussion Questions

1. How have the Supreme Court's decisions regarding the right to counsel changed the American court system? In your opinion, have these been positive or negative changes?

2. Why would critics of the public defender system argue that criminal defendants "get what they pay for"? What are the problems inherent in the public defender system?

3. Evidence suggesting that prosecutors continue to use their peremptory challenges to preserve all-White juries in cases involving African American or Hispanic defendants has led some commentators to call for the elimination of the peremptory challenge. What do you think is the strongest argument in favor of eliminating the peremptory challenge? In favor of retaining it? How would elimination of the peremptory challenge change the criminal trial?

4. What will be the impact of the Supreme Court's decision for making the federal sentencing guidelines voluntary and advisory rather than mandatory? Will these decisions lead to less uniformity and more disparity in sentencing, or will they enable judges to individualize justice in appropriate ways?

5. An important goal of sentencing guidelines was to eliminate unwarranted disparity in sentencing. Given this, how would you explain the fact that research reveals that both the offender's race and ethnicity and the offender's sex influence sentences imposed under state and federal sentencing guidelines?

6. How do specialized or problem-solving courts differ from traditional courts? Why have these courts become so popular in the United States?

Notes

1. *Argersinger v. Hamlin*, 407 U.S. 25 (1972), at 37.

2. A defendant is entitled to counsel at every stage "where substantial rights of the accused may be affected" that require the "guiding hand of counsel" (*Mempa v. Rhay*, 389 U.S. 128 [1967], at 134). These critical stages include arraignment, preliminary hearing, entry of a plea, trial, sentencing, and the first appeal.

3. *McCleskey v. Kemp* (481 U.S. 279 [1987], at 310), quoting *Strauder v. West Virginia*, 100 U.S. 303 (1880).

4. *Strauder v. West Virginia*, 100 U.S. 303 (1880), at 305; *Batson v. Kentucky*, 476 U.S. 79 (1986), at 85.

5. *Swain v. Alabama*, 380 U.S. 202, 212 (1965), at 380.

6. *United States v. Montgomery*, 819 F.2d at 851. The Eleventh Circuit, however, rejected this line of reasoning in *Fleming v. Kemp* (794 F.2d 1478 [11th Cir. 1986]) and *United States v. David* (803 F.2d 1567 [11th Cir. 1986]).

7. *United States v. Vaccaro*, 816 F.2d 443, 457 (9th Cir. 1987); *Fields v. People*, 732 P.2d 1145, 1158 n.20 (Colo. 1987).

8. Also decided at the same time—and with the same result—was *United States v. Fanfan* (125 S. Ct. 12 [2004]).

9. *Gall v. United States*, No. 06-7949, decided December 10, 2007. *Kimbrough v. United States*, No. 06-6330, decided December 10, 2007.

10. Most scholars contend that this punitiveness has not produced the predicted reduction in crime. Conservative advocates of harsh crime control policies claim that locking up increasingly large numbers of felony offenders for increasingly long periods of time has caused the crime rate to fall; however, conceptual and methodological flaws in the "prison 'works'" argument call this conclusion into question. Critics suggest that a more careful examination of the evidence leads to the conclusion that increasing incarceration rates have little, if any, effect on crime rates (see, for example, Austin & Irwin, 2001; Tonry, 1995).

References

Albonetti, C. A. (1997). Sentencing under the federal sentencing guidelines: Effects of defendant characteristics, guilty pleas, and departures on sentence outcomes for drug offenses, 1991–1992. *Law & Society Review, 31*(4), 789–822.

Albonetti, C. A. (2002). The joint conditioning effect of defendant's gender and ethnicity on length of imprisonment under the federal sentencing guidelines for drug trafficking/manufacturing offenders. *Journal of Gender, Race, and Justice, 6*, 39–60.

American Bar Association. (1994). *Standards for criminal justice—Sentencing alternatives and procedures* (3rd ed.). Boston, MA: Little, Brown.

Anderson, J. M., Kling, J. R., & Stith, K. (1999). Measuring interjudge sentencing disparity: Before and after the federal sentencing guidelines. *Journal of Law and Economics, 42*(S1), 271–307.

Anderson, A. L., & Spohn, C. (2010). Lawless in the federal sentencing process: A test for uniformity and consistency in sentence outcomes. *Justice Quarterly, 27*, 362–393.

Ashford, K., & Mosbaek, C. (1991). First year report on implementation of sentencing guidelines, November 1989 to January 1991. Portland, OR: Oregon Criminal Justice Council.

Austin, J., & Irwin, J. (2001). *It's about time: America's imprisonment binge* (3rd ed.). Belmont, CA: Wadsworth.

Beckett, K., & Sasson, T. (2000). *The politics of injustice*. Thousand Oaks, CA: Pine Forge.

Belenko, S. (1998). Research on drug courts: A critical review. *National Drug Court Institute Review, 1*(1), 1–42.

Berman, G., & Feinblatt, J. (2001). *Problem-solving courts: A brief primer*. New York, NY: Center for Court Innovation.

Bright, S. B. (1994). Counsel for the poor: The death sentence not for the worst crime but for the worst lawyer. *Yale Law Journal, 103*, 1835–1883

Bureau of Justice Assistance. (1996). *National assessment of structured sentencing*. Washington, DC: U.S. Department of Justice, Bureau of Justice Assistance.

Bureau of Justice Assistance Drug Court Clearinghouse Project at American University. (2006, July). Sentencing Judges for Drug Court participants who are terminated. *Washington, DC: American University*. Retrieved from http://www.ndcrc.org/sites/default/files/sentencingwithtermination.pdf

Bureau of Justice Statistics. (2006). *State court organization, 2004*. Washington, DC: United States Department of Justice, Bureau of Justice Statistics.

Casper, J. D. (1971). Did you have a lawyer when you went to court? No, I had a public defender. *Yale Review of Law and Social Action, 1*, 4–9.

Casper, J. D., Brereton, D., & Neal, D. (1982). *The implementation of the California determinate sentencing law: Executive summary*. Washington, DC: Government Printing Office.

Cohen, J., & Tonry, M. H. (1983). Sentencing reforms and their impacts. In A. Blumstein, J. Cohen, S. E. Martin, & M. H. Tonry (Eds.), *Research on sentencing: The search for reform* (Vol. *1*, pp. 305–349). Washington, DC: National Academy Press.

Demuth, S., & Steffensmeier, D. (2004). Ethnicity effects on sentencing outcomes in large urban courts: Comparisons among White, Black, and Hispanic defendants. *Social Science Quarterly, 85*(4), 991–1011.

Drug Court Clearinghouse and Technical Assistance Project. (1999). *Looking at a decade of drug courts*. Washington, DC: U.S. Department of Justice.

Engen, R. L., & Steen, S. (2000). The power to punish: Discretion and sentencing reform in the war on drugs. *American Journal of Sociology, 105*(5), 1357–1395.

Everett, R. S., & Wojtkiewicz, R. A. (2002). Difference, disparity, and race/ethnic bias in federal sentencing. *Journal of Quantitative Criminology, 18*(2), 189–211.

Frankel, M. (1972). Lawlessness in sentencing. *University of Cincinnati Law Review, 41*(1), 1–54.

Frase, R. (1997). Prison population growing under Minnesota guidelines. In M. Tonry & K. Hatlestad

(Eds.), *Sentencing reform in overcrowded times: A comparative perspective* (pp. 12–16). New York, NY: Oxford University Press.

Gideon's promise unfulfilled: The need for litigated reform of indigent defense. (2000). *Harvard Law Review, 113*, 2062–2079.

Gottfredson, D. C., & Exum, M. L. (2002). Baltimore City Drug Treatment Court: One-year results from a randomized study. *Journal of Research in Crime and Delinquency, 39*(3), 337–356.

Gottfredson, D. C., Najaka, S. S., Kearley, B. W., & Rocha, C. M. (2006). Long-term effects of participation in the Baltimore City Drug Treatment Court: Results from an experimental study. *Journal of Experimental Criminology, 2*(1), 67–98.

Griffin, T., & Wooldredge, J. (2006). Sex-based disparities in felony dispositions before and after sentencing reform in Ohio. *Criminology, 44*, 893–923.

Hanson, R. A., & Ostrom, B. J. (2004). Indigent defenders get the job done and done well. In G. F. Cole, M. G. Gertz, & A. Bunger (Eds.), *The criminal justice system: Law and politics* (pp. 227–248). Belmont, CA: Wadsworth.

Hofer, P. J., Blackwell, K. R., & Ruback, B. (1999). The effect of the federal sentencing guidelines on interjudge sentencing disparity. *Journal of Criminal Law & Criminology, 90*(1), 239–321.

Huddleston, C. W., III, Freeman-Wilson, K., Marlowe, D. B., & Roussell, A. (2005). Painting the current picture: A national report card on drug courts and other problem solving court programs in the United States. Washington, DC: National Drug Court Institute.

Inciardi, J. A., McBride, D. C., & Rivers, J. E. (1996). *Drug control and the courts*. Thousand Oaks, CA: Sage.

Kennedy, R. (1997). *Race, crime, and the law*. New York, NY: Vintage Books.

Knapp, K. A. (1987). Implementation of the Minnesota guidelines: Can the innovative spirit be preserved? In A. von Hirsch, K. A. Knapp, & M. Tonry (Eds.), *The sentencing commission and its guidelines* (pp. 127–141). Boston, MA: Northeastern University Press.

Kramer, J. H., & Lubitz, R. L. (1985). Pennsylvania's sentencing reform: The impact of commission-established guidelines. *Crime & Delinquency, 31*(4), 481–500.

Kramer, J. H., & Steffensmeier, D. (1993). Race and imprisonment decisions. *Sociological Quarterly, 34*(2), 357–376.

Kramer, J. H., & Ulmer, J. T. (1996). Sentencing disparity and departures from guidelines. *Justice Quarterly, 13*(1), 81–106.

LaFrentz, C., & Spohn, C. (2006). Who is punished more harshly? An examination of race/ethnicity, gender, age and employment status under the federal sentencing guidelines. *Justice Research & Policy, 8*(2), 25–56.

Marvel, T. B., & Moody, C. E. (1995). The impact of enhanced prison terms for felonies committed with guns. *Criminology, 33*(2), 247–281.

Mauer, M. (2006). *Race to incarcerate* (2nd ed.). New York, NY: New Press.

McIntyre, L. (1987). *The public defender: The practice of law in the shadows of repute*. Chicago, IL: University of Chicago Press.

Moore, C. A., & Miethe, T. D. (1986). Regulated and unregulated sentencing decisions: An analysis of first-year practices under Minnesota's felony sentencing guidelines. *Law & Society Review, 20*(2), 253–277.

Mustard, D. (2001). Racial, ethnic and gender disparities in sentencing: Evidence from the U.S. federal courts. *Journal of Law and Economics, 44*(1), 285–314.

Myrdal, G. (1944). *An American dilemma: The Negro problem and modern democracy*. New York, NY: Harper.

National Association of Drug Court Professionals. (1997). *Defining drug courts: The key components*. Washington, DC: Bureau of Justice Assistance, U.S. Department of Justice.

Serr, B. J., & Maney, M. (1988). Racism, peremptory challenges and the democratic jury: The jurisprudence of a delicate balance. *Journal of Criminal Law & Criminology, 79*(1), 1–65.

Spohn, C. (2000). *Thirty years of sentencing reform: The quest for a racially neutral sentencing process*. Washington, DC: U.S. Department of Justice.

Stacey, A. M., & Spohn, C. (2006). Gender and the social costs of sentencing: An analysis of sentences imposed on male and female offenders in three U.S. District Courts. *Berkeley Journal of Criminal Law, 11*(1), 43–76.

Steen, S., Engen, R. L., & Gainey, R. R. (2005). Images of danger and culpability: Racial stereotyping, case processing, and criminal sentencing. *Criminology, 43*(2), 435–468.

Steffensmeier, D., & Demuth, S. (2000). Ethnicity and sentencing outcomes in U.S. federal courts: Who is punished more harshly? *American Sociological Review, 65*(5), 705–729.

Steffensmeier, D., & Demuth, S. (2006). Does gender modify the effects of race-ethnicity on criminal sanctioning? Sentences for male and female White, Black, and Hispanic defendants. *Journal of Quantitative Criminology, 22*(3), 241–261.

Steffensmeier, D., & Hebert, C. (1999). Women and men policymakers: Does the judge's gender affect the sentencing of criminal defendants? *Social Forces, 77*(3), 1163–1196.

Steffensmeier, D., Kramer, J., & Streifel, C. (1993). Gender and imprisonment decisions. *Criminology, 31*(3), 411–446.

Steffensmeier, D., Ulmer, J., & Kramer, J. (1998). The interaction of race, gender, and age in criminal sentencing: The punishment cost of being young, Black, and male. *Criminology, 36*(4), 763–797.

Stith, K., & Cabranes, J. A. (1998). *Fear of judging: Sentencing guidelines in the federal courts*. Chicago, IL: University of Chicago Press.

Stolzenberg, L., & D'Alessio, S. J. (1994). Sentencing and unwarranted disparity: An empirical assessment of the long-term impact of sentencing guidelines in Minnesota. *Criminology, 32*(2), 301–310.

Tonry, M. (1995). *Malign neglect: Race, crime, and punishment in America*. New York, NY: Oxford University Press.

Tonry, M. (1996). *Sentencing matters*. New York, NY: Oxford University Press.

U.S. General Accounting Office. (1997). *Drug courts: Overview of growth, characteristics, and results*. Washington, DC: U.S. General Accounting Office.

U.S. Sentencing Commission. (1991a). *The federal sentencing guidelines: A report on the operation of the guidelines system and short-term impacts on disparity in sentencing, use of incarceration, and prosecutorial discretion and plea bargaining*. Washington, DC: Author.

U.S. Sentencing Commission. (1991b). *Special report to Congress: Mandatory minimum penalties in the federal criminal justice system*. Washington, DC: Author.

U.S. Sentencing Commission. (2004). *Fifteen years of guidelines sentencing: An assessment of how well the federal criminal justice system is achieving the goals of sentencing reform*. Washington, DC: Author.

Walker, S. (1993). *Taming the system: The control of discretion in criminal justice, 1950–1990*. New York, NY: Oxford University Press.

Washington State Sentencing Guidelines Commission. (1992). *A decade of sentencing reform: Washington and its guidelines, 1981–1991*. Olympia, WA: Author.

Williams, M. (2002, January). A comparison of sentencing outcomes for defendants with public defenders versus retained counsel in a Florida circuit court. *Justice Systems Journal, 23*, 249–257.

Wishman, S. (1986). *Anatomy of a jury: The system on trial*. New York, NY: Penguin Books.

Wright, R. F. (1998). Managing prison growth in North Carolina through structured sentencing. *National Institute of Justice, Program Focus Series*. Washington, DC: U.S. Department of Justice, National Institute of Justice.

THE JUVENILE
JUSTICE SYSTEM

Randall G. Shelden

Founded in 1899 in Chicago and Denver, a new court promised that children's "best interest" would be served, as it was based upon the old English doctrine of *parens patriae* (for more detail, see Shelden, 2008, chapter 5). The new laws that defined delinquency and predelinquent behavior were broad in scope and quite vague, covering the following: (1) violations of laws also applicable to adults; (2) violations of local ordinances; (3) such catchalls as "vicious or immoral behavior," "incorrigibility," truancy, "profane or indecent behavior," "growing up in idleness," "living with any vicious or disreputable person," and many more. The third category would eventually be known as *status offenses*.

The juvenile court system rapidly spread throughout the country, following the lead of Chicago and Denver. Juvenile institutions, such as industrial and training schools and reform schools, continued to develop and expand. Until the 1960s, there were relatively few structural changes within the juvenile justice system. However, serious problems emerged from the very start, not the least of which was an obvious class, race, and gender bias. Indeed, the vast majority of youth brought into the juvenile court have been drawn from the ranks of the poor and racial and ethnic minorities (Shelden, 2008).

Although the most common disposition of cases processed through the juvenile court is probation, many young offenders end up placed somewhere other than within their own home. Most spend at least some time locked up in a secure facility, most commonly called a *detention center*. This subject is treated in the following section.

Juvenile corrections include several different types of out-of-home placements of which the courts can make use. Some of these institutions are public (i.e., run by state or local governments), and others are privately funded. They can be further subdivided into short-term confinement (usually ranging from a few days to a couple of months) and long-term confinement (ranging from 3 or 4 months to 1 or 2 years).

DETENTION CENTERS

Detention is the most common temporary holding facility for juveniles. Here is where youths are placed pending a court hearing to determine whether or not they should be released. Despite the reforms of the past half-century, conditions in many of the nation's detention centers remain horrible. This is especially true for the growing numbers of youth with serious mental health problems. Among the recent scandals surrounding detention centers was when two Pennsylvania judges were convicted of sending more than 5,000 children to one of two privately operated detention centers in return for kickbacks that amounted to more than $2.6 million. The judges had helped the detention centers obtain a county contract worth $58 million. They then guaranteed the operators a steady income by providing a steady stream of juveniles, mostly for very minor offenses (Chen, 2009; "Judges Sentenced Kids for Cash," 2009; Ecenbarger, 2012).

One of the most problematic features of detention centers is the large number of youths with serious mental health problems. The most recent estimates have found that from 67% to 70% of youths in all juvenile facilities (detention and juvenile prisons) "meet criteria for at least one mental health disorder" and that "79% of youth who met criteria for at least one mental health disorder actually met criteria for two or more diagnoses." Further, "over 60% of these youth were diagnosed with three or more mental health disorders" (Shufelt & Cocozza, 2006). Another survey found that more than one third of juveniles in detention and almost half of females "had felt hopeless or thought about death in the 6 months before detention," while about 10% had thought about suicide and the same percentage actually attempted suicide (Abram et al., 2008). Another survey found that about 11% of the males and 30% of the girls were diagnosed with major depression and just over half of both males and females were diagnosed with "conduct disorders" (Fazel et al., 2008; see also, ACT 4 Juvenile Justice, 2010).

A 2004 report by the U.S. Senate's Governmental Affairs Committee concluded "thousands of children with mental illnesses await needed community mental health services in juvenile detention centers across the country" (Bazelon Center for Mental Health Law, 2004). One expert testified that "juvenile detention facilities lack the resources and staff to confront this problem; yet, corrections is being forced to shoulder the burden of the nation's failure to properly diagnose and care for children with mental or emotional disorders." The report identified 698 correctional facilities. Three-quarters (524) responded to a survey in 2003, including facilities in every state except New Hampshire. In 33 states, juveniles with mental health problems were held even though there were no charges against them.

Among the key findings from the report included the fact that the rate of suicide was 4 times higher than in the general juvenile population, that it is extremely expensive ($100 million per year to house youth waiting mental health placement), and detention centers are overwhelmed, unable to cope with the situation (Associated Press, 2004). Writing in the *New York Times* Solomon Moore says that "jails and juvenile justice facilities are the new asylums" (Moore, 2009).

More recent reports continue to note the thousands of youths with mental health problems sitting in detention centers. Not surprisingly, the costs to keep such youth in detention are greater than other youths. A California study of 18 counties found that the cost per youth was $18,000 greater than other youth; the study also noted that the costs of drugs administered to such youth amounted to an average of $4,387 per month (Justice Policy Institute, 2009).

One of the worst states (and there are many) is Mississippi. In March of 2010, the Southern Poverty Law Center filed suit against the state charging that

(1)   Mississippi discriminates against children with mental illness by unlawfully separating them from their families and communities and by forcing them to cycle through psychiatric institutions that fail to provide adequate services; (2) The state ignores the ongoing needs of children with mental illness by failing to provide federally mandated and medically necessary home- and community-based mental health services (Southern Poverty Law Center, 2010).

SPECIAL ISSUES FACING THE JUVENILE JUSTICE SYSTEM

The juvenile justice system cannot be discussed honestly without reference to two glaring problems: gender and race.

Status Offenses and the Double Standard

Since the beginning of the juvenile court, one of the biggest issues has been the vagueness of status offenses. Much of this vagueness stems from the differential application of such offenses, especially the use of a double standard for males and females who are brought within the juvenile court jurisdiction (Chesney-Lind & Shelden, 2014). Today, status offenses involve such behaviors as truancy, violating curfew, running away from home, and "incorrigibility" (often called by other names, such as "beyond control" and "unmanageable"). The ambiguity of such statutes gives those in authority a tremendous amount of discretionary power, which often leads to arbitrary decisions based on subjective value judgments imbued with class, race, and (of course) sexual bias.

From the very start of the juvenile court, girls particularly were victimized by the ambiguity of status offenses and the resulting double standard of treatment. Studies of early family court activity reveal that almost all of the girls who appeared in these courts were charged with immorality or waywardness (Chesney-Lind, 1971; Schlossman & Wallach, 1978; Shelden, 1981).

The sanctions for such misbehavior were extremely severe. For example, the Chicago family court sent half of the girl delinquents but only a fifth of the boy delinquents to reformatories between 1899 and 1909. In Milwaukee, twice as many girls as boys were committed to training schools, while in Memphis, females were twice as likely as males to be committed to training schools (Schlossman & Wallach, 1978; Shelden, 1981). In Honolulu between 1929 and 1930, more than half of the girls referred to juvenile court were charged with "immorality," which meant there was evidence of sexual intercourse; 30% were charged with "waywardness." Evidence of immorality was vigorously pursued by arresting officers and social workers alike through lengthy questioning of the girls and, if possible, of males with whom they were suspected of having sex. Girls were twice as likely as males to be detained for their offenses and spent 5 times as long in detention, on average, as their male counterparts. They were also nearly 3 times more likely to be sentenced to the training school. Well into the 1950s, half of those committed to training schools in Honolulu were girls (Chesney-Lind, 1971).

Subsequent studies of the juvenile justice system continued to find evidence of this double standard continuing throughout the 20th century and into the current century (for a complete review, see Chesney-Lind & Shelden, 2014). For example, an investigation by the Southern Poverty Law Center found that 75% of the girls at the Columbia Training School for Girls in Mississippi had been committed for status offenses, probation violations, or contempt of court (Southern Poverty Law Center, 2008). The suit "exposed brutal conditions at the prison, including the painful shackling of girls for weeks at a time. One girl was choked by a guard. Another girl was groped and fondled while in isolation." As a result the institution was closed (Southern Poverty Law Center, 2008).

One recent study by Human Rights Watch documented what is done to girls within the juvenile penal system of New York State. Their report, which focused on two training schools for girls, concluded that "far too often, girls experience abusive physical restraints and other forms of abuse and neglect, and are denied the mental health, educational, and other rehabilitative services they need. Because of the facilities' remote locations, confined girls are isolated from their families and communities" (Human Rights Watch, 2006, p. 3). The report further notes that

a disproportionate number of girls confined in New York are African-Americans from families who have lived in poverty for generations, with parents or other close relatives who themselves have been incarcerated. In many cases, these girls fall into juvenile facilities through vast holes in the social safety net, after child welfare institutions and schools have failed them. In the wake of legal reform in 1996, girls who commit "status offenses" such as disobedience and running away from home are no longer supposed to be placed in custody, but such offenses—and the related issue of involvement with child welfare agencies because of parental abuse and neglect—continue to function as gateways through which particularly vulnerable children are drawn into the juvenile justice system. (Human Rights Watch, 2006, p. 4)

The report was most critical of the agency responsible for overseeing these institutions, the New York State Office of Children and Family Services (OCFS). The report tersely adds that

> although OCFS is charged with rehabilitating children over whom it takes custody, it often fails to serve, and even to protect, confined girls, and this failure continues because there is little or no meaningful oversight of conditions in OCFS facilities. This last point is critical. Internal monitoring and oversight of the facility are, to put it charitably, dysfunctional, and independent outside monitoring is all but nonexistent. As a result, the conditions in the Tryon and Lansing facilities addressed in this report are shrouded in secrecy and girls who suffer abuse have little meaningful redress . . . we have found OCFS to be among the most hostile juvenile justice agencies we have ever encountered. (Human Rights Watch, 2006, pp. 3–4)

The report documents rampant abuse and the use of force on girls, including a "forcible face-down 'restraint' procedure intended for emergencies but in fact used far more often. In a restraint, staff seize a girl from behind and, in a face-down posture, push her head and entire body to the floor. They then pull her arms up behind her and hold or handcuff them. We found that the procedure is used against girls as young as 12 and that it frequently results in facial abrasions and other injuries, and even broken limbs." They also documented cases of sexual abuse by staff, including three cases of sexual intercourse with the girls. Also, the girls "are bound in some combination of handcuffs, legshackles, and leather restraint belts any time they leave the facility" (Human Rights Watch, 2006, pp. 5–6). They "are also subject to frequent strip-searches in which they must undress in front of a staff person and submit to a thorough visual inspection including their genitals" (Human Rights Watch, 2006, pp. 5–6). Throughout the report, there are documented incidents of human rights violations at both institutions, including violations of "United Nations Standard Minimum Rules for the Treatment of Prisoners," plus violations of New York State laws.

RACE, THE WAR ON DRUGS, AND REFERRALS TO JUVENILE COURT

It is impossible to talk about juvenile court processing without reference to race and, especially in recent years, drug offenses. Race often plays an indirect role in that it relates to offense, which, in turn, affects the police decision to arrest. Race may also relate to the *visibility* of the offense. This is especially the case with regard to drugs. There is abundant evidence that the War on Drugs has targeted African Americans on a scale unprecedented in U.S. history (Provine, 2007; Tonry, 1995; Walker, Spohn, & DeLone, 2007).

The juvenile arrest rate for both races for heroin and cocaine possession was virtually the same in 1965. By the 1970s, the gap had begun to widen and continue to grow until the current era, where a huge gap remains (Shelden, 2012), as noted later.

Regardless of whether race, class, or demeanor is statistically more relevant, one fact remains: Growing numbers of African American youths are finding themselves within the juvenile justice system. They are more likely to be detained, more likely to have their cases petitioned to go before a judge, more likely to be waived to the adult system, and more likely to be institutionalized than their White counterparts (Walker, Spohn, & DeLone, 2007, p. 144). On the bright side, there has been some progress in decreasing disproportionate minority representation within the juvenile justice system nationally (Davis & Sorensen, 2010).

One often overlooked source of racial bias is in child welfare case processing and how it relates to juvenile justice processing. One study examined data on child maltreatment cases covering a 30-year period in Los Angeles and found that the child welfare system is a major source of African American overrepresentation in the juvenile justice system. Delinquency cases that began within the child welfare system were found to be far less likely to receive probation or other alternatives to incarceration (Ryan et al., 2007).

Some believe that the overrepresentation of minority youth is a result of their committing more crimes than Whites. However, self-report surveys and surveys on drug use showing that Whites are more likely than minorities to use illegal drugs contradict that belief. The differential is more likely the result of police policies (e.g., targeting low-income, mostly minority neighborhoods) or the location of some offenses (especially drug use) in more visible places. Regardless of the reasons, studies have shown race to be a very important factor (Walker, Spohn, & DeLone, 2007). One of the most recent studies focused on Kentucky, where it was found that at each stage of the process, Whites were treated more leniently than minorities. As cases move further and further into the system, the disadvantages of minority status increases (Cowell et al., 2009).

Race and Detention

One of the most important decisions within the juvenile court is whether or not to detain a youth. Such decisions are usually based on written court policies. The three typical reasons for detention are (1) the youth may harm self or others or may be subject to injury by others if not detained; (2) the youth is homeless or a runaway or has no parent, guardian, or other person able to provide adequate care and supervision; and (3) it is believed that, if not detained, the youth will leave the jurisdiction and not appear for court proceedings.

It could be argued that detention should be reserved for youth who are charged with serious crimes. This is not the case, however (Sickmund et al., 2013). The distribution according to offense is shown in Table 20.1. As shown here, about one fourth of those detained are charged with a serious violent crime (24%), while "technical violations" (violation of a court order or violation of probation or parole, which does not include a new offense, as these are the "most serious offenses") constitute 22%.

Race figures prominently in the decision to detain. The same data shown in Table 20.1 are presented in Table 20.2 but expressed as rate per 100,000 juveniles. Here, the racial discrepancies are clear. Regardless of offense, African American youths are far more likely to be detained than their White counterparts. Indeed, for all delinquent offenses, Black youths are about 5 times more likely to be detained, while for violent index crimes, the ratio is almost 10:1.

The most severe disposition is commitment to an institution. Once again, race appears to be a big factor. Regardless of the offense, both African American and Hispanic youth have the highest rates of commitment. For all delinquent offenses, the ratio is about 5:1; for violent index crimes, the ratio is 6.5:1. Hispanic youth have the second-highest rate in all offense categories, just ahead of Whites but far below Blacks. In the 1960s, the following phrase surfaced: "If you're white, you're all right; if you're brown, stick around; if you're black, stay back." This seems to apply to these data.

This is not to suggest that everyone connected with the juvenile justice system is racist and practices discrimination, although stereotypes about youth from certain race or class backgrounds definitely exist. Part of the problem is institutional, in that such negative stereotypes are deeply embedded in our culture. Juvenile courts and police departments are largely staffed by Whites. The widespread poverty and joblessness affecting minority communities result in the lack of available resources (e.g., alternatives to formal court processing) to deal with crime-related issues and the general failure of schools. Many studies have reported that prior record, instant offense, and previous sentences are among the most important factors in determining the final disposition (for a review see Shelden, 2012).

TABLE 20.1 ■ **Juveniles in Detention by Offense, Sex, and Race (Percentage Distribution), 2015**

	Detained	Sex		Race/Ethnicity					
Most Serious Offense	Total	Male	Female	White	Black	Hispanic	American Indian	Asian	Other
Total	100%	100%	100%	100%	100%	100%	100%	100%	100%
Delinquency	97%	98%	93%	94%	98%	98%	94%	100%	90%
Person	37%	38%	32%	32%	40%	36%	30%	55%	36%
Violent Crime Index*	26%	28%	15%	17%	30%	28%	14%	37%	21%
Other Person	11%	10%	18%	14%	10%	8%	16%	18%	14%
Property	19%	20%	17%	19%	21%	17%	18%	13%	20%
Property Crime Index**	16%	17%	12%	16%	19%	13%	13%	11%	18%
Other Property	3%	3%	4%	4%	3%	3%	5%	2%	2%
Drug	5%	5%	5%	6%	4%	6%	6%	5%	4%
Public order	13%	13%	9%	11%	14%	12%	13%	8%	12%
Technical violation	23%	21%	30%	26%	19%	27%	27%	19%	19%
Status offense	3%	2%	7%	6%	2%	2%	6%	0%	10%

Source: Sickmund, M., Sladky, T. J., Kang, W., and Puzzanchera, C. (2017). "Easy Access to the Census of Juveniles in Residential Placement." Available online at http://www.ojjdp.gov/ojstatbb/ezacjrp/

*Includes criminal homicide, violent sexual assault, robbery, and aggravated assault.

**Includes burglary, theft, auto theft, and arson.

Note: U.S. total includes 1,593 juvenile offenders in private facilities for whom state of offense was not reported and a handful of youth who committed their offense in a U.S. territory but were being held in a U.S. mainland facility. Visit the EZACJRP methods section for more information about unknown state of offense.

TABLE 20.2 ■ Juveniles in Detention by Offense, Sex, and Race (Rate per 100,000 Juveniles), 2015

	Detained							
	Sex			Race/Ethinicity				
Most Serious Offense	Total	Male	Female	White	Black	Hispanic	American Indian	Asian
Total	50	81	17	25	153	50	74	7
Delinquency	48	80	16	23	150	49	69	7
Person	18	31	6	8	61	18	22	4
Violent Crime Index*	13	23	3	4	46	14	10	3
Other Person	6	8	3	4	15	4	12	1
Property	10	16	3	5	32	8	13	1
Property Crime Index**	8	14	2	4	28	7	9	7
Other Property	2	2	1	1	4	2	4	0
Drug	2	4	1	1	5	3	5	0
Public order	6	11	2	3	22	6	10	1
Technical violation	11	17	5	6	29	13	20	1
Status offense	2	2	1	1	3	1	4	0

Source: Sickmund, M., Sladky, T. J., Kang, W., and Puzzanchera, C. (2017). "Easy Access to the Census of Juveniles in Residential Placement." Available online at http://www.ojjdp.gov/ojstatbb/ezacjrp/

*Includes criminal homicide, violent sexual assault, robbery, and aggravated assault.

**Includes burglary, theft, auto theft, and arson.

Note: The rate is the number of juvenile offenders in residential placement per 100,000 juveniles ages 10 through the upper age of original juvenile court jurisdiction in each state.

Note: U.S. total includes 1,593 juvenile offenders in private facilities for whom state of offense was not reported and a handful of youth who committed their offense in a U.S. territory but were being held in a U.S. mainland facility. Visit the EZACJRP methods section for more information about unknown state of offense.

Note: Rates for "All racial/ethnic groups" include juveniles identified in the CJRP as "Other" race, most of whom were individuals with multiple race identification. Rates are not presented separately for these "Other" race juveniles because there is no comparable reference population available.

Note: Detained juveniles include those held awaiting a court hearing, adjudication, disposition, or placement elsewhere.

Note: The "Hispanic" category includes persons of Latin American or other Spanish culture or origin regardless of race. These persons are not included in the other race/ethnicity categories.

THE RACIAL COMPOSITION OF JUVENILE INSTITUTIONS

The percentage of incarcerated youth who are racial minorities has risen steadily over the years. The national percentage of minorities in training schools was 23% in 1950, 32% in 1960, 40% in 1970, 60% in 1989, and 66% in 1997, then dropping to 63% in 2006 but increasing to 66% in 2011. One of the reasons White youth constitute the lowest percentage is that so many are confined in private facilities. This is no doubt because most of the costs are paid by family members, usually through their insurance (for details on these rates, see Shelden, 2012, Chapter 12).

Not surprisingly, the overall *rate* of incarceration was considerably higher for minorities. Table 20.3 reveals stark contrasts. The rate for Blacks for all offenses (343) is 3 times higher than Whites (134) and almost 5 times the rate for Hispanics (79). For violent index crimes, there is a huge difference, as the rate for Blacks (104) is 6.5:1 over Whites (16) and about 3 times greater than Hispanics (38).

A Notorious Example: The California Youth Authority

A large number of states have been plagued by scandals concerning the juvenile justice system, especially youth correctional institutions. Texas, Ohio, Florida, South Dakota, Oklahoma, Indiana, Maryland, Hawaii, Arizona, and Mississippi are among those states in which scandals have erupted and lawsuits have been filed (Dexheimer, 2007). The case of the California Youth Authority looms as one of the most significant.

The California Youth Authority (CYA) was created with the passage of the Youth Corrections Authority Act of 1941. The law created a three-person commission, mandated the acceptance of all youths under the age of 23 who had been committed to various prisons and already existing youth facilities, and appropriated $100,000 to run the CYA for 2 years. Until the early 2000s, this system consisted of 11 youth "correctional institutions," 11 forestry camps, 59 detention facilities, and several dozen "probation camps" scattered all over the state. At this time there were about 10,000 youths housed within its 11 institutions.

Partly as a result of several recent scandals (more about that will follow), there was a reorganization of the California Department of Corrections and the CYA became the Division of Juvenile Justice (DJJ) within the new Department of Corrections and Rehabilitation in 2005.[1] As of this writing (October 2013), there are fewer than 700 youth in three institutions. Part of the investigation into conditions within the CYA revealed the enormous costs of running these institutions. A detailed report noted that the yearly cost for one youth came to $234,029 (Macallair, Males, & McCracken, 2009).

TABLE 20.3 ■ Offense Profile of Committed Residents by Sex and Race/Ethnicity for United States (Rate per 100,000 Juveniles), 2015

Most Serious Offense	Committed	Sex		Race/Ethnicity				
	Total	Male	Female	White	Black	Hispanic	American Indian	Asian
Total	100	168	29	60	275	89	185	15
Delinquency	94	161	25	55	263	86	168	14
Person	38	65	10	21	112	33	59	6
Violent Crime Index*	27	49	4	15	83	24	39	4
Other Person	11	16	6	7	29	10	20	2
Property	23	40	5	13	68	20	48	3
Property Crime Index**	19	34	4	10	58	16	41	3
Other Property	4	6	1	2	10	3	7	0
Drug	6	9	2	5	10	6	12	1
Public order	12	22	2	8	34	11	21	2
Technical violation	15	24	6	9	40	16	28	2
Status offense	5	7	4	5	12	3	17	1

Source: Sickmund, M., Sladky, T. J., Kang, W., and Puzzanchera, C. (2017). "Easy Access to the Census of Juveniles in Residential Placement." Available online at http://www.ojjdp.gov/ojstatbb/ezacjrp/

*Includes criminal homicide, violent sexual assault, robbery, and aggravated assault.

**Includes burglary, theft, auto theft, and arson.

Note: The rate is the number of juvenile offenders in residential placement per 100,000 juveniles ages 10 through the upper age of original juvenile court jurisdiction in each state.

Note: U.S. total includes 1,593 juvenile offenders in private facilities for whom state of offense was not reported and a handful of youth who committed their offense in a U.S. territory but were being held in a U.S. mainland facility. Visit the EZACJRP methods section for more information about unknown state of offense.

Note: Rates for "All racial/ethnic groups" include juveniles identified in the CJRP as "Other" race, most of whom were individuals with multiple race identification. Rates are not presented separately for these "Other" race juveniles because there is no comparable reference population available.

Note: Committed juveniles include those placed in the facility as part of a court-ordered disposition.

Note: The "Hispanic" category includes persons of Latin American or other Spanish culture or origin regardless of race. These persons are not included in the other race/ethnicity categories.

Beginning in the 1980s, a series of reports surfaced condemning practices within the CYA (DeMuro & DeMuro, 1988; Lerner, 1982, 1986). Each of these reports documented extreme brutality and the lack of meaningful treatment within these institutions. The third and final report found that the CYA institutions "are seriously overcrowded, offer minimal treatment value despite their high expense, and are ineffective in long-term protection of public safety" (DeMuro & DeMuro, 1988, p. 11). Nothing significant was done about the problem.

In June 1999, the Youth Law Center (San Francisco) began investigating allegations that some CYA wards were being denied food as punishment. In September, the inspector general of California released a report about "Friday Night Fights" (where correctional counselors forced wards to fight each other) at the Heman G. Stark Youth Correctional Facility. In December, the *Los Angeles Times* reported that wards at the Paso Robles Youth Correctional Facility were being handcuffed around the clock, sometimes for several days at a time. In May 2000, the Youth Law Center filed a federal lawsuit (*Wilber v. Warner*) against the CYA for the failure of the CYA to license its inpatient medical and mental health services, as required by state law.

In 2002, another lawsuit was filed against CYA in *Farrell v. Harper*, alleging "inhumane conditions" and pointing out that "rehabilitation is impossible when the classroom is a cage and wards live in constant fear of physical and sexual violence from CYA staff and other wards." A follow-up lawsuit (*Farrel v. Allen*) contended that the CYA is inflicting "cruel and unusual punishment" on its wards, in violation of the Eighth Amendment. Meanwhile, it was reported that there had been 13 suicides within CYA institutions since 1996, and between 2001 and 2003, there were 56 attempted suicides.

A report by the Legislative Analyst's Office of California in 2004 stated,

> A significant amount of the educational program at various institutions is delivered in temporary buildings. These temporary buildings inherently have a rather limited useful life, and have functional deficiencies such as inadequate security and ineffective air conditioning at institutions located in warm climates. The location of some of these temporary buildings is also an issue because they are often located a distance from housing units, requiring intensive staff supervision of ward movements. (California Legislative Analyst's Office, 2004)

Meanwhile, the press was getting involved. A series of reports in the *Los Angeles Times* revealed cases of extreme brutality, suicides, horrible physical conditions, and the CYA's almost total failure to live up to its mission statement. One report quoted Dan Macallair, a 20-year veteran of juvenile justice work, who stated, "The California Youth Authority is a dinosaur . . . based on a 19th century model. The institutions need to be torn down" (Warren, 2004c). Another report focused on the cages used within some classrooms. The CYA called them "secure program areas," ostensibly to protect both youth and teachers from violent acts. The *Los Angeles Times* reported that "the cages essentially are large boxes in which wards are supplied with a chair and desk, and teachers instruct them through a barrier of metal mesh or chain link" (Leovy & Chong, 2004).

Still another news report of two more deaths within a CYA institution (Bell & Stauring, 2004) revealed "excessive rates of violence; inadequate mental health care and educational services; overuse of isolation cells; and deplorable conditions, including feces spread all over some of the cells. Some boys were being forced to sit or stand in cages while attending classes, a 'normal' situation in the state's Kafkaesque system." The report further stated that "more than nine out of 10 CYA 'graduates' are back in trouble with the law within three years of their release."[2]

In December 2004, the lawsuit was settled (now known as *Farrell v. Cate*), and the CYA was ordered to implement a plan to reduce violence and use of force. One result of the suit was the changing of the name of the CYA to the Division of Juvenile Justice (DJJ). In March 2006, the Safety and Welfare Planning Team, a panel of state-approved correctional experts, found DJJ was "not a system that needs tinkering around the edges, this is a system that is broken almost everywhere you look" (Murray et al., 2006, p. 1). Moreover, the team concluded that the state's juvenile facilities had "[become] like adult prisons" (Murray et al., 2006, p. 22). Among its list of 17 significant problems, the team reported "high levels of violence and fear," "antiquated facilities unsuited for any mission," "an adult corrections mentality," "hours on end when many youths have nothing to do," and "poor re-entry planning and too few services on parole" (Murray et al., 2006, p. 1).

Unfortunately, the agreement did not go far enough. As noted in a 2005 report (Anderson, Macallair, & Ramirez, 2005), "What the agreement does not explicitly require, however, is that the CYA close any of its existing eight facilities as part of its new juvenile justice model for the state. These prison facilities are large, remote, outdated, dangerous, and cannot provide the right environment within which to conduct rehabilitative programming."

The CYA was ordered to develop what was called the Ward Safety and Welfare (S&W), Mental Health and Rehabilitation plan. In September 2007, Barry Krisberg (who was appointed as a "Special Master" to oversee the consent decree) filed a "DJJ Progress on the Standards and Criteria of the Safety and Welfare Remedial Plan." He wrote that "at this point, my judgment is that DJJ has not complied with the spirit and intent of the S&W standards and criteria. The current state of the custody classification process in DJJ does not meet nationally-accepted professional standards."

In October 2008, a judge ruled that DJJ had failed to implement the S&W plan and noted that "by its own witness' admission, however, DJJ has written only 12 policies in the last year out of the 800 necessary for implementation of the remedial plans—and not all of those even relate to the remedial plans. DJJ has neither a date to develop the remaining policies nor a date to set a date to develop them."

Gradually, the state began to order the closing of several CYA institutions, starting with two in July 2008, and then, in August 2009, another one was closed. Finally, in 2011, two more were closed. Then, in September 2011, Krisberg issued his 19th report, where he noted that there were "insufficient service provision for youth in restrictive programs" and noted that there was frequent use of force (with chemical agents) toward youth with mental health problems.

The most recent developments have been rather dramatic, for the newly elected Governor Jerry Brown has proposed in the new budget "the elimination of the youth prison system," plus the release of several thousand low-risk adult prisoners who would be transferred to county-run jails. This is according to a report from the Legislative Analyst's Office (2012). The juvenile offenders will be housed in county-run facilities near where they live. In other words, the last five existing juvenile prisons will be closed permanently, saving several millions dollars per year (di Sa, 2011). There is currently some debate about whether or not counties can handle the influx of new youth offenders (Bundy, 2011). It remains to be seen what the outcome will be. Nevertheless, the very idea of closing down the remaining institutions of the former CYA represents one of the most—if not the most—significant changes in juvenile justice ever.

THE FUTURE OF THE JUVENILE COURT

In the years since the Supreme Court began reviewing issues related to juvenile justice (e.g., *In re Gault*), there has been a great deal of discussion concerning the role of the juvenile court. Should it be abolished, should it adhere strictly to a legalistic framework (e.g., due process considerations), or should it focus more on its original *parens patriae* principles? Many have challenged as counterproductive the movement toward treating young offenders as adults (Feld, 1999); besides, certification has not had very many positive results, which is one reason its use has declined in recent years (Shelden, 2012, pp. 385–388). The Supreme Court ruling in *Roper v. Simmons* demonstrated that young offenders need to be treated more leniently because there are significant differences between adolescent and adult reasoning processes (Shelden, 2012, pp. 360–362).

There is no question that there should be a separate system for young offenders, but it should be one that would adhere to principles consistent with that of restorative justice. Restorative justice is based on the idea that the only way to rid oneself of hurt and anger is through forgiveness. The object is to cease further objectification of those who have been involved in the crime—the victim, the offender, the families connected to these two individuals, and the community at large (Sullivan & Tifft, 2000).

My position is summed up nicely in one of the classic critiques of the juvenile court by Supreme Court justice Abe Fortas, when he wrote in *Kent v. United States*

(383 U.S. 541, 1966) that "the child receives the worst of both worlds; that he gets neither the protection accorded to adults nor the solicitous care and regenerative treatment postulated for children" (quoted in Shelden, 2012, p. 354).[3] Let us have a Court that gives youth both the protection of the Bill of Rights *and* the care and treatment that should be available to all children.

Discussion Questions

1. How do you explain the persistence of the double standard despite the many changes brought about by the women's movement of the past several decades?

2. Why do you think that race remains such a critical issue within the juvenile justice system?

3. Reports have consistently found little difference in drug usage among the different races, yet Blacks continue to be vastly overrepresented within the juvenile justice system for drug offenses. Explain this.

4. What do you think accounts for the persistent abuse within such juvenile institutions as the California Youth Authority?

5. Do a Google search of other states, and find some examples of other scandals centering on juvenile detention centers and correctional institutions.

6. Do you agree with the author's recommendation concerning the future of the juvenile court? Why, or why not?

Notes

1. Much of the information in this section has been obtained from the following: Center on Juvenile and Criminal Justice, "Juvenile Corrections Reform in California." Retrieved on October 19, 2013, from http://www.cjcj.org/Education1/California-s-Farrell-Litigation.html.

2. Numerous additional reports appeared in the *Los Angeles Times* and other newspapers in the state (Warren, 2004a, 2004b; Warren, Leovy, & Zamichow, 2004; Leovy & Chong, 2004; de Sá, 2004).

3. *Kent v. United States* was the first juvenile court case heard by the U.S. Supreme Court; a minor's waiver from the jurisdiction of a juvenile court to that of an adult court was reviewed. For more detailed discussion, see Shelden (2012, Chapter 11).

References

Abram, K. M., Choe, J. Y., Washburn, J. J., Teplin, L. A., King, D. C., & Dulcan, M. K. (2008). Suicidal ideation and behaviors among youths in juvenile detention. *Journal of the American Academy of Child and Adolescent Psychiatry, 47*, 291–300.

ACT 4 Juvenile Justice, A Campaign of the National Juvenile Justice & Delinquency Prevention Coalition. (n.d.). *Fact sheet: Mental health and substance abuse needs.* Retrieved from http://www.bazelon.org/pdf/Act4JJfactsheet6-09.pdf

Anderson, C., Macallair, D., & Ramirez, C. (2005). *CYA warehouses: Failing kids, families, and public safety.* Oakland, CA: Books Not Bars. Retrieved on October 19, 2013, from http://www.prisonpolicy.org/scans/cya_warehouses.pdf

Associated Press. (2004, July 7). Report: Mentally ill teens 'warehoused' in jails. Retrieved on October 17, 2013 from: http://www.nbcnews.com/id/5387015

Bazelon Center for Mental Health Law. (2004, July 7). *Thousands of children with mental illness warehoused in juvenile detention centers awaiting mental health services.* Retrieved on October 19, 2013 from, http://www.bazelon.org/LinkClick.aspx?fileticket=sKFPwea2dVg%3D&tabid=328

Bell, J., & Stauring, J. (2004, May 2). Serious problems festering in juvenile justice system require serious reforms. *Los Angeles Times.* Retrieved on October 19, 2013, from http://articles.latimes.com/2004/may/02/opinion/oe-bell2

Buchen, L. (2013). California's Division of Juvenile Facilities: Nine years after Farrell. San Francisco, CA: Center on Juvenile and Criminal Justice. Retrieved on October 19, 2013, from http://www.cjcj.org/uploads/cjcj/documents/state_of_djf.pdf

Bundy, T. (2011, January 22). Can counties handle young offenders on their own? *Bay Citizen News.* Retrieved on October 19, 2013, from http://www.baycitizen.org/crime/story/can-counties-handle-young-offenders-own

California Legislative Analyst's Office. (2004, May). *A review of the California Youth Authority's infrastructure.* Retrieved from http://www.lao.ca.gov/2004/cya/052504_cya.htm. Retrieved October 20, 2009.

California Legislative Analyst's Office. (2012). Governor's proposal to complete juvenile justice realignment. Retrieved on October 19, 2013, from http://www.lao.ca.gov/handouts/crimjust/2012/Completing_Juvenile_Realignment_03_22_12.pdf

Center on Juvenile and Criminal Justice. (2011). *Closing California's Division of Juvenile Facilities: An analysis of county institutional capacity 2009–2010.* Retrieved on October 19, 2013, from http://www.cjcj.org/uploads/cjcj/documents/Closing_Californias_Division_of_Juvenile_Facilities.pdf

Chen, S. (2009, February 23). Pennsylvania rocked by 'jailing kids for cash' scandal. CNN. Retrieved from http://www.cnn.com/2009/CRIME/02/23/pennsylvania.corrupt.judges/index.html

Chesney-Lind, M. (1971). *Female juvenile delinquency in Hawaii.* Unpublished master's thesis, University of Hawaii.

Chesney-Lind, M., & Shelden, R. G. (2014). *Girls, delinquency, and juvenile justice* (4th ed.). New York, NY: Wiley-Blackwell.

Colwell, P., Grieshop-Goodwin, T., & Swann, A. (2009). *Opportunities lost: Racial disparities in juvenile justice in Kentucky and identified needs for system change.* Jeffersontown, KY: Kentucky Youth Advocates. Retrieved on October 18, 2013, from http://www.louisvilleky.gov/NR/rdonlyres/52FB78DC-C5CC-4C3E-977E-99D65B79878D/0/KYAIssueBrief.pdf

Davis, J., & Sorensen, J. R. (2010). Disproportionate minority confinement of juveniles: A national examination of Black–White disparity in placements. *Crime & Delinquency.* Retrieved on October 19, 2013, from http://cad.sagepub.com/cgi/rapidpdf/0011128709359653v1.pdf

DeMuro, P., & DeMuro, A. (1988). *Reforming the California Youth Authority.* Bolinas, CA: Common Knowledge Press.

de Sá, K. (2004, February 12). Judge orders moratorium on sending juveniles to CYA until review. *San Jose Mercury News,* 1B.

de Sá, K. (2011, January 14). Brown calls for elimination of youth prison system and shifting of state prisoners to county jails. *San Jose Mercury News.* Retrieved on October 19, 2013, from http://www.mercurynews.com/san-mateo-county/ci_17091138?nclick_check=1

Dexheimer, E. (2007, April 29). Scandal and reform: A familiar cycle in agencies that deal with juvenile delinquents. *Austin American-Statesman.* Retrieved October 19, 2013, from http://www.texaspolicy.com/sites/default/files/documents/2007-04-29-AAS-ML.pdf

Ecenbarger, W. (2012). *Kids for cash: Two judges, thousands of children, and a $2.6 million kickback scheme.* New York, NY: New Press.

Fazel, S. H., Doll, M., & Langstrom, N. (2008). Mental disorders among adolescents in juvenile detention and correctional facilities: A systematic review and metaregression analysis of 25 surveys. *Journal of the American Academy of Child & Adolescent Psychiatry, 47,* 1010–1019.

Feld, B. C. (1999). *Bad kids: Race and the transformation of the juvenile court.* New York, NY: Oxford University Press.

Human Rights Watch. (2006). *Custody and control conditions of confinement in New York's juvenile prisons for girls: Summary.* Retrieved on October 18, 2013, from http://www.hrw.org/sites/default/files/reports/us0906webwcover.pdf

Judges sentenced kids for cash (editorial). (2009, January 28). Retrieved from http://www.philly.com/philly/opinion/inquirer/20090128_Editorial_Judges Sentenced.html.

Justice Policy Institute. (2009, May). *The costs of confinement: Why good juvenile justice policies make good fiscal sense.* Retrieved on October 17, 2013, from http://www.justicepolicy.org/images/upload/09_05_REP_CostsOfConfinement_JJ_PS.pdf

Leovy, J., & Chong, J. (2004, February 6). Youth Authority to review use of cages. *Los Angeles Times.* Retrieved on October 19, 2013, from http://articles.latimes.com/2004/feb/06/local/me-cage6

Lerner, S. (1982). *The CYA report: Conditions of life at the California Youth Authority.* Bolinas, CA: Common Knowledge Press.

Lerner, S. (1986). *Bodily harm: The pattern of fear and violence at the California Youth Authority.* Bolinas, CA: Common Knowledge Press.

Macallair, D., Males, M., & McCracken, C. (2009). *Closing California's Division of Juvenile Facilities: An analysis of county institutional capacity.* San Francisco, CA: Center on Juvenile and Criminal Justice.

Moore, S. (2009, August 10). Mentally ill offenders strain juvenile system. *New York Times.* Retrieved on October 17, 2013, from http://www.nytimes.com/2009/08/10/us/10juvenile.html?pagewanted=all&_r=0

Murray, C., Baird, C., Loughran, N., Mills, F., & Platt, J. (2006). *Safety and welfare plan: Implementing reform in California.* Sacramento, CA: California Department of Corrections and Rehabilitation, Division of Juvenile Justice. Retrieved from http://www.cdcr.ca.gov/news/docs/djj_safety_and_welfare%20plan.pdf

Provine, D. M. (2007). *Unequal under law: Race in the war on drugs.* Chicago, IL: University of Chicago Press.

Ryan, J. P., Herzb, D., Hernandeza, P. M., & Marshall, J. M. (2007). Maltreatment and delinquency: Investigating child welfare bias in juvenile justice processing. *Children and Youth Services Review, 29,* 1035–1050.

Schlossman, S., & Wallach, S. (1978). The crime of precocious sexuality: Female delinquency in the progressive era. *Harvard Educational Review, 8,* 65–94.

Shelden, R. G. (1981). Sex discrimination in the juvenile justice system: Memphis, Tennessee, 1900–1917. In M. Q. Warren (Ed.), *Comparing male and female offenders.* Newbury Park, CA: Sage.

Shelden, R. G. (2008). Controlling the dangerous classes: A history of criminal justice in America (2nd ed.). Boston, MA: Allyn and Bacon.

Shelden, R. G. (2012). *Delinquency and juvenile justice in American society* (2nd ed.). Long Grove, IL: Waveland Press.

Shufelt, J. L. & Cocozza, J. J. (2006). *Youth with mental health disorders in the juvenile justice system: Results from a multi-state prevalence study.* National Center for Mental Health and Juvenile Justice. Retrieved on October 19, 2013, from http://ncmhjj.com/pdfs/publications/PrevalenceRPB.pdf

Sickmund, M., Sladky, T. J., & Kang, W. (2008). *Census of juveniles in Residential Placement Databook.* Retrieved from http://www.ojjdp.ncjrs.gov/ojstatbb/cjrp

Southern Poverty Law Center. (2008). *J. A. et al. v. Barbour et al.* Retrieved on October 18, 2013, from http://www.splcenter.org/get-informed/case-docket/ja-et-al-v-barbour-et-al

Southern Poverty Law Center. (2010, March 10). SPLC sues Mississippi over mental health system for children on Medicaid. Retrieved on October 17, 2013, from http://www.splcenter.org/get-informed/news/splc-sues-mississippi-over-mental-health-system-for-children-on-medicaid

Sullivan, D., & Tifft, L. (2000). *Restorative justice as a transformative process.* Voorheesville, NY: Mutual Aid Press.

Tonry, M. (1995). *Malign neglect: Race, crime, and punishment in America.* New York, NY: Oxford University Press.

Walker, S., Spohn, C., & DeLone, M. (2007). *The color of justice: Race, ethnicity, and crime in America* (4th ed.). Belmont, CA: Cengage.

Warren, J. (2004a, February 3). Youth prison system unsafe, unhealthful, reports find. *Los Angeles Times*. Retrieved from http://articles.latimes.com/2004/feb/03/local/me-youth3

Warren, J. (2004b, February 4). Disarray in juvenile prisons jolts capital. *Los Angeles Times*. Retrieved from http://articles.latimes.com/2004/feb/04/local/me-cya4

Warren, J. (2004c, September 22). Shut down state youth prisons, experts say. *Los Angeles Times*. Retrieved from http://articles.latimes.com/2004/sep/22/local/me-cya22

Warren, J. (2005, February 1). For young offenders, a softer approach. *Los Angeles Times*. Retrieved from http://articles.latimes.com/2005/feb/01/local/me-cya1

Warren, J., Leovy, J., & Zamichow, N. (2004, February 17). A daily lesson in violence and despair. *Los Angeles Times*. Retrieved from http://articles.latimes.com/2004/feb/17/local/me-cya17

21

WHY ARE THERE SO MANY MENTALLY ILL IN THE CRIMINAL JUSTICE SYSTEM?

Jennie K. Singer and Chelsea M. Johnson

Over the past several decades, the mentally ill have become more visible in our cities. They can be seen wandering the streets, sometimes disheveled and talking to themselves. There are too many people with severe mental illnesses who have nowhere to go and do not get the treatment that might help them to live safe and meaningful lives. If we turn back the clock to the 1960s, we did not have a "homeless problem" as most individuals with severe mental illness were living in mental hospitals. Although hospitals segregated and isolated the mentally ill, frequently subjecting their patients to backward and brutal "treatments," they provided stability, community, and, most importantly, food, shelter, and medical care (Torrey, 2014). Reformers like Dorothea Dix, who lived in the 19th century, lobbied for a more humane way to treat the mentally ill by integrating them back into society with enough care and support. A vision of federally funded mental health clinics focusing on bringing the severely mentally ill to be treated in their own homes was developed during the Kennedy presidency, but this ambitious plan failed to get proper funding and was quietly disbanded during the Nixon years. Additionally, while these federal programs would have done much (if funding had remained) for our stable mentally ill population, they were shown to fail those clients who had the most severe mental illnesses. With both populations (severe and stable mentally ill individuals) lacking proper treatment options, more and more resources have dried up as economic downturns have led to shrinking budgets nationwide. As we walk down an urban street decades later, we see large numbers of homeless mentally ill men and women living in tent cities or sitting on the pavement on a dirty sidewalk. With nowhere to go and no treatment for their symptoms, many turn to illegal substances to get rid of negative voices in their heads and to help ease their massive anxiety. Without proper housing or treatment, the severely mentally ill become caught up in the criminal justice system.

PREVALENCE OF
MENTALLY ILL OFFENDERS

There has been a striking increase in the number of mentally ill inmates in both federal and state prisons and jails over the past several years, although there have been declining correctional populations since 2002. According to the Bureau of Justice Statistics (Carson, 2018) an estimated 6,741,400 individuals were supervised by adult correctional systems (including jails, prisons, parole, and probation) in the United States at the end of 2015. The population decreased 1.7% during 2015, dropping below 6.8 million for the first time since 2002. By the end of 2015, about 1 in 37 adults (or 2.7% of all adults) in the United States were under some form of correctional supervision, the lowest rate since 1994. Most of these individuals are supervised in the community. State and federal prisons held an estimated 1.51 million prisoners by the end of 2016. This is 1% less than the end of 2015 and 7% less than the peak at the end of 2009. This population includes a large proportion of individuals with serious mental illnesses, such as schizophrenia, bipolar disorder, and major depression[1] (Eno Louden et al., 2008). It is important to understand the extent of how many offenders with mental illness are in the criminal justice system because of their extra needs for treatment and services beyond that of the average offender.

Using a formula for severe mental illness for recently booked jail inmates, the prevalence rates for males were 14.5% and 31.0% for women (Stedman, Osher, Robbins, Case, & Samuels, 2009). When applied to the 13 million annual jail admissions in 2007, there were approximately 2 million annual jail bookings of persons with serious mental illness. Stedman et al. (2009) explain that this number is only approximate, as several disorders, such as anxiety or post-traumatic stress, are not taken into account when addressing mental illness in a correctional setting.

According to James and Glaze (2006), 56% of state prisoners, 45% of federal prisoners, and 64% of jail inmates were identified as having a mental health problem, based on data gathered from personal interviews with state and federal prisoners in 2004 and local jail inmates in 2002. The definition of mental health problems was more broadly defined for these interviews as a recent history or symptoms of a mental health problem within 12 months of the interview, as well as a diagnosis or treatment for any mental health disorder in the *Diagnostic and Statistical Manual of Mental Disorders*, fourth edition (DSM-IV). Some estimates of mentally ill inmates in prisons and jails are lower than these calculations because some prisons (such as in the state of California) only treat some mental disorders, such as major mood or psychotic disorders, and do not treat other disorders, such as anxiety disorders, unless they are severe enough to warrant treatment because the inmate is experiencing painful symptoms that require urgent care. Mental disorders are 3 times more prevalent in criminal justice settings as they are in the general population (Teplin, 1994; Teplin, Abram, & McClelland, 1996).

Prevalence rates of substance abuse in the mentally ill range from 50% (Drake, Bartels, Teague, et al., 1993; Kessler, Nelson, McGonagle, et al., 1996) to about 80% (Wolff, Diamond, & Helminiak, 1997) depending on how the researchers define substance use (current use or use at some point in their lives). James and Glaze (2006) found that 74% of state inmates and 76% of jail inmates who met criteria for a mental health problem met criteria for substance abuse or dependence. Additionally, James and Glaze found that almost 63% of state inmates with mental disorders used drugs in the month prior to their arrest, compared with 49% of state inmates with no mental disorder. The connection between mental illness and substance abuse is an extremely important one because substance abuse among offenders with mental illness increases the likelihood of these offenders experiencing problems such as homelessness and escalating involvement with the criminal justice system (i.e., Hartwell, 2004).

ARE JAILS AND PRISONS THE NEW MENTAL HOSPITALS, OR ARE WE CRIMINALIZING MENTAL ILLNESS?

The severely mentally ill (SMI) were treated in long-term, publicly funded mental hospitals up until the 1960s (Markowitz, 2010), at which time the number of available beds started to decline. According to a research report from the Treatment Advocacy Center (2017), the discovery of chlorpromazine (Thorazine®) in the 1950s made it possible to control psychiatric symptoms of many individuals with serious mental illness, which was a major impetus to the emptying of state psychiatric hospitals. This decrease took place when the U.S. population—and thus the need for psychiatric beds—was doubling.

According to the National Institute of Mental Health estimates (National Institute of Mental Health, 1990), in 1960, there were about 314 beds available per 100,000 persons, or about 563,000 beds in U.S. state and county psychiatric facilities. By 1990, there were only 98,800 beds, or 40 per 100,000 persons, and by 2005, there were only 17 beds per 100,000 persons, despite estimates that with population growth, 50 beds per 100,000 would provide minimal coverage for mental health needs in the United States (Torrey, Kennard, Eslinger, Lamb, & Payle, 2010). Markowitz (2010) described three main reasons for this decline in hospital beds: the development of psychiatric medications (such as Thorazine®), which were able to stabilize symptoms for the first time; a shift in how people felt about confining the mentally ill for extended periods of time; and a shifting of the cost burden of care from the states to the federal government, followed by severe budget cuts that greatly underfunded the care of mental health treatment.

As a result of these changes, the SMI population is frequently admitted to in-patient hospital settings but is then quickly stabilized and released, most of the time by general hospitals instead of specialized psychiatric hospitals (Markowitz, 2010). Unfortunately, SMI are frequently released too quickly because the standards for involuntary commitment have become extremely strict and without adequate follow-up care in the community (Weinstein, 1990). Lamb, Weinberger, and Gross (2004) point out that the Lanterman-Petris-Short Act (which went into effect in California in 1969) brought about a major change in the commitment laws, which eventually resulted in every state changing their commitment laws as well. The new, tougher commitment laws made it necessary for an individual with SMI to have imminent dangerousness (to self or others) as mandatory for a now shorter period of determinate hospitalization. Hospitalized persons also have access to attorneys now, allowing them to challenge their commitments. All of these changes have made long-term hospitalizations a thing of the past. SMI, now almost unable to be hospitalized and rarely given the level of care needed to sustain them successfully in the community, are given the long-term care they need in the criminal justice system (Lamb et al., 2004).

Markowitz (2010) sees the deinstitutionalization of the SMI as directly contributing to the increase of this population in the criminal justice system. SMI have migrated to disorganized neighborhoods and have experienced a lack of symptom management and an increase in homelessness due to a pervasive lack of care, all of which enhance the risk of the SMI becoming involved in crime. Stigma and social rejection limit the SMI's job, housing, and social networking opportunities, which takes away potential protective factors while increasing the risk of violent behaviors. Care is limited due to a lack of resources in the community (Lamb et al., 2004). Another reason cited for the increase of SMI in the criminal justice system is the belief that police can better deal with deviant behaviors that scare society (Laberge & Morin, 1995; Jemelka, Trupin, & Chiles, 1989), along with society's lack of tolerance for the mentally ill (Lamb & Weinberger, 1998).

Lurigio (2011) points out that police frequently arrest SMI to help provide them with treatment, meals, or shelter from inclement weather. Fitzpatrick and Myrstol (2011) disagree, stating that SMI are more likely to be homeless and abusing substances and thus might be jailed by police as an effort to manage society's rabble or offensive nonviolent people who are merely guilty of misdemeanors.

Lurigio writes that when an individual with SMI is arrested, convicted, and incarcerated, it is because s/he has committed a criminal act. Although there has been a documented increase in SMI in jails and prisons, some researchers have not found evidence of a shift from state mental hospitals to the criminal justice system (Steadman, Monahan, Duffee, Hartstone, & Rohhins, 1984; Teplin & Voit, 1996). Lurigio (2011) pointed out that the rise in the percentage of incarcerated SMI from 1950 to 2000 has been both modest and predictable in light of how much the overall population of incarcerated individuals has increased over this time period. Frank and Glied (2006) found that while the percentage of SMI fell 23% in public psychiatric institutions during that time period, the number of SMI increased only 4% in correctional institutions between 1950 and 2000.

However, the American Psychiatric Association (2004) and others (i.e., Fellner, 2006; Treatment Advocacy Center, 2007) have declared that correctional facilities have become the primary mental health institutions in the United States. Adams and Ferrandino (2008) stated that the three largest psychiatric institutions in the country are the Los Angeles County Jail, New York City Rikers Island, and the Cook County Jail in Chicago. The numbers of mentally ill, particularly severely mentally ill, in the criminal justice system have been increasing in most states over time (Adams & Ferrandino, 2008; National Institute of Corrections, 2001). According to the American Psychiatric Association (2004), the most common mental illnesses found in the inmate population in both the United States are depression, schizophrenia, and bipolar disorder.

A main issue that is brought out in the literature is that there are some SMI who are less likely to offend, and these individuals are generally treatment compliant, have more community supports, and are less likely to be involved with illegal drugs or substance abuse. These SMI are also generally less prone to have personality disorders, antisocial personality disorder in particular. Those SMI who have issues with substance abuse have been caught up in the war against drugs and have been swept into the criminal justice system along with drug users without any mental illness. There is a group of SMI who are treatment resistant and who do not have social support. This group has a tendency to end up in disorganized and lower income neighborhoods with more access to illegal drugs (Clear, Byrne, & Dvoskin, 1993; Swanson, Estroff, Swartz, Borum, Lachicotte, Zimmer, & Wagner, 1997; Swartz, Swanson, Hiday, Borum, Wagner, & Burns, 1998) and more criminal activity. Lurigio (2011) states that the crime control policies and increased police presence in lower income neighborhoods, paired with the tendency for individuals with SMI to also have issues with substance abuse, has greatly elevated their entry into the criminal justice system.

An additional point made in the literature is that the SMI who have substance abuse issues, as well as antisocial thinking patterns, have been shown to have criminal thinking styles and to have the same risks of criminal behavior as those in the criminal justice system who do not have SMI (i.e., Walters, 2003). Those individuals who have SMI, substance abuse, and antisocial personality disorder are more at risk for violent crimes (Harris & Lurigio, 2007). Some studies indicate that merely having a mental disorder increases the probability that one will commit a crime (Fazel & Danesh 2002; Hodgins 1992; Hodgins et al., 1996; Wallace et al., 2004). In particular, schizophrenia, especially when paired with substance abuse, is associated with an elevated risk of criminal behavior (Arseneault et al., 2000; Fazel et al., 2009; Lafayette et al., 2003; Link et al., 1992; Mullen et al., 2000; Munetz et al., 2001) and even violent behavior (Arseneault et al., 2000; Brennan et al., 2000; Eronen et al., 1996; Fazel & Grann, 2006; Lindqvist & Allebeck, 1990; Swanson et al., 1990; Swanson et al., 2006; Walsh et al., 2002). What is particularly difficult for those with SMI is that they need a higher level of care than is typically available in the community. When SMI lack a supportive family member to care for them, they are unable to follow complicated treatment protocols, make appointments and keep them, keep track of when medications are running low, and make sure that they eat and sleep appropriately. Without support, they are at high risk for out-of-control and paranoid behaviors that frequently land them in the criminal justice system. Sadly, even SMI with willing family members sometimes will not accept help when offered. Once in the system, it is so hard to follow the rules (both in and out of the institution) that they become stuck in the revolving door of incarceration, release, and reincarceration (i.e., Hefley, 2009; Navasky & O'Connor, 2009; Stephey, 2007).

According to a research study from the Treatment Advocacy Center (2017), several past studies have shown that many individuals with serious mental illness who have committed major crimes had been arrested and/or psychiatrically hospitalized multiple times prior to their crime. This group of repeat offenders makes up only 2% of all individuals with serious mental illness, and this small group causes a grossly disproportionate share of the problems and consumes a large amount of public resources.

One study used data from the Clinical Antipsychotic Trials of Intervention Effectiveness (CATIE), a large medication trial that compared first and second generation antipsychotic medications with 1,460 individuals with schizophrenia over a period of 18 months to study the mentally ill in the criminal justice system (Greenberg, Rosenbeck, Erickson, Desai, Stefanovics, Swartz, Keefe, McEvoy, & Stroup, et al., 2011). This prospective study examined a variety of information, including sociodemographic characteristics to find out what were predictors of involvement with the criminal justice system over the first year of the experiment. Greenberg et al. found that self-reported conduct disordered behavior before the age of 15, being younger and male, symptoms of akathisia (a neurological side effect of medication causing a feeling of inner restlessness), and both self-report and toxicological measures of drug use were significant and independent predictors of criminal justice involvement. Comorbid drug use was found to be one of the strongest risk factors for violence and criminal activity for persons with schizophrenia, in congruence with prior research (Cuffel et al., 1994; Fowler et al., 1998; Swanson et al., 2006; Wallace et al., 2004). This study did not find that severe symptoms of schizophrenia were a risk factor for increased violence or criminal conduct.

Another study examined the prevalence of criminal thinking in 265 male and 149 female incarcerated mentally disordered offenders (Morgan, Fisher, Duan, Mandraccia, & Murray, 2010). They found that 92% of the study participants were diagnosed with a serious mental illness such as schizophrenia, schizoaffective disorder, delusional disorder, other psychotic disorder, bipolar disorder, major depressive disorder, or other mood disorder. Mentally disordered offenders were found to have the same amount of criminal thinking (as measured by scores on the Psychological Inventory of Criminal Thinking Styles [PICTS] and Criminal Sentiments Scale–Modified [CSS-M)]) as offenders with no mental disorders. This finding is similar to other studies done by Walters and colleagues (i.e., Walters, 1995, 2011; Walters & Geyer, 2005). Morgan et al. (2010) concluded that mentally ill offenders appear to think and process information like criminals and that they did not offend mainly as a function of their mental illness. These offenders have been found to be both criminal and to have a severe mental illness. Gross and Morgan (2013) further explored this hypothesis and found that mentally ill individuals who had been hospitalized but had no involvement with the criminal justice system experienced less severe symptoms and had much lower levels of criminal thinking (as measured by the PICTS) than the mentally ill who had been hospitalized and did have a history of criminal justice involvement. Girard and Wormith (2004) found that SMI had higher scores on a commonly used and valid risk instrument, the Level of Service Inventory/Case Management Inventory (LS/CMI), than offenders with no mental illness. Risk factors measured by the LS/CMI include lack of education, employment and housing, and substance abuse. These risk factors positively correlate with criminal recidivism. SMI who have these risk factors, including an antisocial personality, are far more at risk for becoming involved in the criminal justice system than those with mental illness who do not have these risk factors (Gross & Morgan, 2013).

In summary, although there are researchers who do endorse the hypothesis that the mentally ill have migrated from the now almost-defunct state mental hospitals to prisons and jails, some research seems to indicate that is not the case. The war on drugs, harsh crime control policies, and the downward spiral that takes many SMI to disorganized and crime-prone neighborhoods with weak social supports and negligible treatment services combines with other empirical risk factors, leading the SMI into the criminal justice system in greater and greater numbers. Comorbid substance abuse, along with antisocial and possibly criminal thinking, puts a group of SMI in the same category as criminals without SMI but with a higher propensity for violence and recidivism. Morgan et al. (2010) make the salient point that mentally disordered offenders in the criminal justice system need rehabilitative treatment that not only addresses their mental health but also their criminogenic risks/needs, or those concerns that relate to a decrease in the individual's risk of committing a crime. For example, sad mood is an uncomfortable symptom but is not one that is correlated with criminal behavior. Thus, sad mood is not a criminogenic risk/need. However, command hallucinations, or voices that tell an SMI to do something (such as hurt someone), are a risk for violence and thus must be addressed to reduce the individual's risk.

However, even though the criminal justice system potentially holds both SMI who are criminals with mental illness as well as those who truly need long-term hospitalization or a higher level of care than is available in the community, the prisons and jails in the United States have indeed become "de facto" mental hospitals (Holton, 2003; Wilson & Draine, 2006). There is a consensus that people with SMI are overrepresented in the criminal justice system and that despite best efforts, correctional facilities are not the best treatment settings for SMI (Council of State Governments, 2002). Prins (2011) states that there is a group of SMI who are resistant to or unable to utilize community treatment and would reside in in-patient psychiatric hospitals if enough beds existed. Prins argues that even though the idea of reinstitutionalizing SMI in mental facilities sounds abhorrent to some, it is less negative than what is happening today: reinstitutionalizing SMI in the prisons and jails, which have become our new mental health system (Holton, 2003; Wilson & Draine, 2006). According to Rich, Wakeman, and Dickman (2011), the increase of mentally ill in the criminal justice system is due to the "War on Drugs" and United States' failure to treat substance addiction and mental illness as medical conditions that lead people to engage in behaviors that can result in incarceration.

THE SMI STAY LONGER IN JAILS AND PRISONS

As discussed previously, an individual with SMI has a much greater odds of ending up in jail than being hospitalized (Morrissey et al., 2007). After being arrested, a person with SMI is more likely to be detained in jail, as opposed to being released on their own recognizance or having their cases dismissed (Council of State Governments, 2005). Once in jail, those with SMI stay incarcerated 2.5 to 8 times longer than those without mental illness. McNiel, Binder, and Robinson (2005) found that a substantial number of people detained in jail are homeless and that a large proportion of this population had co-occurring mental disorders and substance abuse. Homeless persons who are jailed are held longer than offenders who have housing with similar demographics and crimes.

The Council of State Governments (2002) found that parole board members, possibly lacking confidence in community resources for SMI serving prison sentences, having misconceptions about mental illness, or fearing negative public reactions, may be more likely to let offenders with SMI serve the maximum prison sentence allowable by law. According to Ditton (1999), SMI were more likely to serve longer sentences than were other inmates, with the average being 12 extra months. Fields (2006) found that in Oklahoma, SMI were less likely to be paroled than those who were not identified as having a mental illness.

The large number of SMI in jails and prisons present a serious problem in behavior management for correctional staff, second only to overcrowding (Gibbs, 1983). The National Commission on Correctional Health Care (NCCHC, 1999) developed standards of care and treatment, administrative, personnel issues, support services, special needs and services, health records, and medical and legal issues that guide prison administrators in meeting the comprehensive needs for the SMI in their care (National Institute of Corrections, 2004). Elements of the NCCHC stipulations for care and treatment include immediate screening for mental health problems by a qualified health professional, timely appointments with a qualified professional when requested, prison procedures in place for psychiatric emergencies and suicide attempts, and treatment plans for seriously mentally ill and developmentally disabled inmates (NIC, 2004).

Fellner (2006) acknowledged that most prison systems provide correctional officers with minimal mental health training and that officers generally do not understand the nature of mental illness or how psychiatric symptoms impact behavior. This issue has led most officers to assume that most negative behaviors are manipulative and that SMI violate rules on purpose. The tension between correctional officers and SMI are created from the difficulty (or impossibility) of coordinating the needs of SMI with staff concerns of safety, power, and control in the institutional setting (Fellner, 2006). Adams and Ferrandino (2008) point out that inmates' pathology, such as experiencing hallucinations and delusions, can prevent them from understanding the rules, and they may break rules without realizing that rules were broken in some circumstances.

Despite obvious challenges, some correctional staff training programs have proven to be effective. Parker (2006) stated that the National Alliance of Mentally Ill in Indiana worked with Indiana University to develop a 10-hour curriculum to teach correctional officers about mental illnesses. After the Secure Housing Unit in Wabash Valley Prison implemented this program, use-of-force incidents by officers and battery with bodily fluids by inmates both decreased. Dvoskin and Spiers (2004) advocate the use of treatment teams where clinical and custody staff interact and share information to benefit the offender with SMI. These authors cite their personal experiences and older studies as a basis for believing that correctional staff can perform many of the roles and duties of clinicians when necessary (such as evenings and weekends when clinical staff are unavailable). This type of collaboration, accompanied by training, they assert, can help correctional staff have helpful, as opposed to harmful, interactions with SMI and will ultimately provide the SMI with the best care.

Regardless of how well trained the correctional staff, SMI will break prison rules and regulations. Punishment in prison settings frequently consists of being sent to segregated housing and, when repeated violence is involved, to a supermax prison setting. NIC (2004) guidelines state that although SMI must be punished, caution must be exercised to avoid exacerbating their psychiatric symptoms. Requirements and guidelines include extra checks on inmates with SMI, special policies and procedures for managing violent behavior and restraints, a full mental health evaluation, and monitoring and treatment if SMI are placed in a supermax facility (APA, 2000; NCCHC, 1999; NIC, 2004). Despite careful monitoring, psychologists have written of their concerns that when SMI are housed in supermax prison settings, serious psychological problems can be made worse. Additionally, symptoms can emerge, even for those inmates with no history of SMI, with isolation causing depression and anxiety (Bottoms, 1999; Ditton, 1999). When SMI are placed in housing where they are isolated and locked down up to 23 hours per day, they can decompensate or experience a psychiatric breakdown (APA, 2000; Human Rights Watch, 2003). Another issue cited by the Human Rights Watch is that because of the strict rules in segregation and in supermax prison settings, the only treatment readily available for SMI, now at their most vulnerable to mental health symptoms, is generally psychiatric medication.

THE SMI IN THE COMMUNITY: MORE DIFFICULTY ON PROBATION OR ON PAROLE?

The burgeoning probation population includes a substantial proportion of probationers with SMI (Eno Louden, Skeem, Camp, & Christensen, 2008). These probationers present unique challenges to probation supervisors, as SMI frequently have a difficult time following the standard conditions of probation, such as maintaining employment (Orlando-Morningstar, Skoler, & Holliday, 1999). SMI are often required to take medication or participate in treatment as an additional or "special" condition of probation (Skeem, Emke-Francis, & Eno Louden, 2006). Perhaps for these reasons, Eno Louden et al. (2008) surmise that probationers with SMI are twice as likely to fail on supervision as probationers without SMI (Dauphinot, 1996).

A main issue when SMI reenter the community from prison is that offenders generally leave prison without a reentry plan, except for parole supervision. Some SMI are sent into the community with no parole supervision because they are kept in prison until their prison term expires. Unlike jail, which typically consists of confinement that lasts under 1 year, leaving prison represents an intense life transition, and those with SMI are paroled with few rehabilitative resources or behavioral health supports (Garland, 2001; Marlowe, 2006; Petersilia, 2003).

According to Beck (2000), 80% of parolees are assigned to a parole officer upon release; the remaining 20% will serve their full sentence term and therefore will not receive supervision. Offenders who are no longer under parole supervision are generally not willing to participate in rehabilitative services. Further, parole officers generally have high caseloads, which can allow parolees to abscond (Beck, 2000; Bonzcar, 1999). Additionally, parolees who do not engage in supportive systems or treatment programs have greater chances of reoffending and recidivating; a full two thirds of all released parolees will be rearrested within 1 year (Prins, 2009). This leaves both society and the criminal justice system with a lack of community safeguards and increasing prisoner admissions.

SMI released from prison face a multitude of difficulties. Most offenders with mental illness leave correctional institutions without a reentry plan beyond parole supervision. Additionally, parolees with SMI are left with few rehabilitative resources and behavioral health supports to reestablish stable lifestyles that address work, education, and substance abuse deficiencies (Garland, 2001; Marlowe, 2006; Petersilia, 2003). Other problems facing SMI upon release include socioeconomic barriers, such as lacking health insurance or government benefits; little or no family support; ineligibility for subsidized housing, food stamps, or other government assistance if they have been convicted of a felony; and difficulty finding employment, as well as harboring the stigma of being incarcerated and having an SMI (Hoge, 2007; Peters, 1993). Having to cope with a severe mental disorder while dealing with multiple obstacles postrelease may lead SMI to supervision failure (Skeem & Louden, 2006).

The Human Rights Watch report (2003) states that it is short sighted for states to cut costs by removing programs that help SMI with reentry after prison because "without good discharge planning and post-release programs, seriously mentally ill prisoners are likely to cycle endlessly between prison and the community, their illnesses worsening, and chances increasing that they will end up in the high security units within the prison system" (p. 201). Human Rights Watch recommended partnerships between departments of corrections and other state agencies, postrelease treatment, early enrollment in Medicaid or other health coverage, and early prerelease counseling, all with proper funding allotted. "In an era in which the United States incarcerates hundreds of thousands of seriously mentally ill men and women in its prisons, it serves neither the mentally ill nor the broader community to shortchange the transitional programs that could serve to break these linkages between mental illness and imprisonment in 21st century America" (Human Rights Watch, 2003, p. 201).

Several studies have demonstrated the propensity for SMIs on probation or parole (or in psychiatric hospitals) to become incarcerated and to recidivate, mainly as a result of technical violations. Solomon, Draine, and Marcus (2002) monitored 250 clients of an urban psychiatric probation and parole service for 12 months. They found that 85 clients with SMI (34%) were incarcerated in the 12 months. Of the 85, 44 (18%) were incarcerated for a new offense and 41 (16%) were incarcerated for a technical violation. Solomon et al. found that those offenders reincarcerated for technical violations were over 6 times more likely to have had intensive case management services. The authors concluded that intensive case management puts clients with SMI at risk for reincarceration for technical violations. However, they found that when SMI participated in treatment, the added supervision reduced their likelihood of being reincarcerated.

The Colorado Division of Criminal Justice (CDOCJ, 2008) reported that in Colorado, inmates with SMI were less likely than inmates without SMI to have a transitional community corrections placement following their release from prison: 28% of inmates with SMI were placed in community corrections during their incarceration, as compared with 36% of inmates without SMI. Among SMI, technical violations rather than new crimes are increasingly responsible for prison admissions. SMI were found to have higher-than-average recidivism rates. At 3 years postrelease, return rates to CDOC were 49% for offenders with some degree of mental illness, 58% for offenders with moderately severe to severe mental illness, and 47% for those without any mental disorder. The CDOCJ (2008) reported that people with SMI are 64% more likely to be arrested than those without SMI who committed the same crime (Olson, 2001). Cycling through the mental health, substance abuse, and criminal justice systems is a fairly common occurrence for offenders with SMI (CDOCJ, 2008).

A large recidivism study in Utah compared SMI and non-SMI offenders on parole and found that of the 9,245 offenders released from prison between 1998 and 2000, 23% ($N = 2,112$) of the sample met the criteria for SMI (Cloyes, Wong, Latimer, & Abarca, 2010). Cloyes et al. found that when controlling for demographics, condition of release, offense type, and condition of return (new offense versus a technical violation), the median time for all SMI offenders returning to prison was 385 days versus 743 days for all non-SMI offenders, or almost 1 year sooner. The authors concluded that the difference in recidivism rates appeared to be due to clinical symptoms and resource use. Cloyes et al. (2010) argued that their findings have serious implications for a "reinstitutionalization" movement, or the repeated incarceration of people with SMI, which incurs profound economic and human costs (p. 183). In their sample, 85% of their SMI sample committed technical violations versus 15% who committed new offenses. Most of the SMI (87% of the women and 84% of the men) were released to parole, and following the conditions of parole were extremely difficult for this population.

Another large study found that during the year 2005–2006, 11.5% of patients ($N = 4,544$) in a public mental health system (out of a total $N = 39,463$ patient records) were incarcerated in the county jail system (Hawthorne, Folsom, Sommerfeld, Lanouette, Lewis, Aarons, Conklin, Solorzano, Lindamer, & Jeste, 2012). Hawthorne et al. found that risk factors for incarceration included prior incarcerations; co-occurring substance abuse; homelessness; diagnoses of schizophrenia, bipolar disorder, or other psychotic disorders; and being male, having no Medicaid insurance, and being African American. Protective factors included being older than 45, having Medicaid beneficiaries, and being Latino, Asian, or another non-Euro-American racial ethnic group. Patients who received immediate outpatient treatment or case management services were less likely to be incarcerated within 90 days.

Since SMI are at a higher risk of initial incarceration and then recidivism upon reentry, what can help this population stay in the community once they have been put on probation or have been released from jail or prison? According to Lamb, Weinberger, and Gross (2004), several factors can help SMI released to the community. First, SMI need continuous rather than episodic care because regular monitoring can help SMI control violent impulses and inappropriate expressions of anger. This is especially true of SMI with a history of violent behavior (Dvoskin & Steadman, 1994). A case manager can help the SMI population find appropriate housing with enough support so that they can be compliant with treatment, medication, and other conditions of parole or probation. An appropriate housing arrangement, such as a board and care facility, can also help the SMI with rehabilitation programming and transportation to outside programs to help them achieve optimal functioning (Lamb et al., 2004). Ideally, each SMI would have a treatment team, as well as involved family members or other sources of social support—an extremely important part of an SMI's care. The family member who has been victimized by an SMI also needs guidance and support. The family member should be able to recognize when an SMI is experiencing a period of decompensation (where their symptoms of mental illness get much worse) and be given ways to protect themselves while enabling patients with SMI to get help for their symptoms and legal situation.

In recent years, several programs for SMI have shown great promise in helping this difficult population remain in the community with a high enough level of functioning to remain clear of the criminal justice system. While these programs are few and far between, they are enough to provide hope in this seemingly dismal situation. The New Freedom Commission on Mental Health (2003) suggested that three main responses are needed: (1) diversion programs that keep people with SMI out of the criminal justice system; (2) institutional services for people with SMI who do need to be in correctional facilities; (3) transition programs that facilitate the successful reentry of people with SMI to the community (p. 6).

Steadman and Naples (2005) found seven published empirical studies that examined program outcomes of jail diversion programs. They found that jail diversion reduces the time that SMI spend in jail without compromising public safety. One diversion approach that has been studied more than the rest is the crisis intervention team model (CIT). Developed by the Memphis, Tennessee, police department in 1988, it is now used widely in Colorado and in 35 states. Police officers are trained in crisis intervention and in de-escalation techniques, with the goal of diverting SMI at the first point of contact with the police. Trained officers help SMI connect with mental health resources and community treatment (CDOCJ, 2008). Data provided in the state of Colorado shows that 3 out of 4 four CIT calls resulted in a transport to treatment. Almost 1 in 5 calls resulted in successful de-escalation of the situation so that no transport to treatment was required, and a referral to community services was given instead (Pasini-Hill & English, 2006). CDOCJ (2008) reported that the core component of CIT is the development of cooperative relationships among community agencies.

Another model that has shown promise is Assertive Community Treatment (ACT). Also known as the Program of Assertive Community Treatment (PACT), this program combines treatment, rehabilitation, and support services in a multidisciplinary team typically made up of professionals from a variety of disciplines, such as psychiatry, nursing, and addiction counseling (CDOCJ, 2008). The ACT team is mobile and operates 24 hours a day, 7 days per week to provide services to SMI. Staff help SMI to find housing and employment and help with legal problems. Research has shown that ACT helps to reduce hospitalizations, although it was not consistent in reducing arrests and jail time (Morrissey & Meyer, 2007).

However, more forensically oriented programs, similar to ACT for SMI (called FACT for Forensic ACT), have emerged in recent years and have produced better results regarding keeping SMI out of the criminal justice system (Morrissey & Meyer, 2005). FACT teams specifically target SMI with prior arrests, accept referrals from criminal justice agencies, recruit criminal justice agencies as partners, use court sanctions to encourage SMI to participate, and encourage probation officers to be part of the FACT team (Cusack, Morrissey, Cuddeback, Prins, & Williams, 2010). Preventing rearrest is an explicit goal of the FACT team. Unfortunately, the FACT team is expensive, and thus, some criminal justice agencies opt for less expensive resources, such as intensive case management, even though some evidence suggests that FACT can reduce more arrests, jail days, and hospitalizations (Lamberti et al., 2001; McCoy et al., 2004), while other research found no difference in types of intensive care for SMI (Solomon & Draine, 1995). Cusack et al.'s (2010) study found that when comparing SMI treated by a FACT team versus treatment as usual (TAU), FACT led to fewer bookings and a greater likelihood of staying out of jail each year, even though FACT did not result in a shorter jail time if FACT participants were booked into jail. Also, FACT participants had fewer days of hospitalization compared with TAU participants. Cusack et al. stated that while FACT is costly ($8,000 more in per person outpatient service costs compared with TAU costs in the first 12 months), when reduced costs are factored in for less jail stays and inpatient stays, FACT services were only $3,520 more per person. Cusack et al. concluded that more empirical evidence is necessary before more jurisdictions would be willing to pay the higher cost for FACT.

Another community option for the SMI is the Modified Therapeutic Community (MTC) for offenders with mental illness and chemical abuse disorders. The community structure of the traditional Therapeutic Community is retained, but modifications for the mentally ill include increased flexibility, decreased intensity, and greater individual treatment care. Mental health needs and treatment are mixed with substance abuse treatment approaches for this dually diagnosed population (Sacks, Sacks, & Stommel, 2003). Community aftercare focusing on relapse prevention, medication, symptom management, and basic life skills are part of the program's approach. Sacks et al. (2003) evaluated Colorado MTC programs, where inmates with co-occurring SMI and substance abuse were randomly assigned to either the prison-based MTC or usual mental health services. Inmates completing the MTC could choose to enter the aftercare program in the community or receive other services. Sacks et al. found that inmates who participated in the prison-based MTC program had significantly lower recidivism rates than the control group (9% compared with 33%). Inmates who participated in both the prison-based MTC and the community-based aftercare had significantly lower recidivism rates (5% compared with 33%) and rates of criminal activity related to alcohol or drug use (30% compared with 58%) than members of the control group (Sacks et al., 2003). Sacks et al. reported that the longer an SMI was in treatment (such as an additional 2 months of treatment), the greater the likelihood that they would not be reincarcerated (2 months would lower the likelihood by 17%).

Supported housing and supported employment can also help SMI stay connected to the community and be less likely to recidivate. Roman, McBride, and Osborne (2006) state that while there are not many rigorous evaluations of supportive housing for forensically involved SMI, outcome data from a small number of individual and statewide programs show positive results in how supported housing can help SMI avoid recidivating. Roman et al. (2006) report that the statewide Shelter Plus Care program in Maryland, which provides SMI with rental assistance when they are released from jail, reports jail recidivism rates of less than 7%. Housing reentry programs for SMI are typically designed with a focus on treatment and a supportive peer community.

Supported employment programs are an evidence-based practice that help SMI find and keep meaningful work (CDOCJ, 2008). While there are ample studies of how supported employment helps non–criminal-justice-involved SMI, there is less evidence that this program can help forensically involved SMI out of prison or jail (Anthony, 2005). McGurk and Mueser (2006) state that although research has shown that supported employment has worked for people with SMI over other vocational programs, SMI in these programs tend to work very minimal hours. In their study of nonforensically involved clients with schizophrenia, they found that cognitive functioning becomes more important as a predictor of competitive work outcomes over time (the study took place over 4 years) for clients participating in supported employment programs. Initially, factors such as motivation are more important in locating employment, while those with higher cognitive functioning were more likely to stay employed.

One study used an experimental design to examine the effects of an integrated psychiatric and vocational service intervention at seven sites nationwide (Cook, Lehman, Drake, McFarlane, Gold, Leff, Blyer, Toprac, Razzano, Burke-Biller, Blankertz, Shafer, Pickett-Schenk, & Grey, 2005). Cook et al. found that SMI who received the program were more than twice as likely to be meaningfully employed as the control group 2 years after participating in the program. There were positive outcomes for the few SMI who had been arrested in the 3 months prior to the program, even though the program was not focused on criminally involved SMI.

Parole supervision and release present complicated issues and predicaments. Most inmates have been released to parole systems that provide few services and almost guarantee failure. Therefore, it is important to acknowledge and expand on prisoner reentry initiatives *especially* those proven to be successful. Positive changes may greatly improve prisoner reentry, as well as reduce the revolving-door syndrome and collateral consequences parolees face throughout (Seiter, 2003).

CONCLUSION

The United States has inadvertently made jails and prisons the most likely place SMI will receive psychiatric treatment by systematically shutting down state-funded psychiatric facilities and rehabilitation programs, failing to create a community treatment system with appropriate supports and by lacking a basic understanding of mental illness as a treatable medical disorder. The cyclical involvement parolees experience in the criminal justice system continues to devastate community cohesion and adds to homelessness, unemployment and poverty. Furthermore, stigma and fear surround those who are dysfunctional, which lead to a society lacking in ability and knowledge. Police officers, possibly uneducated and untrained in mental illness, confront severely mentally ill individuals in often hostile situations where circumstances and individual discretion leave minimal options. Such an unyielding dilemma initiates SMI into the "revolving door" of a system not meant to deal with their criminal mental state, one that is scary, stressful, and full of rules that are confusing and difficult to manage. Mentally disordered individuals are incarcerated longer, typically disregarded as to reentry planning, and are paroled to communities where resources and support are often lacking.

Although working with SMI will be a continual challenge for both society and mental health services, evidence-based treatment and community programs will not only improve their mental state and well-being but can also reduce their criminal behavior. Many programs are already being implemented nationwide with varying degrees of success. If the most successful evidence-based programs, including promising practices, are replicated across the United States, then we can be hopeful that things will improve for the mentally ill in our country.

Discussion Questions

1. What are the main reasons why the severely mentally ill were moved out of long-term care in mental hospitals and into the community starting in the early 1960s?

2. What are some of the reasons that the severely mentally ill are more likely to be arrested and brought to jail than to a mental hospital if they are in a mental health crisis?

3. Why are the severely mentally ill generally incarcerated longer than non–mentally ill inmates in jails and in prisons?

4. What are the most challenging things for the severely mentally ill living in jails or prisons versus those under community supervision? Why are these activities so challenging for this population?

5. Can you describe a few programs that have been shown to stabilize or otherwise help the SMI to cope in prison or to stay out of trouble in the community?

Note

1. Major mood disorders include depression (very low mood that can lead to suicidal behavior) and bipolar disorder (periods of intense highs and lows that can lead to suicidal behavior, agitation, and poor judgment).

The main psychotic disorder is schizophrenia, and symptoms include auditory hallucinations (hearing voices), delusions or strange beliefs, and difficulty distinguishing reality from fantasy.

References

Adams, K., & Ferrandino, J. (2008). Managing mentally ill inmates in prisons. *Criminal Justice and Behavior, 35*(8), 913–927.

Anthony, W. A. (2005). Psychiatric rehabilitation and the science of possibilities. *Psychiatric Rehabilitation Journal, 28*(4), 313–314. doi:10.2975/28.2005.313.314

Arseneault, L., Moffitt, T. E., Caspi, A., Taylor, P. J., & Silva, P. A. (2000). Mental disorders and violence in a total birth cohort: Results from the Dunedin Study. *Archives of General Psychiatry, 57*(10), 979–986.

Beck, A. (2000). *Prisoners in 1999.* Washington, DC: Bureau of Justice Statistics.

Bonzcar, T. P., & Glaze, L. E. (1999). *Probation and parole in the United States.* Washington, DC: U.S. Department of Justice, Bureau of Justice Statistics.

Bottoms, A. E. (1999). Interpersonal violence and social order in prisons. *Crime and Justice, 26,* 205.

Brennan, P. A., Mednick, S. A., & Hodgins, S. (2000). Major mental disorders and criminal violence in a Danish birth cohort. *Archives of General Psychiatry, 57*(5), 494–500.

Carson, E. A. (2018). *Prisoners in 2016.* Washington, DC: U.S. Department of Justice, Office of Justice Programs, Bureau of Justice Statistics. Retrieved from https://www.bjs.gov/content/pub/pdf/p16.pdf

Clear, T. R., Byrne, J. M., & Dvoskin, J. A. (1993). *The transition from being an inmate: Discharge planning, parole, and community-based services for offenders with mental illness.* Washington, DC: National Coalition for the Mentally Ill in the Criminal Justice System.

Cloyes, K. G., Wong, B., Latimer, S., & Abarca, J. (2010). Time to prison return for offenders with serious mental illness released from prison: A survival analysis. *Criminal Justice and Behavior, 37*(2), 175–187.

Colorado Division of Criminal Justice. (2008). What works: Effective recidivism reduction and risk-focused prevention programs. A Compendium of Evidence-Based Options for Preventing New and Persistent Criminal Behavior. Prepared by the RKC Group, Roger Przybylski.

Cook, J. A., Lehman, A. F., Drake, R., McFarlane, W. R., Gold, P. B., Leff, H. S., . . . Grey, D. D. (2005). Integration of psychiatric and vocational services: a multisite randomized, controlled trial of supported employment. *American Journal of Psychiatry, 162*(10), 1948–1956.

Council of State Governments. (2002). Criminal justice/mental health consensus project. Retrieved August 15, 2002, from http://www.consensus project.org

Cuffel, B. J., Shumway, M., Choujian, T. L., et al. (1994). A longitudinal study of substance use and community violence in schizophrenia. *Journal of Nervous and Mental Disease, 182,* 704 –708.

Cusack, K. J., Morrissey, J. P., Cuddeback, G. S., Prins, A., & Wiliams, D. M. (2010). Criminal justice involvement, behavioral health service use, and costs of forensic assertive community treatment: A randomized trial. *Community Mental Health Journal, 46*(4), 356–363.

Dauphinot, L. (1996). *The efficacy of community correctional supervision for offenders with severe mental illness.* Unpublished doctoral dissertation, University of Texas at Austin.

Ditton, P. M. (1999). *Mental health and treatment of inmates and probationers.* Washington, DC: Bureau of Justice Statistics. Retrieved from http://bjs.ojp .usdoj.gov/index.cfm?ty=pbdetail&iid=787

Drake, R. E., Bartels, S. J., Teague, G. B., Noordsy, D. L., & Clark, R. E. (1993). Treatment of substance abuse in severely mentally ill patients. *Journal of Nervous and Mental Disorders, 181*(10), 606–611.

Dvoskin, J. A., & Spiers, E. M. (2004). On the role of correctional officers in prison mental health. *Psychiatric Quarterly, 75*(1), 41–59.

Dvoskin, J. A., & Steadman, H. J. (1994). Using intensive case management to reduce violence by mentally ill persons in the community. *Hospital and Community Psychiatry, 45,* 679–684.

Eno Louden, J., Skeem, J., Camp, J., & Christensen, E. (2008). Supervising probationers with mental disorder: How do agencies respond to violations. *Criminal Justice and Behavior, 35,* 832–847.

Eronen, M., Hakola, P., & Tiihonen, J. (1996). Mental disorders and homicidal behavior in Finland. *Archives of General Psychiatry, 53*(6), 497–501.

Fazel, S., & Danesh, J. (2002). Serious mental disorder in 23,000 prisoners: A systematic review of 62 surveys. *Lancet, 359,* 545–550.

Fazel, S., Gautam, G., Linsell, L., Geddes, J. R., & Grann, M. (2009). Schizophrenia and violence: Systematic review and meta-analysis. *PLoS Medicine, 6*(8), e1000120.

Fazel, S., & Grann, M. (2006). The population impact of severe mental illness on violent crime. *American Journal of Psychiatry, 163*(8), 1397–1403.

Fellner, J. (2006). A corrections quandary: Mental illness and prison rules. *Harvard Civil Rights-Civil Liberties Law Review, 41,* 391–412.

Fields, G. (2006). No way out: Trapped by rules the mentally ill languish in prison. *Wall Street Journal,* A1.

Fitzpatrick, K. M., & Myrstol, B. (2011). The jailing of America's homeless: Evaluating the rabble management thesis. *Crime & Delinquency, 57*(2), 271–297.

Fowler, D., Garety, P., & Kuipers, E. (1998). Understanding the inexplicable: An individually formulated cognitive approach to delusional beliefs. In C. Perris & P. D. McGorry (Eds.),

Cognitive psychotherapy of psychotic and personality disorders (pp. 129–146). Chichester, UK: Wiley.

Frank, R. G., & Glied, S. A. (2006). *Better but not well: Mental health policy in the United States since 1950.* Baltimore, MD: Johns Hopkins University Press.

Garland, D. (2001). *Mass imprisonment: Social causes and consequences.* Thousand Oaks, CA: Sage.

Gibbs, J. J. (1983). Problems and priorities: Perceptions of jail custodians and social service providers. *Journal of Criminal Justice, 11,* 327–349.

Girard, L., & Wormith, J. (2004). The predictive validity of the Level of Service Inventory-Ontario Revision on general and violent recidivism among various offender groups. *Criminal Justice and Behavior, 31,* 150–181. doi:10.1177/0093854803261335

Greenberg, G., Rosenheck, R. A., Erickson, S. K., Desai, R. A., Stefanovics, E. A., Swartz, M., . . . Stroup, T. S. (2011). Criminal justice system involvement among people with schizophrenia. *Community Menta Health Journal, 47*(6), 727–736.

Gross, N. R., & Morgan, R. D. (2013). Understanding persons with mental illness who are and are not criminal justice involved: A comparison of criminal thinking and psychiatric symptoms. *Law and Human Behavior, 37*(3), 175–186.

Harris, A., & Lurigio, A. J. (2007). The mentally ill as perpetrators of violence: A brief review of research and assessment strategies. *Aggression and Violent Behavior, 12,* 542–551.

Hartwell, S. W. (2004). Comparison of offenders with mental illness only and offenders with dual diagnosis. *Psychiatric Services, 55,* 145–150.

Hawthorne, W. B., Folsom, D. P., Sommerfeld, D. H., Lanoutte, N. M., Lewis, M., Aarons, G. A., . . . Jeste, D. V. (2012). Incarceration among adults who are in the public mental health system: Rates, risk factors, and short-term outcomes. *Psychiatric Services, 63*(1), 26–32.

Hefley, D. (2009). Mentally ill often adrift in the criminal justice system. *The Herald.* Everett, WA.

Hodgins, S. (1992). Mental disorder, intellectual deficiency, and crime: Evidence from a birth cohort. *Archives of General Psychiatry, 49,* 476–483.

Hodgins, S., Mednick, S. A., Brennan, P. A., et al. (1996). Mental disorder and crime: evidence from a Danish birth cohort. *Archives of General Psychiatry, 53*, 489–496.

Hoge, S. K. (2007). *Providing transition and outpatient services to the mentally ill released from correctional institutions.* New York, NY: Springer.

Holton, S. M. B. (2003). *Managing and treating mentally disordered offenders in jails and prisons.* Thousand Oaks, CA: Sage.

Human Rights Watch. (2003). *Ill-equipped: U.S. prisons and offenders with mental illness.* New York, NY: Author.

Jamelka, R., Trupin, E., & Chiles, J. A. (1989). The mentally ill in prisons: A review. *Hospital and Community Psychiatry, 40*(5), 481–491.

James, D. J., & Glaze, L. E. (2006). *Mental health problems in prison and jail inmates.* Washington, DC: Bureau Of Justice Statistics. Retrieved from www.ojp.usdoj.gov/bjs/pub/pdf/mhppji.pdf

Kessler, R. C., Nelson, C. B., McGonagle, K. A., Edlund, M. J., Frank, R. G., & Leaf, P. J. (1996). The epidemiology of co-occurring addictive and mental disorders: Implications for prevention and service utilization. *American Journal of Orthopsychiatry, 66*(1), 17–31.

Laberge, D., & Morin, D. (1995). The overuse of criminal justice dispositions: Failure of diversionary policies in the management of mental health problems. *International Journal of Law and Psychiatry, 18*(4), 389–414.

Lafayette, J. M., Frankle, W., Pollock, A., Dyer, K., & Goff, D. C. (2003). Clinical characteristics, cognitive functioning, and criminal histories of outpatients with schizophrenia. *Psychiatric Services, 54*(12), 1635–1640.

Lamb, R. H., & Weinberger, L. E. (1998). Persons with severe mental illness in jails and prisons: A review. *Psychiatric Services, 49*, 483–492.

Lamb, R. H., Weinberger, L. E., & Gross, B. H. (2004). Mentally ill persons in the criminal justice system: Some perspectives. *Psychiatric Quarterly, 75*, 107–126.

Lamberti, J. S., Weisman, R. L., Schwarzkopf, S. N., Price, N., Ashton, R. M., & Trompeter, J. (2001).

The mentally ill in jails and prisons: Towards an integrated model of prevention. *Psychiatric Quarterly, 72*, 63–77.

Lindqvist, P., & Allebeck, P. (1990). Schizophrenia and crime: A longitudinal follow-up of 644 schizophrenics in Stockholm. *British Journal of Psychiatry, 157*(3), 345–350.

Link, B. G., Andrews, H., & Cullen, F. T. (1992). The violent and illegal behavior of mental patients reconsidered. *American Sociological Review, 57*(3), 275–292.

Lurigio, A. J. (2011). Examining prevailing beliefs about people with serious mental illness in the criminal justice system. *Federal Probation: A Journal of Correctional Philosophy and Practice, 75*(1).

Markowitz, F. E. (2010). Mental Ilness, crime, and violence: Risk, context, and social control. *Aggression and Violent Behavior, 16*, 36–44. doi:10.1016/j.avb.2010.10.003

Marlowe, D. B. (2006). When "what works" never did: Dodging the "scarlet m" in correctional rehabilitation. *Criminology & Public Policy, 5*(2), 339–346.

McCoy, M. L., Roberts, D. L., Hanrahan, P., Clay, R., Luchins, D. J. (2004). Jail linkage assertive community treatment services for individuals with mental illnesses. *Psychiatric Rehabilitation Journal, 27*, 243–250.

McGurk, S. R., & Mueser, K. T. (2006). Strategies for coping with cognitive impairment in supported employment. *Psychiatric Services, 57*, 1421–1429.

McNiel, D. E., Binder, R. L., & Robinson, J. C. (2005). Incarceration associated with homelessness, mental disorder, and co-occuring substance abuse. *Psychiatric Services, 56*(7), 840–846.

Morgan, R. D., Fisher, W. H., Duan, N., Mandracchia, J. T., & Murray, D. (2010). Prevalence of criminal thinking among state prison inmates with serious mental illness. *Law and Human Behavior, 34*(4), 324–336.

Morrissey, J. P., & Meyer, P. (2005). *Extending ACT to criminal justice settings: Applications, evidence and options.* Paper presented at the Evidence-Based Practice for Justice-Involved Individuals: Assertive Community Treatment Expert Panel

Meeting, Bethesda, MD. Retrieved from http://gainscenter.samhsa.gov/text/ebp/Papers/ExtendingACTPaper.asp

Morrissey, J. P., Meyer, P., & Cuddeback, G. (2007). Extending ACT to criminal justice settings: Origins, current evidence and future directions. *Community Mental Health Journal, 43*, 527–544. doi:10.1007/s10597-007-9092-9

Mullen, P. E., Burgess, P., Wallace, C., Palmer, S., & Ruschena, D. (2000). Community care and criminal offending in schizophrenia. *Lancet, 355*(9204), 614–617.

Munetz, M. R., Grande, T. P., & Chambers, M. R. (2001). The incarceration of individuals with severe mental disorders. *Community Mental Health Journal, 37*(4), 361–372.

National Commission on Correctional Health Care. (1999). *Correctional mental health care: Standards and guidelines for delivering services.* Chicago, IL: Author.

National Institute of Corrections. (2001). *Provision of mental health care in prisons.* Washington, DC: Department of Justice.

National Institute of Corrections. (2004). *Correctional health care: Addressing the needs of elderly, chronically ill, and terminally ill inmates.* Washington, DC: Department of Justice.

National Institute of Mental Health. (1990). *Clinical training in serious mental illness* (DHHS Publication No. ADM 90-1679). Washington, DC: U.S. Government Printing Office.

Navasky, M. (Producer & Director), & O'Connor, K. (Producer & Director). (2009). *The released* [Motion picture]. Boston, MA: Frontline.

New Freedom Commission on Mental Health. (2003). *Achieving the promise: Transforming mental health care in America.* Final Report. DHHS Pub. No. SMA-03-3832. Rockville, MD: Author.

Olsen, D. P. (2001). Protection and advocacy: An ethics practice in mental health. *Journal of Psychiatric and Mental Health Nursing, 8*(2), 121–128.

Orlando-Morningstar, D., Skoler, G., & Holliday, S. (1999). *Handbook for working with mentally disordered defendants and offenders.* Washington, DC: Federal Judicial Center.

Parker, G. (2006). *Mental illness in jails & prisons: An overview for correctional staff.* Retrieved April 9, 2008, from http://www.in.gov/indcorrection/news/030106suicidesummitjailsprisons.ppt

Pasini-Hill, D., & English, K. (2006). *Crisis intervention teams: A community-based initiative elements of change* (10th ed.). Denver, CO: Office of Research and Statistics, Division of Criminal Justice.

Peters, R. H., & Hills, H. A. (1993). *Inmates with co-ocuring substance abuse and mental health disorders.* Seattle, WA: National Coalition for the Mentally Ill in the Criminal Justice System.

Petersilia, J. (2003). *When prisoners come home: Parole and prisoner reentry.* New York, NY: Oxford University Press.

Prins, S. J. (2011). Does transinstitutionalization explain the overrepresentation of people with serious mental illnesses in the criminal justice system? *Community Mental Health Journal, 47*(6), 716–722. doi:10.1007/s10597-011-9420-y

Prins, S. J., & Draper, L. (2009). *Improving outcomes for people with mental illnesses under community corrections supervision: A guide to research-informed policy and practice.* New York, NY: Council of State Governments Justice Center.

Psychiatric Services in Jails and Prisons. (2001). A task force report of the American Psychiatric Association (2nd ed.). *Psychiatric Services, 52*(8), 1114.

Rich, J. D., Wakeman, S. E., & Dickman, S. L. (2011). Medicine and the epidemic of incarceration in the United States. *New England Journal of Medicine, 364*, 2081–2083.

Roman, C. R., McBride, E. C., & Osborne, J. (2006). *Principles and practices in housing for persons with mental illness who have had contact with the justice system.* Washington, DC: Urban Institute.

Sacks, S., Sacks, J. Y., & Stommel, J. (2003). Modified TC for MICA inmates in correctional settings: A program description. *Corrections Today,* 90–99.

Seiter, R. P., & Kadela, K. R. (2003). Prisoner reentry: What works, what does not, and what is promising. *Crime and Delinquency, 49*(3), 360–388.

Skeem, J., Emke-Francis, P., & Eno Louden, J. (2006). Probation, mental health, and mandated treatment: A national survey. *Criminal Justice and Behavior, 33,* 158–184. doi:10.1177/0093854805284420

Skeem, J., & Eno Louden, J. (2006). Toward evidence-based practice for probationers and parolees mandated to mental health treatment. *Psychiatric Services, 57*(3), 333–342.

Solomon, P., & Draine, J. (1995). Subjective burden among family members of mentally ill adults: Relation to stress, coping, and adaptation. *American Journal of Orthopsychiatry, 65*(3), 419–427.

Solomon, P., Draine, J., & Marcus, S. C. (2002). Predicting incarceration of clients of a psychiatric probation and parole service. *Psychiatric Services, 53*(1), 50–56.

Steadman, H. J., Monohan, J., Duffee, B., Hartstone, E., & Robbins, P. C. (1984). The impact of state mental hospital deinstitutionalization on U.S. prison populations, 1968–1978. *Journal of Criminal Law and Criminology, 75,* 474–490.

Steadman, H. J., & Naples, M. (2005). Assessing the effectiveness of jail diversion programs for persons with serious mental illness and co-occuring substance use disorders. *Behavioral Sciences and the Law, 23,* 163–170.

Steadman, H. J., Osher, F. C., Robbins, P. C., Case, B., & Samuels, S. (2009). Prevalence of serious mental illness among jail inmates. *Psychiatric Services, 60*(6), 761–765.

Stephey, M. J. (2007). De-criminalizing mental illness. *Time.*

Swanson, J., Estroff, S., Swartz, M., Borum, R., Lachicotte, W., Zimmer, C., & Wagner, R. (1997). Violence and severe mental disorder in clinical and community populations: The effects of psychotic symptoms, comorbidity, and lack of treatment. *Psychiatry, 60*(1), 1–22.

Swanson, J. W., Holzer, C. E., Ganju, V. K., & Jono, R. T. (1990). Violence and psychiatric disorder in the community: Evidence from the Epidemiologic Catchment Area surveys. *Hospital & Community Psychiatry, 41*(7), 761–770.

Swanson, J. W., Swartz, M. S., Van Dorn, R. A., Elbogen, E. B., Wagner, H. R., Rosenheck, R. A., . . . Lieberman, J. A. (2006). A national study of violent behavior in persons with schizophrenia. *Archives of General Psychiatry, 63*(5), 490–499.

Swartz, M. S., Swanson, J. W., Hiday, V. A., Borum, R., Wagner, R. H., & Burns, B. J. (1998). Violence and severe mental illness: The effects of subtance abuse and nonadherence to medication. *American Journal of Psychiatry, 155,* 226–231.

Teplin, L. (1994). Psychiatric and substance abuse disorders among male urban jail detainees. *American Journal of Public Health, 84,* 290–293.

Teplin, L., Abram, K. M., & McClelland, G. M. (1996). Prevalence of psychiatric disorders among incarcerated women. *Archives of General Psychiatry, 53,* 505–512.

Teplin, L., & Voit, E. (1996). *Criminalizing the seriously mentally ill: Putting the problem in perspective.* Durham, NC: Carolina Academic Publishers.

Torrey, E. F. (2014). *American psychosis: How the federal government destroyed the mental illness treatment system.* New York, NY: Oxford University Press.

Torrey, E. F., Kennard, A. D., Eslinger, D., Lamb, R., & Pavle, J. (2010). *More mentally ill persons are in jails and prisons than hospitals: A survey of the states.* Mental Illness Policy Org. Retrieved from http://mentalillnesspolicy.org

Wallace, C., Mullen, P. E., & Burgess, P. (2004). Criminal offending in schizophrenia over a 25-year period marked by deinstitutionalization and increasing prevalence of comorbid substance use disorders. *American Journal of Psychiatry, 161,* 716–727.

Walsh, E., Buchanan, A., & Fahy, T. (2002). Violence and schizophrenia: Examining the evidence. *British Journal of Psychiatry, 180,* 490–495.

Walters, G. D. (1995). The Psychological Inventory of Criminal Thinking Styles: Part I. Reliability and initial validity. *Criminal Justice and Behavior, 22,* 307–325.

Walters, G. D. (2003). Predicting institutional adjustment and recidivism with the Psychopathy

Checklist factor scores: A meta-analysis. *Law and Human Behavior, 27*, 541–558.

Walters, G. D. (2011). The latent structure of life-course-persistent antisocial behavior: Is Moffitt's developmental taxonomy a true taxonomy? *Journal of Consulting and Clinical Psychology, 79*, 96–105.

Walters, G. D., & Geyer, M. D. (2005). Construct validity of the Psychological Inventory of Criminal Thinking Styles in relationship to the PAI, disciplinary adjustment, and program completion. *Journal of Personality Assessment, 84*, 252–260.

Weinstein, R. M. (1990). *Mental hospitals and the institutionalization of patients. Research in community and mental health, vol. 6* (pp. 273–294). Greenwich, CT: JAI Press.

Wilson, A. B., & Draine, J. (2006). Collaborations between criminal justice and mental health systems for prisoner reentry. *Psychiatric Services, 57*, 875–878. doi:10.1176/appi.ps.57.6.875

Wolff, N., Diamond, R. J., & Helminiak, T. W. (1997). A new look at an old issue: People with mental illness and the law enforcement system. *Journal of Mental Health Administration, 24*(2), 152–165.

22

WRONGFUL CONVICTIONS IN THE UNITED STATES

Kim Schnurbush

"Injustice anywhere is a threat to justice everywhere."

—Martin Luther King Jr.

According to *Black's Law Dictionary*, a wrongful conviction is considered a "grossly unfair outcome in a judicial proceeding, as when a defendant is convicted despite a lack of evidence on an essential element of a crime" (Garner, 2000, p. 811). Wrongful convictions can also be cases where a person is found guilty, but due to the actual offender's confession, the true perpetrator is found. Wrongful conviction cases can also be discovered when new evidence is introduced that was not available at the trial. It can also be a case where a court dismisses charges, acquittal after a second trial, or acknowledgement of innocence after an inmate has died in prison (Huff, Rattner, Sagarin, & MacNamara, 1986). An exoneration, on the other hand, is when a person convicted of a crime is later proven to be innocent by a court.

According to the Bill of Rights of the United States Constitution, criminal defendants are provided with the right to be free from unreasonable search and seizure; a speedy trial; a jury of peers; an attorney when facing felony charges; be adjudicated without regard to race, gender, or religious preference; the right to due process; and the right to the presumption of innocence until proven guilty by a criminal court.

Such confidence in our criminal justice system assumed that constitutional protections are always paramount and safeguards always implemented. Over the past several decades, U.S. officials have embarked on a 'war on crime,' resulting in increases in arrests, convictions, and the use of severe penalties. (Chen, 2000, pp. 4–5)

Because of the "war on crime," many citizens equate arrests with their need for the pursuit of justice. The struggle between the pursuit of justice by law enforcement and the need to satiate the general public's need for a pursuit of justice can create conflict and, in some cases, criminally convicting the wrong person for a litany of reasons.

SCOPE OF WRONGFUL CONVICTIONS

When an offender who committed a crime or crimes is arrested and convicted, it is said that "justice has been served." In cases of wrongful convictions, however, the problem is twofold. When a person is wrongfully convicted and his or her freedom is removed when imprisoned, that person's constitutional rights have been violated. Also, when the wrong person is convicted, the guilty party runs free, placing the public at risk of further harm (Huff, Rattner, & Sagrin, 1996, p. xxiii). Generally, the more arrests are made, the more comfortable the public feels, as the general public believes that a high level of arrests equals justice being served. With this "war on crime," however, there is an increased possibility that an innocent person will be arrested, rushed through the system, and wrongfully convicted, all to quiet public's anxiety about increasing public safety and that "justice be done" (Chen, 2000, pp. 4–5).

Criminal justice professionals and academic scholars agree that although the actual numbers may appear low, approximately 1% of felony convictions, or approximately 100,000 felony convictions per year, are wrongful convictions (Gross, Jacoby, Matheson, Montgomery, & Patil, 2005; Zalman, Smith, & Kiger, 2008). The number for misdemeanor crimes, however, is likely to be much higher, although that research is not currently available (Huff et al., 1996).

Murder cases have the highest clearance rate due to both the allocated police resources and crime severity (Gross et al., 2005). Because of the high stakes involved in murder cases, police are likely to offer plea bargains to codefendants and to involve informants, if available, in order to solve the case. Additionally, they are more likely to cut corners, withhold evidence, and falsify evidence (Gross et al., 2005) in order to close a case and restore confidence in the community.

HISTORY OF WRONGFUL CONVICTIONS IN THE UNITED STATES

The study of wrongful convictions is in its infancy. Spoken by Justice Learned Hand in *United States v. Garrison* (1923), "Our procedure has always been haunted by the ghost of an innocent man convicted. It is an unreal dream" (Huff et al., 1996, p. 4). Since society determined the need for blame and punishment, wrongful convictions have existed. However, very little attention has been placed on the study of wrongful convictions and their causes until the past few decades. The availability of DNA testing in criminal cases in the mid-1980s, the Illinois Moratorium, publication of the book *Actual Innocence* by Scheck and Neufeld (1992), and the call for justice by Senator Webb have all increased attention placed on the phenomenon of wrongful convictions, placing a spotlight on an area that had previously only known darkness.

Salem Witch Trials

One of the first time periods where we saw wrongful convictions en masse was during the Salem Witch Trials. Between 1692 and 1693, over 150 people, mostly women, were falsely accused of practicing witchcraft, leading to mass hysteria in the surrounding communities (Huff et al., 1996). While in prison, five of the accused died due to poor prison conditions, and 29 people were found guilty of practicing witchcraft. Nineteen of the 29 people were hanged, most of them women. One man was crushed to death by boulders when he refused to admit to being a witch (Hill, 2002; LeBeau, 1997).

The Scottsboro Boys

In 1927, two White women had been riding a train illegally with nine African American teenagers, then called "Negroes." The women did not want to get in trouble for riding the train illegally, so they claimed they had been raped. Shortly after claiming they had been raped, three White women were kidnapped, raped, and shot to death. Due to faulty eyewitness testimony, complicated by the recent murders of the three White women, all nine of the African American boys who were riding the train illegally were found guilty of rape by an all-White jury and sentenced to death. Now coined the "Scottsboro Boys," the boys had spent a total of 104 combined years in prison for crimes that never occurred when the two White accusers admitted their false accusations against the nine African American boys (Huff et al., 1994). The errors contributing to the wrongful convictions included public fear and a racially charged atmosphere (Huff et al., 1994).

First Study of Wrongful Convictions

The first known study of wrongful convictions was conducted by Edward Borchard in 1932 (Reusink & Free, 2007). Borchard studied 65 wrongful conviction cases and concluded that the United States system of justice was fallible (Leo, 2005; Reusink & Free, 2007). The United States criminal justice system operates on the presumption of innocence, or being innocent until proven guilty, coined by English lawyer Sir William Garrow (Moore, 1997). The prosecution must prove guilt of the accused beyond a reasonable doubt (Meuller, 2009). Criminal defendants are entitled to their *Miranda* rights, along with due process, each implemented to make sure defendants are treated fairly in the pursuit of justice. If the accused is found guilty beyond a reasonable doubt, he or she can be found guilty in a criminal court. For those innocents caught in the judicial web, however, the results can be disastrous. "Few problems can pose a greater threat to free, democratic societies than that of wrongful conviction—the conviction of an innocent person" (Huff et al., 1986, p. 518). It was not until the advent of DNA testing in criminal cases that the phenomenon of wrongful convictions came to light.

DNA Testing

It was not until 1989 that DNA was used to exonerate someone of a felony conviction (Leo, 2005; Medwed, 2005). Gary Dotson, convicted of raping a woman in 1977, was found guilty and sent to prison for a rape he did not commit. It took over a decade for the victim to come forward to tell the truth, as she was riddled with guilt for fabricating the story that Dotson had raped her because she had become pregnant with her own boyfriend and needed a "cover story," so she falsified the report against Dotson. Although a rape examination was performed on the victim, DNA testing was not available at the time of the crime. In 1989, when testing was performed in the Dotson case, DNA evidence showed that Dotson was not the perpetrator, and he was eventually released from prison.

Much of the current exoneration rate can be attributed to the advances in DNA technology. With advances in DNA technology and crime lab testing and the 2000 Illinois Moratorium, the fallibility of the criminal justice system finally started to appear (Gaumgartner et al., 2007; Huff, 2002; Ruesink & Free, 2007). Whereas much of the general public tends to believe DNA evidence is available at all crime scenes, that is far from the truth. According to Scheck et al. (2000), DNA evidence is available only in about 20% of violent crime scenes and can only be found in bodily fluids, skin, hair, and so forth and is most likely to be evident in the crimes of rape and murder because of the close physical contact with the victim or victims. "Ninety-six percent of the known exonerations of individual defendants since 1989 were either for murder—60% for rape or sexual assault—36%. Most of the remaining fourteen cases were crimes of violence—six robberies, two attempted murders, a kidnapping and an assault—plus a larceny, a gun possession case and two drug cases" (Gross et al., 2005, pp. 528–529).

For many defendants, two challenges exist surrounding DNA testing, availability and evidence and cost. Additionally, challenges exist with collection, handling, and storing of evidence, if not done properly. For example, at the Houston,

Texas, crime lab, 185 cases were put into jeopardy when DNA lab technician Peter Lentz resigned after an internal investigation found evidence of lying on official documents, improper procedure, and tampering with official records (Rogers, 2014). Evidence can also be lost through improper procedures and even contamination in crime labs as well. If situations like that occur and DNA evidence is contaminated, it can no longer be tested, so any chance an innocent person sitting in prison could be freed is lost forever. Backlogs of cases, such as in Houston, Texas, where over 4,000 rape kits were waiting for processing, many of which had sat in evidence longer than the offenders were in prison (Pinkerton, 2009), can also present problems, as even if DNA evidence is collected, it may never be tested. Situations such as natural disasters can also wreak havoc with stored DNA evidence. When Hurricane Harvey hit the Houston area in 2017, personnel in the Harris County Sheriff's Office had to move over 15,000 pieces of evidence from criminal cases. Although they moved a substantial amount of evidence, there were 11 cases impacted in the move, and unfortunately, that evidence was lost or damaged forever (Abrahams, 2017).

Because so few cases actually have DNA evidence available, very few wrongful conviction cases are even brought to light. Inmates lucky enough to have their case reviewed by a wrongful conviction organization, such as the Innocence Project or the Western Center on Wrongful Convictions, are few and far between. Unfortunately for the others, they will remain incarcerated for the remainder of their sentence. According to Bedau and Radelet (1987), "The coincidences involved in exposing so many of the errors and the luck that is so often required suggest that only a fraction of the wrongfully convicted are eventually able to clear their names" (p. 70). According to Gross et al. (2005), a large percentage of noncapital cases are never examined because no one seriously entertains the defendant's innocence or investigates the case since their sentences are less severe.

Compared with other social issues, very little attention has been placed on wrongful convictions until the past few decades. The United States Supreme Court concluded in *United States v. Wade* (1967) that the "annals of criminal law are rife with instances of mistaken identification" (Christianson, 2004, p. 28). Not until the advent of DNA testing, however, did the spotlight get placed on wrongful convictions and exonerations as DNA provided scientific proof of a defendant's innocence if DNA was available. Only about 20% of violent felony cases have DNA evidence, however, so DNA testing was merely a step up from the fingerprints and blood serology that was historically available in criminal cases. "Forty-six states—except Alabama, Alaska, Massachusetts, and Oklahoma—now provide access to post-conviction DNA testing. Three of four remaining states—Alabama, Alaska, and Massachusetts—have introduced legislation to provide access, and Nevada, New York, Ohio and Texas have introduced additional measures to further increase access" (Innocence Project, n.d.). In 2009, the National Academy of Sciences recommended standardization of DNA testing to assure standards are consistent across the nation. In addition, 26 states have instituted reform on DNA handling, to include collection and cataloging of biological samples at crime scenes (Innocence Project, n.d.).

Illinois Moratorium

In 2000, Illinois governor George Ryan stated, "I cannot support a system which, in it's administration, has proven to be so fraught with error and has come so close to the ultimate nightmare, the state's taking of an innocent life" (Associated Press, 2000). Since *Gregg v. Georgia* (1976) reinstated the death penalty, Illinois had experienced 13 exonerations and 14 executions. Governor Ryan said he could not be sure of the guilt of someone on death row in Illinois, and "Until I can be sure that everyone sentenced to death in Illinois is truly guilty, no one will meet that fate" (Associated Press, 2000). Governor Ryan placed a moratorium on executions in Illinois, appointed a commission to study the death penalty in Illinois, and commuted all Illinois death sentences to life prior to leaving office 2 years later (Zalman, 2006, p. 471).

Justice for All Act of 2004 and the Innocence Protection Act

Four years following the Illinois Moratorium, the Justice for All Act of 2004 was signed into law and outlined rules and procedures for any federal inmate applying for DNA testing. The act also provides for state funding for both prosecution and defense improvements in capital cases to include training, improving the quality of trials, and assisting the families of murder victims (Justice for All Act). In the same year, the Innocence Protection Act was passed, which increased the compensation amount for those wrongfully convicted of federal crimes from $100,000 per year for death row inmates and $50,000 per year for non–death row inmates (Leahy, 2004). Additionally, Attorney General Janet Reno authorized a Department of Justice study to examine convictions, specifically those based upon eyewitness error (Connors et al., 1996; Doyle, 2005, pp. 169–187; Technical Working Group for Eyewitness Evidence, 1999). The book *Actual Innocence* was published as well, exploring multiple exoneration stories and explaining specific errors in wrongful conviction cases (Zalman, 2006).

WRONGFUL CONVICTION/ EXONERATION CASE EXAMPLES

History and statistics outline issues in linear form, lending a general understanding to the issue at hand; however, there is nothing more powerful when considering cases of wrongful convictions and exonerations than to explore specific cases. In doing so, the true impact on humanity is understood.

Kirk Bloodsworth

Kirk Bloodsworth, a former Marine, was the first person to be sentenced to death and exonerated with DNA evidence in the United States. In 1984, Bloodsworth was 22 years old and was arrested for the murder and rape of a 9-year-old girl found in the woods in Maryland. She had been beaten with a rock, sexually assaulted, and strangled to death. Bloodsworth was arrested based on an anonymous phone call indicating he looked like the police sketch shown on television that day; however, Bloodsworth was only 6 feet tall, had red hair, and weighed over 200 pounds. The description of the perpetrator was a 6 foot 5 inch tall, thin, tan man with curly blonde hair and a bushy mustache. Despite the discrepancy in description, Bloodsworth was arrested and tried for the horrific crimes. At his trial, five witnesses testified that Bloodsworth was seen with the victim; however, two of those witnesses were not able to identify Bloodsworth in the police lineup. Bloodsworth was convicted of rape and murder based upon eyewitness testimony. No physical evidence connected Bloodsworth to the crime (Innocence Project, n.d.).

In the early 1990s, Bloodsworth heard about DNA testing, which was still relatively new. He believed it could prove his innocence, and the prosecution finally agreed to test DNA available from the rape kit, to include the victim's underwear and shorts, and a stick found at the scene. After an independent lab tested the DNA, replicate testing was performed by the FBI, which produced the same results. Bloodsworth was innocent. After spending nearly 9 years in prison, two of those years facing execution on death row, Bloodsworth was released from prison in December 1993. "If it could happen to me, it could happen to anybody," Bloodsworth has said many times. After being exonerated, Bloodsworth became an advocate for the wrongfully convicted, published a book titled *Bloodsworth*, became the advocacy director for a Philadelphia-based coalition of death row exonerees who work to end capital punishment called Witness to Innocence, and was an integral part of abolishing Maryland's death penalty. In addition, Bloodsworth introduced the Innocence Protection Act of 2003, which establishes funding for DNA testing for those inmates claiming innocence (Innocence Project, n.d.).

Ronald Cotton

Ronald Cotton spent over 10 years in prison for a July 1984 incident involving two counts each of rape and burglary of a woman named Jennifer Thompson-Cannino. Cotton was sentenced in 1985 to life, plus 54 years. In July 1984, a man broke into Jennifer Thompson-Cannino's apartment and sexually assaulted her. Later that night, the same man broke into another apartment and sexually assaulted another woman. While Thompson-Cannino was being sexually assaulted, she said she studied the perpetrator's face, and "I was just trying to pay attention to a detail, so that if I survived . . . I'd be able to help the police catch him" (Innocence Project, n.d.).

In the police lineup, Thompson-Cannino chose Cotton as the rapist and said she was 100% sure he was the perpetrator. Evidence presented at trial included a flashlight found in Cotton's home that was similar to the one used in the attacks and rubber from one of Cotton's shoes that was consistent with shoe rubber found at the scene of the Thompson-Cannino attack. In January 1985, Cotton was found guilty by a jury of one count of rape and one count of burglary. In a second trial 2 years later, Cotton was found guilty in November 1987 of both rapes and burglaries. Cotton was sentence to life in prison, plus 54 years (Innocence Project, n.d.).

Cotton was unsuccessful at having his case overturned in several appeals, but in 1995, his case was given a major break. The Burlington (VT) Police Department turned over all evidence in the case, to include DNA evidence of the assailant. Testing showed Cotton was not the perpetrator, and when the results were provided to the district attorney, the defense motioned to have all charges dismissed. Cotton was cleared of all charges and released from prison in June 1995 (Innocence Project, n.d.).

Cotton's first job postrelease was at LabCorp, the company used to test the DNA evidence. He also got married, had a child, bought some land, and received $110,000 in compensation from the state for his wrongful conviction.

Upon his release, Thompson-Cannino and Cotton met for the first time in person. She said, "I just started to sob. I looked at him and said, 'If I spent every minute of every hour of every day for the rest of my life telling you that I'm sorry, can you ever forgive me?' He did the one thing that I never imagined. He started to cry and he said, 'Jennifer, I forgave you years ago.'" The two are good friends and travel around the country to spread the word about how easily wrongful convictions can occur and to share their ideas for system reform, particularly those involving eyewitness identification procedures, in hopes of preventing future injustices for others (Innocence Project, n.d.).

Michael Morton

Michael Morton spent 25 years in prison for the murder of his wife before being exonerated. In 1986, Morton, both a husband and a father, managed a supermarket in Texas. In August 1986, Morton celebrated his birthday at a restaurant with his wife Christine and their 3-year-old son. On August 13, 1986, Morton left a note on their bathroom vanity saying he was disappointed Christine declined to be intimate with him the night before but that he loved her. Morton left for work around 5:30 a.m. that day. Later that day, Christine was found dead in their bed. She had been brutally bludgeoned to death with a weapon made of wood, and their bed sheets were stained with both blood and semen. One day later, a bloody bandana was found at a construction site approximately 100 yards away from the Morton's house (Innocence Project, n.d.).

During the police investigation, Morton's neighbors said a man had repeatedly parked a green van behind the Morton household and walked to the nearby woods. Christine's mother told the police that the Morton's son Eric had been present during the murder and told his grandmother that the murderer was a "monster," but that "daddy was not home" during the murder. The police investigation revealed that Christine was missing a credit card, and it was used in a San Antonio, Texas, jewelry store and that a San Antonio police officer said he could identify the woman who tried to use the credit card. Morton's defense attorneys claimed none of the above evidence was turned over to them at trial (Innocence Project, n.d.).

When Morton's defense attorneys learned the chief police investigator in the case was not going to be called at trial, they suspected the prosecution was attempting to conceal exculpatory evidence. They raised their concern at the trial, and the judge ordered the prosecution to overturn all reports by the investigating officer so a thorough review could be conducted by the defense. Evidence about Morton's son's eyewitness account, the green van, and the credit card being used in San Antonio were missing from the documents provided to the defense (Innocence Project, n.d.).

The prosecution laid their entire case on the hypothesis that because Christine had refused to have sex with Michael the night of his birthday that he beat her to death in their bed. No witnesses or physical evidence tied Michael Morton to the murder, but he was convicted of Christine's murder in February 1987 and sentenced to life in prison (Innocence Project, n.d.).

In 2005, the Innocence Project and a law firm, Raley & Bowick, filed a motion for DNA testing of items found at the crime scene. The court granted permission for the testing but excluded the bloody bandana found near the home. Testing could not exclude Morton as the source of the DNA collected from the bed because he and his wife Christine shared their marital bed. In 2011, Morton was finally granted DNA testing on the bandana and hair found on the bandana, which revealed both Christine's and an unknown perpetrator's DNA. The DNA from the unknown male was run through the CODIS (Combined DNA Index System, a DNA database) databank and matched a convicted California felon named Mark Norwood. At the time of the murder, Norwood had a criminal record in Texas and was living in Texas as well. Further investigation into Norwood revealed his hair was also found at the home of another murder victim in Travis County, Texas, named Debra Masters. Similar to Christine Morton, Masters was found bludgeoned to death in her own bed, but the murder of Masters occurred a full 2 years after the murder of Christine Morton, when Michael Morton was in prison. After spending nearly 25 years in prison, Michael Morton was released and exonerated for the murder of his wife Christine. Morton moved in with his parents after his release, but 2 years later married a woman he met in church. Like Bloodsworth and Cotton, Morton spends much of his time working as an advocate for the wrongfully convicted.

During the postconviction DNA litigation, Morton's attorneys filed a Public Information Act request, which revealed the prosecution had withheld documents proving Morton's innocence at trial. The Innocence Project filed a brief on Morton's behalf, and the Texas Supreme Court ordered an unprecedented Court of Inquiry to determine whether the former prosecutor, Ken Anderson, had committed official misconduct. The Inquiry revealed Attorney Anderson had violated the law by concealing evidence and charged him with contempt. In a plea deal, Anderson agreed to serve a 10-day jail sentence, resigned from his position as a district court judge, and permanently surrendered his law license. No other prosecutor, to date, had ever been held criminally responsible for misconduct (Innocence Project, n.d.).

WRONGFUL CONVICTION ORGANIZATIONS/MOVEMENTS

Because of the rise of attention on wrongful conviction cases and the work both advocates and wrongful conviction organizations perform every day, more people are becoming aware of the fallibility of the United States criminal justice system. There is no perfect system; however, the tides are turning for those who have been wrongfully convicted. Individual advocates, organizations, and even universities with law clinics are popping up across the nation. The one hope for all of these individuals and organizations is for the general public to realize that the "war on crime" has caused a tsunami effect of wrongful convictions, all in the pursuit of "justice." In an attempt to raise awareness and educate the public, wrongful conviction organizations have made available to the public information surrounding wrongful convictions, and there is even an international day of awareness.

Wrongful Conviction Day is an international day to raise awareness of the causes and remedies of wrongful conviction and to recognize the tremendous personal, social, and emotional costs of wrongful convictions for innocent people and their families. Wrongful Conviction Day began as an effort of the Innocence Network, an affiliation of organizations dedicated to providing pro bono legal and investigative services to individuals seeking to prove innocence of crimes for which they have been convicted, working to redress the causes of wrongful convictions, and supporting the exonerated after they are freed. For more information, see www .intlwrongfulconvictionday.org.

The listing that follows is just a sampling of organization websites available with the purpose of advocating for the wrongfully convicted. If you have further interest in wrongful convictions, a simple search in any web browser of "wrongful convictions" will result in a rich list of organizations, movements, and personal webpages, most of which focus on advocating for the wrongfully convicted and educating the public on criminal justice failure and ideas for system reform.

- Center on Wrongful Convictions: www.law.northwestern.edu/ wrongfulconvictions

- Justice Denied: www.justicedenied.org

- The Innocence Project: www.innocenceproject.org

- Innocence Network: www.innocencenetwork.org

- The National Center for Reason and Justice: www.ncrj.org

- Seeking Justice for the Innocent: www.seekingjusticefortheinnocent.com

CONCLUSION

If asked, many American's will say they believe the United States has the best system of justice in the world. The majority of the time, our system of justice works, as it should. It is meant to seek truth and justice, punish offenders, and make communities a safer place to live and work. No system is 100% effective though, and when errors are made, those errors can be disastrous.

Imagine one day you are on your way home from work, school, church, or even your child's soccer game, and you are pulled over by the police. As you search for your license and registration, you wonder why you were stopped. Instead of the expected "license and registration, please," you are ordered to step out of your vehicle, and you are arrested. From that moment on, whether you are innocent or guilty of whatever crime or crimes you are being charged with, your life has forever changed. What do you think about when you are being transported to the county jail in the police cruiser? What about when you enter the jail and get searched and all of your possessions are taken from you? What about when you sit in booking waiting to be fingerprinted and to have your picture taken for the publicly available mug shot? For the first few hours or days, how do you believe you will deal with the situation? Who will you call for your one and only phone call? Who will take care of your children? Who will take care of your pets? Who will call your boss to inform that you will not be in to work? Who will tell your professors you will be missing classes? Who will tell your parents, wife, husband, boyfriend, girlfriend, partner, and/or friends that you have been arrested and you are sitting in jail? Who will pay those bills you have due? Who will pay your rent or mortgage? *What will you be thinking?* All of those thoughts will fill your mind as you sit in your cell. Are you guilty, or are you one of the thousands who will be wrongfully convicted this year? Think about it. You are only *one* of 100,000 people who will be wrongfully convicted this year. Like Kirk Bloodsworth, Ronald Cotton, and Michael Morton, you may be one of the unfortunate people to be caught up in the judicial web of a wrongful conviction case in the future. No system of justice is infallible. What if you are next?

Discussion Questions

1. What do you think about the statistic that 100,000 people will be wrongfully convicted of felonies this year? Do you think that's too high? Too low? Why?

2. Which part of the history of wrongful convictions interests you the most? Why?

3. Which of the case studies, Kirk Bloodsworth, Ronald Cotton, or Michael Morton, impacts you the most? Why?

4. What you do think you would believe about a criminal justice system that wrongfully convicted you?

5. What do you believe should happen to those police officers and/or prosecutors who are found to have withheld evidence (or similar) in a criminal case where someone ends up being wrongfully convicted? Should police officers and prosecutors be held to a higher standard than general citizens when it comes to professional conduct? Explain your answer.

6. Do you believe people should be found guilty if all that is available is eyewitness testimony? Are there any exceptions? Explain your answer.

7. What can you, as a general citizen, do to reduce the numbers of wrongful convictions in your community?

References

Abrahams, T. (2017, September 27). Evidence in several criminal cases destroyed by Harvey. ABC13 Eyewitness News.

Associated Press. (2000, January 31). *Illinois puts executions on hold [Web log post]*. Retrieved from http://www.abcnews.com

Bedau, H., & Radelet, M. (1987). Miscarriages of justice in potentially capital cases. *Stanford Law Review, 40,* 21–179.

Carlos v. Superior Court, 672 P.2d 862 (1983).

Chen, H. H. (2000, April 19). U.S. prison population hits all-time high [Web log post]. Retrieved from http://www.abcnews.com

Christianson, S. (2004). *Innocent: Inside wrongful conviction cases.* New York, NY: New York University Press.

Connors, E., Lundregan, T., Miller, N., & McEwan, T. (1996). *Convicted by juries, exonerated by science: Case studies in the use of DNA to establish innocence after trial* (NCJ 161258). Washington DC: National Institute of Justice.

Garner, B. A. (Ed.). (2000). *Black's law dictionary* (Abridged, 7th ed.). St. Paul, MN: West Group.

Gregg v. Georgia, 428 U.S. 153 (1976).

Gross, S. R., Jacoby, K., Matheson, D. J., Montgomery, N., & Patil, S. (2005). Exonerations in the United States, 1989 through 2003. *Journal of Criminal Law & Criminology, 95,* 523–560.

Hill, F. (2002). *Hunting for witches: A visitor's guide to the Salem witchcraft trials.* Boston, MA: Commonwealth Editions.

Huff, C. R., Rattner, A., Sagarin, E., & MacNamara, D. E. J. (1986). Guilty until proven innocent: Wrongful conviction and public policy. *Crime Delinquency, 32,* 518–544.

Huff, C. R., Rattner, A., & Sagarin, E. (1996). *Convicted but innocent: Wrongful conviction and public policy.* London, UK: Sage.

Innocence Project. (n.d.). Retrieved from www .innocenceproject.org

Innocence Protection Act, S. 2073, 106th Congress (2000).

Justice for All Act, P. L. 108-404 (2006).

LeBeau, B. (1997). *The story of the Salem witch trials.* Upper Saddle River, NJ: Prentice-Hall.

Leo, R. A. (2005). Rethinking the study of miscarriages of justice: Developing a criminology of wrongful conviction. *Journal of Contemporary Criminal Justice*, *21*(3), 201–223.

Medwed, D. S. (2005). Looking foreword: Wrongful convictions and systemic reform. *American Criminal Law Review*, *42*, 1117–1121.

Miranda v. Arizona, 384 U.S. 436 (1966).

Moore, C. (1997). *The Law Society of Upper Canada and Ontario Lawyers, 1797–1997*. Toronto, ON: University of Toronto Press.

Pinkerton, J. (2009, October 2). 7 years after scandal, backlog still plagues HPD crime lab. *Houston Chronicle*.

Public Information Act, No. 104-231 Stat. 3048 (1996).

Rogers, B. (2014, June 18). Scores of cases affected after HPD crime lab analyst ousted. *Houston Chronicle*.

Ruesink, M., & Free, M. D., Jr. (2007). Wrongful convictions among women: An exploratory study of a neglected topic. *Women & Criminal Justice*, *16*(4), 1–23.

Scheck, B., & Neufeld, P. (1992). *The Innocence Project: Understand the causes*. Retrieved from http://www.innocenceproject.org

Scheck, B., Neufeld, P., & Dwyer, J. (2000). *Actual innocence*. New York, NY: Doubleday.

United States v. Wade, 388 U.S. 218 (1967).

Zalman, M. (2006). Criminal justice system reform and wrongful conviction: A research agenda. *Criminal Justice Policy Review*, *17*(4), 468–492.

Zalman, M., Smith, B., & Kiger, A. (2008). Officials' estimates of the incidence of "actual innocence" convictions. *Justice Quarterly*, *25*, 72–100.

CORRECTIONS

PART V

23

THE PHILOSOPHICAL AND IDEOLOGICAL UNDERPINNINGS OF CORRECTIONS

Anthony Walsh and Ilhong Yun

WHAT IS CORRECTIONS?

Corrections is a generic term covering a wide variety of functions carried out by government agencies (and, increasingly, by private ones) having to do with the punishment, treatment, supervision, and management of individuals who have been convicted of crime. These functions are implemented in prisons, jails, and other secure institutions, as well as in community-based agencies, such as probation and parole departments. As the term implies, the whole correctional enterprise exists to correct, amend, or put right the criminal behavior of its clientele. This is a difficult task because that which must be corrected has festered for many years, and offenders often have a psychological, emotional, or financial investment in their current lifestyles (Andrews & Bonta, 2007).

THE THEORETICAL UNDERPINNINGS OF CORRECTIONS

Ever since humans have devised rules of conduct, they have wanted to break them. This is the reason that Nathaniel Hawthorne (1850/2003) opened his classical book *The Scarlet Letter* with these words: "The founders of a new colony, whatever

Utopia of human virtue and happiness they might originally project, have invariably recognized it among their earliest practical necessities to allot a portion of the virgin soil as a cemetery, and another portion as the site of a prison" (p. 1). Hawthorne is reminding us of two things we cannot avoid—death and human moral fallibility—and that we must make provisions for both. However, most of us conform to the rules of our social groups most of the time and feel shamed and guilty when we violate them, but traveling the straight and narrow road does not always come naturally. Control theorists tell us that the real question is not why some people commit crimes but rather why most of us do not. After all, crime affords immediate gratification of desires with little effort: "money without work, sex without courtship, revenge without court delays" (Gottfredson & Hirschi, 2002, p. 210). We must learn to curb our appetites for immediate gratification and learn self-control as the social emotions—guilt, shame, embarrassment—merge with lessons taught us to become our consciences.

In our earliest days, parents chastise us for doing things that we have an urge to do: throw temper tantrums, hit our siblings or steal their cookies, bite the cat's tail, and so on. Later on, teachers scold us, peers ostracize us, and employers fire us if we do not behave according to the rules. These chastisements are examples of informal social control used to achieve peace and predictability in our relationships with others. The more heavy-handed punishment handed out by the state is formal social control exercised against those who have not learned to behave well via informal control methods. In short, we have to learn to be good children and good citizens, and we learn that only when we realize that our wants and needs are inextricably bound up with the wants and needs of others and that they are best realized by cooperating with others who want the same things.

A SHORT HISTORY OF CORRECTIONAL PUNISHMENT

The earliest known written code of punishment is the Code of Hammurabi, created about 1780 BC. This code expressed the concept of *lex talionis* (the law of equal retaliation, or "an eye for an eye, a tooth for a tooth"). These laws codified the natural inclination of individuals harmed by another to seek revenge, but they also recognize that personal revenge must be restrained if society is not to be fractured by a cycle of tit-for-tat blood feuds. To avoid this, the state took responsibility for punishing wrongdoers. Nevertheless, state-controlled punishment was typically as uncontrolled and vengeful as that which any grieving parent might inflict on the murderer of his or her child. Prior to the 18th century, human beings were considered born sinners because of the Christian legacy of original sin. Cruel tortures, used on criminals to literally "beat the devil out of them," were justified by the need to save sinners' souls.

The practice of brutal punishment began to wane in the late 18th century with the beginning of the Enlightenment, which was essentially a major shift in the way people viewed the world and their place in it. It was also marked by the narrowing of the mental and emotional distance between people. Enlightenment thinkers questioned traditional values and began to embrace humanism, rationalism, and science, values that ushered in the beginnings of a belief in the dignity and worth of all individuals. This view would eventually find expression in the law and in the treatment of criminal offenders.

The first person to apply Enlightenment thinking to crime and punishment was the English playwright and judge Henry Fielding (1707–1754). Fielding's book, *Inquiry Into the Causes of the Late Increase of Robbers* (1751/1967) set forth his thoughts on the causes of robbery, called for a "safety net" for the poor (free housing and food) as a crime prevention strategy, and campaigned for alternative punishments to hanging. Many of his suggestions were implemented and were apparently successful (Sherman, 2005).

THE EMERGENCE OF
THE CLASSICAL SCHOOL

Enlightenment ideas led to a school of penology known as the *classical school*. More than a decade after Fielding's book, the Italian philosopher and politician Cesare Beccaria (1738–1794) published a manifesto for the reform of European judicial and penal systems titled *On Crimes and Punishment* (1764/1963). Beccaria did not question the need for punishment but believed that laws should be designed to preserve public order, not to avenge crime. Punishment should be proportionate to the harm done to society, should be identical for identical crimes, and should be applied without reference to the social status of offenders or victims. Punishment must be certain and swift to make a lasting impression on the criminal and to deter others. To ensure a rational and fair penal structure, punishments for specific crimes must be decreed by written criminal codes and the discretionary powers of judges curtailed.

Beccaria's work was so influential that many of his reforms were implemented in a number of European countries within his lifetime (Durant & Durant, 1967, p. 321). His reform ideas tapped into and broadened the scope of such emotions as sympathy and empathy among the intellectual elite of Europe. Alexis de Tocqueville (1838/1956, Book III, Chapter 1) noticed the diffusion of these emotions across the social classes, beginning in the Enlightenment with the spreading of egalitarian attitudes, and attributed the "mildness" of the American criminal justice system to the country's democratic spirit. We tend to feel empathy for those whom we view as being like us, and empathy often leads to sympathy, which may translate the vicarious experience of the pains of others into active concern for their welfare. With cognition and emotion blended into the Enlightenment ideal of the basic unity of humanity, justice became both more refined and more diffuse (Walsh & Hemmens, 2007).

Another prominent figure was the British lawyer and philosopher Jeremy Bentham (1748–1832). His major work, *Principles of Morals and Legislation* (1789/1948), is essentially a philosophy of social control based on the principle of utility, which prescribes "the greatest happiness for the greatest number." The proper function of the legislature is to promulgate laws aimed at maximizing the pleasure and minimizing the pain of the largest number in society. If legislators are to legislate according to this principle, they must understand human motivation, which for Bentham (1948) was easily summed up: "Nature has placed mankind under the governance of two sovereign masters, pain and pleasure. It is for them alone to point out what we ought to do, as well as to determine what we shall do" (p. 125). This was the Enlightenment concept of human nature: hedonistic, rational, and endowed with free will. Classical explanation of criminal behavior and how to prevent it are derived from these three assumptions.

Bentham devoted a great deal of energy (and his own money) to arguing for the development of prisons as substitutes for torture, execution, or transportation. He designed a prison in the 1790s called the *panopticon* ("all-seeing"), which was to be a circular "inspection house" enabling guards to constantly see their charges, thus requiring fewer staff. Because prisoners could always be seen without seeing by whom or when they were being watched, the belief was that the perception of constant scrutiny would develop into self-monitoring. Bentham felt that prisoners could be put to useful work to acquire the habit of honest labor.

THE EMERGENCE OF POSITIVISM

Classical thinkers were armchair philosophers, whereas positivist thinkers took upon themselves the methods of empirical science, from which more "positive" conclusions could be drawn. Positivists believe that human actions have causes and that these causes are to be found in the uniformities that precede those actions. While early positivists were excessively deterministic, they slowly moved the criminal justice system away from a singular concentration on the criminal act as the sole determinant of punishment to an appraisal of the characteristics and circumstances of the offender as an additional determinant. Others, such as Raffaele Garofalo (1885/1968), believed that because human action is determined, the only things that should be considered at sentencing are offenders' "peculiarities" and the danger they pose to society. Garofalo's proposed sentences ranged from execution for *extreme criminals* (psychopaths), to transportation to penal colonies for *impulsive* criminals, to simply changing the law to deal with *endemic criminals* (those who commit "victimless crimes").

THE FUNCTION OF PUNISHMENT

The desire to punish those who have harmed us or otherwise cheated on the social contract is as old as the species itself. Punishment aimed at discouraging cheats is observed in every social species of animals, which leads biologists to conclude that punishment of cheats is an evolutionarily stable strategy designed by natural selection for the emergence and maintenance of cooperative behavior (Fehr & Gachter, 2002). Indeed, neuroimaging studies using PET and fMRI scans provide hard evidence that positive feelings accompany the punishment of those who have wronged us and that negative feelings evoked when we are wronged are reduced. These studies showed that when subjects were able to punish cheats, they had significantly increased blood flow to areas of the brain that responded to reward, suggesting that punishing those who have wronged us provides emotional relief and reward for the punisher (de Quervain et al., 2004; Fehr & Gachter, 2002). Perhaps we are hardwired to "get even," as suggested by the popular saying, "Vengeance is sweet."

Sociologist Emile Durkheim (1893/1964) also argued that crime and punishment are central to social life. Crime is socially useful, argued Durkheim, because by shocking the collective conscience, it serves to clarify the boundaries of acceptable behavior, and punishing criminals maintains solidarity because the rituals of punishment reaffirm the justness of the social norms. Durkheim recognized the inborn nature of the punishment urge and that punishment serves an expiatory role, but he also recognized that we can temper the urge with sympathy. He observed that over the course of social evolution, humankind had largely moved from retributive justice (characterized by cruel and vengeful punishments) to restitutive justice (characterized by reparation). Both forms of justice satisfy the human urge for social regularity by punishing those who violate the social contract, but repressive justice oversteps its adaptive usefulness and becomes socially destructive. Repressive justice is driven by the natural passion for punitive revenge that "ceases only when exhausted . . . only after it has destroyed" (Durkheim, 1964, p. 86). Durkheim (1964) goes on to claim that restitutive justice is driven by simple deterrence and is more humanistic and tolerant, although it is still "at least in part, a work of vengeance" . . . since it is still "an expiation" (pp. 88–89).

THE OBJECTIVES OF CORRECTIONS

The five major objectives or justifications for the practice of punishing criminals are described next.

Retribution

Retribution is a *just deserts model*, which demands that criminals' punishments match the degree of harm they have inflicted on their victims. This is the most honestly stated justification for punishment because it both taps into our most primal urges and posits no secondary purpose for it, such as the reform of the criminal. California is among the states that have explicitly embraced this justification in their criminal codes (California Penal Code Sec. 1170a): "The Legislature finds and declares that the purpose of imprisonment for a crime is punishment" (cited in Barker, 2006, p. 12). This model of punishment avers that it is right to punish criminals, regardless of any secondary purpose that punishment may serve, simply because justice demands it.

Durkheim recognized that the urge to punish is inherent in human nature and that it serves to soothe, pacify, and even provide pleasant feelings for those witnessing it, vicariously or otherwise.

On a similar note, in his written opinion in *Furman vs. Georgia* (1972) in which the United States Supreme Court invalidated Georgia's death penalty statute, Mr. Justice Stewart wrote the following about retribution (punishment that is justly deserved for its own sake):

> I cannot agree that retribution is a constitutionally impermissible ingredient in the imposition of punishment. The instinct for retribution is part of the nature of man, and channeling that instinct in the administration of criminal justice serves an important purpose in promoting the stability of a society governed by law.
>
> When people begin to believe that organized society is unwilling or unable to impose upon criminal offenders the punishment they "deserve," then there are sown the seeds of anarchy—of self-help, vigilante justice, and lynch law.

Some of us may consider retribution to be primitive revenge and therefore morally wrong, but retribution as presently conceived is constrained revenge, curbed by proportionality and imposed by neutral parties bound by laws mandating respect for the rights of individuals against whom it is imposed. Logan and Gaes (1993) go so far as to claim that only retributive punishment "is an affirmation of the autonomy, responsibility, and dignity of the individual" (p. 252). By holding offenders responsible and blameworthy for their actions, we are treating them as free moral agents, not as mindless rag dolls blown around by the capricious winds of the environment.

Deterrence

Deterrence justifies punishment by assuming that it will prevent crime. The principle that people respond to incentives and are deterred by the threat of punishment is the philosophical foundation behind all systems of criminal law. Deterrence may be either specific or general.

Specific deterrence refers to the effect of punishment on the future behavior of people who experience the punishment. For specific deterrence to work, it is necessary that a person make a conscious connection between an intended criminal act and the punishment suffered as a result of similar acts committed in the past. If that person fails to make the connection, it is likely that he or she will continue to commit crimes. Committing further crimes after being punished is called *recidivism*, or "falling back" (into criminal behavior). Nationwide, about 33% of released prisoners recidivate within the first 6 months after release, 44% within the first year, 54% by the second year, and 67.5% by the third year (Robinson, 2005, p. 222).

The effect of punishment on future behavior depends on its certainty, celerity (swiftness), and severity. In other words, there must be a relatively high degree of certainty that punishment will follow a criminal act, the punishment must be administered soon after the act, and it must be harsh. Unfortunately, the wheels of justice grind excruciatingly slowly today, with many months passing between the criminal act and the imposition of punishment; so much for celerity. This leaves the law with severity as the only element it can realistically manipulate, but it is unfortunately the least effective element. Studies from the United States and the United Kingdom find substantial negative correlations (as one factor goes up, the other goes down) between the likelihood of conviction (a measure of certainty) and crime rates but much weaker ones (albeit in the same direction) for the severity of punishment (Langan & Farrington, 1998).

The effect of punishment on future behavior also depends on the *contrast effect*, which is the distinction between the circumstances of the possible punishment and the usual life experience of the person who may be punished. For people with little or nothing to lose, an arrest may be perceived as little more than an inconvenient occupational hazard, but for those who enjoy a loving family and the security of a valued career, the prospect of incarceration is a nightmarish contrast. Like so many other things in life, deterrence works least for those who need it most.

General deterrence refers to the preventive effect of the threat of punishment on the general population; it is thus aimed at *potential* offenders. The punishments meted out to offenders serve as examples to the rest of us of what may happen if we violate the law. The existence of a system of punishment for law violators deters a large but unknown number of individuals who might commit crimes if no such system existed.

What is the bottom line? Are we putting too much faith in the ability of criminals and would-be criminals to calculate the cost–benefit ratio of engaging in crime? Although many violent crimes are committed in the heat of passion or under the influence of mind-altering substances, there is evidence underscoring the classical notions that individuals do (subconsciously at least) calculate the ratio of expected pleasures to possible pains when contemplating a course of action. Gary Becker (1997) dismisses the idea that criminals lack the foresight to take punitive probabilities into consideration when deciding whether or not to continue committing crimes. He says, "Interviews of young people in high crime areas who do engage in crime show an amazing understanding of what punishments are, what young people can get away with, how to behave when going before a judge" (p. 20).

Some reviews of deterrence research indicate that legal sanctions do have "substantial deterrent effect" (Nagin, 1998, p. 16), and some have claimed that increased incarceration rates account for about 25% of the variance in the decline in violent crime over the last decade or so (Rosenfeld, 2000; Spelman, 2000). Paternoster (2010) cites a number of studies demonstrating that 20% to 30% of the crime drop from its peak in the early 1990s is attributable to the approximately 52% increase in the imprisonment rate in the United States. As he put it, "There is a general consensus that the decline in crime is, at least in part, due to more and longer prison sentences, with much of the controversy being over how much of an effect" (p. 801). Of course, this leaves 70% to 80% to be explained by other factors. Unfortunately, we cannot determine if we are witnessing a *deterrent* effect (Has violent crime declined because more would-be violent people have perceived a greater punitive threat?) or an *incapacitation* effect (Has violent crime declined because more violent people are behind bars and thus not at liberty to commit violent crimes on the outside?). Paternoster (2010) concludes his review of the deterrence literature by stating, "Finally, while there may be disagreement about the magnitude, there does seem to be a modest inverse relationship between the perceived certainty of punishment and crime [as certainty goes up, crime goes down], but no real evidence of a deterrent effect for severity, and no real knowledge base about the celerity [swiftness] of punishment" (p. 818).

Incapacitation

Incapacitation refers to the inability of criminals, while incarcerated, to victimize people outside prison walls. Its rationale is aptly summarized in James Q. Wilson's (1975) remark, "Wicked people exist. Nothing avails except to set them apart from innocent people" (p. 391). The incapacitation justification probably originated with Enrico Ferri's (1897/1917) concept of social defense. To determine punishment, notions of culpability, moral responsibility, and intent were to be subordinate to an assessment of offenders' strength of resistance to criminal impulses, with the express purpose of averting future danger to society. Ferri reasoned that the characteristics of criminals prevented them from basing their behavior on rational principles, so they could be neither deterred nor rehabilitated, and therefore, the only reasonable rationale for punishing offenders is to incapacitate them for as long as possible.

It goes without saying that incapacitation works, at least while criminals are incarcerated. Elliot Currie (1999) uses robbery rates to illustrate this point. He states that in 1995, there were 135,000 inmates in state and federal institutions whose most serious crime was robbery and that each robber, on average, commits five robberies per year. Had these robbers been left on the streets, they would have been responsible for an additional 135,000 × 5, or 675,000, robberies, on top of the 580,000 actual robberies reported to the police in 1995. Similarly, Wright (1999) estimated that imprisonment averted almost 7 million offenses in 1990.

A further example is the Italian government's Collective Clemency Bill (CCB), passed in 2006, ordering the release of one third of Italy's prisoners (about 22,000) with 3 years or less left to serve. This would be equivalent to the U.S. releasing 756,000 inmates. The CCB resulted from budgetary and overcrowding concerns and gave criminologists an excellent chance to gauge the effects of incapacitation by tracking released inmates. Buonanno and Raphael's (2013) analysis of released convicts found that the incapacitation effect was between 14 and 18 extra crimes committed per year per criminal. (They only included theft and robbery arrests in their analysis.)

Prison overcrowding was eliminated, and prison authorities saved an estimated 245 million euros ($316 million), so the policy "worked." But what about the impact on society? Buonanno and Raphael (2013) estimated that crime costs were between 466 million and 2.2 billion euros, or between approximately $606 million and $2.9 billion. They state, "Overall, the pardon falls far short of passing cost–benefit analysis determining a 'social' cost between 10 and 60 thousand euros per prisoner per year" (p. 2463). Although this economic analysis shows a huge financial loss to society attributable to the CCB, it does not take into consideration other social costs of crimes committed by released prisoners, such as the emotional and physical costs of being victimized and the general feeling of the inadequacy of the state to protect its citizens.

Rehabilitation

To rehabilitate means to restore or return to constructive or healthy activity. Whereas deterrence and incapacitation are primarily justified philosophically on classical grounds, rehabilitation is primarily a positivist concept. The rehabilitative goal is to change offenders' attitudes so that they come to accept that their behavior was wrong, not to deter them by the threat of further punishment. The difficulty with rehabilitation is that it asks criminals to return to a state that many (obviously, not all) of them have never been in (habilitation). But we keep on trying to rehabilitate criminals because what helps the offender helps the community. As former U.S. Supreme Court chief justice Warren Burger noted, "To put people behind walls and bars and do little or nothing to change them is to win a battle but lose a war. It is wrong. It is expensive. It is stupid" (in Schmalleger, 2001, p. 439).

Correctional scholars are always mindful of the "nothing works" position of those who demand too much of rehabilitative efforts. Many correctional programs did not work in the past for a variety of reasons: They relied on nondirective methods that were inappropriate for offenders; they sought to change behaviors unrelated to crime; they used programs that were not intensive enough; and they used inadequately skilled staff to run them. Correctional scholars are somewhat more upbeat about rehabilitation today, given a range of new treatment modalities (Latessa, Cullen, & Gendreau, 2002; Walsh, 2006).

Reintegration

The goal of reintegration is to use the time criminals are under correctional supervision to prepare them to reenter the free community as well equipped as possible. In effect, reintegration is not much different from rehabilitation, but it is more pragmatic, focusing on concrete programs like job training rather than attitude change.

In 2004, 503,200 adult convicts entered American prisons, and 483,000 left them (Glaze & Palla, 2005), and 1 in 5 will leave with no postrelease supervision, rendering parole "more a legal status than a systematic process of reintegrating returning prisoners" (Travis, 2000, p. 1). With the exception of convicts who max out, then, prisoners will be released under the supervision of a parole officer who is charged with monitoring offenders' behavior and helping them to readjust to the free world. The longer people remain in prison, the more difficult it is for them to readjust to the outside world.

Table 23.1 provides a summary of the key elements of the five punishment philosophies. Their common goal, of course, is the prevention of crime.

THE PAST, PRESENT, AND FUTURE OF CORRECTIONS

Many features of corrections' past still manifest themselves in the current correctional landscape, albeit in modified forms. Recent decades have seen an increase of

TABLE 23.1 ■ Summary of Key Elements of Different Correctional Perspectives					
	Retribution	**Deterrence**	**Incapacitation**	**Rehabilitation**	**Reintegration**
Justification	Moral; just deserts	Prevention of further crime	Risk control	Offenders have correctable deficiencies	Offenders have correctable deficiencies
Strategy	None; offenders simply deserve to be punished	Make punishment more certain, swift, and severe	Offenders cannot offend while in prison. Reduce opportunity.	Treatment to reduce offenders' inclination to reoffend	Concrete programming to make for successful reentry into society
Focus of Perspective	The offense and just deserts	Actual and potential offenders	Actual offenders	Needs of offenders	Needs of offenders
Image of Offenders	Free agents whose humanity we affirm by holding them accountable	Rational beings who engage in cost–benefit calculations	Not to be trusted but to be constrained	Good people who have gone astray; will respond to treatment	Ordinary folk who require and will respond to concrete help

a type of jail similar to Bentham's panopticon in terms of its design and efficiency (Tartaro, 2002). Frequently termed the *new generation jail*, the podular architecture permits continual surveillance with a minimal number of guards. In new generation jails, individual housing units are placed around an open area where a guard is permanently located. Inmates are allowed to move freely throughout the unit, but continual supervision of the movement is imposed by the centrally located guard. To maximize efficiency by reducing unnecessary movement and costs, all needed services—meals, phones, visits, counseling, showers, laundry, and so forth—are directly offered within the unit.

The call for prison labor by early reformers as a way to reform criminals shaped the history of American corrections significantly, although the original rehabilitative rationale has largely been replaced by profits. In the United States, the Auburn system eventually outlasted the rival Pennsylvania system, largely due to the greater profits generated by the former's adoption of the congregate labor system, under which prisoners are able to pay for their own keep (Hawkins & Alpert, 1989).

Although inmate labor has been a central feature of prisons, it was not until the 20th century that prison industries flourished. During this period, the emerging *contract labor system* was implemented in many prisons nationwide. In this system, prison administrators contract with private firms, offering inmate labor in exchange for profits. The operation of prison industries was actively pursued, with the implicit notion of prisoner reform through disciplined work habits. This system hit a major roadblock during the Great Depression. Fearing the competition of inmate labor, labor unions successfully lobbied the legislature to curtail prison industries, and many of these legislative restrictions are still in force today. However, renewed emphasis on the rehabilitative merits of labor has recently brought about some regulatory relaxation. At the present time, goods produced in prison are mostly sold to public agencies, such as mental institutions or schools. Prison industries restore millions of dollars to state economies and contribute to rehabilitative relief from the boredom of prison life.

Diverse views still exist concerning what corrections is expected to accomplish, but the prevailing views of the public often become the basis for determining correctional objectives. With the advent of the Great Depression, the focus on retribution gave way to the goal of rehabilitation. The Great Depression drove many otherwise respectable people to poverty, suicide, and crime, owing to factors beyond their control. The age-old explanation of criminal behavior as a violation of free will did not seem to hold true anymore, and the time was ripe to look to what the positivists had to say about crime causation. The new *medical model* began to view inmates as individuals in need of help and treatment rather than moral failures. The old chain gangs and striped uniforms yielded to psychological diagnosis and counseling. Proof of rehabilitation became the basis of inmate release, therefore indeterminate sentences and parole replaced determinate sentences.

Much to the dismay of supporters of the medical model, however, proof of rehabilitation was sparse. Instead, beginning in the tumultuous 1960s, the criminal justice landscape was painted by rising crime rates and unabated recidivism. Eventually, the public's disillusionment with the ideal of rehabilitation and the general conservative mood of the 1980s saw the return of the just deserts model. The public's mounting demand to "get tough" on criminals resulted in longer and mandatory sentences. Early releases through parole were increasingly supplanted by fixed sentences, and many institutions became "no-frills" prisons divested of TVs, recreational facilities, and educational and vocational opportunities (Finn, 1996). Chain gangs, lockstep marching, and striped uniforms reappeared in some localities. The dubious fame of the United States as the nation with the highest incarceration rate is the direct corollary of this correctional model.

SUMMARY

- Corrections is designed to punish, supervise, deter, and rehabilitate criminals. It is also the study of these functions.

- Although it is natural to want to exact revenge when people wrong us, to allow individuals to pursue this goal is to invite a series of tit-for-tat feuds that may fracture a community. The state has thus taken over responsibility for punishment. Over time, the state has moved to forms of punishment that are more restitutive than retributive, which, while serving to assuage the community's moral outrage, temper it with sympathy.

- Much of the credit for the shift away from retributive punishment must go to the great classical thinkers, such as Fielding, Beccaria, and Bentham, all of whom were imbued with the humanistic spirit of the Enlightenment period. The view of human nature (hedonistic, rational, and possessing free will) held by these men led them to view punishment as primarily for deterrent purposes, that it should only just exceed the "pleasure" (gains) of crime.

- Opposing the classical notions of punishment are those of the positivists, who rose to prominence during the 19th century and who were influenced by the spirit of science. Positivists rejected the classicists' philosophical stance regarding human nature and declared that punishment should fit the offender rather than the crime.

- The objectives of punishment are retribution, deterrence, incapacitation, rehabilitation, and reintegration, all of which have come into and out of favor and back again over the years.

- Retribution is simply just deserts—getting the punishment you deserve, no other justification needed.

- Deterrence is the assumption that people are prevented from committing crimes by the threat of punishment.

- Incapacitation means that criminals cannot commit further crimes against the innocent while incarcerated.

- Rehabilitation centers on efforts to socialize offenders in prosocial directions while they are under correctional supervision so that they will not commit further crimes.

- Reintegration refers to efforts to provide offenders with concrete, usable skills that will provide them a stake in conformity.

- From the pursuit of correctional administrative efficiency emerged the construction of new generation jails and the wide use of sophisticated electronic devices. Traditionally, prison administrators made extensive use of inmate labor for monetary gain. Due to the opposition of labor unions and regulations imposed by the legislature, however, prison industry has dwindled during the second half of the 20th century.

- The rehabilitation-oriented medical model of corrections largely gave way to the justice model during the 1980s. Instead of treatment and rehabilitation, the justice model emphasizes just deserts and being tough on criminals.

Discussion Questions

1. Discuss the implications for a society that decides to eliminate all sorts of punishment in favor of forgiveness.

2. Is it good or bad that we take pleasure in punishment, and what evolutionary purpose does it serve?

3. Discuss the assumptions about human nature held by the classical thinkers. Are we rational beings, seekers of pleasure, and free moral agents?

4. Discuss the assumptions underlying positivism in terms of the treatment of offenders.

References

Andrews, D., & Bonta, J. (2007). *The psychology of criminal conduct* (5th ed.). Cincinnati, OH: Anderson.

Barker, V. (2006). The politics of punishing: Building a state governance theory of American imprisonment variation. *Punishment & Society, 8,* 5–32.

Beccaria, C. (1963). *On crimes and punishment* (H. Paulucci, Trans.). Indianapolis, IN: Bobbs-Merrill. (Original work published 1764)

Becker, G. (1997). The economics of crime. In M. Fisch (Ed.), *Criminology 97/98* (pp. 15–20). Guilford, CT: Dushkin.

Bentham, J. (1948). *A fragment on government and an introduction to the principles of morals and legislation* (W. Harrison, Ed.). Oxford, UK: Basil Blackwell. (Original work published 1789)

Buonanno, P., & Raphael, S. (2013). Incarceration and Incapacitation: Evidence from the 2006 Italian

Collective Pardon. *American Economic Review*, *103*, 2437–2465.

Currie, E. (1999). Reflections on crime and criminology at the millennium. *Western Criminology Review*, *2*(1). [Online]. Retrieved on October 20, 2009, from http://wcr.sonoma.edu/v2n1/currie.html

de Quervain, D., Fischbacher, U., Valerie, T., Schellhammer, M., Schnyder, U., Buch, A., & Fehr, E. (2004). The neural basis of altruistic punishment. *Science*, *305*, 1254–1259.

de Tocqueville, A. (1956). *Democracy in America* (H. Hefner, Ed.). New York, NY: Norton Books. (Original work published 1838)

Durant, W., & Durant, A. (1967). *Rousseau and revolution*. New York, NY: Simon and Schuster.

Durkheim, E. (1964). *The division of labor in society*. New York: Free Press. (Original work published 1893)

Fehr, E., & Gachter, S. (2002). Altruistic punishment in humans. *Nature*, *415*, 137–140.

Ferri, E. (1917). *Criminal sociology*. Boston, MA: Little, Brown. (Original work published 1897)

Fielding, H. (1967). *Inquiry into the causes of the late increase of robbers*. Oxford, UK: Oxford University Press. (Original work published 1751)

Finn, P. (1996). No-frills prisons and jails: A movement in flux. *Federal Probation*, *60*(3), 35–44.

Furman v. Georgia, 408 U.S. 153 (1972).

Hawkins, R., & Alpert, G. (1989). *American prison systems: Punishment and justice*. Englewood Cliffs, NJ: Prentice Hall.

Glaze, L., & Palla, S. (2005). Probation and parole in the United States, 2004. *Bureau of Justice Statistics Bulletin*. Washington, DC: U.S. Department of Justice.

Gottfredson, M., & Hirschi, T. (2002). The nature of criminality: Low self-control. In S. Cote (Ed.), *Criminological theories: Bridging the past to the future* (pp. 210–216). Thousand Oaks, CA: Sage.

Langan, P., & Farrington, D. (1998). *Crime and justice in the United States and England and Wales, 1981–1996*. Washington, DC: Bureau of Justice Statistics.

Latessa, W., Cullen, F., & Gendreau, P. (2002). Beyond correctional quackery—Professionalism and the possibility of effective treatment. *Federal Probation*, *66*, 43–50.

Logan, C., & Gaes, G. (1993). Meta-analysis and the rehabilitation of punishment. *Justice Quarterly*, *10*, 245–263.

Nagin, D. (1998). Criminal deterrence research at the onset of the twenty-first century. *Crime and Justice: A Review of Research*, *23*, 1–42.

Paternoster, R. (2010). How much do we really know about criminal deterrence? *Journal of Criminal Law and Criminology*, *100*, 765–823.

Robinson, M. (2005). *Justice blind: Ideals and realities of American criminal justice*. Upper Saddle River, NJ: Prentice Hall.

Rosenfeld, R. (2000). Patterns in adult homicide. In A. Blumstein & J. Wallman (Eds.), *The crime drop in America* (pp. 130–163). Cambridge, UK: Cambridge University Press.

Schmalleger, F. (2001). *Criminal justice today* (6th ed.). Upper Saddle River, NJ: Prentice Hall.

Sherman, L. (2005). The use and usefulness of criminology, 1751–2005: Enlightened justice and its failures. *Annals of the American Academy of Political and Social Science*, *600*, 115–135.

Spelman, W. (2000). The limited importance of prison expansion. In A. Blumstein & J. Wallman (Eds.), *The crime drop in America* (pp. 97–129). Cambridge, UK: Cambridge University Press.

Stinchcomb, J. (2005). *Corrections: Past, present, and future*. Lanham, MD: American Correctional Association.

Tartaro, C. (2002). Examining implementation issues with new generation jails. *Criminal Justice Policy Review*, *13*, 219–237.

Travis, J. (2001, May). But they all come back: Rethinking prisoner reentry. *Sentencing and Corrections: Issues for the 21st Century*. Washington, DC: U.S. Department of Justice, National Institute of Justice.

Walsh, A. (2006). *Correctional assessment, casework, and counseling* (4th ed.). Upper Marlboro, MD: American Correctional Association.

Walsh, A., & Hemmens, C. (2007). *Law, justice, and society: A sociolegal approach*. New York: Oxford University Press.

Wright, R. (1999). The evidence in favor of prisons. In F. Scarpitti & A. Nielson (Eds.), *Crime and criminals: Contemporary and classic readings in criminology* (pp. 483–493). Los Angeles, CA: Roxbury.

COMMUNITY CORRECTIONS

Rehabilitation, Reintegration, and Reentry

Ming-Li Hsieh

At this time, more than 6.6 million adult inmates are under the control of correctional systems in the United States. Within that population, an estimated 4.6 million offenders are assigned to community supervision, representing over two thirds (68%) of all who are subject to correctional sanctions (Kaeble & Glaze, 2016). And even though the number of probationers and parolees has decreased slightly in the past 10 years, the prevalence rates of community corrections sentences have been relatively stable from the years 2007 to 2015 (Kaeble & Glaze, 2016). Given this most recent data, community corrections is undoubtedly the backbone of offender supervision in this country. Community sentencing, whether it is considered a progressive reform in our justice system or an alternative to incarceration, is now the primary form of punishment. Despite continued debate over its appropriateness as a sanction, community correction appears to be the most common disposition in our justice system given the limited resources available for any other option.

The structure of community corrections operations reflects the inherent conflicts in managing local programs with significant state and even federal influence. For example, in a decentralized environment, the administration of community corrections varies across over 400 separate court, county, and state agencies (Kaeble & Bonczar, 2017). The disparate bureaucracies and coercive umbrella of legislation, regulation, and funding initiatives profoundly impact day-to-day supervision plans for offenders in the community. Consequently, the delivery of effective street-level services (Lipsky, 2010) within the rapidly changing priorities of law enforcement, court personnel, and prison and jail authorities is often compromised and undermined in community corrections.

The success of any community corrections effort is often associated with the philosophical punishment purposes of conventional corrections (Materni, 2013). The outcomes depend on the particular goals that are embraced in a specific community corrections environment. These goals would obviously vary by micro-level supervision and macro-level administration decision making. In general, those who support a deterrence model will look for decreases in both self- and official reports of the offender's criminal activity. Evidence of rehabilitation would include abstaining from drug and alcohol use, steady employment, and consistent payments toward supervision and services.

Incapacitation-oriented proponents would closely supervise repeat offenders and expect the reduction of violent and property offenses committed by so-called "career criminals" in the community. Retributive orientations, on the other hand, would expect the offender to have suffered for his or her offenses and, as with deterrence, to have taken steps to avoid more punitive sanctions in the future.

THE COMMON FORMS OF COMMUNITY CORRECTIONS

The concept of community corrections includes a broad array of legal alternatives to incarceration. Although most forms have traditionally involved monitoring the offender who resides at home, program options also include halfway houses, residential treatment, electronic tracking, and cyber-monitoring. Today, advances in technology have changed the way community corrections officers perform their jobs, permitting more flexibility and remote supervision. In addition, contemporary public administration models rely more on networking and coordinating funded projects with schools, law enforcement, and civic leaders in the area. Both juvenile and adult justice systems employ these measures, and some do so as part of deferred adjudication, in which participants' records will be erased or expunged if the term of service under community supervision is successfully completed. The most common forms of community corrections, however, are probation and parole.

Probation is usually judicially administered through the county or city, although separate systems are most often maintained for juveniles and adults. For some time now, probation has been the most common sentence imposed by judges directly for both misdemeanors and felonies (Petersillia & Turner, 1993). A probated sentence is the setting aside of a comparable prison term under a "conditional contract," although probation can also be a combined sentence, especially after a period of incarceration (Kaeble & Bonczar, 2017), commonly referred to as shock incarceration. Probationers account for more than 80% of those on community supervision. And while approximately two thirds of probationers who exit the system do so because they have completed or have been released from supervision, the percentage of those who exit probation because they are reincarcerated has hovered around 15% in recent years (Herberman & Bonczar, 2015).

A term of probation is initiated with a contract that sets out specific constraints or conditions that the offender must adhere to in order to avoid the possible revocation of his or her release. These conditions may include working; attending school; participating in treatment; paying various fines, restitution, and court costs; and avoiding high-risk people, places, and activities. In other words, violations of the terms, as recorded by a supervising probation officer, may mean that the probation is revoked, and the offender will then serve the entire sentence in prison. However, recent efforts have created a continuum of punitive options as progressive or intermediate sanctions that might better control offenders' behavior on probation, reduce infractions, and perhaps eliminate the need to revoke the probated sentences of those who violate their terms and conditions.

Parole is a term used to describe a period of supervision in the community for felons following early release from prison during which the state continues to monitor the behavior of the parolee until the complete expiration of the defendant's full-sentence term. Like probation, parole is the conditional release in which the offender agrees to follow conditions and rules enforced by a parole officer. During the parole period, an offender may be subject to curfews, drug tests, and unannounced visits by the assigned case supervisor. Any violations that occur during the period of parole supervision may subject the parolee to revocation, whereby he or she would be sent back to prison to serve the entire remaining years within institutions. According to the Bureau of Justice Statistics, the number of offenders entering the parole population increased in 2015, representing the first increase in 7 years. That year, an estimated 875,500 offenders made up the parole population (Kaeble & Bonczar, 2017), and while the number of those entering and exiting the system rose that year, reincarceration rates among parolees have been relatively stable over the years (Herberman & Bonczar, 2015).

Although more states are limiting the number of paroles and reducing the number of cases eligible to go before the parole board or increasing the time between parole hearings, more offenders are being released on a variation of parole called *mandatory release* or *mandatory supervision*. This is a legal status that usually reflects that inmates have served sufficient actual time along with accrued good-time credit to constitute the full length of their sentences. Release is then required by law; offenders remain under the jurisdiction of the state until the time by which they would have served the entire sentence without good-time credit. This means that if a person has served 2 years in prison and has accumulated 2 years of good-time credit through good behavior, he or she may be released from a 4-year incarceration term. However, the offender will be supervised by a parole officer in the community until the remaining 2 years (the good-time credit portion) have been served. When offenders have "maxed out," meaning that they have served the maximum sentence even minus good-time credit, they will receive an *expiration release*, whereby they will no longer be supervised in the community.

For newly released inmates, halfway houses are a popular option, as they provide a more gradual release from custody. This alternative allows offenders to remain in a more structured environment until their transition to independent living and working arrangements is functioning smoothly. Likewise, prerevocation facilities, relapse centers for drug addicts, and state jails may provide enough structured support and intensive monitoring to control offenders and avoid the need to return them to the more costly prison environment.

PROBATION: PROGRESSIVE REFORM AND THE PROMISE OF REHABILITATION

While the concept of probation can be traced to the English corrections system, the term *probation* appears to have been coined by the American philanthropist John Augustus (Rothman, 1980). Augustus, who focused his efforts on helping the more undesirable elements of Boston society, created a system that allowed offenders, particularly alcoholics, to remain in the community under his strict supervision and to engage in work apprenticeships and mentoring. Probation as a sanction was also extended to juvenile offenders with the creation of the Juvenile Court in 1899.

The corruption of the original intent of this rehabilitative venture is seen in its widespread application to most offenders, not just those who appear motivated to reform. In addition, probation moved from providing a residential type of supervision to one that sends the offender back into a potentially high-risk environment. The most recent statistics show that the majority (57%) of probationers are convicted of felony crimes and only two-fifths of probationers have committed misdemeanor or petty offenses (Kaeble & Bonczar, 2017). What appear to be high failure rates may be explained by the attempt to make a very intensive sentence, constructed for a relatively select group, applicable to all at very low levels of programming.

It is not surprising that in the process of moving more offenders toward community sanctions and in our overreliance on the application of one-size-fits-all treatment programs, we grew more pessimistic about the effectiveness of a medical model in corrections. Martinson's controversial 1974 essay, "What Works?— Questions and Answers About Prison Reform" (better known as "Nothing Works"), reflected the public's concern that rehabilitation efforts were not effective enough and, consequently, resulted in the suspension of programming in favor of more conservative models of deterrence and harsh punishment. As a result, more offenders were released from prisons without any treatment, which undoubtedly diminished their prospects for success in society. Still, corrections officials persisted in finding ways to divert offenders and avoid building more prisons. In California, counties were offered subsidies so that they would send fewer serious offenders to state facilities. At local levels, corrections administrators struggled to find more effective community-based components and formulas that would prescribe how much treatment and supervision were needed at what point in time for each type of offender.

As part of the attempt to create new varieties of probation services, officials in the late 1970s and early 1980s experimented with shock probation and intensive supervision. For shock probation, offenders were sent to prisons for a short time, usually less than 180 days, and then judges would release them to a term of probation, believing that they had been "shocked" into good behavior by the harsh realities of prison, much like juveniles exposed to prisons in the *Scared Straight* programs.

Efforts to provide intensive supervision were based on research that seemed to indicate that when offenders with the highest risk and needs levels receive the most intensive interventions, then reductions in recidivism were more likely to be realized (Reichert, DeLong, Sacomani, & Gonzales, 2016). Still, in other studies, intensive supervision efforts seemed to yield higher levels of revocation and reincarceration (Hyatt & Barnes, 2017), perhaps because probationers were being watched too closely (Turner, Petersilia, & Deschenes, 1992) or because supervising agencies were not able to sustain the surveillance efforts called for at this level. As one group of experts concluded (Lutze, Johnson, Clear, Latessa, & Slate, 2011), alternative sanctions do not appear to be working, and offenders recidivate because communities of reentry are unable to support the level of jobs and community-based services required by probationers. The lack of economic investments that would sponsor human capital and thus enhance community capacity can be cited as one of the most complex reasons for the failure of community supervision today.

PAROLE AS REWARD OR RELIEF

The earliest forms of parole were viewed as an indication that the offender was not only contrite and remorseful but prepared to engage in productive citizenship. Inmates who best demonstrated literacy, discipline, job skills, and a deep appreciation of the habits of industry were carefully selected for the privilege of early release. This designation was not only a personal reward for conforming to American values but a lesson to other inmates about the benefits of the assimilation of mainstream values. The period of postincarcerative supervision was considered an opportunity to ensure, under the watchful eye of the state, that the offender made a successful transition into the community.

Under the framework of indeterminate sentences, parole has been considered as keeping with the goal of treatment and rehabilitation toward offenders throughout the progressive period in corrections and before entire correctional policies moved toward the punitive model attributed to the influence of Martinson's (1974) study. In the early 1900s, parole was criticized for its appearance of being "soft" on crime, the use of unstructured discretionary release, and poor performance outcomes, in part, perhaps, because of unrealistic expectations about the criminal population. These views are still relevant today. By 2002, the federal government and 16 states had abolished discretionary release by parole boards, and some other states had restrictions on the use of discretionary parole for certain offenses or directly limited the use of discretion with parole-eligible populations (Petersilia, 2003). In an assessment of public perceptions on parole innovation, Rothman (1980) explained that "parole became the whipping boy for the failures of law enforcement agencies to control or reduce crime. Whenever fears of a 'crime wave' swept through the country, or whenever a particularly senseless or tragic crime occurred, parole invariably bore the brunt of attack" (p. 159).

The popularity of get-tough politicians has resulted in a wide range of increasingly harsh laws, restrictive parole policies, and barriers to release that seem to preclude officers and supervisors who work directly with inmates on a daily basis from utilizing their experience and expertise (DeMichele & Payne, 2012). Although validated assessments that can be objectively scored have become a major factor in the release decision, probation and parole officers fear that such generalized approaches do not allow them to include their instincts and experiences with specific offenders and offender populations. It has been argued that it may be difficult for correctional systems to operate a systematically cohesive and empirically driven program of risk and needs assessment and release. In particular, the potential negative impact of release mechanisms may be found where there is almost exclusive reliance on standardized risk and needs assessment instruments to guide release decisions, and where case managers may attempt to subvert the outcomes or override the assessment scores.

Miller and Maloney (2013) found that almost half of practitioners filling out prediction tools did so by either manipulating the data entered or reaching formal conclusions that were inconsistent with data included in the instrument. Nonadherence to tool recommendations and overrides of case management decisions appear to reflect philosophy discrepancies between professional judgment and structured-instrument assessment and pessimism and cynicism of tool effectiveness in the field (Lyoung & Wormith, 2011), as do other compliance issues related to evidence-based supervision training (Bonta et al., 2011).

CONCERNS REGARDING STAKES: RISK ASSESSMENT AND PREDICTION

For both probation and parole, the essence of community corrections and programming does not simply rest on the effective rehabilitation and fair treatment of the offender but also addresses the mandate for public safety and crime control. In other words, what is at stake for community corrections is the requirement of balancing the dynamic relationship between risk and harm to the public, to the victims, and even to the supervising agency with an offender's release. For example, notorious offenders who have high public profiles seem to cause more political harm if they recidivate, as compared to lesser known and less serious offenders, because of the widespread anger and fear created by the publicity. Understandably, their cases must be weighed in terms of those stakes, as well as according to the normal concept of risk (Williams, McShane, & Dolny, 2000). Stakes also include losses that may occur as a result of serious reoffending that remains undetected by the justice system.

Given these concerns with stakes, applying the most sophisticated and proper risk assessment and prediction mechanisms on offenders has become an essential strategy in *actuarial justice*, through which we are able to identify, classify, and manage dangerous groups aggregately and systematically in corrections (Feeley & Simon, 1992). The distinguishing feature of this new mechanism is to assess an individual's recidivism propensity by using "actuarial language of probabilistic calculations and statistical distributions" (p. 452). The goals then would be to (1) guide rational practices associated with levels of supervision, dosages of treatment, tailored case management plans, and even to monitor criminality periodically with reassessment and (2) to phase out practitioners' clinical judgments that do not involve scientific- and statistic-based modules for risk prediction and criminality assessment which, in turn, will further the march toward evidence-based decision making (Feeley & Simon, 1992).

Traditionally, clinical risk assessments have been used to determine the probability of offending based on professional judgments in the form of classification and prediction. Clinical assessments are more subjective and more individualized and take longer to complete than actuarial versions. Actuarial assessments, however, are objective and standardize prediction procedures. They involve statistical models and risk factor tools that predict behavior based on how others have acted in similar situations and/or an individual's similarity to various factor groupings. For large groups of offenders, meta-analyses have provided strong evidence to support that actuarial assessment is superior to clinical assessment in terms of estimating future criminality and criminal recidivism (Grove, Zald, Lebow, Snitz, & Nelson, 2000).

With an actuarial tool, offenders' characteristics are inventoried, and risk is determined by the extent to which they possess various risk factors associated with recidivism. Risk prediction is conventionally based on static and dynamic factors that contribute to crime (Andrews & Bonta, 2010). Static variables are those that do not change (i.e., prior offense history and age at first offense). Dynamic factors represent issues or characteristics that may change, such as job stability and living arrangements. The current trend of evidence-based correctional policies indicates expanding the framework of using actuarial risk assessment instruments involves applying and matching the risk-need-responsivity (RNR) principles with services, interventions, programming, and supervision, allocating resources efficaciously, preventing chronic offending, and increasing public safety (Hanson et al., 2017).

Despite the trend toward the use of actuarial risk and needs assessment in probation and parole, there remains a persistent gap between promise and practice (Burrell, 2017). The effective implementation approaches of RNR principles or actuarial risk assessment instrument selections are often problematic within agencies. Not all leaders are knowledgeable about the utility and limitations of risk and needs assessment and instruments. Policy makers may also be unfamiliar with how to mobilize the resources or the corresponding organizational change necessary to implement new risk and needs assessment models. Moreover, rapid changes in leadership may mean that one administration is not able to fully complete implementation or oversight of the transformation in organizational culture or overcome the challenges of staff commitment.

WORSE THAN PRISON?

Public safety is a major concern any time offenders remain in the community. Conservative attacks by more punitive lawmakers often restrict the use of community supervision and narrow the potential pool served by these alternative sanctions. *Truth-in-sentencing* laws passed over the last decade have increased the proportion of actual sentences served in prison and have limited the accrual of good-time credit toward early release. Realistically, however, the current capacity of prisons will not allow more significant portions of sentences to be served. This issue is often overlooked when more conservative, punitive laws are passed.

Underlying the fight against expanding the community corrections base is a perception that probation and parole sanctions are soft on criminals, easy to serve, and not painful enough to be a deterrent. However, studies of offenders' perceptions toward the alternative sentence in the community and the punitiveness of prison have indicated that serving terms behind bars may be considered preferable to serving alternative sanctions. These findings directly challenge public impressions of community corrections as lenient punishment (Jones, 1996).

In *Profiles from Prison* (2003), Michael Santos describes an offender who returned to prison to serve his final year rather than have his family suffer through the impositions and intrusions of constant surveillance. In this case, the parolee had to call for a recorded message each day to see if he was scheduled for a urinalysis, even though he had no prior drug use history or offenses. He also had to regularly attend anger management classes, Alcoholics Anonymous, and Narcotics Anonymous for 90 minutes each per week. He had to pay a fee for these meetings, as well as miss work to attend them, which resulted in lower earnings. In addition, the offender reported to his parole officer monthly and filled out detailed records of all his finances and activities, including purchases made by his wife and children. His supervising officer made surprise weekly visits to his workplace and his home, sometimes at 5:30 in the morning when the family was asleep. The offender, Billy, describes the strain that parole put on his family. Billy told Santos that for him and his wife, living under the parole officer's microscope for five years seemed worse than another six-to-twelve months of imprisonment . . . Our marriage was strong. But the stress associated with supervised release was too much . . . The stress threatened to break us up. I just wanted out. And if that meant going back to prison for a while, that's what I was willing to do. It was the only way I could get my life back. (p. 53)

Even though some offenders view longer and more intensive levels of community supervision (Petersilia & Deschenes, 1994), electronic monitoring (Wood & Grasmick, 1999; Wood & May, 2003; Spelman, 1995), and boot camp (Wood & Grasmick, 1999) as harsher than prison, others argue that intermediate sanctions are still less restrictive and not as harsh as incarceration (Martin, Hanrahan, & Bowers, 2009). These studies all send a similar message—in which the majority of community alternatives to incarceration lean toward punitive sanctions and a tough-on-crime philosophy rather than the lenient treatment of offenders. The importance of community supervision conditions also impacts the offender's performance in the social arenas of life at home and at work.

REINTEGRATION AND REENTRY

Every year, more than 600,000 prisoners are released from federal and state facilities (Carson & Anderson, 2016), and another 9 million are released from jails (Yoon & Nickel, 2008). Although rearrest rates vary by state enforcement levels, caseloads, and revocation policies, three quarters of state prisoners come into contact with police for committing a new crime within 5 years of release, and almost half of them either violate their parole or probation condition within 3 years of release (Durose, Cooper, & Snyder, 2014). Data indicate that these offenders will most likely be returned to prison within a relatively short period of time. Ironically, as conditions for community release become stricter and supervision becomes more punitive, revocations may be blamed as a factor that contributes to increased prison crowding (Caplow & Simon, 1999). More enforcement of probation and parole contracts also has the effect of net widening, drawing more of those released back into the system (Phelps, 2013). Thus, the mechanism used to relieve institutional crowding seems to have become its major contributor.

Fortunately, officials can reform and revise criteria to make success more probable through meaningful reentry programming. This is especially important, as some recent research has indicated that people who are granted a discretionary release from prison seem to have lower rates of recidivism than those who complete their entire term incarcerated and "max out" (Schlager & Robbins, 2008). One example of the opportunity to reduce recidivism rates is the Second Chance Act of 2007. This federal legislation provides support for reentry initiatives that attempt to rehabilitate offenders by equipping them with the necessary skills to become law-abiding, productive citizens for postrelease life. In fiscal year 2017, a total of 36 million grants were funded to 68 jurisdictions across the states for providing promising reentry services and programs (National Reentry Resource Center [NRRC], 2017).

Program evaluations have demonstrated that reentry programming, such as faith-based (Duwe & King, 2012) and family-based (Miller, Miller, & Barnes, 2016) programs, substance abuse (Hsieh & Hamilton, 2016) and sex offender treatment (Lösel & Schmucker, 2005), housing assistance (Hamilton, Kigerl, & Hays, 2015), cognitive-behavioral therapies (Pearson, Lipton, Cleland, & Yee, 2002), and educational and vocational training (Wilson, Gallagher, & MacKenzie, 2000) could produce positive treatment outcomes and effectively reduce recidivism. These evidence-based practices are built on the crucial features of program effectiveness and suggest that successful interventions should address criminogenic needs and risk levels. They should also be voluntary and include processes to assess program design, implementation, quality, and fidelity. In addition, they should deliver an institution-to-community continuum of care and service.

Despite the many programs that demonstrate positive results, barriers still remain preventing offenders from successfully transitioning back into society. Officials agree that large caseloads, limited resources, and the lack of specialized training on the part of criminal justice agents reduce the chances of meaningful outcomes (Byrnes, Macallair, & Shorter, 2002). Highly trained justice professionals are one of the keys to ensuring that offenders in transition fully benefit from reentry programs. Offenders most likely to recidivate are those with low levels of education and a general lack of social support, including shelter, food, employment assistance, clothing, and substance abuse and mental health treatment. Because offenders exhibit mental health disabilities at a rate 3 times that of the general population, the demand for services often creates a strain on communities' already overburdened health care systems (Skeem, Emke-Francis, & Louden, 2006).

Legislative barriers must also be discussed as difficult challenges that newly released offenders have to face. Unexpected collateral consequences of criminal convictions may jeopardize someone's civil rights, such as the ability to vote or own a firearm. The negative effects of a conviction may also extend to a ban on public assistance, driver's licenses, adoptive and foster parenting, and other restrictions in an ex-offender's daily life (Legal Action Center [LAC], 2004). Certain crimes, such as distribution of drugs, may restrict someone with a felony record from accessing certain government services otherwise available for the needy. Federal education grants, welfare, food stamps, public housing, and certain types of jobs (e.g., childcare, nursing, etc.) often exclude those with certain offense histories (Byrnes et al., 2002). Likewise, supplemental security income (SSI) recipients may lose benefits if they violate certain parole conditions. Offenders may also be excluded from jobs that require them to be bonded and to obtain driver's licenses (Travis, 2002).

FACTORS ASSOCIATED WITH COMMUNITY SUPERVISION SUCCESS AND FAILURE

Effective community supervision is dependent on the collaborative work of a wide variety of corrections agents. Given their interdependence, it can be said that there is an exchange relationship between bureaucratic organizations, the offender's responses, and the roles of the officer. The elements of this complex relationship can be viewed as a mixed triangle (Klockars, 1972), where each of these domains, separately or collectively, are responsible for service delivery, the quality of treatment, and the reinforcement of public health and safety. Throughout the research literature, these factors continue to be associated with the traditional "treatment-control dilemma" in community supervision and "its resolution in the revocation decision," both of which determine whether the reentry process will be successful (Klockars, 1972, p. 552).

From the bureaucratic perspective, the American Probation and Parole Association ([APPA], 1991) has indicated that when the concept of time and case priority in terms of risk classification has been taken into account under the workload model, the supervision caseload assigned to officers affect their attitudes toward street-level bureaucracy. There is no single magic number about how many offenders could be handled effectively by an officer but "it is a necessary force" to consider for effective and promising supervision (DeMichele, 2007, p. 20). Optimal caseloads, it has been suggested, should remain "small."

Evidence-based practices show that for high-risk and intensive cases or for moderate-risk or low-risk offenders, each officer should handle 20–30, 50–60, and 120–200 cases, respectively (APPA, 1991; Burrell, 2006). A multicity study revealed that probationers were less likely to be rearrested or commit a new crime under community supervision when officers managed a relatively smaller caseload (Jalbert et al., 2011). When officers have more time to build positive bonds and rapport with offenders, they are more effective in their use of discretion and can better implement organizational goals and case management strategies that would be tailored to an individual offender's needs.

With large caseloads and limited resources being the norm within organizations today, the way in which officers carry out their duties is a significant part of community supervision. Officers have had a long history of role conflicts acting as both a social worker focusing on rehabilitation and a peace officer emphasizing law enforcement practices (Hsieh, Hafoka, Woo, van Wormer, Stohr, & Hemmens, 2015). Leaning too much toward either side would make it difficult to fulfill the new role of "case manager." This role allows one to span the two more conventional roles and to match the offender's level of criminogenic risk to his or her individual needs with intervention and monitoring plans.

Theoretically, as officers reconcile these roles and new functions, they will be able to move toward a more balanced practice, which is a promising community supervision approach (Miller, 2015). Officers who adopt this balanced approach may experience a higher likelihood of successful behavior change among offenders (Taxman, 2008). In fact, from a legislative perspective, there are 28 states that legally prescribe adult (Hsieh et al., 2015) and 40 states that legally prescribe juvenile probation supervision functions (Hsieh et al., 2016) toward this approach. This model encourages officers to integrate law enforcement–oriented, therapeutic and individual case adjustment, and management and risk and needs assessment tasks into community supervision.

Research has found several demographic background traits that have been consistently correlated with success and failure in community supervision. These include offense history, substance use and abuse, age, marital and employment status, as well as gender. Offenders with a history of criminality, particularly property offenders, have long been associated with probation and parole failure (Morgan, 1994; Petersilia, Turner, Kahan, & Peterson, 1985; Stahler, Mennis, Belenko, Welsh, Hiller, & Zajac, 2013; Sims & Jones, 1997; Whitehead, 1991). Alcohol and drug use also appear to predict recidivism. In addition, alcohol and drug treatment that is initiated but not completed may also result in a high rate of recidivism. Alcohol and drug treatment that addresses the motivation for committing crimes seems more likely to predict community supervision success (Gottfredson, Najaka, & Kearley, 2003).

Age appears to be a consistent predictor of probation success or failure, as younger offenders and those who begin their criminal activity at a younger age appear to be at greater risk for recidivism (Irish, 1989; Williams et al., 2000). The theoretical literature suggests that those more likely to reoffend typically have fewer social bonds than offenders who have more social bonds. Further, having a job and living with a spouse would influence criminality (Farrington, 1988). Carmichael, Gover, Koons-Witt, and Inabnit (2005) found that age, race, and the use of alcohol and drugs were predictors of parolee success in a sample of 503 female offenders. Also, Whites and older females were most likely to complete their sentences successfully. Females who did not indicate a history of drug or alcohol use and those who successfully addressed such problems were more likely to succeed on supervision.

Overall, it appears that most community supervision revocations are the result of technical violations, as opposed to a new offense (Carmichael et al., 2005). According to Sims and Jones (1997), technical violations surpass both major and minor violations. Gray, Fields, and Maxwell (2001) examined offenders who received probation violations, the reasons for probation violation, and the time to violation. The 30-month study of 1,500 probationers found that most technical probation violations occurred during the first 3 months of supervision.

One of the major difficulties in interpreting studies on community corrections outcomes, however, is the different definitions of recidivism that are used. Events that trigger revocation vary in levels of seriousness or degrees of probability that a violation actually took place. Some researchers measure arrest, reconviction, incarceration, absconding, and any probation or parole violations, as well as probation suspension or revocation. While most use arrest, this is often a subjective outcome that depends, to some extent, on law enforcement resources, probation and parole supervision policies, and court workloads.

Studies at both macro and micro levels have indicated that stereotypes about race and dangerousness may lead to harsher sentences (those that do not include community supervision), as well as to higher rates of probation and parole revocations (Huebner & Bynum, 2008). In examining racial disparities in corrections, for instance, we know that among the 2.2 million inmates incarcerated, African Americans currently account for 35% of the prison population (Carson & Anderson, 2016) and 35% of the jail population (Minton & Zeng, 2016). However, African Americans make up only about 13% of the United States' population. The Sentencing Project (2017) has argued that the War on Drugs dramatically increased the incarcerated population and that mandatory minimum sentences produced longer prison terms for convicted drug offenders. These drug policies appear to have had a much more punitive impact on Black and ethnic inmates as they disproportionately represented three fourths of the total sentenced drug offenders in federal prisons (Taxy, Samuels, & Adams, 2015).

In order to address the inequities of past drug policies, particularly those that disparately impacted African Americans, President Barack Obama signed the Fair Sentencing Act in 2010. This legislation was developed to minimize the sentencing disparities between simple possession of crack and powder cocaine. Awareness of disproportionate minority confinement has directed attention toward finding ways to control discretion in the community corrections process that might introduce bias and discriminate against segments of society. The U.S. Sentencing Commission's recent decision to address crack/powder cocaine sentencing disparities by revising the sentencing guidelines and making those revisions retroactive may mean that many minority defendants are now eligible for parole or release. The development of a number of ethnically and culturally based programming initiatives has also created opportunities to meet the needs of minority youth in the community.

ONGOING DEBATES AND POLICY IMPLICATIONS

Community corrections continues to be a controversial component of the justice system, perhaps because of its attempt to balance meaningful correctional measures with fair sentences, affordable policies and practices, and victims' rights. Moreover, sensationalized media accounts of some crimes feed panics that create assumptions about risk and violence that perpetuate the need for harsher punishments. This punitively oriented penal attitude may further result in roadblocks on the path to changing public views about appropriate conditions of community supervision, as well as the technologies available to enforce them.

Although many issues are ultimately settled by the courts, legal officials continue to divide the priorities of the system into control and reform. Conditions in either category must be rationally related to a correctional goal and must be clear, reasonable, and constitutional.

Recently, the courts have found that probationers could not be compelled to enroll in religiously oriented treatment programs like Alcoholics Anonymous (AA; *U.S. v. Myers*, 1994; *Warner v. Orange County Department of Probation*, 1994), nor can they be forced to participate in publicly humiliating displays of guilt (*People v. Hackler*, 1993). While there is agreement that a wider range of strategies must be available, authorities, as well as the public, must be careful about the potentially damaging effects of any requirements and understand the discretionary rationale behind decision making.

As trends indicate, harsher sentencing strategies and more assertive victims' rights measures may make it more difficult for some offenders to be assigned community corrections options. For example, in some jurisdictions, the sentencing of youthful offenders to adult facilities has become routine rather than an occasional product of judicial discretion. In these states, the transfer of juvenile offenders to adult courts is the result of statutorily defined net widening whereby legislators have "increased the set of crimes that qualified an adolescent for transfer, lifted age restrictions, and added statutory exclusion and prosecutorial discretion as methods" to respond to public safety concerns and tough-on-crime control ideology (Mulvey & Schubert, 2012, p. 2). On the other hand, responding to scandals and abuses in the juvenile corrections system in Texas, the 2012–2013 legislative appropriations bill specifically set aside funding for new diversion programs for youthful offenders. The goal was to provide resources for juvenile probation services locally that would reduce the population of the trouble-plagued Youth Commission (Texas Juvenile Justice Department, 2012).

Saving children from a life of crime through early intervention and rehabilitation should be reaffirmed, it has been argued, because punishment and punitive models do not work well and even cause additional harm (Cullen & Jonson, 2012). Still, debates between retribution and rehabilitation doctrines in the community treatment and supervision of juvenile offenders continue. Arguments include the "actor vs. the act" thesis, adult system and juvenile system practices, and a host of issues related to "age" in terms of behavioral responsibility, accountability, changeability, stability, and treatability.

An emerging new philosophy in community corrections is community justice. Community justice recognizes that the outcome of collective community input, involvement, initiatives, and endeavor can effectively repair harm, restore the quality of community life, prevent both crime and noncrime problems, and maintain social order (Karp & Clear, 2000). This model uses an array of community-level interventions, innovative projects, and programs to reintegrate offenders by addressing the needs of victims in a corrections process that restores community. The community justice framework has received considerable attention and support among practitioners and policy makers. Since 2009, over $475 million in federal funding has been spent across the country to increase resources for the creation and implementation of reentry and justice programs that would facilitate inmates returning from incarceration to safely and successfully reintegrate into the community (Bureau of Justice Assistance [BJA], 2017). A significant portion of the funding has focused on continued aftercare for those released after undergoing mental health or substance abuse treatments in prison. Programs were also developed around work readiness, family reunification, and mentoring services (Listwan, Jonson, Cullen, & Latessa, 2008).

An important contribution to the development of meaningful corrections services and policies would be rigorous program evaluations. Such studies should identify the best evidence-based practices and continue to refine new experimental options. To date, many services and policies appear to have significantly lowered recidivism rates, but a consistent body of results must be analyzed to convince offenders that a true second chance really does exist and to assure citizens that reductions in prison crowding through community corrections is a safe investment.

The reality of the revolving door between community and prison also has led Congress to pass pieces of legislation aimed at increasing success in local corrections programming. For example, the 2003 Serious and Violent Offender Reentry Initiative directed funds to programs nationwide that would develop best practices for dealing with high-risk juvenile and adult offenders at release. Another example found in California, a historic piece of legislation signed by Governor Brown appears to have significantly reduced that state's prison population. California's Public Safety and Realignment Act of 2011 transferred the custody of low-level and nonserious offenders to the county for both jurisdiction and funding. Early reports seem to indicate that lower recidivism rates may reflect the greater reentry and reintegration potential in this arrangement (California Department of Corrections and Rehabilitation, 2013). In addition, national prisoner statistics indicate that over half of the reductions in the United States prison population can be attributed to California's new mandates (Carson & Golinelli, 2013).

It would be fair to say that despite our continued efforts in developing effective community corrections models, we still lack not only rigorous assessments of existing programs but also clarification of the concepts of reentry, restorative justice, and community justice. Although community justice has similar features to restorative justice, there may still be philosophic conflicts among practitioners, the community, and stakeholders, especially if we do not have clear distinctions between the two models in terms of definitions, goals, missions, objectives, and outcomes. And as discussed earlier, we must acknowledge the fears of the public, which, to some degree, continue to support the punitive sanctions of a conventional crime control ideology. It appears that we must work toward disentangling the concept of "criminal" justice from "community" justice and broaden public views about justice in general. This is obviously worth further explorative and explanatory research in the near future.

From cumulative research and the experiences of everyday corrections personnel, the Pew Center on the States (2008) noted several feasible and practical strategies for successful supervision and reentry in community corrections across jurisdictions in the future. According to the Pew report, policy implications should continue to focus on the following areas:

- Probation and parole agencies should clearly define missions, goals, outcomes, and benchmarks for performance measurement. Develop a series of evaluation plans in terms of formative, process and implementation, outcome and impact evaluation that assess the relationship between inputs and outputs within organizations for further modification and improvement on success recidivism reduction.

- Under the RNR doctrine (Andrews & Bonta, 2010), tailor supervision conditions for probationers and parolee based on "three Rs." First, supervision conditions should be *realistic* and doable and not overestimate attainable objectives. This means that in the process of supervision plan design, officers and offenders should work together to build a realistic case plan by considering bureaucracy, resources, limitations, and offender's valuable input collectively rather than a one-way contract controlled by a bureaucrat's discretion. Second, the supervision plan should be *relevant* and fit the individual risks and needs. In doing so, agencies should employ reliable and valid actuarial risk assessment instruments and classify cases into appropriate risk and needs levels followed by monitoring, interventions, programming, and service. Third, strategies imposed by officers or program selection should be *research-based* practices that have demonstrated the effective propensity of behavior change and recidivism reduction and positive reintegration outcomes.

- Officials should mobilize resources to target high-risk offenders for effective supervision and rehabilitation outcomes. While this would result in less supervision and programming for low-risk offenders, it would possibly prevent them from being too strictly followed and too easily revoked as they adjust to monitoring requirements. Probation and parole agencies should also frontload resources for high-risk offenders in the first few weeks and months of supervision following releases from incarceration. This might better engage them in various services (e.g., substance abuse program, mental health treatment, housing, and employment assistance) and stabilize and adjust an offender's pro-social life.

- Providing incentives and rewards for offenders who meet supervision plans and goals to positively motivate their buy-in and compliance with conditions. For instance, low-risk probationers and parolees would be able to earn progress toward discharge, reduce a term or intensity of supervision, defer a monthly payment, or remove restrictions (e.g., curfew) based on their performance on assigned conditions. This may also save more agency resources and could even concentrate additional assistance and service to high-risk offenders.

- Punishment could be used by officers to respond to conditional violations, but again, penalties should be graduated by level of risk and behaviors and clearly set out in contract terms. Incarceration should be considered the last resort, used only for the most serious infractions. Minor violations should be handled with lower levels of restrictions and interventions. This system would be more consistent with the idea of community justice without compromising goals and outcomes.

- For efficiently and effectively managing cases, agencies should reduce the time and costs associated with officers' travel and use place-based supervision. Also, officers should supervise offenders where they live and build relationships with the local community and with people (e.g., family, friends, employers, community leaders, and priests) who know them. Emphasis should be placed on enhancing social bonds and social capital as informal social controls for long-term positive behavioral change.

Source: Pew Center on The States. (2008). *Putting public safety first: 13 strategies for successful supervision and reentry.*

CONCLUSION

Community corrections serves a critical function in bridging institutional effectiveness and public safety. Without effective transitional and reintegration approaches for reentry, offenders may pose further threats or cause additional harm to the community and disrupt the social order. In other words, the coming together of supportive supervision and offender compliance with probation and parole terms is the key to the overall success and failure of the criminal justice system.

In addition, it is imperative that the system strives to remove any roadblocks that former prisoners face. From statutory regulations to social reforms, there are areas of discord that we should reconcile and refine. Former prisoners will eventually "graduate" from community supervision and aftercare plans and attempt to rebuild their lives in order to become more productive members of society. However, legal barriers may still deny them to access social benefits and public assistance that would help them attain economic security and stability when they struggle for material support (LAC, 2004). Meeting basic survival needs and creating channels of upward mobility over time is a promising strategy to prevent ex-offenders from returning to prison (Harding, Wyse, Dobson, & Morenoff, 2015).

Legislators and stakeholders should resolve the obstacles of civil disabilities and expand the scope of opportunities for former prisoners to develop positive social interactions.

The barriers newly released offenders face often include the more subtle labels and stigmas about ex-convicts that make it difficult to truly integrate into a community. Stereotypes are difficult to overcome, and it is still unclear how probation and parole officers can help to prepare an offender to overcome public biases and to remain positive and confident prior to and after release. Former inmates who anticipate a greater level and perceive a greater level of stigma and discrimination from community members are more likely to have postrelease adjustment problems, which would reduce the likelihood of the successful reentry outcomes (Moore, Stuewig, & Tangney, 2016). Hence, innovative initiatives are needed to address labeling and stigmas so that they will not sabotage the efforts of community corrections.

Successful reentry for any offender relies on collective justice and the concept of community reinvestment at both the micro and macro level. To see that this takes place, we must make continuous improvements in three areas. First, we should redirect policy makers and correctional agencies to design promising tactics for ensuring better long-term outcomes rather than short-term behavior change. Second, we must provide adequate training for officers so that they might develop balanced and meaningful case plans. Such plans will help offenders obtain independence, legitimate survival skills, and appropriate coping mechanisms, as well as problem-solving and rational decision-making abilities. All of these traits are necessary in the process of becoming law-abiding citizens. Third and finally, we must commit to a schedule of accurate risk assessment and the provision of effective programming that will provide the necessary continuum of care for minimizing the likelihood of future reoffending.

Discussion Questions

1. What is the purpose of community corrections in this country today, and what are the strengths and weaknesses of the concept in general?

2. What are some of the barriers faced by offenders who have recently been released from prison? How can we address them effectively?

3. Many people seem to want to lock up more and more people for longer periods of time. How do we select offenders for community supervision programs so that we stay within our current budgets?

4. How realistic is the argument some offenders make that community supervision is worse than prison?

5. What changes would you make in the operation of community supervision programs in your area, and how, specifically, would you engage the community in this process?

References

American Probation and Parole Association. (1991, Summer). Caseload standards: APPA issues committee report. *Perspectives*, 34–36.

Andrews, D. A., & Bonta, J. (2010). *The psychology of criminal conduct* (5th ed.). New Providence, NJ: LexisNexis Group.

Bonta, J., Bourgon, G., Rugge, T., Scott, T.-L., Yessine, A. K., Gutierrez, L., & Li, J. (2011). An experimental demonstration of training probation officers in evidence-based community supervision. *Criminal Justice and Behavior, 38*(1), 1127–1148.

Bureau of Justice Assistance. (2017). Second Chance Act (SCA). *Retrieved on* November 23, 2017, from https://www.bja.gov/ProgramDetails .aspx?Program_ID=90

Burrell, B. (2006). *Caseload standards for probation and parole*. American Probation and Parole Association. Retrieved on November 23, 2017, from https://www.appa-net.org/eweb/docs/APPA/ stances/ip_CSPP.pdf

Burrell, W. D. (2017). Risk and needs assessment in probation and parole: The persistent gap between promise and practice. In F. S. Taxman (Ed.), *Handbook on risk and need assessment: Theory and Practice* (pp. 23–48). New York, NY: Routledge.

Byrnes, M., Macallair, D., & Shorter, A. (2002). *Aftercare as afterthought: Reentry and the California Youth Authority*. San Francisco, CA: Center on Juvenile and Criminal Justice.

California Department of Corrections and Rehabilitation. (2013). *Realignment report: A one-year examination of offenders released from state prison in the first six months of Public Safety Realignment*. Sacramento, CA: Author.

Caplow, T., & Simon, J. (1999). Understanding prison policy and population trends. *Crime and Justice, 26*, 63–120.

Carmichael, S., Gover, A., Koons-Witt, B., & Inabnit, B. (2005). The successful completion of probation and parole among female offenders. *Women and Criminal Justice, 17*, 75–97.

Carson, E. A., & Anderson, E. (2016). *Prisoners in 2015* (NCJ 250229). Washington, DC: Bureau of Justice Statistics.

Carson, E. A., & Golinelli, D. (2013). *Prisoners in 2012* (NCJ 243920). Washington, DC: Bureau of Justice Statistics.

Cullen, F. T., & Jonson, C. L. (2012). Four correctional lessons. In F. T. Cullen & C. L. Johnson (Eds.), *Correctional theory: Context and consequences* (pp. 205–229). Thousand Oaks, CA: Sage.

DeMichele, M., & Payne, B. K. (2012). Measuring community corrections' officials perceptions of goals, strategies, and workload from a systems perspective. *Prison Journal, 92*(3), 388–410.

DeMichele, M. T. (2007). *Probation and parole's growing caseloads and workload allocation: Strategies for managerial decision making*. Retrieved on November 23, 2017, from https://www.appa-net .org/eweb/docs/appa/pubs/SMDM.pdf

Durose, M. R., Cooper, A. D., & Snyder, H. N. (2014). *Recidivism of prisoners released in 30 States in 2005: Patterns from 2005 to 2010* (NCJ 244205). Washington, DC: Bureau of Justice Statistics.

Duwe, G., & King, M. (2013). Can faith-based correctional programs work? An outcome evaluation of the InnerChange Freedom Initiative in Minnesota. *International Journal of Offender Therapy and Comparative Criminology, 57*(7), 813–841.

Farrington, D. P. (1988). Studying changes within individuals: The causes of offending. In M. Rutter (Ed.), *Studies of psychosocial risk: The power of longitudinal data* (pp. 158–183). Cambridge, UK: Cambridge University Press.

Feeley, M., & Simon, J. (1992). The new penology: Notes on the emerging strategy of corrections and its implications. *Criminology, 30*(4), 449–474.

Gottfredson, D., Najaka, S., & Kearley, B. (2003). Effectiveness of drug treatment courts: Evidence from a randomized trial. *Criminology and Public Policy, 2*, 171–196.

Gray, M., Fields, M., & Maxwell, S. (2001). Examining probation violations: Who, what, and when. *Crime and Delinquency, 47*, 537–557.

Grove, W. M., Zald, D. H., Lebow, B. S., Snitz, B. E., & Nelson, C. (2000). Clinical versus mechanical prediction: A meta-analysis. *Psychological Assessment, 12*(1), 19–30.

Hamilton, Z., Kigerl, A., & Hays, Z. (2015). Removing release impediments and reducing correctional costs: Evaluation of Washington State's Housing Voucher Program. *Justice Quarterly, 32*(2), 255–287.

Hanson, K. R., Bourgon, G., McGrath, R. J., Kroner, D., D'Amora, D. A., Thomas, S. S., & Tavarez, L. P. (2017). *A five-level risk and needs system: Maximizing assessment results in corrections through the development of a common language.* New York, NY: National Reentry Resource Center.

Harding, D. J., Wyse, J. J. B., Dobson, C., & Morenoff, J. D. (2014). Making ends meet after prison. *Journal of Policy Analysis and Management, 33*(2), 440–470.

Herberman, E. J., & Bonczar, T. P. (2015). *Probation and parole in the United States, 2013* (NCJ 248029). Washington, DC: Bureau of Justice Statistics.

Hsieh, M.-L., & Hamilton, Z. K. (2016). Predicting success in residential substance abuse interventions: New Jersey's pre-release incarceration alternatives. *Criminal Justice Policy Review, 27*(2), 182–202.

Hsieh, M.-L., Hafoka, M., Woo, Y., van Wormer, J., Stohr, M. K., & Hemmens, C. (2015). Probation officer roles: A statutory analysis. *Federal Probation, 79*(3), 20–37.

Hsieh, M.-L., Woo, Y., Hafoka, M., van Wormer, J., Hemmens, C., & Stohr, M. K. (2016). Assessing the current state of juvenile probation practice: A statutory analysis. *Journal of Offender Rehabilitation, 55*(5), 329–354.

Huebner, B., & Bynum, T. (2008). The role of race and ethnicity in parole decisions. *Criminology, 46,* 907–937.

Hyatt, J. M., & Barnes, G. C. (2017). An experimental evaluation of the impact of intensive supervision on the recidivism of high-risk probationers. *Crime and Delinquency, 63*(1), 3–38.

Irish, J. F. (1989). *Probation and recidivism: A study of probation adjustment and its relationship to post-probation outcome.* Mineola, NY: Nassau County Probation Department.

Jalbert, S. K., Rhodes, W., Kane, M., Clawson, E., Bogue, B., Flygare, C., & Guevara, M. (2011). *A multi-site evaluation of reduced probation caseload size in an evidence-based practice setting.* Cambridge, MA: Abt Associates Inc.

Jones, M. (1996). Voluntary revocations and the "elect-to-serve" option in North Carolina probation. *Crime and Delinquency, 42*(1), 36–49.

Kaeble, D., & Bonczar, T. P. (2017). *Probation and parole in the United States, 2015* (NCJ 250230). Washington, DC: Bureau of Justice Statistics.

Kaeble, D., & Glaze, L. (2016). *Correctional populations in the United States, 2015* (NCJ 250374). Washington, DC: Bureau of Justice Statistics.

Karp, D. R., & Clear, T. R. (2000). Community justice: A conceptual framework. In C. M. Friel (Ed.), *Boundary changes in criminal justice organization* (pp. 323–368). Washington, DC: National Institute of Justice.

Klockars, C. B. (1972). A theory of probation supervision. *Journal of Criminal Law, Criminology, and Police Science, 63*(4), 550–557.

Legal Action Center. (2004). *After prison: Roadblocks to reentry.* New York, NY: Legal Action Center.

Lipsky, M. (2010). *Street-level bureaucracy: Dilemmas of the individual in public service.* New York, NY: Russell Sage Foundation.

Listwan, S. J., Jonson, C. L., Cullen, F. T., & Latessa, E. (2008). Cracks in the penal harm movement: Evidence from the field. *Criminology and Public Policy, 7*(3), 423–465.

Lösel, F., & Schmucker, M. (2005). The effectiveness of treatment for sexual offenders: A comprehensive meta-analysis. *Journal of Experimental Criminology, 1,* 117–146.

Luong, D., & Wormith, J. S. (2011). Applying risk/need assessment to probation practice and its impact on the recidivism of young offenders. *Criminal Justice and Behavior, 38,* 1177–1199.

Lutze, F. E., Johnson, W., Clear, T., Latessa, E., & Slate, R. (2012). The future of community corrections is now: Stop dreaming and take action. *Journal of Contemporary Criminal Justice, 28*(1), 42–59.

Martin, J. S., Hanrahan, K., & Bowers, J. H., Jr. (2009). Offender's perceptions of house arrest and electronic monitoring. *Journal of Offender Rehabilitation, 48*, 547–570.

Martinson, R. (1974). What works? Questions and answers about prison reform. *Public Interest, 35*, 22–54.

Materni, M. C. (2013). Criminal punishment and the pursuit of justice. *British Journal of American Legal Studies, 2*, 263–304.

Miller, J. (2015). Contemporary modes of probation officer supervision: The triumph of the "synthetic" officer? *Justice Quarterly, 32*(2), 314–336.

Miller, J. M., Miller, H. V., & Barnes, J. C. (2016). Outcome evaluation of a family-based jail reentry program for substance abuse offenders. *Prison Journal, 96*(1), 53–78.

Miller, J., & Maloney, C. (2013). Practitioner compliance with risk/needs assessment tools: A theoretical and empirical assessment. *Criminal Justice and Behavior, 40*(7), 716–736.

Minton, T. D., & Zeng, Z. (2016). *Jail inmates in 2015* (NCJ 2503945). Washington, DC: Bureau of Justice Statistics.

Moore, K. E., Stuewig, J. B., & Tangney, J. P. (2016). The effect of stigma on criminal offenders' functioning: A longitudinal meditational model. *Deviant Behavior, 37*(2), 196–218.

Morgan, K. D. (1994). Factors associated with probation outcome. *Journal of Criminal Justice, 22*, 341–353.

Mulvey, E. P., & Schubert, C. A. (2012). *Transfer of juveniles to adult court: Effects of a broad policy in one court*. Washington, DC: Office of Juvenile Justice and Delinquency Prevention.

National Reentry Resource Center. (2017). *U.S. Department of Justice announces FY2017 Second Chance Act awards to support reentry initiatives for adults and youth*. Retrieved on November 23, 2017, from https://csgjusticecenter.org/nrrc/posts/department-of-justice-announces-fy2017-second-chance-act-awards-to-support-reentry-initiatives-for-adults-and-youth

Pearson, F. S., Lipton, D. S., Cleland, C. M., & Yee, D. S. (2002). The effects of behavioral/cognitive-behavioral programs on recidivism. *Crime and Delinquency, 48*, 476–496.

People v. Hackler, 13 Cal. App. 4th 1049 (1993).

Petersilia, J. (2003). *When prisoners come home: Parole and prisoner reentry*. New York, NY: Oxford University Press.

Petersilia, J., & Turner, S. (1993). Intensive probation and parole. *Crime and Justice: A Review of Research, 17*, 281–335.

Petersilia, J., & Deschenes, E. P. (1994). Perceptions of punishment: Inmates and staff rank the severity of prison versus intermediate sanctions. *Prison Journal, 74*(3), 306–328.

Petersilia, J., Turner, S., Kahan, J., & Peterson, J. (1985). Executive summary of Rand's study, "Granting Felons Probation: Public Risks and Alternatives." *Crime and Delinquency, 31*, 379–392.

Pew Center on the States. (2008). *Putting public safety first: 13 strategies for successful supervision and reentry*. Retrieved on November 23, 2017, from http://www.pewtrusts.org/en/research-and-analysis/reports/0001/01/01/putting-public-safety-first

Phelps, M. S. (2013). The paradox of probation: Community supervision in the age of mass incarceration. *Law Policy, 35*, 51–80.

Rothman, D. (1980). *Conscience and convenience: The asylum and its alternatives in progressive America*. Boston, MA: Little, Brown.

Santos, M. (2003). *Profiles from prison: Adjusting to life behind bars*. Westport, CT: Praeger.

Schlager, M. D., & Robbins, K. (2008). Does parole work?—Revisited. *Prison Journal, 88*(2), 234–251.

Sims, B., & Jones, M. (1997). Predicting success or failure on probation: Factors associated with felony probation outcomes. *Crime and Delinquency, 43*, 314–327.

Skeem, J. L., Emke-Francis, P., & Louden, J. (2006). Probation, mental health, and mandatory treatment. *Criminal Justice and Behavior, 33*, 158–184.

Spelman, W. (1995). The severity of intermediate sanctions. *Journal of Research in Crime and Delinquency, 32*(2), 107–135.

Stahler, G., Mennis, J., Belenko, S., Welsh, W., Hiller, M., & Zajac, G. (2013). *Predicting recidivism for released state prison offenders: Examining the influence of individual and neighborhood characteristics and spatial contagion on the likelihood of reincarceration.* Bethesda, MD: National Institute on Drug Abuse.

Taxman, F. S. (2008). No illusions: Gender and organizational change in Maryland's proactive community supervision efforts. *Criminology and Public Policy, 7*(2), 275–302.

Taxy, S., Samuels, J., & Adams, W. (2015). *Drug offenders in federal prison: Estimates of characteristics based on linked data* (NCJ 248648). Washington, DC: Bureau of Justice Statistics.

Texas Juvenile Justice Department. (2012). *Community Juvenile Justice Appropriations, Riders and Special Diversion Programs.* Texas Juvenile Justice Department. Retrieved on December 9, 2017, from https://www.tjjd.texas.gov/publications/reports/AnnualReportFundingandRiders2012-12.pdf

The Sentencing Project. (2017). *Trends in U.S. corrections.* Washington, DC: The Sentencing Project.

Travis, J. (2002). Invisible punishment: An instrument of social exclusion. In M. Mauer & M. Chesney-Lind (Eds.), *Invisible punishment: The collateral consequences of mass imprisonment* (pp. 15–36). New York, NY: W. W. Norton.

Turner, S., Petersilia, J., & Deschenes, E. P. (1992). Evaluating intensive supervision probation/parole (ISP) for drug offenders. *Crime and Delinquency, 38*(4), 539–556.

U.S. v. Myers, 864 F. Supp. 794 (1994).

Warner v. Orange County Department of Probation, 870 F. Supp. 69 (1994).

Whitehead, J. T. (1991). The effectiveness of felony probation: Results from an eastern state. *Justice Quarterly, 8*, 523–543.

Williams, F. P., McShane, M. D., & Dolny, M. (2000). Developing a parole classification instrument for use as a management tool. *Corrections Management Quarterly, 4*(4), 45–56.

Wilson, D. B., Gallagher, C. A., & MacKenzie, D. L. (2000). A meta-analysis of corrections-based education, vocation, and work programs for adult offenders. *Journal of Research in Crime and Delinquency, 37*, 347–368.

Wood, P., & Grasmick, H. (1999). Toward the development of punishment equivalencies: Male and female inmates rate the severity of alternative sanctions compared to prison. *Justice Quarterly, 16*(1), 19–50.

Wood, P., & May, D. (2003). Racial differences in perceptions of severity of sanctions: A comparison of prison with alternatives. *Justice Quarterly, 20*(3), 605–631.

Yoon, J., & Nickel, J. (2008). *Reentry partnerships: A guide for states and faith-based and community organizations.* New York, NY: The Council of State Governments, Justice Center.

RESTORATIVE JUSTICE IN THEORY

Lois Presser and Kyle Letteney

When we have been harmed by another, we typically seek justice. But what is justice? According to the restorative justice perspective, justice is repair of harms, with the offender as the main agent of repair. The harms requiring repair are considered both concretely and broadly. For example, restorative justice requires attention to the medical bills that an assault victim might have accumulated. But the victim's fears and self-doubt must also be addressed. Harm to *relationships* is taken especially seriously. Restorative justice stresses the victim's and the offender's relationships with each other and with other members of their communities. And so, in the restorative justice perspective, repair is seen as best facilitated by dialogue—key tool of human relationship that it is.

In practice, restorative justice is various things. Restorative justice programs include community service orders for offenders, school-based antibullying interventions, victim–offender dialogue, and meetings where Mothers Against Drunk Driving confront persons convicted of driving while intoxicated. Restorative justice clearly means different things to different people. The expression *restorative justice* gets pressed into the service of various goals, such as community building, rehabilitation of offenders, and victim healing. The fact of wide interpretation is a boon if one's goal is to gain support for a "restorative justice" program. It is a problem, however, if one's goal is to design a *focused* program—one whose measures of performance are agreed upon by all stakeholders. The purpose of this chapter is to clarify what restorative justice is and how it is *supposed to* work—that is, to review theories of restorative justice. Along the way, we identify certain key controversies surrounding restorative justice in theory and in practice. These concern whether restorative justice should ever intentionally harm offenders, whether participants should be forced to participate, whether certain interpersonal crimes are inappropriate for restorative justice practices, and whether restorative justice reproduces societal inequalities.

WHAT IS RESTORATIVE JUSTICE?

"So what are we actually here for today? Can I ask you?"[1]

We define a restorative justice program as any organized practice in which people, especially laypersons, participate by talking with one another, that focuses on a specific (pattern of) harm, stands opposed to harm, and is based on an understanding of justice as harm reduction. Clearly, these foci extend to harms that are not treated within the criminal justice system, such as political crime and school misconduct, hence the potentially broad scope of restorative justice (Umbreit & Armour, 2011). According to Presser and Van Voorhis (2002), the core processes of restorative justice are dialogue, relationship building, and communication of moral values. A restorative justice program generally aims to facilitate all three processes.

Essential and Desirable Features

The expression *restorative justice* was first applied in the 1970s to interventions with low-level property offenders that entailed encounters between the offender and her or his victim (Zehr, 1995). Restorative justice is still frequently associated with face-to-face dialogue, but the latter must not be overstated. Dialogue may not occur, or it may occur via letters—as between incarcerated offenders and their victims. Expressions of apology and forgiveness are generally associated with restorative justice, but they are not essential, even as such expressions—if genuine—can be uniquely helpful in rebuilding a relationship in the aftermath of harm.

Correctional treatment programs are designed to change offenders. But the potential targets of restorative justice are *all* those affected by crime: victims, offenders, and communities, whom Bazemore (1997) refers to as the "three clients" of restorative justice (p. 43). The healing of victims and communities is at least as important as any correctional impact that the intervention might have on the offender.

Is restorative justice simply a more traditional, premodern kind of justice? Ancient responses to crime were focused on the harms caused (Zehr 1995). Dialogue, relationship building, and communication of moral values prevailed. Laypersons "ran the show"; governments had not yet codified and commandeered social conflicts (Christie, 1977; Weitekamp, 1996). Hence, restorative justice borrows from traditional responses to crime. However, restorative justice proponents are not necessarily opposed to state sponsorship of responses to crime. For example,

Van Ness and Strong (2006) include in their vision of restorative justice a role for the state in ensuring order: It has "both the power and mandate" to do so (p. 47). If the holism and individualization of restorative justice is incompatible with the bureaucratization of contemporary Western criminal justice (McAlinden 2011), restorative justice is nonetheless consistent with the nominal purpose of the formal system: to stem harm.

A Place for Retribution and Control?

Some ancient societies, while focused on harm and not law violation, nonetheless sought to *harm* the offender—to exact retribution, and the same is true for indigenous societies today (Daly, 2002). The intent to harm would seem inconsistent with today's restorative justice. But the in/compatibility of restorative justice and retribution has been contested.

Both restorative justice and retribution focus on harms due to crime. They share the same end—to achieve justice—as opposed to the crime control sought by other rationales of punishment (i.e., deterrence, incapacitation, and rehabilitation). Both are concerned with victims. Indeed, survey research conducted by Huang et al. (2012) finds that "when respondents gave priority to the need for victim voice and amends, they were both more supportive of restorative justice and of punitive justice" (p. 304). Zehr (2002) observes, "Both retributive and restorative theories of justice acknowledge a basic moral intuition that a balance has been thrown off by a wrongdoing" (p. 59). Yet whereas retributivists would correct the balance through imposition of pain, restorativitists would correct it through acknowledgement and repair of harms. In addition, restorativists consider the harms that the offender has experienced, which may or may not have instigated the offending behavior.

Bazemore and Schiff (2001, pp. 64–65) frame the difference another way: Retribution has the offender taking responsibility but passively and retrospectively, as she or he must pay in the same measure as her or his past action harmed the victim. Restorative justice looks both backward and forward, holding the offender responsible for what she or he did but also encouraging the active, future responsibility to make amends.

Whether or not restorative justice, in *practice*, precludes infliction of harm remains controversial. Some scholars contend that restorative justice is not incompatible with retribution. Based on her own careful research, Daly (2002) writes,

> I have come to see that apparently contrary principles of retribution and reparation should be viewed as dependent on one another. Retributive censure should ideally occur before reparative gestures (or a victim's interest or movement to negotiate these) are possible in an ethical or psychological sense. Both censure and reparation may be experienced as 'punishment' by offenders (even if this is not the intent of decision-makers), and both censure and reparation need to occur before a victim or community can 'reintegrate' an offender into the community. (p. 60)

Duff (2002) likewise makes a case for "restoration through punishment." He writes, "The wrongdoer should be pained by the censure of his fellow citizens: if he is not pained, their censure has failed to achieve its intended result" (p. 96).

Restorative justice proponents specify that censure, however harsh, involves declarations that the offense *but not the offender* is bad (Barton, 2003, p. 23). The reasons for this principle mainly have to do with crime control and are discussed in the next section. At the same time, in the restorative justice ideal, victims are encouraged to express the full range of their thoughts and feelings. Thus, the "disciplining" of censure within restorative justice encounters is *potentially* at odds with its deference to victims. What victims might want to say does not always accord with restorative justice ideals or theories.

Arrigo and Schehr (1998) observe that the protocol and language of restorative justice constrain what participants can say: "Limiting potentially hostile outbursts from victims (and offenders) is essential to the reconciliation and restitution process" (p. 649). For Barton (2003), however, a high degree of structure during the victim–offender conference ensures that all participants speak (relatively) free of intimidation: He believes that structure ultimately empowers. Braithwaite (2002) observes that "at least compared to courtroom processes, restorative justice does better in terms of recognition and empowerment" (p. 133). We believe that the disagreements over harm and control in restorative justice encounters reflect deep questions concerning the very nature of harm and control and whether these are even avoidable in human interaction. To what extent can social control be avoided in human encounter? What is harm, and can we avoid doing harm as we attempt to change harmful ways?

Restorative justice is *not* a return to ancient justice practices because it orients to an *ideal* of nonharm and usually works with or within a government justice system. It follows that restorative justice seeks order *and* peace, crime control, *and* healing experience (Van Ness & Strong, 2006).

HOW IS RESTORATIVE JUSTICE SUPPOSED TO WORK?

> "Sometimes it is like you are getting picked at. Like they are picking away at you but it is for the good. . . . And then other times it is like I have a whole circle, a whole network of people that are willing to help me and volunteer their time to come and do this, and I appreciate it."[2]

We turn now to theories of restorative justice.[3] What is restorative justice supposed to accomplish, and how? In an earlier essay, the first author suggested that restorative justice "works" by *being* an experience of justice (Presser, 2004). It need not achieve some other thing. Still, when people ask if restorative justice "works," they are generally asking if it helps in reducing crime. The corresponding theoretical question is, How is restorative justice *supposed to* reduce crime? But equally

TABLE 25.1 ■ Theories of Restorative Justice Effects		
Theories of Crime Reduction	*Theories of Victim Healing*	*Theories of Community Building*

important questions are, How is restorative justice *supposed to* help victims heal, and how is restorative justice *supposed to* help build communities?

These questions are equally important; as such, we depict the corresponding theories laterally and not hierarchically in Table 25.1. Yet it is certainly the case that theories of crime reduction receive the lion's share of attention, so we begin with these.

Theories of Crime Reduction

A restorative justice practice may reduce crime at either individual (micro) or societal (macro) levels. That is, individual participants might change in ways that reduce criminal behavior, *or* crime rates might fall because a restorative justice practice changes something about culture or social structure. What follows is a selective review of given explanations of how restorative justice practice might reduce crime.[4]

John Braithwaite's (1989) reintegrative shaming theory is most often cited to explain how restorative justice practice might reduce reoffending. Reintegrative shaming involves affirming and insisting upon conventional standards of behavior by the (would-be) offender. Reintegrative refers to the mode of communication—the "shamed" person is treated as a member of the collective—and to the practical reintegration that may follow from the shaming, including, for example, help finding or keeping a job. The offense, not the (would-be) offender, is condemned. In this way, she or he gets a lesson on how to behave without being and feeling alienated from those giving the lesson.

Reintegrative shaming theory is a macro, meso, and micro level theory of crime. On the macro level, cultures that do reintegrative shaming should have lower rates of crime. In other words, reintegrative shaming supposedly prevents crime. The same is said to hold true for groups (meso level): Group members are influenced by others' experience of reintegrative shaming. On the micro level, offenders who are subject to reintegrative shaming should change their wayward patterns of behavior. That is, reintegrative shaming supposedly reduces recidivism. Commonly used restorative justice practices, especially those that convene community members *and* victims *and* offenders like family group conferencing and peacemaking circles, involve both practical and symbolic gestures of reintegrative shaming (Braithwaite, 2002).

Closely related to reintegrative shaming theory are Lawrence Sherman's (1993) defiance theory and Tom Tyler's (2006) legitimacy theory. Generally stated, these two theories propose that people obey the law to the extent that they view the law and its enforcers as legitimate. Sherman (1993) further specifies that people's obedience to law is conditioned by bonds to its enforcers. To the extent that restorative justice practices involve affirmation of the law by persons whom the offender respects, then according to these theories, we should expect greater conformity with law following such practices.

Barton (2003) proposes that restorative justice works by intervening in moral disengagement. In offending against another, a person "will tend to silence their conscience by means of various internal mechanisms of moral disengagement" (Barton, 2003, p. 50). Of course, the assumption here is that offenders have a conscience or sense of morality that proscribes doing what they did, an assumption not inconsistent with the optimistic attitude restorative justice proponents tend to hold concerning human nature. Barton refers to Albert Bandura's four mechanisms of moral disengagement by which the perpetrator of a harmful deed silences her or his conscience: morally justifying the deed, reducing one's personal responsibility, denying the harmfulness of the deed, and derogating the victim. These mechanisms are roughly comparable to Sykes and Matza's (1957) techniques of neutralization, and interventions to disable their use among known offenders are already featured in cognitively oriented correctional interventions (Andrews & Bonta, 2001). Barton's thinking is that encountering victims—and seeing and hearing what the crime did to them—is *uniquely* disabling to these means of disengaging. He proposes, "When victims tell offenders face-to-face about the harm the offenders' actions have caused, offenders' internal mechanisms of disengagement are seriously challenged and, in most cases, reversed" (Barton, 2003, p. 50).

Barton's theory of crime reduction based on moral engagement pertains exclusively to restorative justice programs that convene victim–offender encounters. Theories that emphasize strain (Agnew, 1992) and deficient social control (Hirschi, 1969) as the causes of offending pertain to those restorative justice programs that do not involve encounter but address offender needs. For example, a restorative justice program might intervene in offending patterns to the extent that the program contributes to the development of "competencies" among offenders (see Bazemore, 1991). A community member might offer job training and a job to the participant who perpetrated a property crime. This participant may thus gain the social capital that can serve as a hedge against future offending.

Finally, restorative justice practices may reduce reoffending by helping the offender to tell a new story about herself or himself. The dialogue featured in many restorative justice practices invites a renarrating of the past and a redemptive script for the future, which Maruna (2001) has identified as conducive to desistance from crime. Theories of narrative—in the social sciences and in literary studies— suggest that "one's story" is actually a collaborative production and that we act based on our stories (Bruner, 1990; Presser, 2009). As Braithwaite (2006) writes, "In restorative justice conferences, after each individual has their stories listened to, new stories that allow new identities are coauthored by a plurality of stakeholders in the injustice" (p. 428).

Note that each of the foregoing theories engages with some or all of the concepts of the dominant criminological theories, such as strain, learning, control, and labeling theories. As suggested earlier in regard to strain and control theories, the dominant theories can thus also explain restorative justice effects on criminal behavior. In addition, restorative justice practices can be seen as reinforcing positive conduct (social learning theory) or undermining "criminal" labels (labeling theory). However, the theories previously reviewed (e.g., theories of reintegrative shaming or revised narratives) go beyond the mainline theories in explicitly assigning causal roles to dialogue, relationship building, and communication of moral values. They are, in that sense, more true to what restorative justice aims to do.

Theories of Victim Healing

Victim healing is central to restorative justice. The goals of crime reduction and control ought not overshadow the goal of healing (Presser, Gaarder, & Hesselton, 2007). It follows that theories of restorative justice must give pride of place to theories of victim healing.

How is restorative justice practice supposed to help victims heal? The answer depends on what healing is thought to consist in. In some cases, healing can be tangible, such as compensation for destroyed or stolen property or recovery from broken bones sustained during a robbery. The restitution agreements made via a restorative justice practice, if kept, thus can help in healing. Restitution can be used to replace property or to pay medical bills.

Victims generally experience a need for *emotional* healing. This is as true for victims of many property crimes as it is for victims of violence (Deem, Nerenberg, & Titus, 2007). Restorative justice stands to promote victim healing far more than interventions associated with criminal justice, which are largely neglectful of victims (see Kelly & Erez, 1997) and may even revictimize them. Judith Herman (1997) squarely makes this argument: "If one set out by design to devise a system for provoking intrusive post-traumatic symptoms, once could do not better than a court of law" (p. 72). Some crime victims are especially ill-treated by police officers, prosecutors, and/or judges. These include victims of rape and battering—crimes that, by their threat, oppress all women. But Daly and Stubbs (2006) note that use of restorative justice practices to address such crimes might provide the offender with a forum for further manipulation or abuse and possibly communicate that the crime is not serious enough to warrant punishment such as the formal system metes out (see also Stubbs, 2010). Yet these scholars also consider the *potential* for restorative justice to give victims a voice and an opportunity for validation of harms, which formal justice systems, at their best, have not.

Bracketing these contrasting potentialities, we turn again to theories. Several theories can be advanced as to how restorative justice might emotionally heal victims. We identify three, which concern communication of the victim's worth, social reintegration of victims, and communication about moral (dis)order.

With acknowledgement of the crime and its effects and assurances that it was wrong, restorative justice participants would convey the basic worth of the victim. According to the late philosopher Jean Hampton (1988), the essential degradation of criminal victimization lies in its implicit or explicit message that the victim is less than the offender. The positive promise of retribution, she finds, is that it degrades the offender and thus counters the message that the victim is less than the offender.

Hampton observes that punishment has come to signify the victim's worth to the punishing collective. But punishment need not be the signifier of the victim's worth. Instead of bringing the offender down to the level that he or she has brought the victim, we could do something to raise the victim up. It need not be the "ticker tape parade" that Hampton playfully suggests, but we could do far more to communicate, emphatically and publicly, that the victim should not have been hurt as she or he was. That message is clearest if the offender expresses remorse and apologizes. But even hearing an offender's relative or a neighbor say, "That should not have happened to you," can be restorative. Hampton's philosophy of retribution thus works as a theory of victim healing via restorative justice, especially those restorative justice programs that invite community members to participate.

Trouble lies in the possibility that restorative justice participants do not convey a message of victim worth—a message that they did not deserve to experience what they did. Rather, encounters might provide the offender or community members with a forum for reaffirming her, his, or their disrespect toward the victim. Such a hazard gives us pause when considering the circumstances under which victims should meet with offenders and their supporters. The generally accepted guideline of *voluntary* participation, of both victims and offenders, is geared toward avoiding that hazard. Other guidelines pertaining to the order of speech in encounter programs (Barton, 2003); the screening of offenders (Presser & Lowenkamp, 1999) and victims; and the exclusion of certain crimes (e.g., battering) where disrespect is an entrenched feature of the victim–offender relationship, are relevant here as well. In our view, however, because honest dialogue cannot be scripted in advance, the risk that dialogue will cause further trauma cannot be *completely* eliminated.

Crime can leave victims feeling alone, with isolation compounding the experience of degradation (Herman, 1997). Restorative justice programs that bring community members together, such as family group conferences and community circles, can assist victims in reconnecting with other people. Barton (2003) is explicit about the restorative justice goal of victim reintegration. The victim's experience of reintegration relies not merely on "getting together" with other people. It relies also on telling one's story and having one's story taken as truth, discussing one's needs and getting help in meeting them, and expressing emotions and having those emotions acknowledged. As Herman (1997) writes, "Recovery can take place only within the context of relationships; it cannot occur in isolation" (p. 133).

Finally, restorative justice programming may reaffirm a sense of moral order for the victim. Crime can undermine victims' erstwhile belief that the world makes sense and that they control what happens to them. As a result, many victims feel confused and helpless (Herman, 1997). A victim–offender conference, where one confronts and questions the wrongdoer (e.g., "Why me?"), can recover a sense of an orderly world and personal power in that world. Alternatively, the conference may reveal that one actually had and has limited control over one's experiences (e.g., the victim was randomly chosen), and *this* might be a source of comfort (i.e., the victim did nothing wrong) or even spiritual enlightenment (Zehr, 2001). As spiritual writer Eckhart Tolle (2005) explains, "The eruption of disorder into a person's life, and the resultant collapse of a mentally defined meaning, can become the opening into a higher order" (p. 196).

Theories of Community Building

From some perspectives, the essence of restorative justice is in community building or change. The expression "restorative community justice" is common (e.g., Bazemore & Schiff, 2001; Young, 1995). Clear and Karp (1999) subsume their discussion of restorative justice under that of community justice. And Sullivan and Tifft (2005) call for a restorative justice that transforms unjust social structures.

In the short run, a restorative justice conference brings people together to address a problem of common concern. As Nils Christie (1977) is famous for noting, interpersonal conflicts are the stuff with which healthy interpersonal relationships are forged. When government agents deal with citizens' conflicts for them, as is the case in developed societies, communities are weakened (see also McKnight, 1995).

In the long run, the values of restorative justice might infuse our society culturally (Harris, 1991). The restorative justice emphasis on harms and needs might influence public policies, including but not limited to criminal justice policies. If injustice is tolerance of unmet needs, then courtrooms might take more seriously the injustice of, say, constricted economic choice that causes poverty and despair. Yet some charge restorative justice with simply reproducing societal inequalities. How so? If a restorative justice program is an adjunct of the criminal justice system, it will usually take the state's designations of "victim" and "offender" as given and not question them (Presser & Hamilton, 2006). As discussed previously, unimpeded, a restorative justice conference might provide a new forum for the offender to bully or to show disrespect toward the victim. Cultural differences among participants might engender failures of communication and mutual understanding during conferences (Albrecht, 2010). Or the scripting of restorative justice dialogue might adhere to institutionalized inequalities, as when young offenders must abase themselves before adult victims (Arrigo & Schehr, 1998).

Observing that generally held values may be oppressive and thus that "justice" often requires transformation and not just restoration, Hudson (2003) states that restorative justice encounters can "not only perform the norm-affirming expressive role of adversarial criminal justice; it can also perform an additional, norm-creating role" (p. 444). Hudson sees the potential for restorative justice dialogues as resembling Habermas's "ideal speech situation," with all "participants expressing their viewpoints and needs" and being heard (p. 444). The restorative justice philosophy is compatible with Collins's (1981) view of social structures as aggregations of human encounters. Thus, restorative justice is indeed compatible with and might even promote change to societies.

CONCLUSIONS

This chapter examined the nature of restorative justice and theories of how restorative justice works. Studies of restorative justice are usually concerned with restorative justice as a means to reducing the reoffense rates of participating offenders. In fact, restorative justice sets its sights on far more than recidivism reduction because it serves victims *and* community members *and* offenders. As we have seen, several theories explain how restorative justice might achieve its goals. The next step is many careful program evaluations, both to discover what programs are accomplishing, if anything, and to discover how.

Discussion Questions

1. Why is dialogue important to restorative justice practice?

2. What theories best explain how restorative justice might help victims to heal?

3. What theories best explain how restorative justice might help reduce crime?

4. What theories best explain how restorative justice might help build communities?

5. What are the factors restorative justice planners should consider when planning victim–offender encounters?

6. Could harming offenders be compatible with doing restorative justice? Explain.

7. How could restorative justice practices reproduce societal inequalities?

8. How could restorative justice practices transform societies and communities?

Notes

1. Question posed by father of young offender, during a victim–offender mediation session concerning vandalism. The excerpt is taken from Presser and Hamilton's (2006) study of a victim–offender mediation program with young offenders.

2. Comment by domestic violence offender concerning a sentencing circle in Minnesota (Gaarder, 2008).

3. The chapter focuses on theories that *explain* potential *effects* of restorative justice practice.

However, theories, in general, do not merely explain; they also discern the nature of things (Abend, 2008). That is, a theory can outline what a thing *is*. Theories that speak to the nature of restorative justice include (but are not limited to) theories of justice and the state, social movements, dialogue and democracy, the nature of conflict, and the nature of power.

4. See Chapter 4 in Braithwaite (2002) for an excellent discussion.

References

Abend, G. (2008). The meaning of "theory." *Sociological Theory, 26*(2), 173–199.

Agnew, R. (1992). Foundation for a general strain theory of crime and delinquency. *Criminology, 30*(1), 47–88.

Albrecht, B. (2010). Multicultural challenges for restorative justice: Mediators' experiences from Norway and Finland. *Journal of Scandinavian Studies in Criminology and Crime Prevention, 11*(1), 3–24.

Andrews, D. A., & Bonta, J. (2001). *The psychology of criminal conduct* (3rd ed.). Cincinnati, OH: Anderson.

Arrigo, B. A., & Schehr, R. C. (1998). Restoring justice for juveniles: A critical analysis of victim–offender mediation. *Justice Quarterly, 15*(4), 629–666.

Barton, C. K. B. (2003). *Restorative justice: The empowerment model.* Sydney, Australia: Hawkins Press.

Bazemore, G. (1991). New concepts and alternative practice in community supervision of juvenile offenders: Rediscovering work experience and competency development. *Journal of Crime and Justice, 14*(2), 27–52.

Bazemore, G., & Schiff, M. (2001). *Restorative community justice: Repairing harms and transforming communities.* Cincinnati, OH: Anderson.

Braithwaite, J. (1989). *Crime, shame, and reintegration.* Cambridge, UK: Cambridge University Press.

Braithwaite, J. (2002). *Restorative justice and responsive regulation.* New York, NY: Oxford.

Braithwaite, J. (2006). Narrative and "compulsory compassion." *Law & Social Inquiry, 31*(2), 425–446.

Bruner, J. (1990). *Acts of meaning.* Cambridge, MA: Harvard University Press.

Christie, N. (1977). Conflicts as property. *British Journal of Criminology, 17*(1), 1–15.

Clear, T. R., & Karp, D. R. (1999). *The community justice ideal: Preventing crime and achieving justice.* Boulder, CO: Westview.

Collins, R. (1981). On the microfoundations of macrosociology. *American Journal of Sociology, 86*(5), 984–1014.

Daly, K. (2002). Restorative justice: The real story. *Punishment & Society, 4*(1), 55–79.

Daly, K., & Stubbs, J. (2006). Feminist engagement with restorative justice. *Theoretical Criminology, 10*(1), 9–28.

Deem, D., Nerenberg, L., & Titus, R. (2007). Victims of financial crime. In R. C. Davis, A. J. Lurigio, & S. Herman (Eds.), *Victims of crime* (3rd ed.). Thousand Oaks, CA: Sage.

Duff, R. A. (2002). Restorative punishment and punitive restoration. In L. Walgrave (Ed.), *Restorative justice and the law.* Devon, UK: Willan.

Gaarder, E. (2008, June 6). *Sentencing circles and domestic violence: Examining a pilot project in Minnesota.* Paper presented at the Justice Studies Association Annual Meeting, Fairfax, VA.

Hampton, J. (1988). The retributive idea. In J. G. Murphy & J. Hampton (Ed.), *Forgiveness and mercy.* Cambridge, UK: Cambridge University Press.

Harris, M. K. (1991). Moving into the new millennium: Toward a feminist vision of justice. In H. E. Pepinsky & R. Quinney (Eds.), *Criminology as peacemaking* (pp. 83–97). Bloomington: Indiana University Press.

Herman, J. L. (1997). *Trauma and recovery: The aftermath of violence—From domestic abuse to political terror* (2nd ed.). New York, NY: BasicBooks.

Hirschi, T. (1969). *Causes of delinquency.* Berkeley: University of California Press.

Huang, H.-F., Braithwaite, V., Tsutomi, H., Hosoi, Y., & Braithwaite, J. (2012). Social capital, rehabilitation, tradition: Support for restorative justice in Japan and Australia. *Asian Criminology, 7,* 295–308.

Hudson, B. (2003). Restorative justice: The challenge of sexual and racial violence. In G. Johnstone (Ed.), *A restorative justice reader: Texts, sources, context.* Devon, UK: Willan.

Kelly, D. P., & Erez, E. (1997). Victim participation in the criminal justice system. In R. C. Davis,

A. J. Lurigio, & W. G. Skogan (Eds.), *Victims of crime* (2nd ed.). Thousand Oaks, CA: Sage.

Maruna, S. (2001). *Making good: How ex-convicts reform and rebuild their lives.* Washington, DC: American Psychological Association.

McAlinden, A.-M. (2011). "Transforming justice": Challenges for restorative justice in an era of punishment-based corrections. *Contemporary Justice Review, 14*(4), 383–406.

McKnight, J. (1995). *The careless society: Community and its counterfeits.* New York, NY: Basic Books.

Presser, L. (2004). Justice here and now: A personal reflection on the restorative and community justice paradigms. *Contemporary Justice Review, 7*(1), 101–106.

Presser, L. (2009). The narratives of offenders. *Theoretical Criminology, 13*(2), 177–200.

Presser, L., Gaarder, E., & Hesselton, D. (2007). Imagining restorative justice beyond recidivism. *Journal of Offender Rehabilitation, 46*(1/2), 163–176.

Presser, L., & Hamilton, C. A. (2006). The micropolitics of victim offender mediation. *Sociological Inquiry, 76*(3), 316–342.

Presser, L., & Lowenkamp, C. T. (1999). Restorative justice and offender screening. *Journal of Criminal Justice, 27*(4), 333–343.

Presser, L., & Van Voorhis, P. (2002). Values and evaluation: Assessing processes and outcomes of restorative justice programs. *Crime and Delinquency, 48*(1), 162–188.

Sherman, L. (1993). Defiance, deterrence, and irrelevance: A theory of the criminal sanction. *Journal of Research in Crime and Delinquency, 30,* 445–473.

Stubbs, J. (2010). Relations of domination and subordination: Challenges for restorative justice in response to domestic violence. *UNSW Law Journal, 33,* 970–111.

Sullivan, D., & Tifft, L. 2005. *Restorative Justice: Healing the Foundations of Our Everyday Lives,* 2nd edition. Monsey, NY: Willow Tree Press.

Sykes, G. M., & Matza, D. (1957, December). Techniques of neutralization: A theory of delinquency. *American Sociological Review, 22,* 664–670.

Tolle, E. (2005). *A new Earth: Awakening to your life's purpose.* New York, NY: Plume.

Tyler, T. R. (2006). *Why people obey the law.* Princeton, NJ: Princeton University Press.

Umbreit, M. S., & Armour, M. P. (2011). Restorative justice and dialogue: Impact, opportunities, and challenges in the global community. *Washington University Journal of Law & Policy, 36,* 65–89.

Van Ness, D., & Strong, K. H. (2006). *Restoring justice: An introduction to restorative justice* (3rd ed.). Cincinnati, OH: LexisNexis/Anderson.

Walgrave, L., & Aertsen, I. (1996). Reintegrative shaming and restorative justice: Interchangeable, complementary or different? *European Journal on Criminal Policy and Research, 4*(4), 67–85.

Wietekamp, E. G. M. (1996). The history of restorative justice. In G. Bazemore & L. Walgrave (Eds.), *Restorative juvenile justice: Repairing the harm of youth crime.* Monsey, NY: Criminal Justice Press.

Young, M. A. (1995). *Restorative community justice: A call to action.* Washington, DC: National Organization for Victim Assistance.

Zehr, H. (1995). *Changing lenses: A new focus for crime and justice.* Scottsdale, PA: Herald Press.

Zehr, H. (2001). *Transcending: Reflections of crime victims.* Intercourse, PA: Good Books.

Zehr, H. (2002). *The little book of restorative justice.* Intercourse, PA: Good Books.

GARBAGE IN, GARBAGE OUT?

Convict Criminology, the Convict Code, and Participatory Prison Reform

Alan Mobley

The prison experience and its aftermath have been the subjects of much study and description. In different ways and with varying degrees of success, scholars (e.g., Clemmer, 1958; Jacobs, 1977; Johnson, 2002; Stern, 1998; and Sykes, 1958), journalists (e.g., Conover, 2000; Earley, 1992), and current and former prisoners (e.g., Abbott, 1981; Cleaver, 1968; Hassine, 1999; Irwin, 1970, 2005; and Jackson, 1970) have sought to chronicle the pain, degradation, and emotional devastation of incarceration. In spite of these efforts, I am inclined to believe that much remains to be told. Although I have confidence in the possibility that sensitive people can achieve a conceptual understanding of "doing time" without having to experience prison for themselves, I respectfully maintain that an intellectual understanding of prison is not enough.

Someday, humans may have the ability to download sensate experience directly, but until that day, it seems that the best I can do is to analogize. Instead of laboring to induce empathy, I will try to convey some of the learning we have acquired as a result of occupying—indeed, embodying—the convict perspective. I passed 10 years in prison and 5 more on parole. My collaborators tally decades more behind bars, and some remain there still. The analogy that presents itself as most like the psychological cesspool of prison is the locker room: a high school or college locker room for male athletes.

In your mind's eye, fill out the room, if you will, with damp and sweat, stench and soiled belongings. Now, put in place a large number—too large for the room—of opposing athletes. Watch some gamely strut and posture while others withdraw into the self-imposed isolation of daydreams and consuming, reflexive thought. Feel the hypermasculinity manifested in shouted expletives and grunting sexual innuendo. Observe the sophomoric humor and carelessly displayed bodily functions.

Think of those participating in the antics as World Wrestling performers. See their legendary menace and outrageous, provocative acts. Now consider, quite seriously, that they are not acting, that they see their individual performances as competitive, as vital to their integrity and personal safety. Consider that they view one another as lethal threats. Throw in one or two officials who are paid to keep an eye on things but who make going home safely every night their top priority. Now, finally, go ahead and step into the locker room yourself, and seal the door behind you. How do you feel? If you have conscientiously engaged in this exercise, you now have a reasonable approximation of prison. Enjoy your stay.

MASS INCARCERATION IN AMERICA

From 1970 to 1988, the prison population in the United States tripled (Bureau of Justice Statistics, 1989). In the next 12 years, it tripled again, threatening to fill prisons faster than states could build them (Lynch, 2000). The incarceration business is said to employ 747,000 people and involve over $37 billion in expenditures (Jacobson, 2005, pp. 67–70). California now spends more on prisons than on the state university system. The electoral passage of Proposition 21 in California, which allows prosecutors to try accused criminal perpetrators 14 years old and above as adults, has at least symbolically impacted the state's prisons by bringing children—disproportionate numbers of minority children—into the adult justice system.

Advocates for the rights of racial minorities are alarmed at this new development, since overcrowding and racial segregation may worsen prevailing conditions both in prisons and in mostly minority neighborhoods. The life chances of African American and Latino males are already diminished by their frequent interaction with the criminal justice system (Miller, 1996; Western, 2007). Across the country, they are overrepresented in the new cohorts of specially selected penal detainees (Mauer, 1999; Mauer & King, 2007). Critics of the expanding prison–industrial complex complain that offender incapacitation is just the latest punitive twist in the continuing legacy of America's hot and cold running fascination with race-based social engineering (Clear, 2007; Gordon, 1999).

Criticisms of penal expansion and its variations are not new. Auerhahn (1999) convincingly shows that the underlying rationales supporting incapacitation have been repeatedly challenged on conceptual, ethical, and methodological grounds. Even the chief architect of selective incapacitation, the Rand Corporation's Peter

Greenwood (with colleague Susan Turner, 1987), later disputed the efficacy of profiling and targeting selected groups for incarceration.

Some proponents of penal incapacitation responded to criticism by crediting the policy with lowered crime rates in U.S. cities and towns. Officially compiled crime rates do show that some categories of major crimes are down 15% to 20% and more (Austin et al., 2009; Lichtblau, 1999). It is uncertain to what extent we can credit the decrease in crime to the increase in the number of the incarcerated.

The so-called War on Drugs has brought other groups into prison besides the traditionally oppressed minorities. Among them are the middle class. These convicts have had some impact on the prison system, and the system has deeply affected them. Some have gone on to make the study of prison their lifework. Most of these are reformers. Their energy, it is said, comes from the poignant observation that "you can take the man out of prison, but it's hard to take the prison out of the man." Some of these folks, mostly male, mostly of European American extraction, have grouped together under the banner of convict criminology.

CONVICT CRIMINOLOGY

It is fair to say that convict criminology was brought into being by the War on Drugs. Although the large majority of people swept into prisons by the wars on drugs and crime have been minority, poor, and poorly educated, another subgroup has been brought along, mostly for the ride, it seems. This group, mostly of European American extraction and middle class, found itself imported into a world of strange customs and moral codes. The prison experience itself, far from being routine and an accepted rite of passage, was bizarre. Some individuals within this group began to look upon the prison as an object of study and brought the culture of prison into their inquiry as well. They have become known, at least in their initial foray into research and publishing, as convict criminologists. The form and function of prisons in America was taken up as their first object of study.

Convict criminology began as an organizing effort to bring the human back into prison scholarship. In the mid-1990s, agitated by a curriculum void of any indication that those persons referred to as criminals, inmates, and offenders were also flesh-and-blood human beings, Chuck Terry and I—two University of California, Irvine, graduate students—met regularly to share strong coffee and even stronger opinions reflecting their convicted perspective.

Soon, Chuck and I realized that what we saw in their course materials as the dehumanization of justice system clients existed at an even more profound level at professional conferences. As intense immersions in the thought, politics, and personalities of a profession, these professional conferences were both repulsive and alienating for us. From these intense experiences came our desire to step beyond conventional criminology and make our own way. I soon began to pursue social justice activism, prison reform, and fieldwork-based scholarship. Chuck, however, sought out other academics who shared an incarcerated past. His research revealed several former prisoners teaching criminal justice and sociology at U.S. universities. As he began to share his misgivings over criminological study and practice, these new colleagues responded with a litany of their own concerns.

Sparked by the collective sentiment, Chuck wanted change. Rather than continue to toil in relative isolation among the conventionally minded, he thought that the ex-con criminologists ought to take a tip from Narcotics Anonymous (a group to which he belonged) and form a mutual-aid support group. When one of his graduate school advisors suggested he organize a panel of ex-con academics for the upcoming American Society of Criminology (ASC) meeting, he did the legwork. As luck would have it, his advisor also happened to be on the conference organizing committee and could see to it that the panel was seated. So, out of frustration, comradeship, and with logistical help from a sympathetic insider, convict criminology was born (Terry, 2003).

Convict criminology was announced as a "new school" in a 2001 issue of the journal *Social Justice* (Richards & Ross, 2001). An edited volume titled "Convict Criminology" was released in 2003 (Ross & Richards, 2003). As defined, "Convict Criminology represents the work of convicts or ex-convicts, in possession of a Ph.D. or on their way to completing one, or enlightened academics and practitioners, who contribute to a new conversation about crime and corrections" (Ross & Richards, 2003, p. 6).

Several principles were declared as core to this new school. Among them were the failure of prisons, the value of taking an insider perspective, the centrality of ethnography, and the preeminence of noted penologist and ex-convict John Irwin.

Irwin is the author of several prominent works of penology (Irwin, 1970, 1980, 1985, 2005; Irwin & Austin, 2000) that have achieved the status of classics in the field. His work combines social analysis with descriptive statistics and ethnography. For his latest book, *The Warehouse Prison*, Irwin gained access to California state prisons, where he assembled groups of convicts with whom he met over a 2.5-year period. Irwin credits them with contributing significantly to the book. The group "shared ideas, descriptions, and analyses of prisoner behavior and relationships. These 'experts' read and critiqued drafts of most of the book's chapters. They [10 prisoners] have served a total of 207 years in prison" (Irwin, 2005, p. ix).

Following Irwin's lead, convict criminologists offer an often blistering critique of U.S. penal justice and mainstream criminology. Often, the two are lumped into one lucrative, self-perpetuating machine (see Ross & Richards, 2003). Convict criminologists use their academic credentials to argue for their own analytical abilities, if not their objectivity, and burnish their pasts as further validation of the insights and recommendations they offer. They challenge the standard bearers of the mainstream to let them in and heed their words, and to an extent, they have been successful. Since the first conference panel in 1997, convict criminology has grown tremendously. The group now boasts many very well-attended panels at criminology's flagship conference and other national and regional meetings, dozens of journal articles and books, a website (see www.convictcriminology.org) that offers everything from consulting services to advice for prisoners wanting to attend college, and, most importantly, many new cohort members. In short, convict criminology is productive and growing.

As might be expected, countercriticism has come from the criminological mainstream. The *New York Times* quoted one prominent criminologist as implying that convict criminologists lack objectivity, asking, "What convict criminologist is going to say people are in prison because they have low self-control and lower I.Q. scores?" (St. John, 2003, p. 7). The prominent mainstream criminologist goes on, "There's a tendency among convict criminologists to say, 'Because I've been there, I know and you don't. Being there gives you access to some information, but not all the information. It illuminates and it distorts" (St. John, 2003, p. 7).

A more subtle form of critique is the exclusion of convict criminology from the discipline's leading journals. This does not surprise the convict criminologists, however, as they see their exclusion as further proof of scholarly complicity with a negligent (and perhaps malign) government in furthering a mutually beneficial prison–industrial complex (see Ross & Richards, 2003, pp. 18, 41, 349). John Irwin sets the tone in the preface to *Convict Criminology* when he states the need for a convict perspective within the larger, ill-informed discipline: "Not only do we have to push, we have to guide them" (Ross & Richards, 2003, p. xviii).

The prison is one place where all agree that convict criminologists can serve as useful guides. In what follows, we discuss the legendary convict code and its more recent variation (for the traditional treatment of the "inmate code," see Sykes & Messinger, 1960).

THE CONVICT CODE

Modern American prisons are largely self-contained establishments operating behind barbed-wire-topped fences and razor wire rolls. Within the confines of penal institutions, prisoners live, work, and play, providing all manner of services necessary for the continued safety, security, and sanitation of their community. Off hours are passed in leisure activities not so different from the outside world's. Prisoners read; watch television; engage in sports, games, and hobbies; eat junk food; and sleep. A prisoner's incarcerated life is lived in a compressed, communal lifestyle, no doubt much altered from whatever manner of living the imprisoned knew when free (see Wacquant, 2001, and Anderson, 1998, for different views on the exclusivity of the prison experience).

Prior to the introduction of congregate-style prisons, prisoners passed their days in silence and solitude. Meals were taken, labor performed, and all activities carried out within each individual prisoner's cell. No particularly new mode of living was imparted to prisoners; they were simply expected to utilize the time their sentences allowed to make peace with themselves and with God. Reaching the goal of inner peace was more than some prisoners could manage, however, and methods of incarceration were implemented that were essentially like those used today.

Adapting to limited personal autonomy, enforced material and heterosexual deprivation, and the rigors of communal living among strangers necessitated the development of norms, rules, and roles appropriate to the peculiar world of the prison. Solitary confinement had made for peacefully running prisons, and the shift to prisoners working together to perform institutional tasks was rough. Congregate living did ease high rates of suicide and insanity among prisoners, but it replaced those hazards with violence. Frustrated convicts spent their rage upon one another, finally settling into regular patterns of transactions, exchanges, and interactions that permitted each prisoner an opportunity to survive according to his strength and cunning. Two rules, in particular, emerged as conducive to peaceful, individualized communal living: "Do your own time" and "Don't snitch."

Both of these rules mainly concern the effects of prisoner actions on other prisoners. "Doing your own time" entails not bothering others, while "not snitching" means not involving officials or other convicts in one's private affairs. Our contention here is that these two behavioral guidelines are not only obsolete and in disuse but, through a lingering sense of their continuing validity, actually serve to undermine the ability of prisoners to rehabilitate themselves. A new basis for interaction between incarcerates, between prisoners and staff, and between prison society and the outside world can interrupt our prisons' current spiral toward stupefaction or anarchy and serve the best interests of all who participate in good faith.

The Original Convict Code

The convict code is a short set of principles that serve as guidelines for interactions between convicts, convicts and jailers, and convicts and the outside world. The convict code recognizes that each prisoner has different goals and desires to fulfill within a highly circumscribed environment of scarce resources. The convict code also encourages each prisoner to acknowledge the commonality of circumstances all prisoners face. No matter what a prisoner chooses to do with his or her time, all are subjected to the same limitations that coerced, unisexual incarceration brings.

By explicitly identifying the predicaments of imprisonment as universal to all convicts while simultaneously admitting the validity of diverse individual pursuits among the prisoner population, the convict code of conduct was intended to provide for peaceful, individualized, communal living.

Rule 1: Do Your Own Time

The vague but fundamental rule "Do your own time" typifies the code. "Do your own time" implies the uncomfortable fact that each convict is essentially alone. Each was judged alone, sentenced alone, admitted to prison alone, and will be released completely alone. The criminal justice system places other individuals in extremely close proximity and in remarkably similar circumstances to each convicted individual, but the salient point of imprisonment, time to be served, belongs/applies to each individual alone. Because of this simple fact, that each prisoner's sentence (or "time") is his or hers to serve alone, each individual in prison is separate from the start. The question is not, How and when do we get out? It is, How can I get out?

Obtaining release appears to be a main goal of nearly all prisoners. The actions in which a convict chooses to engage can often either speed or delay the release process, however. Participation in activities that can prolong a prisoner's sentence, such as fights, killings, escape attempts, or drug use, is therefore a highly personal decision affecting the decision maker, his confederates, and possibly victims. Being drawn into such situations unexpectedly is a convict's worst nightmare. As defense against this possibility, a high degree of external awareness is advisable at all times.

"Doing your own time" means one should mind one's own business so as not to become involved in the potentially dangerous escapades of others. Strengthening oneself as a preventative measure against possible victimization is a second goal of this rule. When a convict follows the suggestion, "Do your own time; don't let the time do you," he is careful not to let the deprivations of prison life get him down. When prisoners mope around in an attitude of self-pity, the chances of becoming entangled in confrontations with staff and other prisoners are greatly increased. A convict is a person who practices self-defense with the utmost vigilance. A convict can take a breather and relax when he goes home.

Safety

The issue of personal safety is the only issue that rivals obtaining release as a convict's priority. The convict code tries to restrict one's exposure to dangerous situations to those situations one willingly enters. For example, if a prisoner enters into a gang relationship for personal safety, drug accessibility, or any other reason, certain obligations are acquired. If a gang member is peacefully walking down a hallway and happens to see a fellow gang member being physically assaulted by one or more assailants, she or he is obligated to immediately enter the fray on the side of the compatriot. Such an action could result in injury or death immediately or in the future or in an increased sentence should injury or death occur to another involved in the conflict. A prisoner knowingly assumes this sort of obligatory risk when voluntarily entering into a gang relationship. A prisoner who is unaffiliated with the gang, who walks by and witnesses the same incident, is under no obligation to put himself or herself at risk. In fact, the convict code demands that bystanders be totally detached and not even look toward any event outside each one's immediate personal interest.

The prohibition against "rubbernecking," or looking at things or people beyond one's previously established parameters of legitimate interest, exists for two reasons. The first, essentially, "What you don't know can't hurt you," alludes to the precariousness of witnessing any illegal act. If a passerby witnesses illegal or improper actions, that person can be seen as a possible informant and therefore threatens the perpetrators by his or her very existence. Strong feelings of mistrust born of personal or vicarious experience involving the treachery of informants, or "snitches," can build to the point of confrontations and preemptive violence. It is also standard procedure for the prison administration to segregate or "lock up" witnesses to serious events in order to interrogate them more effectively. If one fails to witness the activities of others, however, one bypasses exposure to such unpleasant involvements.

Privacy

A second reason why rubbernecking is derided is simple privacy. Prisons are designed so that most every prisoner action occurs in a public—or at least a visible—space. There are windows in every door, lights never go completely off, and even the toilet stalls are open to view, the doors having been removed. In such a potentially degrading environment, where a total lack of privacy for inhabitants is institutionalized, prisoners must look to one another for whatever bits of privacy there are to be had. After all, usually only one or two officers patrol each living unit at any one time. Nearly every eye observing any prisoner's actions, therefore, belongs to a fellow convict. If prisoners have the consideration and discipline not to allow their eyes to wander into areas outside their immediate, legitimate concern, some vestige of personal privacy is possible for each individual. Not surprisingly, having a greater degree of privacy is often considered a more pleasant, dignified, and safer manner of living.

Personal Responsibility

Surviving the prison experience as comfortably as possible and allowing others to do the same is basic to the code. Each imprisoned individual is granted the right to say and do as he pleases. With this right comes the further implication that one's actions, because he or she has freely chosen, is representative of his or her intentions. Prisoners' words and actions are assumed to demonstrate their thoughts, and others form judgments accordingly. Failure to defend his or her words or actions when challenged sends a message that he or she is weak and can be exploited easily.

Exploitation

The nature of communal living, as well as the administration's perceived need to force all actions and interactions of prisoners into open spaces, guarantees tension over utilization of scarce resources. This tension is often prevented from becoming hostile and potentially dangerous competition by the implicit threat of retaliation against aggression. Retaliation against aggressors can be carried out by the offended party or by someone acting as his or her proxy. The possibility of retaliation by the state may be just as deterring as unsanctioned violence.

If a prisoner is caught engaging in overt aggression by an officer or through the use of informants, privileges can be taken away and sentences lengthened. Prisoners acting aggressively to hoard resources or intimidate others are looked upon as intentionally challenging those chosen as victims. The convict code holds the aggressor responsible for his or her actions and thus liable to retaliation for encroachment on the rights of others. The code also provides for victims to rightfully seek revenge.

Actually, the convict code stipulates that those acting as aggressors must themselves be victimized by their victims. The manner of such retaliation should be disproportionately greater than the original offense. Those who fail to defend themselves, their speech, or their property violate the code. Compliant victims unwilling to retaliate against aggressors forfeit their "respect," that is, their right to expect others to treat them in accordance with the code. Victims who do not stand up for themselves are seen as both weak and failing to abide by the code's directions. In short, the convict code condones the exploitation of those who are unwilling or unable to defend themselves.

Opportunities to exploit others without fear of retaliation are rare in prison, so those who seek victims are drawn to individuals who have revealed a willingness to be victimized. If the degradation inflicted by "wolves" upon a "mark" becomes too great, the mark often seeks protection in the formal structure, either by requesting to be segregated (locked up) or by informing on victimizers so that they are segregated.

Rule 2: Don't Snitch

The use of informants by police agencies is responsible for a majority of arrests. In exchange for lesser sentences, money, or other considerations, individuals with knowledge of others' criminal culpability often provide incriminating evidence to police. Nearly all prisoners serving time in prison were convicted with the aid of informants, often former friends. As the conviction and incarceration experience is perceived to be the wellspring of a prisoner's troubles, individuals responsible for incarcerating others are particularly despised by convicts. Police officials and officers of the court are usually viewed quite unfavorably, but government informants, people ostensibly acting as criminals but actually helping law enforcement build cases against outlaws, are generally hated.

Many convicts presume that one small benefit of imprisonment is separation from informants. Everyone in close-custody prisons (fenced and guarded facilities) is there for conviction of a felony considered serious, a conviction most often made possible by the cooperation of an informant. Prisoners thus feel they should have some things in common: an identity as convicts, similar deprivations, and status as victims of informants. When a prisoner is identified as an informant, therefore, it causes a fissure in the social bond of prisoner society.

Life outside frequently permits individuals to let their guard down and be themselves. Prison life does not. With essentially no privacy and surrounded by mostly hostile or apathetic strangers, prisoners have no "backstage" in which to relax. The assumed presence of snitches within prisons influences convicts to cloak their acts with respect to how they may appear to others. Even if a prisoner is not doing anything significantly deviant, chances are she or he could be set up as another's "fall guy." Additionally, each prisoner knows that hardly a day goes by when she or he does not commit some sort of infraction of prison rules, and most prisoners have personal property in violation of known statutes. Even if the nature of one's deviance falls short of provoking severe official sanctions, such as segregation or additional time, just the prospect of being hassled by guards and having one's lifestyle disrupted is bothersome and threatening.

To illustrate this point, prisoners who possess items considered "serious" contraband— knives, syringes, tattoo guns, and so forth—usually do not store such things in their designated personal territory. Contraband is routinely tucked into hidden spots in public places, territory over which no single prisoner has responsibility or control. This sort of precaution against prosecution presupposes the eventuality of detection. Though snitches ensure that no one gets away with anything for long, if one avoids being caught red-handed with illicit goods, disciplinary action by the prison administration cannot usually be taken.

Prisoners who do not routinely engage in serious deviance still check their living areas for signs of tampering. Intrusion by guards, thieves, or setup artists trying to plant evidence is not uncommon. In self-defense against loss of property or additional punishment, prisoners routinely police their primary personal territories. The fact that prisoners feel compelled to take precautions against theft or entrapment reveals the high level of mistrust present in captive society.

Thieves and snitches form an antisocial aggregate most responsible for the breakdown of community values in prison. Together, they create an atmosphere of defensiveness and suspicion that is perpetuated because each group feeds off the other. For example, thieves operate with near impunity because they know that snitches indirectly protect them. If a thief is caught by a prisoner and violence ensues, the victim of the theft will be punished by authorities as harshly as the thief. The convict code is supposed to protect the anonymity of both thieves and revenge-seeking victims of theft so that retribution against thievery can occur without official intervention. Snitches bring officials into privacy disputes and therefore undermine enforcement of the code.

Victims of thieves and snitches often see the wisdom of cutting their losses and simply writing off stolen articles and incidences of disrespect. Silent acceptance of ostensibly prohibited conduct has always occurred in prison. When, for example, the perpetrator of a proscribed act is an especially feared individual or one particularly well supported by a strong group, discretion on the victim's part becomes the wiser part of valor.

Snitches benefit from thieves in equal measure to the covert assistance given. When a rash of break-ins raises tensions, and the administration needs an arrest to quiet things, snitches provide the information. Those apprehended often avoid serious punishment because actual physical evidence of their guilt is rarely discovered. Snitches, however, still get credit from officials for cooperating at significant personal risk.

The existence of informants on the outside and snitches inside works to absolve individuals of a measure of responsibility for their own actions. Where dealings between individuals are based on at least some level of trust and expectation of mutual profit, activities involving bureaucratized structures revolve around procedures, laws, and regulations. Individual responsibility is replaced by systematized expediency where benefit accrues to the bureaucracy. Snitches bring third parties—police agents—into private affairs. The power relationship of any interaction between prisoners is fundamentally altered by including the bureaucracy. Involving the formal prison structure in informal private dealings takes the responsibility for outcomes and consequences away from prisoners and places it in the hands of hostile administrators. Instead of trust and mutual benefit, prisoner interactions become forced, shaped by suspicion and fear.

Bringing the prospect of negative sanctions and lengthened incarceration to another's door is antithetical to the convict code. "Squealing" by prisoners compels officials to enter situations they could not otherwise involve themselves in. Since police agents dispense negative sanctions almost exclusively, little chance exists for prisoners to benefit from their inclusion in prisoner affairs. Snitching, squealing, and informing thus make a mockery of Rule 1, "Do your own time." For this fundamental reason, the proscription against snitching has always held a prominent position in the convict code. Snitching has traditionally been met with the most severe informal sanctions, including removal from the general population of prison society—one way or another.

FACTORS UNDERMINING THE CONVICT CODE/FORMAL STRUCTURE

As stated previously, the two traditional premises underlying the convict code of conduct are "Don't squeal on other prisoners" and "Do your own time" (i.e., mind your own business). The second principle implies that it is forbidden to disturb anything other than oneself, one's relationships, and one's possessions. For example, bothering others by noisy or intrusive behavior is considered wrong. Listening in on, or "burglarizing," others' conversations or looking at what others are doing ("rubbernecking") are likewise inappropriate. Taking or in any way upsetting others' possessions or modes of lifestyle, called "routines," is forbidden as well.

Previous studies and anecdotal evidence suggest that belief in the validity of these elements of the informal convict code were once fairly universal in U.S. prisons, especially higher security prisons. Popular adherence to the code's dictates, however, has probably never been as consistent as hard-core convicts would like to believe. By and large, episodes of violence resulting from deviations from the code have kept alive the notion that the code is still a valid expression of prisoner ideals and a reliable guideline for prisoner action. The relative rarity of violent incidents in prison, as compared with the generally high level of disrespectful behavior, however, illustrates how seldom the code is actually enforced.

Several factors have arisen in recent years to help break whatever real effectiveness the code once had. First, unprecedented growth in prison construction now enables authorities to more easily transfer prisoners between facilities and isolate prison leaders. Frequent transfers dilute prisoner solidarity, remove leaders from leadership positions, pacify prisoners by keeping them either farther from home or closer to it, and remove the threat of such negative social sanctions as ostracism and violent attacks, violations of conduct codes once promised. Authorities now have the luxury of rewarding informants and punishing the rebellious through facility designation.

A second factor leading to the code's demise is the professionalization of correctional occupations. Authorities' unwillingness to allow prisoners to enforce informal codes and police themselves has removed an important ingredient of power from prisoner groups. Enforcement of informal rules through violence is no longer tacitly or implicitly permitted. Enforcers are now themselves harshly punished through additional time incarcerated and segregation from general population. Code enforcers are also transferred to other facilities as punishment for their informal roles. Their sacrifices for the common good are then unknown, unrecognized, and therefore unrewarded in unfamiliar, far-flung facilities.

The growing number of institutions in most prison systems has enhanced the trend toward professionalization of increasingly sought-after careers in corrections, as well as exposing the presence of individual code enforcers and informal leadership structures. Informants who reveal the secrets of captive society to officials can be protected by the anonymity of submergence in an ocean of inmates at one of any number of prisons. Bureaucratic tendencies to centralize expanding prison systems and staff institutions with better trained personnel stem largely from the same causes that have boosted incidences of snitching. The criminalization of drug use and the prioritization of law enforcement resources against drugs criminals—known in recent years as the Drug War—is the central factor influencing the prison industry and the dissolution of the convict code itself.

Self-Concept

The rise of drug sales and consumption in the 1980s and 1990s led certain individuals into criminality who otherwise possessed mainstream sensibilities. Stringent drug law enforcement prompted by political pressures brought many of these users and/or dealers into contact with the criminal justice system. The experience of being taken from one's environment, stripped of possessions, separated from friends and family, and labeled a criminal often has a dramatic and apparently enlightening effect on offenders guilty of consensual crimes. Drug profiteers were often trying to reach approved societal goals but used inappropriate means to do so. (Criminology has long recognized this phenomenon. See Akers, 1997; Sykes & Messinger, 1960.) For individuals who have no real "outlaw" mentality, after feeling the power of negative social sanctions, the shift back to a more complete agreement with legal, socially approved norms is not difficult to envision.

Whether from upper-, middle-, or lower-class backgrounds, offenders without genuine criminal self-concepts typically adapt to the incarceration experience by throwing themselves on the mercy of the criminal justice system and begging for release. Their common strategy is to prove to law enforcement officials that a terrible mistake has been made and a valuable lesson learned. The convict code, therefore, has little force or meaning for prisoners without criminal self-concepts. This self-styled "noncriminal" tries to impress officials by cooperating in every way. He works hard for nominal pay, keeps his living area up to prescribed standards, acts respectfully toward staff, withdraws from illicit elements of prison life, and informs, either baldly or surreptitiously, on other prisoners.

In medium- and lower-security institutions, these mostly Caucasian, noncriminal drug users and entrepreneurs compose a substantial aggregate. The presence of such a large segment of prisoners disinterested in adherence to the convict code calls into question the code's relevance as a functioning normative system. Following the code's prescriptions once guaranteed prisoners' personal safety. In today's largely nonviolent medium- and lower-security institutions, however, adapting one's behavior to an existent prison subculture has become unnecessary. The threat to personal safety and the subculture itself have been invalidated by the introduction of relatively large numbers of uninitiated prisoners acting independently and unilaterally who are interested in only one thing: going home.

Gangbangers

Gangbangers are another large group of prisoners who fail to abide by the principles of the convict code. Interestingly, on the surface, gangbangers are almost exact opposites of the mostly Caucasian, noncriminal drug user and/or entrepreneur. Gangbangers are primarily African Americans from homogeneous inner-city social environments. They appear to have completely assimilated criminal identities and consider doing time just another part of the criminal lifestyle. Like noncriminals, however, gangbangers have no use for the convict code. They care little what members of the general population think or do. Their alliances and allegiance are uniformly tied to outside gangs operating inside prison walls. So many young inner-city African American males are incarcerated that one's homeboys can be found in any penal institution. Young gangsters, therefore, need not trouble themselves to adapt their behavior to a prison subculture.

With their homeboys, gangsters compose a distinct subculture themselves, whether on the streets or in prison. They "look out for," or protect, their own, live an almost familial lifestyle, and rarely so much as speak to prisoners outside their own set. No loyalties exist toward prisoners in general or to the ideal of a united convict society. Gangbangers "run with" their "dogs" from "the 'hood," meet up with each other in the joint, then plan to reunite again on home turf. No involvement with outsiders is needed or apparently desired.

This fragmentation of incarcerated African Americans into distinct gangs, whether Crips, Bloods, or others, mirrors a similar move made by Chicanos in the 1960s. Racial and ethnic minorities have long tended to congregate in large prison gangs. (For reflections on a firsthand examination of racial tensions in California prisons, see Irwin, 1980.) Neighborhood economic and protection associations merged with others of the same race in prison in order to provide a larger membership, greater economic power, and individual security. Particularly in large state prison systems, the formation of race-based groups led to strict voluntary racial segregation. Incidences of personal differences often escalated into tit-for-tat warfare, with a seemingly endless supply of gang "soldiers" ready to avenge attacks on "brothers." In self-defense, Whites were forced to form similar associations, dropping, in the name of survival, the cliquishness typical of intra-Caucasian behavior.

Today, some state systems, such as California's, have had to adopt the extraordinary practice of designating certain prisons as the territory of certain gangs. Where once wings of particular prisons were segregated by race, now entire prisons are integrated racially but segregated according to gang affiliation. Internecine rivalries apparently arose around the struggle for control of prison groups. Leaders of smaller street gangs were reluctant to surrender their power and authority just because they were incarcerated. As more and more members of individual gangs were incarcerated, however, gang leaders saw less need to join larger, prison-based racial associations. Street gangs thus reformed within prison yards, with competition for traditional rackets soon flaring and then evolving into hostile and often violated truces.

Intraracial unity is no longer the norm in prison, except in times of extreme interracial conflict. Prisoners brought into the penal system by increased law enforcement pressure on urban areas and mandatory prison terms for crack cocaine crimes look to alliances formed in neighborhoods for guidance, protection, and provision of material resources in prison.

The task of initiating prisoners into the prison subculture, once accomplished by means of a generalized code of conduct, is now successfully completed for a large number of prisoners by reliance on preprison affiliations. Whether they are Native Americans associating exclusively with members of their own tribe; voluntarily segregated gang members; old-timers, bank robbers, and dope fiends hanging out on the compound telling lies; or noncriminal drug entrepreneurs reverting to precriminal behavior patterns and beliefs, a majority of today's prisoners no longer need to feel accepted by a generalized inmate subculture. The convict code of conduct, therefore, which exists for the explicit purpose of initiating prison neophytes into captive society, is functionally obsolete.

A NEW CODE

Today's convict would be well advised to admit several things and react accordingly. First, society has developed a habitual intolerance for deviance. Increased frustration with unsolved social problems has led politicians and the public to scapegoat societal out-groups as responsible. Political rhetoric that decried intolerance and punishment-laden responses to deviance born of inequality, although often heard during national election campaigns of past generations, has been dropped from public discourse. To pacify a frightened and worried public, policy makers continue to resort to higher levels of policing, criminalization of deviant behavior, and incarceration. Even though fiscal shortfalls will result in early releases for some prisoners and the elimination of parole supervision for others, this exercise in budgetary pragmatics should not be mistaken for a new, liberal wave in incarceration practices. In fact, reactionary measures and increased unpleasantness for prisoners should be anticipated. Budget cuts mean reduced programs and services for prisoners, and hard times tend to bequeath hard time.

Second, because policy makers have an apparent mandate to use whatever means are necessary to curb crime, factors contributing to the demise of the convict code will intensify in magnitude. More corrections infrastructure will be built, more professionalization of correctional occupations will occur, more noncriminal offenders and gang-oriented criminals will be incarcerated, and increased competition in overcrowded institutions for scarcer material resources will further splinter captive populations and promote the formation of antagonistic prison groups.

Third, due to these factors, prison officials now hold all the cards in their dealings with medium- and lower-security prisoners. Penal administrators will only be strengthened by prisoner uprisings. Any show of protest against social or penal policies will be met by harsher conditions, justified by the public's unwillingness to face and deal with social problems or the offspring of those problems. America's problem children are to be incarcerated for the foreseeable future because no one sees any long-term solutions.

Fourth, the high level of mistrust in prisons will intensify between prisoners themselves and between prisoners and politicians. Harsher sentencing and mandatory minimum prison terms for drug crimes have taken the carrot from government's traditional carrot-and-stick program. Prisoners of past years have had a glimmer of hope for early release through the parole mechanism. Even if apprehended, convicted, and sentenced, felons knew that, with good behavior, time incarcerated could be cut drastically. The pressure to inform on colleagues in order to avoid prison was there, but it was not nearly as strong as it is today, when little hope exists for meaningful sentence reduction.

The fate of prisoners and prison society depends partly on prisoners themselves. If convicts insist on perpetuating antagonism among themselves and toward prison staff, they play right into the hands of custody-oriented penal administrators. The structural antagonism between incarcerates and staff has reached its intended goal and serves only the interests of career bureaucrats, politicians, and corrections unions. Individual prisoners are not well served by prisons filled with tension and removed from mainstream culture nor are their families, communities, or victims and surely not the public. Convict criminology suggests that all groups can best be served if each is permitted a meaningful voice in the justice reform process. We hope that this chapter has provided some evidence for the value of the convict perspective.

Discussion Questions

1. Why do you think incarceration rates have continued to climb in spite of falling crime rates? Is this a reasonable state of affairs?

2. What might you consider to be the pros and cons of convict criminologists in the classroom? What value do you place on experience in your own education?

3. What do you see as the appropriate role (if any) for prisons in a free society?

4. Many commentators take note of the distinct racial composition of U.S. prisons and jails. To what do you attribute the overrepresentation of racial minorities? What, if anything, should be done about it?

Note From the Author

This paper was prepared with the assistance of many current and former prisoners, particularly my friend and colleague, Chuck Terry. The collaborative nature of the project suggests to the named author that he honor his unnamed colleagues through the use of "we" throughout the narrative. We also acknowledge the patient assistance of Paul Jesilow, William Granados, Michael Braun, and the editors and peer reviewers of this volume in the preparation of this paper.

References

Abbott, J. H. (1981). *In the belly of the beast: Letters from prison.* New York, NY: Vintage Books.

Akers, R. (1997). *Criminological theories: Introduction and evaluation.* Los Angeles, CA: Roxbury.

Anderson, E. (1998). *Code of the street: Decency, violence, and the moral life of the inner city.* New York, NY: W. W. Norton.

Auerhahn, K. (1999). Selective incapacitation and the problem of prediction. *Criminology, 37,* 703–733.

Austin, J., Clear, T., Duster, T., Greenberg, D. F., Irwin, J., McCoy, C., . . . Page, J. (2007). *Unlocking America: Why and how to reduce America's prison population.* Washington, DC: JFA Institute.

Bureau of Justice Statistics. (1989). *Prisoners in 1988.* Washington, DC: U.S. Government Printing Office.

Clear, T. (2007). *Imprisoning communities.* London, UK: Oxford University Press.

Cleaver, E. (1968). *Soul on ice.* New York, NY: McGraw-Hill.

Clemmer, D. (1958). *The prison community.* New York, NY: Rinehart.

Conover, T. (2000). *Newjack: Guarding Sing Sing.* New York, NY: Random House.

Earley, P. (1992). *The hot house: Life inside Leavenworth Prison.* New York, NY: Bantam Books.

Gordon, A. F. (1999). Globalism and the prison industrial complex: An interview with Angela Davis. *Race and Class, 40,* 145–157.

Greenwood, P., & Turner, S. (1987). *Selective incapacitation revisited: Why the high-rate offenders are hard to predict.* Santa Monica, CA: Rand.

Hassine, V. (1999). *Life without parole: Living in prison today* (2nd ed.). Boston, MA: Roxbury.

Irwin, J. (1970). *The felon.* Englewood Cliffs, NJ: Prentice Hall.

Irwin, J. (1980). *Prisons in turmoil.* Boston, MA: Little, Brown.

Irwin, J. (1985). *The jail.* Berkeley, CA: University of California Press.

Irwin, J. (2005). *The warehouse prison: Disposal of the new dangerous class.* Los Angeles, CA: Roxbury.

Irwin, J., & Austin, J. (2000). *It's about time: America's imprisonment binge.* Belmont, CA: Wadsworth.

Jackson, G. (1970). *Soledad brother.* New York, NY: Coward-McCann.

Jacobs, J. B. (1977). *Stateville.* Chicago, IL: University of Chicago Press.

Jacobson, M. (2005). *Downsizing prisons: How to reduce crime and end mass incarceration.* New York, NY: New York University Press.

Johnson, R. (2002). *Hard time: Understanding and reforming the prison.* Belmont, CA: Wadsworth.

Lichtblau, E. (1999, May 17). Crime rates continue record 7-year plunge. *Los Angeles Times,* A1.

Lynch, T. (2000, February 20). All locked up. *Washington Post,* B07.

Mauer, M. (1999). *Race to incarcerate.* New York, NY: New Press.

Mauer, M., & King, R. (2007). *A 25-year quagmire: The "War on Drugs" and its impact on American society.* Washington, DC: The Sentencing Project.

Miller, J. (1996). *Search and destroy: African-American males in the criminal justice system.* Cambridge, UK: Cambridge University Press.

Richards, S. C., & Ross, J. I. (2001). The new school of convict criminology. *Social Justice, 28*(1), 177–190.

Ross, J. I., & Richards, S. C. (2003). *Convict criminology.* Belmont, CA: Wadsworth.

Stern, V. (1998). *A sin against the future.* Boston, MA: Northeastern University Press.

St. John, W. (2003, August 9). Professors with a past. *New York Times,* 7. (Quoting University of Cincinnati criminal justice professor Francis Cullen).

Sykes, G. (1958). *The society of captives.* Princeton, NJ: Princeton University Press.

Sykes, G., & Messinger, S. (1960). The inmate social system. In R. Cloward et al. (Eds.), *Theoretical studies in social organization of the prison.* New York, NY: Social Science Research Council.

Terry, C. M. (2003). From C-block to academia: You can't get there from here. In J. I. Ross & S. C. Richards (Eds.), *Convict criminology.* Belmont, CA: Wadsworth

Wacquant, L. (2001). Deadly symbiosis. *Punishment and Society, 3*(1), 95–133.

Western, B. (2007). Mass imprisonment and economic inequality. *Social Research, 74*(2), 509–542.

INDEX

ABOUT THE EDITORS

Dan Okada is a professor in the Division of Criminal Justice at California State University Sacramento. He has professed criminal justice at Long Beach State University and Marist College (in Poughkeepsie, New York). He is past editor-in-chief of *Contemporary Justice Review* and is a past president of Justice Studies Association, with both efforts promoting social, transformative, and restorative justice and peacemaking criminology. His work revolves around juvenile and restorative justice, while his play centers on doing as little harm to others as possible.

Mary Maguire is the associate dean of the College of Health and Human Services at California State University Sacramento where she previously served as a professor and the chair of the Division of Criminal Justice and the director of the Center for Justice and Policy Research. Her research interests include moral panic and public policy, as well as issues related to the incarceration movement in the United States, including drugs, race, class, and programs for those at risk for offending. Selected publications include *A False Sense of Security: Moral Panic Driven Sex Offender Legislation, Corrections in California: The California Department of Corrections and Rehabilitation*, and *The Prevalence of Mental Illness in California Sex Offenders on Parole: A Comparison of Those Who Recidivated With a New Sex Crime Versus Those Who Did Not*. In addition to *Critical Issues in Crime and Justice*, she has three editions of *Annual Editions: Drugs, Society, and Behavior*. She served as the book review editor for *Contemporary Justice Review* and is the past president of the Western Society of Criminology. In addition to numerous student programs, Dr. Maguire started a Project Rebound site, a prison-to-university pipeline, at Sacramento State and continues to advance issues of justice and equity.

Alexa Sardina is an assistant professor in the Division of Criminal Justice at California State University California. Her research interests include sex offender motivation, offense cycles, and the use of restorative justice models in cases of rape and sexual assault. Her recent work has been published in the *Journal of Offender Rehabilitation* and *International Journal of Offender Therapy and Comparative Criminology*.

ABOUT THE CONTRIBUTORS

Janice Ahmad is an associate professor in the Department of Criminal Justice at the University of Houston–Downtown. Dr. Ahmad's research interests include police management, citizen involvement in policing, women in policing, crime victims, and program evaluation. Dr. Ahmad earned her PhD in criminal justice from Sam Houston State University.

Cyndi Banks is an emeritus professor of criminology and criminal justice from Northern Arizona University where she served over the years as dean of University College and chair and faculty within the Department of Criminology and Criminal Justice. She is currently associate vice president of student success at Capilano University in Vancouver, Canada. She has 25 years experience of research and project implementation in developing countries in the fields of juvenile justice, probation, justice policy, and children's rights. She has worked as a criminologist in Papua New Guinea, Bangladesh, Iraq, Kurdistan, Timor Leste, South Sudan, and Myanmar and is the author of numerous articles and books including *Criminal Justice Ethics: Theory and Practice*, currently working on its 5th Edition; *Comparative, International, and Global Justice: Perspectives from Criminology and Criminal Justice*; *Youth, Crime and Justice*; *Developing Cultural Criminology: Theory and Practice in Papua New Guinea*; *Alaska Native Juveniles in Prison*; and, most recently, *Punishment in America*.

Casey Branchini, MHS, is a PhD candidate at the Johns Hopkins Bloomberg School of Public Health (Department of International Health). Before pursuing her PhD, Ms. Branchini Risko worked at the U.S. Department of State, Office to Monitor and Combat Trafficking in Persons (J/TIP) where she served as a monitoring and evaluation specialist for programs addressing human trafficking in more than 10 countries, including Thailand, Cambodia, Afghanistan, Lebanon, Guatemala, Haiti, and Brazil. Her dissertation focuses on the intersection between health and human rights violations among migrant workers in Kuala Lumpur, Malaysia. Ms. Branchini Risko has extensive research experience in the areas of disaster response and humanitarian aid throughout other countries in Asia and beyond. Most recently, she worked as a coinvestigator on studies estimating the prevalence of forced marriage and childbearing among Burmese women trafficked to China, as well as on the health impact of human rights violations among North Korean children.

Meda Chesney-Lind, PhD, teaches women's studies at the University of Hawaii. Nationally recognized for her work on women and crime, her testimony before Congress resulted in national support of gender-responsive programming for girls in the juvenile justice system. In 2013, the Western Society of Criminology named an award after her honoring "significant contributions to the fields of gender, crime and justice" and made her the inaugural recipient. Most recently, she has been elected president of the American Society of Criminology; her term will begin in 2019.

John P. Crank, PhD, is professor emeritus of criminology and criminal justice at the University of Nebraska, Omaha. He is the author or coauthor of eight books and 56 articles in peer-reviewed journals. His most recent book, *Global Warming, Violence, and Crime* (with Linda Jacoby), was published by Lexis/Nexis in the spring of 2014. He has received the ACJS outstanding book award for *Imagining Justice* and was nominated for that award for *Mission-Based Policing* (with Rebecca Murray, Mark Sundermeier, and Dawn Irlbeck).

Leah E. Daigle, PhD, is professor in the Department of Criminal Justice in the Andrew Young School of Policy Studies at Georgia State University. Her most recent research has centered on repeat sexual victimization of college women and the development and continuation of victimization across the life course. She is coauthor of *Criminals in the Making: Criminality Across the Life Course (2nd ed.)* and *Unsafe in the Ivory Tower: The Sexual Victimization of College Women*, which was awarded the 2011 Outstanding Book Award by the Academy of Criminal Justice Sciences, and author of *Victimology: A Text/Reader* and *Victimology: The Essentials*. Her research has also appeared in peer-reviewed journals, including *Justice Quarterly*, *Victims and Offenders*, *The Journal of Quantitative Criminology*, and *The Journal of Interpersonal Violence*. She was awarded the 2014 Andrew Young School of Policy of Studies Excellence in Teaching Award.

James C. (Buddy) Howell worked at the federal Office of Juvenile Justice and Delinquency Prevention in the U.S. Department of Justice for 21 years (1974–1995), mostly as director of research and program development. He also served as deputy administrator of OJJDP (1977–1984). He currently is senior research associate with the National Gang Center in Tallahassee, Florida, where he has researched youth and street gangs for the past 20 years. Buddy has published more than 100 works on juvenile justice, youth violence, and gangs, including eight books. His gang books are titled *The History of Street Gangs in the United States* (Lexington Books, 2015), and *Gangs in America's Communities*, 3rd ed. (Sage Publications, 2018, coauthor: Elizabeth Griffiths).

Megan Qually Howell, MCJ, is a data analyst with the North Carolina Department of Public Safety since 2005. Megan has carried out several statewide policy studies on topics including youth gang activity, youth violence prevention, school crime and violence, juvenile justice policies and practices, juvenile diversion, and disproportionate minority contact. In her role as an analyst, Megan assists with development of statewide and local initiatives, periodic agency reports, legislative reports, grant programs, and collaborations with external researchers. She also has responsibility for data quality assurance and management information system improvements.

Ming-Li Hsieh, PhD, is an assistant professor in the Criminal Justice Program at the University of Wisconsin–Eau Claire and is a research fellow of the Washington State Institute for Criminal Justice. Her research includes corrections and program evaluation, risk assessment instruments, crime control policies, and comparative criminal justice. Her recent work has been published in *Criminal Justice Policy Review, International Criminal Justice Review, Journal of Interpersonal Violence*, and *Feminist Criminology*, among others.

Dawn M. Irlbeck is associate professor of sociology at Creighton University where she facilitates the criminal justice policy track as well as the Nebraska State Victims Assistance Academy administrated by Creighton University. Her primary research interests include policing and minority communities, racial profiling, and Latino police officers. She recently published (with John Crank, Rebecca Murray, and Mark Sundermeier) *Mission-Based Policing*, which was nominated for the Academy of Criminal Justice Sciences 2012 Outstanding Book Award.

Chelsea M. Johnson received her BS in criminal justice at California State University Sacramento and has focused her research in the areas of recidivism, criminogenic behavior, substance abuse, mental illness, motivation, and resilience. She earned her MA in psychology of education, and she is working as a high school teacher at an all-Hispanic, Title 1 charter school in the North Bay of California. She is currently pursuing her PhD in educational psychology, studying the psychological approach to achievement in underprivileged social groups.

Connie M. Koski received her PhD in criminology and criminal justice from the University of Nebraska at Omaha and is currently an assistant professor of criminology and criminal justice at Longwood University in Farmville, Virginia. Her primary research interests include crime, criminal justice, and immigration; neighborhoods and crime; police–community relations; race/ethnicity and criminal justice; and qualitative methods. Dr. Koski's work has been published in the *Journal of Criminal Justice, Police Practice and Research: An International Journal*, and the *Journal of Criminal Justice Education*, and she is an author (S. Cox, B. Fitch, C. Koski, and D. Massey) of the forthcoming *Introduction to Policing, 4th edition* (Sage).

Peter B. Kraska, PhD, is professor and chair of graduate studies and research in the School of Justice Studies at Eastern Kentucky University. He is a leading scholar in the areas of criminal justice theory, police and criminal justice militarization, and research methods. He has published a number of books, including *Criminal Justice and Criminology Research Methods, Theorizing Criminal Justice: Eight Essential Orientations*, and *Militarizing the American Criminal Justice System: The Changing Roles of the Armed Forces and Police*. Dr. Kraska's research has also been published in a number of leading journals, including the *British Journal of Criminology*, *Social Problems*, *Justice Quarterly*, and *Policing and Society*. Dr. Kraska's work has received national and international attention; it has been featured in media outlets such as *The Economist*, *Washington Post*, BBC, *New York Times*, *Wall Street Journal*, *Huffington Post*, National Public Radio, Peter Jennings's *World News Tonight*, and the PBS News Hour. His recent research interests include making theoretical sense of the emergence of underground cage-fighting, the trend to legalize through medicalization the use of performance enhancing drugs (PEDs), and a continuation of study into the blurring distinction between criminal justice and the military in the wars on drugs and terrorism.

Kyle Letteney received his BA degree in criminal justice with a minor in sociology at Rochester Institute of Technology. From 2011 to 2013, he worked with the Center for Public Safety Initiatives in Rochester, New York, conducting research on state-level narcotic laws and community empowerment projects. He is currently working on his MA in sociology at the University of Tennessee. His research interests include restorative justice in contemporary society, the social impacts of law, structural violence, and mass incarceration.

C. Augustus "Gus" Martin is a professor of criminal justice administration at California State University, Dominguez Hills, where he regularly teaches a course on the subject of terrorism and extremism. He has also served as associate vice president for human resources management, acting associate dean of the College of Business Administration and Public Policy, associate vice president for faculty affairs, and chair of the Department of Public Administration & Public Policy. He began his academic career as a member of the faculty of the Graduate School of Public and International Affairs, University of Pittsburgh, where he was an administration of justice professor. Prior to joining academia, Dr. Martin served as managing attorney for the Fair Housing Partnership of Greater Pittsburgh, special counsel to the attorney general of the U.S. Virgin Islands, and legislative assistant to Congressman Charles B. Rangel of New York.

Alan Mobley is an associate professor of criminal justice and public affairs at San Diego State University. He teaches courses on restorative justice, community-based service learning, and law and society. His academic career began with sporadic attendance at several California community colleges. Later, while in federal prison for cocaine convictions, he earned a BS in economics from Regents College of the University of the State of New York and an MA in sociology from Vermont College. After a decade of incarceration, he was released to 5 years parole. He received a doctorate in criminology, law, and society from the School of Social Ecology at the University of California, Irvine. His work engages interdisciplinary convict criminology, including participatory action research on mass incarceration, shame and trauma, and restorative practices. His recent writing appears in *Museums and Social Issues*, *Western Criminology Review*, *Eurovista*, *Contemporary Justice Review*, *Peace Review*, and the *Journal of Critical Animal Studies*.

Stephen L. Muzzatti is an associate professor of sociology at Ryerson University in Toronto, Canada, specializing in the areas of crime and inequality. He has published work on crimes of globalization, consumerism and violence, animal studies, the news media, the Italian-Canadian community, working-class identities, and motorcycle culture. He is also an expert in arson and demolition. Dr. Muzzatti previously served in several executive capacities for the American Society of Criminology's Division on Critical Criminology and is currently a departmental representative for the Canadian Sociological Association.

Johnny Nhan is graduate director and associate professor of criminal justice at Texas Christian University. His research interests lie at the intersection of technology and crime. He has written on a variety of cybercrime topics, including issues of policing, law, and the role of the public in controlling the online environment. His book, *Policing Cyberspace: A Structural and Cultural Analysis*, was published in 2010.

Thomas Nolan has been an associate professor in criminal justice at Boston University, the State University of New York at Plattsburgh, and Merrimack College. He was a senior policy advisor at the Office of Civil Rights and Civil Liberties in the Department of Homeland Security in Washington, DC, and a 27-year veteran (and former lieutenant) with the city of Boston police department. Tom is regularly sought out for his expertise and commentary on policing and civil rights and civil liberties issues by local, national, and international media—print, radio, television, and the Internet. Tom's book, *Perilous Policing: Navigating the Dangerous Straits*, will be published in 2019.

Dan Okada earned his doctorate at the University of Maryland (GO Terps!) and his undergraduate degree at the University of California Berkeley (GO Bears!). He is a professor of criminal justice at California State University Sacramento. He is a Vietnam veteran whose work centers on juvenile delinquency and juvenile justice and attempts at promoting restorative justice. He is conducting interviews of survivors of the Japanese American incarceration experience during World War II.

David L. Parry is a professor of criminal justice at Endicott College in Beverly, Massachusetts, where he has taught for over 20 years, offering courses in nearly all core criminal justice subject areas and mentoring hundreds of undergraduates through empirical senior thesis projects. The editor of *Essential Readings in Juvenile Justice* (Pearson Prentice Hall, 2005), he has directed research projects examining delinquent behavior, the operation of state and local juvenile justice systems, and the interaction of police, court, and correctional agencies with youth in numerous jurisdictions across the United States. After completing his undergraduate education at UCLA, Dr. Parry earned his PhD in the School of Criminal Justice at the University at Albany, State University of New York.

Lois Presser is professor of sociology and associate head of the Department of Sociology at the University of Tennessee. Her research explores social harm, narrative, and restorative justice. She is the author of *Been a Heavy Life: Stories of Violent*

Men (2008) and *Why We Harm* (2013) and the forthcoming *Inside Story: How Narratives Drive Mass Harm* and coeditor of *Narrative Criminology: Understanding Stories of Crime* (2015) with Sveinung Sandberg.

Maggie Reid is a PhD candidate in the joint Communication and Culture program at Ryerson University. She is a media practitioner, having worked in both radio and television production. She has been an active participant in communications policy through both advocacy work as well as regulatory interventions to the CRTC. Her dissertation research focuses on shifts in journalistic identity and labor practices for freelance journalists in a digital context. She has published academic works as well as pieces for j-source, IP Osgoode, and CWA Canada.

Alexa Sardina is an assistant professor at California State University Sacramento. Her scholarship focuses on the motivations and justifications of female child sex offenders with special attention given to the situational contexts within which child sexual abuse occurs. In 2000, she cofounded the It Happened to Alexa Foundation, which provides support for survivors of sexual assault during the criminal trial process. At the Association for the Treatment of Sexual Abusers, she has presented on research that combines her experience as a sex offender expert and rape survivor to encourage the perspective of "survivor scholars." She hopes this will bring a fresh perspective to sex crimes policy, sex offender assessment and treatment, and aid in treatment efforts for survivors and offenders.

Kim Schnurbush is an assistant professor of criminal justice at California State University Sacramento. She received her bachelor of arts degree from the University of New Hampshire, her master's degree from Fitchburg State University, and her PhD in criminal justice from Sam Houston State University. She worked for 14 years in the criminal justice system, in a combination of law enforcement and corrections. Dr. Schnurbush also has 10 years of teaching experience at the university level and specializes in teaching drug abuse, law enforcement, and corrections classes, and her research currently centers on wrongful convictions and the death penalty. She is a member of Alpha Phi Sigma, American Correctional Association, the American Society of Criminology, and the Academy of Criminal Justice Sciences.

Randall G. Shelden is professor of criminal justice, University of Nevada–Las Vegas, where he has been a faculty member since 1977. He is also a senior research fellow with the Center on Juvenile and Criminal Justice in San Francisco. He received his master's degree in sociology at Memphis State University and PhD in sociology at Southern Illinois University. He is the author or coauthor of the following books: *Criminal Justice in America: A Sociological Approach*; *Girls, Delinquency and Juvenile Justice* (4th edition), with Meda Chesney-Lind (which received the Hindelang Award for outstanding contribution to Criminology in 1992); *Youth Gangs in American Society* (4th ed.), with Sharon Tracy and William B. Brown; *Crime and Criminal Justice in American Society* (with William Brown, Karen Miller, and Randall Fritzler, 2nd edition, Waveland Press); *Controlling the Dangerous*

Classes: The History of Criminal Justice (3rd edition, Waveland Press); *Delinquency and Juvenile Justice in American Society* (3rd edition, Waveland Press, forthcoming); *Juvenile Justice in America: Problems and Prospects* (Waveland Press, coedited with Daniel Macallair); and *Our Punitive Society* (Waveland Press). He is also the author of more than 50 journal articles and book chapters on the subject of crime and justice. He has also written more than 100 commentaries appearing in local and regional newspapers. He is the coeditor of the online *Justice Policy Journal*. His website is www.sheldensays.com. His e-mail is shelden@unlv.nevada.edu.

Jennie K. Singer received her PhD in clinical psychology from the California School of Professional Psychology, San Diego. She is a licensed forensic psychologist and a professor in the Division of Criminal Justice at California State University Sacramento. Dr. Singer is also the director of the Center for Justice and Policy Research, where she works to evaluate regional rehabilitation programs and government agencies' programming for offenders. Dr. Singer has worked in state and federal departments of corrections as both a psychologist and a clinical supervisor, and she currently assesses adolescent and adult offenders for court-ordered psychological evaluations. She has published edited books, chapters, and articles on the mentally ill, sex offenders, and offender rehabilitation programs. She has also published chapters in psychological textbooks in the area of special education, intellectual assessment, and juvenile delinquency.

Cassia Spohn is Foundation Professor and director of the School of Criminology and Criminal Justice at Arizona State University. She has a PhD in political science from the University of Nebraska–Lincoln. Prior to joining the ASU faculty in 2006, she was a faculty member in the School of Criminology and Criminal Justice at the University of Nebraska at Omaha for 28 years. She is the author or coauthor of seven books, including *Policing and Prosecuting Sexual Assault: Inside the Criminal Justice System* and *How Do Judges Decide? The Search for Fairness and Equity in Sentencing*. Her research interests include prosecutorial and judicial decision making; the intersections of race, ethnicity, crime, and justice; and sexual assault case processing decisions. In 2013 she received ASU's Award for Leading Edge Research in the Social Sciences and was selected as a fellow of the American Society of Criminology.

Richelle S. Swan is professor of sociology and criminology and justice studies at California State University, San Marcos. She teaches a number of classes related to delinquency, crime, law, and social justice. Her current research projects focus on a number of topics related to the intersection of crime, law, and in/justice. Recent scholarship examines juvenile delinquency, the impact of gang injunction laws on Southern Californian communities, the legal consciousness of undocumented young adults, popular culture, and social constructions of crime.

Helen Taylor-Greene, PhD, is professor emeritus in the Department of Administration of Justice in the Barbara Jordan-Mickey Leland School of Public

Affairs at Texas Southern University in Houston, Texas. She served as interim graduate program director and taught both traditional and online graduate courses. She is the author, coauthor, and coeditor with Dr. Shaun L. Gabbidon of *Race and Crime*, 3rd ed. (2013, Sage) and *Race and Crime: A Text Reader* (2011, Sage). She also served as lead coeditor of the *Encyclopedia of Race and Crime* (2009, Sage) with Dr. Gabbidon. Dr. Taylor Greene is the 2014 recipient of the 2014 W. E. B. Du Bois Award from the Western Society of Criminology. In 2011, she received the Academy of Criminal Justice Science's Outstanding Mentor Award.

Gennaro F. Vito is a professor in the Department of Criminal Justice at the University of Louisville. He also serves as a faculty member in the Administrative Officer's Course at the Southern Police Institute. He holds a PhD in public administration from The Ohio State University. He is a past president and fellow of the Academy of Criminal Justice Sciences and a recipient of their Bruce Smith Award. He has published journal articles on such topics as capital sentencing, police consolidation, police traffic stops, policing strategies for drug problems in public housing, attitudes toward capital punishment, and the effectiveness of criminal justice programs, such as drug elimination programs, drug courts, and drug testing of probationers and parolees. He is the coauthor of nine textbooks in criminal justice and criminology, including *Criminology: Theory, Research and Practice* (Jones & Bartlett) and *Organizational Behavior and Management in Law Enforcement* (Prentice Hall).

Anthony Walsh received his PhD in criminology from Bowling Green State University, Ohio, after 25 years in the real world as a marine, police officer, and probation officer. He teaches criminology, statistics, and corrections at Boise State University, Idaho. He is the author, coauthor, or editor of 38 books and over 150 journal articles or book chapters. His primary interests are biosocial criminology and the philosophy of science. His latest book is *The Gavel and Sickle: The Supreme Court, Cultural Marxism, and the Assault on Christianity*.

Ilhong Yun is an associate professor in the Department of Police Administration at Chosun University in South Korea. He earned his doctorate in criminal justice from Sam Houston State University. He has field experience as a police officer for 12 years in South Korea and his 30 research articles have been published in the *Journal of Interpersonal Violence*, *Journal of Criminal Justice*, *Policing*, and other academic journals. Currently, his research interests lie in the area of biosocial criminology, comparative criminal justice, and policing.